BRUCE R. HOPKINS' NONPROFIT LAW DICTIONARY

BRUCE R. HOPKINS

T0320071

WILEY

Library of Congress Cataloging-in-Publication Data:

Hopkins, Bruce R., author.
  Bruce R. Hopkins' nonprofit law dictionary / Bruce R. Hopkins. – 1
      pages cm. – (Wiley nonprofit law, finance and management series)
  ISBN 978-1-118-99608-9 (hardback)
  ISBN 9781119057079 (ePDF)
  ISBN 9781119057116 (ePub)
  1. Nonprofit organizations–Law and legislation–United States–Dictionaries.
  2. Nonprofit organizations–Taxation–Law and legislation–United States–Dictionaries.
  3. Law–United States–Dictionaries.   I. Title.   II. Title: Nonprofit law dictionary.
  KF1388.A68H665 2015
  346.73'06403–dc23   2015005233

Printed in the United States of America

10 9 8 7 6 5 4 3 2 1

This Dictionary is dedicated to my youngest granddaughter, Sadie Marie Ash, who will be nearly twelve years of age when it is published. The book is dedicated to her because she is a logophile. (When she first learned of this project, she offered to help me write the Dictionary but was chagrined to learn it would contain only law words and phrases, which, she ruefully admits, she is not quite (or yet) ready to absorb.) When I realized Sadie was interested in words, beginning around four or five, I set about to teach her some polysyllabic doozies. I succeeded in some instances, although I still cannot determine what approach leads to success. Some words she retains and sometime uses; some drift away. She reports her favorite word at this time is incognito but cannot explain why. Another is sommelier, which is a byproduct of my efforts to get her to say "Opus One" when a restaurant waitperson would ask her what she wanted to drink. Other words that have managed to stick are ambiguous, imperative, loquacious, metaphor, micturate, and palindrome. The Dictionary will give her much more to work on. I must close this dedication now and return to my current task, which is to insert zeitgeist into Sadie's young brain.

CONTENTS

PREFACE

Anyone familiar with the Wiley series of publications on law, accounting, management, and fundraising for nonprofit organizations knows that your author has a passion for writing about the federal and state laws applicable to charitable and other types of nonprofit organizations. One of the reasons for this compulsion is the challenge of capturing—and then keeping up with—this vast body of complex and intricate rules, particularly in the federal tax area. Thanks to Congress and the state legislatures, the Internal Revenue Service, and other government agencies, there is always a wide range and deep flow of topics to write about.

There is another challenge underlying the zeal for this type of writing. It is what I call the "interpretive" function. That is, it is not enough to simply write summaries of the law and keep those summaries current—the challenge is to write in a way that the nontechnical reader (as well as many lawyers and accountants who do not often dwell on the subjects) can understand. This observation is not meant to be denigrating to someone who is not a tax lawyer or an accountant; it is simply recognition of the fact that the law is so convoluted and mangled, and so filled with cross-references and unintelligible phraseology, that the average person needs an interpreter to wade through it. To state the matter less delicately, some of these laws are not readily understandable at first reading.

Some quotations from the Internal Revenue Code illustrate the point. Here is the language Congress selected when it amended the income expenditure requirements for private operating foundations:

> Notwithstanding the provisions of subparagraph (A), if the qualifying distributions (within the meaning of paragraph (1) or (2) of subsection (g)) of an organization for the taxable year exceed the minimum investment return for the taxable year, clause (ii) of subparagraph (A) shall not apply unless substantially all of such qualifying distributions are made directly for the active conduct of the activities constituting the purpose or function for which it is organized and operated.

This is the last sentence of IRC § 4942(j)(3).

Next is Congress' description of the criteria that a private foundation must meet to pay a 1 percent excise tax (rather than the general 2 percent) based on investment income:

> A private foundation meets the requirements of this paragraph for any taxable year if (A) the amount of the qualifying distributions made by the private foundation during such taxable year equals or exceeds the sum of (i) an amount equal to the assets of such foundation for such taxable year multiplied by the average percentage payout for the base period, plus (ii) 1 percent of the net investment income of such foundation for such taxable year, and (B) such private foundation was not liable for tax under section 4942 with respect to any year in the base period.

This is section 4940(e)(2) of the Internal Revenue Code.

Here is my favorite example of the point, and I will even provide a clue in advance, which is that this passage "describes" a qualification that a charitable organization must meet if it wishes to be classified as a supporting organization with respect to a social welfare organization, a labor organization, or a trade or professional organization:

> For purposes of paragraph (3), an organization described in paragraph (2) shall be deemed to include an organization described in section 501(c)(4), (5), or (6) which would be described in paragraph (2) if it were an organization described in section 501(c)(3).

This sentence (which is the last one in section 509(a)(3) of the Internal Revenue Code) and other words and phrases are explained more clearly in this book. These items cover corporate and tax terms (and many others) that apply specifically in the realm of tax-exempt and other nonprofit organizations.

The purpose of these books and the monthly newsletter is to meet these three challenges: to capture all of the pertinent law, write summaries of it in a meaningful, understandable way, and to keep with all changes to the law. It is chiefly an educational purpose.

There are many ways to provide education in a written form. The approach of the other Wiley books that I have written has been to describe the law by subject matter (tax-exempt organizations, charitable giving, fundraising, and so forth). But there are many concepts that apply to more than one of these fields.

I have been struggling to find a way to bring all of these fields into one publication, where the subject matter can still be addressed at a technical level. One way to do this is a dictionary of the terms comprising the law of nonprofit organizations. This is a tool designed to aid the reader of other books or periodicals when he or she comes across a word or phrase that is not understandable.

I am not out to join the ranks of Noah Webster or Henry Campbell Black (the latter being the author of *Black's Law Dictionary*); rather, the purpose of this volume is to supplement the educational and interpretative functions of other books in the Wiley series. Indeed, in addition to the definition of a word or phrase, a cross-reference leads to one or more of the other Wiley books where the reader can find more detailed information on the subject.

The exercise of preparing this book has changed me. I find that I have become somewhat of an amateur lexicologist or even a philologist. Sometimes, while working on this volume late at night, numbed by mental fatigue, I became concerned with abecedarianism. Even in the darkest hour, however, I remained convinced that this book is an afflatus.

As I indicated earlier, I see myself in this process as a dragoman. I was forced to turn in the manuscript of this book when I did, lest the editors accuse me of barmecide. I wanted to call these brief remarks the "Prolegomena," but they made me stay with "Preface." This process, to my colleagues' dismay, has caused me to become a word-grubber.

It is best that I cause an aposiopesis and say that, for those of you in the nonprofit world who are straining with the burden of government regulation and enforcement, I hope the *Nonprofit Law Dictionary* helps bring more understanding to the process and to pathways for relief.

Bruce R. Hopkins
May 2015

HOW TO USE THIS DICTIONARY

The purpose of this book is to provide useful definitions of all of the terms in the law pertaining to nonprofit organizations.

The definitions in this book are written so as to explain the legal terms to those who are not schooled in the law, as well as to lawyers. Each term used in a definition that is defined elsewhere in the Dictionary is **boldface**. Where a definition involves a section of the Internal Revenue Code, that section of the code is referenced.

Nearly every definition is coded to one or more books by the author (in some instances, as co-author), all published by John Wiley & Sons. This information is provided so that the reader desiring more information about a body of law represented by a particular term or phrase is guided to the book or books where the subject is discussed in greater detail.

The codes for these books are as follows:

Code	Title
LI	*Bruce R. Hopkins' Nonprofit Law Library*
AU	*IRS Audits of Tax-Exempt Organizations*
FR	*The Law of Fundraising, Fifth Edition*
HC	*The Law of Tax-Exempt Healthcare Organizations, Fourth Edition*
EO	*The Law of Tax-Exempt Organizations, Eleventh Edition*
AR	*The New Form 990: Law, Policy, and Preparation*
GV	*Nonprofit Governance: Law, Practices & Trends*
CU	*Nonprofit Law for Colleges and Universities: Essential Questions and Answers for Officers, Directors and Advisors*
RE	*Nonprofit Law for Religious Organizations: Essential Questions and Answers*
PF	*Private Foundations: Tax Law and Compliance, Fourth Edition*
PG	*Planning Guide for the Law of Tax-Exempt Organizations: Strategies and Commentaries*
SM	*Starting and Managing a Nonprofit Organization: A Legal Guide, Sixth Edition*
AS	*The Tax Law of Associations*
CG	*The Tax Law of Charitable Giving, Fifth Edition*
UB	*The Tax Law of Unrelated Business for Nonprofit Organizations*
CL	*Tax-Exempt Organizations and Constitutional Law: Nonprofit Law as Shaped by the U.S. Supreme Court*

A

abatement

In general, the word "abatement" means an alleviation, lessening, mitigation, or reduction of something. More technically, the **IRS** has the authority to "abate" all of the **first-tier taxes** underlying the **private foundation** rules, other than those concerning **self-dealing**; the penalties underlying the **political expenditures** rules; the penalties underlying the **intermediate sanctions** rules; the penalties underlying the rules concerning **hospitals' failures**; and the penalties underlying the **donor-advised funds** rules. These abatable taxes are known as **qualified first tier taxes**. Additional rules apply in connection with the potential for abatement of **second-tier taxes** when there is a **correction** (**IRC** §§ 4961, 4962). [EO §§ 12.4, 21.10; PF §§ 1.10, 5.15(f), 6.7(d), 9.10(b), 13.1, 13.7].

absolute percentage limitation

The phrase "absolute percentage limitation" refers to a provision of a state **charitable solicitation act** (or local **law** equivalent) containing a percentage, which, when applied to the total expenses of a **charitable organization**, results in an amount of money that is less than the organization's **fundraising costs**. The organization's fundraising costs are consequently deemed, by operation of law, to be deemed **unreasonable**, thus preventing the organization form **soliciting charitable contributions** in the jurisdiction. The use of this type of percentage limitation was struck down by the U.S. Supreme Court as a violation of the **free speech rights** of the soliciting charitable organizations. [FR § 4.3; SM p. 152].

abuse of discretion

The phrase "abuse of discretion" arises in the context of court review of a decision by an **administrative agency** or an **appellate court** review of a decision by a **lower court**. Both government agencies and lower courts generally have broad discretion in formulating their decisions. When these fact-finders and decision-makers, however, arrive at a conclusion of **law** that is inconsistent with the **facts and circumstances** that were before the agency or lower court, the reviewing court can find an abuse of discretion and overrule that decision.

Bruce R. Hopkins' Nonprofit Law Dictionary, First Edition. Bruce R. Hopkins.
© 2015 Bruce R. Hopkins. Published 2015 by John Wiley & Sons, Inc.

A

abusive tax shelter

The phrase "abusive tax shelter" means a partnership or other entity, an investment plan or arrangement, or any other plan or arrangement, in connection with which a statement is made by a person with respect to the allowability of **a tax deduction** or a **tax credit,** the **excludability** of any income, or the securing of any other tax benefit by reason of holding an interest in the entity or participating in the plan or arrangement which the person knows or has reason to know is false or **fraudulent** as to any **material** matter. Abusive tax shelter also refers to instances in which there is **a gross valuation overstatement** as to any material **matter** (**IRC** § 6700(a)). [EO § 28.17(a)] (also **Tax shelter**).

accountable care organization

The Department of Health and Human Services has established a Medicare Shared Savings Program that promotes accountability for care of Medic are beneficiaries, improves the coordination of Medicare fee-for-service items and services, and encourages investment in infrastructure and redesigned care processes for high-quality and efficient health care service delivery. Groups of health care service providers, including **tax-exempt organizations**, and suppliers that have established a mechanism for shared **governance** and that meet criteria specified by the HHS are eligible to participate as "accountable care organizations," which essentially are networks designed to reduce health care costs, under the MSSP. [HC § 13.5; EO § 7.6(m); SM pp. 5, 230].

accountable plan

An "accountable plan" is a reimbursement or other expense allowance arrangement that satisfies the requirements of the **federal tax law** by including the elements of business connection, substantiation, and return of amounts that are in excess of substantiated expenses (**IRC** § 62(c)). Reimbursements that are not pursuant to an accountable plan are forms of **gross income** and likely are **automatic excess benefit transactions**. [GV § 6.3(r); CU Q 7.28; SM pp. 279–280; LI Q 6.28].

accountant

The word "accountant" is used to describe an individual whose profession is the preparation, inspection, and **auditing** of the books and records of other individuals and **organizations.** Most **nonprofit organizations** use the services of an accountant, both in the preparation of their books and records, including preparation of the appropriate **annual information return**, and in the audit phase. [AR § 7.2(d)(2); SM pp. 26, 27, 81, 241] (also **Certified public accountant; Generally accepted accounting principles; Public accountant**).

accounting method

The term "accounting method" is used to describe one of the methods by which a **for-profit organization** or a **nonprofit organization** keeps its books and records. **It** is by this method that the organization determines its **revenue** and **expenses** (both **deductible** and nondeductible) and thus its **net income,** as well as its **assets**, **liabilities**, and **fund** balance. One of the principal differences among accounting methods is the timing of **recognition** of an item of income and expense (**IRC** § 446). [AR § 7.2(d)(1); PF §§ 2.7(b), 6.5, 12.3(e), 15.4(a), 15.5, 15.6(a); CG §§ 2.10, 6.14; CU Q 17.54; UB § 11.5(a); SM p. 155] (also **Accrual method of accounting; Cash basis method of accounting**).

accounting period

An organization's "accounting period" is the period of time comprising twelve months, such as the calendar year or a **fiscal year**, that corresponds to its **tax year**. [CG § 2.9; UB § 11.5(b)] (also **Annual accounting period**).

accounting period, change of

A **tax-exempt organization** may decide to change its **accounting period**. This is done by a timely filing of its **annual information return** with the appropriate **IRS** Center for the **short period** (occasioned by the change in the period) for which the return is required, indicating on the return that a change of accounting period is being made. Generally, if an organization is not required to file an annual information return or a **tax return** reflecting **unrelated business income**, it is not necessary to otherwise notify the **IRS** that a change of accounting period is being made. If, however, an organization has previously changed its annual accounting period at any time within the ten calendar years ending with the calendar year that includes the beginning of the short period resulting from the change of an accounting period, and if the organization had a filing requirement at any time during the ten-year period, it must file an application for a change in accounting period (**Form 1128**) with the appropriate **IRS** Center. [PF § 10.4(c); CU Q 17.57; RE Q 12.1].

accounting standards

See **Generally accepted accounting principles**.

accreditation

The term "accreditation" refers to a form of **credentialing**, by which an **organization** reviews the **programs** and other activities of other organizations for a particular purpose and approves (or disapproves) the organization by using a set of criteria known to all of the organizations being reviewed. For example, an accrediting organization will periodically review **colleges** to determine whether they should continue to be accredited as **educational organizations** or to initially accredit such an **institution**. An organization may also accredit programs of other organizations. Most accrediting organizations are **tax-exempt organizations** and will be classified as **charitable organizations** where the organizations being accredited are charitable organizations, or where the programs being accredited are **operated** by organizations that are charitable organizations. [CU Q 5.45] (cf. **Certification**).

accrual, of income

See **Accrue**.

accrual method of accounting

The "accrual method of accounting" is a **method of accounting** by which items of **income** and **expense** are recognized at the time a **right** to receive income and/or an obligation for an expense arises (**IRC** § 446(c) (2)).

A **corporation** that reports its **taxable income** using the accrual method of accounting may, at its **election**, **deduct charitable contributions** paid within two and a half months after the close of its **tax year,** as long as the **board of directors** of the corporation authorized the making of the charitable contribution during the tax year and the charitable contribution is made after the close of the tax year of the corporation and within the two-and-a-half-month period (**IRC** § 170(a)(2)). [CG § 2.10] (also **Cash basis method of accounting**).

accrue

The word "accrue" generally means either to come into existence or to accumulate something. The term is used as part of the **federal tax law** that **excludes** from **gross income** forms of income accrued by a state or a **political subdivision** of a state, or the District of Columbia, where the income is derived from any public utility or the exercise of any **essential governmental function**, or forms of income that accrued to the government of any possession of the United States or any political subdivision of such a possession (**IRC** § 115). [EO § 19.21(b)].

accuracy-related penalty

The **federal tax law** contains several "accuracy-related penalties," many of them having direct applicability to **tax-exempt organizations** and **charitable** giving to them. These penalties apply to acts of **negligence** in the tax context (**IRC** § 6662(b)(1)), disregard of tax **rules** and **regulations** *(id),* a **substantial understatement** of **income tax** (**IRC** § 6662(b)(2)), a **substantial valuation misstatement** in the income tax setting (**IRC** § 6662(b)(3)), a **substantial estate tax valuation understatement** (**IRC** § 6662(b)(5)), and a **substantial gift tax valuation understatement** *(id).* The penalty is 20 percent of the portion of an underpayment of tax required to be shown on a **tax return** (**IRC** § 6662(a)). [CG § 10.14].

achievement award

A **private foundation grant** to an individual made in recognition of an achievement generally does not require prior approval of the **IRS**. The selection criteria must be fair and serve one or more **charitable** purposes. These grants do not require that the monetary award be expended for a particular purpose or that the recipient perform a specific action. [PF § 9.3(b)].

acknowledgement

For purposes of the **corporate sponsorship** rules, an "acknowledgment" may include exclusive sponsorship arrangements; logos and slogans that do not contain qualitative or comparative descriptions of a company's products, services, or facilities; a list of the company's locations, telephone numbers, or Internet address; value-neutral descriptions, including displays or visual depictions, of a company's product line or services; and a company's brand or trade names and product or services listings. (also **Contemporaneous written acknowledgement**).

acquisition indebtedness

The term "acquisition indebtedness" is used in the context of the rules pertaining to the computation of **unrelated debt-financed income**. Acquisition indebtedness, with respect to **debt-financed property,** means the unpaid amount of (1) the indebtedness incurred by an **organization** in acquiring or improving the property, (2) the indebtedness incurred before any acquisition or improvement of the property if the indebtedness would not have been incurred but for the acquisition or improvement, and (3) the indebtedness incurred after the acquisition or improvement of the property if the indebtedness would not have been incurred but for the acquisition or improvement and the incurring of the indebtedness was **reasonably** foreseeable at the time of the acquisition or improvement (**IRC** § 514(c)(1)).

There are some **exceptions** to these rules. One is that the phrase acquisition indebtedness does not include indebtedness that was necessarily incurred in the performance or exercise of an organization's **tax-exempt purpose** or function (**IRC** § 514(c)(4)). Another is that the term does not include an obligation to pay an **annuity** that (1) is the sole **consideration** issued in **exchange** for property if, at the time of the exchange, the **value** of the annuity is less than 90 percent of the value of the property received in the exchange, (2) is payable over the life of one individual who is living at the time the annuity is issued, or over the lives of two individuals living at that time, and (3) is payable under a **contract** that does not guarantee a minimum amount of payments or specify a maximum amount of payments and does not provide for any adjustment of the amount of the annuity payments by reference to the **income** received from the transferred property or any other property (**IRC** § 514(c)(5)). Further, the term generally does not include indebtedness incurred by a **qualified organization** in acquiring or improving any **real property** (**IRC** § 514(c)(9)). [UB § 5.4(a); EO § 24.9(c); HC § 24.21(b); PF §§ 6.2(f), 11.4(a)–(c); CG § 14.6; SM p. 175].

act

An "act" is the product of a **bill** or resolution passed by a legislature. It is **statutory law.** [EO § 22.2].

act of god

The phrase "act of God" is used to describe an incident involving natural forces that cannot be prevented by human beings, such as flooding, hurricanes, and tornadoes. Most **contracts,** including **insurance** policies, contain a provision relieving one or more parties from **liability** where damages are due to an act of God, rather than a direct act (or failure to act) on the part of a party to the **agreement**.

action

The word "action" is a technical term for a lawsuit. It is, thus, a proceeding in a court where one **person** has instituted litigation against another person for something done or not done, or to protect a **right**. The word is used in the sense of one person bringing an "action" against another. This term can also be used in connection with an **administrative proceeding**.

A

The word is also used in connection with the **expenditure test**. In defining the word "**legislation**," the test uses the word "action." That use defines the term "action" as being limited to the introduction, amendment, enactment, defeat, or repeal of **acts**, **bills**, resolutions, or similar items (**IRC § 4911(c)(3)**). [EO § 22.2(b)] (also **Actionable; Cause of action**).

action on decision

An "Action on Decision" is a document prepared by the **IRS** that contains an analysis of a court opinion and the decision by the Office of Chief Counsel as to the future steps the **IRS** should take with respect to it, such as opting to appeal the decision.

action organization

An **organization** is an "action organization" if a **substantial** part of its activities involves attempting to **influence legislation** by **propaganda** or otherwise. Also, an organization is an action organization if it participates or intervenes, **directly or indirectly,** in any **political campaign** on behalf of or in opposition to any **candidate** for **public office**. Further, an organization is an action organization if it has these characteristics: (1) its main or **primary** objective or objectives (as distinguished from its **incidental** or secondary objectives) may be attained only by legislation or a defeat of proposed legislation, and (2) it advocates or campaigns for the attainment of these primary objectives as distinguished from engaging in **nonpartisan analysis, study, or research** and making the results of those nonpartisan activities available to the public. In determining whether an organization has these characteristics, ail of the surrounding **facts and circumstances**, including the **articles of organization** and all activities of the organization, are considered. [EO §§ 4.5(b), 22.3(c)(i), 23.1; HC §§ 7.1(b), 7.4(b), (f); AR § 1.6(d); CU Q 8.5, Q 9.4; SM pp. 186, 198; LI Q 7.5, Q 8.4].

actionable

A matter is "actionable" when it involves one or more legitimate bases for a lawsuit (an **action**).

active conduct

The term "active conduct" is used to describe a situation in which a **tax-exempt organization** is engaged in the **operation** of a **program**, as contrasted with the funding of a program that is operated by another organization. An illustration of this is the "active conduct" requirement that is part of the **income test** that a **private operating foundation** must meet. Under that test, funds must be expended by the private operating foundation itself (the active conduct), rather than by or through one or more **grantee** organizations. The rules concerning **medical research organizations** contain a requirement that these entities be directly engaged in the continuous active conduct of **medical research** in conjunction with a **hospital**. [EO § 7.6(d); HC § 5.1(b); PF § 3.1(d)] (also **Significant involvement**).

activist organization

The term "activist organization" is used to describe an **organization** that engages in advocacy activities, such as demonstrations, boycotts, strikes, picketing, and litigation, and is not an **action organization**. [EO § 23.2(f)].

activities, bundle of

In many ways, a **nonprofit organization** can be regarded as a bundle of activities. Some of these activities are **program**, some are administration or management, and some are **fundraising**. Other activities may be **lobbying** or **political campaign activities** (which may be program), or **unrelated business** activities.

Essentially, when the **IRS audits** a **tax-exempt organization**, it is reviewing each of the activities in this bundle. The law in this regard is particularly developed in the unrelated business income context. Thus, the law states that an activity does not lose identity as a **trade or business** merely because it is carried on within a larger aggregate of similar activities or within a larger complex of other endeavors that may, or may not, be related to the **exempt purposes** of the organization (**IRC** § 513(c)). This is known as the **fragmentation rule**.

With the authority of this rule, the **IRS** is empowered to fragment a tax-exempt organization's operation, administered as an integrated whole, into its component parts in search of an unrelated trade or business or other disqualifying activity. [EO § 24.2(f); UB § 2.3; SM p. 172] (also **Functional accounting**).

activities conducted outside the United States

The phrase "activities conducted outside the United States," for purposes of **Form 990**, Schedule F, include grantmaking, other **program** services, **fundraising**, the conduct of **unrelated trade or business**, **program-related investments**, other investments, or maintaining offices, **employees**, or **agents** in particular regions outside the U.S. [AR Chap. 13].

activities, measurement of

As a consequence of the controversy concerning the permissible extent of **political campaign activities** that may be undertaken by **tax-exempt social welfare organizations**, there is interest in the methodology (or methodologies) to be used in measuring the activities of these organizations. This quantification needs to be developed because, in addition to defining permissible (and impermissible) political campaign activity, the federal tax law must stipulate how much of this activity is allowable. This matter goes beyond the confines of political campaign activity and the activities of exempt social welfare organizations, however, and will encompass all activities of all **tax-exempt organizations**.

The current approach of the **IRS** in this regard is to allocate expenditures to an exempt organization's various functions, thereby assigning a percentage of these expenditures to each function. Sometimes, the agency also ascribes percentages on the basis of time expended by an organization's **directors**, **trustees**, **officers**, **employees**, **volunteers**, and **agents**. A third approach used by the **IRS** is to analyze the way in which the organization describes itself in its dealings with the **public**. (also **Primary purpose text**).

activities test

Increasingly, the **IRS** is applying an "activities test" to determine whether a **nonprofit organization** qualifies for **tax exemption** in accordance with the **federal tax law**. This test is usually applied in a **noncharitable** context. As the test's name implies, it is used to ascertain whether an organization is sufficiently performing activities in conformity with the prescription of the particular exemption. (also **Operational test**; **Primary purpose test**).

actual controversy

One of the requirements for bringing an **action** in accordance with the **declaratory judgment** rules (concerning the **tax** status of **charitable organizations** and **farmers' cooperatives**) is that the case must involve an "actual controversy" (**IRC § 7428**). This means that there must be a **bona fide** issue of law between the organization and the **IRS** and that the organization is in existence and prepared to litigate the issue or issues between the parties. [EO § 27.6(b)(i)].

actuarial tables

The U.S. Department of the Treasury prepares "actuarial tables" for a variety of uses, including the determination of the **value** of **income interests** and **remainder interests** for purposes of computing **charitable contribution deductions**. (**IRC § 7520(a)(1)**) These tables must be prepared using the most recent mortality experience available (**IRC § 7520(c)(3)**). The tables must be revised at least once every ten years to take into account the most recent mortality experience available as of the time of the revision (*id.*). In this setting, these tables are often termed "valuation tables." They reflect the use of certain **interest** rates and **adjusted payout rates**. [CG §§ 11.3, 11.4].

actuary

An "actuary" is an individual who computes elements, such as risks and rates, according to probabilities on the basis of certain facts. Actuaries prepare **actuarial tables** (sometimes termed "experience tables") to determine statistical items such as **insurance** rates, pension rates, and premiums. In the context of **planned giving**, actuaries prepare tables of **factors**, used to determine the **charitable contribution deduction**; these tables are prepared by actuaries in the U.S. Department of the Treasury (**IRC § 7520(a)(1)**). [CG §§ 11.3, 11.4].

ad hoc

"Ad hoc" is a Latin term meaning "for a particular purpose." It is generally used in reference to an **ad hoc committee**.

ad hoc committee

The term "ad hoc committee" is used to describe a **committee**, such as one established by a **nonprofit organization**, formed to function only for a specific purpose and often only for a specific time (as opposed to a **standing committee**).

addition to tax

Some **penalties** in the **federal tax law** that are particularly relevant to **tax-exempt organizations** and **charitable** giving to them are framed as "additions to tax." Thus, there is an **addition to tax** for a failure to timely file a **tax return** (for example, a **Form 990-T**) (**IRC § 6651(a)(1)**).

This addition to tax is 5 percent of the amount of the tax due if the failure is for not more than one month, with an additional 5 percent for each additional month or fraction of a month during which the failure continues, not exceeding 25 percent in the aggregate.

There is an addition to tax for a failure to timely pay a tax shown due on a tax return (**IRC** § 6651(a)(2)). This addition to tax is 0.5 percent of the amount of the tax due if the failure is for not more than one month, with an additional 0.5 percent for each additional month or fraction of a month during which the failure continues, not exceeding 25 percent in the aggregate.

There also is an addition to tax for a failure to timely pay any amount in respect of any tax required to be shown on a tax return that is not shown (**IRC** § 6651(a)(3)). This addition to tax is 0.5 percent of the amount of the tax due if the failure is for not more than one month, with an additional 0.5 percent for each additional month or fraction of a month during which the failure continues, not exceeding 25 percent in the aggregate.

These additions to tax of 0.5 percent may be increased to 1 percent where the failure continues after notice and demand for payment is given by the **IRS** (**IRC** § 6651(d)). They are not to be applied, however, in instances where the failure is due to **reasonable cause** and not due to **willful neglect**.

There are explicit penalties imposed on tax-exempt organizations and/or their **managers** that are enumerated in the **Internal Revenue Code** in the portion referencing additions to tax. These are the penalties for failure to file an annual information return (**IRC** §§ 6652(c)(1)(A) and (B)), for failure to provide public access to an **annual information return** (**IRC** § 6652(c)(1)(C)), failure to provide public access to an **application for recognition of exemption** (**IRC** § 6652(c)(1)(D)), failure by certain **trusts** to file an **information return** (**IRC** §§ 6652(c)(2)(A) and (B)), failure to file an information return reflecting a **liquidation, dissolution, termination,** or **substantial contraction** of a tax-exempt organization (*id.*), failure by an **estate** or trust to pay **estimated income taxes** (**IRC** § 6654(1)), failure by a tax-exempt organization to pay estimated **unrelated business income taxes** (**IRC** § 6655(g)(3)), and failure by a **private foundation** to pay estimated **net investment income taxes** (*id.*).

additional hospital exemption requirements

Congress, as part of enactment of the **Pension Protection and Affordable Care Act**, enacted an array of additional requirements for eligibility for **tax-exempt status**, as **charitable** entities, for **hospital organizations**. These requirements pertain to **community health needs assessments, financial assistance policies, limitations on charges,** and **billings and collections** (**IRC** § 501(r)). [HC § 26.10; EO § 7.6(b)].

additional tax

The term "additional tax" is synonymous with the term **"second-tier tax,"** as these taxes are applied in the **private foundation, black lung benefits trust, intermediate sanctions,** and **political expenditures** settings (**IRC** §§ 4941(b), 4942(b), 4943(b), 4944(b), 4945(b), 4951, 4952, 4955(b), 4958(b)). [EO §§ 12.4, 18.5, 21.10, 23.3; PF §§ 5.15(d), 6.7(c), 7.6, 8.5, 9.10(c); HC § 4.9(a)(vi); SM pp. 90–91].

A

adjunct theory

The term "adjunct theory" means, in essence, that an **organization** that is an adjunct of another organization takes on the **tax law** characteristics of the other entity. Under this theory, an organization can be **tax-exempt** because it bears a close and intimate relationship to another organization that is tax-exempt. This doctrine, however, does not have broad application, in that it cannot be used to sidestep the prerequisites for tax exemption that an organization must meet under the **statutory** rules. [EO § 7.13(b)].

adjusted basis

The phrase "adjusted basis" is used to define a **basis** in a **property** that has been adjusted to reflect true economic **gain** or **loss** in the **disposition** of the property. (**IRC** § 1011) Generally, basis is adjusted for **expenditures**, receipts, losses, or other items properly chargeable to a capital account (other than for certain **taxes** (**IRC** § 266) or other carrying charges and circulation expenditures (**IRC** § 173)) (**IRC** § 1016). Basis is also adjusted for the following items, to the extent the allowable items resulted in a reduction of tax: exhaustion, wear and tear, obsolescence, **amortization,** and **depletion.** [CG § 2.14(b)].

adjusted gross income

The term "adjusted gross income" means **gross income** less certain **expenses,** such as alimony payments, certain moving expenses, and certain **business** expenses (**IRC** § 62(a)). Thus, adjusted gross income is gross income that is adjusted to take into account certain costs of acquiring or transferring income. The reason for the concept of adjusted gross income is to provide a fair basis for the allowance of noneconomic personal expense **deductions.** Thus, adjusted gross income is gross income after adjusting for the economic costs of generating revenue to the **taxpayer.** [CG § 2.4] (also **Contribution base**).

adjusted net income

For purposes of the rules concerning **mandatory payout** by **private foundations,** the term "adjusted net income" means the excess (if any) of (1) the private foundation's gross income for the **tax year** (determined using certain income **modifications**) over (2) the sum of the **deductions** (determined using certain **deduction modifications**) that would be allowed to a taxable **corporation** for the tax year (**IRC** §§ 4942(f)(1), 4942(j)(3)(A)(i)). This term is also used in connection with the **income test** with respect to **private operating foundations** and the payout requirement for **Type III non-functionally integrated supporting organizations.** [PF §§ 3.1(d), 12.1(b), 15.7(g)].

adjusted payout rate

The term "adjusted payout rate" is used in the context of **charitable remainder trusts** to mean adjustments in the factors used to calculate the **charitable contribution deduction** where there is a variation in the payout sequence other than an **income interest** payment at the end of each tax year or, in the case of a **charitable remainder unitrust,** where there is a valuation of **trust assets** on a day other than the day at the end of the year. [CG § 12.12].

administration, power of

See **Power of administration**.

administrative

The term "administrative" is derived from the words "administer" and "administration." The term is used in government parlance to describe the function of an **entity** that has the task of implementing (administering) a body of **statutory law**. A U.S. Supreme Court justice wrote that, "[a]lthough modern administrative agencies fit most comfortably within the Executive Branch, as a practical matter they exercise legislative power, by promulgating **regulations** with the force of law; executive power, by policing compliance with those regulations; and judicial power, by adjudicating enforcement actions and imposing sanctions on those found to have violated their rules." (also **Administrative agency**).

administrative agency

An "administrative agency" is a unit of government that has some form of regulatory and/or **rule**-making authority. For example, the **IRS** is an administrative agency, as are the **Federal Election Commission** and the U.S. Postal Service. A U.S. Supreme Court justice wrote that, "[a]lthough modern administrative agencies fit most comfortably within the Executive Branch, as a practical matter they exercise legislative power, by promulgating **regulations** with the force of law; executive power, by policing compliance with those regulations; and judicial power, by adjudicating enforcement actions and imposing sanctions on those found to have violated their rules." [FR §§ 3.1(k), 4.6].

administrative allowance

The term "administrative allowance" is used to define the amount of money a **tax-exempt organization** is to receive from an **insurance** company or broker for its efforts in assisting with the marketing and sale of insurance products to its **members**. This type of payment is likely to constitute **unrelated business income,** unless it can be structured as a **royalty**. [UB § 9.4(b); EO §§ 24.5(e)(ii), 25.1(g)].

administrative hearing

An "administrative hearing" is a type of **administrative proceeding**, in which facts are adduced, such as by the testimony of witnesses, usually in the context of development of a **rule** or **regulation**.

administrative law

The body of **law** known as "administrative law" is law created by an **administrative agency** as the result of the promulgation of **regulations**, **rules**, forms, and the instructions to forms, and

A

the issuance of decisions. For example, the **IRS** creates administrative law when it promulgates regulations, **revenue rulings**, **revenue procedures**, and the like.

administrative proceeding

An "administrative proceeding" is a proceeding conducted by an **administrative agency.** In the proceeding, the agency must comport with its own **rules** and **regulations,** as well as applicable **statutory law** and **constitutional law.** For example, when the **IRS** conducts a hearing on a proposed regulation or rule, or in connection with a specific issue, the hearing is an administrative proceeding.

administrative record

In a **declaratory judgment** case, concerning the **tax** status of a **charitable organization** or a **farmers' cooperative**, the court involved generally will confine its review of the case to the scope of facts contained in the "administrative record." That is, the court usually will not conduct a trial at which new evidence may be presented. This limitation is not followed, however, where the matter concerns the revocation of the **tax-exempt status** of an organization. The administrative record is that body of evidence consisting of facts submitted by the organization involved and developed by the **IRS**; third parties may not submit material for the administrative record. [EO § 27.6(b)(iv)].

administrative remedy

The concept of "administrative remedies" is the range of forms of relief (remedies) available to a **person** when that person is involved in a proceeding before an **administrative agency.** Before taking the particular matter into court, the person must **exhaust** his, her, or its administrative remedies. [EO § 27.6(b)(ii)].

administrative remedies, exhaustion of

See **Exhaustion of remedies**.

administrator

An "administrator" is an individual appointed by a court to resolve the affairs of another individual who died **intestate**.

advance

The **federal tax law** uses the word "advance" as a synonym for the word "promote" (as in **promotion of health** and **promotion of social welfare),** principally to describe categories of **charitable organizations.** The term thus means "to move forward" or "to progress." [EO §§ 7.6, 7.8-7.11; SM p. 34].

advance approval of grants

The **federal tax law** requires a **private foundation**, when it is planning a **program** of **grants** to individuals for travel, study, or similar purposes, to obtain from the **IRS** advance approval of its grant-making procedures (**IRC** § 4945(g)). To secure this approval, a private foundation must demonstrate, to the satisfaction of the **IRS**, that (1) its grant procedure includes an objective and nondiscriminatory selection process, (2) the procedure is **reasonably** calculated to result in performance by the **grantees** of the activities that the grants are intended to finance, and (3) the private foundation plans to obtain reports to determine whether the grantees have performed the activities that the grants are intended to finance. No single procedure or set of procedures is required. Procedures may vary, depending upon factors such as the size of the private foundation, the amount and purpose of the grants, and whether one or more recipients are involved. Generally, a private foundation that has filed its procedures with the **IRS** can implement them within forty-five days, unless the **IRS** has acted **adversely** in the interim. [PF § 9.3(a)].

advance ruling

When a **private foundation** seeks to **terminate** its **private foundation status** on the ground that it will be operating as a **publicly supported charity,** the organization must receive an advance ruling and meet the requirements of the publicly supported charity rules for an advance ruling period of sixty months. [PF § 13.4].

advancement organizations

Organizations that are **tax-exempt** because they are **charitable** entities include those that **advance education**, **advance science**, and **advance religion**. [EO §§ 7.8-7.10; SM p. 34].

advantages of tax exemption

See **Tax exemption, advantages of.**

adverse

The **IRS** issues **determination letters** and **rulings.** When these pronouncements provide the **person** requesting them with a response that the person did not want, the pronouncements are said to be "adverse." (also **Favorable**).

adverse determination

A **nonprofit organization** may make **application** to the **IRS** for **recognition** of its **tax-exempt status**. If the **IRS** concludes that the organization qualifies for **tax exemption**, it will issue a **favorable determination letter** or **ruling**. If, however, the **IRS** decides to the contrary, it will issue an "adverse determination," perhaps triggering the process of **administrative** appeals and **litigation**. [EO § 27.1].

adverse party

For purposes of the **grantor trust** rules, an "adverse party" is a **person** having a **substantial beneficial interest** in a trust that would be **adversely** affected by the exercise or nonexercise of the **power** which he, she, or it possesses with respect to the trust (**IRC** § 672(a)). [CG § 3.8].

A

adverse possession

The term "adverse possession" means a method of acquisition of **title** to an item of **property** by possession of it for a period of time, set by **statute**, and under certain other conditions. (also **Usucaption**).

advertising

As to **law** in the **nonprofit organization** context, the most comprehensive definition as to what constitutes "advertising" is found in the **corporate sponsorship** rules. There, the term means any message or other programming material that is broadcast or otherwise transmitted, published, displayed, or distributed, and that promotes or markets a **trade or business**, or any service, facility, or product. Advertising includes messages containing qualitative or comparative language, price information, or other indications of savings or value, an endorsement, or an inducement to purchase, sell, or use any company, service, facility, or product. Also, any **communication** that is a **business listing** is likely to be regarded as "advertising." The **net income** from advertising by a **tax-exempt organization** is generally subject to tax as **unrelated business income**. Some forms of "advertising" are acts of **fundraising**. [UB §§ 6.5(a), 6.5(b); EO §§ 24.5(h), 24.6; HC § 24.17; AS § 5.8; CG § 3.1(g); SM pp. 172, 286] (also **Acknowledgment**).

advertising income

Net income derived by a **tax-exempt organization** from the sale of **advertising** is, almost always, **taxable** as a form of **unrelated business income** (IRC § 513(c)). The **federal income tax regulations** contain detailed rules for calculation and reporting of this type of income. It is the view of the **IRS** that all forms of advertising income are taxable; that is, this view holds that it is not possible for a tax-exempt organization to have **related income** from advertising. [EO § 24.5(h); UB § 6.5].

advice of counsel

The term "advice of counsel" means advice provided by a **lawyer**, usually in writing, preceded by a full disclosure of the factual situation. (also **Reasoned written legal opinion**).

advisory committee

An "advisory committee" is a group of individuals who provide policy or technical input in connection with the programs of a **tax-exempt organization**. This committee is, however, separate from the organization's **governing body** and thus does not have a formal role in the organization's **governance**. [SM p. 18].

advisory letter

The **IRS** has the authority to, when concluding its examination of a **tax-exempt organization**, issue an "advisory letter" concerning one or more aspects of the organization's operations where there may be endangerment of **exempt status** or other compliance issues. [AU §§ 5.32(a), 5.33(b)].

advisory opinion

An "advisory opinion" is an interpretation of the **federal** election **laws** issued by the **Federal Election Commission**.

advocacy

"Advocacy" is active espousal of a position, a point of view, or a course of action. It can include **lobbying**, **political campaign activity**, demonstrations, boycotts, **litigation**, and various forms of **programmatic advocacy**. [EO Chaps. 22, 23; UB § 9.7(d); PG Chap. 5, p. 342; FR § 4.3(e)].

advocacy communications or research materials

The **expenditure test** contains rules concerning situations where expenses for what are initially nonlobbying **communications** can subsequently be characterized as **grass-roots lobbying** expenditures where the materials or other communications are later used in a lobbying effort. For this result to occur, the materials must be "advocacy communications or research materials." These materials are any communications or materials that both refer to and reflect a view on **specific legislation** but that do not, in their initial format, contain a direct encouragement for recipients to take action with respect to **legislation**. Where these communications or materials are subsequently accompanied by a direct encouragement for recipients to take action with respect to legislation, the communications or materials themselves are treated as grass-roots lobbying communications unless the **primary** purpose of the **organization** in undertaking or preparing the communications or materials was not for use in lobbying. In the absence of this primary purpose, all **expenses** of preparing and distributing the communications or materials will be treated as **grass-roots expenditures**; in the case of subsequent distribution of the materials by another organization, however, the characterization of expenditures as grass-roots lobbying expenditures under this rule applies only to expenditures paid less than six months before the first use of the communications or materials with a direct encouragement to action. [EO § 23.9; SM p. 203].

advocacy organizations

An "advocacy organization" is an **entity** that has **advocacy** as its **primary purpose**. An **organization** can be an advocacy organization without being an **action organization**. [EO Chaps. 17, 22, 23, § 13.3].

affiant

An "affiant" is an individual who makes and executes an **affidavit**.

affidavit

The term "affidavit" means a written legal document that contains a statement of an individual, executed under oath and attested to by a notary public or some other authorized individual. An affidavit may be used in **litigation** or in an **administrative proceeding** in lieu of testimony.

affiliate

The word "affiliate" means a close connection or close association; it basically is synonymous with "associate" or "auxiliary." The term is often used to describe a class of **members** of an **organization** that are not "voting members" (or otherwise not "regular" members), but nonetheless have some interest in the purposes and programs of the organization. The term is also used to describe a relationship between two or more organizations; an affiliation usually is a looser arrangement than that evidenced by a **parent** and **subsidiary** relationship or that of organizations in a **joint venture**. [HC § 34.3(e)] (also **Affiliated group**; **Affiliated organization**).

affiliated group

The term "affiliated group" is used in conjunction with the **expenditure test**. Generally, under this test, two organizations are deemed "affiliated" where one organization is bound by decisions of the other on legislative issues pursuant to its **governing instrument**, or where the governing board of one organization includes enough representatives of the other to cause or prevent action on legislative issues by the first organization (**IRC** § 4911(1)(2)). Where a number of organizations are affiliated, even in **chain fashion**, all of them are treated as one group of affiliated organizations. If, however, a group of autonomous organizations controls an organization, but no one organization in the controlling group alone can control that organization, the organizations are not considered an affiliated group by reason of the second of these definitions (**IRC** § 4911(f)(1)). [AR §§ 9.1(e), 9.2(b); EO § 22.3(d)(viii); HC § 7.1(f)] (also **Interlocking directorate**).

affiliated organization

An **organization** is "affiliated" with another organization if the two entities are related in some manner. The concept of affiliation is broader than that of **control**, although controlled organizations are obviously affiliated. The **law** of **tax-exempt organizations** contains several instances of situations involving affiliated entities, including organizations that are part of a **group** for purposes of tax exemption, **supporting organizations** in relation to one or more **supported organizations**, related organizations such as a **trade association** and a related **foundation**, a national organization with affiliated organizations that all participate as **beneficiaries** of a **pooled income fund**, and organizations that are members of an **affiliated group**, as that term is used as part of the **expenditure test** rules. [AR §§ 7.2(a)(1), 7.2(b)(19), 15.2(c), (i)(7); EO § 22.2(d)(vii), Chaps. 28–30; CU Q 1.42, Q 1.43, Q 2.66, Q 4.6; SM pp. 190–191 (also **Association-related foundation**; **Group exemption**).

affiliated organization, policy as to

The **IRS**, on the **Form 990**, suggests that the filing organization, if it has one or more **affiliated organizations**, have a policy as to standardization of activities and practices, given the entities' common **mission** and goals, and the public perception that the organizations are all part of one entity. [GV §§ 4.1(i), 6.3(h); AR §§ 5.1(i)(4), 5.2(a)(8)].

affinity

The word "affinity" means an inherent likeness or agreement between things; when individuals are involved, it refers to a group with common interests or objectives (affinity groups). Many **clubs,** such as those of individuals interested in a particular hobby, are affinity groups. **Organizations** of individuals with a common heritage, base of employment, or some other common experience (such as alumni **associations**) are affinity groups.

affinity card

An "affinity card" is a credit or debit card issued only to members of an **affinity** group; the card bears the **organization's** name, logo, and/or some other unifying symbol. Many **nonprofit organizations** use these cards as **fundraising** opportunities; the **for-profit organization** that is receiving a profit from the use of the card by the consumers who are **members** of the affinity group agrees to pay a percentage of its profit to the nonprofit organization. If this arrangement is properly structured, these payments constitute **royalties,** so that the income the nonprofit organization receives from its affinity card program is not taxable as **unrelated business income**. If, however, the organization is significantly involved in promotion of the program, the consequence may be taxation of the revenue. [EO § 25.1(g); FR §§ 5.7(b)(vi), 5.18(d); SM p. 178].

affinity group

See **Affinity**.

affirmative action

The concept of "affirmative action" is the taking of positive ("affirmative") steps and measures to eradicate the results of previous forms of **discrimination**; it is the basis for programs that benefit individuals in a particular class (defined using factors such as race or gender) because of past discrimination against other individuals in the same class. Affirmative action is based on the **constitutional law** principle of **equal protection**. The U.S. Supreme Court has held that, while discrimination generally is constitutionally impermissible, it may be engaged in when a legitimate state interest is being pursued and short of any violation of the **Fourteenth Amendment**.

It was in this spirit that the law evolved to the point where a **private educational institution** that has racially discriminatory policies cannot qualify for **tax-exempt status** or **charitable donee status** under the **federal tax law** as a **charitable organization.** While that approach has not been completely taken with respect to other forms of discrimination, the law is developing a comparable **federal public policy** against support for institutions that engage in gender-based discrimination. This body of law to date has concerned equal access to places of public accommodation (defined to include some **nonprofit membership organizations**) and organizations' **free speech** rights and **right of** association. [EO § 6.2(e); CL § 1.8(d)].

agency

The word "agency" is used to define a relationship between two **persons**: a **principal** and an **agent**. The word also includes a segment of a **governmental unit**. [EO § 24.3(b); PF § 15.5(d)] (also **Bureau; Bureau or similar agency**).

agent

An agent is a **person** who acts on behalf of, and under the authority of, a **principal**. The acts of an agent are considered those of the principal and thus are attributed to the principal. For example, a court has held that, in determining whether an **unrelated business** is **regularly carried on**, the functions of a service provider with which a **tax-exempt organization** has **contracted** may be attributed to the **exempt organization** on the ground that the service provider was acting as an agent of the organization. Likewise, **charitable contributions** may be made by means of an agent. [EO § 24.3(b); FR § 5.7(b)(v); CG §§ 3.2, 10.2].

agreed case

An "agreed case" is a circumstance where an **IRS** examination has closed, with the **tax-exempt organization** involved agreeing to the **IRS**'s position as to a change in **exempt status, public charity** status, and/or **tax liability**, with the exempt organization signing the appropriate waiver and acceptance forms. [AU §§ 5.32(a), 5.33(g), (i)] (cf. **Partially agreed case, Excepted agreed case, Unagreed case**).

agreement

An "agreement" essentially is the same as a **contract**, although it may reflect an arrangement between **persons** that is less formal than a contract.

aggregate principle

In accordance with the "aggregate principle," the activities of a **partnership** or other form of **joint venture** are considered to be the activities of the partners or members of the venture. Thus, the operations of a joint venture that includes a **tax-exempt organization** are attributed to the exempt organization when it is being evaluated pursuant to the **operational test**. This can be a harsh and undesirable outcome, particularly where the exempt organization lacks **control** over and/or has a small interest in the venture. The **IRS** is signaling, by means of developments in the **accountable care organization** context, that it may not apply the principle if the nonexempt activities that would otherwise be attributed are **insubstantial**. [EO § 4.5(c); UB § 8.11; CU Q 15.58; HC § 16.1(a); SM p. 231].

aggregate tax benefit

For purposes of the **termination tax,** the phrase "aggregate tax benefit" means the total tax benefits that have resulted from the **charitable status of a private foundation** (IRC § 507(d)(1)). These benefits are the sum of three items. One is the aggregate increases in **tax** that would have been imposed with respect to all **substantial contributors** to the private foundation if **deductions** for all **contributions** made by these contributors to the private foundation after February 28, 1913, had been disallowed. Another is the aggregate increases in tax that would have been imposed with respect to the **income** of the private foundation for **tax years** beginning alter December 31, 1912, if it had not been a **tax-exempt organization** and, in the case of **a trust,** if its deductions had been limited to 20 percent of the **taxable income** of the trust. The third is **interest** on these increases in tax from the first date on which each increase would have been due and payable to the date on which the **organization** ceases to be a private foundation. [PF § 13.6].

aggregation rule

The "aggregation rule" arises in the context of the general requirement that an **information return** be filed by a **charitable organization** when it **disposes** of **charitable deduction property** within three years of the date of the **gift** (**IRC** § 6050L). This reporting obligation is not required with respect to an item of charitable deduction property disposed of by **sale** if the **appraisal summary** signed by the **donee** with respect to the item contains, at the time of the donee's signature, a statement signed by the **donor** that the **appraised value** of the item does not exceed five hundred dollars. The aggregation rule requires that items that form a set (for example, a collection of books written by the same author, components of a stereo system, or a group of place settings of a pattern of silverware) must be considered one item. Nonpublicly traded securities are also treated as one item. [CG § 24.10].

agricultural organization

The term "agricultural organization" means an **entity** that is **organized** and **operated primarily** in activities related to **agriculture**. This type of organization may qualify for **tax-exempt status** pursuant to the **federal income tax** rules (**IRC** § 501(a), by reason of **IRC** § 501(c)(5)). [EO § 16.2; AS § 1.6(d); UB § 9.5; AU § 7.1(f); PF § 15.9; SM pp. 41, 55].

agriculture

For purposes of the **federal tax law** concerning **tax exemption** for **agricultural organizations,** the term "agriculture" includes the art or science of cultivating land, harvesting crops or aquatic resources, or raising livestock (**IRC** § 501(g)). A nearly parallel definition in the postal laws defines the word "agriculture" as including the art or science of cultivating land, harvesting crops or marine resources, or raising livestock. (39 U.S.C. § 3626(d)).

This distinction in the two definitions, where one uses the term "aquatic," while the other uses the term "marine," has led to a bit of an anomaly. The word "aquatic" means "of or pertaining to water"; the word "marine" means "of or pertaining to the sea." Thus, an organization engaged in or associated with the harvesting of only fresh (non-salt) waters will acquire classification as an agricultural organization for federal tax purposes but (if these definitions are taken literally) will fail to be categorized as an agricultural organization for postal law purposes (that is. it will be ineligible for preferential postal rates). The postal law is unclear as to the proper classification of an organization that harvests both fresh and salt waters. [EO § 16.2].

aiding and abetting

The **federal income tax law** includes a **penalty** for "aiding and abetting" an **understatement of** tax **liability**. This penalty is imposed upon a **person** who (1) aids or assists in, procures, or

A

advises with respect to, the preparation or presentation of any portion of a **return**, **affidavit**, claim, or other document, (2) knows or has reason to believe that the portion will be used in connection with any **material** matter arising under that body of law, and (3) knows that the portion (if used) would result in an understatement of the liability for tax of another person (**IRC § 6701(a)**). This penalty may be applied in the context of aiding and abetting a person to **overvalue** an item of **property** for purposes of computing a **charitable contribution deduction.** [CG § 10.14(d)].

allocation

In the law concerning **nonprofit organizations,** the principal use of the term "allocation" is in the context of allocating an **expense** to two or more categories of outlays. The term, however, can be used in other senses, such as an allocation of time by an individual to two or more organizations and allocation of **basis** in **property** to a **gift** portion and to a **sale** portion (as is done in the instance of a **bargain sale**). (also **Allocation of basis**; **Allocation of expenses**).

allocation of basis

In the instance of a **bargain sale,** there must be allocated to the **contributed** portion of the **property** involved the portion of the **adjusted basis** of the entire property that bears the same ratio to the total adjusted basis as the **fair market value** of the contributed property bears to the fair market value of the entire property. In other words, in the case or a bargain sale, the basis in the property involved must be allocated to the gift portion and the sales portion of the property. [CG § 9.19(b)].

allocation of expenses

A single **expense** by a **nonprofit organization** can relate to two or more functions of the organization, in which case the expense may be **allocated** to those functions for purposes of determining **net income** (or **net expenses**) of each function. For example, in the case of a **charitable organization,** an expense may be allocable part to **program** and part to **fundraising.** As another example, an expense may be allocable part to program and part to **lobbying.** Essentially, the **law** on this point is that an allocation of expenses must be **reasonable** and consistent. In certain instances, however, such as a **nonmembership lobbying communication** that has a **nonlobbying purpose,** the law precludes an allocation. When an allocation is made, the nature of the allocation must be reflected on the organization's **annual information return.** Further, expenses are often allocated in computing net income from a **related activity** of a **tax-exempt organization** and from an **unrelated business** conducted by the organization, where a facility or other **property** is used in both functions. It is the view of the **IRS** that the allocation must be made on the basis of a twenty-four-hour period (including the period of no use), rather than on the basis of actual use.

The **expenditure test** contains two allocation of expense rules for lobbying **communications** that have a lobbying and a nonlobbying purpose. One rule requires that the allocation be reasonable. This rule applies to an **electing public charity's** communications primarily with its **members**. More than one half of the recipients of the communication must be members of the electing public charity for this rule to apply. The other allocation rule is for nonmember communications. Where a nonmembership lobbying communication also has a nonlobbying purpose, an organization must include as lobbying expenditures all costs attributable to those parts of the communication that are on the "same specific subject" as the lobbying message. [EO §§ 22.3(d)(ii), 24.11; HC § 18.4(b); PF §§ 10.4, 12.1(c); AU § 5.19(g)] (also **Functional method of accounting**).

allocations of income and deductions among taxpayers

The **IRS** has broad authority to undo a **taxpayer's tax** planning by readjusting the facts to state and reflect more correctly the taxpayer's tax position. This authority empowers the **IRS** to closely scrutinize transactions between mutually **controlled parties**. This process is known as "allocation" (or **reallocation**) of items of **income, deductions**, and **credits**; it is done where necessary to prevent the evasion of taxes or to ensure the clear reflection of each taxpayer's income (**IRC § 482**). The **IRS** can use this authority to reallocate, in the context of **charitable contributions,** in order to adjust (reduce) a claimed **charitable contribution deduction**. Further, this rule is utilized in the context of determining whether payments to **controlling organizations** are **reasonable**, for purposes of a special rule by which these payments may not be treated as **unrelated business income** (**IRC § 512(b)(13)(E)**). [EO §§ 29.6, 30.7(d); CG § 10.10] (also **Reallocation of charitable contribution deduction, by IRS**).

allowable distribution period

The phrase "allowable distribution period" is used in the **federal tax law** concerning **mandatory payouts** by **private foundations**. It means the period beginning with the first day of the first **tax year** following the tax year in which the incorrect **valuation** of assets occurred and ending ninety days after the date of mailing of a **notice of deficiency** for the involved. It may be extended by a period of time that the **IRS** determines is **reasonable** and necessary to permit a distribution of undistributed income (**IRC § 4942(j)(2)**). [PF § 6.7(c)].

allowable lobbying

A **charitable organization** (other than a **private foundation**) may engage in a certain amount of **lobbying** of one or more legislative branches without loss or denial of **tax-exempt status**. The amount that is allowed is an amount that is less than a **substantial** amount. There are two bodies of **law** concerning the determination of what is substantial in this context: the **substantial part test** and the **expenditure test**. [EO § 22.1].

alter ego

The term "alter ego" is used to describe a **corporation**, where the separate identity of the corporate **entity** is **disregarded** and it is treated as being the same as or part of another **person** (usually, an individual). This doctrine is often applied where a party seeks to hold an individual **liable** for a corporation's debts. (also **Corporate veil, piercing the; Sham transaction**).

alternative minimum tax

The **federal tax law** includes an "alternative minimum tax" (**IRC §§ 55-59**). This **tax** is termed an "alternative" tax because it may have to be paid instead of the "regular" **income tax**. It is

A

called a "minimum" tax because it is designed to force a person of wealth to pay some federal tax, notwithstanding the sophistication of his or her tax planning.

The tax is applied to many of a person's **items of tax preference** (**IRC** § 57). In general, beginning January 1, 1987, through December 31, 1992, the **appreciation element** inherent in a **charitable contribution** of **appreciated property** was considered an item of tax preference for purposes of this tax; this tax preference item was termed the **appreciated property charitable deduction** (former **IRC** § 57(a)(6)). There was an exception from the alternative minimum tax concerning contributions made in a tax year beginning in 1991 or made before July 1, 1992, in a tax year beginning in 1992, in the case of contributions of **tangible personal property** (former **IRC** § 57(a)(6)(B)). The inclusion of the appreciated property charitable deduction as a tax preference item, however, was permanently repealed by a provision in the **Omnibus Budget Reconciliation Act of 1993**. [CG §§ 2.18, 10.6].

amateur athletic organization

A **nonprofit organization** can qualify as an "amateur athletic organization" where its purpose is to foster national or international amateur sports competition (as long as no part of its activities involve the provision of athletic facilities or equipment) (**IRC** §§ 170(c)(2)(B), 501(c)(3), 2055(a)(2), 2522(a)(2)). When these rules are complied with, the organization qualifies (assuming it otherwise qualifies) as a **charitable organization**. [EO § 11.2; AU § 7.1(h)].

amateur sports organization

See **Amateur athletic organization**.

American Jobs Protection Act of 2004

Enactment of the "American Jobs Protection Act of 2004" brought **federal tax law** changes and additions in connection with the **charitable gift appraisal rules**, the charitable giving recordkeeping rules, the **tax law** treatment of certain leasing arrangements involving **tax-exempt organizations**, and the tax-exempt organizations **tax shelter rules;** plus, it extended the **declaratory judgment** procedures to **farmers' cooperatives**, modified the **unrelated business income** limitation on investment in certain small business investment companies, introduced rules concerning the treatment of **charitable contributions** of intellectual property and vehicles, increased reporting for **noncash contributions**, added an **exclusion** from unrelated business income for **gain** or **loss** on the sale or exchange of certain **brownfield properties**, and extended the **IRS user fee** program. [EO §§ 25.1(o), 26.1(d), 27.5(b)(i), 28.15(h); CG §§ 9.27, 9.28, 21.1, 21.5, 24.7; FR §§ 5.9, 5.14(c), 5.14(h), 5.14(k), 5.17; HC § 31.2(d)].

American National Red Cross Governance Modernization Act of 2007

The principal purpose of the American National Red Cross Governance Modernization Act of 2007 was to amend the congressional charter of the American National Red Cross to modernize its structure and enhance the ability of its board of governors to support the organization's mission. The legislation, however, includes a checklist of responsibilities and duties of **nonprofit boards** in general, particularly those of **public charities**. [GV §§ 2.1(a)-2.1(d), 2.1(g), 3.1, 3.11, 5.2(a), 5.4(a), 5.4(b), 6.1(a), 7.1; EO § 5.6(e); AU § 3.1(o); CU Q 5.11; RE Q 2.14; SM p. 94].

American Recovery and Reinvestment Act of 2009

The legislation titled the American Recovery and Reinvestment Act of 2009 facilitated **tax-exempt status** for **regional health information organizations**, and brought adjustments in the **federal tax law** for state-sponsored **qualified tuition programs** and **voluntary employees' beneficiary associations**. [EO §§ 7.6(k), 18.3, 19.19(a); HC § 19.5].

American Taxpayer Relief Act of 2012

Enactment of the American Taxpayer Relief Act of 2012 brought extension of the special rules pertaining to **charitable gifts** from retirement accounts, concerning payments to **controlled organizations**, for gifts of book **inventory**, and expanding the charitable gift percentage limitations applicable to **farmers** and **ranchers**. [EO § 30.7(d); CG §§ 9.3(i), 9.7(j), 9.10(e)].

amnesty program

The general definition of the word "amnesty" is a forgiving (or pardoning or overlooking) of an offense. An amnesty program, then, is an activity (usually by a **government agency**) by which a violation of law is pardoned, in exchange for an alteration in or cessation of a particular behavior. An illustration of an amnesty program in the **tax-exempt organizations** context was the determination by the **IRS** to allow **tax-exempt hospitals** to reveal and discontinue **joint ventures** with physicians, where the joint venture acquired the net revenue stream of a department of the hospital, because of the decision of the **IRS** that that type of joint venture constituted **private inurement** on a per se basis. [HC §§ 25.6, 25.7].

amount involved

The term "amount involved" is used in connection with the **private foundation rules** concerning **self-dealing**. For purposes of the **excise tax** on **self-dealing**, the "amount involved" means, with respect to an act of self-dealing, the greater of the amount of money and the **fair market value** of the other **property** given or the amount of money and the fair market value of the other property received (**IRC** § 4941(e)(2)). In the case of certain services, however, the amount involved is the excess compensation (*id.*). The same definition is used in connection with the rules concerning self-dealing applicable to **black lung benefit trusts** (**IRC** § 4951(e)(2)). [PF § 5.15(b); EO § 18.5].

ancillary joint venture

The phrase "ancillary joint venture" means a **joint venture** that, from the standpoint of a participant in the venture, such as a **tax-exempt organization**, something less than primary operations of the participant are in the venture. [EO § 31.4; HC § 22.11; UB §§ 8.15(a), 8.15(b); AR § 11.1(f)(3)(F)); AS § 7.5; CU Q 16.61, Q 16.62; PG pp. 161–164; SM pp. 229–230].

animals, prevention of cruelty to

A **nonprofit organization** can qualify for **tax-exempt status** as a **charitable organization** when it is **organized** and **operated exclusively** for the prevention of cruelty to animals. [EO § 11.1].

announcement, IRS

The **IRS** frequently issues "announcements," which are usually notices of upcoming events (such as **administrative hearings)** and other procedural matters. These announcements are published in the IRS' biweekly **Internal Revenue Bulletin**. [EO App. A; AU § 2.10].

annual accounting period

An **organization's** "annual accounting period" is essentially its **tax year. Income** and **expenses** are reported for **federal income tax** purposes on the basis of the **taxpayer's** annual **accounting period** (**IRC** § 441(a),(b)). [CG § 2.9] (also **Fiscal year**).

annual distribution

The **federal tax law** requires certain types of **organizations** to make a distribution of **income** or **property** with respect to each of its **tax years**. A **private foundation** must comply with the **annual mandatory distribution** requirement. Other **charitable organizations,** such as certain **supporting organizations**, **medical research organizations**, and **private operating foundations,** also have payout requirements. [PF Chap. 6, §§ 3.1(d), 15.3(c), 15.7(g); EO §§ 7.6(d), 12.3(a), 12.3(c), 12.4(b)].

   Split-interest trusts, such as **charitable lead trusts**, **charitable remainder trusts**, and **pooled income funds** have payout requirements (in some instances, more frequently than annually). A **charitable gift annuity contract** also involves a payout requirement. [CG Chaps. 12, 13, 14, 16].

annual dues

The term "annual dues" means the amount an **organization** requires a **member** to pay in order to be recognized by the organization as a member for an annual period. The term is used in conjunction with the rules by which an **agricultural organization** or a **horticultural organization** determines whether it is automatically **exempt** from the reporting and notice requirements otherwise applicable to it by reason of the law denying a **business expense deduction** for the payment of dues allocable to certain **lobbying activities** and **political campaign activities** (**IRC** § 162(e)(1)). [EO §§ 22.6(a), 22.6(b), 23.7, 25.2(l)].

annual exclusion

The term "annual exclusion" is used in the context of the **federal gift tax**. The annual exclusion currently is $14,000. This amount is indexed for inflation (**IRC** § 2503). It means that a gift of $14,000 or less is not subject to gift taxation; it also means that, as to a gift in excess of $14,000, the first $14,000 is not taxable. Each gift by a **donor** to a separate **donee** is subject to an annual exclusion. There is no limit on the number of **donees** that may receive gifts of money and/or **property** that are covered, in whole or in part, by the annual exclusion. Only **present interests are** considered for purposes of the annual exclusion. The annual exclusion is irrelevant in the case of **charitable contributions** and contributions to **political organizations**, because these gifts are **excluded** from gift taxation in their entirety. [CG § 8.2(h); EO § 17.0].

annual giving program

Many **charitable organizations** have an "annual giving program." The basic concept of these programs is to recruit **new donors** and renew prior donors; these **contributions** provide for the annual operating needs of the organization. Most of these programs require staff and a volume of **volunteer** leaders and workers. Charitable organizations frequently conduct two or more forms of annual **solicitation** within a twelve-month period, the effect of which is contact of the same audience with multiple requests within a year. [FR § 2.2(a)].

annual information return

Most **nonprofit organizations** that are **exempt** from **federal income taxation** must file an "annual information return" with the **IRS** (**IRC** § 6033(a)(1)). The **return** filed by the larger exempt organizations is **Form 990**. Most **smaller tax-exempt organizations** file **Form 990-EZ** (although the smallest of organizations submit a **Form 990-N**); **private foundations** file **Form 990-PF**; and **black lung benefit trusts** file **Form 990-BL**. Some tax-exempt organizations annually file **tax returns**. Thus, **political organizations** file **Form 1120-POL** and **homeowners' associations** file **Form 1120-H**. Most organizations with **unrelated business income** file **Form 990-T**. Tax-exempt organizations must make copies of their annual information returns accessible to the public during normal business hours. The annual information return of a charitable organization contains considerable information about **fundraising;** some states permit a charitable organization to file a copy of its annual information return as the basis for compliance with the requests for financial information contained in the states' **charitable solicitation act**. [EO Chap. 28; FR Chap. 6; GV Chap. 4, §§ 3.13, 8.8(a); CU Chap. 17; RE Q 9.1, Q 9.8; AS §§ 10.1, 10.5; UB §§ 11.3(a), 11.3(c); PG pp. 193–220, 222–227, 236, 237, 347, 448; SM pp. 109–117] (also **Notice**).

annual report

The term "annual report" is used in several ways. It may refer to the annual report a **nonprofit organization** may have to file with one or more states, either by application of a state's **nonprofit corporation** act and/or **charitable solicitation act**. It may refer to a document that a nonprofit organization prepares for the benefit of its **membership** or other **constituency**, such as its **donors**. The term may refer to an annual financial statement prepared by the **accountants** for a nonprofit organization. Or, the term may be loosely used to make reference to an organization's **annual information return**. [FR § 3.4; CU Q 18.36; SM pp. 126–127].

annuitant

An "annuitant" is a **person** (usually an individual) who is receiving an **annuity**. [CG §§ 12.2(a)–12.2(c), 14.1, 16.2; SM pp. 235–236, 238].

annuitor

An "annuitor" is a **person**, such as a **charitable remainder annuity trust** or a **charitable organization**, that is paying an **annuity**. [CG §§ 12.2(a), 14.1, 16.2; SM pp. 235–236, 238].

A

annuity

The term "annuity" means an amount of money, fixed by **contract** between the **annuitor** and the **annuitant,** that is paid annually, either in one sum or in installments (such as semiannually or quarterly). An annuity is payable over a stated period, usually (particularly in the **charitable** giving context) over the life of an individual (who may or may not be the **donor**). In **consideration** for the annuity, the annuitor is paid a stipulated amount (often termed a **premium),** usually as a single payment but possibly in prior installments. An annuity may be paid by a **charitable remainder annuity trust** or a **charitable lead** trust, or by a **charitable organization** by reason of a **charitable gift annuity** agreement. [EO §§ 3.2(e), 25.1(f); CG §§ 12.2(a), 14.1, 16.2; UB §§ 3.6, 5.4(e)(ii); SM pp. 235–236, 238].

annuity interest

An "annuity interest" is an **income interest** that is structured as payments of an **annuity**. [CG §§ 5.4(b), 5.7(a), 9.23, 16.2].

annuity starting date

The phrase "annuity starting date" is used in the context of the **charitable gift annuity**. For an **immediate payment charitable gift annuity**, the annuity starting date is the date on which the annuity was purchased. In the case of a **deferred payment charitable gift annuity,** the annuity starting date is an anniversary date beginning on a stated date in the future. [CG § 14.3(a)].

answer

An "answer" is a document, filed by one or more **persons** in **litigation,** in response to the filing of a **complaint**. It essentially is a denial by a **defendant** (or defendants) of the allegations made by a **plaintiff;** it may also contain one or more assertions by the defendant against the plaintiff. (also **Counterclaim; Petition**).

anti-abuse rule

An "anti-abuse rule" is a **rule** or **regulation** that is developed by a **government agency** in anticipation of, and to prevent, an abuse of a particular **law**. This type of rule is often created before any actual abuse occurs, because the potential for abuse is so obvious and so great. For example, in the context of the **charitable contribution substantiation rules**, where the **separate contribution** rule exists, the **IRS** has the authority (which it has yet to exercise) to formulate an anti-abuse rule to preclude practices such as the writing of multiple checks on the same date. Likewise, the **quid pro quo contributions** rules contain a **separate payment** rule; again, the **IRS** has the (unexercised) authority to issue an anti-abuse rule to preclude practices such as the writing of multiple checks for the same transaction. [CG §§ 21.3, 22.2].

anti-cascading rule

The "anti-cascading rule" applies in the context of the **federal tax law** that denies a **business expense deduction** for **expenditures** for a variety of attempts to **influence legislation** or engage in **political campaign activities** (IRC § 162(e)(1)). It is possible for more than one **person** to be involved in this type of activity where the **lobbying** or political effort is the same; the "anti-cascading rule" operates to ensure that this **lobbying expense disallowance rule** results in denial of the deduction at only one level (**IRC** § 162(e)(5)(A)).

Thus, in the case of an individual engaged in the **trade or business** of providing lobbying services or an individual who is an **employee** and receives **employer** reimbursements for lobbying expenses, the disallowance rule does not apply to expenditures of the individual in conducting the activities **directly** on behalf of a client or employer. Instead, the lobbying payments made by the client or the employer to the **lobbyist** or employee are nondeductible under the general disallowance rule.

The anti-cascading rule applies where there is a direct, one-on-one relationship between the person and the entity conducting the lobbying activity, such as a client or employment relationship. It does not apply to **dues** or other payments to taxable membership organizations that act to further the interests of all of their members rather than the interests of any one particular member. These organizations are themselves subject to the general disallowance rule based on the amount of their lobbying expenditures. [EO §§ 22.6(a), 23.7; AS §§ 4.2(a)(viii), 4.5(a); HC 18.4(f)].

Anti-Injunction Act

A **federal tax statute**, known as the Anti-Injunction Act, provides that, aside from minor exceptions, "in suit for the purpose of restraining the assessment or collection of any tax shall be maintained in any court by any person" (**IRC** § 7421(a)). This law is designed to facilitate prompt collection of federal tax revenue by preventing **taxpayers** from inundating tax collectors with pre-enforcement lawsuits over disputed sums. The U.S. Supreme Court carved out a narrow exception from this act, in that a pre-enforcement **injunction** against tax **assessment** or collection may be granted only if it is clear that under no circumstances could the government ultimately prevail and if **equity jurisdiction** exists (that is, a showing of irreparable injury, no adequate remedy at **law**, and advancement of the **public** interest). Thus, this act, when applicable, divests courts of subject matter **jurisdiction**. [CL § 8.13; EO § 27.6(a)].

anticipated life expectancy

See **Life expectancy**.

anticipatory income assignment

An "anticipatory assignment of income" occurs in the **charitable giving** setting when a **person** has certain **rights** in the **contributed property** that have so matured that the person has a right to the proceeds from the property at the time the transfer is made. If the transfer is an assignment of income, there may not be a **charitable contribution deduction** based on the **fair market value** of the transferred property; the transferor may be taxable on the proceeds diverted to the **charitable organization**, with the charitable deduction determined as if the gift was of the after-tax income. [CG § 3.1(i)].

antitrust laws

Both **federal** and state **laws** include **statutes**, termed "antitrust laws," that are intended to advance and protect competition in economic marketplaces. At the federal level, the principal statutes are the Clayton Act and the Sherman Act. These laws are directed against

A

combinations, conspiracies, or other collective restraints of trade. The antitrust laws apply in the **nonprofit organization** setting, in instances such as (1) inappropriate **membership** exclusion or expulsion practices, (2) the maintenance of **credentialing** programs, or (3) the enforcement of **codes of ethics** in ways that restrain free competition and trade. [EO § 3.2(f); AS §§ 1.2, 11.6; CL § 3.2(b); CG § 14.8; FR §§ 5.13, 5.19].

apostolic organization

The word "apostolic" means pertaining to or characteristic of an apostle, particularly with respect to the twelve apostles in the Christian religion. Certain **"religious or apostolic" organizations** are **exempt** from **federal income taxation,** even though they are not embraced by the general reference to religious organizations (**IRC** § 501(d)). These entities are religious or apostolic **associations** or **corporations** if the organizations have a **common treasury** or **community treasury,** even if the organizations engage in **business** for the common benefit of their **members.** The members of this type of communal organization include (at the time of the filing of their **tax returns**) in their **gross income** their pro rata shares, whether distributed or not, of the **taxable income** of the organization for the year; these amounts are treated as **dividends**. [EO § 10.7; AU § 7.1(aa); RE Q 3.12, Q 9.8; AS § 1.6(p)].

applicable disposition

The term "applicable disposition" means any sale, exchange, or other disposition by the **donee** of **applicable property** (1) after the last day of the **tax year** of the **donor** in which the property was **contributed** and (2) before the last day of the three-year period beginning on the date of the contribution of the property, unless the donee makes a certification as to use of the property (**IRC** § 170(e)(7)(B)). [CG § 4.6(c)].

applicable federal rate

The **IRS**, each month, publishes the "applicable federal rate," which is a rate of interest used for a variety of **federal income tax** purposes. The valuation of **partial interests** in **property** is the subject of federal legislation, which created a mechanism for determining rates of return (**IRC** § 7520). This legislation addresses the method for valuing an **annuity**, any interest for life or a term of years, or any **remainder** or reversionary interest, for **income**, **estate**, or **gift** tax purposes. Under this approach, the **value** of these interests is determined by using (1) a floating interest rate equal to 120 percent of the applicable federal rate (**IRC** § 1274(d)) in effect for the month in which the valuation date falls and (2) life contingencies in mortality tables prescribed by the **IRS**. [CG § 11.1; HC § 28.3(d)].

applicable property

The term "applicable property" means **charitable deduction property** that is **tangible personal property** the use of which is identified by the **donee** as **related** to its **exempt purpose** and for which a **charitable deduction** in excess of the **donor's basis** in the property is allowed (**IRC** § 170(e)(7)(C)). [CG § 4.6(c)].

applicable tax-exempt organization

For purposes of the **intermediate sanctions rules**, the phrase "applicable tax-exempt organization" means any organization that (without regard to any **excess benefit**) is a **tax-exempt charitable organization** (other than a **private foundation**), an **exempt social welfare organization**, or an exempt **health insurance issuer**, and any organization that was so exempt at any time during the five-year period ending on the date of the **excess benefit transaction** (IRC § 4958(e)). [EO § 21.2; HC § 4.9(a)(i); AS 3.8(b); SM p. 59].

application for recognition of exempt status

The **IRS** has developed four forms constituting "applications for **recognition** of **exempt status**." These forms are useable by nearly all types of **tax-exempt organizations;** the forms are **Form 1023, Form 1023-EZ, Form 1024,** and **Form 1028**. Most categories of tax-exempt organizations, however, are not required to file any of these forms; nonetheless, an organization not required to file may file if it wishes to receive recognition by the **IRS** of its tax exemption. The organizations that must file an application to be tax-exempt are most **charitable organizations** (IRC § 508(a)), certain **consumer counseling organizations** (IRC § 501(q)(3)), **qualified health insurance issuers** (IRC § 501(c)(29)(B)(i)), and certain **employee benefit organizations** (IRC § 505(c)(1)). [EO Chap. 26; CU Q 3.31–Q 3.38; HC § 8.1; AS § 2.15; PG pp. 42–53, 235–236; SM pp. 66–71, 74–75; LI Q 2.13, Q 2.25, Q 2.27, Q 2.47–Q 2.57] (also **Self-declarer; User fee**).

appointment, power of

A "general power of appointment" over **property** is the power to appoint property to oneself, one's **estate**, creditors, or the creditors of the estate (**IRC** § 2514(c)). [CG §§ 8.2(d), 8.3(a)].

appraisal

An "appraisal" is an objective estimation of the **fair market value** of an item of **property**. In the case of many **charitable contributions** of property, the **substantiation requirements** mandate a **qualified appraisal** of the property. [EO §§ 20.5(c), 32.7(b); CG §§ 10.1, 21.5; FR § 5.14(k); HC § 31.2(d); PF § 14.6(c); RE Q 13.28; PG pp. 246–250; SM pp. 139–141; LI Q 12.31, Q 12.32] (also **Valuation of property**).

appraisal summary

In the case of **charitable contributions** of **property** for which a **qualified appraisal** is required, an "appraisal summary" must be attached to the **donor's tax return** on which a **charitable contribution deduction** with respect to the property is first claimed or reported. This appraisal summary must be on a form prescribed by the **IRS** (**Form 8283,** Section B), and signed and dated by the charitable **donee** and the **qualified appraiser** (or appraisers). The **law** requires the inclusion of certain information in an appraisal summary. [CG § 21.5; FR § 5.14(k); SM p. 139].

appraisal summary, partial

See **Partial appraisal summary.**

appraiser

An "appraiser" is an individual hired to make an **appraisal**. Property valuations are necessary, for **charitable contribution deduction** purposes, in the instance of many charitable **gifts** of property. [CG § 21.5(b); FR §§ 5.14(k), 5.17] (also **Appraisal summaries**; **Qualified appraiser**).

appreciated

See **Appreciation**.

appreciated property

An item of **property** is termed an "appreciated property" where the property has **appreciated** in **value**. This type of property is often an ideal subject for a **charitable gift,** in that the **charitable contribution deduction** is based on the **fair market value** of the property, with no **recognition** of any **capital gain**. [CG §§ 5.2, 7.1; PF §§ 14.2, 14.4(b), 15.1; FR § 5.14(c); SM pp. 135, 233].

appreciation

"Appreciation" is a term that refers to the increase in the **value** of an item of **property**. This occurs where the value of a property is greater than the owner's cost of acquisition (the, or part of the, **basis**) of the property. Almost always, appreciation is composed of two elements: real and nominal changes in the value of property. One of these elements, real appreciation, reflects the true increase in economic value of the property. The other element, nominal appreciation, reflects the relative effect in the change in the value of money, rather than a change in the inherent value of the property. Whatever the amount of appreciation is, it is often referred to as the **appreciation element** in the property. In the case of **capital gain property,** the term sometimes used is **capital gain element**.

   Over time, then, the value of an item of property may change. This should be considered in relation to the fact that the **federal income tax** system utilizes an **annual accounting period** for purposes of accounting for and taxing of income. Each year, a **person** may have an increase or decrease in wealth due to the real and/or nominal change in the value of the property being held. The federal income tax system does not attempt to track, measure, and tax economic **gain** or **loss** annually. Instead, gain or loss is accounted for only where there is the occurrence of some transactional event—a **sale**, **exchange**, or other **disposition** of property. The tax on gains or losses, then, is a transactional tax, not a tax on economic improvement (appreciation). [CG §§ 2.14(e), 4.2] (also **Appreciated property**).

appreciation element

The "appreciation element" in an item of **property** is the amount by which the **fair market value** of the property at a point in time exceeds the **adjusted basis** in the property. [CG §§ 2.14(e), 4.2] (also **Appreciated property**).

appropriate data as to comparability

In connection with application of the **rebuttable presumption of reasonableness**, an **authorized body** has "appropriate data as to comparability" if, given the knowledge and expertise of its **members**, it has information sufficient to determine whether the terms and conditions of a transaction or arrangement are **reasonable**. [EO § 21.9(b); CU Q 7.19].

appropriate high-level Treasury official

The phrase "appropriate high-level Treasury official" refers to the individual within the **IRS** who has the authority to initiate a **church tax inquiry** and/or a **church tax examination**. The existing definition in the **IRC** is not operative because it has never been updated to reflect the reorganization of the **exempt organizations** function of the **IRS** in 1999. Proposed regulations to define the term were issued in 2009 but have not been finalized (**IRC** § 7611(h)(7)). [EO § 27.7(c)].

appropriate state officer

For purposes of the law authorizing disclosures of certain proposed actions involving **charitable organizations** and certain other **tax-exempt** organizations to state officials, the phrase "appropriate state officers" means states' **attorneys general**; states' tax officers; in the case of exempt charitable organizations, other state officials charged with oversight of these organizations; and, in the case of other categories of exempt organizations, heads of agencies designated by the states' attorney general who have the primary responsibility for overseeing the **solicitation** of funds for **charitable** purposes. These individuals must be notified of a refusal by the **IRS** to **recognize** the **tax-exempt status** of a charitable organization, of the fact that the organization is out of compliance with the **federal tax** rules concerning charitable organizations, or of the mailing of a notice of deficiency in connection with certain **taxes.** Also, they may inspect and photocopy filed statements, records, reports, and other information relating to the qualification for, or denial or loss of, tax exemption by a charitable organization as are relevant to any determination under state law (**IRC** § 6104(c)(6)(B)). [EO § 27.10].

appropriations bill

An "appropriations" bill is an item of **legislation** passed by the U.S. Congress to obligate federal funds in support of government programs that previously have been created by means of enactment of an **authorization bill**. While an appropriations bill is **law** in a general sense, it is usually not law in the sense that it contains rules of conduct applicable to one or more persons. Nonetheless, the funding underlying this latter type of law is the function of appropriations bills.

arm's length

The phrase "arm's length" is used to describe a distance between two or more **persons** where none of the persons has a close or intimate relationship with another of these persons. The phrase was born of the view that each of the parties would stand apart from the other—at least as far as the length of a human being's arm.

arm's length relationship

An "arm's length relationship" is a relationship between two persons that is at **arm's length.** It is a relationship in which authentic bargaining can take place. Some relationships, such as those between **insiders** or otherwise constituting **self-dealing,** do not reflect an arm's length relationship. Nonetheless, insiders or other **related parties** may have a relationship, including an **arm's length transaction,** that is at arm's length.

arm's length transaction

An "arm's length transaction" is a transaction involving two or more **persons** where each of these persons is functioning at **arm's length** in relation to the others. For example, the actual selling price of an **asset** that is **sold** in an arm's length transaction is considered to be the true **value** of the asset. The **private foundation** rules were enacted because Congress concluded that an arm's length standard between private foundations and their **disqualified persons** was inadequate. [EO § 20.0; PF Chap. 5; CG § 2.14].

art, gift of

A work of art may be the subject of a **charitable contribution**. In general, the **federal income tax charitable contribution deduction** for a **gift** of a work of art is equal to the **fair market value** of the **property** at the time of the gift. There are, however, exceptions to this rule. One of them pertains to contributions of art that was created by the **donor;** in this case, the deduction is confined to the donor's **basis** in the property (**IRC** §§ 170(e)(1), 1221). Another exception pertains to the fact that a work of art may be put to an **unrelated use** by the charitable recipient, in which case the deduction is confined to the donor's **basis** in the property (**IRC** § 170(e)(1)(B)(i)). [AR §§ 3.1(h), 3.2(h), 11.1(c), 19.1(d)(1), 19.2(b); CG §§ 9.1(a), 24.7(b)(2); SM pp. 114–115] (also **Fractional interest in art**).

art, loan of

Certain transfers are **excluded** from the definition of a **taxable gift** for **federal gift tax** purposes. One of these exclusions involves a loan of any work of art that is archaeological, historic, or creative **tangible personal property**. The **law** excludes from this tax loans of art made to a **tax-exempt charitable organization** and used for its **exempt purposes** (**IRC** § 2503(g)). [AR § 11.1(c)(2); CG §§ 8.2(g), 9.1(c)].

articles of incorporation

The phrase "articles of incorporation" is used to describe the document filed with the appropriate state authority to establish a **corporation**; this is the case irrespective of whether the corporation is **nonprofit** or **for-profit**. Thus, articles of incorporation are the **articles of organization** used to create a corporate entity. [EO § 4.2; GV § 1.2(a); RE Q 2.16; PG pp.; SM pp. 8–9, 68–69, 313; LI Q 1.12, Q 1.40].

articles of organization

The phrase "articles of organization" is used to describe the document by which an **organization** is created. It is the document that is the subject of the **organizational test**. The articles of organization of a **nonprofit organization** should contain a variety of provisions, including those stating the organization's name and purposes; whether there will be **members** and, if so, the qualifications and classes of them; the members of the initial **board of directors** (or **board** of trustees); the **registered agent** and **incorporators** (if a **corporation**); the **dissolution** or **liquidation** procedure; and the requisite language (if any) referencing the appropriate **tax** law (**federal** and state) requirements and prohibitions. Some states require special language in the articles of organization to enable the directors and **officers** of the entity to utilize statutes providing **immunity** from **personal liability** for acts or failures to act in connection with service to the organization. [EO §§ 4.2, 4.3, 4.3(c); PF §§ 1.6, 1.7, 15.7(c); AR §§ 2.1(b), 2.2(a); GV § 1.2(b); RE Q 1.8, Q 2.16: PG pp. 4–5; SM p. 6; LI Q 1.40] (also **Articles of incorporation; Constitution; Declaration of trust; Trust agreement**).

artificial person

The **law** is applicable to **persons,** and it distinguishes between **natural persons and** "**artificial** persons." The latter are, in essence, fictions; they are not real in the tangible sense. The principal legal fictions that are artificial persons are **corporations**, **estates**, **partnerships**, **limited liability companies,** and **trusts**. These **entities** are considered by the **law** to be distinct and separate from the individuals who form and/or manage them.

arts, promotion of

"Promotion of the arts" is a category of **charitable** purpose that can be the basis for **tax exemption** (under **IRC** § 501(a) by reason of **IRC** § 501(c)(3)) for a **nonprofit organization**. Arts can be promoted in many ways, including operation of a theater, training of artists, and promotion of public appreciation of one of the arts. [EO § 7.12; CG § 3.2(b)].

ascending liability

A **nonprofit organization** may incur a legal **liability**, thus causing another nonprofit **entity** to also be liable. For example, a **chapter** of a national organization may cause the national entity to be liable as well; this is termed "ascending liability." [SM p. 105].

ascertainability

An **estate tax charitable contribution deduction** is likely to be defeated if the **value** of the charitable interest is not "ascertainable" as of the death of the **decedent**, so that it can be severed from noncharitable interests. This rule is at issue if there is vague language in the **will** and/or a substantial amount of discretion vested in the personal representative or a **trustee**. The U.S. Supreme Court stated that the standard must, to be ascertainable, "fixed in fact and capable of being stated in definite terms of money." [CG § 8.7].

assembly, freedom of

The U.S. Constitution, in the **First Amendment,** provides that Congress may not pass a **law** that abridges the **right** of the people to assemble peaceably. This constitutional protection extends to forms of **advocacy,** such as **demonstrations** and rallies. These activities, however, may not be conducted in a way that is illegal or contrary to **public policy**. [EO §§ 6.2(a), 23.2(g); CL §§ 1.8(a), 8.8].

assessment, of tax

An "assessment" of **tax** is made by the **IRS** by recording the tax liability of the **taxpayer** in its records. Several types of assessments exist. The most common form of tax assessment occurs when a taxpayer files an income tax **return** showing a tax due; this is known as a "summary assessment." An amount of tax due (that is, not paid) is a "tax deficiency." To start the process of collection of a tax deficiency, the **IRS** is required to send the taxpayer a **notice of deficiency**. (**IRC** §§ 6201(a)(1), 6203) [EO § 28.2(a)(vi); PF § 5.15(g)] (also **Jeopardy Assessment; Termination assessment**).

asset

An "asset" is an item of **property,** irrespective of whether the property is **real property**, **tangible personal property,** or **intangible personal property**. [EO §§ 11.8(d), 12.4(a), 15.6, 20.5(c), 21.4(a); PF §§ 13.1, 13.3, 13.5, 13.6, 16.5; CG § 2.16(a); HC §§ 4.4(g), 21.3(b); AR Chap. 7, §§ 3.1(k), 3.2(k); CU Q 2.47] (also **Capital asset; Ordinary asset**).

asset test

One of the tests a **private foundation** may satisfy to qualify as a **private operating foundation** is an "asset test" (**IRC** § 4942(j)(3)(B)). This test requires that **substantially all** (at least 65 percent) of the foundation's **assets** be active-use assets of any of these types: (1) program assets devoted **directly** to the active conduct of its **tax-exempt** activities, to one or more **functionally related businesses,** or both; (2) stock of a **corporation** that is **controlled** by the foundation, the assets of which are 65 percent or more so devoted; or (3) a combination of the foregoing two categories. [PF §§ 3.1(e), 3.1(f); EO § 12.1(b); SM p. 87].

assets, diversion of

For purposes of annual reporting to the **IRS**, a "diversion of assets" is an unauthorized conversion or use of the **organization's assets,** including **embezzlement** or theft. [GV § 4.1(f); AR § 5.2(a)(5)].

assign

In **law,** the word "assign" means to transfer. For example, unless the document prohibits it, a **person** obligated under a **contract** may assign his, her, or its **rights** and responsibilities under the **agreement to** a person not then **a** party to the contract. In another example, an **annuitant** may assign his or her **rights** under an **annuity** contract to the **annuitor or** another entity in return for **a lump sum** payment or installment payments. [CG §§ 3.1(i), 5.5(b)].

Assistant Commissioner (Employee Plans and Exempt Organizations)

There is, within the **IRS**, an Assistant Commissioner (Employee Plans and Exempt Organizations). The function of this individual is to supervise and direct the "Office of Employee Plans and Exempt Organizations." He or she is responsible for carrying out such functions as the **Secretary of the Treasury** may prescribe with respect to **administrative** matters pertaining to the **federal tax law** of **tax-exempt organizations** and **employee** plans (**IRC** § 7802(b)(1)). [EO § 2.2(b)].

associate member

A **person** is an "associate member" of a **nonprofit organization** where the person's is a **member** solely for the purpose of receiving a specific service, such as insurance coverage. [EO § 24.5(e)(iii)].

associate member dues

The term "associate member dues" means **dues** paid by an **associate member** of a **tax-exempt organization**. This type of dues payment may be subject to **unrelated business taxation.** [EO §§ 24.5(e)(iii), 25.2(l); UB §§ 4.8, 9.4(c)].

association

An "association" is an **organization** that has **members**; the organization may be **incorporated or unincorporated**. Usually, these members have a common business, professional, or trade interest, and the purpose of this type of association (often, a **business league**) is to promote that interest. This type of association is likely to qualify for **tax-exempt status** under **federal** law (**IRC** § 501(a), by reason of description in **IRC** § 501(c)(6)). Some associations are formed for **advocacy** purposes; these are also likely to be tax-exempt (by reason of **IRC** § 501(c)(4)). Other associations are **organized** and **operated** for **charitable, educational, and/or scientific** purposes (often termed **societies**); these **entities** are likely to be tax-exempt as well (by reason of **IRC** § 501(c)(3)). Still other organizations of this nature are organized and operated for **social** and recreational purposes (usually termed **clubs**); these are tax-exempt (by reason of **IRC** § 501(c)(7)). [AS § 1.1; EO Chap. 14; UB §§ 9.4, 10.11; SM pp. 40–41; CL § 8.3; CG §§ 2.8, 3.3(a); LI Q 1.50] (cf. **Union**).

association, freedom of

An element of the **constitutionally** provided **freedom of speech** is the "freedom of association." This is the **right** of **persons** to associate for the advancement of some purpose. This right, however, like most, can be abridged when to do so involves a legitimate **state interest**. For example, **nonprofit membership organizations** are compelled to accept women as regular members— in advancement of eradication of gender-based discrimination—by direction of states' human rights acts, notwithstanding the organizations' associational rights. [CL § 1.9; EO § 1.7; CG § 1.3(c)] (also **Expressive association, freedom of; Intimate association, freedom of**).

association of churches

An "association of churches" is **tax-exempt** under the **federal tax law** as a **religious organization** and is not a **private foundation**. The historical meaning of this type of **entity** is a cooperative undertaking by **churches** of the same denomination. A **tax-exempt organization**, the **membership** of which is comprised of churches of different denominations. has been held by the **IRS** to qualify as an association of churches (**IRC** §§ 170(b)(1)(A)(i), 509(a)(1)). [EO § 10.4; AR § 1.1(b); RE Q 3.7] (also **Convention of churches; Institution**).

A

association-related foundation

An "association-related foundation" is just that: a **foundation** that is **related** to an **association**. In the typical instance, the association is a **tax-exempt organization** (IRC § 501(a), by reason of **IRC** § 501(c)(6), as is the foundation (**IRC** § 501(a), by reason of **IRC** § 501(c)(3)). The usual mechanism for the relatedness factor is the **interlocking directorate**.

The usual purpose of an association-related foundation is to take advantage of the tax attributes of each **entity**. For example, a **contribution** to an association is not deductible as a **charitable gift** (unless the association is a **charitable** organization), but a contribution to a foundation is so deductible. Similarly, a **private foundation** is not likely to make a **grant** to an association (again, unless it is a charitable entity), but a private foundation may make a grant to an association-related foundation.

The typical association is likely to be made up of a blend of **membership** service (**IRC** § 501(c)(6)) functions and charitable, **educational**, **scientific**, and/or similar (**IRC** § 501(c)(3)) functions. The ideal is to fund the membership services with **dues** and similar association **revenue**, and fund the charitable activities with gifts and grants. There are two models for this approach. One is for all charitable and like activities to be undertaken by the foundation, initiated there and/or transferred to it from the association; the foundation would fund these activities. The other approach is for all charitable and like activities to remain in the association; the foundation would be a **fundraising** vehicle and would make grants **restricted** for charitable programs to the association.

This approach also works where the association is a **social welfare** (**IRC** § 501(c)(4)) organization or is a **social club** (**IRC** § 501(c)(7)). There may be one or more rationales for utilizing a related foundation even where the association is a charitable (**IRC** § 501(c)(3)) entity.

This type of related foundation is rarely a private foundation; it is usually a **publicly supported organization** or a **supporting organization**. [AS §§ 8.8(a)-8.8(h); EO §§ 12.4(b), 12.4(c); PF §§ 15.4–15.7; SM pp. 80–85].

associational test

The "associational test" is a court-created standard defining what it means to be a **church** for **federal tax law** purposes. This test requires at least a place of worship, a congregation, and regular **religious** services. [EO §§ 10.3(b), 10.3(c); RE 3.4].

astroturf

The word "astroturf " is used as a term of derision, by members of a legislature, to describe a **grass-roots lobbying** effort that is so obviously staged or coordinated by professional **lobbyists** (such as the use of printed postcards) as to not truly reflect the sentiments of a segment of the **public**. [EO §§ 22.3(b), 22.3(d)(i)].

assumption of liability

An "assumption of liability" by an **insider** with respect to a **tax-exempt organization**, if not **valued** as being **reasonable**, can be a form of **private inurement**. [EO § 20.5(e); HC § 4.4(e); AS § 3.4(b)(v)].

attempt to influence

The **federal tax law** provides that, for an **entity** to qualify as a **tax-exempt**, **charitable organization**, no **substantial part** of its activities may constitute attempts to **influence legislation** (IRC § 501(c)(3)). Thus, inasmuch as the proscription applies to "attempts" to influence legislation, the ultimate success of the effort is irrelevant. [EO § 22.3] (also **Lobbying**).

attempt to influence legislation

See **Influence legislation**.

attentiveness requirement

To qualify, a **non-functionally integrated Type III supporting organization** must meet an "attentiveness requirement," which means that the **supported organization** is attentive to the operations of the supporting organization during a year if, in the year, at least one of the following requirements is satisfied: (1) the supporting organization distributes to the supported organization amounts constituting at least 10 percent of the supported organization's total financial support (or perhaps the support of a **division** of the organization) received during the supported organization's last tax year ending before the beginning of the supporting organization's tax year, (2) the amount of support received from the supporting organization is necessary to avoid interruption of the conduct of a particular function or activity of the supported organization, or (3) the amount of support received from the supporting organization is a sufficient part of the supported organization's total support (or perhaps that of a division)to ensure attentiveness. [PF § 15.7(g)].

attorney

The term "attorney" is usually used to refer to a **member** of the legal profession who is licensed to practice law. A lawyer is often referred to as an "attorney." While technically that designation is correct—in that the term "attorney" means no more than a "representative"—it does not convey the fact of the formal training of and services provided by a lawyer. A compromise term is "attorney-at-law." One individual can make another individual an "attorney" simply by executing a **power of attorney**.

attorney general

An "attorney general" is the chief legal officer of a government. The U.S. government has an Attorney General, who is the head of the Department of Justice; each of the states has an attorney general as well. In many states, the administration and enforcement of the charitable solicitation act is in the office of the **attorney general**. (Colloquially, a state's attorney general is often referred to as the "AG"; some are of the view that those initials stand for "aspiring governor.). [FR § 3.19].

attribution considerations

Where an **organization** so **controls** the affairs of another organization, to the point that the latter is merely an extension of the former, the controlled **entity's** functions will likely be attributed

A

to the controlling entity so that the controlled entity will not be regarded as a separate entity for **federal tax law** purposes. This can happen, for example, where one organization is **directly** involved in the day-to-day management of the other organization. [EO §§ 30.2, 32.1(d); AR §§ 21.1(b), (c)].

auction

An "auction" is an event at which there are **sales** of items of **property** and/or services to the highest bidder for each item. An auction is frequently used by a **tax-exempt charitable organization** as a **fundraising event**. As a general rule, a payment made to a charitable organization at a fundraising auction by one acquiring the property (the highest bidder) is not a **gift**; rather, it is the purchase of the item and thus there is no **charitable contribution deduction** for the payment (although a **business expense deduction** may be available). State law may require that the organization that is conducting the auction collect the appropriate **sales tax** and remit it to the state. [CG § 9.13; FR § 8.8].

audit

The word "audit" has three meanings. One is the review of an **organization's** books and records and the preparation of a financial statement by an **accountant** (usually a **certified public accountant**). The second meaning is an examination of an organization's books, records, and operations by the **IRS** to determine whether the organization is in compliance with the **federal tax laws** and whether it has properly reported and paid all **taxes** due; this definition of an "audit" also extends to examinations by state and local tax authorities. In this regard, there are special rules to which the **IRS** must adhere when auditing a **church** (**IRC** § 7611). The third meaning is an examination of an organization's books, records, and operations by a **lawyer** and the rendering of a letter of opinion as to the organization's compliance with federal and state laws (termed a **legal audit**). [AU Chap. 1, §§ 3.0, 3.3; GV Chap. 9; EO § 27.6; PF §§ 2.7(d), 27(e); HC §§ 36.1–36.3; PG Chap. 12; SM pp. 294–296, 306–307].

audit committee

The term "audit committee" means a committee, generally established by the **governing body** of an **organization**, with the responsibilities of overseeing the organization's financial reporting process, monitoring the choice of accounting policies and principles, monitoring internal control processes, and/or overseeing hiring and performance of any external auditors. [GV §§ 3.4(b), 4.2(e), 5.10, 6.3(u); AU § 7.2(d)(2)].

audit guide

An "audit guide" is a document developed to provide accounting standards and reporting procedures. Audit guides are published by the American Association of Certified Public Accountants; these include guides for **hospitals**, **colleges**, **universities**, and **voluntary** health and welfare **organizations**. Other organizations publish audit guides.

audit guidelines

The **IRS,** from time to time, issues "audit guidelines" to assist its agents in the various field offices in the conduct of their examinations (**audits**) of **tax-exempt organizations**, when these reviews involve specialized areas of the **law**. [HC §§ 7.1(c), 36.3; CG § 23.1; FR § 5.1].

audit lottery, winning of

The phrase "winning the audit lottery" is a euphemism for selection by the **IRS** of a **person** for examination by the agency. [AU §§ 3.2, 5.2; GV § 8.17; SM pp. 302–304].

authority

The word "authority" is used by **lawyers** to describe the body of **law** that supports their position with respect to a particular set of facts. To some extent, the term is synonymous with the concept of **precedent**. That term, however, is usually used in connection with court opinions; "authority" can also include **statutes**, **regulations**, **rules**, **agency rulings**, and (sometimes) scholarly articles.

authorization bill

An "authorization bill" is an item of **legislation** passed by the U.S. Congress that creates **law**. The term is often used when the legislation "authorizes" a government program. Funding for these laws is separately legislated, in an **appropriations bill**. This terminology may also be used at the state level.

authorized body

An "authorized body" is an **independent board** or an independent **committee** of a **governing body** that has been so designed in connection with the **rebuttable presumption of reasonableness**. [EO § 21.9(a)].

automatic excess benefit transaction

An economic benefit may not be treated as **consideration** for the performance of services by a **disqualified person**, in the **intermediate sanctions** context, unless the **applicable tax-exempt organization** providing the benefit clearly indicates its intent to treat the benefit as **compensation** when the benefit is paid (**IRC § 4958(1)(1)(A)**). If this intent is not proven, the services provided by the disqualified person will not be treated as provided in consideration for the benefit for purposes of determining the **reasonableness** of the transaction (even if it is, in fact, reasonable); this is known as an "automatic excess benefit transaction." Grants, loans, payments of compensation, and similar payments by a **supporting organization** to a **substantial contributor** with respect to the organization are also automatic excess benefit transactions (**IRC § 4958(c)(3)**), as are these types of payments from a **donor-advised fund** to a **person** who, with respect to the fund, is a **donor, donor advisor**, or related party (**IRC § 4958(c)(2)**). [EO §§ 21.4(c)-(e); HC § 4.9(a)(iii); AU § 21.1(i); CU Q 6.36, Q 6.37; AS § 3.8(d)(ii)].

auto-revocation

The informal term "auto-revocation" refers to the loss of its **tax-exempt status**, by **operation of law**, when a **tax-exempt organization**, that is required to file an **annual information return** and/or **submit** a **notice**, fails to do so for three consecutive years (**IRC § 6033(j)**). [EO § 28.5].

auxiliary, of church

An "integrated auxiliary of a church" is a **tax-exempt organization** the principal activity of which is **exclusively religious** and which is **controlled** by or associated with a **church** or a **convention** or **association of churches**. This type of auxiliary entity is a **public charity**. [EO § 10.5; CG § 3.4(a); RE Q 3.8; SM p. 80].

average gift size factor

The concept of the "average gift size factor" was developed in the context of efforts to measure the **reasonableness** of the **fundraising costs** of **charitable organizations**. This approach rejects the view that the bottom-line amount of fundraising costs (or a ratio that is produced using that amount) is the appropriate way to determine what is reasonable in this setting. One significant factor affecting fundraising costs is the average size of the **gifts** received in a year by a charitable organization. Thus, it is contended that **disclosure** of a charitable organization's number of gifts—by category of type of **fundraising method** used—is essential for a complete and fair evaluation of the reasonableness of fundraising costs, and that any comparisons of fundraising performance should occur only between organizations with similar **constituencies,** based on a number of factors, particularly average gift size. [FR § 4.1(f)].

average percentage payout

The phrase "average percentage payout" is used in the **federal tax law** concerning circumstances where the **rate** of the **tax** on the **net investment income** of a **private foundation** is one percent. It is defined as being, for the **base period**, the average of the **percentage payouts** for **tax years** in the base period (**IRC § 4940(e)(3)(A)**). [PF § 10.2(a)].

B corporation

Despite the name, the "B corporation" is not a legal form of **entity** but is a business **corporation** that is certified by the B Lab (a **tax-exempt charitable organization**) as a company that is working to solve social and environmental problems. [EO § 4.11(d)].

background file document

The phrase "background file document," with respect to a **written determination**, includes the request for that written determination, any written material submitted in support of the request, and any **communication,** written or otherwise, between the **IRS** and **persons** outside the **IRS** in connection with the written determination (other than a communication between the Department of Justice and the **IRS** relating to a pending civil or **criminal** case or investigation received before issuance of the written determination (**IRC** § 6110(b)(2)). These documents generally are disposed of by the **IRS** within three years from the date they are made available for public inspection (**IRC** § 6110(j)(2)). [EO § 28.9(a)(i); HC § 34.2].

balance

The word "balance" means the remainder of something, usually arrived at following reconciliation of accounts (debits and credits, **assets** and **liabilities**). **Tax-exempt charitable organizations** are required by the **federal tax law to** calculate annually the balance of their assets and liabilities, and to report this item on their **annual information return** (IRC § 6033(b)(4)). [EO § 28.3(g)] (also **Balance sheet**).

balance sheet

A "balance sheet" is the portion of an **organization's financial statement** and/or **annual information return** that states the organization's **balance** of its **assets** and **liabilities**. This balance will either be **net assets** or **net liabilities**, or, if the organization uses fund accounting, the **fund balance**. [AR § 7.2(c); AU § 5.19(h)] (also **Form 990**).

Balanced Budget Act of 1997

By enactment of the Balanced Budget Act of 1997, Congress expanded the Medicare program by adding Medicare Part C, which permits Medicare beneficiaries to receive services covered

Bruce R. Hopkins' Nonprofit Law Dictionary, First Edition. Bruce R. Hopkins.
© 2015 Bruce R. Hopkins. Published 2015 by John Wiley & Sons, Inc.

B

by the Medicare program from a then-new type of health care **entity** termed a **provider-sponsored organization**. This legislation also added a **federal tax law**, stating that a **tax-exempt charitable organization** will retain its exemption if a **hospital** it owns and operates participates in a **joint venture** with a PCO, irrespective of whether the PCO is an **exempt organization** (IRC § 501(o)). [HC § 22.10; EO § 7.6(a)(i)].

bargain sale

A "bargain sale" is a transfer of **property** that is in part a **sale** or **exchange** of the property and in part a **charitable contribution** of the property. Basically, a bargain sale is a sale of an item of property to a **charitable organization** at a price that is less than the **fair market value** of the property, with the seller/**donor** regarding the amount equal to the fair market value of the properly less the amount that is the sale price as a contribution to the charitable organization. In an instance of a bargain sale, there must be an **allocation of basis** between the gift portion and the sales portion of the property. [CG §§ 3.1(c), 9.19; CU Q 12.13; PF § 2.4(c); SM p. 238; LI Q 11.13].

base period

For purposes of the rules by which a **private foundation** is permitted to pay a reduced **tax** on its **net investment income**, the term "base period" means, with respect to a **tax year**, the five tax years preceding the tax year (**IRC** § 4940(e)(4)(A)). [PF § 10.2(a)].

base year

The term "base year" is used in connection with the measuring period of the **expenditure test**, where the **expenditures** of a **charitable organization** are measured to determine the extent the **entity** was **normally** engaged in **legislative activities**. This measuring period is a four-year period; each of the years in the period is a base year. [EO § 22.3(d)(iii)].

basic labor costs

The phrase "basic labor costs," as used in the **gross-up method** of **cost allocation**, means the basic costs of **lobbying labor hours**, except that an **organization** may not treat as zero the lobbying labor hours of personnel who engage in secretarial, maintenance, and similar activities if they engage in **lobbying activities**. Basic costs of lobbying labor hours are **wages** or other similar costs of labor, including guaranteed payments for services. Basic costs do not include **pension**, **profit-sharing**, **employee benefits**, and supplemented unemployment benefit plan costs, as well as other similar costs. [EO § 22.6(a)].

basic research

The **federal tax law** defines the term "basic research" as any original investigation for the advancement of **scientific** knowledge that does not have a specific **commercial** objective, other than basic research conducted outside the United States and basic research in the social sciences, arts, or humanities (**IRC** § 41(e)(7)(A)). [EO § 9.2].

basis

The term "basis" is used to describe the cost incurred to acquire an **asset** (**IRC** § 1012). When an item of **property** is sold or otherwise disposed of at a **gain**, the difference between the total amount **realized** and the gain element is the basis in the property. [CG §§ 2.14(a), 8.2(j), 8.3(d), 9.19(b)] (also **Adjusted basis**; **Capital gain element**; **Stepped-up basis**).

basis adjustment

The amount of a **shareholder's basis reduction** in the **stock** of an **S corporation**, by reason of a **charitable contribution** made by the corporation, is equal to the shareholder's pro rata share of the adjusted basis of the contributed property (**IRC** § 1367(a)(2)). [CG § 6.15].

beautification and maintenance organization

A **nonprofit organization** can qualify for **tax exemption** under the **federal tax law** if its purpose is **community** beautification and maintenance, and the preservation of natural beauty. [EO § 7.11].

beneficial interest

For purposes of defining the category of **disqualified person** known as "**20 percent owners**, where the **entity** involved is an **unincorporated enterprise** (including a **trust**), the term "beneficial interest" includes any **interest** that is outstanding, but not any interest that is obtainable but has not been obtained. The term includes (except in relation to a trust or an **estate**) any **right** to receive a portion of distributions from **profits** of the enterprise or, in the absence of a profit-sharing **agreement**, any right to receive a portion of the **assets** (if any) on **liquidation** of the enterprise, except as a creditor or **employee** (**IRC** § 4946(a)(1)(C)(iii)). A right to receive distribution of profits includes a right to receive any amount from the profits other than as a creditor or employee, whether as a **sum certain** or as a portion of profits realized by the enterprise. Where there is no agreement fixing the rights of the participants in an enterprise, the fraction of the respective interests of each participant in the enterprise is determined by recording the amount of all investments or contributions to the **capital** of the enterprise made or obligated to be made by the participant and dividing it by the amount of all investments or contributions to capital made or obligated to be made by all of the participants. [PF § 4.3].

beneficial title

The term "beneficial title" is used to describe some benefit or advantage that **a person** has with respect to one or more items of **property**, as evidenced by a **contract** or a similar document, or a set of other facts. In this circumstance, another person has **legal title** to the property. (also **Beneficial interest**).

beneficial use

A **person** has "beneficial use" of an item of **property** where the person has the **right** to some form of enjoyment of the property, even though the property is owned by someone else (that is, another person holds **legal title** to the property). The person who is this type of **beneficiary** of the property has a **beneficial interest** in the property.

B

beneficiary

A "beneficiary" is a **person** who is receiving, or is entitled to receive, some form of benefit from an item of **property** (and/or collection of money) held elsewhere. A person may be a beneficiary of a **trust, estate, insurance** policy, an **agency** relationship, or the like. In the **law** of **nonprofit organizations**, the term is usually used to refer to a beneficiary of a **gift**, either **outright** or by **trust**. For example, a person who has an **income interest** in a **split-interest trust** is a beneficiary. [CG §§ 12.1(a), 13.2(b), 14.1, 16.2; HC §§ 28.6, 29.1] (also **Beneficial title; Income interest beneficiary; Remainder interest beneficiary**).

benefit corporation

The term "benefit corporation" is used to refer to a type of hybrid **corporation**, which is an **entity** that has socially responsible and commercial business purposes. This type corporation elects this status, pursuing objectives such as **environmental preservation, promotion of health**, and **advancement** of the arts and sciences. [EO § 4.11(e)].

benefit events

See **Special events**.

benefits

For purposes of the **corporate sponsorship** rules, the term "benefits" (provided to payors) include **advertising; exclusive provider arrangements**; goods, facilities, services, or other privileges; and exclusive or nonexclusive rights to use an **intangible asset** (such as a trademark, patent, logo, or designation) of the **tax-exempt organization**. [EO § 24.6].

benevolent

The term "benevolent" is used to describe a broad range of activities designed to confer benefits, rather than generate profit for private ends. It is generally synonymous with terms such as **eleemosynary**, "humane," and **philanthropic**, and has a meaning that is broader than the term **charitable**. [EO § 6.1(b)].

benevolent organization

Certain **benevolent** life **insurance associations** of a **purely local character** are **exempt** from the **federal income tax** (under **IRC** § 501(a) by reason of **IRC** § 501(c)(12)). These associations basically operate to provide life insurance coverage for their **members**, albeit at cost because of a requirement that income be collected solely for the purpose of meeting losses and **expenses**. This category of **tax exemption** is also available for organizations like benevolent life insurance associations, such as "burial associations" and "funeral benefit associations." [EO § 19.5; AS § 1.6(k); SM p. 44].

bequeath

The word "bequeath" technically means the making of a **gift** of **personal property** by means of a **will**. A bequeathing of item of personal property is a form of **disposition** of the property. Sometimes, the word "bequeath" is used to embrace gifts by will of both personal property and **real property**. (also **Bequest**; **Devise**).

bequest

A "bequest" is a **gift** of **property** by means of a **will**. Technically, the term is used only to describe such a gift of **personal property**. (A gift by will of **real property** is termed a **devise**.) [CG § 8.3; SM p. 244] (also **Bequeath**; **Disposition**; **Legacy**).

bezonian

A "bezonian" is a slightly derogatory term for a fundraiser. When used, the word is likely to more technically connote a beggar.

bifurcation

In the context of the **law** of **nonprofit organizations,** the concept of bifurcation is the assignment of activities to two **organizations**, often **related** to each other. This type of bifurcation is usually done to facilitate compliance with the law, rather than for purely management reasons. Absent law requirements, all of the activities would be housed in one entity. The organizations may both be **tax-exempt**, such as a **charitable** (**IRC** § 501(c)(3)) organization with a related **lobbying** (**IRC** § 501(c)(4)) entity, a **business** or professional (**IRC** § 501(c)(6)) organization with a related (**IRC** § 501(c)(3)) **foundation**, or a tax-exempt organization with a related **title-holding** (**IRC** § 501(c)(2)) company. There may also be bifurcation, so that one organization is tax-exempt and the other is not, such as a tax-exempt organization with a **for-profit subsidiary**. The concept of bifurcation has expanded in many instances, particularly in the health care field, so that there may be dozens of related organizations in a single structure. [EO §§ 29.1, 30.1; PG pp. 92, 133, 134–136, 343; SM p. 86] (also **Spin-off**; **Subsidiary**; **Supporting organization**).

bill

The word "bill" has many meanings in the **law**. One of them is a draft of proposed **legislation**, usually so called after it has been introduced in a legislature.

Bill of Rights

The "Bill of Rights" is the first ten amendments to the U.S. Constitution. These **rights**, against interference by the **federal government**, which may be and often are articulated in state **constitutions,** include the rights of or to **free speech**, **assembly**, practice of **religion**, **due process**, **equal protection** under the **law**, a jury trial for **criminal** offenses, and freedom from **unreasonable** searches and seizures. The substance of the Bill of Rights has been incorporated by the U.S. Supreme Court into the Fourteenth Amendment and thus made applicable to state governments.

Rights provided by the Bill of Rights may be in conflict; in these circumstances, the courts will endeavor to balance them. For example, the **members** of an **organization** have a free speech right of **freedom of association**, but the courts will not let that constitutional right be used to thwart a state's interest in eradicating gender-based discrimination where the organization is a place of public accommodation. Also, even though a **charitable organization** has the free speech right to **solicit contributions**, the states generally can enact and enforce **charitable solicitation acts** in furtherance of their interest in protecting their citizens from **fraud** and other forms of deception (termed the **police power**).

The Bill of Rights does not protect against the interference with these fundamental rights by **persons** in their private capacity, unless the **state action doctrine** is applicable. For example, it has been held that **fraternal organizations,** because of the benefit of their **tax-exempt status** by which the state action doctrine was invoked, may not, on constitutional grounds, engage in racially discriminatory practices. [CL § 1.1(b); EO §§ 1.7, 4.8; FR § 4.2].

billing and collection requirement

To be **tax-exempt**, a **hospital organization** or **hospital facility** must meet a "billing and collection requirement" (**IRC** § 501(r)(6)). This requirement is met where the **entity** does not engage in extraordinary collection actions, with respect to an individual, before the entity has made reasonable efforts to determine whether the individual is eligible for assistance pursuant to the entity's **financial assistance policy**. [HC § 26.10(a)(vi); EO § 7.6(b)(vi)].

bingo game income

"Bingo game income" received by most types of **tax-exempt organizations** is not subject to the **unrelated business income tax** where the game is not conducted on a **commercial** basis and where the game does not violate state or local **law** (**IRC** § 513(f)). Some **charitable organizations** use bingo games as a form of **fundraising**. [EO § 25.2(h); UB § 4.7; FR § 4.3(e); SM p. 176].

Bipartisan Campaign Reform Act of 2002

The Bipartisan Campaign Reform Act of 2002 is the most recent **federal political campaign** financing **law**; it amended the body of law that includes limitations on the amounts and timing of **contributions** and **expenditures** for political campaign purposes, soft money restrictions, establishment and maintenance of **separate segregated funds**, use of political committees, and **disclosure** requirements. Decisions by the U.S. Supreme Court have trimmed the reach of this act. [FR § 5.25; CL §§ 5.0, 5.1; AS § 11.5; CU Q 9.29; EO § 23.2(b)(ii); HC § 7.9; SM p. 197].

black lung benefits law

Under the federal black lung benefits law, a coal mine operator in a state not deemed to provide adequate worker's compensation coverage for **black lung disease** must secure the payment of benefits for which the operator may be found liable, either by means of **commercial insurance** or through self-insuring. Inasmuch as no state laws are currently deemed adequate for this purpose, all operators subject to this **liability** must obtain sufficient insurance or self-insure.

Because this insurance is unavailable or is of high cost, coal mine operators self-insure and do so by means of **black lung benefits trusts**.

Black Lung Benefits Revenue Act of 1977
The Black Lung Benefits Revenue Act of 1977 brought enactment of the rules concerning **tax exemption** for **black lung benefits trusts**. [EO § 18.5].

black lung benefits trust
A "black lung benefits trust" is a **tax-exempt organization** (under **IRC** § 501(a) by reason of **IRC** § 501(c)(21)) that enables a coal mine operator to self-insure for **liabilities** under **federal** and state **black lung benefits laws**. A qualifying black lung benefits trust must be irrevocable, must be established by a written **instrument**, must be organized in the United States, and may be contributed to by any person (other than an **insurance** company). [EO § 18.5; AU § 7.1(y); SM p. 43].

black lung disease
The formal name used in the Internal Revenue Code for "black lung disease" is pneumoconiosis (otherwise known as anthracosis).

blockage discount
The term "blockage discount" is used in the context of **valuing** publicly traded securities. If the amount of the securities is so large that their **fair market value** would be depressed if all of the securities were placed on the market at the same time, that is a factor to be taken into account in determining the value of the securities; this factor is termed "blockage" (or "blockage discount"). A **private foundation**, when valuing its securities for purposes of determining its **minimum investment return**, may not reduce their value, unless and only to the extent that the securities could not be liquidated within a **reasonable** period of time, except at a price less than fair market value, due to (1) the size of the block of the securities, (2) the fact that the securities are those of a closely held corporation, or (3) the fact that **sale** of the securities would result in a forced or distressed sale. (**IRC** § 4942(e)(2)(B)) Even where one or more of the foregoing criteria are met, however, the reduction in value of a private foundation's securities may not exceed 10 percent of their otherwise-determined fair market value (*id.*). [PF § 6.3(d)].

blocker corporation
A **tax-exempt organization** may form a **corporation** in a foreign country for the purpose of facilitating and managing its foreign investing; this type of corporation can be used for liability protection purposes. These entities usually are "controlled foreign corporations." If that is the case, the income received by the controlled foreign corporation must be included, on a pro rata basis, in the gross income of the U.S. shareholders. This income is known as "Subpart F income" (due to the law contained in that portion of the **IRC**). These corporations generally receive only (or nearly all) **passive income**, although some income may be **debt-financed income**. Generally, the income received by the exempt organization from the foreign corporation will

B

be treated as **dividend** income (nontaxable under the **unrelated business income rules**). The process of converting what may be taxable income to the exempt organization to nontaxable income causes the controlled foreign corporation to be informally termed a "blocker corporation." This approach is unsuccessful to the extent the income received by the exempt organization from the foreign corporation is attributable to **insurance income**. If the tax-exempt organization is a **private foundation**, this structure should be tested against the rules concerning **excess business holdings** and **jeopardizing investments** (IRC §§ 512(b)(1), 951, 957). [EO §§ 25.1(b)(ii), (n)].

Blue Cross and Blue Shield

The "Blue Cross and Blue Shield" **organizations** operate forms of prepaid health care plans. These organizations lost their general tax exemption (under **IRC** § 501(a) by reason of **IRC** § 501(c)(4)) in 1986 (by enactment of **IRC** § 501(m)). [HC § 13.1; EO § 28.13(b); SM p. 289] (also **Commercial-type insurance**).

blue sky law

A "blue sky law" is a state **law** regulating the offering and sale of securities. These laws are likely applicable to offers to sell and to sales of interests in and operation of **pooled income funds**. These laws may also apply with respect to **charitable remainder annuity trusts** and **charitable remainder unitrusts**. [FR § 3.22].

board

The word "board" is generally used to describe a group of individuals who are **organized** to provide some official or representative function; it may be a governmental or nongovernmental body. A board usually has some **administrative** or management purpose or responsibility. Examples include a **board of directors**, **board of trade**, **board of trustees**, and a **real estate board**.

board of directors

A "board of directors" is a group of individuals elected or appointed to provide overall policy and management directives to an **organization;** it is the **governing body** of a **nonprofit organization** or a **for-profit organization**, usually a **corporation**. A board of directors may have the authority to elect the organization's **officers**. In the for-profit organization context, these individuals are almost always elected by the organization's stockholders. In the nonprofit organization context, there are three basic models: (1) the directors are elected by the organization's **members**, (2) the board of directors is a **self-perpetuating board**, or (3) the directors are elected (or appointed) by the board of directors of another organization. The board of directors of a **trust** (and sometimes other organizations) is termed a **board of trustees**. [GV §§ 1.3, 1.5, 2.7(n), 3.5(a), 3.10(e), 3.11, 4.1(a), 5.2–5.4, 5.7; EO §§ 5.1(a)–5.1(g), 5.2, 5.3(a), 5.3(b), 5.4, 5.6(h), 20.4(f), 21.9(a), 32.1(b), 32.1(c); AS §§ 3.4(a)(v), 3.4(a)(vii), 11.2, 11.3; CU Q 5.4– Q 5.24; RE Q 2.8, Q 5.2; SM pp. 16–19, 99–100, 258–259, 261–262; PG pp. 2–29; LI Q 1.23, Q 1.38, Q 3.3, 14.18, 14.19] (also **Ex officio positions; Fiduciary; Foundation managers; Interlocking directorate; Organization managers; Related organizations**).

board of trade

A "board of trade" is a **tax-exempt** (under **IRC** § 501(a) by reason of **IRC** § 501(c)(6)) **organization,** the "common business interest" of which is the general economic welfare of a **community**. That is, it is an organization the efforts of which are directed at promoting the common economic interests of all the **commercial** enterprises in a given trade community. **Membership** in a board of trade is voluntary and generally open to all **business** and professional **persons** in the particular community. [EO § 14.4; AS § 2.12] (also **Chamber of commerce**).

board of trustees

A "board of trustees" is essentially the same as a **board of directors**. The term "trustee," however, is most frequently associated with a **charitable** (**IRC** § 501(c)(3)) **organization,** principally a **trust**. Some charitable organizations that are not trusts use the term "board of trustees" rather than board of directors (principally, **private foundations**, **colleges**, and **universities**).

board-designated endowment

See **Quasi-endowment**.

board-restricted funds

The phrase "board-restricted funds" describes funds of an **organization** (usually a **charitable organization**) that its **governing board** has subjected to a **restriction**. Funds of this nature are not regarded as restricted funds, because the governing board can undo the restriction at any time. (also **Donor-restricted funds**).

BOLO

This acronym, which stands for "be on the lookout," gained enormous prominence in the realm of **tax-exempt organizations law** beginning in 2013, when it was learned that certain agents of the **IRS**, while processing **applications for recognition of exemption** filed by **organizations** (particularly those seeking **status** as **exempt social welfare entities**) who are or would be engaged in **political campaign activities,** utilized the BOLO technique by selecting applications for heightened (and often unwarranted) review on the basis of applicants' names and/or policy positions. [EO § 26.1(k)].

bona fide

The term "bona fide" is Latin for "in good faith"; it means an absence of deception. The **law** uses the term to inject into a set of facts a requirement of veracity, authenticity, and/or fairness; it often speaks of the "bona fides" of something. For example, the rule is that a **church** is a **tax-exempt organization**, but, for that rule to apply, the church must be a bona fide one (rather than, for example, a **personal church**). [EO § 10.2(c)].

bond

A "bond" is a document evidencing the existence of a debt; the entity that issued the bond promises to repay the holders of it at the expiration of a stated period, and in the interim

B

to pay a specified **rate** of **interest**. A bond also is an **instrument** issued by a surety guaranteeing the faithful performance of one or more duties (sometimes termed a "performance bond"); these types of bonds are often required of **professional solicitors**, and sometimes **professional fundraisers** and **charitable organizations**, under the states' **charitable solicitation acts**. [AR §§ 3.1(y)–3.1(bb), 3.2(y)-3.2(bb), 17.2(a)(3), 17.2(c)(20); FR §§ 3.6, 8.2, 8.7(f)] (also **Tax-exempt bond**).

bonding requirement

Many of the states' **charitable solicitation acts** include a requirement that various **entities** obtain a **bond** before commencing a **fundraising** activity. This requirement may apply to the **soliciting charitable organization**, to a **professional fundraiser**, and/or to a **professional solicitor**. [FR §§ 3.6, 8.2, 8.7(f)].

bonus

A "bonus" is an amount of **compensation** paid, usually to an **employee**, in addition to an amount of standard compensation (**salary** or **wage**), for the **value** of extraordinary personal services rendered; often, this type of payment is made pursuant to objective and nondiscriminatory criteria. Like compensation paid by most **tax-exempt organizations**, the bonus amount should be **reasonable**. [EO § 20.4(a); HC §§ 25.7, 28.5(a); SM pp. 51–52; LI Q 4.11–Q 4.14].

boost principle

It has been held that an **organization** may achieve **tax-exempt status** pursuant to the **integral part doctrine** only if the relationship of the subject organization to an **affiliated entity** is such that it somehow enhances the organization's own exempt character to the point that, when the boost provided by the affiliate is added to the contribution in the form of activities made by the organization, the organization would be entitled to **exempt status**. This is known as the "boost principle." [HC §§ 9.2(a); 34.7(a); EO § 26.10(a)].

booster club

The term "booster club" means a nonprofit organization that has as its purpose the provision of money and services in support of a youth sports program, such as gymnastics, swimming, or soccer. Traditionally, the **IRS** has regarded these entities as **tax-exempt charitable organizations** on the basis of the fostering of **amateur sports competition**. Some of these organizations have become more aggressive with their **fundraising**, involving the parents involved, who are the **members** of these clubs. In some instances, parents have assessment obligations that can be reduced by means of fundraising and other volunteer activities. Recently, the **IRS** has started taking the position that the resulting economic benefits amount to **private inurement**, causing clubs' exemptions to be revoked. The government has won the only court case on the point. The **IRS** is also finding that unwarranted **private benefit** is being provided to the youth (**IRC** § 501(c)(3)).

boycott

A "boycott," as defined in the **antitrust** context, is a concerted refusal to do business with a disfavored purchaser or seller, so as to affect the behavior of the purchaser or seller. In the context of the **law** of **nonprofit organizations**, the boycott is often a consumer boycott, designed to induce consumers to refrain from purchasing particular goods or services, in protest of or to alter the behavior of the seller of the goods or services. It has been held that a consumer boycott is an appropriate way for a **tax-exempt charitable organization** to advance its purposes. From this perspective, a boycott is a form of **advocacy**. [EO § 23.2(g)].

boys' club

A "boys' club" is a type of **membership association** that often is a **tax-exempt organization**; as the name indicates, membership in this type of club is confined to boys. These clubs are sometimes exempt from one or more requirements of state **charitable solicitation acts**. [FR § 3.5(n)] (also **Girls' club**).

branch

The word "branch" is used to describe a segment of an **organization** or system, usually a non-governmental **entity**. The word tends to be used to describe a segment that is smaller than a department or a division. The principal exception to the foregoing is the division of the **federal,** state, and other governments into an **executive branch**, a **judicial branch**, and a **legislative branch**. [AR § 5.1(i)(4)] (also **Bureau; Chapter; Lodge**).

branch, policy as to

The **IRS**, on **Form 990**, suggests that the filing organization, if it has one or more **branches**, have a policy as to standardization of activities and practices, given the entities' common **mission** and goals, and the public perception that the organizations are all part of one entity. [GV §§ 4.1(i), 6.3(h); AR §§ 5.1(i)(4), 5.2(a)(8)].

breach of contract

A "breach" generally is a breaking of a **law** or obligation, by commission or omission. Thus, a "breach of contract" occurs when a party to the **agreement** fails, without a lawful defense, to perform in accordance with its duty under the **contract**. A breach of contract can lead to damages incurred by the non-breaching party. (also **Specific performance**).

breach of fiduciary responsibility

Directors and **trustees** of **tax-exempt organizations**, particularly **charitable entities**, are **fiduciaries** of these organizations. When a **person** in this capacity violates the **duty of care**, the **duty of loyalty**, and/or the **duty of obedience**, the person is said to have **breached** his, her, or its fiduciary responsibility. [SM Chaps. 8, 25; EO § 5.3; HC § 33.2].

bright-line test

A "bright-line test," an endpoint rarely achieved in the **federal tax law**, is a test that lays down one or more clear standards to facilitate a consistent and predictable conclusion of law. This approach, which shuns subtleties and exceptions (and sometimes **equity**), is thus rarely found in this aspect of the law, despite clamor by those who wish to substitute objective standards for a facts-and-circumstances approach. [e.g., EO § 23.2(b)].

B

brownfield property

A "brownfield property" is a parcel of **real property** where there is a presence of a hazardous substance, pollutant, or contaminant that is complicating the expansion, redevelopment, or use of the property (**IRC** § 512(b)(19)(C)). [UB § 3.16; EO § 25.1(o)].

bundle of activities

See **Activities, bundle of.**

burden

One of the principal uses, in the **nonprofit law** context, of the word "burden" is in connection with **easements**. In the parlance of the law in this area, an easement is said to "burden" the underlying real property. [CG § 9.7(a)].

burden of proof

In every **administrative proceeding** and **judicial proceeding,** the cases considered turn on the facts before the **tribunal**. Before any element of **law** can be applied, the **material** facts must be developed. (A quaint rendition of this requirement is that the facts are "found"; the individual (or individuals) who determines what the facts are is termed a "fact finder.") To develop a fact it must be proved. It is up to one party in a dispute (usually the one initiating the proceeding) to prove the necessary facts. The extent to which facts must be proved depends, at least in part, on the party's "burden of proof." This is the obligation of a party to **substantiate** an allegation of fact—to convince the tribunal (sometimes termed the "trier of facts") as to the truth of the allegation(s) and thus prevail in the **action**.

There are differing standards to be met by a party in meeting this burden of proof requirement. In a **civil** case, the standard is that of a preponderance of the evidence; in a **criminal** case, the standard is beyond a **reasonable** doubt; and in some **equity** cases, the standard is one of clear and convincing evidence. For example, a **private school** that is seeking **recognition of tax-exempt status** must prove, by a preponderance of the evidence, that it does not engage in racial discrimination. [CG § 21.8; AU § 5.20; EO § 21.9] (also **Administrative record; Presumption**).

burdens of government, lessening

See **Lessening burdens of government.**

bureau

The word "bureau" is used to describe a segment of an **agency** or **department** of a government. Essentially, it is an office for the conduct of a specific function. The word has particular meaning in connection with the definition of the **service provider organization**, where the phrase **bureau or similar agency** is utilized.

bureau or similar agency

Under the definition of a **service provider organization**, **public support** includes **gross receipts** from **related** activities received from any "bureau or similar agency" of a

governmental unit, to the extent that the receipts do not exceed the greater of $5,000 or 1 percent of the organization's support for the year (the **1 percent limitation**) (**IRC** § 509(a)(2)(A)(ii)). The phrase "bureau or similar agency" means a specialized operating (rather than policymaking or **administrative**) unit of an **executive branch**, **judicial branch**, or **legislative branch** of government, usually a subdivision of a **department**. For example, an organization receiving gross receipts from both a policymaking or administrative unit, such as the Agency for International Development (AID), and an operational unit of a department, such as the Bureau for Latin America (an operating unit within AID), is treated as receiving gross receipts from two bureaus, with the amount from each separately subject to the $5,000 or 1 percent limitation. [PF § 15.5(d); HC § 5.3(d)].

burial association

An **organization** formed to develop methods of achieving simplicity and dignity in funeral services for its **members**, that is, a "burial association," may be able to qualify for **federal income tax exemption** as a **social welfare organization**. [EO § 13.1].

business

The term "business," in the **law** of **nonprofit organizations**, is broadly construed; it includes nearly any activity carried on for the production of **income**, including professional and trade undertakings. The term is significant in determining whether an organization can qualify as a **tax-exempt business league**.

The term "business" is also pivotal in the context of **unrelated income taxation**, since one of the elements underlying that form of taxation is that the activity involved be a **trade** or **business**. Generally, any activity that is carried on for the production of income from the **sale** of goods or the performance of services is a trade or business for purposes of the unrelated income tax (**IRC** § 513(c)). The courts have grafted another requirement onto the definition, which is that an activity, to be a "business," must be carried on with a **profit objective**.

An activity does not lose identity as a trade or business merely because it is carried on within a larger aggregate of similar activities or within a larger complex of other endeavors that may or may not be related to the tax-exempt purposes of the organization (**IRC** § 513(c)). Additionally, where an activity carried on for **profit** constitutes an unrelated trade or business, no part of that activity may be excluded from classification as a business merely because it does not result in a profit (**IRC** § 513(c)). [UB § 2.2; EO §§ 14.1(b), 24.2; AS § 2.6; CG § 3.4(b); FR § 5.7(a)(i), 5.7(a)(iii), 5.7(b)(i); PG pp. 172–173; SM pp. 171–172] also **Fragmentation rule**; **Related business**; **Unrelated business**).

business, convenience

A "convenience business" is a **business** carried on by an **organization primarily** for the convenience of its **members**, students, patients, **officers**, or **employees**. In the case of a **tax-exempt charitable** (**IRC** § 501(c)(3)) organization or a state **college** or **university**, this type of business is **excluded** from **unrelated business income taxation** (**IRC** § 513(a)(2)). [UB § 4.1; EO § 25.2(b)].

B

business, line of

The phrase "line of business" arises in the context of determining whether an **organization** can qualify as a **tax-exempt business league**, because a business league's activities must be directed to the improvement of business conditions of one or more lines of business. A line of business is a trade, occupation, or profession, entry into which is not restricted by a patent, trademark, or similar device that would allow private parties to restrict the right to engage in the business. [AS § 2.7; EO § 14.1(c), 14.2(a); SM p. 40].

business enterprise

The term "business enterprise" means the **active conduct** of a **trade or business**, including any activity that is **regularly carried on** for the production of **income** from the sale of goods or the performance of services, and that constitutes an **unrelated business** (**IRC** § 4943(d)(3)(B)). A business enterprise does not encompass a **functionally related business**, a **program-related investment**, a business of which at least 95 percent of the **gross income** is derived from **passive** sources, or certain investment **partnerships**. [PF §§ 7.1(a)–7.1(c), 15.1; UB § 6.3(a); AR § 4.1(p)(2)].

business expense deduction

There is a **federal income tax deduction** for **ordinary and necessary** expenses incurred in the conduct of a **business** (**IRC** § 162). Nearly all business expenses, made for **legislative** or **political campaign** efforts, are not deductible (**IRC** § 162(e)(1)). A transfer of funds or property may not be the subject of a business expense deduction if the transfer is in fact a **gift;** to allow a business expense deduction under these circumstances would be to permit evasion of the **percentage limitations**. [CG §§ 2.5(a), 10.7; HC § 7.2].

business judgment rule

A **director** of a **nonprofit organization** has, along with the other directors, broad control over the organization's management and must make decisions involving risk. Pursuant to the "business judgment rule," directors are protected from **liability** in the case of decisions made in good faith where the director is disinterested, **reasonably** informed, and honestly believes the decision to be in the best interest of the organization. This rule assists in determining whether a director has, in making corporate decisions, complied with the **duty of care**. [HC § 33.2(b); PF § 8.2].

business league

A "business league" is a rather antiquated term for what today is known as a trade, **business**, or professional **association** (or **society**). A business league is an **association** of **persons** having some common business interest, the purpose of which is to promote that common interest and not to engage in a regular business of a kind ordinarily carried on for **profit**. Its activities must be directed toward the improvement of business conditions of one or more **lines of business**, as distinguished from the performance of **particular services** for individual persons. **Organizations** that promote the common interests of hobbyists cannot qualify as business leagues.

A qualifying business league is exempt from **federal income taxation** (under **IRC** § 501(a) and by reason of **IRC** § 501(c)(6)). [AS §§ 1.1, 2.4, 2.5(b); EO Chap. 14, §§ 20.9, 22.2(c), 22.6, 23.7, 24.5(e), 29.2(b); HC Chap. 18; CL §§ 1.11, 8.3; CG § 1.3(b); PF §§ 1.6, 15.9; AU § 7.1(m); AR § 3.1(e)(3); CU Q 1.39; PG pp. 117, 122; SM p. 40].

business judgment rule

A **director** of a **tax-exempt organization** has, along with the other directors, broad **control** over the organization's management and must make decisions involving risk. Pursuant to the "business judgment rule," directors are protected from **liability** in the case of decisions made in **good faith** where the director is disinterested, reasonably informed, and honestly believes the decision to be in the best interest of the organization. This rule assists in determining whether a director has, in making corporate decisions, complied with the **duty of care**.

but for test

In general, a "but for test" requires, for compliance with it, that something happen or be undertaken, that would not happen or be undertaken were it not for the role of the **organization** seeking to satisfy the test. For example, one of the ways a **supporting organization** can meet an **integral part test** and thus be considered **functionally integrated** with a **supported organization** is to, among other criteria, engage in one or more **exempt functions** that, but for the involvement of the supporting organization would normally be engaged in by the supported organization. [PF § 15.7(g)].

bylaws

A set of "bylaws" for a **nonprofit organization** is a document containing the rules pursuant to which the organization is **operated**. It is a **governing instrument**, but usually is separate from the instrument by which the organization was created. An organization's bylaws are subordinate to (that is, must be in conformity with) the organization's **articles of organization** and the applicable **law**. [SM pp. 6, 9; PG p. 5; EO §§ 4.2, 4.3; GV § 1.2; RE Q 1.8, Q 2.18; LI Q 1.42] (also **Organizational test**).

C

C corporation

A **corporation,** in the **federal tax law,** may be classified as a "C corporation" when it is **organized** as a **for-profit** corporation. This name is derived from the fact that these corporations are referenced in Subchapter C of the **Internal Revenue Code,** Subtitle A, Chapter 1. A C corporation is any for-profit corporation that is not an **S corporation** (**IRC** § 1361(a)(2)). [CG §§ 2.8, 3.2, 6.14, 24.2, 24.7(a); UB § 8.2] (also **Regular corporation**).

call to action

The phrase "call to action" is used in the context of the rules defining **grass-roots lobbying communications**. One of the elements of that definition is that the communication encourages the recipient of the communication to take action with respect to the **legislation** involved. This is termed a "call to action"; the absence of this type of call often precludes a communication from being considered a grass-roots lobbying communication. [EO § 22.3(d)(i)].

campaign

The word "campaign" is used in the **nonprofit law** context in two ways. One is the effort of a **charitable organization** (and perhaps another type of **tax-exempt organization**) to attract **contributions** and **grants** to be used to further its **tax-exempt purpose;** this is **fundraising**. The other is the effort of a **candidate** for a **public office** to spend money and attract votes; this is the **political campaign.** [FR § 2.2(a); EO § 23.2].

campaign, capital

See **Capital campaign**.

campaign, fundraising

Tax-exempt organizations particularly those that are **charitable** ones, refer to their discrete **fundraising** efforts as **campaigns**. These campaigns are undertakings to raise **contributions** of money and **property** over a projected period of time. The most common of these campaigns is the **capital campaign**. [FR § 2.2(a)].

Bruce R. Hopkins' Nonprofit Law Dictionary, First Edition. Bruce R. Hopkins.
© 2015 Bruce R. Hopkins. Published 2015 by John Wiley & Sons, Inc.

campaign, political

For **federal tax law** purposes, a "political campaign" (a campaign for a **public office** in a public election) is a running for office, or a campaign for office, as that term is generally used. [EO § 23.2(e)].

campaign committee

See **Political campaign committee**.

candidate

The **federal tax law** defines the term "candidate for public office" as an individual who offers himself or herself, or is proposed by others, as a contestant for an elective **public office,** irrespective of whether the office is national, state, or local. There are no clear standards, however, in the federal tax law for determining precisely when an individual becomes a "candidate." An individual is, of course, a candidate once an announcement of his or her candidacy is made. Mere speculation as to a possible future candidacy by someone who is a prominent political figure does not necessarily make that individual a candidate, although some in the **IRS** tend to use that as a standard. Determinations as to whether an individual is a candidate are often made in hindsight. [EO § 23.2(d); AR § 10.1(a)(2); CU Q 9.8].

candidate-related political activity

The **IRS**, late in 2013, issued proposed regulations addressing the matter of permissible and impermissible **political campaign activity** by **tax-exempt social welfare organizations**. This proposal, which attracted a record number of comments (said to be over 150,000), centered on defining eight types of political campaign activity that would not constitute social welfare activity; these types were denominated "candidate-related political activity." These proposed regulations proved to be controversial and unpopular; the **IRS** announced, in the spring of 2014, that the regulations will be revised and reproposed. It is not known at this time whether the concept of candidate-related political activity will be retained. [EO § 23.5].

capital

"Capital" is **property contributed** to or otherwise acquired by an **organization**, which is held by the organization as part of its **asset** base. The term is usually associated with **for-profit organizations** (as being all of its money and property that is used in its operations), although **nonprofit organizations** often require operating capital as well. In the nonprofit law setting, the term used may be **principal** or **corpus**. Sometimes, the fund holding capital is termed an **endowment**. [CG §§ 2.16(a), 7.6(a); EO § 11.9(a); CU Chap. 19].

capital account

A "capital account" is that portion of an **organization's** financial books and records reflecting **capital assets** and **capital expenditures**, as well as any **liabilities** incurred in the process of acquiring the assets and making the expenditures.

capital asset

A "capital asset" is an item of **property** held by a **person**, other than properties such as **inventory** or other stock in trade, or property that is an integral part of a taxpayer's **business** (**IRC § 1221**). It is either a property that has a long **useful life** or is a fixed **asset** used in a **business**. The term has been construed by courts to mean investment property that tends to **appreciate** in **value** over time. When a capital asset is sold, any economic **gain** is termed **capital gain**; this type of **disposition** can also cause a **capital loss**. If a capital asset is the subject of a **charitable contribution**, the **charitable contribution deduction** is often based on the **fair market value** of the property (and the property is frequently referred to as **capital gain property**). [CG §§ 2.16(a), 7.6(a)] (also **Ordinary income property**).

capital campaign

A "capital campaign" involves **solicitations** by a **charitable organization** to obtain **contributions** and **grants** for a special purpose, which is the augmentation of the organization's physical facilities or other **capital assets**. The objective of the campaign is significant to the future of the organization, **major gifts** are required, and start and end dates are followed. This type of campaign is the culmination of years of effort, both in design and consensus surrounding the master project and in development of the **fundraising** team, including **volunteers**. [FR § 2.2(a)].

capital contribution

A "capital contribution" is a contribution of **capital**, in the form of money or **property**, to an **entity**, usually a **for-profit** business, by an owner (such as a **shareholder** or **partner**) or perhaps another **person**, causing the contribution to create an equity interest or increase the person's equity interest in the enterprise. On occasion, however, capital contributions are made to nonprofit organizations. For example, in computing the **gross receipts** of a **tax-exempt social club**, for purpose of determining its ongoing **exemption**, capital contributions are excluded. [EO § 15.3; CG § 2.3].

capital gain

"Capital gain" is the economic return generated by the **sale** or other **disposition** of a **capital asset**. This gain is the amount **realized** on the transaction less the **taxpayer's basis** in the asset (**IRC § 1222**). Most other forms of economic gain are termed **ordinary income**. Historically, capital gain has been accorded preferential tax treatment. [CG §§ 2.14(b); 2.16(b), 2.20; PF §§ 12.1(b), (f), 14.1(b). 14.2, 14.4(a), (c); EO § 25.1(j); AR § 7.2(a)(3)] (also **Appreciation**; **Appreciation element; Capital gain element; Capital gain property; Long-term capital gain; Short-term capital gain**).

capital gain element

When an item of **capital gain property** is **sold** or otherwise **disposed** of, and where the property has **appreciated** in **value,** the amount received on the transaction (usually an amount equal to the **fair market value** of the property) will reflect the amount of the appreciation (**capital**

gain). The portion of the total amount received that reflects the appreciation in value (fair market value less **basis**) is informally known as the "capital gain element." [CG §§ 2.14(b); 2.16(b)].

capital gain exclusion

Generally, excluded from **unrelated business income taxation** are gains from the sale, exchange, or other disposition of **capital gain property** (**IRC** § 512(b)(5)). [UB §§ 2.2(e), 3.10(a), 3.10(b); EO § 25.1(j)].

capital gain property

The phrase "capital gain property" is a shortened version of the term **long-term capital gain property**, which generally is property that, if sold, would give rise to long-term capital gain. When a **donor** makes a **contribution** of capital gain property to a **charitable organization** (that is not a **private foundation**), the **charitable contribution deduction** is generally based on the **fair market value** of the property. [CG §§ 4.3, 4.5].

capital gains tax

A "capital gains tax" is a **tax** imposed on the transfer of a **capital asset**, where the **property** has **appreciated** (gained) in **value**. Thus, this tax is levied on the **appreciation element** in an item of property at the time of its transfer.

capital improvement

The term "capital improvement" means the enhancement of an item of **capital gain property** (most commonly, **real property**) by the making of a **capital expenditure**. Thus, the purpose of a **capital campaign** by a **charitable organization** is the acquisition or improvement of capital.

capital loss

The term "capital loss" refers to the economic loss generated by the **sale** or other **disposition** of a **capital asset**. This loss is the amount **realized** on the transaction less the **taxpayer's basis** in the asset (**IRC** § 1222). Most other forms of economic loss are termed **ordinary losses**. [CG § 2.16(b)].

capitalization

The word "capitalization" means the process of transferring **capital** to an **organization,** either at the time the entity is being organized or subsequently, when the need for additional capital arises. [EO § 30.3(a); UB § 8.5; CU Q 16.17].

care of the needy

In the context of the special rule governing the **deductibility** of certain **charitable contributions** of **inventory,** the phrase "care of the needy" is defined as an alleviation or satisfaction of an existing need of an individual (or individuals) who is **needy**. Since a person may be needy in some respects and not in others, care of the needy must relate to the particular difficulty that causes the person to be needy. For example, an individual whose temporary need arises from a natural disaster may require temporary shelter and food but not recreational facilities. [CG § 9.3(b)].

care of orphans

A way for a **nonprofit organization** to qualify as a **tax-exempt charitable entity** is to provide care for orphans. [EO § 7.15(f)].

carryback

A "carryback" is the application of a **deduction** or **credit** developed in a **tax year** that cannot be used, in whole or in part, to reduce **tax liability** in that year, but which can be applied to reduce tax liability with respect to a previous taxable year (or years). [CG § 2.17].

carryforward

See **Carryover**.

carryover

A "carryover" is the application of a **deduction** or **credit** developed in a **tax year** that cannot be used, in whole or in part, to reduce **tax liability** in that year, but which can be applied to reduce tax liability in a subsequent taxable year (or years). [CG § 2.17].

carryover, charitable contribution deduction

There are limitations on how much of a **federal income tax charitable contribution deduction** an individual or a **corporation** can claim in a **tax year**; these are known as the **percentage limitations**. An amount in excess of one of these deductions may be able to be carried over to one or more subsequent years and be deducted in one or more of those years. Amounts so carried forward are "charitable contribution deduction carryovers." [CG § 2.17; SM pp. 135–136].

case law

The term "case law" is used to describe a body of law on a particular subject as formed by opinions of courts, as contrasted with **statutory law** and **administrative law** (**regulations** and **rules**).

case statement

A "case statement" is a document prepared by a **tax-exempt organization**, usually a **public charity**, in the context of its **fundraising** efforts, explaining its programs and objectives, and stating its appeal for **contributions** and, perhaps, grants. [PG p. 19].

cash basis method of accounting

Under the method of accounting known as the "cash basis method of accounting" (also more formally known as the "cash receipts and disbursements method of accounting"), an item of **income** (and **expense**) is **recognized** to the **taxpayer** when money is received (income) or is paid out (expensed). The same is the case with respect to transfers of property. [CG § 2.10] (also **Accounting method**).

cash distribution test

The "cash distribution test" is the name given to a type of **set-aside** that can be used by a **private foundation** in meeting its **mandatory payout requirement** (**IRC** § 4942(g)(2)(A)). It may be utilized by a private foundation only in its early years. This test is satisfied when the rules of the **suitability test** are met and when the private foundation actually distributes the **start-up period minimum amount** and subsequently actually distributes the **full-payment period minimum amount**. Advance approval from the **IRS** is not required where the cash distribution amount is correctly utilized. [PF §§ 3.1(h), 6.5(d)].

cash surrender value

The "cash surrender value" is the amount that an **insurance** company will pay in exchange for cancellation, prior to the death of the **insured**, of a life insurance policy. A **charitable organization** that owns and is the **beneficiary** of a life insurance policy must make an investment decision, at one or more points in time, as to whether to retain the policy or surrender it for its cash value. Retention of a life insurance policy, where the better investment practice would have been to surrender it, by a **private foundation** can cause a **jeopardizing investment**. [CG §§ 17.2, 17.3].

cause of action

A "cause of action" is one or more facts which can provide a **right** of action in a **person**. (also **Action**).

cause-related marketing

"Cause-related marketing" involves the marketing of products or services to the public by or on behalf of a **tax-exempt organization,** usually a **charitable organization**. This is a **fundraising** technique, although the practice can be, or appear to be, a **commercial** activity or an **unrelated trade or business**. This term is often applied to **commercial co-ventures**. [FR § 5.7(b)(ix); HC § 31.2(i)].

cemetery company

A "cemetery company" is a type of **tax-exempt organization** under the **federal tax law** (by reason of **IRC** §§ 501(a) and 501(c)(13)). This exemption extends to cemetery companies that are owned and **operated exclusively** for the benefit of their **members** and that are not operated for **profit**. A cemetery company generally is one that owns a cemetery, sells lots in it for burial purposes, and maintains these and the unsold lots in a state of repair and upkeep appropriate to a cemetery. This tax exemption also extends to a **corporation chartered** solely for the purpose of the disposal of bodies by burial or cremation. [EO § 19.6; AS § 1.6(l); AU § 7.1(s); AR § 19.1(a)(2); SM p. 44].

central organization

The term "central organization" is used in the context of the rules concerning the **group exemption**. The "central organization" is the **organization** that has formed the group of **entities**, known as **subordinate organizations**, and that has agreed to maintain some form of approved **affiliation** with them, involving their general supervision and **control**. It is usually a national or regional organization. [EO § 26.9; SM p. 78].

certificate of incorporation

When an **organization** incorporates, it files its **articles of incorporation** with the state (or District of Columbia) and receives in return a document certifying that the incorporation process has taken place and the date of incorporation; this document is termed a "certificate of incorporation." (also **Charter**).

certification

The term "certification" has two meanings. One, it is the process a **nonprofit organization** undertakes to recognize (certify) those individuals (not necessarily its **members**) who have received a certain level of competence and proficiency in the field represented by the organization. The certification is usually evidenced by a set of initials that an individual can use following his or her name (e.g., **certified public accountant** or CPA). Certification is an inappropriate activity, according to the **IRS**, for a **tax-exempt charitable organization**; it is, by contrast, an appropriate undertaking for a tax-exempt **business league**.

Two, the word "certification" is used in connection with the extent of **deductibility** of **charitable contributions** of **tangible personal property** that is **applicable property**; it means a written statement that is signed under penalty of perjury by an **officer** of the **charitable donee** and which (1) certifies that the use of the property by the donee was **substantial** and **related** to the donee's **exempt purpose**, and describes how the property was used and how the use furthered the exempt purpose, or (2) states the intended use of the property by the donee at the time of the contribution and certifies that this use has become impossible or infeasible to implement (**IRC** § 170(e)(7)(D)). [EO §§ 13.1, 24.5(q); AS §§ 1.3(c), 1.4, 2.4(c), 2.8; CG 4.6(c)] (also **Accreditation**)).

certified historic structure

A "certified historic structure" is a building or other structure that is (1) listed in the **National Register of Historic Places** or (2) certified by the Department of the Interior to the **Department of the Treasury** as being of historic significance to a registered historic district (**IRC** §§ 47(c)(3)(A), 170(h)(4)(C)). The structure must satisfy this definition, for **charitable contribution deduction** purposes, either as of the date of the transfer or on the due date (including extensions) for filing the **transferor's tax return** for the year in which the transfer is made (**IRC** § 170(h)(4)). [CG § 9.7(c)]).

certified public accountant

A "certified public accountant" is an **accountant** who has been licensed by a state after proving his or her competency by passing an examination, meeting certain **educational** requirements, and, in most states, working for another CPA for a period of time. A CPA is continually accountable to the state. Only a CPA can be a **member** of the American Institute of Certified Public

Accountants. In general, a **nonprofit organization** should retain the services of a CPA when an **audit** is necessary. (also **Public accountant**)).

certiorari

The word "certiorari" is the name of a writ issued by a **higher court** to a **lower court** by which the former is enabled to review the proceedings below to determine if there has been any procedural or substantive irregularities. For example, the U.S. Supreme Court issues a writ of certiorari to a lower **appellate court** when it has decided to review a case.

chain rule

The "chain rule" is applied in the context of defining **organizations** that are **affiliated** for purposes of the **expenditure test**. One of the ways in which this type of affiliation can exist is when the **governing instrument** of an organization requires it to be hound by decisions of another organization on **legislative issues** (IRC § 4911(f)(2)(A)). If one organization is affiliated with each of two or more organizations, these other organizations are considered affiliated with each other. If one organization is affiliated with another organization and that other organization is affiliated with a third organization, the third organization is considered, by operation of the chain rule, affiliated with the first organization. [EO § 22.3(d)(viii)].

chamber of commerce

A "chamber of commerce" is a type of **tax-exempt organization** under the **federal tax law** (by reason of **IRC** § 501(c)(6)). It is an organization the common business interest of which is the general economic welfare of a **community**. That is, it is an organization that directs its efforts at promoting the common economic interests of all the commercial enterprises in a given trade community. By contrast, a **business league** serves only the common business interests of the **members** of a single **line of business** or of closely related lines of business within a single industry. [EO § 14.3; AS § 2.11; SM p. 40].

chapter

A national or regional **nonprofit organization** (usually a **membership entity**) may have groupings of members at a state or more localized level. These groupings are usually termed a "chapter," although they may be called a **lodge** or similar term. Chapters of this nature may be separate legal entities or **integral parts** of the principal organization. [CU Q 1.30–Q 1.32] (also **Charter**).

chapter, policy as to

The **IRS**, on **Form 990**, suggests that the filing organization, if it has one or more **chapters**, have a policy as to standardization of activities and practices, given the entities' common **mission** and goals, and the public perception that the organizations are all part of one entity. [GV §§ 4.1(i), 6.3(h); AR §§ 5.1(i)(4), 5.2(a)(8)].

charitable

The term "charitable" is defined for **federal tax law** purposes to embrace undertakings such as (1) the relief of **poverty**, (2) the **advancement** of **religion**, (3) the advancement of

C

education, (4) the advancement of **science**, (5) **lessening of the burdens of government**, (6) community **beautification** and **maintenance**, (7) the **promotion of health**, (8) the **promotion of social welfare**, (9) the promotion of the **arts**, (10) the promotion of **environmental conservancy**, (11) the promotion of **patriotism**, (12) the promotion. advancement, and sponsorship of recreational and amateur sports, (13) care of orphans. (14) the facilitating of student and cultural exchanges, and (14) maintenance of public confidence in the legal system. In this sense, the term describes one or more of the types of organizations that qualify for **federal law tax-exempt status** by reason of **IRC** § 501(c)(3).

The term "charitable" is also used in another sense: To describe all of the organizations that are described in **IRC** § 170(c)(2) (including **educational**, **religious**, and **scientific organizations**). This is the case because (with the exception of the **public safety testing organization**) all of these organizations are eligible **donees** in relation to the **federal income tax charitable contribution deduction**.

The term "charitable" is frequently given a broader definition for purposes of application of the states' **charitable solicitation acts**, and includes such other ends as **benevolent**, **philanthropic**, and eleemosynary. [EO § 6.1(a), Chap. 7; CG § 2.1; FR §§ 1.1, 2.1; HC § 8.2; SM pp. 33–35].

charitable class

While the concept of a "charitable class" is somewhat outdated, the principle is that the individuals who are to benefit from a purported **charitable** activity must constitute a sufficiently large or indefinite class. Thus, the **beneficiary** of a charitable activity cannot be a single individual; the beneficiaries cannot be specifically named or related to the organization's **founder**. Charitable classes include the poor, the **distressed**, **students**, and (sometimes) the elderly. [EO § 6.3(a); PF § 1.8; CU Q 17.44; HC § 6.1] (also **Private benefit**; **Private inurement**).

charitable contribution

A "charitable contribution" is a **contribution** of money and/or **property** to a **charitable organization**, often resulting in a **charitable contribution deduction**. [CG § 3.1; FR § 5.14(a); EO § 2.3; PF § 1.4(l); CU Q 12.5; AR § 19.1(a)(1); PG pp. 103–104; SM pp. 129–131].

charitable contribution deduction

A "charitable contribution deduction" is one of the **federal tax law's itemized deductions**; it is available for both individuals and **corporations** (and, in some instances, **trusts**). At the federal tax level, there are three charitable contribution deductions; one in connection with the **income tax** (**IRC** § 170), the **estate tax** (**IRC** § 2055), and the **gift tax** (**IRC** § 2522). There are limits as to how much of a charitable contribution deduction an individual or a corporation may have in a year for income tax purposes; often, any excess over one of these limitations is deductible in a subsequent **tax year**. [CG § 1.1; FR § 5.14; SM Chap. 11; EO §§ 2.3, 3.2(b), 24.6(q); PF §§ 3.2, 9.5, 14.1, 14.3, 15.1; GV §§ 1.1(g), 8.14(a); UB §§ 3.18, 11.4(d)(x)] (also **Carryover**, **charitable contribution deduction**, **Percentage limitations**).

charitable contribution deduction, denial of for lobbying activities

A **charitable contribution deduction** is denied (where it would otherwise be available) for a **contribution** to a **charitable organization** that conducts activities involving attempts to **influence legislation** and **political campaign activities** (**IRC** § 162(e)(1)) on matters of direct financial interest to the **donor's trade or business**, if a **principal** purpose of the contribution was to avoid **federal income tax** by securing a charitable deduction for these activities, which would be disallowed under the **lobbying disallowance rule** if the donor had conducted the activities **directly** (**IRC** § 170(f)(9)). [CG § 10.8].

charitable contribution deduction, timing of

See **Timing of charitable contribution deductions**.

charitable deduction

See **Charitable contribution deduction**.

charitable deduction property

The **federal tax law** contains a requirement that, in general, if a **donee** of an item of "charitable deduction property" **sells, exchanges,** or otherwise **disposes** of the **property** within three years of its receipt, the **charitable organization** must file an **information return (Form 8282)** with the **IRS** (**IRC** § 6050L(a)(2)(A)). For this purpose, the phrase "charitable deduction property" means any property (other than publicly traded securities) made in a **contribution** for which an **income tax charitable contribution deduction** was claimed, if the claimed **value** of the property (plus the claimed value of all **similar items** of property contributed by the **donor** to one or more donees) exceeds $5,000 (**IRC** § 6050L(b)). The phrase "charitable deduction property," as also used in the context of **accuracy-related penalties**, means any **property contributed** by a **person** for which an **income tax charitable contribution deduction** was claimed (**IRC** § 6664(c)(4)(A)). [CG §§ 10.14(a), 24.10; FR § 5.14(l); PF §§ 14.2, 14.4(a), 14.4(c), 15.1; HC § 31.2(c)].

charitable donee status

The phrase "charitable donee status" includes the classification of **tax-exempt organizations** that are eligible to receive **contributions** that are **deductible** under the **federal tax law** and/or the **law** of another government. For federal **income tax** purposes, the phrase includes those organizations that are **charitable organizations** pursuant to the tax-exempt organizations rules (that is, those **entities** described in **IRC** § 501(c)(3)) (other than organizations that are **public safety testing organizations**). It also includes, for federal income tax purposes, states, possessions of the United States, political **subdivisions** of a state or U.S. possession, the United States, the District of Columbia, certain **veterans' organizations**, certain **fraternal organizations**, and certain **cemetery companies**. Similar distinctions are made in the context of the federal **estate tax** and **gift tax** charitable contribution deductions. [CG § 3.3; AR § 19.1(a)(2); RE Q 13.1].

charitable family limited partnership

A "family limited partnership" is a **partnership**, comprised of one or more **general partners** and one or more **limited partners**. The partners are confined to members of a family. A **donor contributes** a percentage interest in the partnership to a **charitable organization**, in the form of a limited partnership interest. The **value** of this interest may be the subject of controversy. The **IRS** observed that the "operation of [this type of a] partnership may cross over into the area of clear tax abuse." [CG § 9.26]

charitable gift annuity

A "charitable gift annuity" is a form of **planned gift** that is reflected in a **contract** between the **donor** and the **donee**, where the donor agrees to make a gift and the donee agrees to provide the donor (and/ or someone else) an **annuity**. In this process, the donor is, in essence, engaging in two transactions, albeit with one payment: the making of a gift and the purchase of an annuity. One sum (and/or one or more items of property) is transferred; the amount in excess of that necessary to purchase the annuity is the charitable **gilt** portion. (It is because of the dual nature of the transaction that the charitable gift annuity transfer constitutes a **bargain sale**.) A charitable gift by means of a gift annuity should be contrasted with the charitable gift made by means of a **charitable remainder annuity trust**.

The charitable gift annuity is referenced in the context of defining what is and is not an **acquisition indebtedness** (**IRC** § 514(c)(5)). The issuance of a charitable gift **annuity** is not regarded as the writing of **commercial-type insurance** (**IRC** §§ 501(m)(3)(E), 501(m)(5)). A contemporary use of the charitable gift annuity is in the **tuition annuity program**. [CG Chap. 14; EO §§ 3.2(f), (g), 24.12(c), 27.13(b); PF § 2.4(c); CU Q 12.68, Q 12.93; RE Q 13.11; AS § 9.2(e); SM pp. 238–239; LI Q 11.68, Q 11.93].

Charitable Gift Annuity Antitrust Relief Act of 1995

The "Charitable Gift Annuity Antitrust Relief Act of 1995" was enacted to make it clear that **charitable organizations** using the same **annuity** rate in connection with issuance of **charitable gift annuities** are not violating the **antitrust laws**. [CG § 14.8].

charitable immunity statute

A "charitable immunity state" is a state **law** designed to immunize qualifying **charitable organizations** from various forms of civil liability. These laws, however, do not provide protection in cases of gross negligence, or intentional or willful and wanton misconduct. [RE Q 15.14–15.17].

charitable income fund

A "charitable income fund" is a **fund** maintained by a **charitable organization exclusively** for the collective investment and reinvestment of one or more **assets** of a **charitable remainder trust** or similar trust, a **pooled income fund**, a **charitable lead trust**, a general **endowment fund** or other funds of a charitable organization, or certain other trusts the remainder interests of which are dedicated to or **for the benefit of** one or more charitable organizations, or assets **contributed** in exchange for the issuance of **charitable gift annuities**. [CG § 5.9].

charitable income trust

A "charitable income trust" is a **trust** whereby the **charitable organization** that is the **income interest beneficiary** is only entitled to the income of the trust. There is no income, **gift**, or **estate tax deduction** for this type of gift (because the trust is not one of the required forms). [CG § 16.9] (also **Charitable lead trust**).

charitable lead trust

A "charitable lead trust" is a form of **planned gift** that utilizes a **split-interest trust**. Pursuant to this type of trust, an **income interest** in **property** is **contributed** to a **charitable organization**, either for a term of years or for the life or lives of one or more individuals. The **remainder interest** in the property is reserved to return, at the expiration of the income interest (the "lead period"), to the **donor** or some other **noncharitable beneficiary** or beneficiaries; often the property passes from one generation (the donor's) to another. [CG Chap. 16; EO §§ 2.5, 3.2(g); PF §§ 2.4(c), 6.2(b), 14.5; CU Q 12.67, Q 12.102; RE Q 13.10; AS § 9.2(d); SM pp. 237–238; LI Q 11.67, Q 11.102] (also **Charitable income trust**).

charitable leakage doctrine

The concept of "charitable leakage" is that resources of a **charitable organization** are inappropriately being put to **noncharitable purposes**. The doctrine is essentially, if awkwardly, embodied in the **private inurement doctrine**. [EO § 20.1; HC § 4.1(a); SM pp. 49–50].

charitable lease

A "charitable lease" is a **lease** of **property**, at a nominal rate, to a **charitable organization** where the **lessee** uses the property for charitable purposes. For example, a charitable lease by a **private foundation** can constitute a **qualifying distribution**, with the leased property excluded from the calculation of the private foundation's **minimum investment return**. [PF § 6.5(c)].

charitable organization

The phrase "charitable organization" is used to refer to an **organization** that is eligible to attract **tax-deductible charitable contributions** and an organization that is **tax-exempt** under the **federal tax law** because it is **organized** and **operated** for **charitable** purposes. [EO Chap. 7; PF §§ 1.7, 1.8, 2.6; SM pp. 33–35; CG § 3.1; FR § 2.1; HC § 1.5; CL § 1.8(a); AU § 7.1(b); CU Q 1.38; LI Q 11.67, Q 11.102] (also **Charity**).

charitable remainder annuity trust

A "charitable remainder annuity trust" is a form of **charitable remainder trust** where the **income** payments are in the form of a fixed amount (an **annuity**). There are some other differences between this type of trust and the **charitable remainder unitrust**. A **gift** transaction utilizing a charitable remainder annuity trust should be compared to a transaction involving a **charitable gift annuity**. [CG § 12.2; SM pp. 235–236].

charitable remainder trust

A "charitable remainder trust" is a form of **planned gift** that utilizes a **split-interest trust**. The statutory **law** concerning this type of trust is in **IRC** § 664. This type of trust is one in which has been created a **remainder interest** that is destined for one or more **charitable organizations**. One or more income interests, for noncharitable beneficiaries, are also created in a charitable remainder trust. This type of trust must either be a **charitable remainder annuity trust** or a **charitable remainder unitrust**.

A charitable remainder trust must provide for a specified **distribution** of **income**, at least annually, to one or more **beneficiaries** (at least one of which is not a charitable organization) for life or for a term of no more than twenty years. An irrevocable remainder interest must be held for the benefit of, or be paid over to, the charitable organization. These beneficiaries are the holders of the income interests, and the charitable organization has the remainder interest; these interests are defined with particularity in the charitable remainder trust **instrument**. [CG Chap. 12; EO §§ 19.23, 28.3; PF §§ 1.1, 2.4(b), 6.2(b), 14.5; CU Q 12.65; RE Q 13.8; AS § 9.2(b); UB § 5.4(e)(v); SM pp. 235–236; LI Q 11.65].

charitable remainder unitrust

A "charitable remainder unitrust" is a form of **charitable remainder trust** where the **income** payments are in the form of an amount equal to a fixed percentage of the **fair market value** of the **assets** in the trust. There are some other differences between this type of trust and the **charitable remainder annuity trust**. For example, additional **contributions** can be made to a charitable remainder unitrust, but not to a charitable remainder annuity trust. Also, there are differing types of charitable remainder unitrusts, such as the **income-only unitrust**, the income-only unitrust with a **make-up feature**, and the **flip unitrust**. [CG § 12.3; SM pp. 235–236].

charitable remainderman

A "charitable remainderman" is a **charitable organization** that is the owner and **beneficiary** of a **remainder interest**, usually one arising from a **split-interest trust**. (also **Remainder interest beneficiary**).

charitable risk pool

See **Qualified charitable risk pool**.

charitable sales promotion

The term "charitable sales promotion" means essentially the same as a **commercial co-venture**. [FR §§ 3.2(i), 8.4; CG § 25.4].

charitable solicitation act

Most states have **laws** that regulate the process of **soliciting gifts** for **charitable** purposes. These laws are termed "charitable solicitation acts." They contain registration, reporting, record-keeping, disclosure, **bonding**, and other requirements. These laws apply to many types of **organizations** engaged in **fundraising**, and often also apply to **professional fundraisers**, **professional solicitors**, and **commercial co-venturers**. Other bodies of government, such as those at the county and city levels, often have similar laws, usually generically referred to as "charitable solicitation ordinances." [FR Chap. 7; CG Chap. 25; CL §§ 7.1, 7.2; HC §§ 31.1, 31.1(i); PF §§ 2.5(g), 14.6(e); AR 14.1(f); GV § 1.1(e); SM pp. 127, 147–152; LI Q 12.4, Q 12.5].

charitable spending initiative

The **IRS** announced, in 2009, commencement of a "charitable spending initiative," which the agency characterized as a "long-range study to learn more about sources and uses of funds in the charitable sector and their impact on the accomplishment of charitable purposes." This is a **compliance check** project, essentially applying elements of the **commensurate test**. [EO § 4.7(b); FR § 5.15(d); CU Q 1.36; LI Q 1.47, Q 12.40].

charitable split-dollar life insurance plan

Under the typical arrangement, one or more **charitable contributions** of money were made to a **public charity** the **donee** used some or all of these funds to purchase and pay premiums in connection with a split-dollar life insurance policy. The death benefits were shared between the family members of the insured and the **charitable organization**. Due to criticisms, including charges of unwarranted **private benefit**, the **federal tax law** denies an **income tax charitable contribution deduction** for, an imposes **excise tax penalties** on, transfers associated with use of "charitable split dollar life insurance plans" (**IRC** § 170(f)(10)). [CG: § 17.6; EO § 27.13(d); SM pp. 239–240].

charitable uses, statute of

See **Statute of Charitable Uses**.

charity

The word "charity" is an informal way of referring to a **charitable organization** or to an activity (or the result of an activity) carried on by a charitable organization (as in an "act of charity"). [CG § 3.2(b); HC §§ 6.1, 7.1].

charity care policy

A **tax-exempt hospital's** "charity care policy" should describe how and the extent to which the **organization** will provide **charity care**, and who is eligible for this type of care. [SM pp. 276–277].

charity care standard

The "charity care standard" is a standard of law that once was the basis of **tax exemption** under the federal tax law for nonprofit **hospitals** (by reason of **IRC** § 501(c)(3)). It is premised largely on the view that tax-exempt status for hospitals should be based on the definition of the term **charitable** that emphasizes **relief of the poor**. Under this standard (which frequently is the law in some states), a hospital, to be tax-exempt, must provide a **substantial** portion of its health care services without cost or on a reduced-cost basis. In recent years, this standard has become reflected in and replaced by the **additional hospital exemption requirements**. [HC §§ 3.2– 3.3(a), Chap. 26; EO § 7.6(a); AR §§ 15.1(a), 15.2(d); GV § 6.3(m)] (also **Community benefit standard**).

Charleston Principles

The National Association of State Charity Officials developed guidelines, named the "Charleston Principles," to assist state regulators, **charitable organizations** that **solicit** contributions, and their **fundraisers**, in deciding whether it is necessary to register fundraising efforts in one or more states when the solicitations are made on the organizations' websites and/or by email. [FR §§ 4.13(b), 4.13(c), 8.13; SM pp. 163–166; LI Q 12.16].

C

charter

A "charter" is a document by which a government (usually a state) recognizes the validity of, accepts (because of the satisfaction of **statutory** criteria), and thereby creates an entity (usually a **corporation**). The most common of this process occurs when the **articles of incorporation** of a putative corporation are filed with a **governmental agency**, which in turn issues a **certificate of incorporation**.

The word "charter" is also used to describe the process by which one **nonprofit organization** recognizes another by application of certain criteria, such as a national organization recognizing various other organizations as its **chapters**. [PG p. 16; SM pp. 6–7].

check-the-box regulations

Pursuant to the "check-the-box regulations," an **organization** is either a **trust** or a business **entity**. A business entity with two or more **members** is classified for **federal tax law purposes** as a **corporation** or a **partnership**. A business entity with only one owner is classified as a corporation or is **disregarded**. A corporation includes a business entity organized under a **federal** or state statute, an **association**, or a business entity owned by a state or political subdivision of a state. A business entity that has been determined to be, or claims to be, **exempt** from federal **income taxation** (**IRC** § 501(a)) is treated as having made the election to be classified as an association, which causes the exempt entity to be regarded as a corporation. [EO § 4.1(b)].

Chevron standard

The "Chevron standard" is a U.S. Supreme Court-articulated (in 1984) test of **statutory construction** at the **federal** level, applied by courts in the context of determining the validity of a **regulation**. Pursuant to this test, a court first ascertains "whether Congress has directly spoken to the precise question at issue." "If the intent of Congress is clear," the Court stated, "that is the end of the matter; for the court, as well as the agency, must give effect to the unambiguously expressed intent of Congress." If, however, the statute involved is "silent or ambiguous with respect to the specific issue," the court must determine whether the agency's interpretation (such as by means of a proposed or final regulation) is "based on a permissible construction of the statute." The agency's formulation will be accorded **deference** by the court "unless it is arbitrary or capricious in substance or manifestly contrary to the statute." The Supreme Court (in 2011) expressly held that the Chevron standard applies with respect to tax regulations. [EO App. A; CL § 8.1; SM pp. 338–339].

chief counsel advice memorandum

In the course of preparing a **revenue ruling**, **private letter ruling**, or **technical advice memorandum**, the **IRS** is likely to seek legal advice from its Office of Chief Counsel; the resulting advice is provided by means of a "chief counsel advice memorandum." [EO App. A; AU § 2.10].

child-care organization

A "child-care organization" is a type of **nonprofit organization** that is **tax-exempt** under the **federal tax law** because it is **educational** in nature. The term "educational purposes" includes the providing of care of children away from their homes if substantially all of the care provided by the organization is for purposes of enabling individuals (the children's parents) to be gainfully employed and if the services provided by the organization are available to the public (**IRC** § 501(k)). [EO § 8.8].

children, prevention of cruelty to

The prevention of cruelty to children is a category of activities by which a **nonprofit organization** can acquire **tax exemption** under the **federal tax law** as a **charitable entity** if it is **organized** and **operated primarily** for this type of purpose. [EO § 11.1; SM p. 38].

chilling effect

The phrase "chilling effect" is used to describe the impact of a **law** on the actions of one or more individuals (acting individually or as part of an **organization**), by which the individuals relinquish the exercise of a **right** (usually, a **constitutional** law right) because of fear of prosecution under that law. For example, a **charitable organization** may refrain from exercising its **free speech** right to engage in **lobbying** because of the chilling effect of a law by which it would or might lose its **tax-exempt status** and/or the ability to attract **deductible charitable contributions** because the lobbying it contemplated may be deemed **substantial**. [EO § 22.1].

choice of entity considerations

Tax-exempt organizations have a variety of **entity** forms to select, whether it is the form of entity for the organization itself, a form of entity for a **related organization**, or a form of entity in which it participates as a **stockholder** or **member**. From a **federal tax law** perspective, the two principal issues to consider are the impact on **exempt status** and the potential for generation of **unrelated business income**. A nontax law issue is limitation on liability. [EO § 32.8; UB § 8.2; GV § 1.2(e); CU Q 16.43; AS § 6.10(a)].

church

Constitutional law precepts (principally the **First Amendment**) make a precise definition in the **tax** law of a "church" difficult. Nonetheless, the **IRS**, aided by courts, has formulated a definition of the term. The **IRS's** historical view has been that, to be a church for **federal tax law** purposes, an **organization** must satisfy at least some of these criteria: a distinct legal existence, a recognized creed and form of worship, a definite and distinct ecclesiastical government, a formal code of doctrine and discipline, a distinct **religious** history, a **membership** not associated with any other church or denomination, an organization of ordained ministers ministering to their congregations and selected after completing prescribed courses of study, a literature of its own, established places of worship, regular congregations, regular religious services, **schools** for the religious instruction of the young, and schools for the preparation of its ministers. Recently, however, the **IRS** has been insisting that a **tax-exempt** must have the core attributes of a place of worship, a congregation, and regular religious services. Thus, it is the agency's position that a church conducted by means of the Internet or by telephone cannot be an exempt church. A church is a **public charity**. Churches are usually exempt from the scope of the states' **charitable solicitation acts** (**IRC** §§ 170(b)(1)(A)(i), 509(a)(1)). [**EO** §§ 10.3, 14.2(d), 20.9, 22.2(c), 22.6, 23.7, 25.2(b), 27.6(c), 28.2(b)(i); **RE** Q 3.4; **PF** § 15.3; **CG** §§ 1.3(a), 3.3(a); **CL** § 2.11; **FR** §§ 3.5(a), 7.3(f), 8.7(h); **AR** § 1.1(b); **SM** pp. 39–40, 80, 121, 149, 309–310] (also **Associational test; Institution**).

churches, convention of

See **Convention of churches**.

church records

The term "church records" means all corporate and financial records regularly kept by a **church**, including corporate minute books and lists of **members** and **contributors** (**IRC** § 7611(h)(4)(A)). [**EO** § 27.6(c); **AU** § 6.5; **SM** p. 309].

church tax examination

The phrase "church tax examination" is used in the context of the special rules by which the **IRS** is empowered to **audit** a **church** (**IRC** § 7611). It is any examination for the purpose of making a **church tax inquiry** of **church records** at the request of the **IRS** or of the **religious** activities of a church (**IRC** § 7611(h)(3)). [**AU** Chap. 6; **EO** § 27.6(c); **RE** Q 24.18; **SM** pp. 309–310].

church tax inquiry

The phrase "church tax inquiry" is used in the context of the special rules by which the **IRS** is empowered to **audit** a **church** (**IRC** § 7611). It is any inquiry to a church (other than a **church tax examination**) that serves as a basis for determining whether the **organization** qualifies for **tax exemption** as a church, is engaged in **unrelated activities**, or is otherwise engaged in taxable activities (**IRC** § 7611(h)(2)). This inquiry commences when the **IRS** requests information or materials from a church of a type contained in **church records**, other than routine requests for information or inquiries regarding matters that do not **primarily** concern the tax status or **liability** of the church. [**AU** Chap. 6; **EO** § 27.6(c); **RE** Q 24.17; **SM** pp. 309–310].

chutzpah trust

Tax regulations have been promulgated to prevent abusers of the **charitable remainder trust** rules from designing transactions by which a charitable remainder trust is used to convert **appreciated property** into money while avoiding tax on the **gain** from the **sale** of **assets**. Some of these arrangements were so audacious that the vehicles garnered the informal name "chutzpah trusts." [**SM** p. 236].

circular gift

A "circular gift" is a **gift** transaction embedded in a number of transactions involving several **persons**, usually **organized** and **operated** by the same individual, where a gift is made by the individual or one of the other **entities** to one of the entities in the group; the gift transaction usually lacks economic substance, so that the claimed **charitable contribution deduction** is disallowed. [CG § 3.1(d)].

civic league

A "civic league" is one of the types of **entities** that qualify as a **social welfare organization**. This type of **nonprofit organization** is **exempt** from **federal income tax** (by reason of **IRC §§** 501(a) and 501(c)(4)). Part of the definition of the term "social welfare" embraces "civic betterments and social improvements." It is, generically, a community action organization. [EO § 13.1(a); SM p. 39] (also **Social welfare organization**).

civil law

The "civil law" is that span of the **law** encompassing all matters other than those within the ambit of the **criminal law**. These matters embrace segments of the law such as **contracts** and **torts**. Some subjects of the law entail both civil and criminal aspects, such as civil and criminal **fraud** and civil and criminal law **tax penalties**. Also, violations of the states' **charitable solicitation acts** can involve both civil and criminal law penalties. [FR § 3.21].

claim

In the context of the **federal tax law**, a "claim" pertains to an item of **income**, loss, **deduction**, or **credit** entailing a potential refund of **tax**. A claim in the **tax-exempt organizations** setting may be made by filing a **claim for refund**, an amended return, or other written request for a tax refund. [AU § 5.34].

claim for refund

A "claim for refund" is a document that a **taxpayer** files with the **IRS** seeking a refund of **taxes** paid to the **federal** government. In this document, the taxpayer explains his, her, or its view as to why the refund is due; the **IRS**, of course, may or may not agree. The filing of a claim for refund and the denial of it is a **jurisdictional** prerequisite to a court review of a refund dispute. For example, a **tax-exempt organization** that wishes to contest an **assessment** of an **unrelated business income tax** must first pay the tax, file a claim for refund, have that claim denied, and then timely file the appropriate complaint or petition.

claim of right doctrine

See **Constructive receipt**.

class, charitable

See **Charitable class**.

closing agreement

A "closing agreement" is an **agreement** that the **IRS** enters into with a **person** relating to the **liability** of the person (or of the person or **estate** for whom he or she acts) in respect of any **tax** for a **taxable period** (**IRC** § 7121(a)). This agreement is final and conclusive and, except on a showing of **fraud** or malfeasance, or misrepresentation of a **material** fact, the case may not be

C

reopened, the agreement may not be modified, and any **determination**, **assessment**, refund, **credit**, **abatement**, or the like made in accordance with the agreement may not be modified or annulled (**IRC** § 7121(b)). Closing agreements may be entered into when it is advantageous to have the matter permanently and conclusively closed, or when a **taxpayer** can show that there are good reasons for an agreement and that making the agreement will not be disadvantageous to the **federal** government. In an appropriate case, a taxpayer may be asked to enter into a closing agreement as a condition to the issuance of a **private letter ruling**. Closing agreements are used by the **IRS** in resolving issues as to **tax-exempt status**, such as situations involving **hospitals** involved in certain **joint ventures** with physicians who practice at the hospital. [AU § 1.10; HC § 3.2; CU Q 8.12; SM p. 307].

club

Nearly every "club" is a **nonprofit organization**; these have a **voluntary membership** base of individuals and/or other legal **entities**. Thus, a club is an **association** of **persons**. The purpose of a nonprofit club is usually social or recreational, or to provide sporting facilities. A club can be considered **charitable**, **educational**, **literary**, or **scientific**, depending on its purposes (although it is then often termed a **society**). Examples of nonprofit clubs are country clubs, sporting clubs, flying clubs, and garden clubs. [EO Chap. 15; SM p. 41] (also **Social club**).

coalition

The word "coalition" is used in the context of **lobbying**. It is a grouping of **organizations** and individuals interested in a particular item of **legislation** or provision in an item of legislation. The coalition may use a name and usually operates as if it were a separate organization. Often, once the legislative effort is over, the coalition dissipates.

code

The word "code" is usually used to define a compilation of **laws** on one or more subjects. For **nonprofit organizations**, the most significant of the various **federal** and state codes is likely to be the **Internal Revenue Code**. The word "code" can also apply to an organization's **code of ethics** or similar body of guidelines or rules.

code of ethics

A "code of ethics" is a statement of principles established by a **nonprofit membership organization** and used to affect the professional behavior of its members. Ethical principles are not necessarily the same as **law**; they tend to be loftier and more idealistic. A popular phrase in the nonprofit community is that adherence to "ethics" means "obedience to the unenforceable." The ability of an individual or other **person** to be, or remain, a member of the organization may require compliance with its code of ethics. Occasionally, a provision in a code of ethics can run afoul of the **antitrust** law. [GV §§ 3.10(b), 5.16, 6.3(t); AS §§ 1.3(c), 11.1(a); CU Q 5.30; PG pp. 19–20; SM pp. 101, 280; LI Q 3.28].

Code of Federal Regulations

The "Code of Federal Regulations" is the collection of all of the **regulations** promulgated by various **agencies** of the **federal** government. These regulations first appear in the Federal Register. [EO App. A].

codicil

A "codicil" is a document that is an amendment to a **will**. A codicil normally amends only a portion of a will; it is not used to **dispose** of the entire **estate**. It must be executed with the same formality as a will.

coin-operated gambling device

The phrase "coin-operated gambling devices" is used by the **IRS**, in the context of the definition of the word **gaming**, to include slot machines, electronic video slot or line games, video poker, video blackjack, video keno, video bingo, and video pull tab games.

collateral estoppel

The doctrine of "collateral estoppel" is a rule of **law** that states that the determination of a body of facts as the result of **litigation**, and the consequences in law as to those facts, is binding on the parties to the litigation in any and all subsequent **judicial** proceedings between them. (A contemporary term for this doctrine is "issue preclusion.") This doctrine estops (precludes) one or both of the parties from litigating the same issue or issues between item again. For example, a **tax-exempt organization** litigated the issue as to whether its revenue from the **rental** of mailing lists was **taxable** as **unrelated business income;** it lost. Years later, it litigated essentially the same issue before another court and won; on appeal, the **appellate court** reversed the **lower court**, holding that the court below lacked **jurisdiction** over the case because of the doctrine of collateral estoppel. [EO § 25.2(k)].

college

A college is, under the **federal tax law**, a **tax-exempt educational organization** (IRC § 501(a), by reason of description in **IRC** § 501(c)(3)), and is a **public charity** (IRC §§ 170(b)(1)(A)(ii), 509(a)(I)). A "college" is a **school** of higher learning that grants bachelor's degrees in liberal arts or sciences, although the term is also frequently used to describe undergraduate divisions or schools of a **university** that offer courses and grant degrees in a particular field. Colleges are usually exempt, in whole or in part, from the states' **charitable solicitation acts**. [CU Q 2.11; EO §§ 8.3(a), 12.3(a), 24.5(a); PF §§ 3.5, 15.3; FR § 5.11(a); AR Chap. 12, § 8.1(c)(3); GV §§ 6.4, 7.6; SM pp. 80, 299; LI Q 9.11] (also **Institution**).

combined federal campaign

The "Combined Federal Campaign" (CFC) is a **federal** government **charitable fundraising program** administered by the Office of Personnel Management. The CFC is the only authorized charitable fundraising drive entitled to be conducted in the federal workplace.

C

combined voting power

For purposes of defining the category of **disqualified person** known as **20 percent owners**, where the **entity** involved is a **corporation**, the phrase "combined voting power" includes **voting power** represented by holdings of voting stock, owned actually or constructively (**constructive ownership**), but does not include voting rights held only as a **director** or **trustee** (IRC § 4946(a)(1)(C)(i)). [PF §§ 4.3, 4.5, 5.11; EO § 12.2(c)].

commensurate test

The "commensurate test" is a formulation devised by the **IRS** to determine whether a **charitable organization** (or perhaps another type of **tax-exempt entity**) is carrying on charitable (or other) activities commensurate in scope with its financial resources. This test is applied in cases where organizations, claiming **exempt status**, have **fundraising** and **grantmaking** as their sole activities.

According to the **IRS**, the commensurate test does not lend itself to a rigid numerical distribution formula. There is no fixed percentage of income that an organization (other than a **private foundation** or perhaps a **supporting organization**) must pay out for exempt purposes. The financial resources of any organization may be affected by factors such as start-up costs, overhead, scale of operations, whether labor is **voluntary** or salaried, telephone costs, and postage costs. In each case, therefore, the particular **facts and circumstances** of each organization must be considered. The test requires the **IRS** to ascertain whether a failure by an organization to make real and substantial contributions for exempt purposes is due to **reasonable cause**. [EO §§ 4.7, 7.14; FR §§ 5.1(c), 5.15(b)(iii), 5.26; GV § 8.4(g); CU Q 1.36; UB § 1.6; SM pp. 289–290; LI Q 1.47].

commercial

The word "commercial" is a derivative of the word "commerce." Thus, an **organization** is often considered acting in a "commercial" manner when it is engaged in "commerce." A **for-profit entity** is one that is **operated** in a commercial manner. A **nonprofit organization** may be considered to be operating in a commercial manner when it is engaging in an activity that is also undertaken in the **for-profit sector**. A commercial activity that is undertaken by a **tax-exempt organization** is likely to be regarded as an **unrelated trade or business**. [EO § 4.11(a)(i); HC § 13.1(b); SM p. 5] (also **Commerciality doctrine**).

commercial activity

See **Commerciality doctrine**.

commercial co-venture

A "commercial co-venture" occurs when a **for-profit business** announces to the public that a portion (a specific amount or a specific percentage) of the purchase price of a product or service will, during a stated period, be paid to a **charitable organization**. This term is, in some respects, unfortunate terminology. It suggests that the charitable organization involved is engaged in a co-venture (**joint venture**) with the participating for-profit organization (which is not always the case) and implies that the charitable organization is doing something that is **commercial** in nature. A synonymous term used in some states' **charitable solicitation acts** is **charitable sales promotion**. [FR §§ 3.2(j), 3.8, 5.7(b)(vii), 8.4; CG § 25.4; HC §§ 31.1(d), 31.2(i); SM pp. 151, 242] (also **Cause-related marketing**).

commercial speech

"Commercial speech" is a form of **free speech**; it is contrasted with the higher form of free speech manifested in **fundraising** by **charitable organizations**. Commercial speech, being the subject of economic regulation, need only be tested against a standard of rationality. By contrast, the speech of charitable organizations can survive a free speech challenge only if it is in furtherance of a **state interest** and is regulated by the narrowest of means. [FR § 5.19; SM p. 152].

commercial testing

"Commercial testing" occurs when an **organization** is readying a product for the commercial market; this testing phase is usually the last phase prior to manufacture and **sale** of the product to the public. It is frequently difficult to distinguish between commercial testing and **scientific research**. [EO § 9.2; HC § 24.13] (also **Public safety testing organization**; **Research**; **Technology transfer**).

commercial-type insurance

The term "commercial-type insurance" is used in connection with a rule that states that a **nonprofit organization** cannot be **tax-exempt** as a **charitable organization** or a **social welfare organization** if a **substantial** part of its activities consists of the provision of commercial-type **insurance** (**IRC** § 501(m)). Although this term is not defined in the **Internal Revenue Code**, a Congressional committee report states that commercial-type insurance generally is any insurance of a type provided by commercial insurance companies. There are some statutory exceptions to the term "commercial-type insurance." [EO §§ 24.8, 28.13(b); UB §§ 7.1(b), 7.3; HC §§ 9.2(a), 9.3, 13.1(d); SM p. 284].

commerciality doctrine

The "commerciality doctrine" is one of the single most important elements of the **law** of **tax-exempt organizations**. This doctrine is shaping the contemporary development of the law concerning exempt organizations and is directly affecting the law of **unrelated business income taxation**. The commerciality doctrine, as it relates to the activities of **nonprofit organizations**, is an overlay body of law that the courts have grafted onto the statutory and regulatory rules.

A tax-exempt organization is engaged in a nonexempt activity when that activity is conducted in a manner that is considered "commercial." An activity usually is a **commercial** one if it has a direct counterpart in the realm of **for-profit organizations**. Thus, the doctrine is born of the fact that society in the U.S. is composed of the **business** (for- profit) **sector**, the nonprofit sector, and the governmental sector.

The U.S. is essentially a capitalist society, so the business sector is, in several ways, the preferred sector. While entities in the business sector are seen as being operated for "private" ends (**profits** to owners), with the overall result a capitalist (albeit rather regulated) economy for the society, the nonprofit sector is seen as being operated for "public" ends (the general good of society). Out of these precepts is emanating the view that organizations in the nonprofit sector should not compete with organizations in the business sector.

The commerciality doctrine thus involves a **counterpart test**. An activity conducted by a nonprofit organization, when that activity is also conducted by a for-profit organization, is frequently regarded as a commercial activity. This conclusion then leads to a finding that the commercial activity is a nonexempt or **unrelated activity**, with adverse consequences in law for the nonprofit organization, either as respects its **tax-exempt status** or **unrelated income taxation**. This counterpart approach rests, in part, on the tax policy belief that an economically neutral tax system requires that institutions engaged in similar activities should be subjected to the same tax treatment. Although many types of nonprofit organizations are being subjected to the commerciality doctrine, two examples of contemporary application of the doctrine in the context of developing law are the proper standard of tax exemption for **hospitals** (a **charity care standard** or a **community benefit standard**) and the appropriateness of tax exemption for **credit unions** (that is, whether they should be treated, for tax purposes, as other financial institutions). [EO § 4.11; UB §§ 7.1, 7.2; HC §§ 3.3, 24.24; CL §§ 1.6, 1.10; AR § 7.1(b)(7); CU Q 1.37; RE Q 18.8–Q 18.14; PG pp. 181–183, 346, 347; SM pp. 283–286; LI Q 1.48, Q 13.11, Q 13.12].

commingling requirement

The "commingling requirement" appears in two principal aspects of **federal tax law** concerning **nonprofit organizations**. One of these aspects relates to the law concerning the tax aspects of **social clubs**, which requires that the club have an established membership of individuals, personal contacts, and fellowship. This means that a commingling of the members must play a **material** part in the operation of the organization. This concept is also reflected in the **associational test**, applied to determine if a **religious organization** qualifies as a **church**.

The second of these two requirements is in the law concerning **pooled income funds**, where the law requires that all transfers of money and **property** made by **donors** be commingled with money and property transferred by **other** donors. There is also somewhat of a commingling requirement with respect to **cooperative educational service organizations** and **churches**. [EO §§ 10.3(b), 15.1(b); CG § 13.2(c); SM pp. 37, 41, 236]

Despite its use in these laws, this word is a redundancy. The correct term is "mingling."

commission

A "commission" is a form of payment for services rendered. It is compensation where the amount to be paid, or actually paid, is a factor of the number of transactions or sources of profit to the payor. A commission usually is based on a percentage of something, such as an amount collected. It is distinguished from a fixed amount agreed in advance to be paid for services performed, such as a wage, salary, or fee. The purpose of a commission is to directly tie compensation to results achieved. This is important, for example, in the **fundraising** context, where the **code of ethics** of several professional fundraising **associations** prohibits an individual subject to the code from being compensated by means of a commission. The word "commission" also means the doing of an act; it is a committing of something (as in the commission of a **crime**). **Liability** can attach when a **person** commits an error. [FR § 5.13; HC § 28.5(a)] (also **Omission**; **Reasonable cause**).

Commissioner of Internal Revenue

The "Commissioner of Internal Revenue" is the government official who has the responsibility for administering the **IRS**. This commissioner is appointed by the President, by and with the advice and consent of the U.S. Senate. He **or** she has such duties as may be prescribed by the **Secretary of the Treasury**. [Oversight Board] (**IRC** §§ 7802(b)(1)(C), 7803) [EO § 2.2(a); AU § 2.2].

Commissioner, Tax Exempt Government Entities Division

[EO § 2.2(b); AU § 2.3(a)].

committee

A "committee" is a group of two or more individuals that has the responsibility for formulating policy and programs for an **organization** within a specified sphere of subject matter. In the case of **nonprofit organizations**, committees are usually subsets of the **board of directors** or the **board of trustees**. Under the **law** of some states, most committees created by a **governing board** must consist wholly of directors or trustees. The policy and programs developed by a committee are usually subject to review and approval by the full governing body. Most committees of nonprofit organizations are **standing committees**; these include a **development committee**, **executive committee**, finance committee, and long-range planning committee. A committee formed for a specific purpose and perhaps for a limited time of existence is termed a **special committee**. The word is also applied to a subset of a legislative body, such as committees of the U.S. Congress. [GV §§ 4.2(e), 5.11; CU Q 5.26, Q 5.27, Q 7.39, Q 17.56; SM p. 12] (also **Ad hoc committee**).

committee report

A "committee report" is a document issued by a **committee** of a legislature, that accompanied a **bill** reported out of the committee, and that explains the purpose of the legislation and of the material provisions in the measure. A committee report frequently contains language that itself becomes part of the **law**, either because the language is reflected in **regulations** and/or because it is part of the **legislative history** of the statute(s). Committee reports are often used to divine **congressional intent**.

common fund

The term "common fund" has two definitions in the **federal tax law** setting. One of these definitions is that of a **private foundation** that pools **contributions** received and allows **donors** and their spouses to retain the right to annually **designate** the **charitable organizations** to which the **income** attributable to the contributions is to be given and to designate by deed or **will** the charitable organizations to which the **corpus** of the contributions is to eventually be given. This type of private foundation is termed a "common fund foundation."

The other use of the term "common fund" in the **nonprofit law** setting is to describe an investment vehicle that is used by banks and other financial institutions to pool investments for the benefit of charitable vehicles, such as **pooled income funds**. [PF §§ 3.3, 14.4(a); EO § 12.1(e); CG § 3.3(b)].

common law

The "common law" is court-made **law** (as opposed to **statutory** law, which is enacted by a legislature). Much of the common law as developed by courts in the United States was initially derived from the common law as it had evolved in England. **Equity** law came into being to provide remedies when the common law could not. Today, American common law includes elements of equity law. [HC § 33.2(a)].

common supervision or control

The phrase "common supervision or control" is used as part of the definition of the phrase "supervised or controlled in connection with," which, in turn, is one of the requisite relationships between a **supporting organization** and a **supported organization**. To meet this requirement, the **control** or management of the supporting organization must be vested in the same persons who control or manage the supported organization (**IRC** § 509(a)(3)(B)). [PF § 15.7(f); EO § 12.3(c); SM p. 83].

common treasury

See **Community treasury**.

common trust fund

A bank or other financial institution usually maintains one or more "common trust funds," which are used as investment vehicles for their customers. **Units** in these funds are issued to the entities that have investments in the funds. For example, a bank, as **trustee** of a **charitable remainder trust** or **pooled income fund**, will invest the **assets** of these entities in its common trust fund (or funds). [CG § 13.3(a); PF § 6.3(e)].

communal group

As a general rule, where individuals reside in a communal setting in the context of professing **religious** beliefs, with room, board, and like services provided by the **organization** involved, the result is unwarranted **private benefit** to the individuals, precluding **tax exemption**. Where, however, the facilities and benefits provided are confined to those strictly necessary for communal religious living, exemption may be available. [EO § 10.8].

communication

The word "communication" refers to an effort and a means by which one or more **persons** endeavors to communicate an idea, thought, proposal, and the like. Thus, the term is often used in the **advocacy** context. For example, most forms of **lobbying** are regarded as "communication." [EO § 22.3(b); SM pp. 186–187] (also **Direct lobbying**; **Grass-roots lobbying**; **Self-defense communication**).

communication, lobbying

Inherent in the concept of an attempt to **influence legislation** is the fact that it involves one or more forms of **communication** (such as letters, telephone calls, personal meetings, emails, and Internet postings) to or with legislators, their staff, members of a segment of the public, and the like. Where the lobbying is **direct lobbying**, the communication is known as a **direct lobbying communication**. Where the lobbying is **grass-roots lobbying**, the communication is known as a **grass-roots lobbying communication**. These terms are used particularly in application of the **expenditure test**. [EO §§ 22.3(c)(ii), 22.3(d)(i); SM pp. 186–187].

community

The term "community" is used to describe a fundamental criterion of a **tax-exempt social welfare organization**, which is that the organization cannot operate for the benefit of a select group of individuals but must be engaged in the promotion of the common good and general welfare of those in a "community." It is the view of the **IRS** that, in this context at least, the term "community" has reference to a geographical unit bearing a reasonably recognizable relationship to an area ordinarily identified as a governmental subdivision or a unit or district of this type of subdivision. A somewhat similar standard applies with respect to the tax exemption for **nonprofit hospitals**. The IRS, in a **private letter ruling** issued in early 2015, had occasion to observe that the **agency** has "not found any **authority** for the proposition that the world is a community." [EO § 13.2; SM p. 39] (also **Community benefit standard**; **Homeowners' association**).

community association

See **Homeowners' association**.

community benefit standard

The term "community benefit standard" is used to describe the present-day rationale for the **federal law tax exemption** for **nonprofit hospitals**. This standard is predicated on the fact that one of the definitions of the term **charitable** is the **promotion of health**. Thus, to be tax-exempt at the federal level, a hospital must promote the health of a class of **persons** broad enough to benefit a **community** and be operated to serve a public rather than a private interest. It is not necessary that a nonprofit hospital base its tax exemption on some other standard, such as **relief of the poor**. [HC §§ 3.2, 3.3(a), 6.1–6.3, 26.3; EO § 7.6(a); AR §§ 15.1(a), 15.2(i)(6); GV § 6.3(n)].

community foundation

A "community foundation" is a form of **publicly supported charitable organization** (that is, it is not a **private foundation**) that attracts, receives, and depends on members of the public on a regular, recurring basis. Community foundations are designed primarily to attract large **contributions** of a **capital** or **endowment** nature from a small number of **donors**, with the **gifts** often received and maintained in the form of separate **trusts** or **funds**. They are generally identified with a particular **community** or like geographic area and are controlled by a representative group of individuals from that community or area. [EO §§ 12.1(f), 12.3(b)(iii); PF §§ 3.5, 11.3(d), 15.4(d), (e); CG § 3.3(a); AR § 8.1(d)(8); SM pp. 81–82, 299].

community health needs assessment

The phrase "community health needs assessment" means an assessment that takes into account input from persons who represent the broad interests of the community served by the **hospital facility**, including those with special knowledge of or expertise in public health, and that is made widely available to the public (**IRC** § 501(r)(3)(B)). [HC § 26.10(a)(ii); AR §§ 15.1(a)(3)(C), 15.2(i)(2); EO § 7.6(b)(ii)].

community health needs assessment requirement

A **hospital organization** or **hospital facility** meets the "community health needs assessment requirement," with respect to a **tax year**, only if the organization or facility (1) has conducted a **community health needs assessment** in that tax year or in either of the two tax years immediately preceding that tax year and (2) has adopted an implementation strategy to meet the community health needs identified through the assessment (**IRC** § 501(r)(3)(A)). [HC § 26.10(d); EO § 7.6(b)(ii)].

community treasury

One of the requirements for qualification as an **apostolic organization** is that the entity has a "common treasury or a community treasury" (**IRC** § 501(d)). This means that the **property** of the **entity** may not be held by its **members** individually, but rather in a community capacity, with all members having equal interests in the property. It is a common **fund** maintained by the organization and used for the support of its membership. [EO § 10.7].

community trust

See **Community foundation**.

compensation

The term "compensation" has at least two meanings in the context of **nonprofit law**. The definition most suitable in this setting is a payment (usually of money) for services rendered. Thus, compensation can be in the form of a salary, wage, **bonus**, **commission**, fee, or other type of remuneration, irrespective of whether the recipient is an **employee** or **independent contractor**. Particularly where the payor **organization** is a **charitable** entity, the compensation paid must be **reasonable**. Payment of reasonable compensation is a major element of the rules concerning **private inurement** and **excess benefit transactions**. Where the compensation is not reasonable and the payor organization is a **private foundation,** the payment of the compensation is an act of **self-dealing**. [EO §§ 18.1, 20.4; HC §§ 4.9(a)(iii), 33.6; PF §§ 5.3(a), 5.6(b); FR §§ 5.6, 5.13; AS § 3.4(a)(i); AR §§ 3.1(x), 3.2(x); GV §§ 2.1(d), 3.10(i), 4.2(c), 5.9; CU Q 7.9; RE Q 21.1; SM pp. 51–52; LI Q 4.9, Q 5.24, Q 6.9–Q 6.13]

The other form of "compensation" is the payment of damages to a **person** to make him, her, or it whole, that is, restored to the state of affairs preceding the injury that caused the damages. (also **Deferred compensation**; **Percentage compensation**; **Reasonable compensation**).

compensation, policy as to

The **IRS**, on the **Form 990**, effectively asks whether the filing organization has a policy as to the payment of executive **compensation**. The **IRS** inquires as to the process used for determining compensation, including review and approval by independent **persons**, use of comparability data, and contemporaneous substantiation of the deliberations. Essentially, the **IRS** is trying to determine whether the organization has invoked the **rebuttable presumption of reasonableness**. [GV §§ 4.2(c), 6.3(e); SM pp. 274–275].

competence

An individual possesses "competence" (that is, the ability to act in a competent manner) if he or she has the mental capacity to understand the nature of his or her act. When the term is used in the context of **execution** of a **will** or a **trust**, it also requires an understanding of the nature of the individual's **property** and his or her relationships to **persons** having an **interest** in that property.

competition

In general, the term "competition" is used to describe two or more legal entities participating in the same enterprise, where they are seeking to engage in commerce with third parties to the economic detriment of the other(s). In the **nonprofit law** setting, the term "competition" is most often used to describe the same activity or enterprise that is being engaged in by both a **for-profit** and a **nonprofit** entity. Often, the presence of this type of competitive activity leads to the conclusion that the nonprofit organization is operating in a **commercial** manner, with the result being denial or revocation of **tax-exempt status** or imposition of the **unrelated business income tax** rules. [EO § 24.2(c); HC § 24.2(c); SM pp. 288–289] (also **Commerciality doctrine**; **Unfair competition**).

complaint

A "complaint" is a document by which a lawsuit is initiated; it states the ground (or grounds) that is the basis for the **action.** The response to a complaint usually is an **answer**; other responses include a **counterclaim** and a motion to dismiss. At the **federal law** level, such as in a **declaratory judgment** action by a **tax-exempt organization**, the proceedings that are initiated by a complaint are in the U.S. District Court for the District of Columbia and the U.S. Court of Federal Claims. [EO § 26.5(b)] (also **Defendant**; **Petition**; **Plaintiff**).

completion

For a transaction to constitute a **gift**, including a **charitable** gift, it must be "completed," which means that the **donor** must part with all right, title, and interest in the contributed property. [CG § 3.1(l)].

compliance check

The term "compliance check" means an undertaking by the **IRS** that focuses on a specific entity type or compliance issue in the law of **tax-exempt organizations**. A compliance check

C

may entail a particular type of exempt organization (recent examples include **colleges**, **hospitals**, and **universities**) or a particular issue (such as **compensation**, **self-declaring**, and **group exemptions**). These checks are initiated by the sending of a questionnaire. A compliance check is not an **IRS examination** but it can lead to one. [AU Chap. 4, § 1.6(d); EO § 27.7; HC §§ 36.4, 36.5(a), (c); GV §§ 6.4, 8.17(e); SM pp. 296–297].

compliance period

The tests that a private foundation must satisfy to qualify as a private operating foundation are applied over a "compliance period," which generally is a four-year period that includes the current year and immediately preceding three years. [PF § 3.1(f)].

condition

 Essentially, a "condition" is a requirement. A "condition" usually is a statement in a legal document making the operation of a provision, effectuation of a transaction, or creation of a **right** dependent on the happening of a described event, which may or may not occur. If the event does occur, it will cause a **person** to have a legal obligation to do or not do something. When a condition exists, it is usually attached to something, such as a **contribution**.

Some conditions that are attached to a **charitable gift** help define the charitable use to which the gift is to be put and thus assure a **charitable contribution deduction** for the gift. An illustration of this point is the making of a charitable gift, conditioning its use to the **granting** of **scholarships**. Some conditions accompanying a gift defeat what would otherwise be a charitable deduction because of the substance of the condition. An illustration of this is a gift to a **school** on the condition that it maintain a racially discriminatory admissions policy. Sonic conditions that accompany a gift defeat a charitable deduction because of their very existence if they are **material**; they prevent the gift from being a completed transfer. An example of this is a gill with a condition that makes it quite likely that the gift will revert to the donor or pass to some other noncharitable person or purpose. [CG § 10.4] (also **Conditional gift**; **Condition precedent**; **Condition subsequent**).

conditional gift

A "conditional gift" is a **gift** that is subject to one or more **conditions**. For example, if an individual makes a **contribution** to a **charitable organization**, with the condition that the charity not accept the gift until a facility of the charity is at least one-half constructed, the gift is subject to a **condition precedent**. By contrast, if an individual makes a contribution to a charitable organization, with the condition that the charity must transfer the gift property to a second charity if a facility owned by the recipient charity is not used for a particular purpose, the gift is subject to a **condition subsequent**. [CG § 10.4] (also **Restricted gift**).

condition precedent

A "condition precedent" is a **condition** that must occur before a provision in a document becomes operative, a transaction becomes effective, or a **right** arises. (also **Conditional gift**; **Condition subsequent**).

condition subsequent

A "condition subsequent" is a **condition** that, should the described event occur, a provision in a document becomes operative or inoperative, a transaction is terminated, or a **right** defeated. (also **Conditional gift; Condition precedent**).

C

conduit

The word "conduit." is applied to an **organization** that is a **pass-through entity** with respect to a particular transaction. It is commonly used in the context of the **charitable contribution deduction** rule that a **gift** to a **foreign charity** is not deductible. Some foreign charities establish **controlled charitable organizations** in the United States and **solicit** contributions to them, for the ultimate purpose of having the funds transferred to the foreign charities. Contributions to these U.S.-based **subsidiaries** are deductible as long as these organizations are not merely conduits of the gifts. [CG § 18.3; EO § 29.2(e)]).

conduit foundation

A "conduit foundation" is a **private foundation** that makes **grants** and other **qualifying distributions** that are treated as distributions out of **corpus**, in an amount equal in value to 100 percent of all **contributions** received in the year involved, whether as cash or **property**. [PF §§ 3.2, 14.4(a); EO § 12.1(d); CG § 7.5(a)]).

conference committee

Legislatures use the device of the "conference committee" to reconcile differing **bills** as passed by the two houses of the legislature. (This concept assumes that the legislature is a bicameral (two-house) one, rather than a unicameral (one-house) one.) The measure devised by the conference committee must pass both houses of the legislature (and be signed by the executive) to become **law** (unless a veto is overridden). For example, almost every **federal tax** bill is a product of a conference committee made up of representatives from the House Committee on Ways and Means and the Senate Committee on Finance. A conference committee is supposed to only resolve differences in the two items of legislation, rather than create new provisions; occasionally, however, the latter happens. For example, this was how the rule concerning the **valuation** of securities held by **private foundations** for purposes of the **minimum payout** requirement was created. [EO, App. A])

conference report

A "conference report" is a document accompanying **legislation**; it includes an explanation of that legislation. This type of report is one developed by a **conference committee**. This report often contains interpretations and expansions of the legislation, and usually is an important component (perhaps the most important component) of the **legislative history** of the legislation. [EO, App. A])

conflict of interest

A "conflict of interest" arises when an individual, in a position of authority over an **organization**, is in a position where he or she is on both sides of an actual or potential transaction or

C

other situation and can personally benefit financially from a decision made with respect to the situation. A typical example of this type of conflict is a **lawyer** serving on the **board of directors** of a **nonprofit organization** that is a client; when the lawyer provides legal advice, he or she may not be completely objective because the advice may affect the lawyer personally as well as the organization, causing the nature of the advice to be affected by the conflict. A conflict of interest, however, is not necessarily contrary to **law**; often, this type of conflict is remedied through **disclosure** or consent. It is a common practice of nonprofit organizations to have a written **conflict-of-interest policy**.

For purposes of **annual information return** reporting, it is the view of the **IRS** that the concept of "conflict of interest" does not include questions involving an individual's competing or respective duties to the organization and to another organization, such as by serving on the boards of both organizations, that do not involve a material financial interest of or benefit to the individual. [RE Q 6.2, Q 6.5; AU § 5.6; LI Q 4.53, Q 5.1].

conflict-of-interest policy

A "conflict-of-interest policy" is a **governance** policy that defines the term **conflict of interest**, identifies the classes of individuals within the **organization** that are covered by the policy, facilitates disclosures of information that can help identify conflicts of interest, and specifies procedures to be followed in managing conflicts of interest. [GV §§ 2.1(e), 2.7(i), 4.2(a), 5.17, 6.3(b); AR §§ 5.1(i)(1), 5.2(b)(1), 5.3; EO §§ 5.7(f)(iv), 28.3(e); HC § 4.9; CU Q 5.29; RE Q 6.3; PG pp. 20, 28, 35; SM pp. 111, 272–273; LI Q 3.27, Q 5.7].

congressional intent

"Congressional intent" is the name given the determination by a court or an **administrative agency** as to what the U.S. Congress (or perhaps another legislature) intended when it passed a particular **law**. In some instances, this intent can be discerned from the language of the statute itself. In most cases, however, resort must be made to one or more components of the **legislative history** of the law to find this intent. This is somewhat of a legal fiction, because (in the case of the federal legislature) it is unlikely that the "intent" of 535 individuals is the same; at best, congressional intent means the finding of the intent of a majority of the Congress. As to a technical item of an item of **legislation**, the congressional intent may be that of a majority of the two **committees** that wrote the legislation. [EO, App. A] (also **Deference**).

conservation easement

A "conservation easement" is a **restriction**, placed in perpetuity, on the use that may be made of **real property** that is granted **exclusively** for **conservation purposes**. [CG § 9.7; AR §§ 11.1(b), 11.2(b)].

conservation easement, policy as to

The **IRS**, in the **Form 990**, inquires as to whether the filing **organization** has a written policy regarding how (if it does) it monitors, inspects, responds to violations, and enforces **conservation easements**. [GV § 6.3(k); SM p. 276].

C

conservation purpose

In the context of the **charitable contribution deduction** for a **gift** of **real property** (or an interest in the property) to a charitable **organization** for "conservation purposes," the phrase "conservation purpose" means the (1) preservation of land areas for outdoor recreation by, or the **education** of, the **public**; (2) protection of a relatively natural habitat of fish, wildlife, or plants, or similar ecosystem; (3) the preservation of open space (including farmland and forest land) where the preservation is for the scenic enjoyment of the public, pursuant to a clearly delineated **federal,** state, or local governmental education policy, and will yield a significant public benefit; or (4) preservation of an historically important land area or a **certified historic structure** (**IRC** § 170(h)(4)(A)). [CG § 9.7(c)].

conservation purpose, gift for

A **charitable contribution** made for a **conservation purpose** usually is **deductible** for federal **income tax** purposes. The federal tax law contains special rules for contributions to charity of **real property** (or interests in property) for conservation purposes; these rules concern **qualified conservation contributions**. [CG § 9.7].

consideration

"Consideration" is one of the principal elements of an enforceable **contract**. Consideration is the reason one **person** contracts with another; the contracting party is motivated or impelled by the benefit to be derived from the contract (usually, goods or services) while the **compensation** to be received by the other person is the inducement to the contract for that person. A transaction that is supported by consideration cannot be a **gift**, unless the consideration is less than the amount gifted, in which case only the excess transferred is a gift. The concept of consideration also is a crucial element in the definition of the phrase **excess benefit transaction**. [CG § 3.1(a); EO § 21.4(a); UB § 3.5; SM pp. 59, 131–132] (also **Bargain sale**; **Quid pro quo contribution**).

consortium

A "consortium" is a cooperative venture involving two or more **nonprofit organizations**, where they have banded together to further their **tax-exempt purposes** collectively, often to achieve economy of scale and/or efficiency. Most consortia are separate legal entities but are not tax-exempt. A consortium, however, can be tax-exempt where its programs are inherently **charitable**, **educational**, or the like, or where at least 85 percent of the consortium's revenue is derived from outside sources. [EO § 7.13] (also **Cooperative**; **Joint venture**).

conspicuous and easily recognizable format

The phrase "conspicuous and easily recognizable format" is a standard that must be followed by a **tax-exempt organization** when making a **disclosure** of the fact that **contributions** made to it are not **deductible** as **charitable contributions** under the **federal tax law**. (**IRC** § 6113(a)) The **IRS** promulgated rules that detail the requirements of this format. This standard must also be followed by a tax-exempt organization in creating the disclosure to its **members** of the portion of the **dues** that the organization **reasonably** estimates will be **allocable** to the organization's **lobbying expenditures** and/or **political expenditures** during the **tax year**, to enable the members to comply with the **lobbying disallowance rule** and/or the **political activities disallowance rule** (**IRC** § 6033(e)(1)(A)(ii)). [EO §§ 22.6(b), 23.7, 28.12; CG § 22.3].

C

constituency

Most **tax-exempt organizations** have a "constituency." This body of individuals may be the **members** of an alumni association or the members of a **trade association**. Nearly every **charitable organization** (whether or not it has a membership) has a constituency: those who make **charitable contributions** to it. In some states, when a charitable organization confines its **fundraising** to a defined constituency, it is **exempt,** in whole or in part, from the state's **charitable solicitation act.** [FR §§ 3.5(c), 3.5(h)].

constitution

A "constitution" is the organizing (or creating) document for a **nonprofit organization** other than a **corporation** or a **trust**. It is, then, the **articles of organization** for an **unincorporated association** or similar entity. The term also defines a document used to organize a nation or a state, such as the U.S. Constitution or a state constitution. [EO § 4.2; PG p. 4; RE Q 2.17; SM p. 10; LI Q 1.41].

construction, of statute

See **Statutory construction**.

constructive

The word "constructive" is used to describe a relationship or a thing that does not actually exist but that is imputed to it by a rule of **law**. For example, a **trust** may not formally exist, yet a court may impose one in connection with a set of facts; this is known as a "constructive trust." The word is also used to describe a form of assent, authority, **contract**, delivery, **notice**, or **possession**. (also **Constructive ownership**; **Constructive receipt**).

constructive ownership

"Constructive ownership" takes place when an item of **property** owned by a **person** is deemed by the **law** to be also owned by another person, for one or more purposes, where there is a defined relationship between the two persons. For example, an item of property may be considered owned by both a husband and wife for a particular purpose, even though **legal title** is actually only **vested** in one of them. For purposes of the **rules** concerning certain **20 percent owners** of the **total combined voting power** of a **corporation** (**IRC** § 4946(a)(1)(C)(i)) and the rules concerning corporations owned by certain holders of more than 35 percent of the total combined voting power (**IRC** § 4946(a)(1)(E)), there generally must be taken into account indirect stockholdings that would be considered (under the constructive ownership rules of **IRC** § 267(c)) as constructively owned. For this purpose, however, the constructive ownership rule (**IRC** § 267(c)(4)) is treated as providing that the **members of the family** of an individual are those individuals that are embraced by the term "member of the family" as that term is used in the rules concerning **disqualified persons** (**IRC** § 4946(d)) (**IRC** § 4946(a)(3)).

Likewise, these constructive ownership rules apply for purposes of the rules concerning certain 20 percent owners of the **profits interest** of a **partnership** (**IRC** § 4946(a)(1)(C)(ii)) or of the **beneficial interest** in a **trust** or **unincorporated enterprise** (**IRC** § 4946(a)(1)(C)(iii)), or the rules concerning partnerships owned by certain holders of more than 35 percent of the profits interest (**IRC** § 4946(a)(1)(F)), or the rules concerning trusts or **estates** where more than 35 percent of the beneficial interest is held by certain persons (**IRC** § 4946(a) (l)(G)) (**IRC** § 4946(a)(4)). Further, these constructive ownership rules apply for purposes defining a **disqualified individual** in the context of the requirements for **exempt operating foundations** (**IRC** § 4940(d)(3)(E)). Constructive ownership rules also apply in connection with the **federal tax law** rules concerning **controlling organizations**. [PF §§ 4.3, 7.1(c), 7.2(b); EO §§ 12.2(c)–12.2(g), 21.3, 29.6, 30.7(b)].

constructive receipt

The rule as to "constructive receipt" attributes to a **person** actual receipt of something, when the person has not physically taken possession of the thing, but is in a position to do so at his or her election. For example, if a person is entitled to an item of **compensation** near the end of a **tax year** and requests the putative payor to defer payment until the beginning of the immediately succeeding year, so as to postpone taxation of the compensation, the rule causes the compensation to be properly reported as **taxable income** for the previous year. This is also known as the "claim of right" doctrine. [CG § 3.1(i)].

consultant

A "consultant" is a **person** who provides advice and services to one or more other persons: a consultant is an **independent contractor**, rather than an **employee**. Examples of consultants include **certified public accountants**, **lawyers**, and **professional fundraisers**. [FR §§ 4.10, 8.1(c), 8.2(a)].

consumer products, public safety testing of

The phrase "public safety testing of consumer products" arises in the context of the **law** concerning **nonprofit organizations** because certain organizations that engage in that activity are **tax-exempt** (by reason of **IRC** §§ 501(a) and 501(c)(3)). **Contributions** to these public safety testing organizations, however, are not **deductible** as **charitable gifts**. [EO § 11.3; CG § 3.3(a)].

contact person

The "contact person" is an individual who should be designated, to the **IRS**, as the single point of contact of a **tax-exempt organization** by the organization when facing an **IRS examination**. [AU §§ 3.2(e), 5.18(a)(ii)].

contemporaneous written acknowledgement

The **substantiation rules** that must be satisfied in the instance of **charitable contributions** in excess of $250 require a "contemporaneous written acknowledgement" (**IRC** § 170(f)(8)). This acknowledgement is "contemporaneous" if the **contributor** obtains it on or before the earlier of (1) the date on which the donor files a **tax return** for the **tax year** in which the contribution was made or (2) the due date (including extensions) for filing the return (**IRC** § 170(f)(8)(C)). [CG § 21.3(a); FR § 5.3; HC § 31.2(a) SM pp. 142–144].

contest, will
See **Will contest**.

contingent gift
See **Conditional gift**.

contract

In general, a "contract" is an agreement among two or more **competent persons** that creates, modifies, or eliminates a relationship that is recognized in the **law.** A contract must, to be enforceable, be underlain with **consideration**. A contract is the culmination of an offer by one or more persons followed by an acceptance of that offer by one or more other persons.

The concept of a contract appears throughout the **law** concerning **nonprofit organizations.** For example, **charitable solicitation acts** often dictate the contents of contracts between **charitable organizations** and **professional fundraisers,** and charitable organizations and **professional solicitors**. As another illustration, a contract is the vehicle underlying the **charitable gift annuity**. A **trust agreement** is a contract. A set of **bylaws** of a **membership** organization is a contract between the organization and its members. [FR § 8.6(a); CG § 14.1; SM p. 6].

contract failure

The concept of "contract failure" is found in economic analyses of the differences between **nonprofit organizations** and **for-profit organizations**, where both types of entities are providing an essentially identical good or service. Contract failure arises where consumers may be incapable of accurately evaluating the goods or services promised or delivered and market competition may well provide insufficient discipline for a profit-seeking producer. Under the theory of contract failure, the consuming public selects the nonprofit organization, which operates without a **profit motive** and offers the consumer the "trust element" that the for-profit organization cannot always provide. [EO § 1.6] (also **Halo effect**; **Level playing field**; **Unfair competition**).

contraction

The word "contraction" means the reduction, lessening, or shrinking of something; a more contemporary term is "down-sizing." A **nonprofit organization** achieves "contraction" when it ceases to undertake one or more functions, such as by making a **grant** of the **assets** and other resources underlying a function or by a **spin off** of a function to another organization. (also **Substantial contraction**).

contributed services

A **person** may **contribute** services to a **charitable organization**. A **charitable contribution deduction** is not, however, available for this type of gift. [CG § 9.14] (also **Volunteer**).

contribution

A "contribution" is a transfer of money or **property** where the transfer is voluntary and is motivated by something other than **consideration**. The **federal income tax regulations** (promulgated in amplification of the **business expense deduction** rules) state that a transfer is not a contribution when it is made with a **reasonable** expectation of financial return **commensurate** with the amount that is transferred. The term "contribution" is essentially synonymous with the words **gift** and **donation**. A transaction may be partly a contribution and a **sale** (although discounts provided on sales of goods in the ordinary course of **business** should not be regarded as contributions). A contribution to a **charitable organization** is termed a **charitable contribution**.

For **annual information return** reporting purposes, neither contributions of services (such as the value of donated advertising space, broadcast air time, or discounts on services) nor contributions of use of materials, equipment, or facilities should be reported as contributions. These items are not forms of **public support** nor is there a **charitable contribution deduction** for a **gift** of them. [CG § 3; PF §14.1; HC §§ 1.2, 1.3, 31.2; SM pp. 131–133] (also **Donative intent; In-kind contributions**).

contribution, charitable

See **Charitable contribution**.

contribution, restricted

A "restricted contribution" is a **contribution**, made to a **charitable organization**, where the **gift** is restricted to a use for a specific purpose. Usually, the restriction does not affect the **deductibility** of the contribution; this is certainly the case where the restriction is for a **program** activity of the organization or it is **de minimis**. A **material** restriction for a noncharitable purpose (such as for **lobbying** or an objective that is contrary to **public policy**) defeats any charitable deduction. [CG § 10.4] (also **Contribution, unrestricted**).

contribution, unrestricted

An "unrestricted contribution" is a **contribution**, made to a **charitable organization**, where the **gift** is made for the **donee's** general use, without any **conditions**. [CG § 10.4] (also **Contribution, restricted**).

contribution base

The **deductibility** of **charitable contributions** for a particular **tax year** is confined by certain **percentage limitations**, which in the case of individuals are a function of the **donor's** "contribution base." An individual's contribution base essentially is an amount equal to his or her **adjusted gross income**. Technically, the contribution base is an individual's adjusted gross income computed without regard to any **net operating loss carryback** to the **tax year** involved (**IRC** § 170(b)(1)(F)). [CG § 7.2; FR § 5.14(d); SM p. 134].

contribution year

A **person's** "contribution year" is a **tax year** in which a **charitable contribution** is made.

contributor, substantial
See **Substantial contributor**.

control

Use of the word "control" in the **nonprofit law** context usually refers to control by an **organization** over another. There are three basic models by which this element of control can be manifested: (1) the **interlocking directorate**; (2) use of the **membership** feature, where the controlling organization is the sole member of the controlled organization, and (3) use of stock, where the controlling organization is the sole (or majority) stockholder of the controlled organization.

One or more **persons** control a nonprofit organization if they have the **power** to remove and replace (or appoint, elect, or approve or veto the appointment or election of, if the power includes a continuing power to appoint, elect, or approve or veto the appointment or election of, periodically or in the event of vacancies) a majority of the nonprofit organization's **directors** or **trustees**, or a majority of **members** who elect a majority of the organization's directors or trustees. This power can be exercised **directly** by a **parent** organization through one or more of the parent organization's trustees, directors, officers, or **agents**, acting in their capacity as trustees, directors, officers, or agents of the parent organization. Also, parent organization controls a **subsidiary** nonprofit organization if a majority of the subsidiary's trustees or directors are trustees, directors, officers, **employees**, or agents of the parent.

One or more persons control a stock **corporation** if they own more than 50 percent of the stock (by voting power or **value**) of the corporation.

One or more persons control a **partnership** (including a **limited liability company**) if they own more than 50 percent of the profits or capital interests in the entity. A person also controls a partnership if the person is a managing partner or managing member of a partnership which has three or fewer managing partners or managing members (regardless of which partner or member has the most actual control) or if the person is a **general partner** in a **limited partnership** (regardless of which partner has the most actual control).

One or more persons control a **trust** if they own more than 50 percent of the **beneficial interests** in the trust. A person's beneficial interest in a trust is determined in proportion to that person's actuarial interest in the trust as of the end of the **tax year**.

Other definitions of the term "control" appear in nonprofit law. For example, in the law pertaining to **private foundations**, a **grant** to an organization that is controlled, **directly or indirectly**, by the foundation or one or more **disqualified persons** with respect to it does not constitute a **qualifying distribution** (IRC § 4942(g)(1)(A)). (An exception is available for curtailed **deemed out-of-corpus distributions**.) An organization is controlled if any of these persons may, by aggregating their votes or **positions of authority**, require the **grantee** to make an **expenditure**, or prevent the grantee from making an expenditure, regardless of the method by which the control is exercised or is exercisable. Control of a grantee is determined, in this context, without regard to any **conditions** imposed on the grantee as part of the distribution or any other **restrictions** accompanying the distribution as to the manner in which the distribution is to be used (unless one or more **material restrictions** are involved). That is, for this rules to apply, it is the grantee, not the distribution, that must be controlled by the distributing private foundation. [EO §§ 12.3(c), 29.1, 30.1(c); HC § 24.20(a); PF § 6.5(b); AR § 21.2(b)–(d); SM p. 215; PG pp. 131–132].

controlled entity

A "controlled entity" is an **organization** that is **controlled** by a **controlling organization**. A controlled entity may be a **for-profit entity**, a nonexempt **nonprofit organization**, or a **tax-exempt organization**. Control is this context means (1) in the case of a **corporation**, ownership (by vote or **value**) of more than 50 percent of the stock in the corporation, (2) in the case of a **partnership**, ownership of more than 50 percent of the profits interests or capital interests in the partnership, and (3) in any other case, ownership of more than 50 percent of the **beneficial** interests in the entity (**IRC** § 512(b)(13)(D)). **Constructive ownership** rules (**IRC** § 318) apply in this setting. [EO §§ 29.6, 30.7; UB § 8.8; PF §§ 11.3(b), 12.3(g), 13.5(a), 15.7(k); HC § 4.9(a)(ii); AR Chap. 21, §§ 3.1(pp), 3.2(pp); AS §§ 3.8, 6.1(c), 8.6; SM pp. 218–219].

controlling organization

A "controlling organization" is a **tax-exempt organization** that **controls** a **controlled entity**. The **federal tax law** treats payments of **interest**, **annuities**, **royalties**, and **rent** from a controlled entity to a controlling organization as **unrelated business income** in certain circumstances (**IRC** §§ 512(b)(13)(A), 6033(h)). [EO §§ 29.6, 30.7; HC §§ 14.1(d), 24.20; CU Q 15.60; SM pp. 218–219].

convenience doctrine

As a general rule, the **net income** derived by a **tax-exempt organization** from the **regular** conduct of an **unrelated trade or business** is subject to the **federal income tax**. One of the **exceptions** to this rule is the conduct of a business, in the case of a **charitable organization** or a state **college** or **university**, that is carried on by the organization **primarily** for the convenience of its **members**, **students**, **patients**, **officers**, or **employees** (**IRC** § 513(a)(2)). [UB § 4.1; EO § 25.2(b); HC § 24.18(a); RE Q 18.6; SM p. 175].

convenience of the employer doctrine

The "convenience of the employer doctrine" is a body of **federal tax law** that determines whether the **value** of employment-related items, such as lodging or meals, furnished by an **employer** for **employees** is considered **gross income**. The general concept is that if the employee is required, in the case of lodging, to accept it on the business premises of the employer as a condition of employment or, in the case of meals, they are furnished on the employer's business premises, the value of the items is not taxable (**IRC** § 119). Thus, for example, a president of a **university** is not taxable on the rental value of a university-provided and –based residence.

convention

See **Qualified convention and trade show activity**.

C

convention of churches

A "convention of churches" generally is an **organization** reflecting a cooperative undertaking by **churches** of the same denomination. It may, however, also mean a cooperative undertaking by churches of different denominations. A convention of churches usually qualifies for **tax exemption** (by reason of **IRC** §§ 501(a) and 501(c)(3)) as a **religious** organization. A **tax-exempt** convention of churches is a **public charity** (**IRC** § 170(b)(1)(A)(i)). [EO § 10.4; RE Q 3.7; CG § 3.3(a); AR § 1.1(b); SM p. 80] (cf. **Association of churches**; **Institution**).

conveyance

A "conveyance" is the transfer of title, leasehold interest, or the like in **property** (usually, **real property**) from one **person** (or group of persons) to another person (or group of persons). For example, the **contribution** of an **easement** to a **charitable organization** is a conveyance. [CG § 9.7].

cooperative

In general, a "cooperative" is an **organization** of **persons** formed for the common prosecution of some enterprise, where the **profits** are shared in accordance with the **capital**, labor, or other contribution of each person. Some cooperatives are **tax-exempt organizations**; others are taxable organizations (**IRC** §§ 1381–1388). [EO §§ 3.4, 19.23] (see **Cooperative hospital service organization**; **Cooperative educational service organization**; **Cooperative telephone company**; **Farmers' cooperative**).

cooperative educational service organization

A "cooperative educational service organization" is an **organization** that is **tax-exempt** as a **charitable organization** (by reason of **IRC** §§ 501(a), 501(f), and 501(c)(3)). This type of organization must be **organized** and **controlled** by and composed solely of **members** that are private or public **educational institutions**. It must be organized and **operated** solely to hold, **commingle**, and collectively invest and reinvest the monies contributed to it by each of the members of the organization, and to collect **income** from the investments and turn over the entire amount, less **expenses**, to its members. [EO § 11.5].

cooperative hospital service organization

A "cooperative hospital service organization" is an **organization** that is **tax-exempt** as a **charitable organization** (by reason of **IRC** §§ 501(a), 501(e), and 501(c)(3)). This type of organization must be **organized** and **operated** solely for two or more tax-exempt **member hospitals**, and must be organized and operated on a **cooperative** basis. It must perform certain specified services on a centralized basis for its members; the services must constitute tax-exempt activities if performed on its own behalf by a participating hospital. [HC § 1.5; EO § 11.4; AR § 8.1(c)(5)].

cooperative organization

A "cooperative organization" is an entity that is **organized** and **operated** in accordance with the principles of being a **cooperative**, which are found in both the **common law** and **IRS** ruling policy. Under the former, a cooperative organization exhibits three characteristics: democratic **control** by the **members**, operation at cost, and subordination of **capital**. [EO §§ 3.4, 19.23; HC § 17.1, 17.2; AU § 7.1(r)].

copyright

The law of "copyright" provides protection against infringement for the works of authors and other artists; it enables them to determine the publication of their works. The **federal law** of copyright essentially is **statutory law**, created by the Copyright Act of 1976. A copyright concerning a creation of a **donor** is **excluded** from the definition of a **capital asset**. [CG § 6.6].

corporate foundation

A "corporate foundation" is a **tax-exempt charitable organization** established and **controlled** by a **for-profit business entity**. In almost all instances, a corporate foundation will be a **private foundation**. [PF Chap. 17].

corporate sponsorship fee

A "corporate sponsorship fee" is a sum of money paid to a **tax-exempt organization**, usually a **public charity**, by a **for-profit corporation,** where the organization causes the name of its public entertainment event or other type of **program** to include the name of the payor corporation. Thus, in return for sponsorship of the event, the corporation is publicly recognized as the event's sponsor or one of its sponsors). It originally was the position of the **IRS** that these fees, paid where the for-profit business receives a package of valuable services, constitute **unrelated business income,** in the nature of **advertising** income, to the recipient exempt organization. Conversely, the exempt organizations want to treat these sponsorship payments as **gifts,** with the benefit to the sponsor being a mere **acknowledgment**. Special rules (**IRC** § 513(i)) help determine which position is correct. [EO § 24.6; CG § 23.3; UB § 6.6(a); FR § 5.16(b); HC § 24.17] (also **Sponsorship, corporate**).

corporate veil, piercing the

See **Veil, piercing the corporate**.

corporation

A "corporation" is a legal **entity** (juridical and artificial **person**), almost always a creation of state **law**. A corporation is one of the four types of legal form that can be used in organizing a **nonprofit organization**, and is the most common form of nonprofit organization. (The other three types are the **trust, unincorporated association**, and **limited liability company.**) The principal feature of a corporation is that it usually shields persons (including individuals) from most forms of legal **liability** that may arise during the course of its existence and operation (**IRC** § 7701(a)(3)).

For-profit corporations have owners, usually known as stockholders (or shareholders). These corporations are subject to **tax,** as is usually the case with the stockholders. Thus, there is a potential for double taxation. A nonprofit corporation is likely to qualify for federal **income**

tax exemption; a few states allow a nonprofit corporation to issue (non-**dividend**-paying) stock.

The U.S. Supreme Court, in an opinion issued in 2014, provided an extensive analysis of the meaning of corporations in the law, both in general and in connection with the distinction between nonprofit and for-profit corporations. The purpose of this legal fiction, the Court wrote, "is to provide protection for human beings." A corporation, said the Court, "is simply a form of organization used by human beings to achieve desired ends." It continued: "An established body of law specifies the rights and obligations of the people (including shareholders, officers, and employees) who are associated with a corporation in one way or another. When rights, whether constitutional or statutory, are extended to corporations, the purpose is to protect the rights of these people."

The Court provided three examples of this principle. The extension of Fourth Amendment protection to corporations "protects the privacy interests of employees and others associated with the company." Protecting corporations from government seizure of their property without just compensation "protects all those who have a stake in the corporation's financial well-being." Protecting the free-exercise rights of corporations "protects the religious liberty of the humans who own and control those companies."

The Court wrote that, "[w]hile it is certainly true that a central objective of for-profit corporations to make money, modern corporate law does not require for-profit corporations to pursue profit at the expense of everything else, and many do not do so." It added: "For-profit corporations, with ownership approval, support a wide variety of charitable causes, and it is not at all uncommon for such corporations to further humanitarian and other altruistic objectives." After giving some examples, the Court stated: "If for-profit corporations may pursue such worthy objectives, there is no apparent reason why they may not further religious objectives as well."

The Court stated: "Not all corporations that decline to organize as nonprofits do so in order to maximize profit." It continued: "For example, organizations with religious and charitable aims might organize as for-profit corporations because of the potential advantages of that corporate form, such as the freedom to participate in lobbying for legislation or campaigning for political candidates who promote their religious or charitable goals."

Indeed, "recognizing the inherent compatibility between establishing a for-profit corporation and pursuing nonprofit goals," the Court acknowledged that states "have increasingly adopted laws formally recognizing hybrid corporate forms." "Over half of the States, for instance," the court observed, "now recognize the 'benefit corporation,' a dual-purpose entity that seeks to achieve both a benefit for the public and a profit for its owners." [PG pp. 4–7; SM pp. 6, 8–9; EO § 4.1(a); PF §§ 4.3, 4.5. 11.3(c); CG § 2.8; RE Q 1.8, Q 1.18; CU Q 1.6].

corporation sole

A "corporation sole" is a category of **corporation** (as opposed to a corporation aggregate) that is formed by a single (sole) individual, with successor office holders, having similar powers, accorded the ability to continue the corporation over time. This corporate form is often used by **religious organizations**.

corpus

The term "corpus" has many meanings in the **law**. The meaning most suitable in the **nonprofit law** context, however, is that a "corpus" is the **property** (**assets** or **principal**) held by a **nonprofit organization** to generate **income**. Thus, income (such as **dividends** or **interest**) is different from corpus. Corpus is, for example, the asset base for many types of trusts (including **private foundations**), pension funds, **endowment funds,** and the like. [PF § 1.2; EO § 11.9(a)].

correct

Generally, the word "correct" has the same meaning as when it is used in the **IRC** provisions imposing a **second-tier tax**. The word, however, has special meaning in three **private foundation** second-tier tax contexts: (1) in the **mandatory payout** setting, the word means reducing the amount of the undistributed **income** to zero; (2) in the **excess business holdings** setting, the word means reducing the amount of the excess business holdings to zero; and (3) in the **jeopardizing investment** setting, the word means removing the investment from jeopardy (IRC § 4963(d)). [PF §§ 6.7(c), 7.6, 8.5(c)].

correction

The term "correction" (and **correct**) means, with respect to an act of **self-dealing**, undoing the transaction to the extent possible, but in any case placing the **private foundation** in a financial position not worse than that in which it would be if the **disqualified person** involved was dealing under the highest **fiduciary** standards (IRC § 4941(e)(3)). The term "correction" (and correct) means, with respect to a **taxable expenditure**, (1) recovering part or all of the **expenditure** to the extent recovery is possible, and where it is not possible, certain other corrective action or (2) in the case of a failure to obtain a full and complete report from the **grantee** on how the funds were spent or a failure to make full and detailed reports with respect to the expenditures to the **IRS,** obtaining or making the report (**IRC** § 4945(i)(1)). The term is also used in the private foundation **mandatory distribution** context (**IRC** § 4942(h)(2)).

The words "correction" and **correct** mean, with respect to an **excess benefit transaction**, undoing the **excess benefit** to the extent possible, and taking any additional measures necessary to place the organization in a financial position not worse than that in which it would be if the **disqualified person** were dealing under the highest **fiduciary** standards, except that in the case of a correction of an excess benefit transaction involving a **donor-advised fund**, no amount repaid in a manner prescribed by the **IRS** may be held in a donor-advised fund. In the context of the **political expenditures taxes** rules, these words mean recovering part or all of the political expenditure to the extent recovery is possible, establishment of safeguards to prevent future political expenditures, and, where full recovery is not possible, such additional corrective action as is prescribed in tax **regulations**. (**IRC** §§ 4955(f)(3), 4958(f)(6)). The term is further used in connection with the excise taxes imposed in the **black lung benefits trust** context (**IRC** §§ 4951(e)(3), 4952(e)(1)). [EO §§ 12.4, 18.5, 21.11, 23.3; PF §§ 5.15(a), 6.7(c), 9.10(d); HC § 4.9(a)(vii); AS § 3.8(f); SM pp. 59, 90–91; LI Q 4.61, Q 5.41, Q 6.36].

C

correction period

The term "correction period" means, with respect to a **taxable event**, the period beginning on the date on which the event occurs and ending 90 days after the date of mailing of a **notice of deficiency** with respect to the **second-tier tax** imposed on the taxable event, extended by any period in which a **deficiency** cannot be **assessed** and any other period which the **IRS** determines is **reasonable** and necessary to bring about **correction** of the taxable event (**IRC §** 4963(e)(1)). [PF § 9.10(d)].

cost basis

See **Basis**.

costs, allocation of

A cost experienced by a **nonprofit organization** may have more than one purpose. In that instance, the cost may be allocated to two or more functions and/or two or more organizations. One common instance of this situation is an **expenditure** that is part for **program** and part for **fundraising**; the cost is to be allocated between the two functions. Another example of cost allocation is an expenditure that is part for program and part for **lobbying**. A cost may be incurred by one organization and partially allocated (perhaps for reimbursement purposes) to another, such as a cost incurred by a professional **association** partially for itself and partially for its related **foundation**. Also, where facilities and/or personnel are used both to carry on **exempt functions** and conduct **unrelated business**, the expenses and similar items must be allocated between the two uses on a **reasonable** basis. [EO §§ 22.3(d)(ii), 22.6(a), 24.11; PF §§ 10.4, 12.1(c); UB § 11.2].

counterclaim

A "counterclaim" is a document that may be filed in response to the filing of a **complaint**. It contains the elements of an **answer**, but also states the basis for a separate **cause of action**.

counterpart test

The "counterpart test," which has several variations, is a way of comparing the activity of a **nonprofit organization** and a **for-profit organization**, or perhaps the organizations in their entirety, to determine whether they are essentially identical. One application of the counterpart test is in the setting of the **commerciality doctrine**. Another use of the counterpart test is to determine whether a governmental **entity** has the same characteristics as a **charitable** entity (that is, whether the governmental entity has a counterpart in the nonprofit **sector**); if so, the governmental entity may be able to be **tax-exempt** us a charitable organization, such as a state entity in relation to the **federal tax law**. [EO § 7.14; SM p. 286].

covered executive branch official

The phrase "covered executive branch official" is used in the context of the **lobbying disallowance rule**, which denies a **business expense deduction** for an amount paid or incurred in connection with any **direct communication** with a covered executive branch official in an attempt to influence the official actions or positions of the official (**IRC** § 162(e)(1)(D)). A covered executive branch official is the President of the United States; the vice president of the United States; any officer or **employee** of the White House Office of the Executive Office of the President; and the two most senior-level officers of each of the other agencies in the Executive Office; any individual serving in a position in level I of the Executive Schedule (under 5 U.S.C. § 5312); any other individual designated by the President as having Cabinet-level status; and any immediate deputy or an individual described in the foregoing two categories (**IRC** § 162(e)(6)). [EO § 22.6(a)].

creating document

See **Articles of organization**.

creator of a trust

The "creator of a trust" is the person who caused the **trust** to be formed; synonyms are **settlor** and **grantor**. A creator of a trust is a **substantial contributor** and thus is a **disqualified person** where the trust is a **private foundation** (**IRC** §§ 507(d)(2)(A), 4946(a)(1)(A)). [PF § 4.1].

credentialing

The word "credentialing" means to confer a form of recognition, on the basis of certain criteria, on a **person**. This recognition may be of an individual, which is usually referred to as **certification**. Recognition conferred on an organization or on a **program** of an organization is usually referred to as **accreditation**. [EO § 14.1(g)].

credit, tax

A "tax credit" is an offset for **tax** purposes, dollar for dollar, of an amount expended for a particular purpose, against a tax liability of the payor. A tax credit differs from a tax **deduction** in that, with a deduction, the amount of tax savings is dependent on the **taxpayer's marginal rate** of tax, whereas with a credit, the value of the tax savings is equal for all taxpayers, irrespective of their marginal rate. [CG § 2.23].

credit counseling services

For purposes of the federal tax law authorizing **tax-exempt status** as **charitable organizations** or **exempt social welfare organizations** for **qualifying credit counseling organizations**, the phrase "credit counseling services" means (1) the provision of **educational** information to the public on budgeting, personal finance, financial literacy, saving and spending practices, and the sound use of consumer credit; (2) the assisting of individuals and families with financial problems by providing them with counseling; or (3) a combination of the foregoing activities (**IRC** § 501(q)(4)(A)). [EO §§ 5.6(h), 7.3; UB § 7.4; AR §§ 3.1(i), 3.2(i), 11.1(d)(1); GV §§ 3.9, 6.1(a); SM p. 39].

credit union

A "credit union" is a **member**-owned, **nonprofit cooperative** financial institution formed to permit those in the field of membership specified in its **charter** to pool their savings, lend them to one another, and own the institution where they save, borrow, and obtain related financial services. Members are united by a common bond and democratically operate the credit union in adherence with federal and state regulations. Credit unions are **tax-exempt** under the **federal tax law** (by reason of **IRC** § 501(a) and 501(c)(1) or 501(c)(14)). [EO §§ 4.10(a)(i), 19.7, 24.5(g); CL § 1.12(g); AU § 7.1(t); SM pp. 44, 292; Q 1.51].

crop operations finance corporation

A "crop operations finance corporation" is a type of **tax-exempt organization** under the **federal tax law** (by reason of **IRC** §§ 501(a) and 501(e)(16)). This type of entity is organized by a tax-exempt **farmers' cooperative** or **association** or **members** of these organizations, for the purpose of financing the ordinary crop operations of the members or other producers, and operated in conjunction with this type of an association. [EO § 19.10; AU § 7.1(v); SM pp. 44–45].

cruelty, prevention of

Federal tax law provides **tax-exempt status** (by reason of **IRC** §§ 501(a) and 501(c)(3)) for **organizations** that are **organized** and **operated exclusively** for the "prevention of cruelty to children or animals." [EO § 11.1].

cy pres doctrine

The words "cy pres" are French for "as near." The cy pros **doctrine** is a rule conceived in **equity**, for the interpretation of documents in effectuation of **donor intent**. This doctrine is usually employed to give effect to a **will** or **trust** provision where a strict construction of the document would give rise to an illegal or impossible act. [EO §§ 6.3(f), 6.3(g)].

damages

"Damages" is a form of **compensation** or restitution paid to a **person**, usually as the consequence of **litigation**, for an injury or other loss (suffered personally in the case of an individual or by an **organization,** or occasioned by harm to an item of **property** or violation of some **right**) caused by **commission** of an unlawful act or some unlawful **omission**. Damages can arise as a result of an act or a failure to act by a **nonprofit organization**; sometimes **officers** and/or **directors** of the organization can be found personally **liable** and responsible for damages. (also **Liquidated damages**).

daycare center

See **Child-care organization**.

de minimis

The term "de minimis" is Latin for "insignificant." When used in a **law** context, it refers to an act that is of such insignificance that the law will ignore (**except**) it, even though the act itself constitutes conduct that is in violation of that (or a) law. A de minimis standard underlies most **civil** and **criminal** rules of law. For example, even though it is the position of the **IRS** that, inasmuch as the statutes do not provide any **insubstantiality** threshold, any **private inurement** or (in the case of **charitable organizations**) any **political campaign activity** will lead to loss or **denial** of **tax-exempt status**, courts usually interpret these rules as being subject to a de minimis threshold. Also, the **substantiation requirements** that apply in the context of **deductible charitable giving**, the rules concerning the dissemination of **low cost articles**. and the rules concerning **quid pro quo contributions** have de minimis thresholds ($250, $5, and $75, respectively (adjusted for inflation)). Still another example of a de minimis exception applies in the setting of the **lobbying disallowance rule**, where that rule does not apply to certain **in-house expenditures** for lobbying where the **person's** total amount of these expenditures for a **tax year** does not exceed $2,000 (computed without taking into account general overhead costs otherwise **allocable** to lobbying) (**IRC** § 162(e)(5)(B)(i)). [EO §§ 20.7, 23.2(a), 25.2(j); CG §§ 22.1, 22.2; HC § 18.4; PF § 5.7(c)].

de minimis rule for labor hours

The phrase "de minimis rule for labor hours" is used in defining the term **lobbying labor hours**. This **de minimis rule** provides that an **organization** may treat time spent by personnel on lobbying activities as zero if less than 5 percent of the **person's** time is spent on lobbying activities. **Reasonable** methods must be used to determine if less than 5 percent of a person's time is spent on lobbying activities. [EO § 22.6(a)].

D

deadwood

The word "deadwood" is used to describe provisions of a **code** of **laws** that have expired or have otherwise become extraneous. From time to time, a legislature will review this code and repeal ("clean out") these extraneous provisions; sometimes, however, a provision of law will continue to apply to one or a few **persons**, in which case the legislature will retain that law in another manner. The U.S. Congress has passed **acts** removing deadwood provisions from the **Internal Revenue Code**.

dealer

A "dealer" is a **person** who repeatedly and consistently engages in the buying and selling of items of a type of **property**. Thus, a dealer is engaged in a **business** and **regularly carries on** that business. A **tax-exempt organization** will be **taxed** on the **income** derived from a business activity where it acts as a dealer, unless the business activity is **related** to the **exempt purposes** of the organization. For example, if an exempt organization occasionally sells a parcel of **real property**, it will not be taxed on the resulting proceeds (unless it is a transaction involving application of the **private foundation net investment income** tax); however, if the organization is a dealer in real property, the activity is quite likely to be considered an unrelated trade or business. [UB §§ 2.2(e), 22.2(g); EO § 24.2(h)].

dealer UBTI rule

The "dealer UBTI rule" states that **gains** and **losses** from the **sale**, **exchange**, or other **disposition** of **property** held **primarily** for sale to customers in the ordinary course of a **trade or business** are not **excluded** from **unrelated business taxable income (UBTI)** by reason of the general exclusion for **capital gains** and **capital losses** (IRC § 512(b)(5)). [UB § 3.10; EO § 25.1(j)] (also **Disposal property**).

death tax

See **Estate tax**.

debt collection policy

Tax-exempt hospital organizations are expected to have a written debt collection policy; the policy is expected to contain provisions on the collection practices to be followed for patients who are known to qualify for **charity care** or financial assistance. [GV § 6.3(o); SM p. 277].

debt management plan services

For purposes of the **federal tax law** authorizing **tax-exempt status** as **charitable organizations** or **exempt social welfare organizations** for qualifying credit counseling organizations, the phrase "debt management plan services" means services related to the repayment, consolidation, or restructuring of a consumer's debt, and includes negotiation with creditors of lower interest rates, the waiver or reduction of fees, and the marketing and processing of debt management plans (**IRC** § 501(q)(4)(B)). Otherwise, the provision of debt management plan services is an **unrelated trade or business** (**IRC** § 513(j)). [EO §§ 7.3, 24.5(p)].

debt-financed income

"Debt-financed income" is **income** of a **tax-exempt organization** that is traceable to borrowed funds. Specifically, in computing an exempt organization's **unrelated business taxable income**, there must be included with respect to each **debt-financed property** that is unrelated to the organization's **exempt function**—as an item of **gross income** derived from an **unrelated trade or business**—an amount of income from the property, subject to tax in the proportion in which the property is financed by the debt (**IRC** § 514(a)(1)). [UB Chap. 5; EO § 24.9; HC § 24.21; PF §§ 7.1(b), 11.4; AR § 7.1(b)(4)(C)(i); SM p. 175].

debt-financed property

The term "debt-financed property" means, with certain **exceptions**, all **property** that is held to produce **income** and with respect to which there is an **acquisition indebtedness** at any time during the **tax year** (or during the preceding twelve months, if the property is disposed of during the year) (**IRC** § 514(b)(1)). One of these exceptions is for property where **substantially all** of its use is substantially **related** (aside from the need of the **organization** for income or funds) to the exercise or performance by the organization of its **tax-exempt purpose** or, if less than substantially all of its use is related, to the extent that its use is related to the organization's exempt purpose (**IRC** § 514(b)(1)). [UB § 5.3; EO § 24.9(b); HC § 24.21(a); CG § 14.6; SM p. 175; LI Q 13.35–Q 13.40].

debt financing

"Debt financing" occurs when **a person** acquires an item of **property** by means of (in whole or in part) a borrowing. That is, the person incurs debt in exchange for acquiring the property. (also **Acquisition indebtedness**; **Debt-financed income**; **Debt-financed property**).

decedent

A "decedent" is an individual who has died. (also **Decedent's estate**).

decedent's estate

The term "decedent's estate" is used to describe the money and/or **property** owned (or otherwise having **a right** to) by a **decedent**, prior to his or her death. The term "estate" is often used as a synonym for the term "decedent's estate."

declaration of trust

There are two basic ways in which a **trust** can be formed. One approach is **a trust agreement**; the other is a "declaration of trust." Unlike a trust agreement, a declaration of trust is not a **contract**. Instead, a declaration of trust is a written statement of a **person** unilaterally declaring the creation of a trust. A **pooled income fund** may be established in either of these two manners. [CG § 13.0; SM p. 10].

declaratory judgment

A "declaratory judgment" is a court opinion that expresses a view as to a point of law without ordering the parties involved to do something. **Federal tax law** contains a special rule providing for declaratory judgments as to the **tax-exempt status**, **private foundation status**, or **charitable donee status** of eligible **organizations** (IRC § 7428). [AU §§ 3.13(b), 5.27, 5.33(g); EO § 27.6(b)] (also **Actual controversy**; **Administrative record**; **Determination**).

deduction

A **federal income tax** "deduction" arises when an **expenditure** is made by a **taxpayer** (such as an individual or **corporation**) and the **law** provides that an amount equal to that expenditure may be subtracted from **gross income** in computing **adjusted gross income** or from adjusted gross income in computing **income**. Two common deductions are the **charitable contribution deduction** and the **business expense deduction**. A **tax-exempt organization** is entitled to use certain deductions in computing its **unrelated business income**. [CG §§ 2.5, 2.6, 9.27, 10.10; UB §§ 3.18, 3.19, 11.2; EO §§ 22.6(a), 22.6(b), 24.11; PF §§ 3.2, 9.5, 14.1].

deduction, business expense

See **Business expense deduction**.

deduction, charitable

See **Charitable contribution deduction**.

deduction modifications

The term "deduction modifications" arises in the setting of the definition of **adjusted gross income** for purposes of the requirements for qualification as a **private operating foundation**. These deduction modifications are as follows: (1) no **deduction** is allowable other than all the ordinary and necessary **expenses** paid or incurred for the production or collection of **gross income** or for the management, conservation, or maintenance of **property** held for the production of income, and the allowances for **depreciation** and **depletion**, and (2) the rules concerning expenses in connection with tax-exempt **interest** (IRC § 265) do not apply (IRC § 4942(f)(3)). [PF § 3.1(d)] (also **Income modifications**).

deduction reduction rule

The "deduction reduction rule" requires an individual to reduce the amount of a **charitable contribution deduction**, arising as the result of a **gift** of **property**, from an amount it might otherwise have been (namely, an amount equal to the property's **fair market value**) to a lesser amount (an amount equal to the **contributor's basis** in the property). Thus, the deduction reduction rule is an **exception** to the general rule that the charitable contribution deduction for a gift of property is an amount equal to the fair market value of the property.

There are six deduction reduction rules. One arises in the case of a charitable gift of **ordinary income property**. In this situation, the amount of the charitable contribution for the gift of the property must be reduced by the amount of **gain** that would have been recognized as gain, which is not **long-term capital gain** if the property had been sold by the **donor** at its fair market value, determined at the time of the contribution to the **charitable organization** (IRC § 170(e)(1)(A)). Thus, this deduction reduction rule basically means that a donor's deduction for a contribution of an item of ordinary income property to a charitable organization is confined to the donor's basis in the property.

Another deduction reduction rule applies in the instance of a charitable gift of **tangible personal property** that is put, by the charitable **donee**, to an **unrelated use**. Specifically, where a charitable gift of tangible personal property is made, the amount of the charitable contribution deduction that would otherwise be determined must be reduced by the amount of gain that would have been long-term capital gain if the property contributed had been sold by the donor at its fair market value, determined at the time of the contribution, where the use by the donee of the property is not **related** to its **tax-exempt purpose** (IRC § 170(e)(1)(B)(i)(I)). Thus, in these circumstances, where the contributed property is **capital gain property**, the charitable deduction that would otherwise be determined must be reduced by the amount of the **unrealized appreciation** in **value**.

The third deduction reduction rule applies in the instance of a charitable gift of tangible personal property that is **applicable property** that is disposed of by the **charitable donee** before the last day of the **tax year** in which the contribution was made and with respect to which the donee has not made the requisite **certification** (IRC § 170(e)(1)(B)(i)(II)).

The fourth deduction reduction rule applies where contributions of property are made **to** or **for the use of** a charitable organization that is not a **public charitable organization**. In this situation, when a charitable gift of capital gain property is made, the amount of the charitable deduction that would otherwise be determined must be reduced by the amount of gain that would have been long-term capital gain if the property contributed had been sold by the donor at its fair market value, determined at the time of the contribution, where the gift is to or for the use of a **private foundation** (IRC § 170(e)(1)(B)(ii)). That is, in these circumstances, where the contributed property is capital gain property, the charitable deduction that would otherwise be determined must be reduced by the amount of the unrealized appreciation in value. Thus, the charitable contribution deduction under these circumstances is confined to the donor's basis in the property. This rule does not, however, apply in the case of contributions to **private operating foundations, pass-through foundations**, or **common fund foundations**. Also, this rule does not apply in the case of a contribution of **qualified appreciated stock**.

The fifth deduction reduction rule applies in connection with charitable contributions of patents, most copyrights, trade names, trade secrets, know-how, most software, or similar property, or applications or registrations of this type of property (IRC § 170(e)(1)(B)(iii)).

The sixth deduction reduction rule applies in connection with charitable contributions of a **taxidermy property** which is contributed by the **person** who prepared, stuffed, or mounted the property or by any person who paid or incurred the cost of preparing, stuffing, or mounting the property (**IRC § 170(e)(1)(B)(iv)**).

Once these reduced deductions are determined, the amount that is actually deductible is subject to the **percentage limitations**.

There are other rules entailing reduction of a charitable deduction, such as those pertaining to gifts of **inventory**. [CG §§ 4.4(b), 4.5(a), 4.6(a), 4.6(c), 9.19(c), 9.24, 9.28(b); AR § 19.1(a)(4); SM pp. 136–137].

D

deduction year

A "deduction year" is a **tax year** in which a **tax deduction** is claimed. For example, if a portion of a **charitable contribution deduction** cannot be utilized in a tax year because of a **percentage limitation**, and that remaining portion of the deduction is claimed in the immediately subsequent tax year, that subsequent tax year is the deduction year for the remaining portion of the deduction, while the immediately preceding tax year is the deduction year for the initial portion of the contribution deduction. [CG § 7.4] (also **Contribution year**).

deemed out-of-corpus distribution

In general, a **grant** by a **private foundation** does not constitute a **qualifying distribution** if the **grantee** is **controlled** by the distributing foundation or **disqualified persons** with respect to it (**IRC § 4942(g)(1)(A)**). An **exception** is available for a grant to a **charitable organization** where, not later than the close of the first **tax year** after its tax year in which the grant is received, the organization makes a distribution equal to the amount of the grant, the distribution is generically a qualifying distribution made out of **corpus**, and the private foundation obtains sufficient evidence of compliance with this **rule** (**IRC §§ 4942(g)(3), (h)**). [PF § 6.5(a)].

defendant

The word "defendant" is used in most courts to describe the **person** who is a party to an item of **civil litigation** because the **complaint** names the person as the one against whom the proceeding is initiated. (also **Petitioner; Plaintiff; Respondent**).

deference

The word "deference" is used to mean when and the extent to which a court will uphold a determination of an **administrative agency** of a government, as opposed to substituting a determination of its own or voiding the agency's determination. Generally, a court will "defer" to the expertise of an agency. As a general rule, Congress delegates policymaking responsibilities to an agency and, pursuant to the principle of **separation of powers**, judges are not to substitute their personal policy preferences for the wisdom of government agency officials. The nature of the deference will depend, in part, on the nature of the determination. Often, when the issue is the subject of **litigation**, the determination is in the form of a **regulation**. The U.S. Supreme Court held that, in testing the validity of a federal agency regulation, a court must look first to see whether Congress itself has resolved the issue; if it has, then that is the end of the matter. If not, the court must decide whether the agency's determination is reasonable; if it is, the determination is valid. As to regulations, this type of deference is known as "*Chevron* deference" (so named because of the name of a litigant). Various other types of guidance are subject to looser standards of review, known as "*Skidmore* deference" (likewise so named). The Court held in

2011 that federal tax regulations are reviewable pursuant to the Chevron deference analytical approach. [CL § 8.1; SM pp. 338–339].

deferred compensation

"Deferred compensation" is **compensation** from an **employer** to an **employee**, under circumstances where the compensation is not currently received by the employee but is delayed until a later period. As with any compensation, deferred compensation, particularly when paid by a **charitable organization**, must be **reasonable**. Deferred compensation embraces **retirement plans** and **profit-sharing plans**. Deferred compensation plans are basically divided into **qualified plans** and **nonqualified plans**. [EO § 18.1(c); HC § 28.6; AR §§ 6.2(a)(6), 6.2(c)(12)].

deferred giving

See **Planned giving**.

deferred payment charitable gift annuity

A "deferred payment charitable gift annuity" is a **charitable gift annuity** as to which the payment of the **annuity** begins more than one year from the date that the annuity was issued. [CG § 14.3] (also **Immediate payment charitable gift annuity**).

deferred revenue

The accounting rules concept of "deferred revenue" includes **donor support** of an **organization**, such as **pledges** and **bequests**.

deficiency

The **federal tax law** defines a "deficiency," in the case of **estate taxes, excise taxes, gift taxes**, and **income taxes**, as the amount by which the **tax** imposed exceeds the excess of (1) the sum of the amount shown as the tax by the **taxpayer** on his, her, or its **tax return** (if a return was made by the taxpayer and an amount of tax was shown on it) and the amounts previously **assessed** (or collected without assessment) as a deficiency, over (2) the amount of rebates made (**IRC §** 6211(a)).

Deficit Reduction Act of 1984

The "Deficit Reduction Act of 1984" brought enactment of the **tax-exempt entity leasing rules**.

defined benefit plan

A "defined benefit plan" is a plan established and maintained by an **employer primarily** to systematically provide for the payment of definitely determinable benefits to its **employees** over a period of years, usually life, following retirement. Retirement benefits under a defined benefit plan are measured by and based on various factors, such as years of service rendered by the employee and **compensation** earned by the employee. The benefits are established in advance by a formula; the employer contributions are treated as the variable factor. [EO § 18.1(d)(i)].

defined contribution plan

A "defined contribution plan" is a plan that provides an individual account for each participant and bases benefits solely on the amount contributed to the participant's account and any expense, investment return, and forfeitures allocated to the account. This type of plan defines the amount of contribution to be added to each participant's account. This may be done in one of two ways: by directly defining the amount the **employer** will contribute on behalf of each **employee** or by leaving to the employer's discretion the amount of contribution, but defining the method of allocation. [EO § 18.1(d)(ii)].

delegation of legislative authority

An administrative agency may issue rules and regulations but is required to do so in the context of a policy established by a **legislative body**. Agency rules that accord government officials unbridled discretion to set a policy can be a prior restraint in violation of **free speech** principles. [FR § 4.6].

delivery

In the case of a **charitable contribution**, there must be the requisite "delivery" of the money or **property** that is the subject of the **gift** before the transaction is complete and the opportunity for a **charitable contribution deduction** arises. Where the gift is of property and there are specific rules as to the transfer of title, such as with respect to securities and **real property**, these rules (which include requirements as to delivery) must be adhered to for the charitable deduction to be available. [CG § 3.1(l)].

demonstration

A "demonstration" is a public exhibition in support of or opposition to an issue, policy, and/or individual. It is a way that a **charitable organization** can **advocate** its position, without endangering its **tax-exempt status**, as long as the demonstration is not an act of violence or some other act that is deemed contrary to **public policy**. [EO §§ 6.2(a), 23.2(g)].

denial of tax exemption

The phrase "denial of tax exemption" refers to a process, undertaken by the **IRS** or a court, by which it reviews the **organization** and **operation** of a **nonprofit organization**, and concludes that the **entity** does not merit **tax-exempt status**. [EO §§ 26.1, 27.1].

denominator (of support fraction)

Certain **charitable organizations** avoid classification as a **private foundation** by qualifying as a **publicly supported organization**. There are two principal categories of publicly supported organizations: the **donative publicly supported organization** and the **service provider publicly supported organization**. **Public support** is calculated by means of a **support fraction**.

For the donative publicly supported organization, the denominator of the support fraction consists of (1) **direct contributions** from the public, (2) indirect contributions from the public, (3) **grants** from **governmental units**, (4) net income from **unrelated business** activities, (5) gross **investment income**, (6) tax revenues levied for the benefit of the organization and either paid to or expended on behalf of the organization, and (7) the value of services or facilities (exclusive of services or facilities generally furnished to the public without charge) furnished by a governmental unit to the organization without charge (**IRC** § 509(d)). Excluded from this denominator are **exempt function revenues**, **unusual grants**, **gain** from the **disposition** of **property** that would be considered as gain from the **sale** or **exchange** of a **capital asset**, and the value of **exemption** from any **federal**, state, or local **tax** or any similar benefit.

For the service provider organization, the denominator of the support fraction consists of (1) contributions, (2) grants, (3) **exempt function income**, and (3) the fourth through seventh of the categories of support for donative publicly supported organizations (**IRC** § 509(d)). Excluded from this denominator are the same forms of support for donative publicly supported organizations, other than exempt function revenue. [PF §§ 15.4(b), 15.5; EO §§ 12.3(b)(i), 12.3(b)(iv); SM pp. 80–82].

department
The word "department" is usually used to describe a division of a government, most frequently the **executive branch** of a government. Other segments of executive branches of government tend to be within departments, such as **agencies** and **bureaus**. For example, within the **Department of the Treasury** is an agency, the **IRS**. Occasionally, a segment of **a nonprofit organization** is referred to as a "department." [PF § 15.5(d); EO § 12.3(b)(iv)].

Department of the Treasury
The "Department of the Treasury" has several functions, one of which is the administration and enforcement of the **IRC** (**IRC** § 7801). This function is usually performed by and through the **IRS**. [EO § 2.2(a); AU § 2.1; SM pp. 293–294] (also **Secretary of the Treasury**).

depreciation
"Depreciation" is the decline in **value** of an item of **property** as the consequence of age, use of the property, and improvement in the class of property. [EO §§ 24.11, 28.15(a); PF §§ 10.4(a), 11.4(c), 12.1(b)] (also **Depreciation, deduction for**; **Depreciation, reserve for**).

depreciation, deduction for
The **federal tax law** provides an **income tax deduction** for **depreciation** (**IRC** § 168). The amount of this deduction is dependent, in part, on the life of the property (termed the **recovery period**). The depreciation deduction is the mechanism on which the **tax-exempt entity leasing** rules are based. [EO §§ 24.11, 28.15(a); CG § 2.19].

depreciation, pass-through of
"Pass-through of depreciation" occurs when the **depreciation** that takes place with respect to an item of **property** held by a **person** is attributed to another person because of the second person's relationship to the first. For example, in some circumstances, the depreciation that occurs with respect to property held by a **pooled income fund** is attributed to the **income beneficiaries** of the fund. n these instances, the beneficiaries of the fund may be able to properly claim the **federal tax deduction for depreciation**. [CG § 13.7].

depreciation, reserve for

A "depreciation reserve" is an account established on the books of an **organization** to offset the **depreciation** of its **property**. For example, the **IRS** requires that a depreciation reserve be established and maintained by **pooled income funds**. [CG § 13.7].

D

depreciation recapture

See **Recapture**.

derivative public charity status

"Derivative public charity status" occurs when the **public charity status** of a **charitable organization** is derived from its relationship with another public charity. An illustration is the **supporting organization**.

derivative status

In the **federal tax law**, a classification of an **organization** can be obtained (derived) from the relationship between the organization and another organization. The principal examples of this form of "derivative status" are **derivative tax exemption** and **derivative public charity status**.

derivative tax exemption

A "derivative tax exemption" occurs when the **tax-exempt status** of an **organization** is derived from its relationship with another exempt organization. An illustration is the tax exemption for **title-holding corporations**. [HC § 34.7] (also **Integral part doctrine**; **Vicarious tax exemption**).

destination-of-income test

The rule in the **common law** known as the "destination-of-income test," which was eliminated by **statute** in 1950 (**IRC § 502**), was that an **organization** could qualify as a **tax-exempt charitable entity**, even if it engaged in **commercial business** activity, as long as its **net income** was destined for charitable purposes. [EO § 28.14; UB § 1.9; CG § 3.4(a)] (also **Feeder organization**).

determination

The term "determination" is used to describe one of the requirements for the special **declaratory judgment** action for **charitable organizations** and **farmers' cooperatives**, which is that there must be a final decision by the **IRS** (the determination) affecting the tax qualification of an organization or a failure by the **IRS** to timely make a determination on a qualifying issue (**IRC §§ 7428(a)(1), (2)**). [EO §§ 26.1(c), 27.6(b)(i)].

determination letter

A "determination letter" is a written statement issued by the **IRS** in response to an **application for recognition of tax exemption,** in response to a written inquiry by an individual or organization. The determination letter applies to the particular facts involved and is based on principles and precedents previously announced by the **IRS** National Office. It is issued only when a **determination** can be made based on clearly established rules in the **Internal Revenue Code**, the **federal tax regulations**, a **ruling**, or court decision that the **IRS** has published that specifically answers the question presented. In practice, the term **ruling** is often used when referring to a determination letter, although technically that is incorrect. [EO § 26.1(c); HC § 34.1(a); PF §§ 2.5(c), 15.11(b); CU Q 3.19; RE Q 8.24; LI Q 2.15].

determination year

The term "determination year" is used in defining the measuring period applicable with respect to the **lobbying expenditures** of a **charitable organization** that has elected the **expenditure test**. This measuring period consists of the most recently completed year of the organization and the three **base years** immediately preceding the determination year. [EO § 22.3(d)(iii)].

development

The word "development" is essentially synonymous with the term **fundraising**. To the extent that there is a difference between the two words, "development" entails the long-range planning and acquisition of **contributions**, whereas the term "fundraising" suggests the seeking of a more immediate return of **gift** support. [HC Chap. 14].

development committee

The "development committee" of a **nonprofit organization** (usually a **public charity**) consists of a group of individuals who are responsible (subject to any oversight by the **governing board**) for the overall design, implementation, and monitoring of the **fundraising** efforts of the organization. In most instances, this type of committee is a **standing committee**.

devise

The word "devise" means to make a **gift** of **real property** by means of a **will**. (also **Bequeath**; **Legacy**).

dicta

See **Dictum**.

Dictionary Act

The "Dictionary Act" is a **federal statute** that is to be consulted in determining the meaning of terminology in any federal law, which is binding unless the context of a particular federal statute indicates otherwise. The purpose of this Act is to generally ensure uniformity of the meaning of terms across the spectrum of federal statutory law. The U.S. Supreme Court has stated that this Act is to be followed by it and other courts because "[t]o give th[e] same words a different meaning for each category would be to invent a statute rather than interpret one."

dictum

The word "dictum" is used to describe language in a court opinion that is not necessary in order for the court to arrive at the decision in the case. It is, thus, language in an opinion that is extraneous—merely observations or musings by a court as it develops its holding(s). Technically, dictum does not have any **precedential** value, although in actual practice it is often difficult to separate "dicta" (the plural of dictum) in an opinion from the language constituting the core holding.

D

direct

Some of the principal definitions of the word "direct" are "straightforward," "undeviating," and "straight to the point." This word is often used in the **law** to describe a relationship between two persons that is "straight" or "unbroken." For example, to qualify as a **medical research organization**, the **entity** must be directly engaged in the continuous **active conduct** of **medical research** in conjunction with a **hospital**. [HC § 5.1(b); EO §§ 7.6(d), 12.3(a)] (cf. **Indirect**).

direct contact lobbying

The term "direct contact lobbying" means a meeting, telephone conversation, letter, email message, or similar means of **communication** with a legislator or **covered executive branch official** that otherwise qualifies as a **lobbying activity**. [EO § 22.6(a); PF § 9.1(b)].

direct contact lobbying hours

Notwithstanding the **de minimis rule for labor hours**, an **organization** must treat all hours spent by a **person** on **direct contact lobbying** (as well as the hours that person spends in connection with direct contact lobbying, including time spent traveling) as labor hours allocable to **lobbying activities**. [EO § 22.6(a)].

direct contribution

A "direct contribution" is a **contribution** that was directly given to a **charitable organization**, as contrasted with a **grant** by a government agency or by a **publicly supported organization**, which is considered by the **law** to embody various **indirect** contributions. This concept is part of the set of rules by which **public support** for **organizations** attempting to qualify as **donative publicly supported organizations** is computed. The **annual information return** filed by many **tax-exempt organizations** has a line item for direct contributions. [PF § 15.4(b); EO § 12.3(b)(i); AR § 8.2(b)] (also **Support fraction**).

direct gift

A "direct gift" is a **gift** made **directly** to an organization (usually a **charitable organization**), rather than to an ultimate **donee** by means of an intermediate organization.

direct lobbying

A **communication** with a legislator or government official, or **employee** of either, is a "direct lobbying" communication where the communication refers to **specific legislation** and reflects a view on the legislation. In addition, where the communication is with a government official or employee, the communication is a direct lobbying communication only where the **principal** purpose of the communication is to **influence legislation**. [EO § 22.3(b); HC § 7.1(b); PF § 9.1(b); SM p. 186].

direct mail solicitation

A "direct mail solicitation" is a form of **fundraising** by which (usually large) numbers of **persons** are **solicited** by mail (by means or response advertising") for a **charitable gift**. A direct mail solicitation may be made as part of **a donor acquisition program**, a **donor renewal program**, or both. [FR § 2.2(a)].

direct public support

The phrase "direct public support" means forms of **public support** that an **organization** (almost always a **charitable organization**) derives **directly** from the **public**, either as **contributions** or **exempt function income**. [PF §§ 15.4(b), 15.5] (also **Revenue**).

direct self-dealing

A "direct" act of **self-dealing** occurs when the offending transaction is **directly** between a **private foundation** and a **disqualified person** with respect to the foundation. [PF § 5.3–5.10] (cf. **Indirect self-dealing**).

direct skip

In the context of the rules concerning the **generation-skipping transfer tax**, the term **generation skipping transfer** includes a "direct skip." A direct skip is the transfer of an **interest** in an item of **property** to a **skip person** (**IRC § 2612(c)**). [CG § 8.5].

direct-outgrowth rule

The **IRS** has a policy of not **recognizing tax-exempt status**, particularly as **charitable entities**, to **organizations** that are "direct outgrowths" of **for-profit enterprises**, for that reason alone. This is a peculiar (and often incorrect) rule because the focus should be on the inherent purposes and activities of an organization, rather than whether it is a **successor** to another entity. There is nothing inappropriate about a for-profit company **spinning off** one or more **nonprofit** (and perhaps exempt) activities into a new organization, just as it is quite appropriate for an exempt organization to spin off one or more **unrelated businesses** into a new for-profit organization. [PF Chap. 17].

directly connected

The words "directly connected" are used in the **federal tax law** to describe a close relationship between an item of **income** and an **expense** that must exist if the expense is to be **deductible**. For example, in the **unrelated trade or business** setting, an item of deduction must have a proximate and **primary** relationship to the carrying on of the business. Thus, the term **unrelated business taxable income** means the **gross income** derived by a **tax-exempt organization** from an unrelated trade or business, **regularly carried on** by the organization, less business deductions that are "directly connected" with the carrying on of the trade or business (**IRC** § 512(a)(1)). Likewise, an exempt organization, in computing its **unrelated business income**, must include its share of the gross income from a **partnership** in which it is a **member** derived from the conduct of an **unrelated business** and its share of the partnership deductions that are "directly connected" with this gross income (**IRC** § 512(c)(1)). [UB § 11.2; EO § 24.11] (also **Partnership rule**).

directly or indirectly

The phrase "directly or indirectly" is used frequently in the law, including the **federal tax law,** to embrace behavior or activities that are not only being (or may be) performed by a **person**, but also by someone **related** to that person or under the **control** of that person. An example of this is the distinction between **direct self-dealing** and **indirect self-dealing**. [PF §§ 5.3–5.11; HC § 4.9(a)(iii)].

D

directly further

One of the ways to meet the **integral part test** applicable with respect to **functionally integrated Type III supporting organizations** is to engage in activities **substantially all** of which "directly further" the **exempt purpose** of one or more **supported organizations**. Holding title to and managing exempt-use **assets** are activities that meet the directly further standard. **Fundraising, grantmaking**, and managing nonexempt-use assets are not activities that satisfy the standard. [PF § 15.7(g)].

director

A "director" is an individual who has the policymaking and oversight responsibilities for an **organization**, whether **incorporated** or **unincorporated**. While some organizations are served by only one director, most are served by a group of them, termed a **board of directors**. [GV §§ 1.5, 2.5–2.7, 3.5(a), 3.10(e); EO §§ 5.1, 5.7(f)(2), 20.4(e), 20.4(f), PG pp. 9–14; PF §§ 1.1, 18.3; AR § 6.1(a)(1); CU Q 1.19, Q 1.20; AS §§ 3.3, 3.8(c); SM pp. 16–19] (also **Board of trustees**; **Fiduciary**; **Liability**; **Trustee**).

directors, board of

See **Board of directors**.

directory requirement

A "directory requirement" is a requirement of **law** in a **statute** that may be satisfied by means of the **doctrine** of **substantial compliance**. This type of requirement tends to be procedural in nature. For example, it has been held that the **substantiation rules** pertaining to the need for the services of a qualified appraiser are directory in nature (rather than being **mandatory**), because these rules do not relate to the substance or essence of whether or not a **charitable contribution** was actually made. [CG §§ 12.1(c), 21.5(c)].

disadvantages of tax exemption

An **organization**, as the consequence of being **tax-exempt** in accordance with the **federal income tax law**, may be required to forego certain activities or functions in which it might otherwise engage. Thus, most **exempt organizations** cannot engage in **commercial** activities to a **substantial** extent. Some exempt organizations, particularly **public charities**, are prohibited from engaging in **substantial legislative** activities and/or any **political campaign activities**. The rules applicable to **private foundations** impose a host of limitations and requirements that generally are not otherwise applicable. Tax-exempt status can bring more extensive **annual reporting** requirements than might otherwise be the case. [EO § 3.4].

disaster relief program
See **Qualified disaster, Qualified disaster relief payment.**

disclaim
The word "disclaim" means to repudiate or renounce. It is usually used in connection with a claim or potential **right vested** in a **person**. The person may disclaim this **interest** by rejecting or disavowing it. When this is properly accomplished, the interest is not attributable to the disclaiming person, for **tax** or other **law** reasons.

disclosure
Tax-exempt organizations are subject to a battery of "disclosure" requirements. **Applications for recognition of tax exemption** and **annual information returns** must be made available for public review and disseminated. **Exempt charitable** organizations must disclose their **unrelated business income tax** returns.

In the **charitable giving** setting, information must be disclosed concerning the **contributing** and disposition of gift **property** and **quid pro quo contributions**. Many charitable gifts, to be **deductible**, must be **substantiated**. Disclosure requirements apply to various payments to noncharitable exempt organizations. An exempt organization is required to disclose (when applicable) the fact that information and/or services it is offering are available without charge from the **federal** government. An **exempt organization**, other than a charitable one, generally must disclose to its **membership** a **reasonable** estimate of the portion of the **dues** or other similar amounts that are allocable to **lobbying** and/or **political campaign activities**, to enable the members to comply with the **lobbying disallowance rule** or the **political activities disallowance rule**; this disclosure must be provided at the time of assessment or payment of the dues or other amounts.

An exempt organization other than a **charitable** one, must (with **exceptions**) expressly state in a **fundraising solicitation** by or on behalf of it that **contributions** to the organization are not deductible, as charitable gifts, for federal income tax purposes. Charitable organizations must make a variety of disclosures to be in compliance with some of the states' **charitable solicitation acts**. [AR §§ 1.1(e), 5.1(j), 5.2(c)(2), 14.1(m)(4); EO §§ 27.8, 28.8, 28.9, 28.11, 28.12; CG §§ 22.1–22.3, 25.11; FR §§ 3.11, 3.15, 3.17, 4.1(a), 4.1(c), 4.1(g), 4.3, 5.1–5.5, 5.9(i), 5.14, 8.12; GV §§ 3.12(a), 4.3, 5.14, 8.9; PF § 12.3(b); CU Q 18.2, Q 18.16; AS § 10.3; PG pp. 224–226, 235–252; SM pp. 122–125].

disclosure on demand
See **Point-of-solicitation disclosure**.

disclosure statement
Most **noncharitable organizations** must, in their **solicitation** literature, contain an express statement that contributions to them are not deductible as gifts. [FR § 5.5; CG § 22.3] (See **Disclosure**).

discovery

"Discovery" is a process, undertaken in advance of a trial, by which a party to the **litigation** endeavors to obtain information from one or more **persons**, who may or may not be parties to the litigation. This information includes statements derived by means of one or more depositions, information derived by means of one or more **interrogatories**, and documents. The type of information to be sought is not limited by the rules of evidence and consequently can be quite broad (sometimes termed a "fishing expedition"). The discovery process can be expensive; more than one **lawsuit** initiated against the **federal government** by a **tax-exempt organization** has been abandoned because of the costs of the process. When litigation is instituted by means of the special **declaratory judgment** procedure available to **charitable organizations** and **farmers' cooperatives** (IRC § 7428), discovery is rarely allowed because the evidence in the case usually is confined to facts reflected in the **administrative record**. [EO § 27.6(b)(iv)].

discrimination

By application of the **public policy doctrine**, an **educational organization** may not have a racially discriminatory policy with respect to admissions, faculty, or programs. This rule of **law** is being extended to many types of **charitable organizations**. A prohibition on racial discrimination can be made applicable to a **tax-exempt organization** by reason of the **state action doctrine**. One of the ways in which an organization can be tax-exempt as a charitable entity is to promote **social welfare**, one form of which is the elimination of prejudice and discrimination. An exempt **social club** cannot have a written policy of discrimination on account of race, color, or religion (**IRC** § 501(i)).

Discrimination on the basis of gender is prohibited by law where the tax-exempt organization is considered a place of **public accommodation**. Other forms of discrimination by exempt organizations may be prohibited.

Tax-exempt organizations may be subject to anti-discrimination rules in the context of the provision of **employee benefits**. Some exempt organizations are not subject to the price discrimination laws. [EO §§ 1.7, 4.9(b), 6.2; CL Chap. 6].

disposal property

The term "disposal property" means **real property**, where (1) the property was acquired by a **tax-exempt organization** from a financial institution (as defined in **IRC** §§ 581 or 591(a)) which is in conservatorship or receivership, or the conservator or receiver of the institution (or any **government agency** or **corporation** succeeding to the **rights** or **interests** of the conservator or receiver); (2) the property is designated by the organization within the nine-month period beginning on the date of its acquisition as property held for **sale**, except that not more than one-half (by **value** determined as of that date) of property acquired in a single transaction may be so designated; (3) the sale, **exchange**, or other **disposition** occurs before the later of the date which is thirty months after the date of acquisition of the property or the date specified by the **IRS** in order to assure an orderly disposition of property held by eligible **persons;** and (4) while the property was held by the tax-exempt organization. the aggregate **expenditures** on improvements and development activities included in the **basis** of the property are (or were) not in excess of 20 percent of the net selling price of the property (**IRC** § 512(b)(16)(A)).

Additionally, this type of property must be property which (1) was held by the financial institution at the lime it entered into the conservatorship or receivership, or (2) was **foreclosure property** which secured indebtedness held by the financial institution at that time (**IRC** § 512(b)(16)(B)). This term "disposal property" is used in defining an **exception** to the **dealer UBTI rule**. [UB § 3.10; EO § 25.1(j)].

disposition

The term "disposition" is used to describe a relinquishment or transfer of something from one **person** to another. The **federal tax law** frequently makes reference to the disposition of **property**, such as by means of an **estate** or by **gift**.

disqualified holder

The term "disqualified holder" is used in the context of the **rules** concerning the taxation of **income** of **tax-exempt organizations** as **unrelated business income**, when that income may be **unrelated debt-financed income**. The term means a shareholder or **beneficiary** of a **multi-parent title-holding company**, where the shareholder or beneficiary is not an **educational institution**, a **supporting organization** of an educational institution, or a **pension trust** (**IRC** § 514(c)(9)(F)(iii)). A multi-parent title-holding company is a **qualified organization** (**IRC** § 514(c)(9)(C)(iii)) and thus is entitled to the benefits of the **exception** from the unrelated debt-financed income rules for income derived from debt-financed investments in **real property** (**IRC** § 514(c)(9)(A)), where certain restrictions are satisfied (**IRC** § 514(c)(9)(B)). Thus, the purpose of the "disqualified holder" rule is to prevent the benefits of this exception from flowing through the title-holding company to its shareholders or beneficiaries (unless those organizations are themselves "qualified organizations" (**IRC** §§ 514(c)(9)(C)(i), (ii)). This purpose is accomplished by deeming the holder's pro rata share of the items of income from the company to be unrelated business income (**IRC** §§ 514(c)(9)(F)(i)(I), (ii)(I)); the holder's pro rata share of related **deductions** are also taken into account (**IRC** §§ 514(c)(9)(F)(i)(II), (ii)(II)). [UB § 5.4(f); EO § 24.9(c)].

disqualified individual

For purposes of the definition of an **exempt operating foundation**, the term "disqualified individual" means, with respect to any **private foundation**, an individual who is (1) a **substantial contributor** to the foundation; (2) an owner of more than 20 percent of the **total combined voting power** of a **corporation**, the **profits interest** of a **partnership**, or the **beneficial interest** of a **trust** or other **unincorporated enterprise**, which is a substantial contributor to the foundation; or (3) a **member of the family** of an individual described in the foregoing two categories (**IRC** § 4940(d)(3)(B)). [PF § 3.1(i)].

disqualified organization

For purposes of the **expenditure test**, a **tax-exempt organization** is a "disqualified organization" (and thus ineligible to elect use of the test) if it is a **church** or certain other **religious organizations** or a **member** of an **affiliated group** if one or more members of the group is one of these organizations (**IRC** § 501(h)(5)). [EO § 22.3(d)(vi)].

D

disqualified person

In connection with the **intermediate sanctions** rules, the term "disqualified person" has many meanings. In this context, a disqualified person is, with respect to a transaction, (1) a **person** who was, at any time during the five-year period ending on the date of the transaction, in a position to exercise **substantial influence** over the affairs of the **organization** involved; (2) a **member of the family** of an individual in the first category; (3) a **35-percent controlled entity** of a disqualified person or family member; (4) a person described in any of the three preceding categories with respect to a **supporting organization** and **organized** and **operated exclusively** for the benefit of, to perform the functions of, or to carry out the purposes of the **applicable tax-exempt organization**; (5) which involves a **donor-advised fund**, any person who is a **donor**, a **donor advisor**, a member of the family of a donor or donor advisor, or a 35 percent controlled entity with respect to the foregoing persons; and (6) which involves a **sponsoring organization**, any person who is an **investment advisor** with respect to the organization (**IRC** § 4958(f)(1)).

A "disqualified person" also is a person standing in one or more particular relationships with respect to a **private foundation**. The types of disqualified persons are **substantial contributors**, **foundation managers**, certain **20 percent owners**, **family members**, certain **corporations**, certain **partnerships**, certain **trusts**, certain **estates**, certain other private foundations, and certain government officials (**IRC** § 4946).

In the context of the **donor-advised fund** rules, a "disqualified person" is a donor, a donor advisor, a member of the family of an individual who is a donor or donor advisor, or a 35 percent controlled entity (**IRC** § 4943(e)(2)). [PF Chap. 4, §§ 1.4(c), 1.9, 17.4, 23.4; EO §§ 11.8(b), 12.2, 21.3; FR § 5.6(b)(ii); HC §§ 4.2(a), 4.9(a)(ii), 4.9(b), 7.4(d); AR § 8.1(l); CU Q 6.53; AS §§ 3.8(c), 3.9; PG pp. 71–72; SM pp. 59, 82; LI Q 4.54–Q 4.59, Q 6.2, Q 6.6, Q 6.7].

disqualified person restriction

The term "disqualified person restriction" is used in the context of defining circumstances where an **exception** from the **law** treating **income** from **debt-financed property** as **unrelated business taxable income**, is available to **qualified organizations** that make debt-financed investments in **real property** (**IRC** § 514(c)(9)(A)). Under this exception, income from investments in real property is not treated as income from debt-financed property. This exception is available only where six restrictions are satisfied (**IRC** § 514(c)(9)(B)). One of them is the "disqualified person restriction," which, through 1993, provided that, in the case of a **pension trust**, the seller or **lessee** of the property may not be a **disqualified person** (**IRC** § 514(c)(9)(B)(iv)). Nonetheless, a limited leaseback of debt-financed property to a disqualified person is permitted. The exception applies only where (1) no more than 25 percent of the leasable floor space in a building (or complex of buildings) is leased back to the disqualified person and (2) the lease is on **commercially reasonable** terms, independent of the sale and other transactions (**IRC** § 514(c)(9)(G)). [UB § 5.4(f); EO § 24.9(c)].

disqualified supporting organization

The phrase "disqualified supporting organization" means, with respect to any distribution, (1) any **Type III supporting organization** that is not a **functionally integrated** Type III supporting organization and (2) any **Type I supporting organization**, **Type II supporting organization**, or a functionally integrated Type III supporting organization if (a) the **donor** or any person designated by the donor for the purpose of advising with respect to distributions from a **donor-advised fund** (and any related parties) directly or indirectly **controls** a **supported organization** of the organization or (b) the **IRS** determines by **regulations** that a distribution to the organization is otherwise inappropriate (**IRC** § 4966(d)(4)). [PF § 8.12; CG § 23.4; EO § 11.8(b)].

disqualifying lobbying expenditure

The **federal tax law** imposes **excise taxes** with respect to an **organization** that once was a **tax-exempt charitable organization** but had that status revoked because of one or more "disqualifying lobbying expenditures" (**IRC** §§ 4912(a), 4912(b)). [EO § 22.4].

disregard

The word "disregard" is used in connection with the **federal tax law accuracy-related penalty** applicable in the case of a "disregard" of **rules** or **regulations** (**IRC** § 6662(b)(1)). In this setting, the word includes any careless, reckless, or intentional disregard (**IRC** § 6662(e)). [CG § 10.14(a)].

disregarded entity

The word **disregard** includes the concept of ignoring something. Thus, for **federal tax law** purposes, a wholly owned **organization** can be ignored ("disregarded") for tax law purposes; that is, the entity is not treated as a separate organization. An example of this is a **single-member limited liability company** of which a **tax-exempt organization** is the sole member. [EO §§ 4.1(b), 32.6; AR §§ 3.1(nn), 3.2(nn), 6.1(a), 21.1(h), 21.1(a); PF § 6.5(a); HC § 35.3(c); CG § 10.9(b); CU Q 16.5, Q 16.18; AS § 6.10(b); SM pp. 22–23, 230–231] (also **Check-the-box regulations**).

dissolution

A **nonprofit organization** may terminate its existence or have its existence terminated; when it does so, it "dissolves." Usually, this is done by action of the **board of directors** or **board of trustees**, either by ceasing operations or merging into another organization. If there is a **membership**, consent of the members will be necessary. Dissolution can occur by adherence to a provision in the **articles of organization** or by **operation of law**. [EO § 4.3(b); AR Chap. 20, §§ 3.1(ll), 3.2(ll)] (also **Liquidation**).

dissolution clause

A **charitable organization** must, by direction of the **organizational test**, have a provision in its articles of organization that states that, on dissolution, the **assets** and **income** of the organization must be distributed for one or more charitable purposes, or to the **federal** government or to a state or local government for a public purpose. This provision is known as a "dissolution clause." [EO § 4.3(b); PF § 1.9; RE Q 2.21; LI Q 1.39, Q 1.44].

distressed

One of the ways to be a **tax-exempt organization** on the basis of having **charitable** purposes is to engage in activities that relieve the condition of individuals who are "distressed." An individual may be physically, emotionally, and/or financially distressed. [EO § 7.2; SM p. 33].

D

distributable amount

The term "distributable amount" is used in connection with the **mandatory distribution** requirement imposed on **private foundations**. The term means, with respect to any private foundation for any **tax year,** an amount equal to four elements. The first is the sum of the **minimum investment return**. The second is amounts received or accrued as repayments of amounts that were taken into account as a **qualifying distribution** for any tax year. The third is amounts received or accrued from the **sale** or other **disposition** of **property** to the extent that the acquisition of the property was taken into account as a qualifying distribution for any tax year. The fourth is any amount **set aside** to the extent that it is determined that the amount is not necessary for the purposes for which it was set aside (**IRC** § 4942(f)(2)(C)). The total of these amounts is reduced by the sum of the **income taxes** and the tax on **net investment income** imposed on the foundation (**IRC** § 4942(d)).

The term "distributable amount" is also used in connection with the payout requirement imposed on **non-functionally integrated Type III supporting organizations**. This amount, for a tax year, is an amount equal to the greater of 85 percent of the organization's **adjusted net income** or 3.5 percent of the **fair market value** of the organization's non-**exempt**-use **assets**. [PF §§ 6.1, 6.4, 12.2(i), 15.7(g); EO § 12.4(b); HC § 5.10; SM p. 89].

distribution, mandatory

The term "mandatory distribution" is used to generally refer to the requirement in the **federal tax law** that a standard **private foundation** distribute (or pay out), with respect to each year, at least a minimum amount of money and/or **property** for **charitable purposes** (IRC § 4942). Other entities, such as **non-functionally integrated Type III supporting organizations, charitable remainder trusts, pooled income funds**, and **charitable lead trusts**, also are subject to mandatory distribution requirements. [PF §§ 6.1, 6.4, 12.2(i), 15.7(g); EO § 12.4(b); CG §§ 12.2(a), 12.3(a), 13.2(a), 16.2; HC § 5.10; SM p. 89] (also **Distributable amount; Minimum investment return; Set-aside; Qualifying distribution**).

divestiture

The term "divestiture" in the **law** of **nonprofit organizations** is most frequently used to refer to the rules requiring a **private foundation** to divest itself of **excess business holdings**. [PF §§ 7.1(d), 7.2(a), 7.2(d), 7.6; EO § 12.4(c); SM p. 89].

dividend

A "dividend" is a share allotted to each of one or more **persons** who are entitled to share in the **net profits** (or **net earnings**) generated by a **business** undertaking. The payment of dividends is a primary illustration of **private inurement**. For the most part, dividends are not taxable to **tax-exempt organizations** as **unrelated business taxable income**. [CG §§ 2.20, 3.1(k); EO §§ 25.1(b), 25.1(n); UB § 3.2; PF §§ 10.3(d), 11.2, 12.1(b)].

division

A "division" of a **nonprofit organization** is a part, or one of several parts, into which the organization has been divided for **administrative** or other purposes. [EO § 26.10(b)] (also **Department; Disregarded entity**).

doctrine

A "doctrine" is a set of principles or a body of teachings on a particular subject. Thus, there is frequent reference to precepts such as the **private inurement** doctrine and the **commerciality** doctrine.

doctrine of substantial compliance

See **Substantial compliance, doctrine of**.

document retention and destruction policy

The **IRS**, in the **Form 990**, asks whether the filing **organization** has a written "document retention and destruction policy," describing this type of policy as one that identifies the record retention responsibilities of staff, **volunteers, board members**, and others for maintaining and documenting the storage and destruction of the organization's documents and records. All organizations, including those that are **tax-exempt**, are subject to the **Sarbanes-Oxley Act's** provisions regarding document destruction. [GV §§ 3.10(j), 4.2(b), 5.19, 6.3(d); AR §§ 5.1(i)(2), 5.2(b)(2), 5.3; CU Q 5.31; SM p. 111; LI Q 3.29].

doing business

A **nonprofit organization** may be headquartered in one state, yet have programs or other operations in one or more other states. As to those other states, the organization is a **foreign organization** and is required to **register** with them because it is "doing business" in the other jurisdiction or jurisdictions. Some states mandate by **statute** that **fundraising** in a state is doing business in that state. [PG pp. 3, 23, 24, 221; FR §§ 3.20, 5.9(f), 8.11; CU Q 1.12; LI Q 1.19].

domestic fraternal society

The **federal tax law** provides **tax-exempt status** (**IRC** § 501(a), by reason of description in **IRC** § 501(c)(10)) to a "domestic fraternal society" or order or **association** operating under the **lodge system**, if its **net earnings** are devoted **exclusively** to **charitable** purposes and if it does not provide for the payment of life, sick, accident, or other benefits to its **members**. [EO § 19.4(b); PF § 1.6; AU § 7.1(o); AS § 1.6(i); SM pp. 42–43; CL §§ 1.12(f), 6.6].

domestic organization

The term "domestic organization," in the context of **nonprofit law**, is used to describe an **organization** that is **organized** and/or **operated** in a particular jurisdiction (such as a state). As to all other similar jurisdictions in which it is **doing business**, it is a **foreign organization**. [PG pp. 3, 23, 24, 221; SM p. 11].

donate

See **Contribute**.

donated goods

The term "donated goods" refers to various types of items of **tangible personal property** that are **donated** to **charitable organizations**. This term is often used in connection with **gifts** of **inventory** and **gifts in kind**. [CG §§ 9.1–9.3, 9.24, 9.25, 9.27].

donated goods exception

The "donated goods exception" is a reference to the rule that the concept of **unrelated trade or business** does not encompass a business, conducted by a **tax-exempt organization**, that constitutes the selling of merchandise, **substantially all** of which has been received by the organization by means of **contributions** (**IRC** § 513(a)(3)). [UB § 4.3; EO § 25.2(c); SM p. 175].

D

donated services

An individual may **donate** his or her services to a **charitable** or other **organization** (thus acting as a **volunteer**). There is no **charitable contribution deduction** for this type of **gift**. The recipient organization may not report the **value** of these services as amounts received as contributions. [CG § 9.14].

donation

In general, the word "donation" is synonymous with the word **contribution** or the phrase "making of a **gift**." In practice, however, a donation is usually considered to be a gift of money of a relatively small amount or of items of **property** having a relatively small **value** (such as used clothing).

donative intent

A rule of **law** that is irregularly used is the requirement that, for a payment to qualify as a **gift**, it must be motivated by detached or disinterested generosity. This is known as "donative intent." Often, however, the contemporary practice is not to focus on donative intent but rather to determine whether the transaction involves an **exchange** having an inherently reciprocal nature or otherwise involves a **quid pro quo**. [CG §§ 3.1(a), 9.7(h); FR § 5.4; SM pp. 132, 144].

donative publicly supported organization

A **charitable organization** can avoid **private foundation** status by qualifying as a **publicly supported organization**. One of the categories of publicly supported organization is the "donative" charity (**IRC** § 509(a)(1)). In general, a donative publicly supported organization is a charitable **entity** that **normally** receives a **substantial** part of its **support** (other than **income** from the conduct of an **exempt function**) from a **governmental unit** or from **direct** or **indirect contributions** from the **public** (**IRC** § 170(b)(1)(A)(vi)). [PF §§ 15.4–15.6; EO § 12.3(b)(i); AR § 8.1(d)(1); HC § 5.2; SM pp. 81–82] (also **Community foundation; Facts and circumstances test**).

donee

A "donee" is a recipient of a **donation**, the transferee of a **donor**. A recipient of a **charitable contribution** is a **charitable donee**. [CG § 3.3(b); SM pp. 133–134].

donor

A "donor" is the maker of a **donation**, a transferor to a **donee**. [CG § 3.2] (also **Contributor**).

donor acquisition

"Donor acquisition" is a form of **fundraising** for a **charitable organization** that is designed to **solicit contributions** from **persons** who have not previously contributed to the organization.

Because these persons have no prior relationship with the charitable organization, the process of reaching them is usually expensive (perhaps over 100 percent of the fundraising **expense**). Some contend that this type of solicitation should not be considered fundraising (but rather **friend-raising**). [FR § 2.2(a)].

donor advisor

A "donor advisor" is a **person** appointed or designated by a **donor** to advise a **sponsoring organization** on the distribution or investment of amounts held in the **donor's donor-advised fund** (**IRC** § 4966(d)(2)(A)(iii)). [EO § 11.8; PF § 16.9; CG § 23.4; AR § 11.2(a)].

donor base

The term "donor base" is often used to refer to what is, in essence, an **asset** of an **organization**: the group of **persons** (individuals, **corporations**, and/or other **entities**) who regularly make **contributions** to the organization. These donors are often acquired by means of a **donor acquisition program**.

donor list

A "donor list" is a register of **contributors** to an **organization**; it is a listing of the **persons** comprising an organization's **donor base**. A donor list is an **asset**; these lists may be **rented**, **exchanged**, and/or **sold**; however, there may be **unrelated business income tax** consequences to such a transaction. [EO § 28.7(k); UB § 4.10].

donor recognition

Donor recognition" occurs when the **donee organization** provides something to or for a **donor** in response to the making of a payment that the donee would prefer to treat as a **gift**. Where the **value** of the recognition is not **substantial**, it will not prevent the payment from being considered a gift. The provision of substantial valuable marketing and/or other services by an organization in return for support of it in the form of funding, however, is likely to constitute **unrelated business income**. [CG § 3.1(g); EO §§ 24.5(h), 24.6; UB §§ 2.7(e), 6.5(a), 6.6; FR § 5.16(b)] (also **Advertising**, **Corporate sponsorship**).

donor renewal

"Donor renewal" is the process of **solicitation** by an **organization** of **gifts** from **persons** who have previously **contributed** to the organization (that is, by those who comprise its then-existing **donor base**). Generally, because of the prior relationship between donor and **donee**, the **fundraising costs** associated with a donor renewal program are substantially less than the costs incurred in relation to a **donor acquisition program**.

donor-advised fund

A "donor-advised fund" is a fund or account that is separately identified by reference to **contributions** of a **donor** or donors, is owned and controlled by a **sponsoring organization**, and with respect to which a donor (or any person appointed or designated by the donor) has, or reasonably expects to have, **advisory privileges** in connection with the distribution or investment of amounts held in the fund or account by reason of the donor's status as a donor. A fund or account is not a donor-advised fund if it makes distributions only to a single identified organization or governmental entity or with respect to which, under certain circumstances, a person with advisory privileges advises as to which individuals receive **grants** for travel, study, or other similar purposes. The **IRS** has limited authority to exempt a fund or account from treatment as a donor-advised fund (**IRC** § 4966(d)(2)). [PF Chap. 16; EO § 11.8; CG §§ 3.1(f), 23.4; AR § 11.2(a); HC § 4.9(a)(iii); PG pp. 104, 105; SM pp. 206–208; LI Q 10.44].

D

donor-directed fund

A "donor-directed fund" is an account within a **charitable organization** into which a **donor** can place funds (as a **gift**) and retain the **right** to determine what the organization will do with the gift proceeds or **assets**. [EO § 11.8(a); PF §§ 16.1, 16.3; CG § 3.1(f)] (cf. **Donor-advised fund**).

donor-restricted fund

The phrase "donor-restricted fund" is used to describe **contributions** of money (or perhaps **property**) when the **contributors** have placed a restriction on use of the funds by the **donee**. Generally, the recipient organization is legally obligated to abide by the restriction as a consequence of accepting the contribution; the arrangement is, in essence, a **contract** between the donee and the **donors**. [CG § 10.4] (also **Board-restricted funds**).

donor's creation, gift of

An individual may make a **charitable contribution** of an item of **property** that he or she created, such as a painting, a sculpture, or a manuscript. The **charitable contribution deduction** for this type of **gift**, however, is confined to the **donor's cost basis** in the property (**IRC** §§ 170(e)(1)(A), 1221(3)). [CG § 9.12].

dormant shell

Under most circumstances, a **nonprofit organization** regarded by the **IRS** as a "dormant shell" cannot qualify for **tax exemption** because it is not doing anything and thus fails the applicable **operational test**. Occasionally, however, an organization with no **assets** and no current operations will be regarded by the **agency** as eligible for exemption (or continuing exemption) if it has a plan to engage in (or resume) exempt functions, even if at some undefined point in time. [EO § 4.5(a)].

down-payment assistance organization

A "down payment assistance organization" is a **nonprofit organization** that makes **grants** to individuals, usually those who are low-income individuals, to enable them to meet the down-payment requirement when purchasing a **personal residence**. The **IRS** initially regarded these organizations a **tax-exempt charitable entities** but has since generally reversed that position. [EO § 7.5; AR § 11.1(d)(2); SM p. 39].

downward rachet rule

The general **excess business holdings** rule applicable to **private foundations** did not apply to **present holdings**, which were holdings of the foundation as of May 26, 1969. Instead, a

50 percent limitation applied, unless the present holdings amounted to less than 50 percent, in which case that lower percentage applied (**IRC** § 4943(c)(4)(A)(i)). If a private foundation organized before May 26, 1969, reduced its present holdings of a **business enterprise** (including the holdings of **disqualified persons**), it could not again increase those holdings (except that if they fell below the levels applicable under the general rule they could be increased to those levels). This one-way limitation on the amount of present holdings is known as the "downward rachet rule." [PF § 7.2(a)].

D

dual-status governmental entity

The term "dual-status governmental entity" refers to an **organization** that has **tax-exempt status** on the basis of two rationales: it is an organization that is a **governmental unit** and a **tax-exempt charitable organization**. [EO § 26.11].

dual-use facility

A "dual-use facility" is a facility of a **tax-exempt organization** that is used for both **related** and **unrelated business** purposes. **Income** and *expenses* from the dual use must be **allocated** to the two uses on a **reasonable** basis. [UB § 2.7(d); EO § 24.4(d); HC § 24.4(c); PF §§ 6.2(a), 6.2].

due process of law

The U.S. Constitution provides that the **federal** government and the states may not deprive any **person** of life, liberty, or **property** without "due process of law." **Laws** regulating the **fundraising** activities of **charitable organizations** and those who assist them in this regard must afford these persons their due process rights. [CL §§ 1.1(b), 7.5; FR § 4.4; SM p. 152].

dues

"Dues" are fees paid by **members** of an **organization** (usually an **association, society**, or **club**) in exchange for the benefits and services they receive by reason of being members. Thus, unless the value of these benefits and services is **incidental**, the payment of dues is not the making of a **gift**. This is because a dues payment is underlain by **consideration**. Dues payments may be **deductible** as **business expenses**. From the standpoint of the organization, dues revenue (unless it is gifts) is **exempt function revenue**. For **service provider publicly supported charitable organizations**, dues constitute (subject to certain limitations) a form of **public support**. [EO § 25.2(l); AS §§ 2.4(a)(iii), 5.9(p), 10.5(j); AR §§ 9.1(h), 9.2(d); PF § 15.5] (also **Annual dues**).

duty of care

One of the three fundamental duties imposed on **directors** and **trustees** of **tax-exempt organizations**, particularly **charitable entities**, is the "duty of care." This duty means that these **persons** should be **reasonably** informed about the organization's activities, participate in decision-making, and act in **good faith** and with the care of an ordinarily **prudent** person in comparable circumstances. [GV § 1.5(a); HC § 33.2(b); RE Q 2.9; SM p. 103; LI Q 3.10, Q 14.20].

D

duty of loyalty

One of the three fundamental duties imposed on **directors** and **trustees** of **tax-exempt organizations**, particularly **charitable entities**, is the "duty of loyalty." This duty means that **board members** should exercise their power in the interest of the **exempt organization** and not in their personal interest or the interest of another **entity**. [GV § 1.5(b); HC § 33.2(c); RE Q 2.10; SM pp. 103–104; LI Q 3.11, Q 14.21].

duty of obedience

One of the three fundamental duties imposed on **directors** and **trustees** of **tax-exempt organizations**, particularly **charitable entities**, is the "duty of obedience." This duty means that **board members** should comply with applicable **federal**, state, and local **laws**; adhere to the organization's **governing documents**; and be guardians of the organization's **mission**. [GV § 1.5(c); HC § 33.2(d); RE Q 2.11; SM p. 104; LI Q 3.12, Q 14.22].

dyadic interest

The word "dyadic" means twofold, as in relating to a dyad. A "dyad" is two units regarded as a pair. Thus, where a **split-interest trust** is structured to provide an **income interest** or a **remainder interest** to two individuals (usually, spouses), that interest is said to be a "dyadic interest."

dynamic scoring

See **Macroeconomic analysis**.

E

e-postcard

See **Notice**.

early termination, of remainder trust

It is possible for a **charitable remainder trust** to be the subject of an "early termination," when there is an agreement between the **income beneficiaries**, the **trust**, and the **remainder interest beneficiary**. An early termination occurs when this type of trust is terminated before the **income interest(s)** would normally expire. This type of termination can occur under circumstances where the method of allocation of **income** and **assets** of the trust is **reasonable** and not detrimental to the charity involved (to avoid **self-dealing**). The **IRS**, however, has a **no-rule position** as to this type of transaction. [CG § 12.7; PF § 5.13].

earmarking

An amount of money or transfer of **property** is "earmarked" for a purpose where there is an **agreement**, oral or written, by which the transferor of the money or property may cause the transferee to expend amounts to accomplish a particular purpose or where the transferor has directed the transferee to add the money or property transferred to a fund to accomplish a purpose. Earmarking occurs, for example, where a **contribution** is made to a **public charity** under the terms of an agreement that the amount involved will be transferred by the public charity to a **private foundation**, in an attempt to enable the **contributor** to claim a larger **charitable contribution deduction** by reason of a (ostensibly) more generous **percentage limitation**.

As another example, amounts can be transfers that become classified as **direct lobbying expenditures** or **grass-roots lobbying expenditures**. A transfer that is earmarked for direct lobbying purposes, or for direct lobbying and grass-roots lobbying purposes, is regarded as a grass-roots lobbying expenditure in full, unless the transferor can demonstrate that all or part of the amounts transferred were expended for direct lobbying purposes, in which case that part of the amounts transferred is a direct lobbying expenditure by the transferor. [EO §§ 12.1(A), 22.3(d)(i), 22.3(d)(iv), 28.17(a); CG § 18.3; PF §§ 3.2, 14.4(a)] (also **Conduit**).

easement

An "easement" is a **right** with respect to **real property** (or an interest in the property) created by the owner of the property by which another **person** (or persons) has a **beneficial** use of the

Bruce R. Hopkins' Nonprofit Law Dictionary, First Edition. Bruce R. Hopkins.
© 2015 Bruce R. Hopkins. Published 2015 by John Wiley & Sons, Inc.

property. Easements include **conservation**, façade, and scenic ones. It is said that an easement **burdens** the underlying property. An owner of real estate may create an easement in the property and thereafter **contribute** that right to a **charitable organization** and receive a **charitable contribution deduction** for the gift. Nonetheless, the **federal tax law** imposes strict requirements in order for this deduction to be available (e.g., **IRC** § 170(h)). [CG § 9.7].

ecclesiastical law

"Ecclesiastical law" is a body of **law** pertaining to matters of **religion**, usually interpreted by a **church**. This type of law was developed as part of the **common law** in England and was administered by separate ecclesiastical courts.

economic development corporation

See **Local economic benefit corporation**.

Economic Recovery Tax Act of 1981

Enactment of the "Economic Recovery Tax Act of 1981" brought another revision of the **private foundation mandatory distribution** rules, causing the requirement to solely utilize the **minimum investment return rate** of 5 percent (current **law**) (**IRC** § 4942(e)(1)). [PF § 6.8].

economic sham

The term "economic sham" generally describes a transaction that occurred but that exploits a feature of the **Internal Revenue Code** without any attendant economic risk. (Cf. **Sham**).

economic substance

A transaction lacks "economic substance" if it has no **reasonable** prospect of earning a **profit** and was undertaken for no **business purpose** other than to obtain one or more **tax** benefits.

education, advancement of

An **organization** can be **tax-exempt** under **federal law** as a **charitable entity** if it is **organized** and **operated principally** to **advance education**. The advancement of education includes the establishment or maintenance of tax-exempt **educational institutions**, **granting** of **scholarships** and other forms of **student** assistance, establishment or maintenance of institutions such as public libraries and **museums**, advancement of knowledge through **research**, and dissemination of knowledge by publications, seminars, lectures, and the like. [EO § 7.8; CU Q 1.38, Q 2.2, Q 3.6–Q 3.8, Q 11.39; CG § 3.2(b); SM p. 34].

educational

The term "educational" as used for **federal tax law** purposes in the **tax-exempt organizations** context, is defined as, in addition to formal schooling, relating to the instruction or training of the individual for the purpose of improving or developing his or her capabilities or the instruction of the **public** on subjects useful to the individual and beneficial to the community. Education involves at least a rational development of a point of view. [CU Q 2.2–Q 2.9; EO § 8.1; SM pp. 35–36; LI Q 9.1, Q 9.2, Q 9.4] (also **Full and fair exposition test**; **Methodology test**).

educational institution

An **entity** is an "educational institution" if it is a **college, school,** or **university**; other organizations may so qualify as well, such as a **museum**. Educational **institutions** such as colleges, schools, and universities are types of **tax-exempt organizations** (IRC § 501(a), by reason of IRC § 501(c)(3)), or are **governmental units**, and are types of **public charities** (IRC §§ 170(b)(1)(A)(ii), 509(a)(1)). These types of institutions are **exempt**, in whole or in part, from some states' **charitable solicitation acts**. **Income** derived from **research** by these institutions is exempt from the **tax** on **unrelated business income**. These institutions must retain certain records so that they can prove that they do not have any racially **discriminatory** practices. An educational organization is a **qualified organization** under an **exception** to the rules concerning **debt-financed real property**. [CU Q 2.11–Q 2.74; EO §§ 8.3, 12.3(a), 24.5(a); PF § 15.3(b); CG § 3.3(a); FR § 5.11; UB § 9.1; SM p. 35].

educational organization

An **organization** can be **tax-exempt** under the **federal tax law** (IRC § 501(a), by reason of description in IRC § 501(c)(3)) if it is **organized** and **operated principally** for **educational** purposes. [EO Chap. 8; CU Q 2.10; PF §§ 1.4, 1.5, 15.3; CG § 3.2(b); AU §§ 7.1(b), 7.1(f); SM pp. 35–36, 80; LI Q 9.10] (also **Child-care organization**; **Educational institution**).

effective control

In the context of determining whether the 35 percent limitation with respect to **excess business holdings** is applicable, the term "effective control" means possession of the power, whether **direct** or **indirect**, and whether or not actually exercised, to direct the management and policies of a **business enterprise**. It is the actual control that is decisive and not its form or the means by which it is exercisable. [PF § 7.1(d)].

elderly

The "elderly" can be the recipients of **charitable** beneficence, although the elderly do not always constitute a **charitable class**. Nonetheless, where there is an element of **distress** as part of the needs of the elderly, that group of elders will be considered a charitable class. [EO § 6.3(a)] (also **Home for the aged**).

electing public charity

An "electing public charity" is a **public charity** that is eligible to make the **election** in accordance with the **expenditure test** and that has made that election. [EO § 22.3(d)(vi); SM p. 189].

election, doctrine of

If an individual has a free choice between alternatives in the **law** and overtly engages in an act that communicates the choice selected, the individual is bound by the legal consequences of the choice by the "doctrine of election." [CG § 7.7(b)].

election laws, federal

The principal **federal law** governing the conduct of elections and the making of **contributions** to political **candidates** and **organizations** is the Federal Election Campaign Act of 1971, as amended. The federal **tax** law rules pertaining to political organizations and **political campaign activities** is not well-integrated with the federal election law. [EO § 23.2(b)(ii); CL §§ 1.2(e), 5.1; FR § 5.25; AS § 11.5; CU Q 9.28; LI Q 8.28–Q 8.31].

electioneering

A **private foundation** may not (without incurring **penalties**) **participate** or **intervene**, **directly or indirectly**, in a **political campaign** on behalf of or in opposition to any **candidate** for **public office**. An attempt by a private foundation to influence the outcome of a specific public election is loosely termed "electioneering," and any amount paid or incurred by a private foundation for this purpose is a type of **taxable expenditure** (**IRC** § 4945(d)(2)). [PF § 9.2(b)] (also **Voter registration drive**).

elective rules.

Some rules of **law** become applicable to a **person** only when and if the person affirmatively "elects" (chooses) to be subject to the rules. This is the case, for example, with respect to the **expenditure test**. [EO § 22.3(d)(vi); SM p. 189].

electronic filing requirements

Certain large **tax-exempt organizations** are required to electronically file their **annual information returns**. These are exempt organizations with **assets** of at least $10 million and that file at least 250 **returns**, and **private foundations** and **split-interest trusts** that file at least 250 returns. The **IRS** may waive this requirement in cases of undue economic hardship or technology issues. [AR §§ 4.1(f), 4.2(a); EO § 28.7].

eleemosynary

The term "eleemosynary" is used to describe acts of **charity** or other public purposes. It is usually thought of as embracing a wider range of activities than that encompassed by the word **charitable**. The term is not utilized in connection with the **federal tax law**. [EO § 6.1(b)] (also **Benevolent**; **Philanthropic**).

eligible organization

An "eligible organization" is an **organization** that is eligible to pursue **recognition** of **tax exemption** by filing a **Form 1023-EZ**. To be an eligible organization, an **entity** must have **gross receipts** of no more than $50,000 and **assets** of no more than $250,000. The $50,000 threshold applies with respect to projected annual gross receipts in the current **tax year** or the next two years, or annual gross receipts that have exceeded $50,000 in any of the past three years.

This application, however, may not be filed by (in addition to entities over the above thresholds) organizations formed under the laws of a foreign country; organizations that do not have a mailing address in the U.S.; organizations that are **terrorist organizations**, or are successors to, or **controlled** by, a terrorist entity **suspended** from **tax exemption**; organizations that are not **corporations**, **unincorporated associations**, or **trusts**; organizations that are successors to a **for-profit entity**; organizations that were previously revoked or that are successors to a previously revoked organization (other than an organization that was revoked for failure to file or submit a **Form 990 series return** or **notice** for three consecutive years); **churches, conventions of churches,** or **associations of churches; schools, colleges,** or **universities; hospitals** or **medical research organizations; cooperative hospital service organizations; cooperative service organizations** of operating educational organizations; **qualified charitable risk pools; supporting organizations;** organizations that have as a **substantial** purpose the provision of assistance to individuals through **credit counseling activities,** such as budgeting, personal finance, financial literacy, mortgage foreclosure assistance, or other consumer credit areas; organizations that invest, or intend to invest, 5 percent or more of their total assets in securities or **funds** that are not publicly traded; organizations that participate, or intend to participate, in **partnerships** (or entities treated as partnerships) in which they share profits and losses with partners other than exempt charitable organizations; organizations that sell, or intend to sell, carbon credits or carbon offsets; **health maintenance organizations; accountable care organizations** or organizations that engage in, or intend to engage in, ACO activities (such as participation in the Medicare Shared Savings Program); organizations that maintain, or intend to maintain, one or more **donor-advised funds;** organizations that are organized and operated exclusively for **testing for public safety** and that are requesting **public charity** classification; **private operating foundations;** and organizations that are applying for retroactive reinstatement of exemption after being **automatically revoked.** [EO §§ 26.1, 26.2].

embezzlement

An act of "embezzlement" is an act of **fraud,** by which an individual appropriates to his or her use or benefit money or other property entrusted to that individual by another **person,** often in circumstances where the individual is expected to act as a **fiduciary. Private inurement** does not occur when an **insider** engages in embezzlement. [EO § 20.5(k); AS § 3.4(b)(x)].

emergency medical care policy

For purposes of the **financial assistance policy requirement,** an "emergency medical care policy" is a written policy requiring the organization to provide, without discrimination, care for emergency medical conditions to individuals regardless of their eligibility under the entity's **financial assistance policy (IRC § 501(r)(4)(B)).** [HC § 26.10(a)(iv)].

employee

An "employee" is an individual who is hired by and works for an **employer.** The work of an employee is usually performed on the premises of and in the facilities of the employer, using equipment, furniture, and supplies provided by the employer. The hours and conditions of work are usually set by the employer. The **compensation** of an employee is usually cast as a **salary** or **wage.** The compensation of an employee is subject to **income tax** and other types of tax withholdings. The **IRS** will issue a **ruling** as to whether an individual is an employee, as opposed to an **independent contractor;** the agency almost always rules that the individual is an employee. As part of the **audit** process, the **IRS** is likely to examine the practices of a **tax-exempt organization** to determine whether it is properly classifying individuals as employees. [EO § 18.1; PF §§ 4.2, 12.2(e)] (also **Key employee;** cf. **Consultant, Independent contractor**).

employee benefit fund

An "employee benefit fund" is a form of **tax-exempt organization**. It is a **fund**, maintained by an **employer** that holds **assets** and **income** for investment and pays out benefits for the **employees**. There are one or more of these funds underlying **retirement plans**, **pension** and profit-sharing arrangements, **voluntary employees' beneficiary associations**, **black lung benefits trusts**, and the like. [EO Chap. 18; SM p. 43] (also **Employee benefit organization**; **Nonqualified plans**; **Qualified plans**).

employee benefit organization

An "employee benefit organization" is a term used in the **federal tax law** to embrace two types of organizations: the **voluntary employees' beneficiary association** and the **black lung benefits trust**. An employee benefit organization that desires **tax exemption** must timely notify the **IRS** by applying for **recognition of tax exemption** on that basis (**IRC** § 505(c)(1)). [EO §§ 18.1, 18.4, 18.5, 18.6, 26.5; SM p. 43].

employee benefits

The concept of "employee benefits" includes **bonus** programs, **commission** arrangements, **fringe benefits**, **loan** programs, **retirement** programs, and profit-sharing arrangements. These benefit programs are subject to the **doctrines** of **private benefit** and **private inurement**, and the **intermediate sanctions rules**. [EO §§ 18.1, 20.5(f); HC § 25.8; AS § 11.9; UB § 6.2(b); PF § 12.1(b); CG § 1.3].

Employee Retirement Income Security Act of 1974

The body of **law** created on enactment of the "Employee Retirement Income Security Act of 1974" and its amendments imposes requirements as respects **employee** participation in benefit plans, coverage, **vesting** of interests, funding, portability of benefits, **fiduciary responsibility**, **prohibited transactions**, preparation of plan summaries, and annual reporting and disclosure to the Department of Labor and the **IRS**. The Pension Benefit Guaranty Corporation administers a program of plan termination **insurance**. [EO § 18.1(c); AS §§ 11.9(d), 11.9(f), 11.9(g), 11.9(i); HC §§ 4.4(b), 28.6; CG § 9.10(c)].

employee trust

An "employee trust" is a type of **tax-exempt organization** (**IRC** § 501(a), by reason of description in **IRC** § 501(c)(24)). This organization is described in section 409 of the **Employee Retirement Income Security Act of 1974** (as in effect on the date of enactment of the Single Employer Pension Plan Amendments Act of 1986). [EO § 18.7].

employees' association, local

The **federal tax law** provides **tax exemption** for "local associations of employees," which means an **organization** the **membership** of which is limited to the **employees** of a designated **person** or persons in a particular municipality, the **net earnings** of which are devoted **exclusively** to charitable, **educational**, or recreational purposes (**IRC** § 501(c)(4)). [EO §§ 19.3, 25.2(d); SM p. 42].

employer

An "employer" is a **person** who employs the services of one or more individuals, termed **employees**. The employer has the right and the ability to control and direct the performance and outcome of the services of an employee. (also **Independent contractor**).

employer identification number

Every **organization**, whether **nonprofit** or **for-profit**, is required to have an "employer identification number" assigned to it by the **IRS**. This is the case irrespective of whether the organization has any **employees**. This number is obtained by filing **Form SS-4**. [SM pp. 22, 25] (also **Tax-exempt number; Taxpayer identification number**).

employer-related grant

An "employer-related grant" is a **grant**, made by a **private foundation**, to one or more **employees** or children of employees of a particular **employer**. The **IRS** provided guidelines for use in determining whether the grants qualify under the rules concerning grants to individuals and are not **taxable expenditures**. [PF § 9.3(e)].

employment-related common bond

Participants in a **tax-exempt voluntary employees' beneficiary association** are required to share an "employment-related common bond." This relationship can be defined by reference to a common **employer** (or **affiliated** employers), coverage under a collective bargaining agreement, or **membership** in a **labor union**. Employees of one or more employers engaged in the same **line of business** in the **same geographic locale** may be considered to share this type of bond. [EO § 18.3].

encheat

An "encheat" is the **revenue** derived by a **governmental** body from an **escheat**.

encumbered property

An item of **property** is "encumbered" when it is made subject to some form of **liability**. Charges that constitute this type of liability include a **mortgage, lien**, and **easement**. A **contribution** to a **charitable organization** of encumbered property is likely to cause a **bargain sale**. A **gift** of this type of property by means of a **pooled income fund** can trigger the **recognition** of **income** to the **donor**. [CG §§ 9.7(a), 9.19] (also **Debt-financed property**).

endowment fund

An "endowment fund" is a collection of **assets**, held for investment for the benefit of an **organization**, from which the investment **income** is paid to the organization for its **programmatic** or general use. This collection of assets is often referred to as **corpus** or **principal**. An endowment fund may be **restricted** for certain uses by the organization, such as an endowment in support of a particular program, project, or facility. An endowment fund may be an **integral part** of an organization or it may be a separate organization. [EO § 11.9; AR Chap. 7, §§ 3.1(j), 3.2(j), 11.1(e), 11.2(e); CU Q 10.1–Q 10.3; RE Q 13.40, Q 14.19] (also **Permanent endowment**; **Quasi-endowment**; **Temporarily restricted endowment**).

endowment test

The "endowment test" is one of the alternative tests a **private foundation** may use to qualify as a **private operating foundation**. A private foundation will satisfy this test only where it **normally** expended its funds, in the form of **qualifying distributions**, **directly** for the active conduct of its **exempt activities**, in an amount equal to at least two-thirds of its **minimum investment return** (IRC § 4942(j)(3)(B)(ii)). Thus, this private operating foundation **payout requirement** obligates the organization to distribute annually an amount equal to at least 3.5 (2/3 × 5) percent of the **value** of its **noncharitable assets**. The endowment test is appropriate for organizations that actively conduct **charitable** activities (for example, **research**) but the services of which are so great in relationship to assets that the cost of these services cannot be met out of their endowment. [PF § 3.1; EO § 12.1(b); SM p. 87].

enhanced charitable contribution deduction

The phrase "enhanced charitable contribution deduction" is used to reference a **charitable deduction**, the amount of which might be confined to the **donor's basis** in the **contributed property** but which is allowed, due to special circumstances, to the extent of an amount equal to as much as twice the basis in the property. [CG § 9.3].

enjoin

The word "enjoin" means to require or command. In the **law**, the word is used in the setting of an **injunction**, which is an order of a court to a **person** requiring the performance of an act or an abstention from committing an act.

enterprise

The word "enterprise" means a project, an undertaking, or, in some instance, a more formal **business**. The word can be used to describe the entirety of the activities of an **entity** or one or more than one of them. Where the **organization** is **tax-exempt**, consideration may have to be given as to whether the enterprise is a **related** or **unrelated** one. (also **Business enterprise**).

entertainment activities

See **Lobbying**; **Public entertainment activities**; **Social clubs**.

entity

The **law** uses the word "entity" to mean the same as the word **organization**. For example, while the **federal tax law** frequently uses the word "organization" when referring to a **tax-exempt organization**, sometimes it uses the word "entity." This is the case, for example, in connection with the **tax-exempt entity leasing rules**. [EO § 28.16].

entity, choice of

See **Choice of entity considerations**.

entity manager

The term "entity manager" is used, in connection with the **federal tax rules** concerning **tax-exempt entities** that enter into **prohibited tax shelter transactions**, in two ways. In cases involving conventionally defined **tax-exempt organizations, apostolic organizations, charitable donees**, and **Indian tribal governments**, the term means the person with authority or responsibility similar to that exercised by an **officer, director**, or **trustee** of an organization, and, with respect to an act, the person having authority or responsibility with respect to the act. In the case of a **prepaid tuition plan**, the term means the person who approves or otherwise causes the entity to be a party to the transaction (**IRC** § 4965(d)). [EO § 28.17(f)].

entity manager, tax on

If an **entity manager** of a **tax-exempt entity** approves the entity as (or otherwise causes the entity to be) a party to a **prohibited tax shelter transaction** at any time during a **tax year** and **knows** or has reason to know that the transaction is a prohibited tax shelter transaction, the manager must pay a tax for that year. The amount of this tax is $20,000 for each approval or other act causing the participation (**IRC** §§ 4965(a)(2), (b)(2)). [EO § 28.17(f)].

environmental conservancy, promotion of

An **organization** can qualify as a **charitable entity** when it is established to promote "environmental conservancy." Efforts to preserve and protect the natural environment for the benefit of the public serve charitable purposes. [EO § 7.15(a); AR § 15.2(e)(4); SM p. 35].

equal protection doctrine

The U.S. Constitution provides that the **federal** or state governments may not deny to any **person** within its jurisdiction the "equal protection of the laws." This **doctrine** means that a **law** (generally) may not contain **discriminatory** classifications. The doctrine has been applied to the states' **charitable solicitation acts**. [CL §§ 1.1(b), 1.8(b)–1.8(d), 1.11, 7.6; FR § 4.5; SM p. 322] (also **Affirmative action**).

equitable

Generally, something is deemed "equitable" if it is fair or objective. More specifically, it means an application of a rule of **law** in **equity**.

equitable title

The term "equitable title" means a form of **beneficial interest** in an item of **property** held by a **person**, in circumstances in which **equity** considers that person the owner of the property, even though **legal title** is held by another person.

equity

The word "equity" is often associated with justice or fairness. More specifically, a body of **law**—the law of "equity"—developed as an alternative to the **common law**, because the common law with its rigidity could not always provide an adequate (perhaps any) remedy for an injury. Today, the law for the most part has merged the two **doctrines** of law into one system, although there are vestiges of separate equitable principles, such as the laws pertaining to **injunctions**. This word is also used as a synonym for **capital** or **principal**.

equity distribution

The most literal and obvious form of **private inurement** is an "equity distribution": the parceling out of a **tax-exempt organization's net earnings** and/or **assets** to **insiders** with respect to the organization, although it is rare that inurement is this blatant. [EO § 20.5(d); HC § 4.4(a); AS § 3.4(b)(iv)].

ERISA Trust

A **trust** described in § 4049 of the **Employee Retirement Income Security Act of 1974** (as in effect on the date of enactment of the Single-Employer Pension Plan Amendments Act of 1986) is a **tax-exempt organization** (IRC § 501(c)(24)). [EO § 18.7].

escheat

An "escheat" is a transfer of an item of **property** to a government because of a failure of an individual to make provision for the inheritance or other passage (such as to a **charitable organization**) of the property by a **will** or because of lack of a **competent** individual to **inherit** the property. The term is also used to mean this type of property.

essential governmental function

The **federal tax law** concept of **gross income** excludes income derived from the exercise of an "essential governmental function," where the income **accrues** to a state, a **political subdivision** of a state, or the District of Columbia (**IRC** § 115(1)). There is no statutory or generic definition of this phrase; it is broadly construed. [EO § 19.21(b)].

Establishment Clause

The U.S. Constitution provides that the **federal** government may not make any laws respecting the "establishment" of **religion** (**First Amendment**). This provision is known as the "Establishment Clause." [CL §§ 2.1, 2.2, 2.4, 2.5, 2.7–2.9; RE Q 3.2, Q 25.1, Q 25.2; EO § 10.1(a)(ii); FR § 4.7(b); SM p. 321].

estate

The "estate" of an individual is the total collection of all **property** that he or she owns, either outright or **beneficially** or in any other way in which he or she has an **interest** in property, whether **real** or **personal**, **tangible** or **intangible**. The estate of an individual can be assessed at any time, with an accounting for one's final estate at one's death. At the death of an individual, it is the responsibility of the **personal representative** of the estate to marshal all of the **assets** and **liabilities** of the final estate. [CG § 2.8(c); PF § 4.6] (also **Decedent's estate**; **Gross estate**; **Marital deduction**; **Taxable estate**; **Will**).

estate, as disqualified person

An **estate** is a **disqualified person** with respect to a **private foundation** if more than 35 percent of the **beneficial interest** in the estate (including **constructive holdings**) is owned by **substantial contributors**, **foundation managers**, **20 percent owners**, or **members of the family** of any of these individuals or other **persons** (**IRC** § 4946(a)(l)(C)). A comparable rule applies in the **intermediate sanctions** context (**IRC** § 4958(f)(3)(A)(iii)). [PF § 4.6; EO §§ 12.2(g), 21.3].

estate administration exception

The "estate administration exception" is an **exception** to the **private foundation self-dealing rules**, enabling transactions (often purchases) with **disqualified persons** with respect to a foundation involving property held in a **decedent's estate** that is otherwise destined for the foundation, where five requirements are satisfied. [PF § 5.12(a)].

estate tax

The **federal tax law** imposes a tax on **estates** (**IRC** § 2001); this tax is a one-time levy, based on the **value** of the **net estate**. This is a separate tax from the **federal income tax**, although that tax is also applicable on an annual basis to estates. [CG §§ 8.1, 8.3; FR § 5.14(l); PF §§ 1.1, 2.3(a), 14.1(c), 14.2] (also **Death tax**; **Gross estate**).

estate tax charitable contribution deduction

The **federal tax law** provides for a **charitable contribution deduction** for payments made from an **estate** for **charitable** purposes (**IRC** § 2055). These payments must be made at the direction of the **will** and not merely at the discretion of the **personal representative** of the estate. [CG § 8.3(b)].

estoppel

The term "estoppel" is used to describe a bar that precludes an allegation or denial of a fact or set of facts, arising out of prior acts, admissions, or final adjudication of a matter by **law**. For example, when a matter has been **litigated** and a result in facts and law found by a court, neither party to the litigation can subsequently litigate the same matter that was at issue; this is termed **collateral estoppel**.

ethical

The word "ethical" is applied to conduct that is in conformance with certain principles of **ethics**.

ethics

The word "ethics" means a set of rules—perhaps, more accurately, principles—to which **members** of an **organization**, profession, field of business, or the like are expected to adhere. These rules are not necessarily the same as the applicable **law**; indeed, they are usually more grandiose or stringent than those of the law. These principles of conduct are usually stated in a **code of ethics**. [GV §§ 3.10(b), 5.16, 6.3(t); PG pp. 19–20; SM pp. 101, 280].

ex officio

The words "ex officio" are Latin ones meaning "by virtue of the office." The term is used in the **nonprofit law** context to mean a position on a **board of directors** (or **board of trustees**) of an **organization** held by an individual, not because he or she was elected or appointed to that position, but because of another position he or she holds in that organization (such as an **officer** of the organization) or another organization. Ex officio positions are often used by one nonprofit organization as a means of constructing an **interlocking directorate** of another organization for the purpose of **controlling** that other organization. An individual who holds an ex officio position on a board of directors (or board of trustees) has a vote in that body unless the **articles of organization** or **bylaws** of that organization specifically provide to the contrary. [CU Q 1.28; LI Q 1.34].

examination

In the **nonprofit law** context, the word "examination" usually connotes an inquiry into (**audit** of) the operations of a **tax-exempt organization** by the **IRS**, which has developed extensive procedures and guidelines for the conduct of these examinations. [AU Chaps. 1, 3, 5, 7; EO § 27.6].

examination notice date

The term "examination notice date" means the date the **notice** with respect to a **church tax examination** is provided to the **church** (**IRC** § 7611(h)(6)). [AU § 6.7(a); EO § 27.6(c)].

excepted agreed case

An "excepted agreed case" is one where, following an **IRS examination**, a **tax-exempt organization** agrees to one or more proposed adjustments but the examination results are subject to **IRS** review, additional processing, or another condition. [AU § 5.32(a)].

exception

An "exception" is a rule of **law** that stands in contrast to a more general rule of law. For example, certain types of activities are excepted from the general concept of **lobbying**: these include **nonpartisan activities**, analysis of broad social and economic problems, **communications** with **members**, requests for **technical advice**, and **self-defense communications**. [EO §§ 22.3(c)(iii), 22.3(d)(v)].

excess benefit

The term "excess benefit" means the excess referred to in the definition of **excess benefit transaction** (**IRC** § 4958(c)(1)(B)). [EO § 21.4(a)].

excess benefit transaction

In general, the phrase "excess benefit transaction" means a transaction in which an economic benefit is provided by an **applicable tax-exempt organization directly** or **indirectly** to or **for the use of** a **disqualified person**, if the value of the economic benefit provided exceeds the value of the **consideration** (including the performance of services) received for providing the benefit. For these purposes, an economic benefit cannot be treated as consideration for the performance of services unless the organization clearly indicated its intent to so treat the benefit (**IRC** § 4958(c)(1)(A)).

In the case of a **donor-advised fund**, the phrase "excess benefit transaction" includes a **grant**, **loan**, **compensation**, or other similar payment from the fund to a **donor** (or any person appointed or designated by the donor) has, or reasonably expects to have, **advisory privileges** with respect to the fund, a **member of the family** of a donor [or a **donor advisor**], or a 35-**percent controlled entity** with respect to the fund. The term **excess benefit** includes, with respect to an excess benefit transaction involving a donor-advised fund, the amount of a grant, loan, compensation, or other similar payment. In other words, this is a form of an **automatic excess benefit transaction** (**IRC** § 4958(c)(2)).

In the case of a **supporting organization**, the phrase "excess benefit transaction" includes a (1) grant, loan, compensation, or other similar payment provided by the organization to a **substantial contributor** to the organization, a member of the family of a substantial contributor, or a 35-percent controlled entity, and (2) a loan provided by the organization to a disqualified person (other than a **public charity** that is not a supporting organization and certain non-**charitable supported organizations**). For this purpose, the term "excess benefit" includes the amount of a grant, loan, compensation, or similar payment. Thus, this also is a form of an automatic excess benefit transaction (**IRC** § 4958(c)(3)).

To the extent provided in tax **regulations**, the phrase "excess benefit transaction" includes a transaction in which the amount of any economic benefit provided to or **for the use of** a disqualified person is determined in whole or in part by the revenue of one or more activities of the organization but only if the transaction results in **private inurement** not permitted under the rules for **tax-exempt charitable** or **exempt social welfare** entities. In the case of this type of transaction, the "excess benefit" is the amount of the inurement that is not permitted. Thus, this also is a form of an automatic excess benefit transaction (**IRC** § 4958(c)(4)). [EO § 21.4; HC §§ 4.4(b), 4.9(a); FR § 5.6(b)(iii); PF §§ 5.6, 5.8(c), 5.9(b), 5.16, 16.9; AR §§ 3.1(cc), 3.1(dd), 3.2(cc), 3.2(dd), 6.1(b), 18.1(a), 21.1(d); AS §§ 3.8(a), 3.8(d); PG pp. 61–62, 71–76, 333–335; SM p. 59; LI §§ Q 4.34–Q 4.51].

excess business holdings

A **private foundation** is subject to an **excise tax** where any of its holdings of an **interest** in one or more **business enterprises** is an "excess business holding" (**IRC** § 4943). An excess business holding is a holding of an interest in one or more business enterprises where the holding is other than a **permitted holding**.

The excess business holdings rules generally limit to 20 percent the permitted ownership of a **corporation's voting stock** or other interest in a business enterprise that may be held by a private foundation and all **disqualified persons** combined (**IRC** § 4943(c)(2)(A)). If, however, **effective control** of the business enterprise can be shown to be elsewhere (that is, other than by the private foundation and its disqualified persons), a 35 percent limit is substituted for the 20 percent limit (**IRC** § 4943(c)(2)(B)).

These excess business holdings rules are applicable to **Type III supporting organizations**, other than **functionally integrated Type III supporting organizations**. The excess business holdings rules also apply to a **Type II supporting organization** if the organization accepts a **contribution** from a person (other than a **public charity**, which is not a supporting organization) who **controls**, either alone or with **family members** and/or certain controlled entities, the **governing body** of a **supported organization** of the supporting organization. Nonetheless, the **IRS** has the authority to not impose the excess business holdings rules on a supporting organization if the organization establishes that the holdings are consistent with the organization's **tax-exempt status** (IRC §§ 4943(f)(1)–(3), 4943(f)(2)). These rules are also applicable to **donor–advised funds** (IRC § 4943(e)). [PF Chap. 7, §§ 1.4(f), 2.4; EO §§ 11.8(b), 12.3(c), 12.4(c); AR §§ 4.1(p)(1)–4.1(p)(5), 4.1(q), 4.2(k), HC § 5.10; SM p. 89] (also **Delayed divestiture**; **Functionally related business**; **Unusual grant**).

excess lobbying expenditure

The phrase "excess lobbying expenditure," used in the context of the **expenditure test**, means, for a **tax year**, the greater of (1) the amount by which the **lobbying expenditures** made by the **organization** involved during the tax year exceed the **lobbying nontaxable amount** for the organization for the year or (2) the amount by which the **grass-roots expenditures** made by the organization during the tax year exceed the **grass-roots nontaxable amount** for the organization for the year (**IRC § 4911(b)**). [EO § 22.3(d)(iii)].

excessive

The word "excessive" means the exceeding of an appropriate limit. This term is applied with respect to **tax-exempt organizations** in a variety of contexts, such as in connection with the **doctrine** of **private inurement,** where "excessive compensation" is a form of private inurement. Other applications of the term can be seen in such phrases as **excess benefit transaction**, **excess business holding**, and **excess lobbying expenditure**. [EO §§ 12.4(a), 20.4, 21.4(a), 22.3(d)(iii); PF Chap. 7, § 5.1].

exchange

The basic concept of an "exchange" is that a **person** transfers one or more goods or services so as to receive one or more goods or services or money, of approximately equal **value**, in return; where money is not involved, an exchange is a "barter." Usually, an exchange is a **sale**. The **federal tax law**, in its sweep, often uses the phrase "sale or exchange" to be certain that it is applicable to transactions where **consideration** is involved, even though technically the transaction is not a sale. [CG § 2.14(f)].

excise tax

An "excise tax" is a tax imposed on the consumption of something and sometimes on the **sale** of an article. Thus, for example, there are **federal** excise taxes on the consumption of alcohol and tobacco.

There is an excise tax imposed on a **charitable organization's** excess **expenditures** to influence legislation (**IRC § 4911**). There is an excise tax on **disqualifying lobbying expenditures** of certain organizations (**IRC § 4912**). There is an excise tax on **political expenditures** of charitable organizations (**IRC § 4955**). Excise taxes are imposed on **black lung benefit trusts** and sometimes others (**IRC §§ 4951–4953**). Additional excise taxes are imposed in the **intermediate sanctions** and **donor-advised fund** contexts (**IRC §§ 4958(a)**, (b), 4966(a), (b), 4967(a), (b)).

The **federal tax rules** that apply to **private foundations** (**IRC §§ 4940–4948**) have as their underlying **sanctions** or **penalties** various excise taxes. These taxes are applicable with respect to **net investment income** (**IRC § 4940**), acts of **self-dealing** (**IRC § 4941**), inadequate making of **qualifying distributions** (**IRC § 4942**), the presence of **excess business holdings** (**IRC § 4943**), the making of a **jeopardizing investment** (**IRC § 4944**), the making of a **taxable expenditure** (**IRC § 4945**), and the gross investment income derived from U.S. sources by **foreign** private foundations (**IRC § 4948**). The **termination tax** that applies in the private foundation context is not an excise tax, although it can serve as a **third-tier tax** (**IRC § 507**). [PF §§ 1.1, 1.10, 5.15(a)(ii), 5.15(b)–5.15(d), 5.15(f), 5.15(g), 6.7(c), 7.6, 8.4(c), 9.10(b), 13.6, 16.9; EO §§ 11.8(b), 12.4, 13.3, 21.10, 22.3(d)(iii), 22.4, 28.13, 28.16(f); AU §§ 5.33(j), 5.33(k)] (also **Additional tax; First-tier tax; Initial tax; Second-tier tax**).

excludability

The word "excludability" is used to refer to forms of **income** that are excluded from treatment as **gross income**.

excludable rent

The term "excludable rent" means **rent** received by a **tax-exempt organization** under circumstances in which the rent is excluded from taxation as **unrelated business income** (**IRC § 512(b)(3)**). [UB § 3.8; EO § 25.1(h); SM p. 177].

exclusion

The word "exclusion" is used in the **federal tax law** setting to refer to an item of **revenue** that, by **statute**, is **excluded** from **gross income**. For example, the following are some of the items that are excluded from gross income: **gifts** (**IRC § 102**), **interest** on state and local **bonds** (**IRC § 103**), the **rental value** of parsonages (**IRC § 107**), income of states and municipalities (**IRC § 115**), qualified **fellowships** and **scholarships** (**IRC § 117**), certain **employer-provided educational assistance** programs (**IRC § 127**), and certain **fringe benefits** (**IRC § 132**). By contrast, the term **exemption** is used to describe nontaxation of the income of an **organization**, by virtue of the nature of the organization rather than the nature of its income. Nonetheless, most **tax-exempt organizations** are at least potentially subject to taxation, principally the **unrelated business income tax** and/or one or more **excise taxes**). (also **Credit; Deduction**).

exclusion ratio

The "exclusion ratio," a term used in the context of the **charitable gift annuity**, is used to determine the portion of each **annuity** payment that is tax-free because it is a **return on investment**. It is an amount equal to the **investment in the contract** divided by the **expected** return. The portion of the annuity that is tax-free is determined by multiplying the amount of the annuity payment by the exclusion ratio. The balance of the annuity is taxable as **ordinary income**. [CG § 14.2].

exclusively

The term "exclusively" means apart from all others; it is synonymous with "solely." Although the **Internal Revenue Code** provides that **charitable organizations** are those **entities** that are **organized** and **operated** "exclusively" for **tax-exempt purposes** (IRC § 501(c)(3)), however, courts have applied the word as if it were **primarily**, **principally**, or **substantially**. This was done, in part, to accommodate the **unrelated business income tax** structure (inasmuch as a **tax-exempt organization** could not have unrelated income if "exclusively" was interpreted to literally mean "exclusively"). Thus, in this context, the term "exclusively" is a **word of art**. By contrast, when the **supporting organization rules** were written, which state that that type of organization must be organized and operated "exclusively" for one or more **supported organizations**, the **legislative history** of these rules stated that Congress meant the term "exclusively" to mean—literally—"exclusively." There also is an exclusivity requirement with respect to the **charitable contribution deduction** for **gifts** for **conservation** purposes. [EO §§ 4.4, 4.6; PF §§ 15.7(a), 15.7(b); CL §§ 1.6, 1.10; CG § 9.7(d); LI Q 1.46].

execute

One of the meanings of the word "execute" is to sign a document according to whatever formalities the **law** may require (such as notarization of signatures and/or the presence of witnesses). Thus, an individual executes a **contract**, **deed**, **power of attorney**, **trust agreement** or **declaration of trust**, **will**, and the like.

executive branch

The "executive branch" of a government is that segment of government with the responsibility of putting **laws** into effect and of enforcing them. (also **Judicial branch**; **Legislative branch**).

executive committee

Many **nonprofit organizations** have an "executive committee." This type of committee has the responsibility of performing the work of the organization's **board of directors** or **board of trustees** when that body is not in session. Frequently, the executive committee is comprised wholly or principally of the organization's **officers**. Some states' **nonprofit corporation statutes** contain rules specifically applicable to executive committees, such as a limitation on what they can do in the absence of the governing board (the committee cannot **dissolve** the corporation, for example) or requiring that every **member** of the committee also be a member of the organization's governing hoard. An executive committee is a **standing committee**. [GV § 5.11].

executive compensation policy

An "executive compensation policy" is a policy that is designed to ensure that **compensation** paid to its executive staff is **reasonable**. This type of policy should make use of the **rebuttable presumption of reasonableness**. [GV §§ 3.4(c), 6.3(e); AR §§ 5.1(g)(2), 5.1(i), 5.3; HC § 33.5; CU Q 5.35; SM pp. 274–275; LI Q 3.33, Q 6.40].

executive order

An "executive order" is a form of **law** that is issued by the head of an **executive branch** of a government, such as the President of the United States. This type of law may not be inconsistent with an applicable **constitution** or **statutory** law. For example, the **Combined Federal Campaign** was established by executive order.

executive trustee

The informal term "executive trustee" refers to an individual who is serving as a **trustee** (or perhaps **director**) of a **tax-exempt organization**, usually a **charitable entity**, but who has duties and responsibilities that are beyond those normally associated with service as a trustee and encompass those usually undertaken by an **officer** and/or **executive employee**.

executor

An "executor" is an individual who has been selected by another individual (the **testator**) to carry out the directions in the testator's **will**, including distribution of the **property** in the **estate** according to the terms of the will. Although the usage is increasingly rare, a woman who is appointed executor may be known as an "executrix." (also **Personal representative**).

exempt

The word "exempt" means to exclude or except a **person**, **program**, or other thing from a legal requirement, such as payment of a **tax**. (also **Exemption**; **Tax exemption**).

exempt function

An "exempt function" is an activity of a **tax-exempt organization** that is conducted by the organization in advancement of one or more of the purposes for which it obtained **recognition** of **tax exemption**. The term "exempt function" is defined for **political organizations** as the function of **influencing** or **attempting to influence** the selection, nomination, **election**, or **appointment** of an individual to a **federal**, state, or local **public office**, or the election of presidential or vice presidential electors, whether or not these individuals or electors are selected, nominated, elected, or appointed (**IRC** § 527(c)(2)). [EO §§ 17.3, 23.9; SM §§ 45–46].

exempt function asset

The phrase "exempt function asset" is used in connection with the **private foundation mandatory payout** rule. This type of **asset** is one that is used by a foundation directly in the conduct of its charitable program. Exempt function assets are **excluded** from the **minimum investment return** formula. [PF §§ 6.2(c), 6.2(e), 6.5(b)].

exempt function income

The phrase "exempt function income" is used to generally describe **revenue** produced by a **tax-exempt organization** in the course of performance of one or more of its **exempt functions**. In some instances, exempt function income is a form of **public** support. Because of the unique way in which they are **taxed**, the phrase "exempt function income" is particularly significant for **social clubs**, **homeowners' associations**, and **political organizations**; it is defined as **income** in the form of **dues**, charges, and similar amounts paid by the **members** of the **exempt organization** in connection with the purposes constituting the basis for the tax exemption of the organization. [EO §§ 12.3(b)(iv), 15.5, 17.5, 19.14; PF §§ 15.5, 15.6(a); HC §§ 5.3, 24.2(d); PG pp. 85, 190; SM pp. 41, 45–46, 82].

exempt operating foundation

An "exempt operating foundation" is a **private foundation** that is **exempt** from the **tax** on **net investment income** generally imposed on private foundations (by **IRC** § 4940(a)). To be an exempt operating foundation for any year, a private foundation must have the following characteristics: (1) it qualifies as a **private operating foundation**, (2) it has been **publicly supported** for at least ten years, (3) at all times during the year involved, the **governing body** of the private foundation consisted of individuals at least 75 percent of whom are not **disqualified individuals** and was broadly representative of the **public**, and (4) at no time during the year involved did the private foundation have an **officer** who was a disqualified individual (**IRC** § 4940(d)(2)). The purpose of this exemption is to eliminate this tax liability for organizations that are not substantively private foundations, such as **museums** and libraries. [PF §§ 3.1(i), 10.6; EO § 12.1(c); SM pp. 87–88].

exempt organization

The term "exempt organization" is used informally to mean the same as **tax-exempt organization**.

exempt purpose expenditure

The term "exempt purpose expenditure" is utilized in the context of the **expenditure test**, which uses various percentages to measure allowable **lobbying** by **electing public charities**. These percentages are applied against a base number, which is the total of exempt function expenditures for the particular measuring period. In general, an **expenditure** is an exempt purpose expenditure for a **tax year** if it is paid or incurred by an electing public charity to accomplish one or more of the organization's **exempt purposes** (**IRC** § 4911(e)(1)(A)). Among the expenditures that do not qualify as exempt operating expenditures are amounts paid to or incurred for a **separate fundraising unit** of the **organization** or an **affiliated** organization. [EO § 22.3(d)(iii); FR § 5.10; HC § 7.1(c)(ii); SM pp. 189–190].

exemption

The word "exemption" is used to describe something—such as a **person** or a type of **income**—that is excused from application of a **law**. For example, several types of **nonprofit organizations** have an "exemption" from the **federal income tax**. (also **Tax exemption**).

exemption by attachment

The concept of tax "exemption by attachment" is that an **organization** can be **tax-exempt** solely by reason of its **affiliation** or other relationship with (attachment to) another organization that is tax-exempt. In general, the **IRS** rejects this concept, particularly in the context of **health care organizations**. [HC § 34.7(a); EO § 26.10(a)] (also **Derivative exemption**; **Vicarious exemption**).

exemption, recognition of

See **Recognition of tax exemption**.

exemptions from state charitable solicitation laws

Various categories of **organizations** are **exempt**, in whole or in part, from one or more of the state **charitable solicitation acts**. These categories include **schools, colleges, universities, hospitals, veterans' organizations**, and **small organizations**. [FR § 3.5; SM p. 149; CG § 25.7].

exhaustion of remedies

The concept of "exhaustion of remedies" is that a court will not hear a case that was initiated with an **administrative agency** until the **person** bringing the **action** can demonstrate that be, she, or it exhausted his, her, or its remedies at the administrative level. For example, a **charitable organization** cannot initiate the special **declaratory judgment** procedure until and unless it has exhausted its administrative remedies with the **IRS**. [EO § 27.5(b)(ii)].

expected return

The term "expected return" is used in the context of the **charitable gift annuity rules**. The term means the total amount that the **annuitant** is expected to receive, determined by using **actuarial** assumptions. [CG § 14.2] (also **Expected return multiple**).

expected return multiple

The phrase "expected return multiple," used in the context of the **charitable gift annuity rules**, means the appropriate number derived from **actuarial tables**, which varies depending on the **contributor's life expectancy**. This number is based on the age of the **annuitant** to the nearest whole year as of the starting date of the annuity. The number derived from the tables may have to be adjusted to reflect the frequency of the annuity payments. The **expected return** from the annuity arrangement is calculated by multiplying the annual aggregate annuity by the (adjusted) expected return multiple. [CG § 14.2].

expenditure

When used in the accounting or other financial context, the word "expenditure" is employed to describe the disbursement or paying out of money. The term is usually used to describe the disbursement of money for a major item of **property** or investment; thus the term **capital expenditure**. The other types of disbursements of money, such as for operations or minor items of property, tend to be termed **expenses**. Thus, an expenditure for a **capital asset** or investment is not fully **deductible** in the acquisition year (**IRC** § 263), while an expense may be deductible (**IRC** § 162). (also **Business expense; Contribution to capital**).

expenditure, improper

See **Taxable expenditure**.

expenditure responsibility

A **taxable expenditure** includes any amount paid or incurred by a **private foundation** as a **grant** (or **loan** or **program-related investment**) to an **organization** (other than an organization that is not a private foundation), unless the private foundation exercises "expenditure responsibility" with respect to the grant (**IRC** § 4945(d)(4)). A private foundation is considered to be exercising expenditure responsibility as long as it exerts all **reasonable** efforts and establishes adequate procedures to see that the grant is spent solely for the purpose for which it was made, obtain full and complete reports from the **grantee** as to how the funds are spent, and make full and detailed reports with respect to the **expenditures** to the **IRS** (**IRC** § 4945(h)). [PF §§ 1.4(h), 8.3, 9.6, 15.1; CG § 20.4(c); HC § 5.9; AR § 16.1(b); SM pp. 89–90].

E

expenditure responsibility grant

An "expenditure responsibility grant" is a **grant** made by a **private foundation** under circumstances in which the foundation is required to exercise **expenditure responsibility**.

expenditure test

An organization that is **tax-exempt** because it is a **charitable entity** may not devote a **substantial** part of its activities to the carrying on of **propaganda** or otherwise attempting to **influence legislation** (**IRC** § 501(c)(3)). In an effort to provide more specific rules for measuring these restrictions, Congress enacted a body of law known as the "expenditure test." This test **must be elected** by a charitable organization; the organization must be a qualifying **public charity** to make this election. The test entails **percentage limitations** on allowable **lobbying expenditures**, **exempts** certain activities from the definition of **legislative activities**, provides definitions of terms such as **direct lobbying** and **grass-roots lobbying**, and provides for the attribution of lobbying by **affiliated organizations**. [EO §§ 22.2(b), 22.3(d); CU Q 8.6, Q 8.16; HC §§ 7.1(a)–(c); CG § 3.3(b); AR §§ 9.1(e), 9.2(b); PG pp. 111–115; SM pp. 189–191].

expense

An "expense" is a disbursement or outlay of money for a particular purpose. [PF §§ 10.4, 12.1(b); CU Q 2.49] (also **Allocation of expenses**; **Expenditure**).

expense reimbursement policy

The **IRS**, on the **Form 990**, asks whether the filing **organization** follows a written policy regarding payment, reimbursement, or provision of business **expenses** and whether the organization requires substantiation prior to reimbursing or allowing expenses by its top officials. [GV § 6.3(r); SM pp. 278–280] (also **Accountable plan**).

expert witness

An "expert witness" is an individual who serves as a witness in either a **judicial proceeding** or an **administrative proceeding**, who has knowledge about a particular subject, where that knowledge is not normally possessed by the average **person**. Formally, the expert witness is a part of the proceeding for the purpose of providing technical assistance to the court or **administrative agency**. In practice, both parties in a proceeding may each use one or more expert witnesses as part of the process of attempting to prove their case. For example, in a court proceeding concerning the **fair market value** of an item of **property contributed** to a **charitable**

organization, both the **contributor** and the **IRS** are likely to have an expert witness on their side whose testimony will buttress the **value** amount they are advocating. [CG § 10.1(a)].

exploitation rule

The "exploitation rule" applies in the context of the **unrelated business income rules**. The rule is that if a product resulting from the performance of a **tax-exempt function** is utilized or exploited in **business** endeavors beyond that **reasonably** appropriate or necessary for disposition in the state it is in on completion of tax-exempt functions, the **gross income** derived from these additional business activities is regarded as income from the conduct of an **unrelated trade or business**. [UB § 2.7(e); EO § 24.4(e); HC § 24.4(d)].

exposition

An "exposition" is an exhibition or show. Certain types of expositions carried on by certain types of **tax-exempt organizations** are termed "**public entertainment activities**" and are excluded from consideration as an **unrelated trade or business** (IRC §§ 513(d)(1), (2)). [UB § 4.4; EO § 25.2(e)].

expressive association, freedom of

The type of **freedom of association** known as the "freedom of expressive association" is a function of the **right** of **free speech**, which is protected by the **First Amendment** to the U.S. Constitution. The freedom to engage in group effort (such as by and through **nonprofit organizations**) is guaranteed under the **doctrine** of freedom of expressive association and is viewed as a way of **advancing political**, social, economic, **educational**, **religious**, and cultural ends. Government, however, has the ability to infringe on this right when compelling state interests, unrelated to the suppression of ideas and that cannot be achieved through means significantly less restrictive of associational freedoms, are served. [CL § 1.9; EO § 1.7].

E

factor

Fundamentally, a "factor" is one of a group of elements that contributes to the achievement of a particular result. In the context of the **federal tax law** of **charitable giving**, a factor is one of the elements used to calculate a **remainder interest** in a charitable **gift** of money and/or **property**. The factor is a seven-digit number that, when combined with other elements of information (such as the **donor's** age, the **value** of the property, and the nature of the **income interest**) yields the remainder interest amount. [CG § 11.2].

facts-and-circumstances test

The "facts-and-circumstances test" is a way by which a charitable organization can qualify as a donative type publicly supported organization without satisfying all of the general requirements. To meet this test, the organization must demonstrate the existence of three elements: (1) the total amount of governmental and public support normally received by the organization is at least 10 percent of its total support normally received, (2) the organization has a continuous and bona fide program for the solicitation of funds from the general public, governmental units, or public charities, and (3) all other pertinent facts and circumstances, including the percentage of its support from governmental and other public sources, the composition of the organization's governing board, the extent to which its facilities or programs are publicly available, its membership dues rates, and whether its activities are likely to appeal to persons having some broad common interest or purpose. [PF §§ 15.4(c), 15.6(b); EO § 12.3(b)(ii); HC §§ 5.2(b), 7.4(b), 27.5; CG § 3.3(a); AR § 8.1(d)(6); PG p. 91; SM p. 86].

failure by hospital organization, tax on

If a **hospital organization**, to which the **additional hospital exemption requirements** apply, fails to meet the requirement concerning **community health needs assessments** for a **tax year**, an **excise tax** in the amount of $50,000 is imposed on the organization (**IRC** § 4959). [HC § 26.10(a)(ii); EO § 7.6(b)(ii)].

fair

A "fair" is a gathering of exhibitors of items such as livestock, products, and/or equipment, usually accompanied by booths and other places of entertainment and social activities. The

Bruce R. Hopkins' Nonprofit Law Dictionary, First Edition. Bruce R. Hopkins.
© 2015 Bruce R. Hopkins. Published 2015 by John Wiley & Sons, Inc.

conduct of entertainment activities at fairs by qualifying **tax-exempt organizations** is **exempt** from **taxation** as an **unrelated trade or business** (**IRC** §§ 513(d)(1), (2)). [UB § 4.4; EO § 25.2(e)] (also **Expositions**; **Public entertainment activities**).

fair competition

In the context of **nonprofit law**, the concept of "fair competition" is part of the **commerciality doctrine**. The concept concerns the matter of competition between **tax-exempt organizations** and **for-profit organizations**, where both categories of organizations are engaged in identical or similar activities (such as health care, publishing, product sales, or research). The term "fair" arises with respect to the **tax exemption** of the nonprofit organization competitor, which is perceived by the for-profit community as an unfair economic advantage. The for-profit community is of the view that this type of competition would be fairer if the tax-exempt competitors were taxed on the **net income** derived from the **enterprise** or, in some instances, if the tax exemption were removed. [EO § 4.10(a)(i); UB § 7.1(a); HC § 3.3(a); CG § 1.6; SM pp. 288–289] (also **Halo effect**; **Level playing field**).

fair market value

The "fair market value" of an item of **property** (or the **right** to use property) is the price at which the property would change hands between a willing buyer and a willing seller, neither being under any compulsion to buy, sell, or otherwise transfer the property, and both having **reasonable** knowledge of the relevant facts. [CG §§ 2.14, 4.2, 9.7(e), 10.1; EO §§ 20.4(b), 20.5; PF § 6.3; FR § 5.14(h)] (also **Arm's length transaction**; **Value**).

family member

The term "family member" generically means an individual's spouse (taking into account same-sex marriage **law**), ancestors, brothers and sisters (whether whole or half blood), children (whether natural or adopted), grandchildren, great-grandchildren, and the spouses of brothers, sisters, children, grandchildren, and great grandchildren. Two definitions of the phrase **member of the family** are utilized in the law of **tax-exempt organizations** in definitions of the term **disqualified person**; the term is also used in the definition of an **exempt operating foundation** (**IRC** § 4940(d)(3)(D)). [EO §§ 12.2(d), 21.3; PF § 4.4; AS § 3.8(c); SM pp. 59, 82].

farm

Traditionally, a "farm" has been thought of as a parcel of **real estate** devoted to **agriculture**. A farm can also be a parcel of real estate devoted to the growing of animals (rather than just crops) or a body of water where something is grown. Certain **charitable contributions** of **remainder interests** in farms are **deductible** under the **federal tax law** when not **donated** by means of **split-interest trusts**. [CG § 15.2(b)].

farmers' cooperative

A "farmers' cooperative" is a type of **tax-exempt organization** under the **federal tax law** (**IRC** § 521). These **cooperatives** are **farmers'**, fruit growers', or like **associations organized** and **operated** on a cooperative basis for the purpose of (1) marketing the products of **members** or other producers and returning to them the proceeds of sales, less the necessary marketing **expenses**, on the basis of either the quantity or the **value** of the products furnished by them, or (2) purchasing supplies and equipment for the use of members or other persons and turning over the supplies and equipment to them at actual cost plus necessary expenses. With respect to a farmers' cooperative that issues stock, for the cooperative to be tax-exempt, **substantially all** of the capital stock must be owned by producers who market their products or purchase their supplies and equipment through the cooperative. [EO § 19.12; AS § 1.6(q); SM p. 45].

F

farming
See **Agriculture**.

fast-track case settlement program
The **IRS** devised a program, known as the "fast-track case settlement program," that enables **tax-exempt organizations** with issues under **examination** by the **TE/GE Division** to participate in this program to expedite resolution of their cases. [EO § 27.7].

favorable
The **IRS** issues **determination letters** and **rulings**. When these pronouncements provide the **person** requesting them with the response they sought, the pronouncements are said to be "favorable." (cf. **Adverse**).

federal
The word "federal" pertains to a union of states under a central government. The word is used in a **law** setting to mean the same as national. Thus, for these purposes, the word "federal" means the governmental jurisdiction of the United States.

Federal Election Campaign Act
The **law** embodied by the "Federal Election Campaign Act" is the law governing **participations**, including **contributions** and **expenditures**, in **federal** elections. [CL Chap. 5; EO § 23.2(b)(ii); FR § 5.25; AS § 11.5; CU Q 9.29; SM pp. 197, 203] (also **Federal Election Commission**).

Federal Election Commission
The "Federal Election Commission" ("FEC") is the **agency** of the **federal** government that is charged with the responsibility of enforcing the **law** created by enactment of the **Federal Election Campaign Act** and its amendments. One of the functions of the FEC is to issue **advisory opinions**. [AS § 11.5(a), CL § 5.2; SM pp. 30, 125, 197, 202, 203].

federal election laws
See **Election laws, federal**.

federal estate tax
The "federal estate tax" is the **tax** law of the United States that imposes taxes on **taxable estates** (**IRC** § 2001). [CG § 8.1] (also **Death tax**).

Federal Food, Drug, and Cosmetic Act

There are several requirements that have to be satisfied for the special **twice-basis charitable contribution deduction** for **gifts** of **inventory** to be available (**IRC** § 170(e)(3)). One of them is that, where the **donated property** is subject to regulation under the "Federal Food, Drug, and Cosmetic Act," the property must fully satisfy the applicable requirements of that **law** on the date of transfer and for 180 days prior to that date. [CG § 9.3(e)].

federal gift tax

The "federal gift tax" is the **tax law** of the United States that imposes taxes on **gifts** made by various **persons** (**IRC** § 2501). [CG §§ 8.2(b), 8.2(c)].

federal income tax

The "federal income tax" is the **tax law** of the United States that imposes taxes at various **rates** on the **net income** of various **persons** (**IRC** §§ 1, 11).

Federal Insurance Contribution Act

The "Federal Insurance Contribution Act" (often referred to as "FICA") is the body of **federal** law requiring nearly all **employers** and **employees** to make contributions to the Social Security trust fund. [HC §§ 27.1, 27.6(b)].

federal law

"Federal law" means the **law** of the United States.

federal mid-term rate

The "federal mid-term rate" is a **federal rate** published monthly by the **U.S. Department of the Treasury** that is used to determine the issue price (**value**) of certain debt instruments (**IRC** § 1274(d)(1)). This rate is used in calculating the value of an **annuity**, an **interest** for life or for a **term of years**, or a **remainder** or **reversionary** interest; this value is determined by using an **interest rate** (rounded to the nearest two-tenths of 1 percent) equal to 120 percent of the federal mid-term rate in effect for the month in which the **valuation date** falls (**IRC** § 7520(a)(2)). [CG § 11.1].

federal rate, applicable

The "applicable federal rate" is one of three rates: the **federal** short-term **rate** (for debt **instruments** with a **term** of three years), the federal mid-term rate (for debt instruments with a term over three years but not over nine years), and the federal long-term rate (for debt instruments with a term over nine years). The federal short-term rate is the rate determined by the **Department of the Treasury** based on the average market yield (during any one-month period selected by the Department and ending in the calendar month in which the determination is made) on outstanding marketable obligations of the United States with remaining periods to maturity of three years or less. The other two rates are determined in accordance with the principles underlying the federal short-term rate. During each calendar month, the Department determines the federal short-term. mid-term, and long-term rates that apply during the following calendar month (**IRC** § 1274(d)). [CG §§ 11.1, 12.12, 13.11].

federal tax law

In general, the "federal tax law" is that body of **federal law** that consists of the **Internal Revenue Code**, court opinions in **tax** cases, the **tax regulations**, **revenue rulings** and **revenue procedures**, forms and instructions to them, and (although they technically are not of **precedential value**) **private letter rulings**, **technical advice memoranda**, **general counsel memoranda**, and other pronouncements of the **Department of the Treasury** and the **IRS**.

Federal Trade Commission

The "Federal Trade Commission," an **agency** of the **federal** government that enforces the **antitrust laws** and has some jurisdiction in the field of consumer protection, has been discussed as an agency that would administer and enforce a **fundraising** regulation law at the federal level. [AS § 11.6(b); FR §§ 2.6, 5.21, 7.2(c)].

Federal Unemployment Tax Act

The "Federal Unemployment Tax Act" (often referred to as "FUTA") is the body of **federal law** that established a system of unemployment compensation. It is **funded** by a **tax** on **wages** paid to covered **employees** by the **employers** embraced by this system. Employers are allowed **credits** against this tax through participation in state unemployment **insurance** laws. Services performed for a **tax-exempt organization** may be **exempt** from taxation under FUTA. [HC §§ 27.1, 27.6(b)].

federally chartered organization

On occasion, the U.S. Congress will enact a **statute** that provides a "federal charter" for a **nonprofit organization**. Sometimes, this **federal charter** obviates the need for the **organization** to be formed under state **law**. **Veterans' organizations** often are federally chartered. Another example is the American National Red Cross. [GV § 3.11].

federated fundraising campaign

A "federated fundraising campaign" is a community-wide **charitable solicitation** organized to support a large number of **civic**, **social**, and **welfare organizations** in the community with a single annual fund drive. The effort is orchestrated by a **federated fundraising organization;** a campaign period is often observed. These campaigns are usually directed at local businesses for annual **gifts** from them and their **employees**; payroll **deductions** for these gifts are encouraged.

federated fundraising organization

The law in some states defines a "federated fundraising organization" as any federation of independent **charitable organizations** that have voluntarily joined together, including a United Fund or Community Chest, for purposes of raising and distributing money for and among themselves and where **membership** does not confer authority and control of the individual agencies on the federated group organization. [AR § 7.2(a)(1)].

federated group

The term "federated group" is used in the context of the **Combined Federal Campaign**. It is an **entity** that administers a local campaign. (also **Principal Combined Fund Organization**).

fee

One definition of the word "fee" is "payment for services rendered," such as the fee paid to a **lawyer** or a **professional fundraiser**. The word also means a type of ownership of **real property**. An ownership that is absolute and without limitation as to any class of **heirs** is termed a **fee simple** (or, perhaps for emphasis, a "fee simple absolute"); when it is limited to a specific class of heirs, the estate is a "fee tail.".

feeder organization

A "feeder organization" is an **organization** operated for the **primary** purpose of carrying on a **trade or business** for **profit**, where all of its profits are payable to one or more **tax-exempt organizations**. Thus, a feeder organization is a business entity that "feeds" its profits to one or more exempt organizations. A feeder organization generally is not tax-exempt solely because it feeds its profits in this manner (**IRC** § 502). [EO § 28.15; UB § 1.9; SM p. 170] (also **Destination-of-income test**; **Exemption by attachment**).

fellowship

A "fellowship" is a **grant** to an individual, usually from a **charitable organization**, for a specified **tax-exempt** purpose, such as study, publication, or **research**. The term is somewhat synonymous with the concept of a **scholarship**, although a fellowship is a more targeted type of grant and usually is for a more limited period of lime than a scholarship. [CU Q 11.4].

felony

A "felony" is a **criminal** act of serious character; it is an act that is graver than a **misdemeanor**. The punishment for the commission of a felony may be death or imprisonment for a period of longer than one year. It is a felony under the **federal tax law** to, for example, (1) make a declaration knowing it to be perjury, (2) assist in the preparation of a **return** or other **tax** document knowing it to be false, (3) falsify records or conceal **property** in connection with a **closing agreement,** or (4) deliver to the **IRS** any return or other document knowing it to be **fraudulent** or false (**IRC** §§ 7206, 7207). Most of the state **charitable solicitation acts** contain **penalties** by which some violations of these laws are felonies. [FR § 3.21].

fiduciary

A "fiduciary" is a **person** that has special responsibilities in connection with the administration, investment, and distribution of **property**, usually property belonging to someone else (who is often termed a **principal**). This range of duties is termed "fiduciary responsibility." The **federal tax law** defines a "fiduciary" as a guardian, **trustee**, **executor**, **administrator**, receiver, conservator, or any person acting in any fiduciary capacity for any person (**IRC** § 7701(a)(6)). [GV § 1.4; PF §§ 1.1, 18.3; HC § 33.2(f); AU § 5.1(f); RE Q 2.5, Q 2.6, Q 2.15; CU Q 1.24, Q 1.25, Q 1.27; SM pp. 313–317; Q 1.30, Q 1.31, Q 1.33, Q 3.9, Q 3.13].

fiduciary responsibility
See **Fiduciary**.

Fifth Amendment
The "Fifth Amendment" to the U.S. Constitution provides, among other guarantees, that life, liberty, or **property** may not be taken without **due process of law**. [FR § 4.4; EO § 27.6; CL § 1.1(b)].

50 percent limitation
The **deductibility** of one or more **charitable contributions** in any one year is limited by the **federal tax law** by means of various **percentage limitations**. The "50 percent limitation" has three applications. One is that the maximum **federal income tax charitable contribution deduction** for a **tax year** for an individual is 50 percent of the individual's **contribution base** (**IRC** § 170(b)(1)(A)). Another rule is that an individual's charitable contributions made during a tax year to one or more **public charitable organizations**, where the subject of the **gift** is money, are deductible to the extent that the contributions in the aggregate do not exceed 50 percent of the individual's contribution base for the tax year (*id.*). The third of these applications allows an individual contributing **capital gain property** to use the 50 percent limitation where the amount of the contribution is reduced by all of the unrealized **appreciation** in the **value** of the property (**IRC** § 170(b)(1)(C)(iii)). [CG §§ 7.4, 7.5, 7.7; SM p. 135].

filing deadline, annual information return
An **annual information return** and any **tax return** by which a **tax-exempt organization** reports its **unrelated business income** is required to be filed with the **IRS** on or before the fifteenth day of the fifth month following the close of its fiscal year (**IRC** § 6072(e)). [EO §§ 28.2(a)(iv), 28.8; UB § 11.5(c)].

financial assistance policy
For purposes of the **financial assistance policy requirement**, a "financial assistance policy" is a written financial assistance policy that includes eligibility criteria for financial assistance, and whether the assistance includes free or discounted care; the basis for calculating amounts charged to patients; the method for applying for financial assistance; in the case of an entity that does not have a separate billing and collections policy, the actions the organization may take in the event of non-payment, including collections action and reporting to credit agencies;

and measures to widely publicize the policy within the community to be served by the entity (**IRC** § 501(r)(4)(A)). [HC § 26.10(a)(iii); EO § 7.6(b)(iii)].

financial assistance policy requirement

A **hospital organization** or **hospital facility** meets the "financial assistance policy requirement" if the organization or facility establishes a **financial assistance policy** and an **emergency medical care policy** (**IRC** § 501(r)(4)). [HC § 26.10(a)(iii); EO § 7.6(b)(iii)].

financial statement

A "financial statement" is a report of an **organization** showing its financial activity (including **revenue**, **expenses**, and **fund balance**) for a particular period of time (usually a year). One of the purposes of a financial statement is to present an accurate picture of the finances of the organization. Among the most important responsibilities of a **treasurer** of an organization is to see to the preparation of a suitable financial statement. [PG pp. 15–16; SM p. 20].

First Amendment

The "First Amendment" to the U.S. Constitution protects the **right** of **free speech**. The First Amendment is not violated by the limitations on **lobbying** activities imposed on **charitable organizations**. The **doctrine** of **freedom of association** is based on the right of free speech. Some **educational** activities are acts of free speech. The **solicitation** of **charitable contributions** is an act of free speech, which means that charitable **fundraising** can be regulated by government only by means of the narrowest form of regulation. The First Amendment also contains the **religion clauses**. [CL §§ 1.9, 1.11, 2.2–2.4, 5.0, 7.4; FR § 4.3; EO § 10.1; CG § 1.3(c); SM pp. 321–322, 326–327, 330–332].

first-bite rule

See **Initial contract**.

first-class travel

Generically, "first class" means the finest or highest class, grade, or rank. In the context of travel (e.g., by airplane, train, or ship), first class means the most expensive and luxurious class of accommodation. **Form 990**, Schedule J (Part I (concerning questions regarding **compensation**), question 1a requires reporting **organizations** to check one or more boxes if it provided various items to a **trustee**, **director**, **officer**, **key employee**, or **highest compensated employee**. One of these items is "first class travel." The payment by a **tax-exempt organization** for first-class travel, however, is not an item of compensation, irrespective of the status of the payee. [AR § 6.2(c)].

first-tier subsidiary

The phrase "first-tier subsidiary" is a more technical term for (and is synonymous with) the sole word "**subsidiary**." It refers to an **organization** that has a subsidiary relationship to a **parent** organization, with that relationship defined by the element of **direct control** that the parent entity has over the subsidiary. [EO § 30.7(b)] (cf. **Second-tier subsidiary**).

first-tier tax

The term "first-tier tax" is synonymous with the term **initial tax**, as that term is used in the **black lung benefits trust**, **donor-advised fund**, **intermediate sanctions**, **political expenditures**, and **private foundations** settings (**IRC** § 4963(a)). [EO §§ 11.8(b), 12.4, 18.5, 21.10, 23.3; PF §§ 5.15(d), 6.7(c), 7.6, 8.5, 9.10, 10.1, 10.2] (cf. **Qualified first-tier tax**).

fiscal agent

The term "fiscal agent" is used to define the role of a **tax-exempt organization** that manages funds or acts in a similar capacity for another **exempt organization**. The organization that provides this service is a true **agent**, in that the other entity is the principal and has the legal right to control the agent's activities. One common example of this practice is for a **charitable organization** to accept **contributions** on behalf of another organization, the **application for recognition of exemption** of which is pending with the **IRS**, to assure **deductibility** of the contributions. In the context of the **Combined Federal Campaign**, a **Principal Combined Fund Organization** serves as a fiscal agent for the local organizations. (also **Conduit**; **Earmarking**; cf. **Fiscal sponsor**).

fiscal sponsor

The term "fiscal sponsor" is usually used to refer to a **tax-exempt charitable organization** that sponsors a charitable project on behalf of a non-exempt organization, a group of individuals, or an individual. The sponsor receives **tax-deductible contributions** for the project and has the responsibility for spending the donated funds in furtherance of the project. (cf. **Fiscal agent**).

fiscal year

A "fiscal year" is a twelve-month period over which an **organization** keeps its financial books and records. A fiscal year must always end on the last day of a month, other than December (**IRC** § 7701(a)(24)). The fiscal year of the **federal government** ends on September 30. [PF § 2.7(b); CG § 2.9] (also **Annual accounting period**; **Tax year**).

fitness center

A "fitness center" (or similar facility), whether freestanding or operated by a **tax-exempt institution** (such as a **hospital** or **university**), can be an **exempt** organization or program, as a **charitable** undertaking because it **promotes health**. The activity must, to be exempt, be beneficial to the **community**. Otherwise, it will be a nonexempt function or an **unrelated business**. [EO §§ 7.6(h), 24.5(b)(iv); UB § 9.2(d); HC § 24.8].

fixed payment

For purposes of the **intermediate sanctions** rules, a "fixed payment" is an amount of money or other property, specified in a contract, or determined by a fixed formula specified in a contract, which is to be paid or transferred in exchange for the provision of specified services or property. [EO § 21.8; HC § 4.9(a)(iii)].

fixed percentage

The concept of the "fixed percentage" arises in connection with the definition of a **charitable remainder unitrust**. Among the requirements for this type of **trust** is that a "fixed percentage" of the **net fair market value** of the **assets** of the trust, valued annually, must be paid to qualified **income interest beneficiaries**. This fixed percentage must be expressed in the **trust instrument** either as a fraction or as a percentage, and must be payable each year for the specified period. A percentage is "fixed" if it is the same either as to each income beneficiary or as to the total percentage payable each year of the period. [CG §§ 12.1(a), 12.3(a); SM p. 235].

fixed price restriction

The term "fixed price restriction" is used in the context of defining circumstances where an **exception**, from the **law** treating **income** from **debt-financed property** as **unrelated business taxable income**, is available to qualified **organizations** that make debt-financed investments in **real property** (**IRC** § 514(c)(9)(A)). Under this exception, income from investments in real property is not treated as income from debt-financed property.

This exception is available only where six restrictions are satisfied (**IRC** § 514(c)(9)(B)). One of them is the "fixed price restriction," which provides that the purchase price of the real property must be a fixed amount determined as of the date of the acquisition (**IRC** § 514(c)(9)(B)(i)). This rule is relaxed, however, in instances in which (1) a qualified organization acquires the property from a financial institution that acquired the real property by foreclosure (or after an actual or imminent default), or was held by the selling financial institution at the time that it entered into conservatorship or receivership, (2) any **gain recognized** by the financial institution with respect to the property is **ordinary income**, (3) the stated **principal** amount of the seller financing does not exceed the financial institution's outstanding indebtedness (including accrued but unpaid **interest**) with respect to the property at the time of foreclosure or default, and (4) the present **value** of the maximum amount payable pursuant to any participation feature cannot exceed 30 percent of the total purchase price of the property (including contingent payments) (**IRC** § 514(c)(9)(H)). [UB § 5.4(f); EO § 24.9(c)].

fixture

A "fixture" is an item of **property** that, standing alone, would probably be an item of **personal property** but, because it is physically attached to an item of **real property** to such an extent that the removal of it would damage or otherwise diminish the real property the item of property is considered, for purposes of the **law**, part of the real property to which it is attached.

flat fixed fee

The phrase "flat fixed fee" is used in many state **charitable solicitation acts** as part of the definition of the term "**professional fundraiser**." The phrase means that the **fee** involved is an absolute amount, established in advance of the rendering of services (usually by **contract**); it is not a function of the number and/or amount of **contributions** received by the **charitable organization** that is being served by the fundraiser. [FR § 3.2(g); SM p. 149] (cf. **Commission**; **Percentage-based compensation**).

F

flat tax

The concept of a "flat tax" is an **income tax** based on a system that does not contain any tax **deductions, credits, exclusions, exemptions**, or other **tax preferences**. [CG § 1.6; HC § 3.2].

flip charitable reminder unitrust

The "flip charitable remainder unitrust" is one of four allowable forms of **charitable remainder unitrusts**. This type of trust is permitted to convert (flip) once from one of the two **income-exception methods** to the **fixed percentage** method for purposes of calculating the required **unitrust amount**. [CG §§ 12.1(a), 12.3(a), 12.4(h)].

floating easement

One of the types of **qualified real property interests** is the **easement**, which is required to be in perpetuity. That requirement is violated if the **donor** is permitted to change the property subject to the easement; this is a form of "floating easement." [CG § 9.7(a)].

floor

The term "floor" is used in the **tax law** context to mean a threshold that must be exceeded before a particular tax feature (usually a **deduction**) can be utilized. For example, in the **federal tax law**, there is a 2 percent floor on **miscellaneous itemized deductions** (IRC § 67(a)). There are proposals, from time to time, to place a floor under the **federal income tax charitable contribution deduction**.

flow-through entity

A "flow-through entity" is an organization such as a **partnership, limited liability company**, other form of **joint venture**, or an **S corporation**. These **entities** are so named because they are not taxable. Rather, their **tax** items (**income, deductions, credits**, and the like) flow through to the **members** or shareholders. [EO §§ 19.23, 31.1(a), 32.4; UB §§ 8.2, 8.10; CU Q 16.6; PG pp. 150–151; SM p. 136].

flow-through rule

The term "flow-through rule" is used to describe a provision of **law** that causes a rule that initially applies at, or in connection with, one level or **person** to continue or additionally apply to another level or person. For example, the **lobbying disallowance rule** and the **political activities disallowance rule** contains a "flow-through rule" that causes the rules to apply with respect to a portion of **dues** paid to **membership organizations** (IRC § 162(e)(3)). [AS §§ 4.2(b)(i), 4.5(b); EO §§ 22.6(b), 23.7; AR §§ 21.1(a), 21.2(a), 21.2(c), 21.2(f); SM p. 192] (also **Look-through rule**).

fluid recovery principles

Court distribution of damages in the aftermath of a class action lawsuit may entail allocation of the funds to one or more **charitable organizations**. **Cy pres** principles are invoked in this context; this is termed "fluid recovery." [EO § 6.3(g)].

Food and Energy Security Act of 2008

The "Food and Energy Security Act of 2008" is one of a number of items of legislation that extended the special rules for **capital gain real property** and the special rules pertaining to **charitable deductions** for **farmers** and **ranchers**. [CG §§ 9.7(i), 9.7(j)].

football league, professional

A "professional football league" (and many other professional sports leagues) is a **tax-exempt organization** (**IRC** § 501(c)(6)). These **entities** function in the nature of **associations**, with the **members** being **for-profit** sports teams. [EO § 19.20].

for the benefit of

An act of **self-dealing** involving a **private foundation** can occur where a benefit is not provided to a **disqualified person**. This type of act can take place where a private foundation engages in a transaction with one or more persons who are not disqualified persons, where the **income** or **assets** of a private foundation are utilized "for the benefit of" one or more disqualified persons (**IRC** § 4941(d)(1)(E)). [PF § 5.8(c); EO § 12.4(a)].

for the use of

A **person** may make a **contribution** "for the use of" a **charitable organization**, rather than a contribution to a charitable **entity**. This terminology means that the gift is not made **directly** to the charitable organization but is made to another person (which may also be a charitable organization) under circumstances where the **gift** is in essence made in **trust** for the beneficiary charitable organization. A broader interpretation of the term is that a contribution for the use of a charitable organization includes any transfer of money or **property** where it is to a third person but for the benefit of a charitable organization. Contributions for the use of a charitable organization are subject to the **general 30 percent limitation** (**IRC** § 170(b)(1)(B)). [CG §§ 7.13, 10.3].

for the use by transaction

An act of **self-dealing** involving a **private foundation** can occur where a benefit is not provided to a **disqualified person**. This type of act can take place where a private foundation engages in a transaction where **income** or **assets** of the foundation are "used by" a disqualified person (**IRC** § 4941(d)(1)(E)). [EO § 12.4(a); PF § 5.8].

for the use of transaction

An **excess benefit transaction** involving an **applicable tax-exempt organization** can occur where an economic benefit is not provided to a **disqualified person**. This type of transaction can take place where an applicable tax-exempt organization provides an economic benefit for the "use of" a disqualified person (**IRC** § 4958(c)(1)(A)). [EO § 21.7].

for-profit organization

A "for-profit organization" is an **entity** that is **operated** for the financial benefit of its **owners**. The **profits** of the **enterprise** are passed through to them, such as the payment of **dividends** on shares of stock. This is what is meant by the term "for-profit organization"; the term does not relate to profits earned at the entity level but rather at the ownership level. As a general rule, a **tax-exempt organization** may own one or more for-profit organizations. [EO Chap. 30, § 1.1(a); HC Chap. 16, §§ 4.9(b), 8.2; PG p. 60; SM p. 5; CL § 1.3; CG § 1.2; LI Q 1.1] (also **Net earnings**; **Nonprofit organization**; **Private inurement**).

foreclosure property

The term "foreclosure property" means any **real property** acquired by a financial institution (as defined in **IRC** § 514(c)(9)(H)(iv)) as the result of having bid on the property at foreclosure, or by **operation** of an **agreement** or process of **law**, after there was a default (or default was imminent) on indebtedness which the property secured (**IRC** § 514(c)(9)(H)(v)). This term is used in the setting of defining a **qualifying sale**, in connection with part of the **unrelated debt-financed income rules**. [UB § 5.4(f); EO § 24.9(c)].

foreign organization

The term "foreign organization" has two basic meanings. One of them is that it is an **organization** that is **organized** and **operating** in a country other than the United States. A foreign organization may be a **charitable** entity. Some foreign charitable organizations have U.S.-based charitable organizations that are related to and engage in acts of **fundraising** for them. Contributions by U.S. donors to foreign charities are generally not deductible. Foreign organizations are taxed on their **unrelated business income** that is **effectively connected** with the conduct of a **trade or business** in the U.S. and on unrelated income derived from sources within the U.S., even though not so effectively connected (**IRC** § 512(a)(2)).

In the **private foundation law** context, a "foreign organization" is defined as any organization that was not created or organized in the U.S. or any U.S. possession, or under the law of the U.S., any state, the District of Columbia. or any possession of the U.S. Federal law imposes an annual 4 percent **excise tax** on the **gross investment income**, derived by a foreign organization that is a private foundation, derived from sources within the U.S. (**IRC** § 4948(a)).

The second meaning of the term "foreign organization" arises out of use of the term in the state law context. When an organization (**nonprofit** or **for-profit**) is **organized** in one state but is **doing business** in one or more other states, it is considered a foreign organization by the states other than that in which it is organized. [EO § 29.2(e); UB § 6.2(d); PF § 10.5; PG pp. 3, 23–24, 221; AR §§ 13.1(b), 13.2(b); SM p. 11] (cf. **Domestic organization**).

foreign source income

A **look-through rule** characterizes certain "foreign source income," namely, income from insurance activities conducted by offshore captives of **tax-exempt organizations**, as **unrelated business income** (**IRC** § 512(b)(17)(A)). Generally, U.S. shareholders of controlled foreign corporations must include in **income** their shares of the foreign entities' income, including certain insurance income (**IRC** §§ 951(a)(1)(A), 953). In most instances, foreign source income received by **exempt organizations** can be characterized as nontaxable dividends by use of **blocker corporations**. [UB §§ 3.2, 3.15; EO §§ 25.1(b), 25.1(n)].

Form 211

The "Form 211" as developed by the **IRS** is the application by which an informant, having provided information leading to **audit** (and perhaps **revocation** of **tax exemption**) of an **exempt organization**, applies for a monetary award. [AU § 5.3(c)] (also **Referral**).

Form 706

The "Form 706" as developed by the **IRS** is the **federal estate** and **generation-skipping tax return**. This return is generally required of **gross estates** having a **value** in excess of $600,000 (**IRC** § 6018(a)).

Form 730

The "Form 730" as developed by the **IRS** is the monthly return filed by **tax-exempt** and other **organizations** that conduct wagering, lotteries, or are otherwise in the business of accepting wagers, and by which the wagering tax (**IRC** § 4401(a)) is paid. [AR § 14.2(c); AU §§ 5.4(d), 5.18(b)(ii)].

Form 843

The "Form 843" as developed by the **IRS** is the claim for refund of **tax** that may be filed by **tax-exempt organizations** and other **persons**. [AU § 5.34].

Form 851

Generally, the consolidated **return** rules (**IRC** § 1501) are inapplicable with respect to **tax-exempt organizations**. An exception may be available in the case of a **title-holding company** and its **parent exempt organization** (**IRC** § 1504(a)). When it is, a "Form 851" as developed by the **IRS** must be attached to the consolidated return. [UB § 11.5(i)].

Form 872

The "Form 872" as developed by the **IRS** is the consent to extend a **statute of limitations** (that is, extend the period for a **tax assessment**). It is common for a **tax-exempt organization** to execute (or at least be asked to execute) one or more of these consents during the course of an **IRS examination**. [AU §§ 3.10, 5.10, 5.16].

Form 906

The "Form 906" as developed by the **IRS** is the prototype **closing agreement** that is generally used in the **tax-exempt organizations** context. [AU § 1.10(b)].

Form 940

The "Form 940" as developed by the **IRS** is the **employer's** annual federal unemployment tax return, filed by most **tax-exempt organizations** and other employers. [AR § 4.1(e); AU §§ 5.4(d), 5.18(b)(ii), 5.33(b), 7.1(p); SM p. 127].

Form 941

The "Form 941" as developed by the **IRS** is the **employer's** quarterly federal tax return, filed by most **tax-exempt organizations**. [AR § 4.1(e); AU §§ 5.2(a), 5.4(d), 5.18(b)(ii), 5.33(b), 7.1(p); SM p. 127].

Form 945

The "Form 945" as developed by the **IRS** is the annual return of withheld federal income taxes, filed by most **tax-exempt organizations**. [AU § 5.18(b)(ii)].

Form 990

The "Form 990" as developed by the **IRS** is the **annual information return** that the larger **tax-exempt organizations** are required to prepare and file with the **IRS** (**IRC** § 6033(b)). [AR passim; GV Chap. 4, §§ 2.1(e), 3.2(c), 3.13, 3.14(e)–3.14(g), 5.2(b), 5.3(c), 5.10(b), 5.14(a), 5.14(b), 5.15(b), 5.15(c), 5.17(a), 5.17(b), 5.18(b), 5.18(c), 5.19(b), 5.21(a), 5.21(e), 6.0–6.2, 6.3(b)–6.3(d), 6.3(f)–6.3(i), 6.3(k), 6.3(m)–.6.3(o), 6.3(s)–6.3(u), 8.8(a); EO §§ 5.1(b), 5.6(g), 11.9, 12.3(b), 20.4(d), 21.4(c), 22.3(x), 28.1(a), 28.2(a), 28.2(b)(i), 28.3, 28.6, 28.7(a), 30.3(a); PG Chap. 9, pp. 35, 347–348; AU §§ 1.13, 3.1(g), 4.5, 4.9(b), 5.2(a), 5.3(c), 5.4(d), 5.18(b)(ii), 5.18(e), 7.1(bb), 7.3(a), 7.4; CG §§ 24.5, 24.5(a), 24.7(b); FR §§ 5.9(a), 5.9(k), 7.4(a)(i); HC §§ 1.0, 5.5(d), 6.3, 8.1, 8.4, 22.5, 26.7, 26.10(b), 26.10(c), 28.2-28.3(c), 28.4, 30.4(c), 31.2(k), 33.5, 35.4(b), 35.7(b), 36.3(d), 36.5; CU Chap. 17; PF §§ 12.1, 15.4(a), 15.5(c), 15.8(a), 15.8(b), 15.14; RE Q 9.1–Q 9.9, Q 12.1; AS §§ 10.1, 10.5–10.7, 11.1; UB § 11.3; SM pp. 15, 74, 95, 98–102, 109–116, 120, 124, 126, 146, 154–156, 271–272; LI Q 12.52, Q 12.54].

Form 1023

The "Form 1023" as developed by the **IRS** is the form by which an **organization** applies for **recognition** of **tax-exempt status** as a **charitable entity**. The filing of this form is mandatory for nearly all charitable organizations that desire recognition of tax-exempt status (**IRC** § 508(a)). [AR §§ 1.4, 2.1(g), 5.1(j), 5.2(c)(2); EO §§ 3.2, 5.5(c), 5.6(f), 26.1, 26.2, 28.7(b), 32.8(b); HC §§ 8.1, 14.1(e), 21.4(b), 33.3(d), 33.4, 34.1(a), 34.1(d), 35.4(b)(xxvi), 36.3(d); FR § 5.8(c); GV §§ 1.1(a), 3.2(c), 3.14(g), 5.14(a); PF §§ 2.5, 2.6, 12.3(d); RE Q 8.23, Q 8.38, Q 8.50, Q 8.51, Q 8.53–8.64; CU Q 3.51–Q 3.61; AS §§ 8.8(h), 11.1; PG pp. 34, 42–48, 57; SM pp. 15, 66–71, 74–75, 102; LI Q 2.47–Q 2.57].

Form 1024

The "Form 1024" as developed by the **IRS** is the form by which an **organization** applies for **recognition** of **tax-exempt** status as an organization other than a **charitable** entity or **farmers' cooperative**. The filing of this form is mandatory for certain **credit counseling organizations**, certain **health insurance issuers**, and certain **employee benefit organizations** (**IRC** §§ 501(c)(29)(B)(i), 501(q)(3), 505(c)(1)). [AR §§ 1.4, 5.1(j), 5.2(c)(2); EO §§ 3.2, 26.1, 26.5, 32.8(b); HC §§ 34.1(d), 35.4(b); AU § 5.21; RE Q 8.23; AS § 2.15; PG pp. 42, 50–52; SM p. 68] (also **Self-declarers**).

Form 1028

The "Form 1028" as developed by the **IRS** is the form by which a **farmers' cooperative** makes **application** to the **IRS** for **recognition** of **tax-exempt status**. [EO § 26.1; HC § 35.4(b)(xxvi); RE Q 8.23; PG p. 42].

Form 1040

The "Form 1040" as developed by the **IRS** is the **tax return** that most individuals are required to prepare and file with the **IRS** each year, reporting, among other items, **deductible charitable contributions** (IRC § 6012(a)(1)). [AR § 14.1(l)(3); CG §§ 24.1, 24.7(a); EO § 21.4(c); RE Q 22.10].

Form 1041

The "Form 1041" as developed by the **IRS** is the **tax return** for **estates** and **trusts**. [AR §§ 1.5(b), 4.1(t), 4.2(o); AU §§ 5.2(a), 5.33(l), 5.34; CG § 24.5(a); PF § 3.6; SM p. 110].

Form 1065

The "Form 1065" as developed by the **IRS** is the **information return** used to report the **income, gains, losses, deductions, credits**, and the like from operation of a **partnership**, including partnerships with **tax-exempt organizations** as **partners**. This return is also filed by **exempt apostolic organizations**. [EO §§ 28.2(b)(i), 31.6; RE Q 9.8, Q 14.44; CG §§ 24.4, 24.7(a); PF §§ 6.5(b), 11.5; AU § 3.1(g); PG p. 244; SM p. 110].

Form 1096

The "Form 1096" as developed by the **IRS** is the form used to annually transmit certain **federal tax information returns**, such as **Form 1098, Form 1099** series, and **Form W-2G** to the **IRS**. [AR §§ 1.5(e), 4.1(a), 4.2(a); AU §§ 5.4(d), 5.18(b)(ii), EO § 28.3(d); SM p. 127].

Form 1098

The "Form 1098" as developed by the **IRS** is the form used by **charitable organizations** in reporting **contributions** motor vehicles, boats, and airplanes. [CG §§ 24.5(a), 24.8; AR § 4.1(a); PF § 14.2].

Form 1099

The "Form 1099" as developed by the **IRS** is an **information return** that is prepared and provided by an **organization**, including a **tax-exempt organization**, to those who receive funds in excess of $600 from it (other than in the employment context), and filed with the **IRS** (IRC § 6041(a)). [AR § 4.1(a); AU §§ 3.1(g), 5.18(b)(ii), 5.19(f), 5.33(b); EO § 21.4(c); HC § 28.3(d); RE Q 22.10; AS § 10.1(e); SM p. 128].

Form 1120

The "Form 1120" as developed by the **IRS** is the **tax return** that most **corporations** (excluding most **tax-exempt organizations**) are required to prepare and file with the **IRS** each year (**IRC** § 6012(a)(2)). [AR § 14.1(l)(3); CG §§ 24.2, 24.7(a); SM p. 110].

Form 1122

For the first year a consolidated **return** is filed by a **title-holding company**, the entity must attach a "Form 1122" as developed by the **IRS**. [UB § 11.5(i)].

Form 1128

The "Form 1128" as developed by the **IRS** is titled "Application to Adopt, Change, or Retain a Tax Year." [UB § 11.5(b); RE Q 12.1].

F

Form 1139

The "Form 1139" as developed by the **IRS** is titled "Corporate Application for Tentative Refund from Net Carryover Operating Loss," which may be filed by a **tax-exempt organization**. [AU § 5.34].

Form 1254

Action on some **IRS audit** cases, including those involving **tax-exempt organizations**, may have to be suspended to ensure uniform and consistent treatment of the issue(s); this occurs, for example, in connection with cases having nationwide implications. These cases are known as "Form 1254 suspense cases" because they are forwarded to a mandatory review office by means of "Form 1254" as developed by the **IRS**. [AU § 5.30].

Form 2220

The "Form 2220" as developed by the **IRS** is used by a **tax-exempt organization** filing an **unrelated business income tax return** to determine whether the organization owes a **penalty** and, if so, to compute the amount of the penalty. [UB § 11.5(h)(v)].

Form 2297

When a **claim** filed by a **tax-exempt organization** for an **income** or **excise tax** refund is disallowed in whole or in part, the **IRS** examiner will prepare the appropriate paperwork: the **examination** closing letter, report form(s), and agreement form. If the agreed or unagreed portion of a case involves an excise tax, one of the agreement forms is "Form 2297" as developed by the **IRS**. [AU §§ 5.32(b), 5.34].

Form 2758

The "Form 2758" as developed by the **IRS** is used by **tax-exempt organizations** seek an extension of the due date for an **annual information return.** [RE Q 9.11].

Form 2807

A **tax-exempt organization** (like any **person** subject to **tax**) is required to maintain adequate books and financial records (**IRC § 6001**). The **IRS** issues "inadequate records notices" to alert taxpayers that their recordkeeping practices are deficient and must be improved in accordance with the law. When an **IRS** examiner and his or her group manger determine that a notice is appropriate, the examiner will prepare an agreement to maintain adequate books of account and records, and attempt to obtain the **exempt organization's** (or other taxpayer's) execution of the agreement. This agreement is the subject of "Form 2807" as developed by the **IRS**. [AU § 5.25; EO § 28.18].

Form 2848

The "Form 2848" as developed by the **IRS** is the **power of attorney** form and the **declaration of representative** form that an **organization** uses when it is applying for **recognition** of **tax exemption** and is being represented in that regard by a **lawyer, accountant**, or other qualified representative. [EO § 26.1(e); AU §§ 3.4, 3.10, 5.16; PF § 2.5(a); RE Q 8.35; PG p. 42; SM p. 68].

Form 3115

The "Form 3115" as developed by the **IRS** is used by a **tax-exempt organization** filing an **unrelated business income tax return** to change to a method of **valuing** inventory that is permitted for **federal income tax law** purposes. [UB §§ 11.4(g), 11.5(a); AS § 10.1(a)(viii)].

Form 3363

When a **claim** filed by a **tax-exempt organization** for an **income** or **excise tax** refund is disallowed in whole or in part, the **IRS** examiner will prepare the appropriate paperwork: the **examination** closing letter, report form(s), and agreement form. If the agreed or unagreed portion of a case involves an excise tax, one of the agreement forms is "Form 3363" as developed by the **IRS**. [AU §§ 5.32(b), 5.34].

Form 4549

There are a number of situations in which a **tax-exempt organization examination** case will be closed. An examination may close with the **exempt organization** agreeing to the **IRS's** position as to a change in **exempt status**, **public charity status**, and/or **tax liability**, and thus executing the appropriate waiver and acceptance forms. One of these forms is the "Form 4549" as developed by the **IRS**. [AU §§ 5.32(a), 5.32(b), 5.33(c), 5.33(d), 5.33(i), 5.34, 5.35(a)].

Form 4564

Once an **IRS examination** of a **tax-exempt organization** is initiated, the revenue agent(s) involved will begin the process of collecting documents and other information. The formal procedure is for the **IRS** to seek this information by submitting to the **exempt organization** one or more written requests for information, in the form of "information document request." This IDR is the subject of "Form 4564" as developed by the **IRS**. [AU §§ 1.4, 3.2(c), 3.10, 5.4(c), 5.18(a)(v)].

Form 4621

In **examination** cases resulting in proposed changes in a **tax-exempt organization's tax liability**, the proposed changes will be presented in an **IRS** report of examination ("Form 4621" as developed by the **IRS**). [AU §§ 5.32(b), 5.33(c), 5.33(d), 5.33(h), 5.33(k), 5.34, 5.35(a), 5.35(c)].

Form 4720

The "Form 4720" as developed by the **IRS** is the **tax return** by which **public charities, private foundations**, and **charitable remainder trusts**, and/or other **persons** (including **disqualified persons**) pay one or more **excise taxes** (imposed by **IRC** Chapters 41 and 42). [AR §§ 4.1(i), 4.1(m), 4.2(k), 4.2(l); AU §§ 1.13, 5.2(a), 5.4(g), 5.33(b), 5.33(j), 5.33(k), 5.34; EO §§ 21.14, 22.3(d)(iii), 22.4, 23.4, 28.2(a)(iv), 28.9(a)(ii); PF §§ 1.8, 5.15, 6.7(d), 7.6, 9.10(b), 12.2, 12.3(b), 12.3(c), 12.3(e); HC § 35.4(b)(xxvi); RE Q 22.40; AS § 3.8(h); PG p. 75].

Form 4883

In **examination** cases resulting in proposed changes in a **tax-exempt organization's excise tax liability**, the proposed changes will be presented in an **IRS** report of examination ("Form 4883" as developed by the **IRS**). [AU §§ 5.32(b), 5.33(d), 5.34, 5.35(a), 5.35(e)].

Form 5227

Split-interest trusts must annually file an **information return** with the **IRS**. The return is the subject of "Form 5227" as developed by the **IRS**. [AU §§ 5.2(a), 5.4(d), 5.33(l); CG § 24.12; SM p. 128].

Form 5464

In connection with an **IRS examination** of a **tax-exempt organization**, the **IRS** reviewer will prepare a "case chronology record" to inventory various actions taken in connection with the case, contacts made, follow-up dates, and time expended; this record is the subject of "Form 5464" as developed by the **IRS**. [AU § 5.16].

Form 5500

The "Form 5500" as developed by the **IRS** is the principal form by which **employee benefit plans** report to the agency. [SM p. 127].

Form 5701

The "Form 5701" as developed by the **IRS** is the agency's notice of proposed adjustment. [EO § 27.7].

Form 5768

The "Form 5768" as developed by the **IRS** is the form by which a qualified **public charity** makes the **election** to have its **lobbying** activities subjected to the **expenditure test**. [EO § 22.3(d)(vi); CU Q 8.17; PG pp. 112, 340].

Form 5772

As part of the **IRS's** preexamination planning, the **IRS** reviewer involved is required to prepare an "exempt organization workpaper summary," which is a list of procedural and technical reminders. This summary is the subject of "Form 5772" as developed by the **IRS**. [AU §§ 5.17, 5.18(e), 5.33(a)].

Form 5773

As a follow-on to its **Form 5772**, the **IRS** has developed a "workpaper summary continuation sheet," which is used to index the workpapers; document the analysis of books, records, and materials relating to the issues identified for **examination**; and summarize the audit steps. This continuation sheet is the subject of "Form 5773" as developed by the **IRS**. [AU §§ 5.17, 5.18(e), 5.33(a)].

Form 5774

If the **organization** to be **examined** is a **private foundation**, "Form 5774" as developed by the **IRS** is utilized rather than **Form 5772**. [AU §§ 5.17, 5.18(e)].

Form 5788

The **IRS** has **examination** procedures for **private schools**. One of the principal issues that will be visited is whether the school has adopted and operated in accordance with a racially nondiscriminatory policy as to students. To this end, the **IRS** examiner will complete a "private school checksheet," which is the subject of "Form 5788" as developed by the **IRS**. [AU § 7.1(d)].

Form 6018

The "consent to proposed action" is a document used by the **IRS** to secure (if it can) agreement from an **examined tax-exempt organization**, that is eligible to use the special **declaratory judgment** procedure (**IRC** § 7428), as to a proposed status change. This consent form is the subject of "Form 6018" as developed by the **IRS**. [AU §§ 3.10(vi), 5.32(b), 5.33(e), 5.33(g), 5.33(h), 5.35(d)].

Form 6069

The **tax** on excess contributions to **black lung benefit trusts** is paid on a **tax return**, which is the subject of "Form 6069" as developed by the **IRS**. [AU § 5.33(k)].

Form 8109

If a **tax-exempt organization** does not use the electronic **tax** payment system, it must deposit **unrelated business income tax** payments and estimated tax payment with "Form 8109" as developed by the **IRS**. [UB § 11.5(g)].

Form 8274

The "Form 8274" as developed by the **IRS** is the form by which a **church** or a **qualified church-controlled organization** makes an **election** to **exclude** from the **Federal Insurance Contribution Act tax** base remuneration for all services performed for it (other than in an **unrelated trade or business**), with the **employees** of the electing organization liable for **self-employment taxes** with respect to the excluded services. This election may be made only where the **employer** organization states that it is opposed for **religious** reasons to the payment of the tax (**IRC** §§ 3121(b)(8)(B), 3121(w)(1), (2)). [EO § 3.3(h)].

Form 8282

A **charitable organization** that disposes of **charitable deduction property** within three years of its receipt is required to file an **information return**. This return is the subject of "Form 8282" as developed by the **IRS**. [AR §§ 1.5(e), 4.1(l), 4.2(g), 14.3(e)(2), 19.1(t), 19.1(v); AU § 7.6(e); CG § 24.10; FR § 5.14(k); EO § 28.3(d); HC § 35.7(b)(xx); CU Q 18.28–Q 18.31; PG pp. 245–246, 349; SM p. 126].

Form 8283

A **donor** uses "Form 8283" as developed by the **IRS** to report required information concerning the donor's **noncash charitable contributions**. [AR §§ 14.3(e)(2), 19.1(u), 19.1(v), 19.1(y)(1), 19.1(y)(4), 19.2(r); AU § 7.6(e); CG § 24.7(a); PF § 14.6(c); CU Q 18.29, Q 18.30; RE Q 13.28; PG pp. 243–245, 248–250, 349; SM p. 114; LI Q 12.63].

Form 8633

Tax professionals who plan to electronically file **returns** for **tax-exempt organizations** must first submit an electronic e-file application, which is "Form 8633" as developed by the **IRS**. [EO § 28.7(b); AS § 10.1(e)(i)].

Form 8718

The "Form 8718" as developed by the **IRS** is the form used to compute the appropriate **user fee** for a request for a **determination letter** that an **organization** qualifies as a **tax-exempt organization**. [EO § 26.1(d)].

Form 8821

The "Form 8821" as developed by the **IRS** when an **organization** wants to authorize an individual or organization to receive or inspect confidential **tax return** information but does not want to authorize that individual or organization to represent it before the **IRS**. [AU § 3.4].

Form 8822

The "Form 8822" as developed by the **IRS** is used by **tax-exempt organizations** to notify the IRS of their change of address. [AR § 1.4].

Form 8832

The "Form 8832" as developed by the **IRS** is used in implementation of the **check-the-box regulations** as part of the **entity** classification process. [EO § 4.1(b)(i); AS § 6.10(a)].

Form 8868

The "Form 8868" as developed by the **IRS** is the form used to apply for an extension of time to file a **return** due by a **tax-exempt organization**. [EO §§ 28.7(a), 28.8; UB § 11.5(c); AS § 10.1(e); PF § 12.2].

Form 8871

Generally, for an **organization** to be treated as a **tax-exempt political organization**, it must provide **notice** to the **IRS** of its existence (IRC § 527(i)). This notice, which is the subject of

"Form 8871" as developed by the **IRS**, must be electronically submitted no later than twenty-four hours after establishment of the organization. [EO § 26.9; AU § 3.1(g); AS § 4.7(a); CG § 24.5(c); SM pp. 26, 65, 125].

Form 8872

The "Form 8872" as developed by the **IRS** is the return form that most **political organizations** must file if it has accepted a **contribution** or made an **expenditure** for an **exempt function**. The timing of this filing varies. [EO § 28.6; AU § 3.1(g); AS §§ 4.7(a), 10.1(d); CG § 24.5(c); SM pp. 110, 125].

Form 8899

Certain **tax-exempt organizations** that receive **income** as the consequence of receiving a **charitable contribution** of **qualified intellectual property** are required to file with the **IRS** "Form 8899" as developed by that agency. [AR §§ 4.1(n), 4.2(i), 19.1(g)(2); CG §§ 24.5(a), 24.9].

Form 8940

The "Form 8940" as developed by the **IRS** is used to transmit a request for advance approval of **set-asides** to be made in accordance with the **suitability test**, advance approval of **private foundation voter registration activities**, advance approval of private foundation **scholarship** approval, **exemption** from the **Form 990** filing requirements, advance approval as to an **unusual grant**, initial determination of or change in type of **supporting organization**, reclassification of **public charity** or private foundation **status**, or **termination** of private foundation status. [PF §§ 6.5(e), 9.2(c), 9.3(g), 13.1, 13.3, 15.5(c), 15.7(g), 15.8(d)].

Form 8960

The "Form 8960" as developed by the **IRS** is used to compute the **net investment income tax** (**IRC** § 1411) that must be paid by **pooled income funds** and certain **charitable lead trusts**, as well as individuals and **estates**. [CG §§ 2.15(b), 24.12].

Form 13790

The "Form 13790" as developed by the **IRS** is the questionnaire utilized by the agency in launching its **compliance check** of **tax-exempt hospitals**. [HC § 6.3].

Form 13909

The "Form 13909" as developed by the **IRS** is used for the submission of complaints about **tax-exempt organizations**, known as **referrals**, to the **IRS**.

Form 14017

The "Form 14017" as developed by the **IRS** is the application to the **fast-track case settlement program**. [EO § 27.7].

Form 14018

The "Form 14018" as developed by the **IRS** is the most important and useful (and largest) of the agency's **compliance check** questionnaires. This questionnaire was used to extract data concerning the operations of the nation's **colleges** and **universities**. The results were published in an interim report dated May 7, 2010, and a final report dated April 25, 2013. [EO §§ 5.7(c), 8.3(a)(ii), 11.9(a), 11.9(b), 20.4(a); GV § 6.4].

Form 14114

The "Form 14114" as developed by the **IRS** is the agency's "governance check sheet" that its **examination** agents use to gather data about the **governance** practices of **public charities**. [EO § 5.7(f); HC § 33.3(c)].

F

Form 14395

The "Form 14395" as developed by the **IRS** is the **compliance check** questionnaire used by the agency in launching its inquiry of **tax-exempt workers' compensation reinsurance organizations**. [EO § 27.7].

Form 14414

The "Form 14414" as developed by the **IRS** is the **compliance check** questionnaire used by the agency in launching its inquiry into **tax-exempt organizations** that maintain a **group exemption**. [EO § 27.7].

Form 14449

The "Form 14449" as developed by the **IRS** is the **compliance check** questionnaire used by the agency in launching its inquiry of **self-declarers**. [EO § 27.7].

Form i1023

The "Form i1023" as developed by the **IRS** is the interactive **Form 1023**, which uses a computer-based program that guides **entities** that desire to be **tax-exempt charitable organizations** through the **exemption recognition** process. [EO § 26.1(h)].

Form 11-C

Tax-exempt organizations and other **persons** are required to file (when applicable) the occupational tax and registration **return** for wagering. This return is the subject of "Form 11-C" as developed by the **IRS**. [AR § 14.2(c); AU §§ 5.4(d), 5.18(b)(ii)].

Form 870-E

There are a number of situations in which a **tax-exempt organization examination** case will be closed. An examination may close with the **exempt organization** agreeing to the **IRS's** position as to a change in **exempt status**, **public charity status**, and/or **tax liability**, and thus executing the appropriate waiver and acceptance forms. One of these forms is the "Form 870-E" as developed by the **IRS**. [AU §§ 5.32(a), 5.32(b), 5.33(j), 5.34].

Form 886-A

In many **examinations** of **tax-exempt organizations**, the **IRS's** "explanation of items" will be, from the organization's standpoint, the most important of the agency's forms. It is on this form that the **IRS** will write, usually in some detail, its views as to the issues, facts, **law**, the organization's and government's positions, and the government's conclusion(s) as to how the case should be resolved. This explanation is the subject of "Form 886-A" as developed by the **IRS**. [AU §§ 3.10, 5.32(b), 5.33(c), 5.33(d), 5.33(f), 5.33(h), 5.33(i), 5.33(k), 5.34, 5.35(a), 5.35(c), 5.35(d)].

Form 990-BL

The "Form 990-BL" as developed by the **IRS** is the **annual information return** that every **black lung benefits trust** is required to prepare and file with the **IRS**. [EO § 28.2; AU § 5.33(k); PG p. 188; SM p. 110].

Form 990-C

The "Form 990-C" as developed by the **IRS** is the **annual information return** that certain **cooperatives** are required to prepare and file with the **IRS**. [SM p. 110].

Form 990-EZ

The "Form 990-EZ" as developed by the **IRS** is the **annual information return** that most mid-sized **tax-exempt organizations** are required to prepare and file with the **IRS** (IRC § 6033). Generally, organizations with **gross receipts** that are less than $200,000 and total **assets** with a **value** that is less than $500,000 at the end of the reporting year are eligible to file this return. Certain **controlling organizations**, **hospital organizations**, **sponsoring organizations**, and **supporting organizations**, however, are ineligible to file this return; they must file **Form 990**. [AR §§ 1.1(a), 1.1(d), 1.9, 2.2(b), 8.0, 8.1(g)(2), 8.3(b), 14.3(e); EO §§ 28.2(a)(ii), 28.4, 28.6, 28.7(a); HC §§ 35.3(a)(ii), 35.4(b)(xxvi); AU §§ 5.2(a), 5.4(d), 5.18(b)(ii), 7.4; PF §§ 2.7(b), 12.1, 15.8(b); CG §§ 24.5, 24.5(b), 24.5(c); RE Q 9.8, Q 9.9; AS §§ 10.1, 10.7; PG pp. 188, 227, 230, 347; SM pp. 30, 110, 120; LI Q 12.52, Q 12.53].

Form 990-N

The "Form 990-N" as developed by the **IRS** is the **notice** that must be electronically **submitted** each year by **tax-exempt organizations** (other than **private foundations**) with gross receipts of no more than $50,000 (**IRC** § 6033(i)). [AR § 1.1(a); EO § 28.4; CG § 24.5; PF § 12.1; RE Q 8.71; SM pp. 116–117, 121] (also **e-Postcard**).

Form 990-PF

The "Form 990-PF" as developed by the **IRS** is the **annual information return** that all **private foundations** are required to prepare and file with the **IRS** each year (**IRC** § 6033). [AR §§ 1.1(a), 14.3(e); PF §§ 2.7, 12.1, 12.2; AU §§ 3.1(g), 5.2(a), 5.4(d), 5.18(b)(ii), 5.33(j), 5.34; EO §§ 28.2, 28.7(a); HC §§ 5.5(d), 35.3, 35.4(b)(xxvi); CG § 24.5; GV § 4.0; AS §§ 10.1, 10.7; PG pp. 188, 347; SM pp. 110, 119–120].

Form 990-T

The "Form 990-T" as developed by the **IRS** is the **tax return** by which a **tax-exempt organization** reports its **unrelated business taxable income** to the IRS (IRC §§ 6012(a)(2), (4)). [AR

§§ 1.1(a), 1.1(e), 1.5(a), 1.5(e), 1.7, 4.1(g), 4.2(b), 4.2(m), 5.1(j), 5.2(c)(2); UB §§ 11.4, 11.5; AU §§ 1.12, 3.1(g), 5.2(a), 5.3(c), 5.4(d), 5.4(g), 5.18(b)(ii), 5.18(e), 5.33(b), 5.33(i), 5.34; EO §§ 28.2(a)(v), 28.3(d), 28.7(a), 28.8; HC §§ 22.5, 35.3(a)(iii), 35.4(b)(xxvi); AS §§ 10.1, 10.7; PF §§ 2.7(b), 11.5, 12.2, 12.3(b); CG § 24.6; GV §§ 3.14(g), 5.14(a); RE Q 8.15, Q 9.2, Q 9.9, Q 23.30; SM pp. 102, 110, 125. 126; LI Q 13.42].

Form 990-W

The "Form 990-W" as developed by the **IRS** is the form by which estimated **tax on unrelated business taxable income** for **tax-exempt organizations** and the **investment income** tax for **private foundations** is remitted. [AR §§ 1.1(a), 4.1(g); UB § 11.5(e); PF §§ 11.5, 12.2; PG p. 188].

Form 1023-EZ

The "Form 1023-EZ" is a **streamlined application for recognition of exemption that** may be filed by an **eligible organization** seeking recognition of **tax exemption** as a **charitable organization**. This application, which must be filed electronically, is a three-page application, with no attachments required. The application is a series of attestations, consisting of an eligibility worksheet and checking of boxes to attest to compliance with various requirements of law. [EO § 26.1(h)].

Form 1041-A

The "Form 1041-A" as developed by the **IRS** is the **information return** filed by **fiduciaries** of nonexempt **charitable trusts**. This return is used to verify that amounts for which a **charitable deduction** was claimed are devoted to charitable purposes. [AU § 5.33(l)].

Form 1065-B

The "Form 1065-B" as developed by the **IRS** is an **information return** that **partnerships** may have to file with the **IRS**. [CG §§ 24.4, 24.7(a)].

Form 1098-C

The "Form 1098-C" as developed by the **IRS** is used by **donee charitable organizations** to report, to the agency, **contributions (IRC § 528)** of **qualified vehicles** and to provide the **donor** with a **contemporaneous written acknowledgement** of the gift. [AR §§ 1.5(e), 4.1(o), 4.2(j), 19.1(g)(4), 19.2(e); EO § 28.3(d); CG § 24.8; HC § 31.2(f)].

Form 1099-MISC

The "Form 1099-MISC" as developed by the **IRS** is used by an **organization** to report various types of miscellaneous **income** paid to an individual who is not an **employee** of the organization. [AR §§ 6.2(a)(1), 6.2(c)(11)].

Form 1120-H

The "Form 1120-H" as developed by the **IRS** is a **tax return** filed by **homeowners' associations** that **elect** to be **taxed**. [EO §§ 19.14, 26.1; SM p. 110].

Form 1120-POL

The "Form 1120-POL" as developed by the **IRS** is the **annual tax return** that **political organizations** are required to prepare and file with the **IRS** (**IRC** § 6012(a)(6)). [AU §§ 3.1(g), 5.2(a), 5.4(d), 5.4(g), 5.18(b)(ii), 5.34; EO §§ 17.1(b), 17.5, 27.6(a)(ii), 28.5(a), 28.7(a); AS §§ 10.1, 10.5; PG p. 188; SM pp. 30, 110].

Form 4506-A

A **tax-exempt organization** may request a copy of an **annual information return** it has filed with the **IRS**; the form for making this request is "Form 4506-A" as developed by the agency. [RE Q 9.14].

Form 4549-A

Form 4549 is designed to cover an **examination** period of up to three years. If the period is longer, the form the **IRS** uses is its "Form 4549-A. [AU §§ 5.32(b), 5.33(d), 5.33(i), 5.35(a)].

Form 4621-A

Accompanying a **Form 886-A** is the **IRS's** "report of examination," which likely will entail status changes, such as **revocation** of **exemption** or change in status from that of **public charity** to that of a form of **private foundation**. This report is the subject of "Form 4621-A" as developed by the **IRS**. [AU §§ 3.10, 5.32(b), 5.33(c), 5.33(d), 5.33(f), 5.35(d)].

Form 6018-A

The **IRS** developed "Form 6018-A" for use in consent arrangements with **tax-exempt organizations**, where the issue involved is not one embraced by the special **declaratory judgment** rules. That is, this form is used in these circumstances under which **Form 6018** is not appropriate. [AU §§ 5.32(b), 5.33(f), 5.35(d)].

Form 8886-T

A **tax-exempt entity** that files **Form 990** and is a party to a **prohibited tax shelter transaction** must file "Form 8886-T" as developed by the **IRS** for the purpose of **disclosure** of its participation in the shelter. [AR §§ 1.5(e), 4.1(i), 4.2(d); EO § 28.3(d)].

Form SS-4

The "Form SS-4" as developed by the **IRS** is the form by which an **organization** makes application for an **employer identification number**. [EO § 25.1(b); SM pp. 22, 68].

Form SS-8

The "Form SS-8" as developed by the **IRS** is filed with the agency when a private ruling is desired as to the proper **federal tax law** classification of workers (**employees** or **independent contractors**). [HC § 27.5].

Form W-2

The "Form W-2" as developed by the **IRS** is the **information return** that is prepared and provided by an **employer**, including a **tax-exempt organization**, to its **employees**, and filed with the **IRS** each year. [AR §§ 6.2(a)(1), 6.2(c)(11); AU §§ 3.1(g), 5.4(d), 5.18(b)(ii), 5.33(b); EO §§ 21.4(c), 28.6(b); HC §§ 28.3(d), 31.2(g); AS §§ 10.1, 10.7; RE Q 21.2, Q 22.10; SM pp. 127, 141].

Form W-2G

The "Form W-2G" as developed by the **IRS** is an **information return** much like the **Form W-2**, except that its use is confined to the reporting of gambling winnings. [AR §§ 1.5(e), 4.1(a), 4.1(b), 4.2(a), 14.1(l)(3); AU §§ 3.1(g), 5.33(b); EO § 28.3(d)].

Form W-2P

The "Form W-2P" as developed by the **IRS** is an **information return** stating amounts distributed as **annuities** or pension payments. [SM p. 127].

Form W-3

The "Form W-3" as developed by the **IRS** is a transmittal form to accompany the filing of one or more forms in the **Form W-2** series. [AR §§ 1.5(e), 4.1(d), 4.2(a); AU § 5.18(b)(ii); EO § 28.3(d); SM p. 127].

Form W-12

One of the ways a **tax return preparer** can obtain a **preparer tax identification number** is by filing a "Form W-12" as developed by the **IRS**. [EO § 28.3(z); HC § 35.4(b)(xxvi)].

form, change in

A change in organizational form generally is regarded by the **IRS** as the creation of a new legal **entity** requiring the filing of an **application for recognition of exemption** for the successor entity (assuming one is mandated), even though the **organization's** purposes, methods of operation, sources of **support**, and **accounting method** remain the same as they were in its predecessor form. [EO § 28.1(b)].

forfeiture of tax exemption

Generally, there is no procedure for voluntarily forfeiting **tax exempt status**, once the **IRS** has **recognized** the **tax exemption** of an **organization**. The IRS has, however, developed a procedure by which a **dual-status entity** may voluntarily terminate its status as a **charitable** organization. [EO § 26.11].

foundation manager

The **federal tax law** defines a type of **disqualified person**, in the **private foundation law** context, as a "foundation manager" (**IRC** §§ 4946(a)(1)(B), 4946(b)(1)). A foundation manager is an **officer**, **director**, or **trustee** of a private foundation, or an individual having powers or responsibilities similar to one of these three positions. An individual is considered an officer of a private foundation if he or she is specifically so designated under the **governing instruments** of the **organization** or if he or she regularly exercises general authority to make administrative or policy decisions on behalf of the organization. [PF §§ 4.2, 8.4, 9.10(a), 9.10(c), 12.2(e), 13.2; EO § 12.2(b); SM pp. 90–91] (cf. **Entity manager**; **Fund manager**; **Organization manager**).

founder

A "founder" of an **organization** is a (or the) **person** who created the **entity**. Usually, when the organization involved is a **charitable organization**, the founder is also the principal, or the only, **contributor** to it. In the body of **federal tax law** that distinguishes between **publicly supported charities** and **private foundations**, the founder is likely to be a **substantial contributor** and perhaps an **organization manager** or a **foundation manager**. (also **Creator of trust**; **Grantor**; **Settlor**; **Trustor**).

401(k) plan

A "401(k) plan" is a qualified cash or deferred arrangement for the benefit of an **organization's employees**; the term is derived from the provision of the **Internal Revenue Code** that authorizes it (**IRC** § 401(k)). A **tax-exempt organization** may not maintain a 401(k) plan (**IRC** § 401(k)(4)(B)). [EO § 18.1(d)(ii); HC § 4.4(b)].

403(b) plan

A "403(b) plan" is a form of **deferred compensation** arrangement known as a **tax-deferred** or **tax-sheltered annuity**; the term is derived from the provision of the **Internal Revenue Code** that authorizes it (**IRC** § 403(b)). A tax-sheltered annuity is a **defined contribution plan**. Tax-sheltered annuity programs are available only to **employees** of **charitable organizations** and **public educational institutions**. [EO § 18.1(e)].

457 plan

A "457 plan" is a **nonqualified**, unfunded, **deferred compensation plan** available to **employees** of **tax-exempt organizations**; the term is derived from the provision of the **Internal Revenue Code** that authorizes it (**IRC** § 457). [EO § 18.1(f)(i)(iii)].

Fourteenth Amendment

The Fourteenth Amendment to the U.S. Constitution provides that a state may not deprive any **person** of life, liberty, or **property**, without **due process** of law, nor deny to any person within its jurisdiction the **equal protection** of the laws. **First Amendment rights** and other freedoms may not be infringed by the states because these freedoms are ensured by the Fourteenth Amendment; that is, the freedoms secured by the **Bill of Rights** are enforceable against the states by reason of the Fourteenth Amendment. [CL §§ 1.1(b), 2.2, 6.6].

fraction, support

Charitable organizations that are able to avoid classification as a **private foundation** often can do so by qualifying as a type of **publicly supported charitable organization**. There are two principal types of publicly supported organizations; the **donative** type (as described in **IRC** §§ 170(b)(1)(A)(vi) and 509(a)(1)) and the **service provider** type (as described in **IRC** § 509(a)(2)). Public support derived by either type is determined by constructing a "support fraction," the numerator of which is qualifying public support and the denominator of which is qualifying total support.

The numerator of the support fraction for donative type publicly supported organizations consists of **contributions** and **grants** from the **public**, both **direct** and **indirect**, and grants from **governmental units**. Direct gifts and grants constitute public support to the extent that the total amount of contributions or grants from any **donor** or **grantor** (including **attributed gifts**) during the **computation period** does not exceed an amount equal to 2 percent of the organization's total includible support for the period. Donors who are related to one another must share a single 2 percent limitation. Grants from governmental units and/or other donative type publicly supported organizations are forms of indirect public support and are not limited by the 2 percent limitation. The denominator of this support fraction essentially consists of all forms of support other than **exempt function income**.

The numerator of the support fraction for the service provider type of publicly supported organization consists of gifts, grants, and exempt function income from sources other than **disqualified persons**. The limitations inherent in the definition of the term **substantial contributor** are somewhat akin to the rules of the 2 percent limitation of the donative publicly supported charity rules. In addition, **gross receipts** from **related activities** received from any **person** or any **bureau or similar agency** of a **governmental unit** are includible as public support in any **tax year** to the extent that these receipts do not exceed the greater of $5,000 or 1 percent of the organization's support for the year. The denominator of this support fraction includes virtually all types of support (other than contributions of services or contributions of the use of property). [PF §§ 15.4(b), 15.5; EO § 12.3(b); SM pp. 81–82] (also **Denominator of support fraction**; **Investment income test**; **Numerator of support fraction**; **Support**).

fractional interest

A **donor** may make a **contribution** to a **charitable organization** of a portion (fraction) of his, her, or its interest in an item of **property**. There may not be a **charitable deduction** for this type of **gift**. For example, special rules apply with respect to a gift of a fractional interest in an item of art. [CG §§ 9.1(b), 15.3(b); FR § 5.14(h); AR § 19.1(d)(3)] (also **Partial interest**).

fragmentation rule

In a sense, the **federal tax law** views every **tax-exempt organization** as a bundle of activities, each of which is a **trade or business**. The **IRS** is empowered to examine each of the activities in the bundle of activities constituting the organization in search of one or more **unrelated businesses**. Each activity in the bundle can be examined as though it existed wholly independently of the others; an unrelated activity cannot be hidden from **IRS** scrutiny by tucking it in among a host of **related activities** (**IRC** § 513(c)). This rule allowing the **IRS** to analytically fragment an organization in this manner is known informally as the "fragmentation rule." [UB §§ 2.3, 9.3; EO §§ 24.2(f), 29.1; HC § 34.6(b); CG § 3.4(b); FR § 5.7(a)(iii); SM p. 172].

fraternal beneficiary association

A "fraternal beneficiary association" is a type of **tax-exempt organization** (**IRC** § 501(a) by reason of **IRC** § 501(c)(8)). This form of **association** is based on the **lodge system** and provides **membership benefits**. This type of organization may be **exempt** from one or more of the state **charitable solicitation acts**. These organizations can qualify as **charitable donees** where the **gifts** to them are used **exclusively** for **charitable** purposes (**IRC** § 170(c)(4)). [EO § 19.4(a); CG § 1.3(b); AR §§ 14.3(e)(3), 19.1(a)(2); CL §§ 1.12(f), 6.6; PF § 1.6; AS § 1.6(g); SM p. 42].

fraternal society, domestic
See **Domestic fraternal society**.

fraternity
In general, a "fraternity" is a **society** of male **undergraduate students** at **colleges** and **universities** and graduates of these **institutions**, traditionally **organized** and **operated** for **social** purposes. Most fraternities are national **organizations**, with **chapters** throughout the country at various **educational institutions**. The name of a fraternity is usually composed of two or three letters of the Greek alphabet. Some **graduate school** organizations, however, although termed "fraternities," are composed of both men and women **members**. A **nonprofit** fraternity is a form of **social club** and thus is a type of **tax-exempt organization** (**IRC** § 501(a) by reason of **IRC** § 501(c)(7)). [CU Q 3.7, Q 3.8; EO § 7.8] (also **Sorority**).

fraud
"Fraud" is a false representation of a matter of fact, by word or conduct, by means of a misleading statement or by concealment of some fact that should have been disclosed, which deceives another **person** (or persons) and is intended to cause this deceit so that the other person acts on it to his, her, or its legal injury. State fraud laws are used to prosecute instances of false and deceptive **charitable solicitations**. [FR §§ 4.3(g), 8.11; HC §§ 29.2, 36.3(d); CL § 7.4(k)].

fraud, tax penalty for
The **federal tax law** contains a variety of **penalties** for its violation, including the penalty for **fraud** in connection with the filing of **tax returns** or the nonpayment of tax (**IRC** § 6663).

fraudulent
A **person** or a practice is "fraudulent" when he, she, or it is engaging in, or has engaged in, one or more acts involving **fraud**.

Free Exercise Clause
The First Amendment to the U.S. Constitution provides that there may be no law prohibiting the free exercise of **religion**. This "Free Exercise Clause" is one of two **religion clauses** in the **First Amendment** that is directed toward the goal of neutrality of government with regard to the affairs of religion. This clause places limits on the government's ability to regulate religious practices, by means of the **tax** or **fundraising laws** or otherwise. [CL §§ 2.1–2.3; EO § 10.1(a)(i); RE Q 3.2, Q 25.1, Q 25.3; CL §§ 2.1–2.3].

free speech

"Free speech" is a basic human **right**, allowing **persons** to say what they wish and when they wish to say it, with the right abridged by a government only by the narrowest forms of regulation. The act of **soliciting** a **charitable contribution** is an act of free speech. [CL §§ 1.1(b), 5.3, 5.5–5.10, 7.4.; FR § 4.3; SM p. 152].

freedom of association

See **Association, freedom of**.

Freedom of Information Act

The "Freedom of Information Act" provides basic rule for disclosure of federal records. Although this **law** is applicable to the **IRS**, there are several **exceptions** that apply in the **federal tax law** and other contexts. [AU §§ 1.11, 5.16, 5.18(e); EO § 28.9(b)].

freedom of speech

See **Free speech**.

friend of the court

A "friend of the court" is a **person** who provides technical legal assistance to a court by means of an **amicus brief**. This person is usually **advocating** a particular outcome of the case, but is not functioning directly under the direction of a party to the **litigation**, as is the case with an expert witness. The functioning as a friend of the court is one of several ways a **tax-exempt organization** can advocate its policies. [EO § 7.15(d)].

friend-raising

The term "friend-raising" is informally used to refer to the process of acquiring **donors** rather than acquiring **contributions**. Its more formal designation is **donor acquisition**. This distinction is made by those who believe that donor acquisition is not properly considered a form of **fundraising**. [FR § 2.2(a)].

friends organization

The concept of the "friends organization" encompasses a **charitable organization** that solicits and receives **contributions** from U.S. **donors** and expends the funds, in the form of **grants**, on behalf of a charitable organization operating in another country. Contributions to this type of organization are not **deductible**, however, if the U.S. **entity** is merely a **conduit** of the funds. [EO § 29.2(e); CG § 18.3].

fringe benefit

A "fringe benefit" usually is a form of noncash **compensation** paid by an **employer** to **employees**, although it may also entail an outlay of money. **Nonprofit** (including **tax-exempt**)

organizations can provide most forms of fringe benefits to their employees; frequently, the **value** of a fringe benefit is taxable as **additional compensation**. Forms of fringe benefits include various forms of **insurance** (such as health, major medical, disability, and/or travel), entertainment allowances, automobile expenses, moving expenses, parking, attendance at seminars and conventions, **club** memberships, and payment of professional fees (such as physicians' charges for physical examinations, legal expenses, financial planning fees, and stress management costs). Payment of fringe benefits by tax-exempt organizations is subject to the **private inurement doctrine** and the **intermediate sanctions rules**. Certain fringe benefits are **excluded** from the recipient's **gross income** (IRC § 132). [EO §§ 18.1(b), 20.4(a), 21.4(a); HC § 28.5(b); PF § 5.7(c); AR § 6.2(c)(1); CU Q 7.22–Q 7.24, Q 7.33, 7.34].

frivolous income tax return

A "frivolous income tax return" is a **tax return** (or what purports to be a tax return) that (1) does not contain information on which the **substantial** correctness of the self-assessment may be judged or (2) contains information that on its face indicates that the self-assessment is substantially incorrect, and (3) involves conduct due to a position that is frivolous or a desire (that appears on the purported return) to delay or impede the administration of **federal income tax laws** (IRC § 6702).

full and fair exposition test

The "full and fair exposition" test was devised by the **IRS** to differentiate between activities that are **educational** and those that constitute **propaganda**. This standard allows an **organization** to be educational, even though it **advocates** a particular position or viewpoint as long as it presents a sufficiently full and fair exposition of the pertinent facts so as to permit an individual or the public to form an independent opinion or conclusion. [EO §§ 8.1, 8.2; CU Q 2.1, Q 2.2, Q 2.5] (also **Methodology test**).

full-payment period

The phrase "full-payment period" is used in connection with the type of **private foundation set-aside** that meets the **cash distribution test**. The full-payment period of a private foundation is the years of its existence after expiration of the **start-up period**. [PF § 6.5(e)].

full-payment period minimum amount

The phrase "full-payment period minimum amount" is used in connection with the type of **private foundation set-aside** that meets the **cash distribution test**. The full-payment period minimum amount that must be timely distributed, in cash or its equivalent, is at least its **distributable amount**. (This means that, once the cash distribution approach is no longer available because of the passage of time, a private foundation can make set-asides only in conformance with the **suitability test**.) A private foundation has a five-year **carryover** of certain distributions that are in excess of the full-payment period minimum amount (IRC § 4942(g)(2)(D)). [PF § 6.5(e)].

functional accounting

The phrase "functional accounting" is used to describe a method of accounting that is more sophisticated than a mere statement of **revenue** and **expenses**. It requires the reporting **organization** to separately account for revenue and expenses in three discrete categories: **program services**, administration (management and general), and **fundraising**. That is, items of revenue and expenses in these categories must be **allocated** over these three functions and reported as such. The **IRS** has adopted the functional method of accounting as part of the reporting requirements imposed on **tax-exempt organizations** by the obligation to file an **annual information return**. [FR §§ 2.4(a), 4.13, 5.7(b)(iv), 5.9(d), 7.3(d); EO § 28.3(g); AR § 7.2(b); HC § 32.2(k); SM p. 155].

F

functionally integrated Type III supporting organization

The phrase "functionally integrated Type III supporting organization" means a **Type III supporting organization** that is not required, by reason of tax **regulations**, to make payments to **supported organizations** due to the activities of the organization related to performing the functions of, or carrying out the purposes of, the supported organizations (**IRC** § 4943(f)(5)(B)). [PF § 15.7(g); EO § 12.3(c); HC § 5.5(g); SM pp. 82–85].

functionally related business

The term "functionally related business" means (1) a **trade or business** that is not an **unrelated trade or business** or (2) an activity carried on within a larger aggregate of similar activities or within a larger complex of other endeavors that is **related** (aside from the need of the **organization** for **income** or funds) to the **exempt purposes** of the organization (**IRC** § 4942(j)(4)). The **excess business holdings rules** do not apply to holdings in functionally related businesses (**IRC** § 4943(d)(3)(A)). [PF §§ 3.1(e), 6.2(c), 7.3, 7.4, 11.3(b); HC § 5.10; SM p. 89] (cf. **Business enterprise**).

fund

The word "fund" has many meanings. It can mean an accumulation of money and/or **property**, that would be reflected in a line item on a **financial statement** of an **organization**, such as a "reserve fund." It can mean a more formal account within an organization, such as an **endowment fund** or a **donor-advised fund**. It may mean a separate **organization**, usually a **charitable** one, that operates in the nature of an endowment fund or a **private foundation**. The word can be used as a verb, as a synonym of **grant**. [PF § 2.2].

fund balance

The "fund balance" of a **tax-exempt organization** (that uses fund accounting) is the net difference between its **assets** and **liabilities**. [PF § 12.1(e)] (also **Balance; Balance sheet; Net assets**).

fund development officer

A "fund development officer" is a (usually fulltime) **salaried employee** of a **charitable organization** and receives the same standard **employee benefits** as all other employees. The fund development officer designs the organization's **fundraising** program in keeping with the organization's priorities; selects the fundraising methods required to produce the **income** needed; and supervises operations on a daily basis. To make the **development process** work, the development officer must set and meet goals and objectives; identify **committees**; assign functions and manage them successfully; recruit and train leaders and **volunteers**; hire and train staff; write policies and procedures, have them approved, and see that they are followed; prepare budgets and supervise **expenses**: perform and report results and analyses; keep confidential records accurately and discreetly; and design and implement a **donor recognition** system. These individuals may also be called a vice president for development, director of development, director of philanthropy, **professional fundraiser**, or fundraising executive.

fund manager

The term "fund manager" means, with respect to a **sponsoring organization**, an **officer, director**, or **trustee** of the sponsoring organization (or an individual having powers or responsibilities similar to those of officers, directors, or trustees of the sponsoring organization), as well as, in connection with any act (or failure to act), the **employees** of a sponsoring organization having authority or responsibility with respect to the act (or failure to act) (**IRC** § 4966(d)(3)). [EO § 11.8(b); CG § 23.4] (cf. **Entity manager, Foundation manager, Organization manager**).

funded

The word "funded" is used to describe a **plan, trust**, or similar vehicle or **fund** that has **assets** and/or **income** in it. For example, some **deferred compensation plans** are "funded." (cf. **Unfunded**).

fundraiser, professional

See **Professional fundraiser**.

fundraising

In the broadest sense, "fundraising" is the process of **soliciting** and receiving **contributions**, usually for a **charitable organization**. There are several categories of fundraising activities, most notably **direct mail solicitation, in-person solicitation, private foundation grant** solicitation, **telemarketing**, radio and television solicitation, website fundraising, **special events**, and **planned giving**.

The **IRS** defined the term "fundraising" in the context of the **expenditure test**. There, the term is defined as encompassing solicitation of (1) **dues** or contributions from **members** of the organization, from persons whose dues are in arrears, or from the **public**; (2) contributions or grants from businesses or other organizations, including charitable **entities**; and/or (3) grants from a **governmental unit** or any agency or **instrumentality** of a governmental unit.

For **Form 990** reporting purposes, however, the **IRS** has a much more expansive definition of "fundraising." In that context, the term is said to mean activities undertaken to induce potential donors to contribute money, securities, services, materials, facilities, other assets, or time. These activities include publicizing and conducting fundraising campaigns; maintaining donor mailing lists; conducting **fundraising events**, preparing and distributing fundraising manuals, instructions, and other materials; **professional fundraising services**; and conducting other activities involved with soliciting contributions from individuals, foundations, governments, and others. Fundraising activities, in this context, do not include **gaming**, the conduct of a **business** that is **regularly carried on**, or activities **substantially related** to accomplishment of the reporting organization's **exempt purpose** or purposes (other than by raising funds).

There is little consistency as to the proper way to formulate this term. It also appears as "fund-raising" and "fund raising." [FR §§ 4.13, 8.1; EO §§ 24.3(c), 24.5(i), 28.3(n), 28.12; CG § 23.2, Chap. 25; AR Chap. 14, §§ 3.1(r), 3.1(s), 3.2(s), 7.2(b), 14.1(a); UB § 9.6(a); GV § 8.15; CL § 7.4; SM pp. 152–153, 256–257; LI Q 12.1] (also **Separate fund-raising unit**).

fundraising cost

See **Fundraising expense**.

fundraising cost limitation

A "fund-raising cost limitation" is a provision in a state's **charitable solicitation act** that prohibits **charitable organizations** with allegedly "high" **fundraising costs** from **soliciting contributions** in the state. These limitations have been held **unconstitutional** by the U.S. Supreme Court. [FR § 4.3(b); SM pp. 152–153].

fundraising event

The **IRS** defines "fundraising events" to include dinners and dances, door-to-door sales of merchandise, concerts, carnivals, sports events, auctions, casino nights (in which participants can play casino-style games but the only prizes or auction items provided to participants are noncash items that were donated to the organization), and similar events that are not **regularly carried on** that are conducted for the **primary purpose** of raising funds. Fundraising events do not include the conduct of a **business** that is regularly carried on; activities **substantially related** to the accomplishment of the organization's **exempt purposes**; **solicitation** campaigns that generate only contributions, which may involve gifts of goods or services from the organization of only nominal value, or sweepstakes, lotteries, or raffles in which the names of contributors or other respondents are entered in a drawing for prizes of only nominal value; and **gaming**. [FR §§ 5.7(b)(i), 5.9(e); AR §§ 14.1(c), 14.2(b); SM pp. 155–156].

fundraising expense

A "fundraising expense" is the cost of one or more activities that constitute, or are an integral and inseparable part of, a **solicitation**, usually by a **charitable organization**. A fundraising **expense** may be **direct**, such as payments to fundraising **consultants**, **salaries** to **employees** principally involved in fundraising, travel, telephone, facsimiles, postage, and supplies. A fundraising expense may also be **indirect**, such as the salaries of supportive personnel and overhead. [FR §§ 4.1, 4.3(g), 8.1(b), 8.11, 8.14, 9.12(b); AR §§ 7.2(b), 7.2(b)(9); SM pp. 256–257].

fundraising expenses, allocation of

An **organization** may incur an **expense** that is made for a **dual purpose**; a **fundraising expense** can be of this nature. An expense can be part for **program** and part for fundraising; it can also be part for and part for fundraising. When this occurs, the expense must be allocated to its appropriate categories. [FR § 4.1(i); AR § 7.2(b)].

fundraising expenses, disclosure of

Some of the various state **charitable solicitation acts** attempt, using various approaches, to force **charitable organizations** that are engaged in **fundraising** or those who assist them in the fundraising process to disclose the organization's fundraising expenses. Sometimes, the disclosure is to be made to the government, through reporting and/or provisions in a **contract**; sometimes, the disclosure is to the public, either in the form of **disclosure-on-demand** or **point-of-solicitation disclosure**; occasionally, all of these requirements appear in the same law. A charitable organization may be reluctant to disclose fundraising costs, out of fear that they will be regarded as being "too high," resulting in fewer **gifts** or gifts of lesser amounts. Charitable organizations are particularly sensitive to the disclosure of fundraising expenses as a percentage of total expenses. It is contrary to a charitable organization's **free speech rights** for a government to preclude the organization from soliciting funds in the jurisdiction on the basis of the extent of its fundraising expenses. [FR §§ 4.1, 4.3(g), 5.2, 5.5, 7.3(c), 8.11; CU Q 13.26, Q 13.52, Q 18.24, 18.26; SM p. 154].

fundraising expenses, pluralization of

The concept of the **reasonableness** of **fundraising expenses** has led some analysts away from the idea of a fundraising cost being a single number (or percentage) and to a focus on the fundraising expenses for each type of fundraising activity. The effort then is to assess the reasonableness of fundraising expenses on a category-by-category basis. This approach is known as the "pluralization" of fundraising expenses.

The pluralization concept led to the development of guidelines by which a **charitable organization** can evaluate the reasonableness of its fundraising expenses. These guidelines are generally based on two elements: the type of fundraising activity and the **average gift size** for each category. (In some instances, the expenses of **donor acquisition** activities and **special events**— where they are essentially public relations and marketing activities—are excluded from the analysis.) The types of fundraising activities identified in this manner (aside from the two types just referenced) are **donor renewal programs. special events** (that are not primarily public relations or marketing activities), major individual gift **solicitations** (from prior donors), the seeking of **planned gifts**, **capital** and **endowment campaigns**, corporate gift- and **private foundation grant-seeking**, and the seeking of government grants.

The average gift size is divided into categories, such as $1–$10, $10–$24, $25–$100, $100–$1,000, $1,000–$10,000, and amounts in excess of $10,000. The guideline for the reasonableness of fundraising costs is thus determined by blending the two sets of factors. For example, it may be considered reasonable to have a fundraising cost percentage of 75 percent for the raising of gifts from prior donors in the $1–$10 range, but not for the $100–$1,000 range, where the guideline as to what is reasonable may be about 25 percent. Likewise, a fundraising cost percentage of 25 percent may be reasonable for a capital campaign in connection with the seeking of gifts in the $100–$1,000 range, while the appropriate percentage for gifts of $10,000 and above in the same campaign may be about 12 percent.

One of the results of the pluralization approach to the analysis of the reasonableness of fundraising costs is that the single-expense (or percentage) approach (sometimes termed the "bottom-line approach") can be seen to be unfair and misleading. The single-number or percentage approach can be perceived as "too high" when it actually is not or, perversely, can hide unreasonable fundraising costs because the overall number or percentage appears to be reasonable. [FR § 4.1(e)].

F

fundraising expenses, reasonableness of

A **fundraising expense** of a **charitable organization** may be **reasonable** or **unreasonable**. The latter category of fundraising expense is also termed an **excessive** fundraising cost. There is no large consensus as to what is a reasonable (or unreasonable) fundraising cost, nor as to how to make that assessment. [FR §§ 2.2(d), 4.1(b), 4.3(g), 8.11] (also **Fundraising expenses, pluralization of**).

fundraising organization

A **nonprofit organization** the operations of which wholly consist of **fundraising** and grant-making can be eligible for **tax exemption** as a **charitable entity**. A key factor in this determination is the **substantiality** of the grantmaking; this entails application of the **commensurate test**. [EO § 7.14; FR § 5.26].

fundraising policy

Some **good governance standards** exhort **public charities**, and perhaps other categories of **tax-exempt organizations**, to develop and adhere to a "fundraising policy." This type of policy may require that, in fundraising materials, the representations of fact, description of the **organization's** financial condition, and narrative information about events be current and accurate. Some of these policies prohibit the organization from accepting a **gift** from a prospective **donor** that would place a hardship on that **person**. [GV §§ 3.10(g), 6.3(q); CU Q 5.33; SM p. 101] (also **Gift acceptance policy**).

fundraising solicitation

The term "fundraising solicitation" is used in the context of the disclosure requirements imposed on **noncharitable organizations** that **solicit** the **public** for **contributions**. Disclosure must be made, using an **express statement** that is in a "conspicuous and easily recognizable format," of the fact that contributions to the **organization** are not **deductible** as **charitable gifts** for federal income tax purposes (**IRC** § 6113). A fundraising solicitation is any solicitation of gifts made in written or printed form, by television, radio, or telephone (although there is an **exclusion** for letters or calls not part of a coordinated fundraising campaign soliciting no more than ten persons during a calendar year). Despite the clear reference in this law to "contributions and gills," the **IRS** interprets this rule to mandate the disclosure when any **tax-exempt**

organization (other than a charitable one) seeks funds, such as **dues** from **members**. [FR § 5.5; CG § 22.3; EO § 28.12].

future interest

A "future interest" is an **interest** in an item of **personal property** or **real property**, including this type of an interest in a **trust**, that may commence in use or enjoyment at a point in time in the future. [CG § 9.21].

future interest, charitable contribution of

A **charitable contribution** consisting of a transfer of a **future interest** in **tangible personal property** is treated as made only when all intervening **interests** in, and **rights** to the actual possession or enjoyment of, the property have expired or are held by **persons** other than the **donor** or persons **related** to the donor (**IRC** § 170(a)(3)). [CG § 9.21].

F

G

gain

The word "gain" is used to describe an economic increase in the **value** of an item of **property**; the gain is obtained by the owner or other holder of the property on a **sale** or **exchange** of the property. This gain may be due to a true increase in value of the property, inflation, or both. If the property involved is a **capital asset**, the gain is termed a **capital gain**. The experiencing of a gain is, for **tax law** purposes, termed a **realization** of the gain. [CG § 2.14] (also **Appreciation**; **Appreciation element**; **Recognition**).

gainsharing

"Gainsharing" refers to cost-savings sharing programs, adopted at **tax-exempt hospitals**, pursuant to which physicians share **revenue** with the hospitals generated by the provision of cost-effective health care. These programs encourage the efficient utilization of services by enabling physicians to benefit financially. There is risk, however, that these arrangements will trigger the **private inurement** and/or **excess benefit** proscriptions, thereby jeopardizing a hospital's **tax exemption** and/or result in the imposition of **intermediate sanctions**. [HC § 25.5(c)].

games of chance

Some **tax-exempt organizations** operate various forms of gambling as a means of **fundraising**. The **law** refers to these gambling forms as "games of chance." Where the game of chance is **bingo**, an **exception** from the **unrelated business income tax** may be available (**IRC** § 513(f)). The term **unrelated trade or business** does not include any **trade or business** that consists of the conduct of games of chance, conducted after June 30, 1981, which, under state law (in effect as of October 5, 1983), can be conducted only by **nonprofit organizations**; however, this rule is applicable only with respect to the law in the state of North Dakota. [UB § 4.7; AU § 7.7; FR § 6.10; EO §§ 25.2(h), 28.3(n); AR § 14.1(l)(1)].

gaming

The **IRS** defines "gaming," for **Form 990** reporting purposes, as including bingo, pull tabs/instant bingo (including satellite, event, and progressive bingo), Texas Hold-Em Poker and other card games, raffles, scratch-offs, charitable gaming tickets, break-opens, hard cards, banded tickets, jar tickets, pickle cards, Lucky Seven cards, Nevada Club tickets, casino

Bruce R. Hopkins' Nonprofit Law Dictionary, First Edition. Bruce R. Hopkins.
© 2015 Bruce R. Hopkins. Published 2015 by John Wiley & Sons, Inc.

nights/Las Vegas nights (other than events not **regularly carried on** in which participants can play casino-style games but the only prizes or auction items provided to participants are non-cash items that were **donated** to the organization, which events are **fundraising events**), and **coin-operated gambling devices**. [FR § 6.10; EO §§ 25.2(h), 28.3(n); AR § 14.1(l)(1); GV § 8.13(a); SM pp. 113, 181–182].

gems, gift of

Gems may be **contributed** to a **charitable organization**. Because of the various **deduction** promotions (in the nature of **tax shelter** promotions) that have unfolded in recent years, the **IRS** and the courts are quick to assign a **value** to donated gems that usually is not in excess of the amount the donors paid for the gems. [AR § 19.1(l); CG §§ 9.2, 24.7(b)(10)].

genealogical society

A "genealogical society" is a **nonprofit organization** that can be **tax-exempt** as a **charitable** or **educational** organization where it engages in activities such as the conduct of lectures, sponsoring of public displays and **museum** tours, provision of written materials to instruct **members** of the public on genealogical **research**, and compilation of a geographic area's pioneer history. A genealogical society generally cannot be tax-exempt as a charitable or educational organization, however, where its membership is limited to descendants of a particular family, it compiles family genealogical research data for use by its members, and it promotes **social** activities among its members. Nonetheless, this type of family **association** may qualify for tax exemption as a charitable organization if it **advances religion**. [EO § 20.5(h)].

general counsel, IRS, office of

Within the **Department of the Treasury** is an office of "General Counsel for the Department of the Treasury" (**IRC** § 7801(b)(1)). This General Counsel, who is the chief **law** officer of the Department, is appointed by the President of the United States, by and with the advice and consent of the Senate.

general counsel memorandum

A "general counsel memorandum" is a statement of the **federal tax law**, as stated by **lawyers** who are **employees** of the **IRS** (that is, those who are in the office of the Chief Counsel of the **IRS** in its **National Office**), as it applies to a specific set of facts. General counsel memoranda have been replaced by **chief counsel advice memoranda**. [EO App. A].

general partner

A "general partner" is a **partner** in a **partnership**. This type of partner is liable for the acts undertaken and the debts incurred by the partnership; a general partner also is likely to have some or all of the management responsibilities for the partnership. By contrast, a partner who only has an investment interest in a partnership and is not liable for any obligations of the partnership is termed a **limited partner**. There may be more than one general partner in a partnership. A **public** charity or other type of **tax-exempt** organization may be either a general partner or a limited partner in a partnership. [EO § 31.1(a); HC § 22.1; SM pp. 225–226, 242–244] (also **General partnership**; **Joint venture**; **Limited partnership**).

general partnership

A "general partnership" is a **partnership** that has only **general partners**. It is, then, a partnership that does not have any **limited partners**. A general partnership is nearly the same as a **joint venture**. [EO § 31.1(a); UB § 8.9(a); HC § 22.1; CU Q 16.38; SM pp. 225, 242–244] (cf. **Limited partnership**).

general power of appointment

A "general power of appointment" is a **power of appointment** that is exercisable in favor of any **person** whom the one granting the power may select. [CG § 8.2(d)].

general public

Several **federal tax law** provisions (in the **IRC**, **tax regulations**, and elsewhere) make reference to the "general public." This phraseology, however, is a redundancy; the appropriate terminology is simply **public**. (It has been said that members of the general public are members of the public who are worthy of a salute.)

For example, a **publicly supported organization** must, at least annually, compute a **support fraction**. One of the elements of this fraction is the amount of financial support received from the "general public." In the case of the **donative** type of public **charitable organization**, a source of a **contribution** or **grant** is, in general, considered to be from the general public to the extent that the total amount of contributions or grants from a **donor** or **grantor** during the **computation period** does not exceed an amount equal to 2 percent of the organization's total includible support for the period. In the case of a **service provider** type of public charitable organization, a source of a contribution or grant is, in general, considered to be from a **member** of the general public if the support is not from a **disqualified person**. [PF §§ 15.4(b), 15.5(d); EO §§ 12.3(b)(i), 12.3(b)(iv); SM pp. 81–82].

general support grant

The term "general support grant" means a **grant** by a **private foundation** to a **public charity** for the purpose of providing unrestricted financial support to the **grantee**. Thus, with this type of grant, there is no **earmarking** or other targeted grantmaking, such as for **lobbying**. [PF § 9.1(c)] (cf. **Specific project grant**).

general 30 percent limitation

The "general 30 percent limitation" is a **federal tax law** rule, the general import of which is that an individual's **charitable contributions** made during a **tax year**, to one or more **charitable organizations** other than **public charitable organizations**, where the subject of the gift is money, are **deductible** to the extent that these contributions in the aggregate do not exceed 30 percent of the individual's **contribution base** for the tax year (**IRC** § 170(b)(1)(B)(i)). [CG § 7.8; SM p. 135].

general written determination

The phrase "general written determination" means a **written determination** that is not a **reference written determination** (**IRC** § 6110(b)(3)(B)). This type of a document generally is disposed of by the **IRS** within three years from the date on which it was made available for public inspection (**IRC** § 6110(j)(2)).

generation-skipping transfer tax

The "generation-skipping transfer tax" (**IRC** § 2601 et seq.) is one of three **federal taxes** on **transfers**, designed to reach transfers of wealth that are not taxed by the other two transfer taxes, which are the **estate tax** and the **gift tax**. As the name of this tax suggests, it attempts to tax transferred wealth that skips a generation. The rationale underlying this tax is a curbing of a perceived abuse involving the use of **trusts** in estate planning.

Since **decedents'** estates are taxed on the **value** of their **property**, and trusts are only taxed on the **income** they generate, trusts have become convenient depositories for generational wealth. A decedent's wealth (at the first generation) can be transferred to a trust. Typically, the trust retains the trust **principal** (or **corpus**) and distributes **income** to the next generation (the second generation), which typically is the sons and daughters of the decedent. Tax is paid on the trust income but not the trust principal; the trust property is not included in the estates of the decedent's children on their deaths, so there is no estate tax at the second generational level. The trust, on the death of the decedent's children, typically distributes its property to the grandchildren of the decedent (the third generation) free of estate or gift tax. Through this use of a trust, a generation was skipped, along with that generation's estate transfer tax.

A transfer tax is imposed on every generation-skipping transfer. The tax rate is a **flat amount** equal to the maximum **unified** estate and gift tax rate. This tax is not unified with the estate and gift taxes. [CG § 8.5].

geographic locale, same

One of the basic requirements for achievement of **tax exemption** as a **voluntary employees' beneficiary association** is that the **organization** be an **association** of **employees**. Employees of one or more **employers** engaged in the same **line of business** in the "same geographic locale" are considered, by the tax **regulations**, to share an **employment-related common bond** for purposes of an organization through which their employers provide benefits. One court, however, has declared this regulation invalid to the extent of the "same geographic locale" requirement. [EO § 18.3; SM p. 43].

ghoul trust

A "ghoul trust" is a type of **charitable lead trust** where the **charitable income interest** was based on the life of a young individual who was seriously ill, so that the **charitable contribution deduction** was predicated on the individual's normal life expectancy, with the amount passing to charity considerably less. This abusive and artificial inflation of charitable deductions has been corrected by tax regulations. [CG § 16.8(a)].

gift

The word "gift" is generally synonymous with the words "**contribution**" and "**donation**," particularly in the context of **charitable giving**. A gift is a transfer of money and/or **property** by one **person** to another, where there is an absence of **consideration**, in whole or in part, in relation to the amount transferred. If a **charitable organization** is not involved, the usual term for this type of transfer is a "gift." If a charitable organization is the recipient, and the transferor is an individual or individuals, or a nongovernmental entity, the usual term is "contributions." If the transferor to a charitable organization is a **private foundation** or governmental entity, the appropriate terminology is "**grant**." [CG §§ 3.1, 8.2(a); PF §§ 6.2(b), 14.1(b), 14.2, 14.4(a), 14.4(c); FR §§ 5.1(a), 5.14(a); CU Q 12.4; SM pp. 131–133; CL § 8.5; LI Q 11.4] (also **Gift tax**; **Quid pro quo contribution**).

gift acceptance policy

The **IRS**, in the **Form 990**, asks filing **organizations** whether they have implemented a "gift acceptance policy" that requires review of **nonstandard contributions**. [GV § 6.3(j); CG § 24.7(b)(21); AR §§ 19.1(x), 19.2(t); CU Q 12.8; SM p. 276; LI Q 11.8, Q 11.9, Q 12.63].

gift in kind

A "gift in kind" is a **gift** of **property**, usually property that constitutes **inventory** in the hands of the **donor**. This term is almost always used in the context of **charitable giving**. It is sometimes used to describe a gift of services and/or a gift of the use of **property**, although technically this is an inappropriate use of the term. A charitable gift in kind may qualify for the **twice-basis charitable contribution deduction**. [CG §§ 9.3, 9.14, 9.18; FR § 2.2(a)].

gift item

The concept of **unrelated trade or business** does not include a business, conducted by a **tax-exempt organization**, that constitutes the selling of merchandise, **substantially all** of which has been received by the organization by means of **contributions** (**IRC** § 513(a)(3)). This type of merchandise is termed "gift items." [UB § 4.3; EO § 25.2(c); SM p. 175].

gift property

Property may be the subject of a **charitable contribution**; this type of property is sometimes referred to as "gift property." One of the basic elements in determining whether a **charitable contribution deduction** is available for a **gift** of property is the nature of the property that is the subject of the contribution. In many instances, the **tax law** of **charitable giving** differentiates between **personal property** and **real property**, and between **tangible property** and **intangible property**. The **value** of a qualified charitable contribution of an item of property often is its **fair market value**. Gift property may also be transferred from one **person** to another in the absence of any charitable giving. [CG §§ 4.3, 4.5, 7.1; FR § 5.14(c); SM p. 134] (also **Capital gain property**; **Gift tax**; **Ordinary income property**).

gift tax

Pursuant to the **federal gift tax law**, a tax is imposed on the transfer of **property** by gift during a calendar year by any individual (**IRC** § 2501). [CG § 8.2(b); FR § 5.14(l)] (also **Annual exclusion**; **Charitable contribution deduction**).

girls' club

A "girls' club" is a type of **membership association** that often is a **tax-exempt organization**; as the name indicates, membership in these types of **clubs** is confined to girls. These clubs are sometimes **exempt** from one or more state **charitable solicitation acts**. [FR § 3.5(n)] (also **Boys' club**).

give

See **Contribute**.

giving

The word "giving" is used to describe the process of transferring money and/or **property** from one **person** to another when **consideration** does not underlie the transaction. It is utilized with respect to the making of **charitable gifts**, as in "charitable giving." [CG §§ 3.1, 8.2(a)].

giving, pyramid of

The **fund development process** includes the acquisition of **contributors**, the renewal and upgrading of contributors, and maximizing contributors. Each of these phases represents an increased capacity to support **charitable organizations**, but the process starts at the bottom of the "pyramid of giving." Identification of **prospects** from the **public** available to a **charitable organization** is accomplished through the several **annual giving** methods. Each individual contributor's progression up the pyramid requires time for information and interest to develop, as well as a level of personal involvement with the charitable organization (the **friend-raising phase**). Major gift opportunities, while less frequent, are usually centered in **capital campaigns**, and represent a continuing investment in response to a rising commitment and enthusiasm for the **programs** and services of the organization. The ultimate investment decision usually is made last, is frequently the largest gift (perhaps a **planned gift**), and may be transferred to the charitable organization from the contributor's estate. [FR § 2.3].

good faith

The **law** expects a **person** to act in "good faith." This means an act (or a decision to not act) that is not undertaken with the intent to seek an unfair advantage over another or to commit a **fraud**. It embodies the concepts of honesty and sincerity. The **federal tax law** occasionally uses this term. For example, the **contemporaneous written acknowledgement** that is required under the **substantiation rules** for gifts in the amount of at least $250 must include a "good faith estimate" of the **value** of any goods or services (other than an **intangible religious benefit**) provided by the **donee charitable organization** in **consideration** of a **contribution** (IRC § 170(f)(8)(B)(iii)). [CG § 21.3(a); SM p. 145].

good governance standards

Several **nonprofit organizations** and **governmental entities** have promulgated standards of "good governance," primarily directed at **public charities**. These standards, which are not necessarily uniform, address matters such as the duties and responsibilities of the **governing board**, expenditures, fundraising, **law** compliance, and 6 disclosures. [GV Chap. 3; CU Q 5.21, Q 5.46; RE Q 2.1, Q 2.2].

good will

"Good will" is an **intangible asset** of an **organization**. The **value** of good will is a composite of the reputation of the organization (usually derived in turn from the reputation associated with the goods and/or services provided by the organization) in the eyes of its customers, suppliers, and the community generally. This term is used most frequently to describe an asset of a **for-profit business enterprise**. The assumption of **liability** for good will of a for-profit **corporation** by a **tax-exempt organization** can constitute an act of **private inurement**. [EO § 20.5(e); CG § 2.12(d)] (also **Halo effect**).

governance, nonprofit

The matter of "nonprofit governance" has become one of the greatest issues in the law of tax-exempt organizations. Traditionally, this subject has been largely the focus of state law. Recently, however, the IRS has taken on a regulatory role in this area. This has manifested itself principally in the areas of ruling policy (based mainly on the private benefit doctrine) and annual reporting (by means of annual information returns). One of the key ways in which this regulatory function is undertaken is by means of encouraging (and sometimes requiring) the development of governance policies by exempt organizations.

Nonprofit governance generally entails consideration of these elements: The size and composition of **governing boards**, the role of these boards, transactions between board members and the organization, and the compensation of board members. Many of these elements are reflected in **Form 990**, Part VI. [GV passim; EO Chap. 5; CU Chap. 5; HC Chap. 33; AR Chap. 5; SM Chap. 8; CL § 8.7; AU § 3.1(o); RE Q 2.1, Q 2.2; LI Q 3.1, Q 3.2, Q 3.19, Q 14.2, Q 14.3, Q 14.7] (also **Fiduciary responsibility**).

governing board

The term "governing hoard" means the group of individuals that sets policy for, and generally oversees, the activities of an **organization**. The term is usually used to refer to a **board of directors** or a **board of trustees**; in some instances, it refers to an **entity's executive committee**. [EO § 5.1; AR §§ 1.6(f), 5.1(b)–5.1(f); SM pp. 16–19; PG pp. 9–14].

governing instrument

The term "governing instrument" means a document by which an **organization** is **organized** and **operated**. In the **nonprofit organization** setting, the nature and content of this document will vary in accordance with the form of the organization. The document constitutes the **articles of organization** and the document containing the organization's rules of operation, such as **bylaws**. [EO § 4.2; AR § 1.6(b); SM pp. 8–11; PG p. 16; CU Q 5.39] (also **Articles of incorporation**; **Declaration of trust**; **Trust agreement**).

government, branch of

The phrase "branch of government" is usually used to describe a government along functional lines. For example, the government of the United States or of a state is often thought of as consisting of a **legislative branch**, an **executive branch**, and a **judicial branch**. [CL § 1.2(a)].

government, department of

A "department" of a government is a component of that government, usually the largest of its components. The government of the United States, for example, has fourteen departments, such as the **Department of the Treasury**. Departments of government are usually subdivided into bodies such as **agencies** or **bureaus**.

government agency

A government is comprised of component parts bearing names such as "agency," **branch, bureau, department, instrumentality**, and/or **political subdivision**. For example, the **Department of the Treasury** is a **department** of the **federal** government, while the **IRS** is an agency within that department. A determination as to these components can be significant in assessing the extent of **public support** for a **service provider publicly supported organization. Contributions** to government agencies are usually **deductible** as **charitable gifts**. [PF § 15.5(d); EO § 12.3(b)(iv); CG § 3.4(a); CU Q 1.40].

government burdens, lessening of

See **Lessening burdens of government**.

government grant

The term "government grant" means a **grant** from a **governmental unit**. This type of grant, which is usually made to a **charitable organization**, should be distinguished from a government **contract**. Government grants are forms of **public support** for **publicly supported organizations**. [PF §§ 15.4(a), 15.5(d)].

government instrumentality

An "instrumentality of government" is a separate **organization** that functions for or on behalf of a government. That is, it typically has one or more governmental purposes; **control** of the **entity** is usually vested in one or more government authorities. A government instrumentality may be **tax-exempt** by reason of the **doctrine** of **intergovernmental immunity** or, if it has a **clear counterpart** in the realm of **charitable organizations**, as a charitable organization. [EO §§ 7.14, 19.21].

government official

Generally, a "government official" is an individual with policy-making responsibilities for one or more **bodies of government**; to be a government official, an individual must be more than merely an **employee** or the government.

The term "government official" is specifically defined, for purposes of the rules against **self-dealing** involving **private foundations**, as a type of **disqualified person**. For this purpose, the term means (1) an elected public official in the U.S. Congress or executive **branch of government**, (2) presidential appointees to the U.S. executive or judicial branches, (3) certain higher compensated or ranking **employees** in any of these three branches, (4) employees of the U.S. House of Representatives or Senate earning at least $15,000 annually, (5) elected or appointed public officials in the U.S. or District of Columbia governments (including governments of U.S. possessions or **political subdivisions** or areas of the U.S.) earning at least $20,000 annually, or (6) the personal or executive assistant or secretary to any of the foregoing (**IRC** § 4946(c)). [PF §§ 4.8, 5.3(a), 5.10; EO § 12.2(i); AR § 7.2(b)(16)] (also **Covered executive branch official**; **Public office**).

governmental body

A "governmental body" (or, sometimes, "body of government") is a broad, generic term encompassing components of government such as **agencies**, **branches**, **departments**, **instrumentalities**, and **units**.

governmental unit

A "governmental unit" is an **entity**, including a state, a possession of the United States, or any **political subdivision** of either the foregoing or the United States or the District of Columbia (**IRC** § 170(c)(1)). A governmental unit is a **public charity** (**IRC** § 170(b)(1)(A)(v)). [EO §§ 7.14, 12.3(a); AR § 1.1(b); HC § 34.3(e); PF § 15.3; CG § 3.3(a); SM pp. 47, 80, 121; LI Q 1.51].

grandparent organization

See **Superparent organization**.

grant

A "grant" is a transfer of money and/or **property** from one **person** to another, without **consideration**. A grant has essentially the same characteristics as a **contribution**. A grant is usually made by a **charitable organization** (such as a **private foundation**) or by a **government agency** (with the term "contribution" used to describe a similar transfer by an individual or **for-profit organization**). A grant may be to an individual (such as in the form of a **scholarship** or **fellowship**) or to an organization; it may be **restricted** or unrestricted. The usual purposes of a grant are to further a course of study, result in a publication or presentation, or carry out **research**.

If there is consideration underlying the transfer, it is a **contract**. The distinction is that a grant has a **substantial** element of gratuitousness to it, while a contract (that may look like a grant) is for the purchase of services and/or something else by the transferor. A grant is a type of **public support** for a **donative publicly supported organization** or a **service provider publicly supported organization**; revenue from the performance of services pursuant to a contract is public support (in whole or in part) only for a service provider publicly supported organization. [PF §§ 1.1, 1.4(h), 3.1(c); 6.5(a), 6.5(b), 9.1(c), 9.3, 9.2(b), 9.4(d), 9.6(d), 9.6(j); HC §§ 2.2(c), 5.8; AR §§ 7.2(a)(1), 7.2(c)(3), 7.2(c)(18); PG p. 189] (also **Exempt function revenue**).

grant, advance approval of

See **Advance approval of grants**.

grant, employer-related

See **Employer-related grant**.

grant, expenditure responsibility
See **Expenditure responsibility grant.**

grant, matching
See **Matching grant.**

grant, unusual
See **Unusual grant.**

grantmaking policy
Some **good governance standards** state that an **organization** that engages in domestic and/or international grantmaking activities should adopt a policy summarizing the substance of these activities, the potential grantees involved, the application process, and the due diligence the organization will undertake before and after the grant is made. [GV § 6.3(l)].

grantee
A "grantee" is a **person** who is the recipient of a **grant**.

grantor
A "grantor" is a **person** who makes a **grant**. The word is sometimes also used to describe a person who establishes and **funds** a **trust**. [PF §§ 9.4(c), 15.11; CG § 3.8].

grantor trust
A "grantor trust" is a **trust** where the circumstances are such that the **grantor** of the trust is treated, for **federal tax purposes**, as the owner of the trust or a portion of it and thus has the **income** of the trust attributable to him, her, or it (**IRC** § 671). Generally, these circumstances are: (1) where the grantor has retained a reversionary **interest** in the trust, within specified time limits (**IRC** § 673); (2) where the grantor or a **nonadverse party** has certain **powers** over the **beneficial interests** under the trust (**IRC** § 674); (3) if certain **administrative powers** over the trust exist under which the grantor can or does benefit (**IRC** § 675); (4) if the grantor or a nonadverse party has a power to revoke the trust or return the **corpus** of the trust to the grantor (**IRC** § 676); or (5) if the grantor or a nonadverse party has the power to distribute income to or for the benefit of the grantor or the spouse of the grantor (**IRC** § 677). These rules are not applicable with respect to **charitable remainder trusts** or **pooled income funds**. [CG § 3.8; CU Q 12.14; SM p. 236; LI Q 11.14].

grass-roots ceiling amount
The phrase "grass-roots ceiling amount" is used to describe the amount of **lobbying expenditures, normally** made by a **charitable organization** that has **elected** the **expenditure** test, that constitute 150 percent of the **allowable grass-roots lobbying amount**, so that the organization loses its **tax-exempt status** as a charitable entity. [EO § 22.3(d)(iii); HC § 7.1(c); SM p. 190].

grass-roots expenditure

A "grass roots expenditure" is an **expenditure** by a qualifying **charitable organization** for a **grass-roots lobbying communication**. [EO § 22.3(d)(iii); SM p. 190].

grass-roots lobbying

Generally, "grass-roots lobbying" consists of appeals to the public to contact legislators or take other specific action regarding legislative matters. Under the **expenditure test**, grass-roots lobbying is defined as an attempt to influence any **legislation** through an attempt to affect the opinions of the public or any segment of the public (**IRC § 4911(d)(1)(A)**). A **communication** is a grass-roots lobbying communication only where the communication refers to **specific legislation**, reflects a view on the legislation, and encourages the recipient of the communication to take action with respect to the legislation (the latter clement is termed a **call to action**). [EO § 22.3(b); HC § 7.1(b); CU Q 8.7; PF § 9.1(b); SM pp. 189–190].

grass-roots nontaxable amount

The "grass-roots nontaxable amount" for an **organization** for a **tax year** is 25 percent of the **lobbying nontaxable amount** for the organization for that tax year (**IRC § 4911(c)(4)**). [EO § 22.3(d)(iii); HC § 7.1(c); SM p. 190].

gross earnings

An **organization's** "gross earnings" is the totality of its earnings; it is generally akin to "**gross receipts**." (cf. **Net earnings**).

gross estate

The "gross estate" of a **decedent** is all of the **property** owned by the decedent at the date of death, along with all other property to the extent the decedent had an **interest** in the property at death (**IRC §§ 2031, 2032**). [CG § 8.3(a)].

gross income

The term "gross income" means the total income of a person, from whatever source derived, without offset for expenses incurred (**IRC § 61**). The U.S. Supreme Court has written that the concept of gross income includes within its reach all "undeniable accessions to wealth, clearly realized, and over which the taxpayer has complete dominion." [CG §§ 1.6, 2.1, 2.2].

gross investment income

The term "gross investment income," as used in connection with the **law** requiring a **private foundation** to pay a **federal excise tax** on its **net investment income**, means the gross amount of income from **interest, dividends, rent**, payments with respect to **securities loans**, and **royalties**, other than **unrelated business taxable income** (**IRC § 4940(c)(2)**). [PF §§ 10.3, 10.4; HC §§ 5.3(b), 5.3(d)].

gross investment income fraction

The "gross investment income fraction" is the means by which a **service provider publicly supported organization** determines whether it has, at any point in time, **normally** received no more than one-third of its **support** from the sum of **gross investment income** and any excess of the amount of **unrelated business taxable income** over the amount of **tax** on that income (**IRC** § 509(a)(2)(B)). The amount of gross investment income and any net unrelated income received during the **computation period** is the numerator of the fraction; the total amount of support received during the period is the denominator of the fraction. If the organization exceeds this limitation, it cannot qualify as a service provider **entity** during the affected period. [PF § 15.5(a); EO § 12.3(b)(iv); HC § 5.3(b)].

gross receipts

Generally, the term "gross receipts" means the gross **revenue** or **gross earnings** received by an **organization**. An illustration of this is the use of the term as part of the rules concerning the **disclosure of nondeductibility**. Also, the term "gross receipts" has a more specific meaning in the context of the rules defining a **service provider publicly supported organization**. In that setting, one of the **support** rules contains a limitation on allowable gross receipts that can qualify as **public support** (the "**1 percent limitation**"). In that setting, the term "gross receipts" means amounts received from one or more **related** activities in which a specific service, facility, or product is provided to serve the **direct** and immediate needs of the payor. This term further has a more specific meaning in the setting of **tax exemption** for **social clubs**, in that, in applying the **nonmember income test**, the term "gross receipts" means receipts from **normal and usual activities** of the club, such as charges, admissions, membership fees, **dues**, assessments, **investment income**, and normal recurring **capital gain** on investments; the term does not encompass initiation fees and capital contributions. [PF § 15.5(d); EO §§ 12.3(b)(iv), 15.2; HC §§ 5.3(b), 5.3(d)].

gross-up method

The "gross-up method" is a method of **allocation** of **expenses** used by an **organization** in allocating costs to **lobbying activities**, for **purposes** of the rules denying a **business expense deduction** for certain lobbying activities (**IRC** § 162(e)(1)). Under this method, an organization's costs for a **tax year** properly allocable to lobbying activities are 175 percent of its **basic labor costs** plus **third-party costs**. An organization that does not pay or incur **reasonable** labor costs for **persons** engaged in lobbying activities, however, may not use this method. [EO § 22.6(a)] (cf. **Ratio method**; **Section 263A cost allocation method**).

gross valuation misstatement

The term "gross valuation misstatement" means any **substantial valuation misstatement** where (1) the **value** of an item of **property** (or the **adjusted basis** of a property) claimed on a **tax return** is 400 percent or more of the amount determined to be the correct amount of the valuation (or adjusted basis), (2) the price of a property or service (or the use of a property) claimed on a tax return in connection with a transaction between **related persons** is 400 percent or more (or 25 percent or less) of the amount determined under the rules concerning **reallocation of expenses** to be the correct amount of the price, or (3) the transfer price adjustment under those rules where it exceeds $20 million (**IRC** § 6662(h)(2)). [CG § 10.14(a)].

gross valuation overstatement

The term "gross valuation overstatement" means any statement as to the **value** of any **property** or services if (1) the value so stated exceeds 200 percent of the amount determined to be the correct valuation and (2) the value of the property or services is **directly** related to the amount of any **deduction** or **credit** allowable to any participant (**IRC** § 6700(b)(1)). This term is used in the context of defining the **penalty** for the promotion of an **abusive tax shelter**. [CG § 10.14(a)].

ground lease

The term "ground lease" means a form of **lease** of **real property** where the **person** who is leasing the property does so on a long-term basis and constructs and often occupies a building on the land. For example, a **tax-exempt organization** may obtain the use of real property by means of a ground lease and build its headquarters on the site; sometimes, this approach is used rather than a **partnership**. [EO § 31.7].

G

group exemption

An **organization** (such as a **chapter**, local, post, or unit) that is **affiliated** with and is subject to the general supervision or **control** of a **central organization** (usually, a regional or national organization) is regarded as a **tax-exempt organization** solely by reason of its relationship with the central (or parent) organization. Tax-exempt status acquired in this manner is referred to as tax exemption on a "group" basis. The organizations in the group are termed **subordinate organizations**. The **IRS** has developed procedures by which a central organization may obtain a **group exemption letter**. [EO §§ 26.9, 28.2(d); HC § 34.6; CU Q 3.68–Q 3.79; RE Q 8.66–Q 8.74; PG pp. 54–55; SM p. 78; LI Q 2.59].

group exemption letter

The "group exemption letter" is the **determination letter** issued by the **IRS** to a **tax-exempt organization**, recognizing it as a **central organization** and recognizing the scope of the group. [EO § 26.9; HC § 34.6; SM p. 78].

group return

A "group return" is a **Form 990** filed by a **central organization** as to a **group exemption** for two or more of the **subordinate organizations**. [AR §§ 1.4, 5.1(i)(4), 14.1(m)(3)].

guaranteed annuity

A "guaranteed annuity" is an arrangement in accordance with which a determinable amount is paid periodically, but at least annually, for a specified **term** and/or for the life or lives of an individual or individuals, each of whom must be living at the date of transfer and can be **ascertained** at that date. [CG § 9.22(c)].

guaranteed annuity interest

An **income interest** is a "guaranteed annuity interest" only if it is an irrevocable right, pursuant to a **governing instrument** (such as that of a **trust**) to receive a **guaranteed annuity**. [CG § 9.22(c)].

halo effect

The "halo effect" is the name informally given to the positive image and aura surrounding **nonprofit organizations**, particularly **charitable** ones, in the marketplace, causing consumers of goods and services to prefer to purchase them from nonprofit organizations due to the level of trust they engender. (also **Contract failure**; **Level playing field**).

hamartia

A "hamartia" is a defect of character, rising to the level of a significant error or even a sin. A court held that a **donor's charitable contribution deduction** was not available because the **gift** was not accompanied by a **qualified appraisal**. One of the defects in the appraisal report was that the report reflected an appraisal of **property** other than the contributed property. The **lawyer** for the donor argued that "albeit" for that error, the appraisal met the legal requirements. The court rejoined: "That's not a tiny albeit; it's a hamartia—it represents the actual property interest contributed." [CG § 21.5(a)].

harassment campaign

A group of requests for a **tax-exempt organization's application for recognition of exemption** and/or **annual information returns** is indicative of a "harassment campaign" if the requests are part of a single coordinated effort to disrupt the operations of the organization. [EO § 28.10(f); HC § 35.5(a)(vi); FR § 5.9(i); CU Q 18.13; RE Q 8.22; SM p. 124].

harassment campaign exception

A **tax-exempt organization** is generally required to make available for inspection and is required to disseminate copies of its **application for recognition of exemption** and its three most recent **annual information returns** (IRC § 6104(d)). If, however, the **IRS** determines that the organization is the subject of a **harassment campaign** and that compliance with requests that are part of that campaign would not be in the public interest, the organization is not required to fulfill a request that it **reasonably** believes is part of the campaign (IRC § 6104(d)(4)). This rule is the "harassment campaign exception." [EO § 28.10(f); HC § 35.5(a)(vi); FR § 5.9(i); CU Q 18.13; RE Q 8.22; SM p. 124].

Bruce R. Hopkins' Nonprofit Law Dictionary, First Edition. Bruce R. Hopkins.
© 2015 Bruce R. Hopkins. Published 2015 by John Wiley & Sons, Inc.

hardening the target

"Hardening the target" is a bit of witticism used to summarize the various steps a **tax-exempt organization** should take to minimize the likelihood that it will be selected for an **IRS examination** or, if there is an **audit**, shortening its duration. [AU § 3.1; SM pp. 300–302].

health, promotion of

One of the ways an **organization** can achieve classification as a **tax-exempt charitable organization** under the **federal tax law** is to engage in one or more activities that constitute the "promotion of health." The promotion of health as a charitable purpose includes the establishment and maintenance of **hospitals**, clinics, **health maintenance organizations, homes for the aged**, and the like; advancement of medical and similar knowledge through **research**; and the maintenance of conditions conducive to health. [HC §§ 1.7, 3.2; EO § 7.6; CG § 3.2(b); SM pp. 34–35].

H

Health Care and Education Reconciliation Act of 2010

The "Health Care and Education Reconciliation Act of 2010" amended the **Patient Protection and Affordable Care Act**, also enacted in that year. [HC §§ 1.0, 26.11(a); EO § 2.4].

health care organization

"Health care organizations" may have **tax-exempt status** under the **federal tax law** and, if so, are likely to be **public charitable organizations**. These organizations frequently are **exempt**, in whole or in part, from state **charitable solicitation acts**. [HC §§ 3.1, 3.2, 5.1(a), 5.5(g), 20.1, 20.2; EO §§ 7.6, 12.3(a), 31.2(b)(ii); SM pp. 34–35; PF § 15.7(j); CG § 3.3(a)] (also **Health maintenance organization; Home for the aged, Hospital**).

health care sharing ministry

The phrase "health care sharing ministry" means an organization (1) that is **tax-exempt** as a **charitable** entity; (2) the **members** of which share a common set of ethical or **religious** beliefs and share medical expenses among themselves in accordance with those beliefs, regardless of the state in which a member resides or is employed; (3) members of which retain membership even after they develop a medical condition; (4) that has itself (or a predecessor of which has) been in existence at all times since December 31, 1999; (5) members of which have continuously and without interruption shared medical expenses since at least December 31, 1999; and (6) that conducts an annual audit performed by an independent certified public accounting firm in accordance with generally accepted accounting principles, the report of which is made available to members of the **public** on request. Members of this type of ministry are not subject to the individual **health insurance mandate** (IRC § 5000A(d)(2)(B)). [HC § 26.11].

health insurance exchange

States are generally required, by the **Patient Protection and Affordable Care Act**, to establish "health insurance exchanges" for the purpose of making available qualified health plans to individuals and employers who are eligible to purchase insurance through these exchanges.

The exchanges can be operated by a government agency, a **quasi-governmental entity**, or a **nonprofit organization** established by a state. [HC § 13.4; EO § 7.6(l)].

health insurance issuer
See Qualified health insurance issuer.

health insurance mandate
The "health insurance mandate," as introduced by the **Patient Protection and Affordable Care Act**, requires most U.S. citizens to obtain acceptable health insurance coverage (IRC § 5000A). This requirement is enforced by annual tax penalties. An individual is excused from this mandate if he or she is a member of a qualified religious sect or division or for any month he or she is a member of a health care sharing ministry. [HC § 26.11; CL §§ 1.2(e), 1.2(f), 4.5–4.8]].

Health Insurance Portability and Accountability Act of 1996
Enactment of the Health Insurance Portability and Accountability Act of 1996 brought **tax-exempt status** for certain **high-risk individuals health care coverage organizations**, certain **workers' compensation insurance providers**, and certain **workers' compensation reimbursement organizations**. [HC § 13.2; FR § 5.23].

health maintenance organization
A "health maintenance organization" is a **health care organization**; it provides health care services by means of facilities and programs, in a manner comparable to that of a **tax-exempt hospital**. It is a **membership** organization; its services are provided to members on a prepaid basis and to nonmembers on a fee-for-service basis. In most instances, a health maintenance organization handles emergency care cases without regard to whether the **patient** is a member of the organization, and provides care either without charge or at reduced rates to a limited number of indigent patients. Frequently, health maintenance organizations sponsor **educational** programs and **research** efforts to study ways to deliver better health care services. Where certain criteria are met, a health maintenance organization can qualify for federal income **tax exemption** as a **charitable organization** or **social welfare organization**. [HC §§ 6.2, 9.2, 9.5; EO § 7.6(e); AU § 7.1(cc)].

heir
An "heir" is a **person** who inherits some or all of the **estate** of another person, or who is entitled by **law** or by the **will** of another person to inherit money and/or **property**.

heritable
The word "heritable" is used to refer to an item of **property** that is capable of being inherited.

high-risk individuals health care coverage organizations
Certain high-risk individuals health care coverage organizations are **tax-exempt organizations** (**IRC** §§ 501(a) and 501(c)(26)). [EO § 19.15; HC § 13.2].

higher court

The term "higher court" is used to describe a court that is able to receive cases on **appeal** from a **lower court**. For example, in the **federal judicial** system, the ultimate higher court is the U.S. Supreme Court. Yet, in relation to federal courts that initially hear cases, the various U.S. Circuit Courts of Appeal are higher courts. [EO App. A].

higher education, institution of

(See **College**; **University**).

highest compensated employee

The **IRS** defines the phrase "highest compensated employee," for **Form 990** reporting purposes (Part VII, Section A), as one of the five highest compensated **employees** of the reporting **organization** (including employees of a **disregarded entity** with respect to the organization), other than current **trustees**, **directors**, **officers**, or **key employees**, whose aggregate **reportable compensation** from the organization and **related organizations** is greater than $100,000 for the calendar year ending with or within the organization's **tax year**.

highly publicized

The phrase "highly publicized" is used as part of the definition of the term **mass media advertisement**. There, the term is used to identify an item of **legislation** that is "highly publicized," which generally means frequent coverage on television and radio, and in **general circulation newspapers**, during the two weeks preceding the vote by the **legislative** body or **committee**. In the case of state or local legislation, the phrase means frequent coverage in the mass media that serve the state or local jurisdiction in question. Even when legislation receives frequent coverage, it is "highly publicized" only if the pendency of the legislation or the legislation's general terms, purpose, or effect are known to a significant segment of the **general public** (as opposed to the particular interest groups that are **directly** affected) in the area in which the paid mass media advertisement appears. [EO § 22.3(d)(i)].

historically important land area

As used in the context of the **charitable contribution deduction** for **gifts** for **conservation purposes**, a "historically important land area" is (1) an independently significant land area, including any related historic resources that meet the National Register of Historic Places Criteria for Evaluation, (2) any land area within a **registered historic district**, including any buildings on the land area that can **reasonably** be considered as contributing to the significance of the district, or (3) any land area adjacent to a **property** listed individually in the National Register, in a case where the physical or environmental features of the land area contribute to the historic or cultural integrity of the property. [CG § 9.7(c)].

historic preservation

One of the ways an **organization** can qualify as a **tax-exempt charitable organization** is by engaging in activities that **promote social welfare** by reason of combating community deterioration by preserving the historic or architectural character of a community. The **charitable**

contribution deduction is available for **gifts** for historic preservation purposes. [EO § 7.11; CG § 9.7(c); SM p. 35].

historical society

A "historical society" is a **nonprofit organization** that engages in activities such as **research** and the publication of materials concerning the history of a community or some other jurisdiction. These organizations may qualify for **tax-exempt status** under the **federal tax law**. They are sometimes **exempt** from one or more of the state **charitable solicitation acts**. [EO §§ 7.8, 8.5; FR § 3.5(n)].

holding period

A "holding period" is a period of time that must elapse before a rule of **law** is satisfied. For example, an item of **property** must be held for a period of at least one year before any **gain** or **loss** arising from the **sale** or other **disposition** of it constitutes **long-term capital gain** or **long-term capital loss** (assuming the property otherwise qualifies for that **federal tax law** treatment) (**IRC** §§ 1222(3), (4)). [CG § 2.20] (also **Capital gain**; **Capital gain property**).

holographic will

A "holographic will" is a **will** that is written and dated by the hand of the **testator** rather than typed. Like any will, a holographic will must be signed by the testator to be valid.

home for the aged

A "home for the aged" is a form of **health care organization** and thus may be **exempt** from **federal income taxation** as a **charitable organization**. To be tax-exempt, a home for the aged must be **operated** so as to satisfy the primary needs of the aged: housing, health cam, and financial security. [HC §§ 11.2–11.4; EO § 7.6(d)].

homeowners' association

A "homeowners' association" is a form of **tax-exempt organization** under the **federal tax law** (**IRC** § 528). These **associations** are usually established as part of the development of a real estate subdivision, a condominium project, or a cooperative housing project. These **entities** enable their **members** (individual homeowners and the like) to act together in managing, maintaining, and improving areas where they live. The associations' purposes include the administration and enforcement of covenants for preserving the physical appearance of the development, the ownership and management of common areas (such as sidewalks and parks), and the exterior maintenance of **property** owned by the members.

To achieve tax exemption under federal law, a homeowners' association must meet a variety of requirements, including a proscription on **private inurement**. Only **exempt function income** is exempt from taxation. [EO § 19.14; AS § 1.6(s); SM p. 46].

honorary member

A **person** is an "honorary member" of an **organization** when the **membership** was obtained solely as the consequence of a form of recognition or other honor. Usually, this type of member does not have the duties and privileges of a **regular member**.

horticultural organization

The term "horticulture" means the art or **science** of cultivating fruits, flowers, and vegetables. A "horticultural organization," then, is an **organization** that is **organized** and **operated primarily** for horticultural purposes. A horticultural organization is a type of **tax-exempt organization** under the **federal tax law** (IRC § 501(a), by reason of description in **IRC** § 501(c)(6)). For example, a garden club can be a tax-exempt horticultural organization. [EO § 16.3; PF § 15.9; AU § 7.1(l); AS § 1.6(e); SM p. 41].

hospital

A nonprofit "hospital" is a form of **health care organization**. This type of hospital is **tax-exempt** as a **charitable organization** because it is **organized** and **operated primarily** for the purpose of **advancing health**; the provision of health care for the benefit of a **community** is a charitable purpose (**IRC** § 501(c)(3)). A nonprofit hospital is, by virtue of its health care activities, a **public charity** (**IRC** §§ 170(b)(1)(A)(iii) and 509(a)(1)).

To be tax-exempt under **federal law**, a hospital must provide **medical care**, provide medical **education**, and/or engage in medical **research**. It must promote the health of a class of **persons** broad enough to benefit a community, and must be operated to serve a public rather than a private interest; this is known as the **community benefit standard**. Basically, this means that the hospital's emergency room must be open to all, and that health care is provided to all who can pay, either **directly** or **indirectly**. Other factors that indicate that a hospital is operating for the benefit of the public include control of the institution by a **board of trustees** composed of individuals who do not have any direct economic interest in the hospital; maintenance by the hospital of an open medical staff, with privileges available to all qualified physicians, consistent with the size and nature of the activities; a hospital policy enabling any member of the medical staff to rent available office space; hospital programs of medical training, research, and education; and involvement by the hospital in various projects and programs to improve the health of the community. To be **exempt**, a hospital must also satisfy the **additional hospital exemption requirements**. Hospitals are frequently exempt from state **charitable solicitation acts**.

The term "hospital" includes federal government hospitals; state, county, and municipal hospitals that are **instrumentalities** of **governmental units**; rehabilitation institutions; outpatient clinics; extended care facilities; and community mental health and alcohol and drug treatment centers. The term does not include convalescent homes, **homes for the aged**, homes for children, or institutions the primary purpose of which is to train handicapped individuals to pursue a vocation, nor does it include clinics for animals. [HC Chap. 8; EO §§ 7.6, 12.3(a), 24.5(b); AR §§ 3.1(u), 3.2(u), 15.2(c), 15.2(i)(1)(G); PF §§ 15.3, 15.7(j); SM pp. 34–35, 80; FR § 3.5(f); CG § 3.3(a); LI Q 10.4].

hospital facility

A "hospital facility" is a facility that is, or is required to be, licensed, registered, or similarly recognized by a state as a **hospital**. This includes a hospital facility that is operated through a **disregarded entity** or a **joint venture** treated as a **partnership** for **federal tax purposes**. This term does not include hospital facilities that are located outside the U.S. It also does not include hospital facilities that are operated by **entities** organized as separate legal entities from the organization that are taxable as a **corporation** for federal tax purposes (except for **member** entities covered by a **group exemption** included in a **group return** filed by the organization). [HC § 26.10; EO § 7.6(b)(i); AR §§ 15.2(h), 15.2(i)(1)(H)].

hospital failure, tax on

A **hospital organization** that fails to meet the **community health needs assessment** requirement for any **tax year** will have an **excise tax** of $50,000 imposed on it (**IRC** § 4959). [EO § 7.6(b)(ii); HC § 26.10(a)(ii)].

hospital organization

The term "hospital organization" means an organization that operates a facility that is required by a state to be licensed, registered, or similarly recognized as a **hospital**. The **IRS** has the authority to denominate a charitable entity as a hospital organization if the agency determines that the entity has the provision of hospital care as its principal function or purpose constituting the basis for its tax exemption; the **IRS** to date has not exercised this authority. If a hospital organization operates more than one hospital facility, the organization must meet the **additional hospital exemption requirements** separately with respect to each facility. Also, an organization with more than one hospital facility is not treated as being an exempt charitable organization with respect to a facility as to which these requirements are not separately met (**IRC** § 501(r)(2)). [HC § 26.10; EO § 7.6(b)(i)].

hospital management services organization

An **organization** that manages **tax-exempt hospitals** and/or other **exempt** health care **entities** may qualify as an exempt **charitable** organization unless it runs afoul of the **IRS's** position on the relationship between a management entity and **unaffiliated** hospitals. [HC § 19.4].

house counsel

The term "house counsel" (or, occasionally, "in-house counsel") means a **lawyer** who is an **employee** of an **organization** rather than an **independent contractor** with respect to the organization. It is common for the larger of the **nonprofit organizations** to have house counsel, although that does not preclude the hiring of outside counsel for assistance concerning specific areas of the **law**.

household item

In the context of the **federal tax law charitable giving** rules, a "household item" includes furniture, furnishings, electronics, appliances, and linens; the term does not embrace food, paintings, antiques, other objects of art, jewelry, gems, and collections (**IRC** § 170(f)(16)(D)). [CG §§ 9.25, 21.7, 24.7(b)(4); AR §§ 19.1(f)(1), 19.2(d)].

Housing and Economic Recovery Act of 2008

The future of **down-payment assistance** programs and **organizations** was significantly imperiled when the "Housing and Economic Recovery Act of 2008," which bans seller-funded down-payment assistance in connection with Federal Housing Administration–insured mortgages, was enacted. [EO § 7.5].

I

IRC

The term "IRC" means the **Internal Revenue Code** of 1986, as amended.

IRS

The term "IRS" means the **Internal Revenue Service**. (also **Agency**).

identification number

See **Employer identification number**.

illegal activity

An **organization** cannot qualify as a **tax-exempt charitable organization** or an **exempt social welfare organization** (and presumably all other types of **exempt organizations**) under the **federal tax law** if it undertakes one or more activities that are illegal under federal law. Recent examples are the advocacy of polygamy and the distribution of marijuana for recreational or medical use. The **IRS** is of the view that illegal activities, which violate the minimum standards of acceptable conduct necessary to the preservation of an orderly society, are contrary to the common good and the general welfare of the people in a community and thus are not permissible means of advancing the purposes and activities of exempt organizations. [EO § 6.3(i); SM p. 324] (also **Public policy doctrine**).

ill person

The **federal tax law** includes special rules by which a **for-profit corporation** can obtain a **twice-basis deduction** for a **charitable contribution** of **property** constituting its **inventory**. These **gifts** must be used for care of the "ill," **needy**, or **infants**. For this purpose, an "ill person" is a **person** who requires medical care. This includes those suffering from a physical injury, a person with a significant impairment of a bodily organ, a person with an existing handicap, whether from birth or later injury, a person suffering from malnutrition, a person with a disease, sickness, or infection that significantly impairs physical health, a person partially or totally incapable of self-care (including incapacity due to old age). A person suffering from mental illness is included in this definition if the person is hospitalized or institutionalized for the mental disorder, or, although the person is not hospitalized or institutionalized, if the person's mental illness constitutes a significant health impairment. [CG § 9.3(b)].

immediate payment charitable gift annuity

An "immediate payment charitable gift annuity" is a **charitable gift annuity** in which the payment of the **annuity** begins less than one year from the date on which the annuity was issued. [CG § 14.1] (cf. **Deferred payment charitable gift annuity**).

immunity

In general, the **law** provides an "immunity" where it **excludes**, **exempts**, or shields a **person** from a legal obligation. For example, some states have enacted laws that immunize individuals who serve, as **volunteers**, on the **board of directors** or **board of trustees** of a **nonprofit organization** from **officers' and directors' legal liability**. [PG p. 25; SM p. 7].

I

impulse donor

An "impulse donor" is an individual who makes a **charitable contribution** on a whim—perhaps in response to a compelling **solicitation** during a telethon or in a **direct mail** piece; the gift usually is of a relatively small amount of money. The gift normally is not of **property** and the donor is not intending to involve himself or herself with the **donee charitable organization** as a **volunteer**. [SM pp. 129–130].

imputed income

"Imputed income" is **income** that a **person** does not **directly** earn or receive, but that is attributed or assigned (imputed), by **operation of law**, to that person. This concept is most notable in the context of the **federal income tax law**; it is based on the thought that there should not be a **deduction** for a particular **expense** if there is no corresponding item of income. For example, this is one of the policy reasons underlying the denial of a federal income tax **charitable contribution deduction** for the **contribution** of services; the individual who would claim that deduction most likely did not regard as imputed income the **value** of the services provided. Moreover, in a situation of this nature, the imputed income and the "imputed deduction" almost always would end in a **wash**. [CG § 9.14].

in being

The words "in being" mean alive at an ascertainable time; this term is applied, of course, with respect to individuals. For example, in the case of a **charitable remainder trust**, where all or a portion of the **income interest** is to be paid to an individual or individuals, all of them must be living at the time of the creation of the trust. A named **person** or persons may include **members** of a named class, provided that, in the case of a class that includes any individual, all of the individuals are alive at the time of the creation of the trust. This requirement does not apply where the period for which the income interest is to be paid to the class consists solely of a **term of years**. [CG §§ 12.2(d), 12.3(d)].

in terrorem clause

The phrase "in terrorem" is a Latin one meaning "in fear." An "in terrorem clause" is a provision inserted in an **instrument** (usually a **contract** or a **will**) requiring a **person** to do something or refrain from doing something as a **condition** of receiving a benefit under the instrument. The clause derives this name from the fact that the requirement usually is not enforceable; the language is there nonetheless in an attempt to induce (scare) the person into compliance with it.

in-kind contribution

The phrase "in-kind contribution" is not firmly defined in the **federal tax law**. These **contributions** are not of money but are of forms of goods or services, including various forms of **property** (such as a **corporation's inventory**), use of facilities, provision of equipment, and individuals' expertise. Some are of the view that these gifts must be of items that the **donee** would otherwise have to purchase. [CG §§ 9.3, 9.14, 9.18].

I

incidental

The word "incidental" is used in the context of the **federal tax law** to describe a **de minimis** act or level of activity; it is usually meant to define something that is to be disregarded when a rule of law is applied. For example, even though a **tax-exempt public charitable organization** is technically forbidden from engaging in an act constituting **private inurement** or a form of **political campaign activity**, a certain amount of incidental activity of this nature generally will be tolerated by the courts (although perhaps not by the **IRS**). Some bodies of the **federal tax law** tolerate incidental activity, such as the **private benefit doctrine** and the **private foundation self-dealing rules**. A comparable rule of **law** is that, where a benefit to a **donor**, as the result or a **gift** to a **charitable organization**, is incidental, the benefit will not defeat the **charitable contribution deduction**. [EO §§ 20.7, 20.11(b), 23.2(a); CG § 3.1(d); PF § 5.3; HC § 4.1(c)].

incidental and tenuous

The phrase "incidental and tenuous" is used to describe the standard by which a benefit derived by a **disqualified person** from the use by a **private foundation** of its **income** or **assets** will not cause an act of **self-dealing**. It is used to describe a relatively minor benefit, such as enhancement of the general reputation or prestige of a disqualified person by a public acknowledgement of a **contribution** by that **person**. For example, a **qualifying distribution** that results in a naming of an **institution** or **fund** after a **substantial contributor** is incidental and tenuous. [PF § 5.3].

incidents of ownership

The phrase "incidents of ownership" is used to describe the elements of **control** and dominion that comprise the ownership by a **person** of an item of **property**. The phrase is often used when a person is endeavoring, for **law** purposes, to transfer ownership of a property to another, yet does not part with all of the "incidents of ownership." Where this is the case, the **federal tax law** will disregard the transfer, in that true passage of ownership has not occurred. [CG § 17.3].

income

Generally, the amount of money (or **revenue**) received by an individual or other **person** is considered "income." In this sense, the term "income" is the same as **gross income**. Federal and state **law** determines what is and is not income for federal and state (respectively) **tax law** purposes. These bodies of law also provide for a range of tax **credits**, **deductions**, **deferrals**, **exclusions**, and **exemptions** that are used in computing **taxable income**. [CG § 2.1; EO §§ 24.2(e), 25.1(a); PF § 12.1(b)] (also **Adjusted gross income**).

income, accumulated

A **tax-exempt organization** may accumulate its **income**, that is, it may hold the income, such as in a special **fund**, invest it, and spend only the income generated from that investment. In this sense, the initial income is converted to **corpus** or **principal**.

The **private foundation mandatory payment** requirements are inapplicable to certain pre-1969 private foundations that are required by their **governing instruments** to accumulate income. [EO § 11.8; PF § 1.2] (also **Endowment fund**).

income, from for-profit subsidiary

A **tax-exempt organization** may have a **for-profit subsidiary** and receive **income** from the subsidiary. This income may constitute **passive income**, which generally is not subject to the tax on **unrelated business income**. Nonetheless, when otherwise nontaxable passive income is derived from a **controlled** for-profit (and taxable) subsidiary, that income is generally taxed as unrelated income (**IRC** § 512(b)(13)). Thus, when a tax-exempt **parent organization** receives **rent**, **interest**, or most other forms of passive income from a controlled for-profit subsidiary, these revenues generally will be taxable. There are two **exceptions** to this rule. One exception is that when a for-profit subsidiary pays a **dividend** to its tax-exempt organization parent, the dividends are not taxable to the parent organization. The other exception is for the payment of certain **qualifying specified payments**. [EO §§ 29.6, 30.7; UB § 8.8].

income, investment

See **Investment income**.

income, passive

The **federal tax law**, particularly in the context of **unrelated business income taxation**, differentiates between **income** that is actively generated by a **tax-exempt organization** and income that is passively derived by an exempt organization; the latter type of income is termed "passive income." The unrelated business income rules were enacted to ameliorate the effects of **competition** between **exempt organizations** and **for-profit organizations**, by taxing the **net income** of exempt organizations from unrelated business activities. The principle underlying this statute is that the business endeavors must be "active" ones for competitive activity to result. Correspondingly, income derived by an exempt organization in a "passive" manner generally is income that is not acquired as the result of competitive activity and thus should not be taxed. Consequently, most forms of passive income are not taxed as unrelated business income.

Two significant **exceptions** to this rule concern income from **debt-financed property** and income from **controlled subsidiaries**.

Therefore, passive income, such as **dividends**, **interest**, payments with respect to **securities loans**, **annuities**, **royalties**, certain forms of **rent**, income from certain **option-writing activities**, income from certain **interest rate swaps**, and **gain** from the disposition of **capital property**, is generally excluded from **unrelated business taxable income**, along with **directly connected** deductions (**IRC** §§ 512(b)(1)–(3), (5)). [EO § 25.1; UB § 3.1; AR § 21.1(g); PF § 7.1(b); FR §§ 5.7(a)(vii), 5.7(b)(vi); SM pp. 177–178] (also **Modifications**).

income interest

Conceptually, every item of **property** contains within it two types of **interests**. One is an "income interest"; the other is a "**remainder interest**." The income interest in a property is a function of the income generated by the property. A **person** may be entitled to all of the income from a property or some portion of the income—for example, income equal to 5 percent of the **fair market value** of the property (even though the property is generating income at the rate of 7 percent). [CG §§ 5.3, 12.2(a), 12.3(a), 13.2(b), 16.2; CU Q 12.61; SM p. 234].

income modifications

The term "income modifications" is used in the context of defining the **adjusted net income** of a **private operating foundation**. These modifications are as follows: (l) the **exclusion** for **interest** on **tax-exempt bonds** does not apply, (2) **capital gains** and **capital losses** from the **sale** or other **disposition** of **property** are taken into account only in an amount equal to any **net short-term capital gain** for the year, and (3) there is taken into account (a) amounts received or accrued as repayments of amounts that were taken into account as a **qualifying distribution** for any **tax year**, (h) amounts received or accrued from the sale or other disposition of property to the extent that the acquisition of the property was taken into account as a qualifying distribution for any tax year, and (c) any amount **set aside** to the extent it is determined that the amount is not necessary for the purposes for which it was set aside (**IRC** § 4942(f)(2)). [PF § 3.1(d)] (also **Deduction modifications**).

income source test

An **organization**, to qualify for **tax exemption** under the **federal tax law**, as a **benevolent life insurance company**, a **mutual ditch or irrigation company**, a **mutual or cooperative telephone company**, or **like** organization (**IRC** § 501(c)(12)), is required to meet the "income source test." This test requires that at least 85 percent of the **entity's income** consist of amounts collected from its **members** for the sole purpose of meeting losses and expenses. The test requires that this type of **exempt organization**, for each of its **tax years**, combine all sources of income not otherwise excludable (**IRC** §§ 501(c)(12)(B) or (C)) and calculate whether more than 15 percent of that income is derived from nonmembers. [EO § 19.5].

income tax

Federal law imposes a *tax* on the **net income** (or **taxable income**) received by individuals and **organizations** (the latter usually being **for-profit corporations**, **estates**, and **trusts**). In arriving at taxable income, the law begins with **gross income**, then determines **adjusted gross**

income, both ascertained by means of application of various **credits**, **deductions**, **deferrals**, **exclusions**, and **exemptions**. [CG §§ 1.1, 9.10(c)].

income tax return preparer

The term "income tax return preparer" designates a **person** who for **compensation** prepares, or who employs one or more persons to prepare, any **tax return** or any **claim for refund**; the preparation of a **substantial** portion of a return or claim for refund is treated as if it were the preparation of the return or claim for refund (**IRC** § 7701(a)(36)(A)). A person is not an income tax preparer, however, merely because the person (1) furnishes typing, reproducing, or other mechanical assistance; (2) prepares a return or claim for refund of an **employer** (or of an **officer** or **employee** of the employer) by whom he or she is regularly and continuously employed; (3) prepares as a **fiduciary** a return or claim for refund for any person; or (4) prepares a claim for refund for a **taxpayer** in response to a **notice of deficiency** issued to the taxpayer or in response to any waiver of restriction after the commencement of an **audit** of the taxpayer or another taxpayer if a determination in the audit of the other taxpayer **directly or indirectly** affects the tax **liability** of the taxpayer (**IRC** § 7701(a)(36)(B)).

income test

To qualify as a **private operating foundation**, the **entity** must meet an "income test." To satisfy this test, a private operating foundation must annually expend an amount that is equal to **substantially all** of the lesser of its **adjusted net income** or its **minimum investment return**, in the form of **qualifying distributions directly** for the **active conduct** of its **tax-exempt activities** (**IRC** § 4942(j)(3)(A)).

The funds expended must be used by the private operating foundation itself rather than by or through one or more **grantee** organizations. An amount **set aside** by a private operating foundation for a **specific project** involving the active conduct of its **exempt** activities will qualify under the test if the initial setting aside of the funds constitutes a qualifying set-aside. The making or awarding of **grants**, **scholarships**, or similar payments to individual **beneficiaries** to support active exempt programs will qualify the **grantor** as a private operating foundation only if it maintains some **significant involvement** in the programs. [PF §§ 3.1(c), 3.1(d); EO § 12.1(b)].

income trust

See **Charitable income trust**.

incorporate

The word "incorporate" means to create a **corporation**. This term applies whether the corporation is a **nonprofit** or **for-profit organization**. [PG pp. 4–5; SM pp. 8–9, 25; CU Q 1.6, Q 1.11, Q 16.18; RE Q 5.18].

income-exception method

The "income-exception method" is one of the ways that the **payout requirement** for certain **charitable remainder unitrusts** is determined. These trusts are the **net-income charitable remainder unitrust** and the **net-income make-up charitable remainder unitrust**. [CG § 12.3(a)].

incorporator

An "incorporator" is an individual who creates, or participates in the creation of, a **corporation**. State **law** determines the number of incorporators that are required for this purpose; the most common number is three. [PG p. 4; SM pp. 8–9; CU Q 1.10, Q 16.8; RE Q 1.12; LI Q 1.16, Q 1.25].

indemnification

See **Indemnify**.

indemnification clause

See **Indemnify**.

indemnify

The term "indemnify" means to hold harmless; thus, one **person** may "indemnify" another against loss or damage. The **indemnitor** agrees to absorb or otherwise pay for a loss or damage incurred by the other person (or persons), who is the **indemnitee**. Usually, an indemnification is found in a **contract**.

In the context of **nonprofit organizations**, the organization may decide to indemnify its **directors**, **trustees**, and/or **officers** against certain forms of liability incurred while in the service of the organization. This is most frequently done by means of an "indemnification clause" in the organization's **bylaws**. The **nonprofit corporation acts** of some states specify what may or may not appear in an indemnification clause.

A **private foundation** may determine to indemnify its directors, trustees, and/or officers (collectively termed **foundation managers**). The prohibitions on **self-dealing** do not apply to the indemnification by a private foundation of a foundation manager, with respect to his or her defense in a **judicial** or **administrative** proceeding involving either the private foundation **excise taxes** or state laws relating to mismanagement of funds of **charitable organizations**, against most **expenses** (including **lawyers'** fees) if the expenses are **reasonably** incurred by the manager in connection with the proceeding, the manager is successful in defending or settling the proceeding, and the manager has not acted **willfully** and without **reasonable cause** in the matter. [PG p. 25; PF §§ 5.7, 5.8(g); RE Q 5.18; SM p. 7].

indemnitee

A **person** who is the **beneficiary** of an "indemnification" is termed an "indemnitee." (also **Indemnify**).

indemnitor

An "indemnitor" is a **person** who provides an **indemnity**. (also **Indemnify**).

independent contractor

An "independent contractor" is a **person** who provides services to another person under circumstances where the relationship between the parties is not that of **employer-employee** or

principal-agent. For example, accountants, **lawyers**, and **professional fundraisers** are commonly independent contractors. [AR § 6.2(b); FR §§ 2.3–2.5].

independent investor test

The "independent investor test" is a method (in the **for-profit** context) for determining the **reasonableness** of an individual's **compensation** package. This test establishes a **presumption** that an executive's compensation is reasonable if the investors in the company (actual or hypothetical) believe that the return on their investment is reasonable. [EO § 20.4(b)].

independent regulatory agency

An "independent regulatory agency" is an **agency** of a government but is not part of the **executive branch** of that government. For example, the **IRS** is not an independent regulatory agency, because it is part of the **Department of the Treasury**. An example of an independent regulatory agency is the **Federal Election Commission**. [EO § 2.2; FR § 5.25(b)].

independent voting member of a governing body

The phrase "independent voting member of a governing body" means, at all times during an **organization's tax year**, (1) a member who was not **compensated** as an **officer** or other **employee** of the organization or of a **related organization** (except as provided in the religious exception in **Form 990**, Part VI); (2) the member did not receive total compensation or other payments exceeding $10,000 from the organization or from related organization's as an **independent contractor**, other than **reasonable** compensation for services provided in the capacity as a member of the governing body; (3) neither the member, nor any **family member** of the member, was involved in a transaction with the organization (**directly** or **indirectly** through **affiliation** with another organization); and (4) neither the member nor any family member of the member was involved in a transaction with a taxable or **tax-exempt** related organization of a type and amount that would be reportable (**Form 990** or **990-EZ**, Schedule L) if required to be filed by the related organization.

A member of a governing body is not considered to lack independence merely because (1) the member is a **donor** to the organization, regardless of the amount of the **contribution**; (2) the member has taken a bona fide vow of poverty and either (a) receives compensation as an **agent** of a **religious order** or an **apostolic organization** but only under circumstances in which the member does not receive taxable **income**; or (3) the member receives financial benefits from the organization solely in the capacity of being a member of the **charitable** or other **class** served by the organization in the exercise of its exempt function, as long as the financial benefits comply with the organization's terms of membership. [AR §§ 1.6(f), 5.1(d), 5.2(a)(1)].

indirect

The word "indirect" means something that is not **direct** in action or procedure. An example of the use of this word is in the phrases **directly or indirectly** or **indirect public support**.

indirect contributions from the public

The phrase "indirect contributions from the general public" is used in the context of constructing the **support fraction** for **donative publicly supported organizations**. These contributions are those from other donative **charitable organizations** and **grants** from **governmental units**. [PF § 15.4(b)] (also **Indirect public support**).

indirectly
See **Indirect**.

indirect public support
The phrase "indirect public support" refers to financial support that one **organization** receives from another in the form of **grants**, where the **grantor** organization previously received the funds from the **public**, either in the form of **contributions** (such as in the case of **donative publicly supported organizations**) or **taxes** (as in the case of **governmental units**). The concept is that the grantor organization was functioning essentially as a **conduit**, so that the **direct public support** received by the grantor organization has been converted to indirect public support to the ultimate grantee. Indirect public support is a form of **public support**. [PF § 15.4(b)] (also **Direct public support**).

indirect self-dealing
An "indirect act of self-dealing" is a **self-dealing** transaction between a **disqualified person** with respect to a **private foundation** and an **organization controlled** by a private foundation. [PF § 5.11].

individual retirement account, distribution from
An **exclusion** from **gross income** is available for otherwise taxable distributions form a traditional or a Roth individual retirement account in the case of a **qualified charitable distribution**. This exclusion may not exceed $100,000 per **taxpayer** per **tax year** (**IRC** § 408(d)(8)(A)). [CG § 9.10(e)].

individuals, instruction of
One of the ways for a **nonprofit organization** to obtain **recognition** of **tax-exempt status** under the **federal tax law** is for it to be **organized** and **operated primarily** for **educational** purposes. One or the ways in which an organization can be "educational" is to instruct or train individuals for the purpose of improving or developing their capabilities. [EO § 8.4; CU Q 2.2; SM p. 36].

industrial liaison program
An "industrial liaison program" is a **program** undertaken by a **tax-exempt college** or **university** in which the **institution** receives a **fee** from **for-profit businesses** for providing them with **research** data (often before it becomes publicly accessible) and information about faculty members who have expertise that is of interest to the fee-paying business. Much of this research data is in manuscripts written by faculty members, before they are published; these manuscripts are termed "preprints." The colleges and universities that have these programs reward their faculty members who write preprints with "points," which are used by these individuals to acquire office furniture, equipment, travel opportunities, and other amenities. (also **Technology transfer**).

infant

In the context of the **federal tax law** rule concerning the special **twice-basis deduction** for **contributions** by **corporations** of property out of their inventory, the word "infant" is defined as a minor child as determined under the laws of the jurisdiction in which the child resides. [CG § 9.3(b)].

influence

The word "influence" means "to have an impact on," "to alter the thinking and/or behavior of," another person. In the **federal tax law**, this word is used in the rule that limits the amount of **lobbying** that a **charitable organization** may undertake without losing its **tax exemption**. The terms "influencing" **legislation** (or attempting to do so) and "lobbying" are essentially synonymous. [EO § 22.3(b); SM pp. 186–187].

influence legislation

The words "influence legislation" (often preceded by the words "attempts to") mean to engage in **lobbying**. Most categories of **tax-exempt organizations** are not subject to any **federal tax law** limitations as to influencing legislation. An **exempt charitable organization** and an exempt **qualified insurance issuer**, however, may not, as a **substantial** portion of its activities, attempt to influence **legislation** (**IRC** §§ 501(c)(3), 501(c)(29)(B)(iii). Generally, an effort by a **private foundation** to influence legislation is a **taxable expenditure** (**IRC** § 4945(d)(1)). The **business expense deduction** is not available, by operation of the **lobbying disallowance rule**, for any amount paid or incurred in connection with the influencing of legislation (**IRC** §§ 162(e)(1)(A), (C)).

Usually, the concept of influencing legislation relates to the influencing of **members** of a **legislative branch** of government or members of their staff or committee staff. In some instances, however, it can extend to the lobbying of members of an **executive branch** of government and their staff. For example, the **law** comprising the **expenditure test** defines the term "influencing legislation" to mean (1) any attempt to influence any legislation through an attempt to affect the opinions of the public or any segment of the public and (2) any attempt to influence any legislation through **communication** with any member or **employee** of a legislative body, or with any **government official** or employee who may participate in the formulation of the legislation (**IRC** § 4911(d)(1)).

In the context of the lobbying disallowance rule, the term "influencing legislation" means any attempt to influence any legislation through communication with any member or employee of a legislative body or with any government official or employee who may participate in the formulation of legislation (**IRC** § 162(e)(4)(A)).

The expenditure test contains the following exceptions from the term "influencing legislation": (1) making available the results of **nonpartisan analysis, study, or research**; (2) the provision of **technical advice** or assistance (where the advice or assistance would otherwise constitute the influencing of legislation) to a governmental body or to a committee or subdivision of a committee in response to a written request by the body or subdivision; (3) appearances before or communications to any legislative body with respect to a possible decision of the body that might affect the existence of the **organization**, its powers and duties, **tax-exempt status**, or the deduction of contributions to the organization (the **self-defense exception**); (4) communications between the organization and its **bona fide** members with respect to legislation or proposed legislation of direct interest to the organization and its members (with exceptions for certain forms of lobbying (**IRC** § 4911(d)(3)); and (5) any communication with a governmental official or employee, other than (a) a communication with a member or employee of a legislative body (where the communication would otherwise constitute the influencing of legislation) or (b) a communication the **principal** purpose of which is to influence legislation (**IRC** § 49l1(d)(2)). [EO § 22.3; HC §§ 7.1(b), 18.4(a); AS § 4.2(a); PG pp. 107–118, 339–341; SM pp. 186–187] (also **Direct lobbying**; **Grass-roots lobbying**; **Subsequent use rule**).

information item

The term "information item" is used by the **IRS** to encompass information from internal or external sources concerning potential noncompliance with the **federal tax law** by a **tax-exempt organization**. [AU § 1.2].

information letter

An "information letter" is a written statement issued by the **National Office** of the **IRS**. It calls attention to a well-established interpretation or principle of the **federal tax law**, usually without applying it to a specific set of facts. An information letter may be issued if the inquiry indicates a need for general information. It may also be issued when the request does not meet the requirements for requesting a **private letter ruling** and the **IRS** believes that the general information will assist the **person** involved. Occasionally, an important element of the **law** of **tax-exempt organizations** will be announced by means of an information letter.

information return

An "information return" is a **return** filed with the **IRS** for the purpose of supplying that government **agency** with information that it is empowered by **law** to request (technically, returning the requested information). An information return is to be distinguished from a tax return, which is a form filed with the **IRS** for the purpose of reporting tax information and (often) paying a tax. For example, most individuals annually file a tax return (usually **Form 1040**), as do **for-profit corporations** (**Form 1120**). Most **tax-exempt organizations** annually **file** or **submit** an **information return** or **notice** (in the **Form 990** series), although when they are required to report **unrelated business income**, they file a tax return (**Form 990-T**). Other organizations that do not pay taxes file information returns, not tax returns; for example, a **partnership** annually files an information return (**Form 1065**). Forms submitted to the **IRS** in connection with the payment of compensation (principally, **Form W-2** or **Form 1099**) are information returns. [EO §§ 28.2–28.4, 28.8; PF § 12.1; HC §§ 35.3, 35.4; UB §§ 11.3, 11.4; SM p. 110] (also **Annual information return**; various **Forms**).

information return, partnership

If a **partnership** in which a **tax-exempt organization** is a partner **regularly carries on** a **trade or business** that would constitute an **unrelated trade or business** if **directly** carried on by the exempt organization, the exempt organization generally must include its share of the partnership's **income** and **deductions** from the business activity in determining its unrelated income tax liability. This is known as the **look-through rule**.

A partnership generally must furnish to each partner a statement reflecting the information about the partnership required to be shown on the partner's tax return (**IRC** § 6031(b)). The statement must set forth the partners distributive share of the partnership's income, **gain**, **loss**, **deduction**, or **credit** required to be shown on the tax return of the partner, along with any additional information as provided by **IRS** forms or instructions that may be required to apply particular provisions of the **federal tax law** to the partner with respect to items related to the partnership. The instructions accompanying the statement for partners (**Schedule K-1**, **Form 1065**) require the partnership to identify whether any of the partners is a tax-exempt organization.

Also, the partnership must attach a statement furnishing any other information needed by the partner to file its **tax return** or **information return** that is not shown elsewhere on the schedule. In the case of a partnership regularly carrying on a trade or business, the partnership must furnish to the partners the information necessary to enable each exempt partner to compute its distributive share of partnership income or loss from the business (**IRC** § 6031(d)). A partnership itself files an information return (**Form 1065**). [EO § 31.6].

inherent tax rationale

There are a variety of rationales underlying the basis in the **federal tax law** for one or more categories of **tax exemptions**. One of these rationales is the "inherent tax rationale." The essence of this rationale is that the receipt of what otherwise might be deemed **income** by a **tax-exempt organization** is not a **taxable event**, in that the organization is merely a convenience or **means to an end**, a vehicle by which those participating in the enterprise may receive and expend money in much the same way that they would if the money was expended by each of them individually. This rationale underlies the tax exemption for certain **social clubs**, **homeowners' associations**, and **political organizations**. [EO § 1.5] (also **Tax exemption, rationale for**).

inherit

The word "inherit" means to obtain the ownership of an item of **property** as the consequence of the death of an individual. A **person** who receives property in this manner is an **heir**. Property obtained in this fashion is termed an "inheritance." A **charitable organization** can inherit property. (also **Bequest**; **Devise**; **Heritable**; **Legacy**).

inheritance

See **Inherit**.

inheritance tax

An "inheritance tax" is a **tax** under state law on the **value** of money and/or **property** that is received as an **inheritance**. This tax is paid by the recipient **heirs**.

in-house expenditure

The term "in-house expenditure" is used as part of the **de minimis exception** from the **lobbying disallowance rule**. The term means **expenditures** for **lobbying** (such as labor and materials costs) other than payments to a professional **lobbyist** to conduct lobbying for the **organization** and **dues** or other similar payments that are **allocable** to lobbying (such as **association** dues) (**IRC** § 162(e)(6)(B)(ii)). [EO § 22.6(c)].

initial contract

The **intermediate sanctions rules** do not apply to a **fixed payment** made to a **person** pursuant to an initial contract. The term "initial contract" means a binding written contract between an **applicable tax-exempt organization** and a person who was not a **disqualified person** with respect to the organization immediately prior to entering into the contract. [EO § 21.8; HC § 4.9(a)(iv); AR §§ 6.1(b)(14), 6.2(c)(9); AS § 3.8(d)(iii); SM pp. 59–60].

initial tax

The **federal tax law** imposes a variety of **excise taxes** that are termed "initial taxes." (The other levels of these excise taxes are **additional** taxes and, in the **private foundation** law context, the **termination** tax.) These taxes are levied in the **intermediate sanctions**, private foundation, and **political campaign activities limitation** contexts.

Initial taxes are imposed on private foundations and, in some instances, on **foundation managers** for **commissions** or **omissions** such as **self-dealing**, insufficient **payouts**, **excess business holdings**, **jeopardizing investments**, and **taxable expenditures**. There are three levels (or tiers) of these excise taxes. The first of these levels involves the "initial tax."

An initial tax is imposed on each act of **self-dealing** between a **disqualified person** and a private foundation, on the self-dealer at a **rate** of 10 percent of the **amount involved** with respect to the act for each year in the **taxable period** (**IRC** § 4941(a)(1)). Under certain circumstances, where that tax is imposed, a tax of 5 percent of the amount involved may be imposed on the **participation** of a foundation manager in the act of self-dealing (**IRC** § 4941(a)(2)).

An initial tax of 30 percent is imposed on the **undistributed income** of a private foundation, for any **tax year**, that has not been timely distributed in the form of **qualifying distributions** (**IRC** § 4942(a)).

An initial tax is imposed on the excess business holdings of a private foundation in any **business enterprise** for each tax year that ends during the taxable period; the amount of this tax is 10 percent of the total **value** of all of the private foundation's excess business holdings in each of its business enterprises (**IRC** § 4943(a)(1)).

If a private foundation invests any amount in a manner as to jeopardize the carrying out of any of its **tax-exempt purposes**, an initial tax is imposed on the private foundation on the making of the investment, at the rate of 10 percent of the amount so invested for each tax year or part of a year in the taxable period (**IRC** § 4944(a)(1)). Where this tax is imposed, another tax may be imposed on the participation of any foundation manager in the making of the investment (**IRC** § 4944(a)(2)).

An excise tax is imposed on each taxable expenditure of a private foundation, which is to be paid by the private foundation at the rate of 20 percent of the amount of each taxable expenditure (**IRC** § 4945(a)(1)). Another excise tax may be imposed on the agreement of any foundation manager to the making of a taxable expenditure by a private foundation (**IRC** § 4945(a)(2)).

In the intermediate sanctions setting, an initial tax is imposed on an **excess benefit transaction** equal to 25 percent of the **excess benefit**; this tax must be paid by the **disqualified person** involved (**IRC** § 4958(a)(1)). If that tax is imposed, an initial tax equal to 10 percent of the excess benefit is imposed on the **participation** of an **organization manager** in the transaction, **knowing** that it is an excess benefit transaction, unless the participation was not **willful** and was due to **reasonable cause** (**IRC** § 4958(a)(2)).

As to **public charities**, there is an initial tax, imposed for violation of the political campaign activities limitation. This tax, payable by the organization, is 10 percent of the amount of the expenditure (**IRC** § 4955(a)(1)). Another initial tax of 2 1/2 percent of the expenditure may also be imposed on each of the **organization's managers** (**IRC** § 4955(a)(2)). [EO §§ 12.4, 21.10, 23.3; PF §§ 5.15, 6.7, 7.6, 8.5, 9.10; SM pp. 58–60, 90–91, 199–200] (also **Abatement**; **Additional tax**; **First-tier tax**; **Termination** tax).

injunction

An "injunction" is a form of remedy, usually initiated by a court, issued to require a **person** to refrain from continuing to do a particular act. An injunction is a form of legal remedy that was conceived in the **law** of **equity**. Some specific types of injunctions are authorized by statute. For example, the **IRS** has the authority to commence an **action** in **federal** district court to enjoin a **charitable organization** from the making of **political expenditures** and for other relief to ensure that the **assets** of the organization are preserved for **tax-exempt purposes** (**IRC** § 7409). The **agency** also has the authority to obtain an injunction to enjoin the promotion of an **abusive tax shelter** (**IRC** § 7408). The state **charitable solicitation acts** usually provide the regulatory officials involved with the authority to issue, or to induce a court to issue, an injunction restraining a **charitable solicitation** that is being conducted without compliance with the act. Some forms of injunctions are prohibited by statute, such as the **Anti-Injunction Act**. [EO §§ 23.3, 28.16(c); FR § 3.21; SM p. 152] (also **Permanent injunction**; **Preliminary injunction**; **Temporary restraining order**).

inquiry notice date

The term "inquiry notice date" means the date the **notice** with respect to a **church tax inquiry** is provided (**IRC** § 7611(h)(5)). [EO § 27.6(c)].

insider

The **federal law** of **tax-exempt organizations** has appropriated the term "insider" from the federal securities law (which prohibits, among other uses of the term, "insider trading") and applies it in the context of the **private inurement doctrine**. Generally, an insider is a **person** who has a special relationship to the **organization** involved, by which that person can cause application of the organization's funds for the private purposes of the person by reason of the person's exercise of **control** of or influence over the organization. In the setting of **nonprofit organizations** generally, an insider includes an organization's **founder, principal funder, directors, trustees, officers**, and perhaps key **employees** and **members of the family** of the foregoing persons. Specific types of **tax-exempt organizations** have unique categories of insiders because of the fact that the terms "insider" and **disqualified person** are nearly synonymous.

The concept of private inurement, with its emphasis on **inurement** of **net earnings**, contemplates a type of transaction between an exempt organization (usually a **charitable organization**) and an insider, who usually is an individual. Thus, the law concerning charitable organizations speaks of inurement to the benefit of any **private shareholder or individual** (**IRC** § 501(c)(3)). The private inurement doctrine focuses on inappropriate takings or uses of an exempt organization's funds; it does not prohibit payments of **reasonable compensation** to insiders or others. The **IRS** has observed that the prohibition on private inurement, in its simplest terms, "means that a private shareholder or individual cannot pocket the organization's funds except as reasonable payment for goods or services." [EO § 20.3; HC §§ 4.2, 4.3, 21.3(b), 25.1; FR § 5.6(b)(ii); PF §§ 5.1, 5.2; AR § 6.1(a)(1); AS §§ 3.3, 3.5; PG pp. 65–66; SM pp. 50–51; CL §§ 1.4, 1.5; LI Q 4.3, Q 6.2, Q 6.6].

institution

The word "institution" is used in reference to those categories of **charitable organizations** that qualify as **public charities** solely by reason of the nature of their **programs**. These principally include **churches, associations of churches, conventions of churches, colleges, hospitals, medical research organizations**, and **universities**. [EO § 12.3(a); PF § 15.3; CG § 3.3(a); HC § 5.1; PG pp. 84, 86; SM p. 80].

institutional trustee

An "institutional trustee" is a **trustee** that is not an individual but rather an **organization**, such as a bank or trust company.

instrument

An "instrument" is a document, recognized in the **law**, that expresses and reflects the fact of an act. Instruments of this nature include an **agreement** (such as a **trust agreement**), **articles of organization**, a **declaration of trust**, a **contract** for goods and/or services, a **pledge**, and a **will**.

instrumentality, government

A government functions, in part, through the use or instrumentalities." These are separate **organizations** that the government uses to further its policies and programs. Instrumentalities of state governments are either **tax-exempt** under **federal** law by reason of the **doctrine** of **intergovernmental immunity** or have their **income excluded** from taxation by a specific provision in the law for entities that exercise an **essential governmental function** and the income of which **accrues** to a state or local government (**IRC** § 115).

Federal income tax exemption is provided for instrumentalities of the United States government (**IRC** § 501(c)(1)). These organizations must be **corporations** organized under an act of Congress and must be specifically provided tax exemption in a **revenue act**. [EO §§ 7.14, 19.1; SM p. 47].

instrumentality rule

Persons may be benefited as the result of a **tax-exempt charitable organization's** activities and the assistance nonetheless considered to be in furtherance of charitable ends as long as the effect is benefit of a **community** or a **charitable class** rather than merely individual recipients.

In these instances, those benefited are regarded as a means or "instruments" to the accomplishment of a charitable objective. [EO § 6.3(b)].

instrumentality of the united states

An **entity** is an "instrumentality of the United States" if it is an **organization organized** under an act of Congress and has a close structural and operational relationship with the **federal** government. When these entities are **corporations**, they may be **tax-exempt** as long as exemption for them is provided in the **IRC** or a revenue act (**IRC** § 501(c)(1)). [EO § 19.1; SM pp. 41–42].

insubstantial

The word "insubstantial" is synonymous with words such as "slight" and "**de minimis**." For example, under the **federal tax law**, **public charities** can engage in an "insubstantial" amount of **lobbying** without endangering their **tax exemption** (**IRC** § 501(c)(3)), a **tax-exempt organization** can provide a **private benefit** of it is insubstantial, and a **disqualified person** can engage in an act of **self-dealing** with a **private foundation** if the self-dealing is insubstantial. [EO §§ 4.4, 12.4(a), 20.11(b), 22.3(c), 24.1; PF § 5.3; SM pp. 185–186].

insurable interest

A **contract** of life **insurance** (that is, a life insurance "policy") is valid (enforceable) only where there is an "insurable interest" between the **insured** and the **beneficiary**. Basically, a **person** has an insurable interest in the life of an individual where the person who is the beneficiary of the insurance is better off economically with the insured alive rather than dead. Thus, the concept of insurable interest is that the beneficiary would suffer an economic loss if the insured were to die. The idea of insurable interest evolved in the **law** to prevent gambling on individuals' lives. The requirement as to insurable interest stems from the need to avoid extending to the beneficiary the temptation to hasten by improper means the time when he or she will receive the benefits of the insurance policy. The most common example of a relationship involving an insurable interest is the marital relationship; likewise, "key" individuals are often insured by their companies. Absent a **statute** on the point, it is not clear whether there is the requisite insurable interest between an insured and a **charitable organization** that is the owner and beneficiary of the insurance. [CG § 17.4].

insurance

The essence of the concept of "insurance" is that the risk of a **liability** is shifted to at least one third party (the **insurer**), and that the risk is shared and distributed across a group of **persons**. The insurance arrangement is evidenced by a **contract** (the insurance "policy"), which provides that, for a stated price (the "premium." which may be paid incrementally or in a lump sum), the insurer will compensate the other party for specified losses (often termed "risks"). One or more persons may be a **beneficiary** of a policy of insurance on the life of the **insured**. For a policy of life insurance to be valid (enforceable), the beneficiary of the insurance must have an **insurable interest** in the life of the insured.

The concept of insurance arises in the context of the **law** of **tax-exempt organizations**. A **charitable organization** or **social welfare organization** will lose or be denied **tax exemption** if a **substantial** part of its activities consists of the provision of **commercial-type insurance** (**IRC** § 501(m)). Otherwise, the activity of providing commercial-type insurance is treated as an **unrelated trade or business** and the income from it is taxed under the rules pertaining to taxable insurance companies (**IRC** Subchapter L).

For these purposes, the issuance of **annuity contracts** is considered the provision of insurance (**IRC** § 501(m)(4)). These rules, however, do not apply with respect to **charitable gift annuities**, which is defined for this purpose as an annuity where a portion of the amount paid in connection with the issuance of the annuity is allowable as a **charitable contribution deduction** for federal income or **estate** tax purposes, and the annuity is described in the special rule for annuities in the **unrelated debt-financed income law** (**IRC** § 514(c)(5)) (determined as if any amount paid in money in connection with the issuance of the annuity were **property**) (**IRC** §§ 501(m)(3)(E), 501(m)(5)).

The concept of insurance also arises in the tax law of charitable giving. An individual may make a charitable contribution of a life insurance policy. The availability of a charitable contribution deduction for a gift of life insurance to a charitable organization is sometimes uncertain (absent a **statute** on the point) because of the question as to whether there is an insurable interest between the insured person and the beneficiary of the insurance proceeds. [EO §§ 21.13, 24.5(e)(ii), 28.13; CG Chap. 17; PF §§ 5.7, 5.9(c), 6.3(f); FR § 3.22; RE Q 16.1; PG p. 25; SM pp. 7, 284].

insurance company

Certain "insurance companies" are **tax-exempt organizations** (**IRC** §§ 501(a) and 501(c)(15)). An insurance company is an **entity**, more than one-half of the **business** of which during the **tax year** involved is the issuance of **insurance** or **annuity contracts** or the reinsurance of risks underwritten by insurance companies (**IRC** § 816(a)). [EO § 19.9; PG p. 258; SM p. 44].

insurance income

Notwithstanding the general **unrelated business income rules** concerning the **modifications**, any amount included in the **gross income** of a **tax-exempt organization**, as "Subpart F" income, must be included as an item of gross income derived from an **unrelated trade or business** to the extent that the amount so included is attributable to "insurance income." The term "insurance income" generally means income that is attributable to the issuance (or reinsuring) of an insurance or annuity contract and would (subject to certain modifications) be taxed under the general tax rules (**IRC** Chapter 1, subchapter L) pertaining to U.S. insurance companies (**IRC** §§ 512(b)(17), 951(a)(1)(A), 952(a)(1), 953(a)). [EO § 25.1(n); UB § 3.15].

insured

The "insured" is a **person** whose life is the subject of a life **insurance** policy, or who is otherwise covered by a policy of insurance.

insurer

An "insurer" is a **person** who issues, and agrees to perform pursuant to, a **contract** of **insurance**.

intangible

The word "intangible" is used to refer to something that is not **tangible**, that is, it does not have a corporeal or physical existence.

intangible property

An item of "intangible property" is a **property** that is **intangible**, so that it is evidenced by a document (**instrument**) that is reflective of the **value** of the property. The most common type of intangible property is securities, namely, stocks and bonds; other examples of this type of property are **good will** and **promissory notes**. A **charitable contribution** may be made using one or more items of intangible property. [CG § 2.12(d)].

intangible religious benefit

An "intangible religious benefit" is a form of nonquantifiable benefit that is provided to an individual by a **religious organization** (often a **church**) solely in return for a payment made to the organization. This benefit generally may not be **sold** in a **commercial** transaction outside the **donative** context (**IRC** § 6115(b). Examples of this benefit are particular seats during worship services provided to Christians in exchange for pew rents, admission to High Holy Days services for members of the Jewish faith in exchange for the purchase of tickets, special religious services provided to Catholics in return for the payment of Mass stipends, and admission to the temple for Mormons in exchange for special tithes. The requirements of the **charitable gift substantiation rules** and the **disclosure** rules concerning **quid pro quo contributions** (**IRC** §§ 170(f)(8)(B), last sentence, 6115(b) are not applicable to an intangible religious benefit. [CG § 21.3(a); FR §§ 5.3, 5.4; HC § 31.2(a); SM p. 143].

integral part doctrine

In the context of the **law** of **tax-exempt organizations**, the "integral part doctrine" provides **tax exemption** for components of an **organization** that itself is formally tax-exempt. These component entities do not require separate exempt status because they are a part of the larger **entity** and thus derive their tax exemption from it; however, the component entities may appear to function as separate legal entities. Examples of entities that are an integral part of an organization include **colleges** within a **university** and an **endowment fund** within a **museum**. [HC §§ 9.2(a), 34.7; EO §§ 11.8, 26.10; CU Q 2.12].

integral part test

An **organization**, to qualify as a **Type III supporting organization**, must satisfy one of two "integral part tests." The integral part test for **functionally integrated Type III supporting organizations** requires the organization to (1) engage in activities **substantially** all of which **directly further** the **exempt purpose** of one or more **supported organizations**, (2) be the **parent** of each of its supported organizations, or (3) support one or more governmental entities. The integral part test for **non-functionally integrated Type III supporting organizations** entails a **distribution requirement** and an **attentiveness requirement**. [PF § 15.7(g); EO § 12.3(c); HC §§ 5.5(c), 5.5(d); SM pp. 83–84].

integrated auxiliary of a church

An "integrated auxiliary of a church" is, under the **federal tax law**, a **tax-exempt organization** the **principal** activity of which is **exclusively religious**, and which is **controlled** by or associated with a **church**, an **association of churches**, or a **convention of churches**. [EO § 10.5; RE Q 3.8; SM p. 38; LI Q 10.4].

integrated delivery system

One of the types of **organizations** eligible for **tax exemption** as a **charitable organization** because it **promotes health** is the "integrated delivery system." An integrated delivery system is a **health care organization** (or a component **entity** of an affiliated network of providers) created to integrate the provision of **hospital** services with the medical services provided by physicians. Previously, these services were provided (and paid for, by **patients**, their **insurers**, or government programs) separately; the hospital provided its services and facilities (such as diagnostic services, surgery, nursing, emergency care, room, and hoard), while physicians provided medical services to patients by means of private medical practices, admitting and treating patients in hospital facilities. In an integrated delivery system, an entity provides and bills for both hospital and physician services, either itself or by **contract** with another organization. [HC §§ 1.5, 23.2, 25.3; EO § 7.6(f)].

integrated giving

The concept of "integrated giving" refers to a form of **charitable giving** that is deliberately planned as part of the **donor's** overall financial and **tax** affairs, and/or his or her **estate**. [CG §§ 5.1, 5.3; SM p. 130] (also **Planned giving**).

integration

The **IRS** will likely deny **recognition** of **tax exemption** or **revoke exemption** of an **organization** where its management, activities, and/or finances are unduly "integrated" with those of another organization, where the other organization is tax-exempt pursuant to another category of exemption or is a **for-profit entity**. [EO § 30.2] (also **Attribution**).

intellectual property

The term "intellectual property" is applicable to items of **property** such as a **copyright**, patent, or similar process or formula. Unique **federal tax law** rules apply in connection with the **deductibility** of **charitable contributions** of intellectual property. [CG §§ 9.28, 24.7(b)(6), 24.9; FR § 5.14(m); AR §§ 4.1(n), 4.2(i), 19.1(h)(1), 19.1(h)(2); EO § 2.3; AS §§ 9.1(h), 11.8; HC § 31.2(g); RE Q 19.1].

inter vivos

The words "inter vivos" are Latin for "between the living." Thus, the term is applied to a transaction between two (or more) living individuals. For example, a **gift** made during the **donor's** lifetime is said to be an "inter vivos gift".

interest

In the **law**, the term "interest" has many meanings. It can be used to describe the nature of an ownership, in whole or in part, of **property**. Thus, the law speaks of "interests in property," in conjunction with terms such as **right**, **title**, and **estate**. Thus, when a **person** fully owns an item of property, it is said that that person has an "absolute" interest in the property. A person may have a **partial interest** in an item of property. A person may be entitled to ownership, in whole or in part, of property when and if a certain circumstance occurs; it is then said that that person has a **conditional** interest in the property. A person may have **control** over, or some other interest in an item of property that the person does not own (such as a **beneficiary** of a **trust**): a person in this circumstance is said to have a **beneficial** interest in the underlying property.

The term "interest" is also used to describe the **compensation** that one person pays to another for the use of money. The underlying transaction is a **loan**; the person making the loan is the "lender" and the person receiving the money and incurring the obligation to repay it, with interest, is the "borrower." The **rate** of interest is either set by the parties (by **contract**, such as a **note**) or by law; where the law determines that a rate of interest being charged or proposed to be charged is exorbitant or unconscionable, the practice is termed "usury" and is illegal.

A **tax-exempt organization** generally can lend money or borrow money. Particularly if the exempt organization is a **charitable organization**, when borrowing money, it should not pay a rate of interest that is other than a **reasonable** rate. If lending money, the exempt organization should receive a reasonable rate of return, the loan should be for a reasonable term, and the loan should be adequately secured. Some loans are, in essence, forbidden for some exempt organizations, such as a loan that would contravene the **private inurement doctrine** or the **private benefit doctrine**, a loan between an **applicable tax-exempt** organization and a **disqualified person** with respect to it (where the rate is not reasonable), or a loan between a **private foundation** and a disqualified person with respect to it that constitutes **self-dealing**.

Interest received by a tax-exempt organization is usually a form of **passive income**; two **exceptions** are interest income that is **debt-financed income** and interest income received from a **controlled subsidiary**. [AR §§ 7.2(a)(3), 7.2(b)(18); EO § 25.1(c); CG § 5.3; PF §§ 10.3(c), 11.2, 12.1(b); UB §§ 3.3, 11.4(d)(viii)].

interest, conflict of
See **Conflict of interest**.

interest, insurable
See **Insurable interest**.

interest, partial
See **Partial interest**.

interest giving
The term "interest giving" is used to describe **charitable giving** by a **donor** who has an ongoing interest in and an authentic involvement with a **charitable organization**. This type of giving is

usually done on a periodic basis (for example, weekly in the case of a **religious organization** or each year in an **annual giving campaign**). [SM p. 130].

interested person

The concept of the "interested person" arises in the context of **Form 990 Schedule L**, which concerns transactions between **tax-exempt organizations** and those who are "interested persons" with respect to them. In general, this term embraces **trustees, directors, officers, key employees**, and **substantial contributors**. The specifically applicable definition of the term varies, depending on which part of the schedule is involved. [AR Chap. 18; HC §§ 4.9, 33.4].

intergovernmental immunity

The **doctrine** of "intergovernmental immunity" is based on a principle, implicit in the U.S. Constitution, that the **federal** government will not **tax** the states. This immunity from taxation extends to **instrumentalities** that a state may employ in the discharge of its essential governmental duties. [EO § 19.21(a); PF § 1.6].

interlocking directorate

The phrase "interlocking directorate" is used to describe the situation in which the **boards of directors** or **boards of trustees** of two **organizations** are, in whole or in part, comprised of the same individuals. Where the interlock of one of the organizations is such that a majority of its directors are also directors of the other organization, the organization is **controlled** by the other organization. This is a common way for a **parent-subsidiary** relationship between two **nonprofit organizations** to be established. [EO Chaps. 29, 30, § 12.3(c); SM p. 215; PG pp. 131–132].

intermediate sanctions

The term "intermediate sanction" is used to describe a **sanction** that can be imposed on one or more **persons** for a violation of a **federal law** pertaining to a **tax-exempt organization**. This type of sanction usually is an excise tax that is imposed on the person or persons (including the organization itself) who or that caused the violation to occur. The word "intermediate" means a sanction that is more stringent than the **IRS** doing nothing in the face of an offending transaction, such as one involving **private inurement** (or informally issuing a reprimand) and **revoking** the tax-exempt status of an organization (sometimes referred to as a "draconian" outcome).

Present law intermediate sanctions are the excise taxes that are part of the rules concerning **excess benefit transactions**, the rules that are imposed on **public charities** for **excess lobbying expenditures**, and the rules with respect to **political expenditures** by charitable organizations.

The excess benefit transaction rules illustrate the usual statutory scheme. In this setting, there are three of these taxes. One is an **initial tax**, equal to 25 percent of the **excess benefit**, imposed on an excess benefit transaction; this tax must be paid by a disqualified person with respect to the transaction. The second of these taxes, equal to 10 percent of the excess benefit, triggered when the foregoing initial tax is imposed, is imposed on the **participation** of an **organization manager** in the excess benefit transaction, **knowing** that it is an excess benefit transaction, unless the participation is not **willful** and is due to **reasonable cause**; this tax must be paid by the organization manager who participated in the excess benefit transaction. The third of these taxes is an **additional tax** on the disqualified person, equal to 200 percent of the excess benefit involved, which is imposed when the initial tax is imposed on an excess benefit transaction involving a disqualified person and the excess benefit inherent in the transaction is not **corrected** within the **taxable period**; this tax also must be paid by a disqualified person with respect to the transaction.

If more than one person is liable for any of these taxes, there is **joint and several liability**. With respect to any one excess benefit transaction, the maximum amount of tax imposed on management is $20,000 (**IRC** §§ 4958(a), (b), (d)). [EO Chap. 21; GV §§ 4.2(c), 6.3(f), 6.3(g), 6.3(r), 8.4(f); FR § 5.6; HC §§ 3.1, 4.9(a); AS §§ 3.8, 3.9; AR §§ 6.1(b), 19.1(g)(6); CU Q 6.26; RE Chap. 22; PG pp. 28, 61, 62, 71–76; SM pp. 58–60; LI Q 4.27] (also **Excise taxes**).

Internal Revenue Bulletin

The "Internal Revenue Bulletin" is the official publication of the **IRS**. Published weekly, this publication includes the text of proposed and final **federal tax regulations** (published as **Treasury Decisions**), **revenue rulings**, **revenue procedures**, **announcements**, **notices**, and news releases, and reproduces all federal tax opinions from the U.S. Supreme Court, other court opinions with which the **IRS** agrees, **revenue acts**, and congressional committee reports. [EO App. A; HC § 34.1(c); AU § 2.10].

Internal Revenue Code

The "Internal Revenue Code" is the body of **federal tax law** enacted by Congress. It appears as Title 26 of the United States Code. The federal **income tax** rules are the subject of Subtitle A; the **estate tax** and **gift tax** rules are the subject of Subtitle B; the **employment tax** rules are the subject of Subtitle C; the **excise taxes** are the subject of Subtitle D; various other taxes are the subject of Subtitle E; the rules concerning payment and collection of taxes and the like are the subject of Subtitle F; the powers and duties of the Joint Committee on Internal Revenue Taxation of the United States Congress are the subject of Subtitle G; and the financing of presidential election campaigns is the subject of Subtitle H. The Internal Revenue Code is the complete collection of **statutory** tax law, as contrasted with the **administrative** tax law (which is created by the **Department of the Treasury**, including the **Internal Revenue Service**) and the **judicial** tax law, which is created by the courts. The Internal Revenue Code is restated from time to time by Congress; at the present, it is fully known as the "Internal Revenue Code of 1986, as amended." The Internal Revenue Code is referred to throughout this book as the "**IRC**." [EO App. A; HC § 2.1; PF § 1.1].

Internal Revenue Service

The "Internal Revenue Service" is an **agency** of the U.S. government; it is a component of the **Department of the Treasury**. The **principal** function of the Internal Revenue Service is enforcement of the **federal tax laws**. The agency is headed by a Commissioner of Internal Revenue, who is supported by ten Assistant Commissioners. One of these Assistant Commissioners is the Assistant Commissioner (Employee Plans and Exempt Organizations (**IRC** § 7802(b)). It is among the responsibilities of this Assistant Commissioner to enforce the law of **tax-exempt organizations**. The Assistant Commissioner (Technical) enforces the tax law as it relates to **charitable giving**. The Internal Revenue Service is referred to throughout this book as the "**IRS**" or, occasionally, the "agency." [EO § 2.2; HC § 6.3; CU Q 1.46; UB § 10.14; SM pp. 293–294; LI Q 1.55].

Internal Revenue Service Restructuring and Reform Act of 1998

The "Internal Revenue Service Restructuring and Reform Act of 1998" contributed importantly to a massive restructuring of the **IRS** that began in that year. [EO § 2.2(a)].

interstate

The word "interstate" means between or jointly involving states, such as those of the United States. The word is often used in the setting of describing **business** taking place in two or more states (termed "**interstate commerce**").

interstate commerce

"Interstate commerce" is **business** done between **persons** in two or more states. This type of commerce is protected in Article 1, section 8, of the U.S. Constitution (the "Commerce Clause"). Courts have ruled, however, that the states may impose **reasonable** restraints on interstate commerce, where to do so furthers a compelling **state interest**; it is under this rationale that challenges, on this ground, to the constitutionality of state **charitable solicitation acts** have been defeated. The **individual health insurance coverage mandate** was ruled, by the U.S. Supreme Court, to be in violation of the Commerce Clause (although it was upheld as being within Congress's power to **tax**). [CL Chaps. 4, 5; HC § 26.11; FR § 4.2] (also **Police power**).

intervention

The word "intervention" means an involvement or an interference in something. The word is used in the context of the prohibition on **political campaign activity** by **charitable organizations**; the proscription is that a charitable organization may not **participate** or intervene in a political campaign on behalf of, or in opposition to, a **candidate** for **public office** (IRC § 501(c)(3)). [EO § 23.2(b); SM pp. 197–199].

intestate

The word "intestate" means lack of a **will**. Thus, when an individual dies without having made a valid will, it is said that he or she has died "intestate."

intestate succession

The term "intestate succession" means the **disposition** of money and/or **property** of a **decedent**, in accordance with the **law** of a state, where the individual has died **intestate**.

intimate association, freedom of

Two types of **freedom of association** are recognized in the **law**. One of them is the "freedom of intimate association," which is a type of protected association derived from the **right** of personal liberty. [CL § 1.9; EO § 1.7; CG § 1.3(c)] (also **Expressive association, freedom of**).

inure

The word "inure" means to cause to flow through something and become the possession of a **person**. It is used in the **organizational** setting to refer to the transfer of **income** or other resources, earned or otherwise acquired by the **entity**, to those who own or **control** the entity. For example, a **for-profit corporation** will earn a **profit** and pass a portion of that profit along to another person who is a stockholder in the corporation; such a payment is in essence a **dividend** that has inured to the shareholder. This is known as **private inurement**, which under the **federal tax law** is impermissible for many **tax-exempt organizations**. [EO § 20.1; HC § 4.4; PF § 5.1; SM pp. 49–50].

inurement
See **Inure**.

inurement, private
See **Private inurement**.

inventory
"Inventory" is **property** that has been created or purchased by, and subsequently **sold** by, a **business organization**; it is property that has been manufactured by the organization.

inventory, gifts of
The **federal income tax law** contains special rules concerning the determination of the **charitable contribution deduction** in the case of **gifts** of their **inventory** by **corporations**. Under certain circumstances, corporate **donors** can achieve a charitable deduction for an amount equal to the corporation's **cost basis** in the **property**, plus one-half of the **appreciated value** of the property; in any event, this deduction may not exceed an amount equal to twice the property's cost basis (**IRC** § 170(e)(3)). [AR §§ 7.2(a)(2), 7.2(c)(8), 19.1(n); CG §§ 2.13, 9.3, 24.7(b)(10); EO § 2.3; SM p. 137] (also **Twice-basis deductions**).

investment, jeopardizing
See **Jeopardizing investment**.

investment, program-related
See **Program-related investment**.

investment advisor
The term "investment advisor" means, in the context of application of the **intermediate sanctions rules** to a transaction involving a **sponsoring organization**, any person (other than an **employee** of the organization) compensated by the organization for managing the investment of, or providing investment advice with respect to, assets maintained in **donor-advised funds** owned by the organization (**IRC** § 4958(f)(8)(B)).

Investment Advisors Act of 1940
The "Investment Advisors Act of 1940" exempts from its reach (other than its antifraud elements) **charitable organizations** and certain **persons** associated with them in connection with the provision of advice, analyses, and reports. [CG § 5.9].

investment assets

The term "investment assets" means the **corpus** or **principal** of an **organization**, that is, its **assets** that are held for the purpose of producing **investment income**. This type of asset, in the case of a **tax-exempt organization**, generally does not include assets used in the performance of **exempt functions**. Thus, for example, a **private foundation**, in computing its **mandatory payout amount**, has in its **asset base** the **value** of its investment assets but not the value of its **exempt function assets**. [PF § 6.2(c); AR §§ 7.2(c)(11)–(13), 11.2(g), 11.2(h)].

Investment Company Act of 1940

The "Investment Company Act of 1940" exempts from its definition of investment company the **charitable income fund**, although this type of fund is expected to provide to each **donor** to a **charity**, by means of such fund, written information describing the **material** terms of operation of the fund. [CG §§ 5.9, 14.9].

investment income

A **tax-exempt organization** may invest **assets** and receive a return of **income** on the investments. This investment income is usually in the form of **dividends**, **interest**, or **capital gain**; it may also be a **rent** or **royalty**. A **service provider publicly supported charitable organization** is subject to an **investment income test**. For most **exempt organizations**, investment income is not taxed. However, for example, a **private foundation** must pay a tax on its **net investment income**. [PF Chap. 10, §§ 11.2(a), 11.2(b), 12.1(b), 15.5, 15.10; UB § 3.9; EO § 25.1(a)–25.1(i); AR § 7.2(a)(3); SM p. 90].

investment income, tax on

Private foundations are subject to an **excise tax** on their **net investment income**. This tax generally is at the rate of 2 percent (**IRC** § 4940(a)), although in some circumstances the rate is reduced to 1 percent (**IRC** § 4940(e)). Other tax-exempt organizations that may be taxable on their investment income are **social clubs**, **political organizations**, and **homeowners' associations**. [PF §§ 1.10, 3.1(a), 10.1, 10.2, 15.1; EO §§ 15.5, 17.5, 17.6, 19.14; SM pp. 41, 46].

investment income test

An **organization**, to avoid classification as a **private foundation** by being categorized as a **service provider publicly supported charitable organization**, must **normally** receive not more than one-third or its **support** from the sum of **gross investment income** and any excess of the amount of **unrelated business taxable income** over the **tax** on that income (**IRC** § 509(a)(2)(B)). [PF § 15.5(a); EO § 12.3(b)(iv); HC § 5.3(b); SM p. 82] (also **Gross investment income fraction**; **Publicly supported organizations**).

investment plus

In general, in the **unrelated business** context, mere investment activity does not rise to the level of a **trade or business**. A court created the concept of "investment plus," which means that individuals and/or entities go beyond investing and become actively involved in the management and operation of the companies in which they invest. This concept causes the overall bundle of activities to become a taxable business. [EO § 24.2(a)].

investment policy

It is recommended that **charitable organizations** and many other types of **tax-exempt organizations** have an "investment policy." This policy should include the vehicles and properties in which the organization will invest (or, perhaps, not invest) and state the general balance of the portfolio, stipulating the percentages of investments in equities, interest-bearing instruments, foreign investment property, and the like. [GV § 6.3(p); AR §§ 5.1(g)(2), 5.1(i), 5.3; CU Q 5.32; SM p. 277; LI Q 3.30].

involuntary termination of private foundation status

A **charitable organization's private foundation status** may be "involuntarily terminated" if the **IRS** notifies the organization that, because of **willful**, flagrant, or repeated acts or failures to act giving rise to one or more of the private foundation **excise taxes**, the organization is liable for a **termination tax** (**IRC** § 507(a)(2)). [PF § 13.2] (also **Third-tier tax**).

irrevocable

The word "irrevocable" means "not **revocable**"; that is, it is something that is legally incapable of being revoked (undone or taken back). For example, for a **charitable contribution** to be **deductible**, the **gift** must be irrevocable. Likewise, a **trust**, to be a medium of a charitable gift, must be irrevocable. By contrast, a **will** is revocable as long as the **testator** is alive.

issue advocacy

An **expenditure** by a **tax-exempt organization** (other than a **political organization**) for issue (or policy) **advocacy** may be a **political expenditure**, as opposed to, for example, **lobbying**) and thus be an **exempt function** as that term is used in the political organizations setting. [EO §§ 17.4, 23.9; SM pp. 125, 203].

issue development

IRS examiners are responsible for "issue development," which means determining whether the **tax-exempt organization** being examined satisfies the requirements for **exemption**, has correctly reported any **tax liabilities**, is meeting required **notice** and **disclosure** requirements, and/or has filed all required **information returns** and **tax returns**. [AU § 5.19(l)].

issue elevation

The **IRS** employs the term "issue elevation" to mean bringing to the attention of higher-level managers or executives, for their information or decision, an issue, concern, or situation about which the mangers or executives must know in order to faithfully execute the **federal tax law** and properly manage the **Tax Exempt and Government Entities Division**. [AU § 3.8(a)].

itemize

The word "itemize" is used in the **tax** context to refer to the process, engaged in by a **taxpayer**, of claiming, on a **tax return**, one or more **itemized deductions**, including the **charitable**

contribution deduction. Under the **federal tax law**, an individual must make an **election** to itemize for a **tax year**; the election is made on the taxpayer's tax return (**IRC** § 63(e)). [CG § 3.6].

itemized deductions

The **federal tax law** defines the term "itemized deductions" to mean all **deductions** allowable under that law other than the deductions used in determining **adjusted gross income** and the deduction for personal exemptions (**IRC** §§ 151, 63(d)). Some "itemized deductions" are those that are also referred to as "miscellaneous itemized deductions" (**IRC** § 67(b)). The **income tax charitable contribution deduction**, however, although it is an itemized deduction (**IRC** § 170), is not a miscellaneous itemized deduction (**IRC** § 67(b)(4)). By contrast, the **business expense deduction** is both an itemized deduction (**IRC** § 162) and a miscellaneous itemized deduction. Miscellaneous itemized deductions are subject to a **floor** (**IRC** § 67(a)). [CG § 2.5] (also **Itemized deduction limitation**).

items of tax preference

See **Tax preference items**.

jeofaile

A "jeofaile" is a mistake made by a **lawyer**, usually in the course of **litigation**, and admitted to a court, such as by amendment to a pleading. This type of admission is infrequent.

jeopardizing investment

A **private foundation** cannot (without incurring one or more **sanctions**) invest any amount (**income** or **principal**) in a manner that would jeopardize the carrying out of any of its **tax-exempt functions** (**IRC** § 4944(a)(1)); investments of this nature are known as "jeopardizing investments." The **statutory law** is silent as to what constitutes this type of investment, other than to exclude the **program-related investment** from the concept of jeopardizing investments. The **tax regulations**, however, state that an investment is considered to jeopardize the carrying out of the exempt purposes of a private foundation if it is determined that the **foundation managers**, in making the investment, failed to exercise **ordinary business care and prudence**, under the facts and circumstances prevailing at the time the investment was made, in providing for the long- and short-term financial needs of the private foundation to carry out its exempt purposes. No category of investments is treated as a per se violation of these rules; however, the regulations list types or methods of investment that are scrutinized closely to determine whether the foundation managers have met the requisite standard of care and prudence. [PF Chap. 8, §§ 1.4(g), 2.4(d), 15.1; EO § 12.4(d); HC § 5.10; SM pp. 89, 90].

jeopardy assessment

The **IRS** has the authority to make a "jeopardy assessment" in the **income tax**, **estate tax**, and **gift tax** contexts (**IRC** § 6861). This authority is triggered when the **IRS** determines that the **assessment** or collection of a **deficiency** in one or more of these taxes will be jeopardized by delay; this is accomplished by an immediate assessment of the tax(es) due, together with **interest**, additional amounts, and **additions to tax**, coupled with a notice and demand for the amounts due.

Bruce R. Hopkins' Nonprofit Law Dictionary, First Edition. Bruce R. Hopkins.
© 2015 Bruce R. Hopkins. Published 2015 by John Wiley & Sons, Inc.

Jobs and Growth Tax Relief Reconciliation Act of 2003

The "Jobs and Growth Tax Relief Reconciliation Act of 2003" changed the **tax** rates for **dividends** and **capital gains**, which has had an impact on **charitable giving** and rules pertaining to the administration of **charitable remainder trusts**.

joint and several liability

"Joint and several liability" is comparable to **joint liability**, except that each **person** involved in the transaction or arrangement that gave rise to the liability is also fully liable for the entire liability. (In this context, "several" means "individual.") Many of the **federal tax law additions to tax** and **penalties** provide for joint and several liability, such as the addition to tax (in actuality, a penalty) for failure to file an **annual information return**, for failure to make an annual information return accessible to the public, and for failure to make an **application for recognition of exemption** accessible to the public (**IRC** § 6652(c)(4)(B)). The tax on **disqualifying lobbying expenditures** contains a provision for joint and several liability (**IRC** § 4912(d)(3)), as do the taxes on **political expenditures** (**IRC** § 4955(c)(1)). The **private foundation** rules contain joint and several liability provisions as well (**IRC** §§ 4941(c)(1), 4944(d)(1), and 4945(c)(1)), as do the **intermediate sanctions rules** (**IRC** § 4958(d)(1)). [EO §§ 22.4, 23.3, 26.10; PF §§ 5.15(d), 8.5, 9.10(a)].

joint liability

"Joint liability" is a form of liability that is shared by two or more **persons**. For example, liability for the **excise taxes** imposed in the context of **private foundations** often is a joint liability. (also **Joint and several liability**).

joint operating agreement

Generally, the provision of services by a **tax-exempt organization** to another organization, including another **exempt organization**, is an **unrelated business**. One of the exceptions to this rule pertains to situations in which the exempt **entities** are **related**, such as the operation of a health care delivery system by means of a "joint operating agreement." [HC § 21.5; EO §§ 7.6(g), 24.5(k)].

joint venture

A "joint venture" is an **unincorporated business enterprise** undertaken by two or more **persons**, in which **profits** and **losses** are shared. A joint venture is thus much like a **general partnership**; a technical distinction is that a joint venture may be of a more limited scope and/or duration than a partnership. A **tax-exempt organization** may enter into a joint venture with one or more other **exempt organizations** and/or one or more **for-profit entities** without adversely affecting its **tax-exempt status**. Usually, when an exempt organization, particularly a **charitable organization**, becomes involved in a joint venture, it does so in advancement of a tax-exempt purpose. The **look-through principle** applies so that, in this situation, the **revenue** derived by the exempt organization from the joint venture is characterized as **related revenue**. By contrast, an involvement in a joint venture by an exempt organization would lead to loss of tax exemption if the primary purpose of the exempt organization is to participate in the venture and if the function of the venture is **unrelated** to the **exempt purpose** of the exempt organization. [EO §§ 20.11(b), 31.1, 31.3, 31.4–31.6; FR § 5.13; UB §§ 8.9(b), 8.13; HC §§ 22.6, 22.9–22.11; AS §§ 3.6(b), 7.3; AR §§ 6.1(a)(7), 11.1(f), 21.1(f); RE Q 14.29–Q 14.31, Q 14.45–Q 14.48; PF § 7.2(b); CU Q 16.34; PG pp. 149, 150, 344, 345; SM pp. 57–58, 241–242] (also **Accountable care organization; Aggregate principle; Limited liability company**).

joint venture policy

The **IRS**, on the **Form 990**, requests information as to whether the filing **organization** is participating in a **joint venture** and, if so, whether it has adopted a written policy or procedure requiring the organization to evaluate its participation in joint venture arrangements under applicable **federal tax law** and taken steps to safeguard the organization's **tax-exempt status** in connection with the arrangement. [GV §§ 4.2(d), 6.3(f); AR §§ 5.1(i)(3), 5.2(b)(4), 5.3; SM p. 275; LI Q 3.32].

judicial branch

A "judicial branch" is that division of a government that is comprised of the judiciary, that is, its court system. [CL § 1.2(b)].

judicial nomination

The concept of **political activity** includes the function of **influencing** or attempting to influence the selection, nomination, election, or appointment of any individual to any **federal**, state, or local **public** office (**IRC** § 527(e)(2)). This process includes appointments by the president of the United States of individuals to judgeships; these appointments are subject to confirmation by the U.S. Senate.

It is the position of the **IRS** that the function of influencing or attempting to influence the appointment of an individual to a public office, including a judgeship, where confirmation by the Senate is involved, constitutes influencing or attempting to influence **legislation**. [EO §§ 17.1(a), 22.2(a)–(c)].

judicial system

The **law of tax-exempt organizations**, **charitable giving**, **fundraising**, and other aspects of operations of **nonprofit organizations** is shaped by **federal** and state court opinions.

The federal court system has three levels: trial courts (including those that initially hear cases where a formal trial is not involved), courts of appeal (or **appellate** courts), and the U.S. Supreme Court. The federal trial courts include the various district courts (at least one in each state, the District of Columbia, and the U.S. territories), the U.S. Tax Court, and the U.S. Court of Federal Claims. There are thirteen federal appellate courts (the U.S. Courts of Appeal for the First through the Eleventh Circuits, the U.S. Court of Appeals for the District of Columbia, and the U.S. Court of Appeals for the Federal Circuit).

Cases involving these areas of the law for nonprofit organizations issues at the federal level can originate in any federal district court, the U.S. Tax Court, and the U.S. Court of Federal

Claims. Under a special **declaratory judgment** procedure available only to **charitable organizations** and **farmers' cooperatives**, cases can originate only with the U.S. District Court for the District of Columbia, the U.S. Tax Court, and the U.S. Court of Federal Claims. Cases involving these matters are considered by the U.S. courts of appeal and the U.S. Supreme Court.

Each of the states has a judiciary system, usually a three-tiered one modeled after the federal system. Cases involving nonprofit organizations are heard in all of these courts. Most of the state court opinions that are published are those of the highest court of the state (usually, the state supreme court). [EO App. A].

jurisdiction

The word "jurisdiction" has several meanings in the law. Courts, for example, have jurisdiction to hear cases, some with wide-ranging authority but circumscribed in some way, such as by geography (e.g. U.S. district courts) or by subject matter (e.g., the **U.S. Tax Court**). Government agencies have jurisdiction to regulate within their respective spheres of authority (e.g., the **IRS** and the **Federal Election Commission**). Occasionally, challenges to the existence occur. With respect to courts, jurisdiction can be barred by statute (e.g., the **Anti-Injunction Act**), trimmed by statute (e.g., the **declaratory judgment** rules), or found wanting in particular cases (such as disputes lacking the requisite **case or controversy** requirement or parties lacking **standing**). As to government agencies, courts are empowered to determine the boundaries of agencies' authority (jurisdiction), using *Chevron* **deference** standards, although a minority view has it that this is a matter of **separation of powers** and that courts should determine agency jurisdiction on their own.

juvenile delinquency

One of the ways a **nonprofit organization** can qualify for **tax-exempt status** under the **federal tax law** as a **charitable organization** is to have as its purpose the **promotion of social welfare**. Five types of endeavors constitute activities that promote social welfare; one of these types of activities involves efforts to combat community deterioration and juvenile delinquency. Frequently, organizations that work to combat juvenile delinquency do so by promoting sports. [EO § 7.11; SM p. 35]

key employee

For purposes of **Form 990** reporting, a "key employee" of a **tax-exempt organization** is an **employee** of the organization (other than a **trustee**, **director**, or **officer**) who meets the following three tests applied in the following order: the **$150,000 test**, the **responsibility test**, and the **top 20 test**. [AR § 6.1(a)(1); GV § 2.3; PF § 4.3; CU Q 7.3, Q 7.4; PG pp. 17, 193; LI Q 6.3, Q 6.4].

kickback

A "kickback" is a payment by a provider of goods and/or services to an **agent** purchasing them, based on some prearranged portion of the purchase price, as an inducement to the agent to participate in the transaction. (also **Administrative allowance**).

knowing

In certain circumstances, an **initial tax** can be imposed on the **participation** of a **foundation manager** in an act of **self-dealing** when the manager acted while "knowing" that the act was self-dealing (**IRC** § 4941(a)(2)). To satisfy the requirement of "knowing" in this setting, the manager must (1) have actual knowledge of sufficient facts so that, based solely on those facts, the transaction would be an act of self-dealing; (2) be aware that this act may violate the self-dealing rules; and (3) **negligently** fail to make **reasonable** attempts to ascertain whether the transaction is art act of self-dealing or he or she is, in fact, aware that it is this type of an act.

The term "knowing" does not mean "having reason to know." Evidence tending to show that an individual has reason to know of a particular factor or particular rule, however, is irrelevant in determining whether he or she had actual knowledge of that fact or rule. Similar concepts apply in connection with the **jeopardizing investment** and **excess business holdings rules**. In the **public charity** context, the "knowing" standard applies in connection with the **intermediate sanctions rules** and the **tax** regimes pertaining to excessive **lobbying expenditures** and **political campaign expenditures**. [PF §§ 5.15(d), 5.15(e), 8.5(a), 8.5(b), 9.10(a); EO §§ 21.12(b), 21.12(c), 22.4, 23.3; LI Q 4.63, Q 5.48].

Bruce R. Hopkins' Nonprofit Law Dictionary, First Edition. Bruce R. Hopkins.
© 2015 Bruce R. Hopkins. Published 2015 by John Wiley & Sons, Inc.

labor organization

A "labor organization" is a form of **tax-exempt organization** under the **federal tax law** (**IRC** §§ 501(a), 501(c)(5)). The general exempt purpose of a labor organization is the betterment of the conditions of those who are **employees** (usually its **members**) in a particular **trade or business**. Thus, a labor organization basically is an **association** of workers who have combined to protect or promote the interests of its members by bargaining collectively with their **employer** to secure better working conditions, wages, and similar benefits. Labor organizations principally are labor **unions** and councils; they also include labor temples, organizations created by a collective bargaining agreement, and organizations that publish newspapers and magazines in the labor field. [EO §§ 16.1, 24.5(f); AS § 1.6(c); PF §§ 1.6, 15.9; FR § 5.18(b)(iv); AR § 3.1(e)(2); AU § 7.1(k); UB § 9.5; SM p. 41; LI Q 1.50].

last-in, first-out method

The "last-in, first-out method" is a method used by a **business** for tracking its **inventory**. This method (often referred to as LIFO) assumes that the items of inventory last purchased are the first sold. This method has ramifications for the way in which the inventory is **valued**. Since the most recently purchased items of inventory are considered to be the first items sold, the effects of inflation (rising market prices) or deflation (falling market prices) are minimized. [CG §§ 2.13, 9.3(f)].

last will and testament

See **Will**.

laundry services, for hospitals

A **tax-exempt hospital** can provide laundry services for itself without adverse **tax law** consequences, inasmuch as clean laundry is integral to the **promotion of health**. If, however, an exempt hospital provides laundry services for one or more other organizations (tax-exempt or not), the activity is considered an **unrelated trade or business**. A **nonprofit organization** that has as its purposes the provision of laundry services to tax-exempt hospitals cannot qualify as a **charitable organization**. An organization that provides laundry services to exempt hospitals cannot qualify as a **cooperative hospital service organization**. [EO §§ 11.4, 24.5(b); HC §§ 1.5, 17.1, 24.16].

law

The "law" on a particular subject is a set of **rules** governing human conduct. When the word is used, it most often is a reference to laws enacted by a **legislature**, in the form of **statutes**. The word law, however, also encompasses **administrative law** and law made by the courts. As to the **federal tax law**, the law (having precedential value) consists of provisions of the **IRC**, **tax regulations**, **revenue rulings**, **revenue procedures**, and court opinions.

This concept is relevant in the **nonprofit organizations** context, in that the term **legislation** is a derivative of the word "law"; there are limitations on the ability of certain **tax-exempt organizations**, particularly **charitable** ones, to act to **influence** the development of legislation. Thus, if an activity of a legislative body does not involve the writing of legislation, the activity presumably is not **lobbying**. It is the view of the **IRS**, however, that an attempt to influence the confirmation, by the U.S. Senate, of a presidential nominee constitutes, for these purposes, an attempt to influence legislation; this position is based upon the definition of the term "legislation" found in the **expenditure test**. [EO § 22.2; SM pp. 187–188].

law, sources of

For **nonprofit organizations**, the sources of the **law** are manifold. These include the U.S. Congress, state legislatures, **federal** and state administrative agencies (including the **IRS**), and court decisions. The result is a battery of **statutes**, **regulations**, **rules**, and court opinions. Other items, such as **revenue rulings**, **revenue procedures**, and forms and instructions to them, are not formally law. [EO App. A].

law firms, public interest

See **Public interest law firms**.

lawsuit

A "lawsuit" is a proceeding initiated in a court where one or more **persons** seek a remedy, recognized in the **law**, against one or more other persons. (also **Declaratory judgment**; **Defendant**; **Plaintiff**).

lawyer

A "lawyer" is an individual who is licensed to practice law in one or more states. Generally, the role of a lawyer is to advise **persons** as to applicability of **laws,** and provide services to them to assist them in planning in connection with, and complying with, the law. A lawyer in private practice is an **independent contractor** and a lawyer that is **in-house** is an **employee**. [SM pp. 26–27, 30; FR § 2.4; CU Q 1.48, Q 1.49; RE Q 1.5–Q 1.7; LI Q 1.57, Q 5.49] (also **Attorney**; **Power of attorney**).

lead period

The term "lead period" is used in the context of **split-interest trusts**. It is the period of time represented by the first of the two interests (**income interest** or **remainder interest**) in the

L

property in the **trust**. The term is usually used in connection with **charitable lead trusts**, where the period that is the lead period is the period represented by the income interest that is created by means of the trust. [CG § 16.2].

leadership gift

A "leadership gift" is a **contribution**, usually to a **charitable organization**, made by an individual (or a **person** related to the individual) who is a part of the **leadership** of the organization. The contribution is often made at the outset of a **fundraising campaign** (most likely, a **capital campaign**), for the purpose of helping to launch the campaign and to demonstrate the support of the **members** of the organization's **governing body** for the objectives of the campaign. This type of contribution is often a **major gift**.

leakage, charitable

The informal term "charitable leakage" means the operation of a **tax-exempt charitable organization** in a manner that causes unwarranted **private benefit** to be provided. [EO §§ 20.1, 20.11; PF § 5.1; HC §§ 4.1(a), 4.6; SM pp. 49–50, 56–57].

Lean Six Sigma

"Lean Six Sigma" is a methodology used in contemporary management practice to improve an **organization's** performance by removing waste from production processes. The **IRS's exempt organization's** function is employing this methodology by developing ways to, in the words of the **Commissioner, Tax Exempt and Governmental Entities**, "improve processes, reduce taxpayer burden, and capture opportunities to eliminate waste."

lease

A "lease" is a **contract** for the possession of **property** for a defined period; where the property is **real property**, the contract is one that causes the relationship of landlord and tenant. When the term is used as a verb, it is synonymous with the word **rent**.

In the **nonprofit law** context, the term "lease" arises in several contexts; three of these uses are unique to the **law** of **tax-exempt organizations**. One of these uses is in the setting of **private foundations**, where one of the forms of **self-dealing** is the leasing of property between a private foundation and a **disqualified person** (**IRC** § 4941(d)(1)(A)). Nonetheless, the leasing of property by a disqualified person to a private foundation without charge is not an act of self-dealing (**IRC** § 4941(d)(2)(C)).

Another of these unique uses is in the **law** concerning the taxation of **unrelated business income**. Many forms of **passive income** are not subject to taxation as income from an **unrelated trade or business**. For this purpose, forms of passive income include certain rental income (generally of real estate) (**IRC** § 512(b)(3)). Where, however, a tax-exempt organization actively engages in a leasing activity, the activity will be considered an unrelated business, with the income from it subject to tax (unless the leasing activity is **substantially related** to the organization's **exempt purpose** or is not **regularly carried on**).

The third of these unique uses arises under the **tax-exempt entity leasing rules**. These rules are designed to impose limitations (by means of a reduction in the **depreciation deduction**) on the federal tax benefits of leasing property to an exempt organization. These rules apply where the property involved is **tax-exempt use property**; this term means any portion of a property (more than 35 percent) that is leased to an exempt organization by means of a **disqualified lease**. One form of disqualified lease is a lease that occurs after a **sale** (or other transfer of the property) by, or lease of the property from, the exempt organization (or a **related entity**) and the property has been used by the organization (or a related entity) before the sale (or other transfer) or lease (**IRC** § 168(h)(1)(B)(ii)). This is known as a **sale-leaseback**, which is the transaction that caused enactment of the tax-exempt entity rules. [EO §§ 25.1(h), 31.7; UB § 3.8; PF §§ 5.4, 6.5(b), 10.3(e), 11.2; SM pp. 89, 177].

leaseback

A "leaseback" is a transaction where a **person** purchases an item of **property** from another person, and thereafter (usually soon thereafter) the purchaser **leases** the property (back) to the seller. [EO §§ 28.15, 31.7] (also **Tax-exempt entity leasing rules**).

leaseback restriction

The term "leaseback restriction" is used in the context of defining circumstances where an **exception**, from the law treating **income** from **debt-financed property** as **unrelated business taxable income**, is available to **qualified organizations** that make debt-financed investments in **real property** (**IRC** § 514(c)(9)(A)). Under this exception, income from investments in real property is not treated as income from debt-financed property. This exception is available only where six restrictions are satisfied (**IRC** § 514(e)(9)(B)). One of them is the "leaseback restriction," where a limited **leaseback** of debt-financed real property to the seller (or a person **related** to the seller) is permitted. This exception applies only where (1) no more than 25 percent of the leasable floor space in a building (or complex of buildings) is leased back to the seller (or related party) and (2) the lease is on **commercially reasonable** terms, independent of the sale and other transactions (**IRC** § 514(c)(9)(G)). [EO § 24.9(c); UB § 5.4(f)].

leasing rules, tax-exempt entity

See **Tax-exempt entity leasing rules**.

legacy

A "legacy" is a **disposition** of **personal property** by means of a **will**. (also **Bequest**; **Devise**).

legal audit

A "legal audit" occurs when a **lawyer** conducts an examination of the structure and operations of a **nonprofit organization** to determine whether, or the extent to which, the organization is in compliance with federal, state, and local law, including the **federal tax law**. [GV Chap. 9; PG Chap. 12].

legal system, promotion of confidence in

It has been held by a court that an **organization** can qualify for **tax exemption** under the **federal tax law** as a **charitable organization** where it engages in activities that maintain public confidence in the legal system. [EO § 7.15(f)].

legal title

The term "legal title" means a **right** in a person (or persons) to own and possess something; in common parlance, only the word "title" is used. The term is applied, for the most part, in connection with **real property**, although it is also used with respect to some items of **tangible personal property**, such as automobiles. If there are no **encumbrances** on titled property, the title is said to be "clear" (or "good" or "marketable"). Where there is some dispute as to the efficacy of a title, there is said to be a "cloud" on it. (also **Equitable title**).

legatee

A "legatee" is a **person** who is a recipient of a **legacy**.

legator

A "legator" is a **person** who disposed of (or has arranged to dispose of) **personal property** by means of a **legacy**.

legend

The word "legend" is used to describe a statement on a document used by a **charitable organization** to **solicit contributions** that is mandated by a state's **charitable solicitation act**. This legend may state an identifying number for the **entity** or that an annual report about the organization is available. Several states have this type of requirement; thus, for an organization that is soliciting in all of these states, the legend combining all of the requirements can be lengthy. [FR § 3.15; SM p. 149].

legislation

The term "legislation" generally means a product of a legislative body, such as the U.S. Congress, a state legislature, or a local council. The product usually is an act, bill, **resolution**, or similar item (**IRC** §§ 4911(e)(2), 162(e)(4)(B)). It also includes the product of the **public** where there is a procedure such as a referendum, initiative, **constitutional** amendment, or similar procedure (*id.*). While the word "legislation" relates to the making of a law, it is the view of the **IRS** that the legislative process includes consideration by a legislative body of an appointment from the executive body (such as confirmation proceedings in the U.S. Senate with respect to presidential cabinet or judicial nominees). Legislation does not normally include a product of an executive branch of government (such as the promulgation of **rules** and **regulations**), nor does it include a similar product of independent regulatory **agencies**). [EO § 22.2; HC § 7.1(a); CU Q 8.2; PG pp. 108–109; SM pp. 187–188; KI Q 7.2].

legislation, influencing of

See **Action organization**; **Influence legislation**; **Lobbying**.

legislation, influencing of, exceptions to

There are limitations on the extent to which **tax-exempt organizations**, particularly **charitable** ones, can engage in attempts to **influence legislation** (or, stated another way, to engage in lobbying). **Exceptions** are available, however, to these limitations, such as engaging in **nonpartisan activities**, analysis of broad economic and social problems, **communications** to **members**, responding to requests for **technical advice**, and **self-defense communications**. The extent and availability of these exceptions may differ, in relation to whether the charitable organization is subject to the **substantial part test** or has **elected** the **expenditure test**. [EO §§ 22.3(c)(iii), 22.3(d)(v); SM pp. 187, 190].

legislative activities

The term "legislative activities," as used in the **law** of **tax-exempt organizations**, means activities by an exempt organization to **influence** the outcome of a legislative process (that is, the making of **legislation**). Common forms of legislative activity include the provision of testimony before a **committee** of a legislature, **communications** (such as letters, telegrams, facsimiles, emails, and telephone calls) to members of a legislature or their staff or committee staff, the submission of studies and reports, and attempts to influence the **public** to take action as regards legislative matters. Legislative activities are generally categorized as **direct** or **grass-roots** activities. [EO §§ 22.3(c)(i), 22.3(c)(ii), 23.3(d)(i), 23.3(d)(iii); AR Chap. 9, §§ 3.1(d), 3.1(e), 3.2(d), 3.2(e); HC § 7.1(b); PF §§ 9.1, 15.1; RE Q 20.1–Q 20.8; SM pp. 186–187] (also **Lobbying**).

legislative authority, delegation of

An **administrative agency** may find facts and issue **regulations** but must do so in the context of policy established by a **legislative body**, which has standards for guidance of the agency. In the area of free expression, such as **fundraising**, a registration statute placing unbridled discretion in the hands of government officials or **agency** may be unconstitutional as a prior restraint. [FR § 4.6].

legislative-basis rationale

The "legislative-basis rationale" is sometimes used as the **statutory** basis for **tax exemption**, under the **federal tax law**, for an **organization**. For example, a variety of **employee benefit organizations** are tax-exempt, although the exemption is more or less a byproduct of a larger legislative scheme. A lesser example is tax-exempt status for professional **football leagues**, which was enacted as part of the legislation effecting the merger between the National Football League and the American Football League. [EO Chap. 18, § 19.20].

legislative branch

A "legislative branch" is that **division** of a government that is comprised of the bodies of that government that consider and enact **legislation**. Nearly all of the states and the **federal** government have a bicameral (two-house) legislature; the legislative branch of the federal government consists of the House of Representatives and the Senate. [CL § 1.2(a)].

legislative history

The "legislative history" of an item of **legislation** consists of the written record underlying the item, such as **committee reports**, transcripts of floor debates, and technical explanations of the item prepared by a committee of the legislature. A court (in the process of writing an opinion), executive branch **department** or **agency** (in the course of promulgating **rules** and **regulations**), or an independent regulatory agency (also while preparing rules and regulations) may refer to the legislative history of an item of legislation in an effort to interpret the intent of the legislature (**legislative intent**), although technically this use of legislative history is impermissible where the legislative intent is ascertainable from the legislation itself. [EO App. A].

legislative intent

The term "legislative intent" means, of course, the intent of a legislative body in enacting an item of **legislation**. Intense controversy persistently rages over the use of **legislative history**, particularly **committee reports**, in divining the intent of a legislature (at the **federal** level, "congressional intent"). A U.S. Supreme Court justice, well-known for his dislike of use of legislative history to ascertain legislative intent, wrote in a dissent that the Court majority, in citing passages from a committee report in support of its decision, "treats those snippets as authoritative evidence of congressional intent even though they come from a single report issued by a committee whose members make up a small fraction of one of the two Houses of Congress"; he added that "[l]ittle else need be said here about the severe shortcomings of that interpretative methodology." The countervailing view is that these reports indeed reflect congressional intent because they are adopted by the very members of Congress who know the most about the legislation involved, with the other members not having much intent (if any) with respect to the legislation.

L

lending of securities

See **Securities, lending of**.

lessening burdens of government

One of the ways a **nonprofit organization** can qualify for **tax exemption** under the **federal tax law** as a **charitable organization** is to engage in activities that "lessen the burdens of government." This concept relates to the provision of services to a government, such as the maintenance of a public facility (for example, a monument or a park) or the expenditure of funds for a public program (for example, an internship program or a police department reward **fund**). For this category of tax exemption to be available, the organization's activities must be those that a unit of government considers to be its burdens and whether the activities actually lessen a governmental burden. [EO § 7.7; HC §§ 13.5, 19.5; SM p. 34].

lessee

A "lessee" is a **person** who holds an item of **property** (usually **real property**) on the basis of a **lease**. A lessee of real property is a tenant. (also **Lessor**).

lessor

A "lessor" is a **person** who enters into a **lease** with another person. A lessor of real property is a landlord. (also **Lessee**).

letter of credit

A "letter of credit" is a written document, where the writer of the document requests the recipient of the letter to extend credit to the bearer of the document and/or a third **person**. The document is issued by a bank or other financial institution that agrees to honor the request for the funds. A **charitable gift** may be made by means of a letter of credit. [CG § 6.8].

letter ruling

See **Private letter ruling**.

level playing field

The phrase "level playing field" is used in the setting of the controversy between **nonprofit organizations** and **for-profit organizations** concerning alleged **unfair competition**. For-profit organizations often feel that nonprofit organizations have an unwarranted advantage in the marketplace (the selling of goods and services), due to their **tax-exempt status** and the **halo effect**. As to the former, for-profit organizations often believe that non-profit organizations can undercut them in pricing due to the fact that taxes usually are not, for nonprofit organizations, a cost of doing business. Thus, some for-profit organizations urge greater taxation of nonprofit organizations' competitive activities, so as to "level the playing field." Some nonprofit organizations are of the view that the for-profit businesses do not want them on the playing field at all. [SM pp. 283–284].

liability

The term "liability" alone is a broad term in the **law**, and it embraces concepts such as responsibility and obligation: the term is not the same as debt, **loss**, or **damage**, although liability can include these matters.

In the context of **nonprofit organizations**, there may be concern that the organization is liable for something as a matter of law. This type of liability can arise as the result of the **commission** of an act or a failure to commit an act (**omission**). Of course, a nonprofit organization can be liable for debt and, in some instances, **taxes**.

There may also be concern that one or more human beings may be personally liable for something done in the name of, for, or for the benefit of a nonprofit organization. This is an unlikely outcome for those individuals who perform services for the organization as **employees** or **independent contractors**. It may also be unlikely for the nonprofit organization that is formed as a **corporation**. If personal liability is found, however, it is most common for it to be found against one or more **trustees**, **directors**, or **officers** of the organization. Nonetheless, even in these circumstances, liability is usually not found where the individual acted in accordance with the **prudent person standard**.

There are four ways to minimize or even eliminate personal liability in connection with the performance of services to a nonprofit organization, for someone who is being compensated or for a **volunteer**. One, as noted, is for the organization to be created as a corporation, inasmuch as the corporate form can provide a total or partial shield against personal liability. Another is the presence of an **indemnification clause** in the appropriate **governing instrument** of the organization. The third is the purchase of **officers' and directors' liability insurance**. The fourth is application of a state's **immunity statute**. [SM pp. 7, 313–318; PG pp. 24–29; AR Chap. 7, §§ 3.1(k), 3.2(k); CU Q 5.16–Q 5.18; RE Q 15.1–Q 15.17] (also **Joint liability**; **Joint and several liability**).

L

licit

The word "licit" means an act or other outcome that is within the **law**; something that is legal. ("Illicit" is something that is illegal.)

lien

A "lien" is a charge (or claim or **encumbrance**) on an item of **property** as security for a debt. The debt may be satisfied by use (such as **sale**) of the property if it is not otherwise extinguished.

life estate

A "life estate" is an **interest** in **property** (usually, **real property**) that is measured by the life or lives of one or more individuals. The life involved may be that of the individual using the property or the life of another individual. The concept of life estates is an integral one in the law of **planned giving**. [CG § 5.3; SM pp. 233–235] (also **Income interest**).

life expectancy

A "life expectancy" is a period of time, determined by an actuary, that a particular individual is expected (predicted) to live, based on his or her age at the time of the determination. The concept of life expectancies is essential to the process of calculating **income interests** and **remainder interests**. [CG § 11.2].

life income interest

See **Income interest**.

life insurance

"Life insurance" is a form of **insurance** that is reflected in a **contract**, whereby an insurance company agrees to pay a cash benefit (or death benefit), to one or more **beneficiaries**, in the event the insured individual dies while the insurance policy is in force. In general, life insurance may be term insurance or permanent insurance, the latter including whole life insurance. A **charitable contribution deduction** may be available for a **gift** of a policy of permanent life insurance. [CG § 17.6(a); RE Q 13.12; SM pp. 145, 239].

life member

An individual is a "life member" of an **organization** if he or she remains a **member** of the **entity** for the remainder of his or her life without having to pay any additional or subsequent **dues** or **assessments**. In some circumstances, a life member is regarded by the **law** as being the same as a **regular member**, such as in defining a **membership communication** pursuant to the **expenditure test**. [EO § 22.3(d)(v)].

like

An **organization** may qualify for **tax exemption**, under the **federal tax law**, as a **benevolent life insurance company**, a **mutual ditch or irrigation company**, a **mutual or cooperative telephone company**, or **like** organization (**IRC** § 501(c)(12)). The word "like" is limited by the types of organizations that are eligible for this tax exemption. For example, organizations that are like mutual or cooperative telephone companies facilitate communication between their **members** and others, while an organization that facilitates communication between its members' customers (namely, nonmembers) and others is not a like organization. [EO § 19.5(b)].

like kind exchange

A "like kind exchange" of **property** occurs where property held for investment or in a **business** is **exchanged** only for property of a similar character (like kind) to be likewise held for investment or in a business. Any **gain** from a like kind exchange is not (with some **exceptions** and under certain conditions) **recognized** for **federal income tax** purposes. [CG § 2.14(f)].

limitation on charges requirement

A **hospital organization** or **hospital facility** meets the "limitation on charges requirement" if the entity limits amounts charged for emergency or other medically necessary care provided to individuals eligible for assistance under the entity's **financial assistance policy** to not more than the amounts generally billed to individuals who have insurance covering the care, and it prohibits the use of gross charges (**IRC** §§ 501(4), (5)). [HC § 26.10(a)(v)].

limited affiliated group

The phrase "limited affiliated group," as used in the context of the **expenditure test**, means organizations that are **affiliated** solely by reason of provisions in their **governing instruments** that extend **control** only with respect to **national legislation**. Specifically, this type of group consists of two or more organizations where (1) each organization is a **member** of an **affiliated group of organizations**, (2) no two members of this group are affiliated by reason of **interlocking directorates**, and (3) no member of the group is, under its governing instruments, bound by decisions of one or more of the other members on legislative issues other than **national legislative issues**. [EO § 22.3(d)(viii)].

limited control rule

The phrase "limited control" is used in the **law** concerning **affiliated organizations**, which is part of the **expenditure test**. When two or more organizations are **members** of an **affiliated group of organizations**, no two members of the group are **affiliated**, and the **governing instruments** of none of the organizations requires it to be bound by decisions of any of the other organizations on legislative issues other than as to **action** with respect to **acts, bills,** resolutions, or **similar items** by the U.S. Congress, then two rules of law are triggered. One law rule is that, in the case of any organization whose decisions bind one or more members of an affiliated group, **directly** or **indirectly**, the determination as to whether the organization has paid or incurred **excess lobbying expenditures** and the determination as to whether the organization has exceeded the **expenditure limits** is made as though the organization has paid or incurred those amounts paid or incurred by the members of the affiliated group to influence legislation with respect to acts, bills, resolutions, or similar items by Congress. The other rule of law is that, in the case of an organization to which the foregoing rule does not apply but which is a member of an affiliated group, the determination as to whether the organization has paid or incurred excess lobbying expenditures and the determination as to whether the organization has exceeded the expenditure limits is made as though the organization is not a member of an affiliated group (**IRC** § 4911(f)(4)). [EO § 22.3(d)(viii)].

limited liability company

A "limited liability company" is a form of business entity (for-profit or nonprofit) that is a hybrid between a corporation and a partnership. It has the corporate attribute of limited liability for its members, yet it is treated as a partnership for federal tax law purposes unless an election is made. [EO §§ 4.1(b), 4.3(d), 19.23, 26.2(c), 28.2(c), 31.7, 32.4, 32.5, 32.6; HC §§ 22.3, 22.4, 22.6, 30.1(b); AR § 11.1(f)(3)(G); PF §§ 3.1(a), 5.4(e), 6.5; CG § 2.8; RE Q 1.8, Q 1.17, Q 14.32; CU Q 16.40; AS § 6.10(a); UB § 8.9(c); PG pp. 154–156; SM pp. 6, 22–23, 227–228, 230–231] (also **Multiple-member limited liability company**, **Single-member limited liability company**).

limited partner

A "limited partner" is a **partner** in a **partnership** who is essentially only an investor in the business conducted by that partnership. This type of partner is termed a "limited" one in the sense that his, her, or its **liability** in connection with the partnership is limited, with the limitation being confined to the amount of the partner's investment. Limited partners are involved in the partnership to obtain a return on their investment and perhaps to obtain one or more **tax** advantages. A **nonprofit organization** can be a limited partner in a partnership. [EO § 31.1(a); HC § 22.1; SM p. 225].

limited partnership

A **partnership** is a "limited partnership" when it is comprised of both **general partners** and **limited partners**. [EO § 31.1(a); UB § 8.9(a); HC § 22.1; CU Q 16.39; SM p. 225] (cf. **General partnership**).

line of business

The phrase "line of business" is used in the context of defining **tax-exempt business leagues** under the **federal tax law**. A line of business is a trade, occupation, or the like that is open to private parties. Thus, the business league has as its **members** private parties in a particular line of business. The efforts of an exempt business league must benefit a sufficiently broad segment of a business community; these community members are usually in competition with one another. Tax exemption of this nature is not available for an **organization** to aid one group in competition with another within a line of business. [AS §§ 1.1, 2.7, 2.10(b); EO § 14.1(c); SM p. 40].

liquidate

In general, the word "liquidate" means to extinguish or eliminate something. In **law**, to liquidate means to end a **business enterprise** by paying debts, and distributing **income** and **assets**. In this sense, the term is synonymous with **dissolve**. [EO § 4.3(b)] (also **Liquidation**).

liquidated damages

The term "liquidated damages" is usually used to mean reference in a document (most frequently, a **contract**) to a specific sum of money that one **person** will owe to another should there be a breach of the relationship (such as breach of contract).

liquidation

The term "liquidation" is used in the context of the **law** of **tax-exempt organizations** in two ways. One of these ways concerns the circumstances in which an organization is in the process of ceasing its existence and is transferring its **income** and **assets** (that is, liquidating) to one or more other **persons**. When the organization is an exempt **charitable organization**, which is required by the **organizational test** to have a **dissolution clause**, this process of liquidation must be accomplished in adherence to the language in that provision.

The other application of the term "liquidation" in this setting occurs when an exempt organization is liquidating a **for-profit subsidiary**. When this transpires, the exempt organization generally must **recognize** any **gain** or **loss** on the distribution of the **assets** (**IRC** § 337(b)(2)). Nonrecognition treatment is available where the **property** distributed is used by the exempt organization in an **unrelated trade or business** immediately after the distribution, although if the property subsequently ceases to be used in an unrelated business, the exempt organization will be taxed on any gain at that time. [EO §§ 30.8, 32.10(c); AR Chap. 20; HC § 16.2(d); PF §§ 1.9, 13.5; AS § 6.8; UB § 8.7] (also **Dissolution**; **Liquidate**).

liquidity

The concept of "liquidity" refers to the ease with which an item of **property** can be used as a medium of exchange. Money (in a stable economy) is perfectly liquid; **publicly traded securities** are often liquid. Conversely, **real property** is rarely liquid. Property contributed for **charitable** purposes by means of a **pooled income fund** is generally required to be liquid because of the **commingling requirement**. [CG § 2.14].

listed transaction

The term "listed transaction" means a **reportable transaction** that is the same as, or substantially similar to, a transaction specifically identified by the **IRS** as a tax avoidance transaction (**IRC** §§ 4965(e)(1)(B), 6707A(c)(2)). [EO § 28.16(d)].

listing reliance

The **IRS** publishes lists of **charitable organizations** and sometimes other categories of **exempt organizations**, as to their **tax-exempt status** and (when applicable) on which members of the **public** may rely, such as when contemplating **charitable contributions** and desiring **charitable deductions**. [EO § 28.6; CG §§ 3.6, 3.7].

literary organization

One of the ways that a **nonprofit organization** can qualify as a **tax-exempt charitable organization** under the **federal tax law** is to be a "literary" organization. There are, however, no **IRS** rulings or court opinions to this effect. This classification of tax exemption is overshadowed by classification as some other type of charitable **entity**, such as one that functions to **advance education**, or an **educational organization**. [EO § 11.7; SM p. 38].

litigation

A **charitable organization** can advance its **tax-exempt purposes** by instituting "litigation" (that is, the bringing of **actions** in court). In this context, litigation is a part of the organization's **program**, such as that conducted by **public interest law firms** or by other organizations in the tiling of **amicus briefs**. Although litigation is rarely inherently a charitable activity, it is often seen as a **means to an end** in achieving charitable objectives. Nonetheless, this type of litigation may not use tactics or pursue ends that are contrary to a clearly defined and established **public policy** or are violative of **statutory** or **constitutional** law. [EO §§ 7.16(d), 23.2(g)] (also **Declaratory judgment action**; **Third-party litigation**).

livestock

The term "livestock" is defined for **federal tax purposes** to include cattle, hogs, horses, mules, donkeys, sheep, goats, captive fur-bearing animals, chickens, turkeys, pigeons, and other poultry. This definition is used in defining the word **farm**, which in turn is used in the setting of the **charitable contribution deduction** that is available for **gifts** of **remainder interests** in farms. [CG § 15.2(b)].

L

loan

A "loan" is an advance of money (or, sometimes, **property**) in response to a promise to repay it, usually within a stated period of time. In the setting of the **law** of **tax-exempt organizations**, there are two unique uses of the term "loan."

One of these instances is in connection with the law pertaining to **private foundations**, which includes limitations on **self-dealing**. The lending of money or other extension of credit between a private foundation and a **disqualified person** generally constitutes an act of self-dealing (**IRC** § 4941(d)(1)(B)). This rule is inapplicable, however, to the lending of money or other extension of credit by a disqualified person to a private foundation if the loan or other extension of credit is without **interest** or other charge (determined without regard to the **imputed interest rules**) and the proceeds of the loan are used **exclusively** for **charitable purposes** (**IRC** § 4941(d)(2)(B)).

The other specific use of the term "loan" in the exempt organizations context arises in connection with the process utilized by some tax-exempt organizations, termed the **lending of securities**. The **federal tax law** generally provides that **income** from the lending of securities by an exempt organization is exempt from the **tax** on **unrelated business income** (**IRC** § 512(a)(5)). [EO § 25.1(d); PF § 5.5; AR §§ 3.1(ee), 3.2(ee), 7.2(c)(7), 7.2(c)(23), 7.2(c)(24), 18.1(b); HC §§ 4.4(c), 25.5(f), 28.3(d); UB § 3.4; RE Q 21.45; SM pp. 52–53].

loan commitment fee

A "loan commitment fee" is a nonrefundable charge made by a lender to reserve a sum of money with fixed terms for a specified period of time. These charges are to compensate the lender for the risk inherent in committing to make the loan (that is, for the lender's exposure to **interest rate** changes and for potential lost opportunities). A **tax-exempt organization** may receive this type of fee; it is **excluded** from the definition of **unrelated business income** (IRC § 512(b)(1)). [UB § 3.12; EO § 25.1(k)].

lobby
A "lobby" is a corridor, vestibule, or anteroom, in relation to a larger room or hall. Those who **attempt** to **influence legislation** often wait (lurk) in these places, in order to meet legislators as they come and go from their chambers. The word has also come to mean the act of **lobbying** and to describe a group of **persons** who engage in or support lobbying.

lobbying
The term "lobbying" is generally (and loosely) used to describe one or more processes by which a **person** endeavors to influence the outcome of a legislative process, involving foreign, national (**federal**), state, or local **legislation**. This entails either **direct lobbying** or **grass-roots lobbying**. More fully, the term also applies to efforts to influence the outcome of an executive branch **rule**-making or **regulation**-making process; however, the term "lobbying" is usually reserved to describe attempts to influence **members** of a legislative branch and/or their staff. [EO § 22.3; AR §§ 9.1(a), 9.1(e), 9.2(b)(2); HC §§ 7.1, 7.3, 7.6, 18.4(a); AS § 4.2; CG § 10.8; FR § 5.10; CU Q 8.1; PG pp. 107–118; SM pp. 186–187; LI Q 7.1, Q 7.7, Q 7.8] (also **Influence legislation**; **Legislative activities**).

lobbying, direct
See **Direct lobbying**.

Lobbying Disclosure Act of 1995
In addition to the **federal tax law**, Congress has enacted a system of regulation of **lobbying** by **tax-exempt organizations** and other **persons**, which imposes registration and reporting requirements. **Lobbyists** are required to register with the Clerk of the House of Representatives and the Secretary of the Senate. This body of law was substantially amended by the Honest Leadership and Open Government Act of 2007. [EO § 22.10; HC § 7.3; AS § 4.2(b)(i); PF § 9.1(a)].

lobbying, grass-roots
See **Grass-roots lobbying**.

lobbying ceiling amount
The phrase "lobbying ceiling amount" is used to describe the amount of **lobbying expenditures**, **normally** made by a **charitable organization** that has **elected** the **expenditure test**, that constitute more than 150 percent of the **allowable lobbying amount**, so that the organization loses its **tax-exempt status** as a charitable entity. [EO § 22.3(d)(iii); SM p. 190].

lobbying disallowance rule

The "lobbying disallowance rule" operates to disallow a **business expense deduction** for an amount paid or incurred in connection with attempts to **influence legislation** (IRC §§ 162(e)(1)(A), (C)). [EO § 22.6(b); AS § 4.2(b); SM pp. 192–193] (also **Political activities disallowance rule**).

lobbying expenditure

The term "lobbying expenditure," as used in connection with the **expenditure test**, means **expenditures** for the purpose of **influencing legislation** (IRC § 4911(c)(1)). For purposes of the **law** concerning **disqualifying lobbying expenditures**, the term "lobbying expenditure" means any amount paid or incurred by an **organization** in carrying on **propaganda** or otherwise attempting to **influence legislation** (IRC § 4912(d)(1)). [EO §§ 22.3(d)(1), 22.4].

lobbying labor hours

The term "lobbying labor hours," used in the **ratio method** of **cost allocation**, means the hours that the personnel of an **organization** spend on **lobbying activities** during a **tax year**. The organization may use any **reasonable** method to determine the number of labor hours spent on lobbying activities. A reasonable method may treat as zero the lobbying labor hours of personnel engaged in secretarial, maintenance, and similar activities. [EO § 22.6(a)] (also **De minimis rule for labor hours**).

lobbying nontaxable amount

The phrase "lobbying nontaxable amount" is used in the context of the **expenditure test**. The basic permitted annual level of **expenditures** for legislative efforts (**lobbying**) is determined by using a sliding scale percentage of the **organization's exempt purpose expenditures**, as follows: 20 percent of the first $500,000 of an organization's expenditures for an exempt purpose, plus 15 percent of the next $500,000, 10 percent of the next $500,000, and 5 percent of any remaining expenditures (**IRC** § 4911(c)(2)). The total amount spent for legislative activities in any one year by an eligible charitable organization, however, may not exceed $1 million (*id.*). [EO § 22.3(d)(iii); HC § 7.1(c); SM pp. 189–190] (also **Grass-roots nontaxable amount**).

lobbying subsidiary

A "lobbying subsidiary" is a **tax-exempt organization**, usually a **social welfare organization**, that is established by an exempt **charitable organization** for the purpose of conducting **lobbying**. This type of **subsidiary** is used to avoid loss of **tax-exempt status**, because of excessive lobbying activity, by the **parent organization**. [EO § 29.3; HC § 7.3].

lobbyist

A "lobbyist" is an individual who engages in the activity known as **lobbying**, that is, attempting to **influence legislation**. A lobbyist may be compensated for his or her efforts, or may serve as a **volunteer**. Those who lobby for **compensation** are either an **employee** of an **organization** or are retained as a **consultant** (**independent contractor**) by one or more organizations.

local

The word "local," in the context of the **federal law** of **tax-exempt organizations**, is used to mean a particular **community**, place, or district—a single identifiable locality. The term is used in connection with **tax-exempt status** for **local associations of employees** and **benevolent life insurance associations**, the latter of which must be of a **purely local character**. [EO §§ 19.3, 19.5(a)].

local association of employees

Tax exemption is provided under **federal law** for a "local association of employees," the **membership** of which is limited to the **employees** of a designated **person** or persons in a particular municipality, and the **net earnings** of which are devoted **exclusively** to **charitable**, **educational**, or **recreational purposes** (IRC §§ 501(a), 501(c)(4)). [EO § 19.3; AU § 7.1(j); AS § 1.6(b); SM p. 42].

local character, purely

The phrase "purely local character" means being confined to a particular **community**, place, or district, irrespective of political subdivisions, that is, a single identifiable locality. [EO § 19.5(a); SM pp. 42, 44].

local economic development corporation

A "local economic development corporation" is a category of **tax-exempt charitable organization** under the **federal tax law**. These organizations, the **principal** purpose of which is to alleviate poverty, engage in a variety of activities, including investment in local businesses; direct operation of job-training, housing, and other programs; business counseling; and encouragement to established national businesses to open plants or offices in economically depressed areas. [EO § 7.15(e); CG § 3.2(b)].

local legislation

The term "local legislation" means **legislation** of any local council or similar governing body (**IRC** § 162(e)(2)). An attempt to influence local legislation is **excepted** from application of the **lobbying disallowance rule** (*id.*). [EO § 22.6(a)].

lodge system

A "lodge" is a meeting place for **members** of a branch, **chapter**, or the like of a **society** or similar form of **membership organization**. An organization that is **organized** and **operated** in this fashion, and utilizes this type of a facility, is considered to be under the "lodge system." Two types of **nonprofit organizations**, the **fraternal beneficiary society** and the **domestic fraternal society**, must operate under the lodge system as a condition of their **tax exemption**. [EO § 19.4(a); SM pp. 42–43].

long-term capital gain

Federal tax law defines a "long- term capital gain" as a **gain** from the **sale** or other **disposition** of **property** that has been held for more than one year. [CG § 2.16(c); SM p. 134] (also **Capital assets**; **Capital gain**; **Capital gain property**; **Long-term capital gain property**).

long-term capital gain property

The term "long-term capital gain property" means **property** that, if sold, would give rise to **long-term capital gain**. Generally, a **charitable contribution** of long-term capital gain property to a **public charitable organization** gives rise to an **income tax charitable contribution deduction** that is based on the full **fair market value** of the property. [CG §§ 4.3, 7.1; PF §§ 14.1, 14.2, 14.4].

long-term capital loss

Federal tax law defines a "long-term capital loss" as a **loss** from the **sale** or other **disposition** of **property** that has been held for more than one year. [CG § 2.16(c)].

look-through rule

If a **trade or business regularly carried on** by a **partnership**, of which a **tax-exempt organization** is a **member**, is an **unrelated trade or business** with respect to the organization, in computing its **unrelated business taxable income** the organization must, in accordance with the "look-through rule," include its share (whether or not distributed and subject to certain **modifications**) of the **gross income** of the partnership from the unrelated trade or business and its share of the partnership **deductions** that are **directly connected with** the gross income (**IRC** § 512(c)(1)). [EO §§ 24.7, 31.1; UB §§ 6.4, 8.17; PG p. 165; SM p. 175].

loophole

The term "loophole" is used to describe a benefit to a **person** derived from a **law**, not infrequently a **tax** law, usually from a creative interpretation of the law or the exploitation of a meaning of the law in a way unintended by the authors of the law. In its narrowest sense, the term entails the manipulation of a law provision to achieve an outcome that was unintended by the writers of it. When use of a loophole is before a court, the question is whether the court should fix it or leave the matter to the **legislature**. In a 2014 case, a U.S. Supreme Court majority elected to remedy the problem caused by a law loophole, causing a dissenting justice to write: "It is not the role of this Court to identify and plug loopholes. It is the role of good lawyers to identify and exploit them, and the role of Congress to eliminate them if it wishes." The term is also often used in a much broader sense (usually a derogatory one), to embrace all **tax preferences**.

loss

A "loss" is the losing of something; in some instances, it is associated with a form of damage. It is often used in the context of a financial loss. (also **Capital loss**; **Short-term capital loss**).

lottery

A "lottery" is a form of gambling and thus is a **game of chance**; payments are collected and prizes awarded solely on the basis of chance (rather than competence or merit). Some **tax-exempt organizations** use lotteries, either as a **special event** or by means of the mail, as **fundraising opportunities**. While a lottery is almost always an **unrelated trade or business**, the resulting **income** is almost always **exempt** from federal income taxation, either because the lottery is not **regularly carried on** or because the **business** is operated primarily by **volunteers**. Lotteries conducted by exempt organizations are exempt from the **federal excise tax** on wagers and from the strictures of the Organized Crime Control Act. [FR § 2.2(a); EO §§ 24.3, 25.2(a); CG § 3.1(b); SM pp. 172–173, 175].

low-cost article

A "low-cost article" is defined in the **federal tax law** as any article (or aggregate of articles distributed to a single distributee in a year) that has a cost not in excess of $5.00 to the **organization** that distributes the item or on behalf of which the item is distributed (with that amount annually adjusted for inflation) (**IRC** § 513(h)(2)). (This amount for the **tax year** beginning in 2015 is $10.50.) Where certain types of **tax-exempt organizations** engage in certain types of distributions of these articles incidental to the **solicitation** of **charitable contributions**. the activity is not considered an **unrelated trade or business** (**IRC** § 513(h)(3)). [FR § 5.2; UB § 4.9; EO § 25.2(j); HC § 24.18(a); SM pp. 176–177].

low-profit limited liability company

A "low-profit limited liability company" usually is a **for-profit limited liability company**, with one or more taxable **members**, having as its primary purpose accomplishment of one or more **charitable** purposes. [EO §§ 4.11(c), 32.7].

lower court

The term "lower court" is used to describe either a court that initially hears a case (sometimes referred to as the "trial court") or an **appellate court** from which a case can be appealed. For example, in the **federal** system, the principal lower courts are the U.S. District Courts, the U.S. Tax Court, and the U.S. Court of Federal Claims. Yet, in relation to the U.S. Supreme Court, the various U.S. Circuit Courts of Appeal are lower courts. On occasion, a judge or justice of a higher court, referring to a lower court, will identify that court as the court "below."

lump sum

A "lump sum" is a single amount of money. The term is often used accompanied by other words, such as a "lump-sum payment" or a "lump-sum distribution." The term is used in contrast to amounts paid or distributed incrementally, as in installments.

M

macroeconomic analysis

The term "macroeconomic analysis" refers to an approach to assessment, at the **federal** level of government, of the economic impact of **major tax** (and other) **legislation**. This assessment methodology is to be contrasted with the more conventional model, which focuses on whether an item of legislation is revenue neutral. The U.S. House of Representatives incorporated the macroeconomic analysis approach (informally known as "dynamic scoring") into its rules at the beginning of 2015. A paper accompanying this rule change stated that, "[i]nstead of concentrating on the top line—whether it's good for the Treasury—elected officials would [using macroeconomic analysis] concentrate on the bottom line—whether it's good for the taxpayer." Conventional wisdom has it that this approach may facilitate enactment of major tax reduction legislation by showing that the resulting economic growth would substantially reduce their cost to the federal government.

mailing list

A "mailing list" is a compilation of names and addresses of individuals. **Nonprofit organizations** frequently maintain mailing lists, such as lists of their **members** and/or **donors**. As part of this maintenance process, nonprofit organizations may **rent** or **exchange** these lists with other organizations. Where the organizations involved on both sides of one of these rental or exchange transactions are organizations eligible to receive **tax-deductible charitable contributions**, the rental or exchange activity is not regarded as an **unrelated business**. [FR § 5.7(b)(6); EO § 25.2(k); UB § 4.10].

maintenance requirement, pooled income fund

To qualify under the **federal tax law**, a **pooled income fund** must be "maintained" by the same **public charity** to or **for the use of** which the **remainder interest** in the **gift properties** is **contributed** (IRC § 642(c)(5)(E)). This requirement of maintenance is satisfied where the public charity exercises **control**, **directly** or **indirectly**, over the fund. A national organization may maintain a pooled income fund on behalf of its **chapters** or similar auxiliary groups. [CG §§ 13.2(e), 13.9(a); SM p. 237] (also **Multi-organization pooled income fund**).

Bruce R. Hopkins' Nonprofit Law Dictionary, First Edition. Bruce R. Hopkins.
© 2015 Bruce R. Hopkins. Published 2015 by John Wiley & Sons, Inc.

major contributor

A "major contributor" is a **person** who makes a **major gift**, usually to a **charitable organization** in the setting of a significant **fundraising** event, such as a **capital campaign**.

major gift

The term "major gift" means a significant **contribution**, usually to a **charitable organization**, often made at the outset of a **fundraising** campaign, from either an individual or some other legal entity (such as a **corporation**); the amount of this type of **gift** is frequently a substantial portion of the total amount being sought in the campaign. (also **Leadership gift**).

major tax legislation

For purposes of the rules of the U.S. House of Representatives pertaining to **macroeconomic analysis**, the phrase "major tax legislation" means **bills** that would increase the federal deficit by an amount equal to or greater than 0.25 percent of the projected gross domestic product of the United States in any year involved in connection with a bill. The gross domestic product in the government's fiscal year 2014 was about $17.3 trillion, so this threshold for that year was $43 billion.

make-up exception

The "make-up exception" is a phrase that is used in the context of defining qualifying **charitable remainder unitrusts**. The general rule is that a charitable remainder unitrust must pay, not less often than annually, an amount equal to a **fixed percentage** of the **net fair market value** of the **trust assets** (the general **unitrust amount**), determined annually, to an eligible **person** or persons for each **tax year** of the appropriate payment period. A charitable remainder unitrust may, however, be designed so that it pays out only the actual **income** from the trust assets (as long as those amounts are no more than the general unitrust amount); this is the **income-only exception**. Moreover, a charitable remainder unitrust may be structured so that it pays out income in conformity with the income-only exception but is required to, for the years in which income is higher than the general unitrust amount, pay out amounts for prior years so as to make the prior years' payments equal to the general unitrust amount; this is the "make-up exception." [CG § 12.3(a)].

manager, foundation

See **Foundation manager**.

mandatory distribution

See **Mandatory payout requirement**.

mandatory gift

The term "mandatory gift" is one of the classic oxymorons in nonprofit law. These payments arise when a **person** is obligated, by **contract** or **law**, to make a payment to a **charitable organization** or a **governmental unit**, and claims a **charitable contribution deduction** for the transfer. There is no such deduction for this type of payment, however, because it is not a **gift**. The payment may, however, be deductible as a business expense (**IRC** § 162). [CG § 3.1(n)].

mandatory payout requirement

The **federal tax law** contains five "mandatory payout requirements" (or **mandatory** distributions). A principal payout requirement is the **statutory** obligation of a standard **private foundation** to distribute, with respect to each of its years, a certain amount of money and/or **property** for **charitable** purposes (IRC § 4942). In general, the amount that must be annually distributed for charitable purposes is an amount equal to 5 percent of the **value** of the **noncharitable assets** of the foundation. The amount that is required to be distributed is termed the **distributable amount,** and the 5 percent amount is deemed the **minimum investment return.**

There is a mandatory payout requirement applicable with respect to **Type III supporting organizations** that are not **functionally integrated Type III supporting organizations.** Basically, this distributable amount is an amount equal to 85 percent of the supporting organization's adjusted net income.

A **private operating foundation** must meet an **income test.** This test requires that this type of private foundation annually expend an amount equal to **substantially all** of the lesser of its **adjusted gross income** or its minimum investment return, in the form of **qualifying distributions directly** for the **active conduct** of its **tax-exempt** activities. In this setting, the phrase "substantially all" means 85 percent. Thus, where the amount is less than its adjusted gross income, the distributable amount of a private operating foundation is 4.25 percent of the value of its noncharitable assets. There are also mandatory payout requirements for the **conduit foundation** and the **common fund foundation.** [PF Chap. 6, §§ 1.7, 1.8, 3.1–3.3, 15.7(g), 17.6(a); EO §§ 12.3(c), 12.4(b); SM p. 84].

M

mandatory provision

The **federal tax law** contains requirements that mandate certain provisions in certain documents; these are "mandatory provisions." One example of this type of mandate is the requirement in the **organizational test** that the **articles of organization** of a **charitable organization** contain a **dissolution clause.** A similar requirement is the organizational provisions that must be in the articles of organization of a **private foundation** (although these provisions may be imputed by **statutory** law) or a **supporting organization.** Various provisions are also mandatory in the organizational documents of qualifying **charitable remainder trusts, pooled income funds,** and **charitable lead trusts.** Where certain tax results are desired, there are mandatory provisions for **charitable gift annuity contracts.** [EO §§ 4.3(b), 12.1(g), 12.3(c); PF §§ 1.9, 15.7(a); CG §§ 12.9, 14.1].

mandatory requirement

A "mandatory requirement" is a requirement of **law** in a **statute** that must be strictly adhered to in its entirety. It is a legal requirement that cannot be satisfied by means of the **doctrine of substantial compliance.** (cf. **Directory requirement**).

marital deduction

The "marital deduction" is a **federal estate tax law** concept. An unlimited marital deduction is allowed to an **estate** of a **decedent** for the **value** of any **property** transferred to his or her surviving spouse. Some **interests,** however, do not qualify for this marital deduction.

The marital deduction is also a federal **gift tax** law concept. Again, the law provides for an unlimited gift tax deduction for transfers between spouses. This marital deduction, however, is subject to some conditions and limitations. [CG §§ 8.2(k), 8.3(b)].

market failure

The term "market failure" is used to help explain an economic rationale for **nonprofit organizations**. This rationale has it that **for-profit organizations** are easily tempted to raise prices and cut quality; the market is unable to control that phenomenon and thus consumers are disadvantaged, leading to market failure. By contrast, consumers may prefer to purchase goods and services from nonprofit organizations (particularly those that are **tax-exempt**) because they are trusted by reason of the legal constraints under which they operate. (also **Contract failure**; **Halo effect**).

marketing

The goods and services of **nonprofit organizations** often need to be "marketed," just as do those of **for-profit organizations**. Much of this marketing is, in essence, **advertising**. (Excessive marketing can lead to allegations of **commerciality**.) For **charitable organizations** and a few other types of **tax-exempt organizations**, marketing can also be **fundraising**. Fundraising programs frequently are marketed by these organizations, just as are their **tax-exempt functions**; this is particularly the case with respect to **planned giving programs**. [SM pp. 244–249].

market value

See **Fair market value**.

mass media

The **federal tax law** defines the term "mass media" in the context of defining the term "mass media communication." The term "mass media" means television, radio, billboards, and general circulation newspapers and general circulation magazines. [EO § 22.3(d)(i)].

mass media advertisement

A **communication** that is not considered a **grass-roots lobbying communication** under the general definition of that term may nonetheless be characterized as a grass-roots lobbying communication by reason of a rule that is applicable to a limited type of paid advertisement that appears in the **mass media**. This type of communication is a "mass media advertisement." A mass media advertisement that is paid for by a **charitable organization** is **presumed** to be grass-roots lobbying if it (1) is made within two weeks before a vote by a legislative body or **committee** (but not a subcommittee) of a legislative body, on a **highly publicized** item of legislation; (2) reflects a view on the general subject of the legislation; and (3) either refers to the legislation or encourages the public to communicate with legislators on the general subject of the legislation. This presumption can be **rebutted** either by demonstrating that the charitable organization regularly makes similar mass media communications without regard to the timing of legislation (a **customary course of business exception**) or that the timing of the paid advertisement was unrelated to the upcoming vote. [EO § 22.3(d)(i)].

M

matching gift

See **Matching grant**.

matching grant

A "matching grant" is a **grant**, such as from a **private foundation**, that is made by the **grantor** only where the **grantee** is able to raise a stated amount of other funds (such as the same amount as the grant) over a stated period of time. This type of arrangement is sometimes also applied to a gift ("matching gift").

material

The word "material" is used to refer to something of importance or substance. When a set of facts is to lead to a conclusion of **law**, it is essential that all of the "material" facts be marshaled. A fact that is not material (that is, is immaterial) is an **incidental** fact and thus can be ignored (or **disregarded** or considered irrelevant) without undermining the conclusion of law.

material change

The term "material change" is used in the context of a **determination letter** or **ruling** from the **IRS**, including a determination of **recognition of exemption**. These letters and rulings are based on what the **IRS** believes are the **material** facts. If the material facts change, the conclusion of the letter or ruling may be different. In most instances of this nature, the **IRS** expects the **persons** involved to bring the material change in the facts to its attention so that an evaluation can be made as to the ongoing efficacy of the letter or ruling. [AR §§ 5.1(k), 5.2(a)(4); EO § 26.1(c); PG pp. 53, 54, 203; SM pp. 125–126].

material condition

A **donor** may make a **contribution** to a **charitable organization**, in so doing placing one or more **conditions** on the **gift**. In general, if, as of the date of a gift, a transfer for **charitable purposes** is dependent on the performance of some act or the happening of a **precedent** event in order that it might become effective, an **income tax charitable contribution deduction** is not allowable unless the possibility that the charitable transfer will not become effective is **so remote as to be negligible**. If the condition is not so remote, it is a "material condition." Nonetheless, a material condition will not defeat a charitable contribution deduction if the condition that must be satisfied is a restriction as to **program** uses, such as **scholarships**, **research**, or **capital improvements**. [CG § 10.4; SM p. 126] (also **Restricted gifts**).

material diversion of assets

A diversion of a **tax-exempt organization's assets** means an unauthorized conversion or use of the organization's assets other than for the organization's **exempt** purposes, including **embezzlement** or theft. A diversion is considered **material** if the gross dollar amount (disregarding restitution, insurance, or similar recoveries) exceeds the lesser of $250,000 or 5 percent of the lesser of the organization's **gross receipts** for the **tax year** or total assets as of the close of the year. [AR § 5.2(a)(5)].

M

means to an end

The phrase "means to an end" is used to describe one or more ways in which a particular objective may be achieved. The phrase is usually employed where the objective is a legitimate or appropriate one, but the method or methods utilized to carry out the objective are questionable. (It is the basis for the saying that "the end justifies the means.") For example, a **charitable** purpose can be advanced by means (or instruments) that are not inherently charitable; an example is the granting of scholarships notwithstanding the **private benefit** enjoyed by the **grantees**. [EO § 6.3(b)].

mechanical test

The **law** employs the term "mechanical test" to refer to a test or standard that does not require subjectivity to apply it; rather, the test embodies a **rule** in terms of a stated length of time, stated percentage, or the like, so that the test requires merely its (mechanical) application to obtain the required result. For example, the phrase **long-term capital gain property** means otherwise qualifying **property** held for at least one year; the determination of the lapse of one year does not require a subjective analysis. Another example of a mechanical test is the rules defining the term **substantially all** to mean 85 percent; there may be some subjectivity in ascertaining what goes into the base to which the percentage applies, but otherwise the test is mechanically applied. Other mechanical tests are found in the **private foundation mandatory distribution** rules, the private foundation **excess business holdings** rules, and in the rules imposing **percentage limitations** on the **deductibility**, for **federal income tax** purposes, of **charitable gifts**.

One of the more elaborate of the mechanical tests is the series of sliding scale percentages that are applied in determining the amounts of permissible and impermissible **lobbying expenditures** of **qualified charitable organizations** pursuant to the **expenditure test**.

medical care costs

The **federal gift tax law excludes** from taxation transfers of money or **property** made **directly** to a medical care provider for medical care services on behalf of one or more other individuals (typically one or more **family members**) (**IRC** § 2503(e)). [CG §§ 3.3(a), 8.2(g)].

medical research

The **federal tax law** defines the term "medical research" in the setting of defining the term **medical research organization**. For this purpose, the term means the conduct of investigations, experiments, and studies to discover, develop, or verify knowledge relating to the causes, diagnosis, treatment, prevention, or control of physical or mental diseases and impairment of human beings. Medical research encompasses the associated disciplines spanning the biological, social, and behavioral sciences. [HC § 24.13; EO § 7.6(d)].

medical research organization

A "medical research organization" is a **tax-exempt** (**IRC** § 501(a), by reason of description in **IRC** § 501(c)(3)) **charitable organization** that is **directly** engaged in the continuous **active conduct** of **medical research** in conjunction with an **exempt hospital** (**IRC** §

M

170(b)(l)(A)(iii)). A medical research organization is a **public charity** (**IRC** § 509(a)(1)). This type of **organization** need not be formally **affiliated** with a hospital to be considered **primarily** engaged in the active conduct of medical research in conjunction with a hospital. There must be, however, a joint effort on the part of the research organization and one or more hospitals pursuant to an understanding that the organizations will maintain continuing close cooperation in the active conduct of medical research. [HC § 5.1(b); EO §§ 7.6(d), 12.3(a); AR § 6.1(c)(6); PF § 15.3; CG § 3.3(a); SM p. 80; LI Q 10.4] (also **Institution**).

meetings documentation policy

On the **Form 990**, a filing **organization** is asked whether it contemporaneously documented every meeting held or written action undertaken during the **tax year** by the **governing body** and committees. Some **exempt organizations** have responded to that questioning by formally adopting a "meetings documentation policy." [GV §§ 4.1(h), 6.3(g); SM p. 275].

member

Nonprofit organizations are often **organized** as **membership organizations**. A "member" can be an individual or other legal **entity**, such as a **corporation**. The **rights** of members of nonprofit organizations can vary, particularly as to voting. Frequently, the relationship between a membership organization and its members has consequences in **law**, such as whether or not a **communication** concerning **legislation** from the organization is a **membership communication** or when a **charitable** membership organization is **soliciting contributions** solely from its members so as to be **exempt** from one or more of the state **charitable solicitation acts**.

In the context of the definition of a membership communication pursuant to the **expenditure test** rules, a **person** is a member of an organization if the person pays **dues** or makes a **contribution** of more than a nominal amount, contributes more than a nominal amount of time, or is one of a limited number of **honorary members** or **life members** who have more than a nominal connection with the organization and who have been chosen for a valid reason (such as length of service to the organization or involvement in activities forming the basis of the organization's **tax exemption**) unrelated to the organization's dissemination of information to its members. A person who is not a "member" of an organization by reason of this definition may nonetheless be treated as a member if the organization demonstrates to the satisfaction of the **IRS** that there is a good reason for the fact that its membership requirements do not meet the terms of this definition and that its membership requirements do not operate to permit an abuse of these rules. Moreover, a person who is a member of a charitable organization that is a member of an **affiliated group of organizations** is treated as a member of each of the organizations in the group.

Several of the state charitable solicitation acts define the term "member." The principal purpose of this definition is to define the term in relation to the **exclusion** for solicitations that are confined to the membership of the soliciting organization. A typical definition of this nature is that a member is a person to whom, for the payment of fees, dues, assessments, and the like, an organization provides services and confers a **bona fide right**, privilege, professional standing, honor, or other direct benefit, in addition to the right to vote, elect **directors** and **officers**, or hold offices. These definitions usually contain the rule that the concept of membership does not include those persons who are granted a membership on making a contribution as the result of a solicitation. [EO §§ 22.3(d)(v), 25.2(l); UB § 9.4(c); GV § 4.1(g); FR § 4.9] (also **Affiliate member**; **Associate member**; **Regular member**; **Voting member**).

member of the family

The **federal tax law** defines the phrase "member of the family" in the **tax-exempt organization** setting in a variety of ways.

The phrase is used in the context of defining **disqualified persons** in the **federal tax law** pertaining to **private foundations**. One type of disqualified person is a member of the family of an individual who is a **substantial contributor**, a **foundation manager**, or a **20 percent owner** (**IRC** § 4946(a)(1)(D)). A "member of the family" is, in turn, an individual's spouse, ancestors, children, grandchildren, great-grandchildren, and the spouses of children, grandchildren, and great-grandchildren (**IRC** § 4946(d)).

For purposes of the **intermediate sanctions rules**, the phrase "member of the family" is determined in accordance with the definition of the phrase in the private foundation context, except that the members also include the brothers and sisters (whether by the whole or half blood) of the individuals and their spouses (**IRC** § 4958(f)(4)).

The phrase is also used in defining the term **qualified appreciated stock**. That type of stock does not include stock of a **corporation** contributed by a **donor** to a private foundation to the extent that the amount of stock contributed (including prior gifts of stock by the donor) exceeds 10 percent (in **value**) of all of the outstanding stock of the corporation (**IRC** § 170(e)(5)(C)(i)). In making this calculation, the individual must take into account all contributions made by any member of his or her family (**IRC** § 170(e)(5)(C)(ii)). That term is defined as meaning only an individual's brothers and sisters (whether by the whole or half blood), spouses, ancestors, and lineal descendants (**IRC** § 267(e)(4)). [EO §§ 12.2(d), 21.3; PF §§ 4.4, 14.4(b), 15.1; HC § 4.9(a)(ii); CG § 4.5(b)].

membership

A "membership" is a group of **persons** that comprise the **members** of an **organization**. States' **charitable solicitation acts** often provide **exemptions** in circumstances where an **organization** is **soliciting** its **bona fide** membership. The word is also used to describe the state of being a member, for example, an individual who holds a membership in an **association**. The word is further used as an adjective, as in a **membership communication**. [FR § 3.2(f)].

membership communication

Expenditures by a **charitable organization** for a **communication** that refers to, and reflects a view on, **specific legislation**, are not **lobbying** expenditures if (1) the communication is directed only to **members** of the **organization**, (2) the specific legislation to which the communication refers, and on which it reflects a view, is of direct interest to the organization and its members, (3) the communication does not **directly** encourage the member to engage in **direct lobbying** (either individually or through the organization), and (4) the communication does not directly encourage the member to engage in **grass-roots lobbying** (either individually or through the organization). [EO § 22.3(d)(v)].

M

membership fee

The term "membership fee" refers to the **fee** that a **person** must pay to an **organization** in order to become a **member** (usually termed an "initiation fee") and to remain a member (generally, **dues**). Other types of membership fees include periodic and specific assessments. Most membership fees constitute **public support** for the **service provider type of publicly supported charity**. [EO §§ 12.3(b)(iv), 25.2(l); AR §§ 7.2(a)(1), 7.2(a)(2); PF §§ 5.8(e), 15.6(c)].

membership organization

A "membership organization" is an **organization**, almost always a **nonprofit organization**, that has a membership base. **Members** may be either individuals or organizations, or both. Members may have full, partial, or no voting rights; members usually pay **dues** to the organization.

Many types of membership organizations are **tax-exempt**. These entities are often referred to using terms such as **association**, **cooperative**, **league**, **society**, or **union**. These organizations provide services to their members, such as provision of health care services or services to assist them as a member of a **line of business**. Other specific membership organizations include **alumni associations**, **fraternities**, other **fraternal** organizations, **service clubs**, **social clubs**, **sororities**, and **veterans' organizations**. (also **Business league**; **Health maintenance organization**).

mere recognition

The concept of "mere recognition" is applied by the **IRS** in determining the scope and **law** consequences of **donor recognition programs**. Where the essence of donor recognition is **advertising**, the transferor of money and/or **property** is not regarded as a donor but rather as a purchaser of services; the payments then become taxable to the recipient **tax-exempt organization** as a form of **unrelated business income**. By contrast, mere recognition of a donor does not transform a **gift** into a form of taxable advertising revenue. This occurs where a benefactor is acknowledged in a way that normally is **incidental** to the **contribution** and not of sufficient **value** to the **contributor** to constitute a unrelated business. [EO §§ 24.5(h), 24.6; FR § 5.16; CG § 3.1(g)] (also **Corporate sponsorship**).

merger

A "merger" is a transaction in which one or more **organizations** become a part of (that is, "merge" with) another **organization**. The entities that are merging into another one cease to exist; the remaining, **entity** is often termed the "survivor." **Nonprofit organizations** do not engage in mergers as frequently as **for-profit organizations**, but nearly every state **law** provides for mergers of nonprofit entities, particularly **corporations**. The **federal tax law** recognizes mergers of nonprofit organizations as well, such as in the rule addressing the possibility of a merger of two **private foundations** (IRC § 507(b)(2)). [EO § 32.3; AR Chap. 20; HC Chap. 21; PF § 13.5].

method of accounting

Every **nonprofit organization** must have a "method of accounting." This is the means by which an organization maintains records as to its **revenue**, **expenses**, **assets**, and **liabilities**. There are two methods of accounting. One is the "cash receipts and disbursement method," in which revenue is **recognized** when it is received and an expense is recorded when a payment is made (**IRC** § 446(c)(1)). The other is the "accrual method," in which revenue and expenses are recognized when a **right** to receive the revenue or an obligation for an expense arises (**IRC** § 446(c)(2)). [CG § 2.10].

methodology test

The "methodology test" is a standard used by the **IRS** to determine whether an **organization** is engaging in **educational** activities or is disseminating **propaganda**. The outcome of this determination can mean to the denial or loss of **tax-exempt status**. The test has its name in reflection of the point that the method used by an organization in advocating its position, rather than the position itself, is the standard for determining whether an organization has educational purposes. Under this test, the method used by an organization is not considered educational if it fails to provide a factual foundation for the viewpoint or position being advocated or if it fails to provide a development from the relevant facts that would **materially** aid a listener or a reader in a learning process. The test includes various factors that, if present, will likely lead the **IRS** to conclude that the method of **advocacy** used is not educational. [EO § 8.2; CU Q 2.7–Q 2.9; SM p. 36; LI Q 9.7–Q 9.9] (also **Full and fair exposition test**).

Military Family Tax Relief Act of 2003

Enactment of the Military Family Tax Relief Act of 2003 brought the body of law denying **tax exemption** for and **deductibility** of **charitable contributions** to **terrorist organizations** during a **period of suspension**.

mineral interest

See **Qualified mineral interest**.

minimum investment return

The phrase "minimum investment return" is an element of the **mandatory payout requirement** that is applicable to **private foundations**. This requirement is defined as including the **distributable amount**, which is an amount equal to 5 percent of the **value** of the **noncharitable assets** of the foundation; this amount is the "minimum investment return" (**IRC** § 4942(d)(1)). [PF §§ 3.1(d), 6.1, 6.2; EO § 12.4(b); HC § 5.10; SM p. 89].

minister

For obvious **constitutional law** reasons, the law does not include a rigid formula for determining when an **employee** of a **religious organization** qualifies as a "minister." Indeed, some religions do not employ that term. A U.S. Supreme Court justice observed that the Constitution "leaves it to the collective conscience of each religious group to determine for itself who is qualified to serve as teacher or messenger of its faith." Two elements of the term, however, appear to be whether the organization is holding an individual out as a minister and the job duties reflect a role in conveying the organization's message and carrying out its **mission**. [CL § 2.11(b)].

M

ministerial exception

The U.S. Supreme Court recognized a "ministerial exception" to employment discrimination **laws,** based on the Constitution's **Religion Clauses,** writing that **religious organizations** are free to select and dismiss their **ministers** without interference by government. [CL § 2.11(a)].

minor

A "minor" is an individual who has not yet reached an age when he or she is considered to be legally **competent** to assume responsibility for his or her actions. While in this stage of life, an individual is said to be at an age of minority; after that phase, the individual is known as being of an age of majority. The **law,** chiefly state law, provides for various ages as the line of demarcation for these purposes, being the ages of eighteen to twenty-one. (The Twenty-Seventh Amendment to the U.S. Constitution permits those over the age of eighteen to vote in **federal** elections.)

For purposes of the **federal income tax charitable contribution deduction,** there are special rules of deductibility pertaining to gifts of a **corporation's inventory.** One of the requirements of these rules is that the **gift properties** must be used for the care of the **ill, needy,** or **infants.** An "infant" in turn is defined as a minor child as that term is used in the jurisdiction in which the child resides.

In the **federal gift tax** setting, a transfer of money or **property** made pursuant to a qualifying written **marital property** settlement agreement is not regarded as a gift if made for the support of one or more minor children born to the marriage (**IRC** § 2516). [CG § 9.3(b)].

minutes

A document containing a summary of decisions made and other actions taken during the course of a meeting is termed the "minutes." The most common occasion for the taking of minutes is at a meeting of the **board of trustees** or **board of directors** of an **organization.** Minutes are an essential way of recording the history of an organization.

Minutes should be carefully written. These documents are frequently read by outsiders, including government officials. For example, the **IRS** will review the minutes of an organization as part of the **audit** process. The preparation of accurate minutes is one of the few ways in which an organization can create evidence in its favor. [PG pp. 17–19; GV § 4.1(h); SM pp. 21–22, 300; AU § 3.1(f); AR § 5.2(a)(7); RE Q 5.15, Q 12.7, Q 12.8; CU Q 5.40; LI Q 3.38].

misdemeanor

A "misdemeanor" is an act that constitutes a **criminal** offense, albeit an offense that is considered to be of less seriousness than a **felony.** Thus, a misdemeanor is punished by means of **sanctions** that are less severe than those imposed for the commission of a felony. Most of the state **charitable solicitation acts** contain provisions making violations of these laws misdemeanors or felonies. [FR § 3.21].

mission society

A "mission society" is an **entity** sponsored or **affiliated** with one or more **churches** or church denominations, more than one-half of the activities of which are conducted in or directed at **persons** in foreign countries. [EO § 10.6].

mission statement

Many **good governance standards** encourage **charitable organizations** to adopt and adhere to a well-defined "mission statement," which is a brief statement of the organization's purpose. An organization is requested by the IRS to describe its mission in the **Form 990**. [EO § 4.3(c); GV §§ 2.1(a), 3.10(a), 3.14(b), 4.2(e), 5.15, 6.3(a); AR §§ 1.6(a), 1.7, 2.1(d), 2.2(a); CU Q 5.38; PG p. 19; SM pp. 99, 102; LI Q 3.36].

mobile giving

The term "mobile giving" refers to **charitable giving** by means of cellular telephones and participating wireless mobile telephone companies. The **donor** initiates this type of **gift** by a text message; the gift amount is charged to the contributor's next cellular telephone bill. This form of **fundraising** is believed to encourage charitable giving by younger donors.

model law

The term "model law" is used to describe a proposed **law** on a particular subject, drafted by a group in the hope that the proposal, or a significant portion of it, will be enacted into law. Thus, the concept of a model law is most useful where there is a multiplicity of jurisdictions that may need or want such a law (such as the states, counties, or cities). In the setting of **nonprofit organizations**, model laws have been drafted in fields such as **charitable solicitations**, **charitable trusts**, and **nonprofit corporations**. [FR § 8.7].

modification

The term "modification" is used in the **law** of **unrelated business income taxation**. It means certain types of **income** received by or activities engaged in by **exempt organizations**; these forms of income or income from these forms of activities are not taxed. The term "modification" also refers to certain other adjustments in the computation of unrelated business income (**IRC** § 512(b)).

As part of these modifications, nearly all forms of **passive income** escape taxation. This **exemption** generally covers income such as **dividends**, **interest**, payments with respect to the **lending of securities**, **annuities**, **royalties**, most forms of **rent**, **capital gain**, and gain on the lapse or termination of **options** written by the organization (**IRC** §§ 512(b)(1)–(3), (5)).

This concept of modification also prevents taxation of certain types of income derived from the performance of **research** (**IRC** §§ 512(b)(7)–(9)), allows a 10 percent **charitable contribution deduction** to be used in computing unrelated business taxable income (**IRC** § 512(b)(10)), and authorizes a **specific deduction** of $1,000 (**IRC** § 512(b)(12)). [UB Chap. 3; EO § 25.1; HC § 24.18(b)(i); SM pp. 174, 177–178].

mortgage

A "mortgage" results when a lender **loans** money to a borrower for the purposes of enabling the borrower to purchase an item of **property**; the lender retains a security interest in the property until the debt is paid.

The existence of a mortgage can be relevant in applying various **laws** of relevance to nonprofit organizations. For example, a **contribution** of mortgaged property to a **charitable organization** may not give rise to a **charitable contribution deduction** at the time of the **gift**.

Mortgaged property held by a **tax-exempt organization** can give rise to **unrelated debt-financed income**, which is a form of **unrelated business income**. Unrelated debt-financed income is not **excluded** from taxation by reason of the **modifications** that are applied in computing unrelated business taxable income. [EO § 24.9(b); CG § 9.20]. (also **Mortgagee**; **Mortgagor**).

mortgagee

The lender of money in an arrangement giving rise to a **mortgage** is a "mortgagee."

mortgagor

The debtor, in an arrangement involving a **mortgage**, is a "mortgagor."

motion

A "motion" is an application to a court requesting an outcome, such as an order or a ruling. For example, a **party** to **litigation** who wishes to have the lawsuit dismissed would file a "motion to dismiss." A party who wants another party in the lawsuit to be required to do something would file a "motion to compel." A party who wants a judge to rule on the merits of a case in which there (allegedly) is no dispute as to the material facts would file a "motion for summary judgment."

multi-employer pension plan trust

A "multi-employer pension plan trust" is a type of **trust**, **tax-exempt** under **federal law** (**IRC** §§ 501(a), 501(c)(22)) that was established by the sponsors of a multi-employer pension plan as a vehicle to accumulate funds in order to provide withdrawal **liability** payments to the plan. [EO § 18.7; SM p. 43].

multi-factor test

The **private inurement doctrine** mandates that the amount of **compensation** paid by most **tax-exempt organizations** to **insiders** be **reasonable**. **Case law** dictates the criteria to be used in ascertaining the reasonableness of compensation. The factors that may be utilized in a particular case can vary; whatever they are, the standard is known as the "multi-factor test." [EO § 20.4(b); PG pp. 66–68].

multi-organization pooled income fund

A "multi-organization pooled income fund" is a **pooled income fund** that is established and operated in circumstances where more than one **charitable organization** is the ultimate **beneficiary** of the **remainder interest** in money and/or **property** transferred to the fund. [CG § 13.9].

multi-parent title-holding company

A "multi-parent title-holding company" is a type of **organization** that, when various requirements are satisfied, is **tax-exempt** under **federal law** (**IRC** § 501(a), by reason of description in **IRC** § 501(c)(25)). This **entity** is an otherwise qualifying organization that is **organized** and **operated** for the exclusive purposes of acquiring and holding **title** to **real property**, collecting **income** from the property, and remitting all of the **net income** from the property to one or more **qualified tax-exempt organizations** that are shareholders of the organization (if a **corporation**) or are **beneficiaries** of it (if a **trust**). Among the various criteria for tax exemption for this type of organization is the rule that it have no more than thirty-five shareholders or beneficiaries. [EO § 19.2(b); HC § 15.2; AU § 7.1(z); SM p. 42].

multi-member limited liability company

A "multi-member limited liability company" is a **limited liability company** having two or more **members**. In the **tax-exempt organizations** setting, this type of company can have a mix of **exempt** and nonexempt **entities** as members, or it can have a membership comprised entirely of exempt organizations. With either approach, the company can be engaged in exempt activities. Some multi-member limited liability companies can be **recognized** as tax-exempt organizations. [EO §§ 26.2(c), 32.5; UB § 8.12(c); AR § 11.1(f)(3)(G)(i); PG pp. 154–156; SM p. 228] (also **Joint venture**; cf. **Single-member limited liability company**).

museum

A "museum" is a facility for the exhibition and other holding of **properties** such as works of art and **scientific** items. The **organization** that operates the museum is usually a **tax-exempt** organization, with the rationale for the exemption being that the **entity** is an **educational** organization. A museum may be a **publicly supported organization**, a **private operating foundation**, or a standard **private foundation**.

A museum is among the types of organizations that are likely to qualify as a publicly supported organization by means of the **facts and circumstances test**. Museums are generally subject to the states' **charitable solicitation acts**, although a few of these laws provide **exemptions**. [EO §§ 8.3(b), 12.3, 24.5(c); UB § 9.3; FR § 3.5(e); SM pp. 86, 174].

mutual organization

A "mutual organization" is an **organization**, often a **nonprofit** and **tax-exempt** one that has **members** who receive benefits as a matter of **contractual right**. While a mutual organization is thus a form of membership organization, the term "mutual organization" is usually reserved for organizations that provide forms of financial services, such as a mutual **insurance** company or a mutual ditch or irrigation company (**IRC** § 501(a) by reason of description in **IRC** § 501(c)(14)(A)). **Credit unions** (mutual reserve funds) (**IRC** § 501(c)(14)(A)) and some **cooperatives** are regarded as mutual organizations. [EO § 19.5(b); AU § 7.1(r); AR §§ 4.1(s), 4.2(n); SM p. 44].

myopia rule

In computing the holdings of a **private foundation** or a **disqualified person** with respect to a private foundation in a **business enterprise**, any stock or other interest owned, **directly or indirectly,** by or for a **corporation, partnership, estate,** or **trust** is considered as owned proportionately by or for its shareholders, partners, or beneficiaries (**IRC** § 4943(d)(1)). Exempted from this **constructive ownership** rule, subject to certain exceptions, are—pursuant to the "myopia rule"—holdings of corporations that are engaged in an active **trade or business**. [PF § 7.2(c)]

named individuals, gift for
See **Specified individuals, gifts for.**

named organization
Some of the state **charitable solicitation acts** provide **exemption**—usually only from the **registration requirements**—for **organizations** that are identified in these **laws** by name. [FR § 3.5(m)].

national legislation
The term "national legislation" is an element of the definition of a **limited affiliated group**, as that term is used in the **federal tax regulations** pertaining to the **expenditure test**. Although this term is not defined as such, it clearly refers to **legislation** before, considered by, or passed by the U.S. Congress. [EO § 22.3(d)(viii)] (also **National legislative issue**).

national legislative issue
The concept of a "national legislative issue" arises in the context of the **expenditure test**. This test entails rules that apply with respect to **members** of a **limited affiliated group** of **organizations**. The definition of this group includes the requirement that no member of the group is, under its **governing instruments**, bound by decisions of one or more of the other members on legislative issues other than national legislative issues. A "national legislative issue" means **legislation**, limited to action by the U.S. Congress or by the public in any national procedure. [EO § 22.3(d)(viii)].

National Office, IRS
The "National Office" of the **IRS** is the **agency's** headquarters in Washington, D.C. This is where the **Commissioner of Internal Revenue** has his or her office, along with the Assistant Commissioners and other **federal tax** policymakers. [EO § 2.2(a)].

National Railroad Retirement Investment Trust
The National Railroad Retirement Investment Trust, established under the Railroad Retirement Act of 1974, is a **tax-exempt organization** (**IRC** §§ 501(a), 501(c)(28)). [EO § 19.17].

Bruce R. Hopkins' Nonprofit Law Dictionary, First Edition. Bruce R. Hopkins.
© 2015 Bruce R. Hopkins. Published 2015 by John Wiley & Sons, Inc.

National Register

The term "National Register" means the "National Register of Historic Places," which is a listing, maintained by the National Park Service, of the nation's historical and cultural resources (buildings and other sites) that are deemed worthy of preservation. The term is used in defining a **certified historic structure** and in other contexts in connection with the making of **deductible contributions** for **conservation purposes**. [CG § 9.7(c)].

National Taxpayer Advocate

The "National Taxpayer Advocate" heads the Taxpayer Advocate Service, which is an independent office within the **IRS**. The mission of the Service is to help taxpayers resolve problems with the **IRS** and to recommend changes to prevent taxpayer problems. The Advocate's functions are available in the **tax-exempt organizations** context, although that office notes that its assistance "is not a substitute for established **IRS** procedures, such as the formal appeals process." [AU §§ 2.2, 2.12].

natural person

A "natural person" is a **person** who is a human being. Thus, the term distinguishes between individuals and **artificial persons**. (cf., e.g., **Corporation**).

needy person

The **federal tax law** provides special rules for determining the **charitable contribution deduction** for a **for-profit corporation** when it makes **gifts** of **property** that comprise its **inventory** (**IRC** § 170(e)(3)). One of these rules is that the gift property must be used for the care of the **ill**, "needy," or **infants**. The term "needy" is defined by the **tax regulations** to mean a **person** who lacks the necessities of life, involving physical, mental, or emotional well-being, as a result of poverty or temporary distress. Examples of needy persons thus include a person who is financially impoverished as a result of low **income** and lack of financial resources, a person who temporarily lacks food or shelter (and the means to provide for it), a person who is a victim of a natural **disaster** (such as fire or flood), a person who is the victim of a civil disaster (such as a civil disturbance), a person who is temporarily not self-sufficient as a result of a sudden and severe personal or family crisis (such as a person who is a victim of a **crime** of violence or who has been physically abused), a person who is a refugee or immigrant and who is experiencing language, cultural, or financial difficulties, a **minor** child who is not self-sufficient and who is not cared for by a parent or guardian, and a person who is not self-sufficient as a result of previous institutionalization (such as a former prisoner or a former patient in a mental institution. [CG § 9.3(b)] (also **Care of the needy**).

negligence

"Negligence" is the failure to do something that a reasonable person, guided by those considerations that ordinarily regulate the conduct of human affairs, would do, or doing something that a prudent and reasonable person would not do. For purposes of the **federal tax law penalty** for negligence, the term includes any failure to make a **reasonable** attempt to comply with that body of law (**IRC** § 6662(c)). (also **Prudent person rule**).

negligible condition

A **donor** may place one or more **conditions** on the use or application of a **gift**. If a condition is **material**, the **charitable contribution deduction** involved may be defeated. Where, however, a condition is **so remote as to be negligible**, it is **disregarded** for purposes of gift deductibility. [CG § 10.4].

neighborhood land rule

The "neighborhood land rule" is an **exemption** from the **debt-financed property rules** for interim income from neighborhood real property acquired by a **tax-exempt organization** for an **exempt purpose**. Thus, the general rule of this exemption is that the **tax** on **unrelated debt-financed income** does not apply to income from real property, located in the neighborhood of other property owned by an **exempt organization**, which it plans to devote to exempt uses within ten years of the time of acquisition (**IRC** §§ 514(b)(3)(A)–(C)). This rule applies after the first five years of the ten-year period only if the exempt organization satisfies the **IRS** that future use of the acquired land in furtherance of its exempt purposes before expiration of the period is reasonably certain. A more generous fifteen-year rule is available for **churches**; indeed, it is not required that the property be in the neighborhood of the church (**IRC** § 514(b)(3)(E)). [EO § 24.9(b); UB § 5.3(c); HC § 24.21(a); PF § 11.4(b)].

N net assets

The "net assets" of a **tax-exempt organization** consist of the **value** of its **assets** to the extent that that value exceeds the value of its **liabilities**. [PF § 12.1(e)] (also **Fund balance**; **Net revenue**).

net capital gain

The **excise tax** that a **private foundation** must pay on its **net investment income** is also imposed on its "net capital gain." This means that, in computing the tax, a private foundation must include any **gains** or **losses** from the **sale** or other **disposition** of **property** used for the production of **interest**, **dividends**, **rents**, and **royalties** (**IRC** § 4940(c)(4)(A)), less allowable deductions. Any gain or loss from the sale or other disposition of property used for the **charitable purposes** of a private foundation, however, is **excluded** from the computation of this tax. [PF § 10.3(b)].

net earnings

The term "net earnings" is used in conjunction with the proscription on **private inurement**, which is applicable to nearly all categories of **tax-exempt organizations**, **charitable entities**. The **federal tax law** for a charitable organization states, on the point, that it must be organized and operated so that "no part of . . . [its] net earnings . . . inures to the benefit of any private shareholder or individual" (**IRC** § 501(c)(3)). The law has become quite expansive in its interpretation of that phrase; the term is not applied in a literal, accounting sense. Technically, however, the term means **gross earnings** less **expenses**; the concept of private inurement means the transfer of net earnings to the owners of the organization (such as **dividends** paid over to shareholders of a **for-profit corporation**). [EO § 20.2; PF § 5.1; HC § 4.1(b); AS § 3.2; SM pp. 49–50].

net income

The term "net income" means **gross income** less allowable off-setting **expenses**. In this context, the term "**income**" and "**revenue**" are often confused. For example, **tax-exempt organizations**, in preparing their **annual information return**, are permitted to report both gross income and net income from the conduct of **special fundraising events** on the first page of the return; however, there, "net income" is defined as "gross revenue" less direct expenses. [FR § 6.12(b); AR § 14.2(b)].

net income guarantee

The **IRS** identified various physician recruitment incentives that are deemed consistent with the requirements for **tax exemption** for **charitable hospitals**. One of these techniques is the provision of a "net income guarantee" (after **reasonable expenses**) for a limited number of years and in an amount commensurate with relevant regional or national income surveys. [HC § 25.7].

net investment income

The term "net investment income" refers to **gross investment income** less the **expenses** of producing that income. For example, the net investment income of a **private foundation** is defined as the amount by which the sum of its gross investment income and its **net capital gain** exceeds the allowable **deductions** (**IRC** § 4940(c)(1)). For a private foundation, as to this last item, there is allowed all of the **ordinary and necessary** expenses paid or incurred for the production or collection of gross investment or for the management, conservation, or maintenance of **property** held for the production of income (**IRC** § 4940(c)(3)(A)). [PF § 10.4(a); HC § 5.10; SM p. 90] (cf. **Gross investment income**).

net investment income, tax on

The **federal tax law** generally imposes an **excise tax** of 2 percent on the **net investment income** of a **private foundation** (**IRC** § 4940). The term is defined as the amount by which the sum of the **gross investment income** and the **capital gain net income** exceeds the allowable **deductions** (**IRC** § 4940(c)(1)). [PF § 10.1; CG § 2.15(c)].

net liability

The "net liability" of a tax-**exempt organization** consists of the **value** of its **liabilities** to the extent that that value exceeds the value of its **assets**. [AR § 7.2(c)] (also **Fund balance**).

net operating loss

The "net operating loss" of a **person** for a **tax year** is an amount equal to all business **credits**, **deductions**, and the like allowable for the year less the person's **gross income** for the year (**IRC** § 172). [UB § 3.20] (also **Net operating loss carryback**; **Net operating loss carryover**).

net operating loss carryback

The **federal tax law** concerning "net operating loss carrybacks" and excess **charitable contributions** for a **contribution year** can be interrelated. The amount of the excess charitable contribution for a contribution year may not be increased because a net operating loss carryback is available as a **deduction** in the contribution year (**IRC** § 172). [CG § 2.17].

net operating loss carryover

The **federal tax law** concerning "net operating loss carryovers" and excess **charitable contributions** for a **contribution year** can be interrelated. An individual having a net operating loss carryover from a prior **tax year** which is available as a **deduction** in a contribution year must apply a special rule for these carryovers in computing the excess charitable contributions for the contribution year (**IRC** § 172). [CG § 2.17].

net revenue

The term "net revenue" means **gross revenue** less allowable off-setting **expenses**. [AR §§ 7.2(a), 7.2(b)] (also **Net assets**; **Net income**).

net revenue stream

The phrase "net revenue stream" means the **net revenue** that is achieved by an **organization** over a stated period of time (in a sense, a net cash flow) from the **operation** of one or more **enterprises**. It often refers to the net revenue that is attributable to a particular **program** or **department** of the organization. For example, the phrase has been used to describe the net revenue stream of a program or a department of a **tax-exempt hospital**; some hospitals have sold the net revenue streams of some of their departments to **partnerships** that included physicians practicing at the institutions, causing **private inurement** problems. [HC § 4.5] (also **Per se rule**).

newsletter fund

A "newsletter fund" is a **fund** established and maintained by an individual who holds, has been elected to, or is a **candidate** for nomination or election to, any **federal**, state, or local elective **public office**. The newsletter fund is used by the individual **exclusively** for the preparation and circulation of a newsletter concerning his or her services to his or her constituents. This type of fund is a form of **political organization** (**IRC** § 527(g)(1)). [EO § 17.1(b)].

90-percent rule

One of the basic requirements for achievement of tax exemption as a **voluntary employees beneficiary association** is that the **organization** be an **association** of **employees**. Employees of one or more **employers** engaged in the same **line of business** in the **same geographic locale** are considered to share an employment related bond for these purposes. Nonetheless, exemption is not necessarily imperiled merely because the membership of a **VEBA** includes individuals who are not employees, as long as these individuals share the requisite employer-related bond with the employee members. A VEBA is considered to be composed of employees if at least 90 percent of its total membership on one day of each quarter of the VEBA's tax year consists of employees. The **IRS** informally applies this 90-day rule in the context of **local associations of employees**. [EO §§ 18.3, 19.3].

no-rule position, IRS

The **IRS** annually publishes a list of topics, including those in the **tax-exempt organizations** and **charitable giving** areas, on which it will not take a position, that is, not issue a **ruling**.

nonadverse party

For purposes of the **grantor trust** rules, a "nonadverse party" is a **person** who is not an **adverse party** (**IRC** § 672(b)). [CG § 3.8].

noncash contribution

The term "noncash contribution" is used to define a **contribution** to a **charitable organization** where the subject of the **gift** is **property**, **tangible** or **intangible**, other than money. Noncash contributions include gifts of securities, **works of art**, vehicles, intellectual property, and items donated for use in **charity auctions**. Noncash contributions do not include **volunteer** services or **donated** use of materials, facilities, or equipment. These contributions are reported on Schedule M of **Form 990** and **Form 990-EZ**. [CG §§ 10.16, 21.4, 24.7; AR Chap. 19, §§ 3.1(jj), 3.1(kk), 3.2(jj), 3.2(kk), 7.2(a)(1); FR § 6.14; EO § 28.3(t); HC § 35.8].

noncharitable assets

The term "noncharitable assets" is used to describe the **assets** of a **charitable organization** that are not used or held for use **directly** in carrying out the **charitable purpose** of the organization. For example, while the collection of paintings held by a **museum** constitutes **charitable assets**, the securities held by the museum for investment purposes are non-charitable assets. This term is of particular relevance in the context of the **mandatory payout requirement** applicable to **private foundations**, in that only noncharitable assets are taken into account in determining a foundation's **minimum investment return**, which, in turn, in part determines the foundation's annual **distributable amount**. [PF § 6.2; EO § 12.4(b); SM p. 89] (cf. **Exempt function property**).

noncharitable exempt organization

The term "noncharitable exempt organization" is used to refer to an **organization** that is **tax-exempt** under the **federal tax law** but is not a **charitable organization**. These organizations include **social welfare organizations**, **trade associations**, and **veterans' organizations**. Special rules apply in connection with **contributions** and similar payments to these **entities**. [CG §§ 10.9(a), 22.3; EO § 29.5; PF § 12.2(o); AR Chap. 21, §§ 3.1(qq), 3.2(qq), 4.1(t), 4.2(o), 8.1(k); LI Q 12.38].

noncharitable purpose expenditure

The term **taxable expenditure** includes any amount paid or incurred by a **private foundation** for any "noncharitable purpose" (**IRC** § 4945(d)(5)). Generally, under this rule, an expenditure for an activity that, if it were a **substantial part** of the **charitable organization's** total activities, would cause loss of the organization's **tax exemption**, is a taxable expenditure. [PF § 9.8].

nondeductibility, disclosure of

A **tax-exempt organization** that is not a **charitable organization** must include, within each **fundraising solicitation**, an express statement that **contributions** to the organization are not deductible for **federal income tax** purposes (**IRC** § 6113(a)). This statement must be in a conspicuous and easily recognizable format. This disclosure requirement does not apply to (1) a letter or telephone call that is not part of a coordinated **fundraising campaign** soliciting more than ten people in a calendar, year, (2) oral solicitations, such as those made door-to-door, (3) situations where all of the parties being solicited are tax-exempt organizations. (4) general material discussing a **political candidacy** and requesting persons to vote for the **candidate** or support the candidate, unless the material specifically requests either a financial **contribution** or a contribution of **volunteer** services in support of the candidate, and (5) solicitations by organizations with annual gross receipts of $100,000 or less. [EO § 29.5; CG § 22.3; FR § 5.14(o)].

nondiscrimination

The word "nondiscrimination" means an absence of **discrimination**. In this sense, the term relates to discrimination on the basis of age, country of origin, ethnicity, gender, handicap, race, religion, and/ or sexual preference. For example, a **private school** cannot qualify for **tax-exempt status** as a **charitable organization**, nor can it qualify as a **charitable donee**, when it lacks a policy of nondiscrimination on the basis of race with respect to students and faculty. Likewise, a tax-exempt **social club** cannot have a written policy of discrimination on account of race, color, or religion (**IRC** § 501(i)). In the context of **employee benefits**, the **law** requires nondiscrimination as between individuals with varying levels of **compensation**. [CU Q 3.66, Q 3.67; EO §§ 6.2(b)–6.2(e); AR §§ 12.1(d), 12.2(a)(1)].

nonexempt charitable trust

A "nonexempt charitable trust" is a **trust** (1) that is not **exempt** from the **federal income tax** (that is, not exempt by reason of **IRC** § 501(a)), (2) all of the unexpired **interests** in which are devoted to **charitable** purposes, and (3) with respect to which a **charitable deduction** was allowed for **contributions** to it (by reason of **IRC** §§ 170, 545(b)(2), 642(c), 2055, 2106(a),(2), or 2522) or for amounts paid by or permanently **set aside** by it (**IRC** § 642(c)) (**IRC** § 4947(a)(1)). [PF § 3.6; AU §§ 5.33(l), 7.3].

nonexempt organization

A "nonexempt organization" is an **organization** that is not **tax-exempt**, usually meaning not exempt from **federal income taxation**. Some nonexempt organizations do not pay any **tax** because their **gross income** is matched by their **expenses**. For nonexempt **membership** organizations, however, the amount of **deductible expenses** may be less. [EO § 19.24] (also **Allocation of expenses**).

nonexempt purpose expenditure

A "nonexempt purpose expenditure" is an **expenditure** by a **tax-exempt organization** for a purpose other than the advancement of its **tax-exempt purpose(s)**. This type of expenditure

N

is not necessarily violative of the **law** of tax-exempt organizations, however; expenditures for **fundraising** and administration usually are nonexempt purpose expenditures.

nonfixed compensation

The term "nonfixed compensation" refers to types of **compensation**, the terms of which are not fixed, such as revenue-sharing arrangements. [AR §§ 6.1(a)(4), 6.2(b)(8); EO § 21.8] (cf. **Fixed compensation**).

nongovernmental organization

The term "nongovernmental organization" essentially means the same as **nonprofit organization**. The term, however, is favored by many in countries other than the United States.

nonlobbying communication

A "nonlobbying communication" means a **communication** in which the purpose of the communication, as determined by its content or the circumstances of its transmission, is neither a **direct lobbying communication** nor a **grass-roots lobbying communication**. Certain **exceptions** from the concept of **lobbying** have been developed, particularly in the context of the **expenditure test**, and these excepted activities also are nonlobbying communications. [EO § 22.3(d)(ii)] (also **Advocacy communication**; **Membership communication**; **Self-defense communication**).

nonmember charitable organization

For purposes of the law concerning **qualified charitable risk pools**, the phrase "nonmember charitable organization" means any **tax-exempt charitable organization** that is not a **member** of the risk pool and does not benefit, directly or indirectly, from the **insurance** coverage provided by the pool to its members (**IRC** § 501(n)(4)(B)). [EO § 11.6].

nonmember income test

An **organization** endeavoring to qualify as a **tax-exempt social club** must adhere to the "nonmember income test." Pursuant to this test, an exempt club is permitted to receive up to 35 percent of its **gross receipts**, including **investment income**, from sources outside its **membership**, without losing its exempt status. Within this amount, no more than 15 percent of the organization's gross receipts may be derived from the use of the club's facilities or services by the **public**. If a club has outside income in excess of either of these percentage thresholds, all facts and circumstances are taken into account in determining whether the organization qualifies for exempt status. Exempt clubs are not permitted to receive, within these percentage allowances, income from the **active conduct** of **businesses** that entail **nontraditional business activities**. [EO §§ 15.2–15.4].

nonpartisan

The word "nonpartisan" technically means an absence of support for a particular **political** party. The term, however, is also used to embrace a lack of a particular position on a subject; it is somewhat synonymous with the word "objective." (cf. **Partisan**).

nonpartisan activity

A "nonpartisan activity" is an activity that is not supportive of a particular position, objective, or **political party**. Frequently, a **nonpartisan** activity will be a **charitable**, **educational**, or **scientific** activity. (also **Nonpartisan analysis, study, and research**).

nonpartisan analysis, study, and research

The phrase "nonpartisan analysis, study, and research" means a range of activities that are an independent and objective exposition of a particular subject matter. These activities are usually **charitable**, **educational**, or **scientific** in nature. Activities of this type are not considered to be **lobbying activities**, either for purposes of the **substantial part test**, the **expenditure test** (IRC § 4911(d)(2)(A)), or the prohibition on **legislative activities** by **private foundations** (IRC § 4945(e)). [EO §§ 22.3(c)(ii), 22.3(d)(v); PF § 9.1(d)] (also **Full and fair exposition test**).

nonprivate foundation status

A **tax-exempt charitable organization** has "nonprivate foundation status" when (except for **churches** and certain other organizations) the **IRS**, by **determination letter** or **ruling**, has classified it as a form of **public charity**. A charitable organization of this nature is also said to have **public charity status**. [PF § 15.1; EO § 12.3].

nonprofit

The word "nonprofit" is often misunderstood. As applied to an **organization**, it does not mean an **entity** that is forbidden by **law** to earn a **profit**. The word in this context is used to refer to an organization that is not operated for the purpose of generating a profit for owners or those who **control** it. [SM pp. 5–6, 25].

nonprofit corporation act

Nearly every state has a "nonprofit corporation act," a **statute** that provides for the establishment and operation of **nonprofit corporations**, including their rights and duties, the election of **directors** and **officers**, the holding of meetings, and their **dissolution**, **liquidation**, or **merger**. [FR § 3.23; SM pp. 8–9].

nonprofit governance

See **Governance, nonprofit**.

nonprofit organization

The **law** generally provides for two types of **organizations**, other than governmental **entities**; the **for-profit organization** and the "nonprofit organization." The concept of both these organizations is usually a matter of state law. Nearly all **tax-exempt organizations** are nonprofit organizations; the concept of tax exemption is largely a matter of the **federal tax law**. The distinction between the two entities principally pertains to the use of the **profits** derived by the organization.

A for-profit organization is one that is operated for the benefit of its owners; it is operated to generate a profit for them. When a profit is paid to one or more owners by the operating enterprise, the transfer is known in the law as an **inurement** of the profit (also known as **net earnings**). Thus, a for-profit organization is operated so as to generate **gross** earnings and subsequently pay the net earnings over to its owners (such as the payment of **dividends** to the shareholders of a **corporation**). By contrast, generally, a nonprofit organization (particularly one that is **tax-exempt**) is not allowed to engage in forms of **private inurement**; the net profits are to be retained and used by the nonprofit organization for the purposes for which it was organized and is operated. A tax-exempt organization may pay **reasonable** compensation for services rendered, and may engage in other reasonable financial transactions but it usually is not permitted to distribute its profits to those who control or financially support it. [SM pp. 3–4, 5–6, 23, 25, 322–323; EO § 1.1(a); HC §§ 1.2, 28.4, 33.3(b); CL §§ 1.3, 1.5; GV § 1.1(a); RE Q 1.1, Q 1.2; CU Q 1.1; AS § 2.1; UB § 1.4; PG p. 37; LI Q 1.1–1.7, Q 1.12, Q 1.17, Q 1.20, Q 1.21] (cf. **For-profit organization**).

nonprofit sector

U.S. society is, basically, comprised of three sectors, so that the institutions of society are generally classified as governmental, **for-profit**, or **nonprofit entities**. Governmental entities are the **branches**, **departments**, **agencies**, and **bureaus** of the **federal**, state, and local governments; for-profit entities comprise the business sector of society; and nonprofit organizations make up the nonprofit sector. This array of entities is sometimes referred to as **pluralism** of **institutions**. The nonprofit sector is also termed the "independent sector," "**philanthropic** sector," "private sector," "third sector," and "voluntary sector." [EO §§ 1.1(b), 2.1; CG § 1.2; SM pp. 3–5].

nonqualified plan

The **federal tax law** of **employee benefits** distinguishes between **deferred compensation plans** that are **qualified plans** and nonqualified plans. Plans that are "nonqualified" are those that are used to provide supplemental benefits or to avoid the technical requirements imposed upon qualified plans. The federal tax consequences of nonqualified plans vary, depending on whether the plan is **funded** or **unfunded**. Funds in these plans can be considered **constructively received** by the **employees** involved and accessible by creditors of the **employer**. [EO § 18.1(f)].

nonrecognition

"Nonrecognition" is a term of the **tax law** that means that a **person**, although receiving (**realizing**) an item of **gross income**, does not have to "recognize" it (treat it as income for tax purposes), at least not at the time that the income is received. The specific law that provides for this exception is known as a "nonrecognition provision." Examples of nonrecognition provisions are those for **gifts** (**IRC** § 102), certain **scholarships** (**IRC** § 117), and **interest** paid on municipal bonds (**IRC** § 103). [CG § 2.14(f)].

nonrecognition of gain

The phrase "nonrecognition of gain" refers to a circumstance wherein a **gain** from the **sale** or **exchange** of an item of **property** is not **recognized** for **federal tax** purposes. For example, a **tax-exempt social club** may sell some of its **real property** to facilitate a relocation and may reinvest the proceeds in **exempt function property**, within a period beginning one year before the sale date and ending three years after that date; any gain from the sale is recognized only to the extent that the sale price of the old property exceeds the sale price of the new property (**IRC** § 512(a)(3)(D)). [EO § 15.6].

nonstandard contribution

A "nonstandard contribution" basically is a **contribution** of an item that is not reasonably expected to be used to further the **donee's exempt purpose** (aside from the need of the organization for **income**) and for which (1) there is no ready market to which the organization may go to liquidate the contribution and (2) the **value** of the item is highly speculative or difficult to ascertain. [AR § 19.1(x); GV § 6.3(j); CU Q 12.9].

nontraditional business activities

In the context of **tax exemption** for **social clubs**, these clubs must differentiate between traditional and nontraditional activities. Traditional business activities are subject to the 15 percent limitation concerning nonmember use of a social club's facilities or services by the **public** (part of the **nonmember income test**). "Nontraditional business activities" are prohibited (subject to an insubstantial, trivial, and nonrecurrent test), that is, will endanger exemption, whether conducted with club **members** or nonmembers. Thus, a "nontraditional business" is one that does not further the exempt purposes of a club, even if conducted solely in connection with its membership. An illustration of this type of business is the sale of liquor to members for consumption off the club's premises. [EO § 15.2].

normal and usual activities

When a **tax-exempt social club** endeavors to comply with the **nonmember income test**, it must take into account **gross receipts** from "normal and usual activities" of the club. These are activities that a club has traditionally conducted and on which a club's exemption is based. [EO §§ 15.2, 15.3] (cf. **Nontraditional business activities**).

normally

The word "normally" is used in the **federal tax law** to reflect a set of facts arrived at by averaging numerical data over a multi-year period. Thus, with respect to a rule of law, the rule is applied to an average of the activity (usually the receipt or **expenditure** of money) over the particular measuring period. Generally, the word "normally" is used to mean a five-year period.

For example, for a **charitable organization** to qualify as a **donative publicly supported organization**, it must "normally" receive the requisite **public support**; generally, this means that the **support** computations are made using support information for the five **tax years** immediately preceding the year involved (**IRC** § 170(b)(i)(A)(vi)). A comparable rule is used for determining the qualification for **service provider** publicly supported organizations (**IRC** § 509(a)(2)(A)) and for determining, under the **expenditure test**, the amount of **lobbying** that will cause a **public charity** to lose its **tax exemption** (**IRC** § 501(h)(1)).

The word is also used in connection with the $5,000 threshold filing requirement with respect to **annual information returns** (**IRC** § 6033(a)(3)(A)(ii)) and the $50,000 **notification requirement**, and the $5,000 threshold filing requirement with respect to **applications**

for recognition of tax exemption. The word further appears in the federal tax law definition of a **school**, **college**, or **university** (**IRC** § 170(b)(1)(A)(ii)) and of a state college- or university-related foundation (**IRC** § 170(b)(1)(A)(v)).

Still another illustration is the rule in connection with the **expenditure test**, where, if a charitable organization's **lobbying** expenditure "normally" exceed 150 percent of either the **lobbying ceiling amount** or the **grass-roots ceiling amount**, it will lose its tax-exempt status (**IRC** § 501(h)(1). [EO §§ 12.3(a), 12.3(b)(i), 12.3(b)(iv), 22.3(d)(iii), 26.2(b), 28.2(b)(ii), 28.4; PF §§ 15.3(b), 15.3(d), 15.4(b), 15.5(b); HC § 5.3(c); SM pp. 80–82, 189–190].

not-for-profit

The term "not-for-profit" is properly used, at least in the **federal tax law** setting, to describe activities, rather than **organizations**. The activities embraced by this term are those the **expenses** of which do not qualify for the **business expense deduction** (**IRC** § 183); these activities are, essentially, hobbies. The term is often used in place of the term **nonprofit**, although this is technically incorrect. [EO § 1.1(a); CU Q 1.2; RE Q 1.2; SM pp. 5, 25; LI Q 1.8].

note

See **Promissory note**.

notice

The concept of "notice" is the communication of information from one **person** to another, particularly where the **law** requires it. Usually, the requirement is that notice be "actual," that is, an express transmission of information; the law occasionally will create the notice process out of the factual circumstances ("**constructive** notice" or "implied notice." The **federal tax law** contains notice requirements for **tax-exempt organizations**: (1) certain **employee benefit organizations** desiring **recognition of tax exemption** must provide timely notice to the **IRS** of that fact (by filing an **application for recognition** of exemption) (**IRC** § 505(c)); (2) in certain circumstances, a **charitable organization** that desires to **terminate** its **private foundation status** must give the **IRS** timely notice of that fact (**IRC** § 507(a)); (3) most **nonprofit organizations** desiring recognition of tax exemption as a charitable organization must provide timely notice to the **IRS** of that fact (by filing an application for recognition of exemption) (**IRC** § 508(a)); (4) a charitable organization must, if it wants to (and is eligible to) avoid classification as a **private foundation**, give the **IRS** timely notice of that fact (**IRC** § 508(b)); (5) certain **credit counseling organizations** must provide the **IRS** this type of notice (**IRC** § 501(q)(3)); (6) **nonprofit health insurance issuers** must provide this type of notice (**IRC** § 501(c)(29)(B)(i)); and (7) **political organizations** are required to provide special notice (**IRC** § 527(i)). (also **Disclosure**; **Notice, fundraising**).

The word "notice" has still another meaning in the federal law of tax-exempt organizations. A **tax-exempt organization**, the **gross receipts** of which in any **tax year** are below a monetary threshold periodically established by the **IRS** (currently, $50,000) so that it is not required to file an **annual information return**, is required to annually **submit** to the **IRS**, in electronic form, information setting forth the legal name of the organization, any name under which the organization operates or does business, the organization's mailing address and website address

N

(if any), the organization's **taxpayer identification number**, the name and address of a principal **officer**, and evidence of the continuing basis for the organization's exemption from the filing requirements. (**IRC** § 6033(i)) [**EO** §§ 26.2–26.6, 26.9, 28.4; **FR** § 5.9(a); **HC** § 34.3(d); **PF** Chap. 13; **SM** pp. 116–118, 121] (also **e-Postcard**).

notice, fundraising

Some of the states' **charitable solicitation acts** contain requirements that prospective **donors** must be provided with certain information as part of the **solicitation** process. (This type of notice is often termed a "disclosure statement.") [**FR** § 3.7].

notice of deficiency

When the **IRS** determines that there is a **tax deficiency**, the agency usually sends the **taxpayer** a "notice of deficiency." This notice generally is a prerequisite to the **assessment** (and perhaps ultimate collection) of the tax. (**IRC** §§ 6211, 6212).

notification requirement

An **organization**, to qualify as a **Type III supporting organization**, must satisfy a "notification requirement," which means that, for each of its **tax years**, the organization must provide certain documents to each of its **supported organizations**, including a written notice describing the type and amount of all of the support the supporting organization provided to the supported organization during the prior year. [**PF** § 15.7(g)].

N

numerator, of support fraction

To qualify as a **publicly supported organization**, a **charitable organization** must derive a certain percentage of its financial **support directly** or **indirectly** from the **public**. The particular percentage that is required and the rules by which it is created differ, depending on the type of publicly supported organization involved (namely, a **donative publicly supported charitable organization**, a **service provider publicly supported charitable organization**, or a charitable organization that is under the **facts and circumstances test**). The appropriate percentage is determined by the applicable **support ratio**.

The donative publicly supported charitable organization must, to avoid classification as a **private foundation**, **normally** receive a **substantial** part of its financial support from one or more **governmental units** in the form of **grants** and/or **direct** or **indirect contributions** from the public (**IRC** § 170(b)(1)(A)(vi)). The general rule for donative publicly supported organizations is that **normally** at least one-third of their support must be from these qualifying sources; this is the numerator amount of this particular support ratio. Where the facts and circumstances test applies, this percentage for the support ratio may be as low as 10 percent, In computing this numerator amount, **contributions** from individuals, **trusts**, **corporations**, or other legal entities constitute public support to the extent that the total amount of contributions from any **donor** (including related persons) during the **support computation period** does not exceed an amount equal to 2 percent of the organization's total support (excluding **exempt function revenue**) for the period. The 2 percent limitation generally does not apply to support received from other donative publicly supported charitable organizations nor to support from governmental units—these forms of support constitute public support in full. Where the applicable support ratio is satisfied, the organization qualifies as a **public charity** (**IRC** § 509(a)(1)).

The service provider publicly supported charitable organization is an entity that normally receives more than one-third of its support from gifts, grants, **membership fees**, and/or gross receipts from the performance of exempt functions. Amounts that are eligible for the numerator of this support fraction are those that are derived from **permitted sources**, which are governmental agencies, the various **public institutions**, donative publicly supported charitable organizations, and persons who are not **disqualified persons**. Exempt function revenue is included in the numerator of this support fraction to the extent that the receipts from any one source do not exceed the greater of $5,000 or 1 percent of the organization's support for the year involved. There is a limitation on the amount of gifts and grants that can count as public support; it is built into the definition of the term **substantial contributor**. A substantial contributor is any person who contributes or **bequeaths** an aggregate amount of more than $5,000, where that amount is more than 2 percent of the total contributions and bequests received by the organization during its existence up to that time (**IRC** § 507(d)(2)(A)). Where this support ratio is satisfied, the organization qualifies as a public charity (**IRC** § 509(a)(2)). [EO §§ 12.3(b)(i), 12.3(b)(iv); PF §§ 15.4(b), 15.5(d); SM pp. 80–82].

N

O

offer

An "offer" is the initial step in developing a **contract**. It is the extension by a **person** of terms and **conditions** of a proposed bargain, made under circumstances where another person realizes that his, her, or its assent to the proposal is being invited. (also **Delivery**).

Office of Employee Plans and Exempt Organizations, IRS

Within the **IRS**, there is an Office of Employee Plans and Exempt Organizations, which has oversight and audit authority over the nation's **tax-exempt organizations**. This office is headed by an Assistant Commissioner (Employee Plans and Exempt Organizations), which is the only one of thirteen Assistant Commissioners who is authorized in the Internal Revenue Code (**IRC** § 7802(b)). [EO § 2.2(b); SM p. 294].

Office of Management and Budget

The Office of Management and Budget (OMB) is an executive branch **agency** in the **federal** government, which has as its purpose the provision of assistance to the President in the discharge of budgetary, management, and other executive responsibilities. The OMB reviews and approves forms promulgated by various federal agencies, including the **IRS**. This agency also promulgates **rules** concerning the allowable (reimbursable) costs of **grants**, **contracts**, and other agreements between agencies of the federal government and other parties, including **nonprofit organizations**; in this connection, the OMB has issued rules detailing the extent to which costs related to **lobbying** activities are allowable. [EO § 22.1].

Office of Personnel Management

The Office of Personnel Management is responsible for the personnel management functions of the **federal** government (OPM). The OPM has among its functions the administration of the **Combined Federal Campaign**. [AU § 5.4(b)].

officer

The term "officer" is defined to mean an individual who has the duty and responsibility to implement one or more of the policies of an **organization**, the policies having been

Bruce R. Hopkins' Nonprofit Law Dictionary, First Edition. Bruce R. Hopkins.
© 2015 Bruce R. Hopkins. Published 2015 by John Wiley & Sons, Inc.

established by the organization's **board of directors** or **board of trustees**. The officers of an **entity** are generally determined by reference to its **articles of organization**, its **bylaws**, and/or board resolutions. An officer may simultaneously be a member of the board of directors of the same organization; he or she may also be an **employee** of the same organization. Particularly with respect to a **charitable organization**, an officer is a **fiduciary** of the organization he or she serves. An officer position is one of the organization, rather than of its **governing board**. The most common of the officer positions are **president**, **treasurer**, and **secretary**; most state laws, particularly **corporation laws**, provide that the same person cannot simultaneously be president and secretary: this is because frequently documents require the signature of two individuals—those holding the two positions. Other officer positions include one or more **vice presidents**, an **assistant secretary**, and an **assistant treasurer**. The position known as chairperson of the board is usually a position created by the board and is not an officer position in the sense that the person is an officer of the organization.

For purposes of the **private foundation** rules, an officer is a **foundation manager** (and thus a **disqualified person**). Under these rules, an individual is considered an "officer" if he or she is specifically so designated pursuant to the governing instruments of the foundation or if he or she regularly exercises general authority to make administrative or policy decisions on behalf of the foundation. The same is the case in the **intermediate sanctions** context, in defining **organization manager**, and in the **donor-advised fund** setting, in defining **fund manager**.

The rules concerning the filing of **annual information returns** by **tax-exempt organizations** require a listing of the organization's trustees, directors, and officers, and their compensation. For this purpose, an individual who has the responsibilities or powers "similar to" those of officers is regarded as an "officer."

Officers of a **charitable organization** can be liable for **excise taxes** if they knowingly cause the organization to engage in excessive **lobbying** activities or **political campaign** activities. [SM pp. 19–21; PG pp. 14–16; GV § 2.2; AR § 6.1(a)(1); EO §§ 11.8(b), 12.2(b), 21.3, 22.4, 23.3; AS §§ 3.3, 3.8(c); CU Q 5.43; RE Q 5.11, Q 5.12; PF § 4.2; LI Q 1.25] (also **Liability**; **Officers' and directors' liability insurance**).

officers' and directors' liability insurance
"Officers' and directors' liability insurance" is **insurance**, usually purchased by the **organization** which they serve, that provides coverage with respect to a range of **civil law** violations. The purpose of this type of insurance is to shift the risk of **liability** for a **commission** and/or **omission**, which may arise in the context of service to the organization, away from the individual and the organization, and to the **insurer**. [SM p. 7; PG p. 25].

omission
The word "omission" means a failure or a neglect to perform an act that the **law** requires. Where there is a duty to act, an omission can give rise to **liability**. (also **Commission**; **Reasonable cause**).

Omnibus Budget Reconciliation Act of 1987

The "Omnibus Budget Reconciliation Act of 1987" is a package of **tax legislation** enacted by Congress in that year. Its contents include the **contribution solicitation disclosure rules** applicable to **noncharitable organizations** (**IRC** § 6113). [CG § 22.3; FR § 5.5].

Omnibus Budget Reconciliation Act of 1990

The "Omnibus Budget Reconciliation Act of 1990" is a package of **tax legislation** enacted by Congress in that year. Its contents include (1) an increase in the **alternative minimum tax rate** from 21 percent to 24 percent and (2) imposition of a **floor** on **itemized deductions** (including the **charitable contribution deduction**). [CG §§ 2.18, 10.6].

Omnibus Budget Reconciliation Act of 1993

The "Omnibus Budget Reconciliation Act of 1993" is a package of **tax legislation** enacted by Congress in that year. Its contents include (1) reinstatement of the rule that a contribution of **appreciated property** to a **charitable organization** is not treated as a **tax preference item** for purposes of the **alternative minimum tax**, (2) introduction of a **law** requiring **taxpayers** who make a separate charitable contribution of $250 or more for which they claim a **charitable contribution deduction** to obtain written **substantiation** of the gift from the charitable organization (rather than relying **solely** on a cancelled check), (3) introduction of a law requiring any charity that receives a **quid pro quo contribution** exceeding $75 to inform the contributor in writing of the **value** of any goods or services furnished to the contributor by the charity (so that only the excess amount is deductible as a charitable gift), (4) a direction to the U.S. Department of the Treasury to report to Congress within one year on the development of a procedure by which taxpayers may seek an **advance valuation** of certain **property** from the **IRS** prior to donating the property to a charitable organization, (5) disallowance as a deduction as a **business expense** amounts incurred in an attempt to influence federal or state legislation through **communication** with legislative bodies and certain federal executive branch officials, including a **flow-through rule** disallowing the portion of **membership dues** paid to a **trade association** that is attributable to **lobbying**, (6) addition of two **marginal tax rates**, namely, a 36 percent rate applicable to taxpayers with **taxable incomes** in excess of $140,000 (married individuals filing joint returns) and a 10 percent **surtax** on individuals with taxable income in excess of $250,000 (calculated by applying a 39.6 percent rate to taxable income in excess of the threshold), (7) establishment of a 35 percent marginal tax rate on the taxable income of **corporations** in excess of $10 million, (8) reinstitution of the two highest **estate** and **gift tax** rates that expired at the end of 1992, (9) relaxation of certain prior-law limitations relating to **debt-financed property** and **exclusion** from taxation as **unrelated business income** a wider range of debt-financed investments in **real estate**, (10) repeal of the rule that automatically treats income from **publicly traded partnerships** as unrelated business income, (11) allowance for a **tax-exempt title-holding corporation** to receive unrelated business income from the holding of real property up to 10 percent of its **gross income** for the **tax year**, (12) an exclusion from unrelated business income taxation for income from sales of property held for sale in the ordinary course of a **trade or business** by excluding **gains** and **losses** from the sale, **exchange**, or other

disposition of certain real property and **mortgages** acquired from financial institutions that are in conservatorship or receivership, (13) exclusion of certain **option** premiums and **loan commitment fees** from taxation as unrelated business income, (14) denial of the business expense deduction for **club dues,** (15) permanence for the overall limitations on **itemized deductions** for high-income taxpayers, and (16) extension of the **employer-provided educational assistance** program. [CG §§ 10.1(b), 10.6, 21.3, 22.2; EO §§ 15.1(c), 22.6, 24.8, 24.9(c), 25.1(k); HC § 23.2(a)(i)].

$150,000 test

For purposes of the definition of the term **key employee**, the first of three tests that need to be satisfied is the "$150,000 test." This means that the employee received **reportable compensation** from the reporting **organization** and all **related organizations** in excess of $150,000 for the calendar year ending with or within the organization's **tax year**.

1 percent limitation

The "1 percent limitation" is used as part of the definition of **public support** for **service provider organizations**. These organizations can include as public support certain types of **exempt function revenue**, that is, revenue (**gross receipts**) generated from the performance of **tax-exempt functions**. In determining the amount of support that constitutes public support of this nature, gross receipts from **related activities** received from any **person** or from any **bureau** or similar **agency** of a **governmental unit** are includible as public support in any **tax year** to the extent that the receipts do not exceed the greater of $5,000 or 1 percent of the organization's support for the year; this is the "1 percent limitation." [PF § 15.5(d); EO § 12.3(b)(iv); SM p. 82].

O

operated

The **federal tax law** usually determines the eligibility for **tax-exempt status** of a **nonprofit organization** on the basis of how it is "operated." In most instances, particularly in the case of **charitable organizations**, this determination is made by application of an **operational test**. The term "operated" in this sense is synonymous with "managed"; however, the operational considerations in this regard focus **primarily** on **program**, rather than on **fundraising** or **administration**. [EO § 4.5(a); SM p. 170].

operated in connection with

A **charitable organization** that intends to avoid **private foundation status** on the ground that it is a **supporting organization** must stand in one of three basic relationships between or among a supporting organization and one or more **supported organizations**. One of these relationships is encompassed by the phrase "operated in connection with"; this is the **Type III supporting organization** (IRC § 509(a)(3)(B)). The principal distinguishing features of this relationship is that the supporting organization does not support any foreign supported organizations, it satisfies a **notification requirement**, it meets a **responsiveness test**, and it meets one of two **integral part tests**. [PF § 15.7(g); EO § 12.3(c); SM pp. 83–84].

operated, supervised, or controlled by

A **charitable organization** that intends to avoid **private foundation status** on the ground that it is a **supporting organization** must stand in one of three basic relationships between a supporting organization and a **supported organization**. One of these relationships is encompassed by the phrase "operated, supervised, or controlled by" (**IRC** § 509(a)(3)(B)). The distinguishing feature of this relationship is the presence of a **substantial** degree of direction by one or more supported organizations over the policies, **programs**, and activities of the supporting organization—a relationship comparable to that of a **subsidiary** and **parent**. [PF § 15.7(e); EO § 12.3(c); SM pp. 83–84].

operating foundation

For purposes of the rules concerning the **mandatory payout requirements** imposed on **private foundations**, the term "operating foundation" means an **organization** with two principal characteristics. The first is that the organization makes **qualifying distributions directly** for the **active conduct** of its **tax-exempt activities** equal to **substantially all** of the lesser of its **adjusted net income** or its **minimum investment return**. The second is that (1) **substantially** more than one-half of its **assets** are devoted directly to these activities or to **functionally related businesses**, or both, or are stock of a **corporation** that is **controlled** by the private foundation and substantially all of the assets of which are so devoted, (2) it **normally** makes qualifying distributions directly for the active conduct of its tax-exempt activities in an amount not less than two-thirds of its minimum investment return, or (3) **substantially** all of its support (other than **gross investment income**) is normally received from the **general public** and from five or more **tax-exempt organizations** (other than certain private foundations that are **disqualified persons** (**IRC** § 4946(a)(1)(H)). Also, as to this third criterion, not more than 25 percent of its support (other than gross investment income) may be normally received from any one of the tax-exempt organizations and not more than one-half of its support may be normally received from gross investment income (**IRC** § 4942(j)(3)). If the qualifying distributions of an organization for a **tax year** exceed the minimum investment return for the year, however, the rule above ((1)(b)) does not apply unless substantially all of the qualifying distributions are made directly for the active conduct of the organization's tax-exempt activities (**IRC** § 4942(j)(3), last sentence). This is the organization that is also referred to as a **private operating foundation**. [PF § 3.1; EO § 12.1(b); SM p. 87] (cf. **Exempt operating foundation**).

operation of law

The phrase "operation of law" means the establishment or loss of a **right**, obligation, characteristic, or classification in or with respect to a **person** by dint of the direction of a **law**. (By contrast, some rights and the like in a person are created by an act of that person or pursuant to a **contract**.) For example, under the **federal tax law**, a **nonprofit organization** is **tax-exempt** if it meets the criteria of a particular provision describing a **tax-exempt organization**; this occurs by operation of law, rather than by a grant of the **exemption** by the **IRS** (which can, and in some instances must, **recognize** the tax exemption). Also, if an exempt organization fails to file an **annual information return** or **submit** a **notice** for three consecutive years, its exemption is revoked by operation of law. [EO §§ 3.2, 28.5].

operational test

The "operational test" is applied with respect to various types of **tax-exempt organizations** to determine whether the organization is being operated **exclusively** for its exempt purposes. This test is most developed for **charitable entities**, being in the **tax regulations**; nonetheless, the **IRS**, in **private letter rulings**, is expressly applying an operational test in connection with other categories of exempt organizations. For example, an organization, to qualify as a charitable entity, is regarded as operated exclusively for one or more charitable purposes only if it engages **primarily** in activities that accomplish one or more of its charitable purposes. An organization is not regarded as meeting this test if more than an **insubstantial part** of its activities is not in furtherance of an exempt purpose.

The rules for **supporting organizations** have a separate operational test. The requirement in this setting is that the organization must be operated exclusively to support or benefit one or more qualified **supported organizations** (**IRC** § 509(a)(3)(A)). There also are separate operational requirements for **private foundations**. [EO §§ 4.5(a), 12.3(c); AR §§ 1.6(c), 2.1(c), 8.1(h)(2); PF §§ 1.8, 5.2, 15.7(b); HC §§ 5.5(b), 21.3(b); GV § 8.4(c); RE Q 2.22, Q 9.16; CU Q 1.34; SM p. 170; CL § 1.10; LI Q 1.45, Q 10.19] (also **Activities test;** cf. **Organizational test**).

opinion letter

An "opinion letter" is a letter written by a **lawyer** to a client stating a conclusion of **law** based on a set of facts as stated in the letter. The use of an opinion letter arises, for example, in the setting of potential imposition of an **excise tax** on the **agreement** of a **foundation manager** to the making of a **taxable expenditure** by a **private foundation**; this tax may be imposed only when the **initial tax** is imposed on the foundation (**IRC** § 4945(a)(2)), the manager **knows** that the expenditure to which he or she agreed was a taxable expenditure, and the agreement is not willful and not due to **reasonable** cause. A manager's reliance on the advice of legal counsel, given in a reasoned, written legal opinion, may enable him or her to avoid the tax. Another example of the use of a letter of opinion is the reliance a private foundation may have on such a letter when making a **grant** to a **foreign charitable organization**; this type of letter addresses the **tax-exempt status** and **public charity status** of the prospective **grantee** under U.S. **law**. [PF §§ 5.15(e), 8.5(b), 9.5, 9.10(a)].

O

option

A **person** may own an item of **property** and create an "option," by which another person may purchase the property at a certain price at or during a certain time. An option may be created for or transferred to a **charitable organization**. There is, however, no **federal income tax charitable contribution deduction** for the transfer of an option to a charitable organization. Rather, the charitable deduction arises at the time the option is exercised by the charitable **donee**.

A **tax-exempt organization** may derive **income** from the lapse or termination of options that it has written and not pay any **unrelated business income tax** on the income received (**IRC** § 512(b)(5)). [UB § 3.11; CG § 6.9; PF § 6.2(b)].

ordinance

An "ordinance" is a **law** established by a municipal government. [FR § 3.23] (also **Local legislation**).

ordinary and necessary

A payment by a taxable **entity** may be **deductible** as a **business expense** if the outlay is "ordinary and necessary"; this principle applies with respect to the payment of **compensation**. In this setting, the concepts of **reasonable** and ordinary and necessary are essentially identical. [EO § 20.4(b)].

ordinary business care and prudence

The phrase "ordinary business care and prudence" is a standard of conduct against which **business** transactions are tested; the standard looks to the general customs and usages of the **commercial** community. This standard is applied in the **federal tax law** in determining whether a particular investment was a **jeopardizing investment**. [PF §§ 8.1(a), 8.2].

ordinary income

The **federal tax law**, in determining the **tax** consequences of the receipt of **income**, differentiates between "ordinary income" and **capital gain**. The term "ordinary income" refers to the usual receipt of income, such as **wages**, **salaries**, **rents**, **dividends**, and **interest**. Also, there are certain types of **property**, the **sale** or other **disposition** of which gives rise to ordinary income (**ordinary income property**). In most instances, ordinary income and **short-term capital gain** are treated in the same way for tax purposes. Thus, generally, ordinary income is income that is not **long-term capital gain** (IRC § 64). [CG § 2.16(b)].

ordinary income property

"Ordinary income property" is **property** that has **appreciated** in **value**, any portion of the gain on which would give rise to **ordinary income** (or **short-term capital gain**) if the property had been sold by its owner at its **fair market value**. In the context of **charitable giving**, then, ordinary income property is property that, if sold at its fair market value by the **donor** at the time of its **contribution** to a **charitable organization**, would generate a gain that is not **long-term capital gain**. Types of ordinary income property include **inventory**, a work of art in the possession of the artist who created it, a manuscript in the possession of the writer who created it, certain types of stock, and property used in a **trade or business** where gain on its sale would produce ordinary income by reason of the **recapture** rules. There is a special rule in the **federal tax law** regarding computation of the **federal income tax charitable contribution deduction** for gifts of ordinary income property (one of the **deduction reduction rules**). [CG § 4.4; PF §§ 14.1(a), 14.2, 14.4(c); SM p. 134].

ordinary loss

The **federal tax law** defines the term "ordinary loss" as a loss resulting from the **sale** or **exchange** of **property** that is not a **capital asset** (IRC § 65). [CG § 2.16(c)].

organization

The word "organization" is used to describe a **person** other than an individual. Thus, an organization may be a **corporation, estate, partnership, limited liability company, trust,** or **unincorporated association**. (also **Entity**).

organization manager

The term "organization manager" means (1) any **officer, director,** or **trustee** of an **organization** (or individual having powers or responsibilities similar to those of officers, directors, or trustees of the organization) and (2) with respect to any **expenditure**, any **employee** of the organization having authority or responsibility with respect to the expenditure (**IRC** §§ 4912(d)(2), 4955(f)(2)).

The term "organization manager" also means, in the context of the **intermediate sanctions rules**, with respect to an **applicable tax-exempt organization**, an **officer, director,** or **trustee** of the organization, or any individual having powers or responsibilities similar to those of officers, directors, or trustees of the organization (**IRC** § 4958(f)(2)). [EO §§ 21.3, 21.10, 22.4, 23.3; HC § 4.9(a)(ii); SM pp. 59, 189, 200; LI Q 4.56, Q 7.13] (cf. **Foundation manager; Fund manager**).

organization's minutes

See **Minutes**.

organizational risk pool requirements

The phrase "organizational risk pool requirements" refers to the organizational requirements imposed on **qualified charitable risk pools** as a condition of their **tax exemption**. These requirements are that the risk pool (1) is **organized** as a **nonprofit** organization under state law provisions authorizing risk-pooling arrangements for **charitable organizations**, (2) is exempt from any income tax imposed by the state (or will be so exempt after the pool qualifies for federal tax exemption), (3) has obtained at least $1 million in **startup capital** from **nonmember charitable organizations**, (4) is **controlled** by a **board of directors** elected by its members, and (5) has organizational documents that require that each member of the risk pool be exempt charitable organizations, that any member that loses its exemption will immediately notify the pool of the **determination** and its effective date, and that each policy of **insurance** issued by the risk pool provide that the policy will not cover the insured with respect to events occurring after the date the final determination was issued to the insured. An organization does not cease to qualify as a qualified charitable risk pool solely by reason of the failure of any of its members to continue to qualify as an exempt charitable organization if, within a reasonable period of time after the pool is notified of the loss of exemption, the pool takes such action as may be reasonably necessary to remove the member from the pool (**IRC** § 501(n)(3)). [EO § 11.6].

organizational test

The "organizational test" is applied with respect to types of **tax-exempt organizations** to determine whether the organization is properly organized from the standpoint of exemption requirements. This test is more developed in connection with **charitable entities**, being in the tax regulations; nonetheless, the **IRS** is, in **private letter rulings**, more frequently expressly applying an organizational test in regard to other types of exemption organizations. An organization will not meet this test if its **articles of organization** empower it, as more than an **insubstantial** part of its activities, to carry on activities that are not in furtherance of its **tax-exempt purposes**. The rules for **supporting organizations** have a separate organizational test. The requirement in this setting is that the organization must be organized **exclusively** to support or benefit one or more qualified **supported organizations** (**IRC** § 509(a)(3)(A)). There also are separate organizational requirements for **private foundations**. [EO §§ 4.3, 12.1(g), 12.3(c), 17.2; AR §§ 1.6(c), 8.1(h)(1); GV § 8.4(b); HC §§ 5.5(a), 21.3(b); PF §§ 1.9, 15.7(a); CU Q 1.33, Q 4.22; RE Q 2.22; SM p. 170; LI Q 1.11, Q 1.44, Q 10.18] (cf. **Operational test**; also **Activities test**).

organizing document

See **Articles of incorporation**; **Articles of organization**, **Declaration of trust**; **Trust agreement**.

orphan

An "orphan" is generally defined as a **minor** child bereaved by the death of his or her parents. The **federal tax law** provides several ways for an **organization** to be considered a **charitable organization**, for purposes of both **tax exemption** and **charitable donee** status. One of these ways is that an organization can be a charitable one where it provides care for orphans (**IRC** § 501(c)(3)). [EO § 11.1; CG § 3.3(b); SM p. 33].

other adjustment, organization, or reorganization

For purposes of the rules concerning the **termination** of **private foundation status**, the phrase "other adjustment, organization, or reorganization" includes any partial **liquidation** or any other **significant disposition of assets** to one or more private foundations, other than transfers for full and adequate **consideration** or distributions out of current **income**. [PF § 13.5].

other benefits

The **federal tax law** uses the term "other benefits" in the context of defining a **tax-exempt voluntary employees' beneficiary association**. The **principal** function of this type of **entity** is the provision of life, sick, accident, or "other benefits" to appropriate **beneficiaries**. The term includes only benefits that are similar to life, sick, or accident benefits, namely, a benefit that is intended to safeguard or improve the health of a **member** or a member's dependents, or that protects against a contingency that interrupts or impairs a member's earning power. These benefits include vacation benefits, the provision of vacation facilities, reimbursement of vacation **expenses**, subsidization of recreational activities, the provision of child-care facilities for preschool and school-age dependents, and personal legal service benefits. The term does not include the payment of commuting expenses, the provision of accident or homeowner's **insurance** benefits for damage to **property**, the provision of malpractice insurance, the provision of loans to members (except in times of distress), the provision of **pension** and **annuity** benefits payable at the time of mandatory or voluntary retirement, or the provision of savings facilities for members. [EO § 18.3; SM p. 43].

outright

The word "outright" is used to describe a **contribution** where all of the **right**, **title**, and **interest** in money and/or **property** is transferred from the **donor** to the **donee**; that is, the donor does not retain any **material** or **substantial** interest in the **gift** property.

outside counsel

The term "outside counsel" is used to refer to a **lawyer** who is not an **employee** of a client **organization** but who serves the organization as an **independent contractor** (or **consultant**). (cf. **House counsel** (or "in-house counsel").

overriding royalty

An "overriding royalty" is a stated percentage of a **royalty**, where the principal portion of that royalty is payable to a **person** and the overriding royalty is payable to another person. An overriding royalty is subject to the same terms and duration as the underlying royalty. The **modification** by which payments of royalties to a **tax-exempt organization** are **excluded** from **unrelated business income** expressly includes overriding royalties (**IRC** § 512(b)(2)). [EO § 25.1(g); UB § 3.7].

Oversight Board, IRS

The "Internal Revenue Service Oversight Board" is responsible for overseeing the **IRS** in its administration, conduct, direction, and supervision of the execution and application of the nation's internal revenue laws (**IRC** §§ 7802(a), (c)(1)(A)). [EO § 2.2(a)].

overthrow of the government, inciting or advocating

In general, a **demonstration** or similar event can be a **charitable activity**. An activity, however, cannot be charitable if it is illegal or is otherwise contrary to **public policy**. Included within this proscription is the **crime** of **advocating** or inciting the overthrow of a government. [EO § 6.2(a)].

owner, as disqualified person

An owner of more than 20 percent of the total **combined voting power** of a **corporation**, the **profits interest** of a **partnership**, or the **beneficial interest** of a **trust** or **unincorporated enterprise**, any of which is (during the ownership) a **substantial contributor** to a **private foundation** is a **disqualified person** (**IRC** § 4946(a)(1)(C)). [PF § 4.3; EO § 12.2(c)].

P

parens patriae

The words "parens patriae" are Latin for "parent of his country." The term today is used to express the role of a government as a guardian of certain **persons** who are seen (usually by the government) as in need of the protection afforded by the government. For example, the role of the states in administering and enforcing **charitable solicitation acts** is viewed as the provision of protection for citizens who would otherwise be duped, swindled, and defrauded into making **contributions** to entities that are not, in fact, **charitable organizations** or to persons who would not use the **gifts** for **charitable purposes**. [FR § 3.19] (also **Police power**).

parent organization

The term "parent organization" is used to describe an **organization** that, at a minimum, **controls** one or more other organizations and perhaps owns one or more other organizations. These other organizations are known as **subsidiary** organizations (or **subsidiaries**). Where the parent and subsidiary organizations are **nonprofit organizations**, this element of control is usually manifested in **interlocking directorates**, where at least a majority of the members of the **board of directors** of the subsidiary organization are, and/or are selected by, members of the board of directors of the parent organization. In some instances, this element of control is reflected in stock; where the relationship between the parent organization and a subsidiary organization is represented by stock, the parent organization will, in addition to controlling the subsidiary, own the subsidiary (assuming the parent organization owns at least a majority of the stock of the subsidiary organization). It is common for this same result to occur by reason of the fact that the parent organization is the **member** of the subsidiary organization. Special rules may apply to **tax revenue** paid by a subsidiary organization to a parent organization. [EO §§ 12.3(c), 29.1; HC § 20.2] (also **Affiliated organization**; **Control**; **Feeder organization**; **Group exemption**; **Subordinate**; **Supporting organization**).

parsonage allowance

A **gross income** tax **exclusion** is available, in the case of a **minister of the gospel**, for the rental value of a home furnished to the minister as part of his or her **compensation** and for a rental allowance paid to the minister as part of his or her compensation. This allowance is available

---

Bruce R. Hopkins' Nonprofit Law Dictionary, First Edition. Bruce R. Hopkins.
© 2015 Bruce R. Hopkins. Published 2015 by John Wiley & Sons, Inc.

to the extent the minister uses it to rent or provide a home and to the extent the allowance does not exceed the **fair rental value** of the home, including furnishings and appurtenances such as a garage, plus the cost of utilities. A federal district court held that the exclusion in the form of the allowance is unconstitutional as a violation of the Establishment Clause, although that determination was nullified when an **appellate court** ruled that the **plaintiffs** lacked **standing** to bring the **action** (**IRC** § 107). [EO § 10.1(b); CL §§ 2.4, 2.5] (also **Convenience of employer doctrine**).

partial interest

An item of **property** is—conceptually—comprised of two types of **interests**: one or more **income interests** and one or more **remainder interests**. Since these interests each constitute less than the totality of the interests in the property, they are termed "partial interests." This concept underlies many forms of **planned giving**. When a **donor** makes an **outright gift** of an item of property, he, she, or it **contributes** all of his, her, or its interest in the property. A donor may, however, contribute only an income interest or a remainder interest in an item of property. Usually, the medium that is used to "split" a property into these interests is a **split-interest trust**. [CG § 5.3; SM pp. 233–234].

partial interest gift

A "partial interest gift" is a **gift** to a **charitable organization** or other **person** of less than the **donor's** entire interest in an item of **property** (or money); it is a gift of a **partial interest**. [CG §§ 5.3, 9.23; PF §§ 14.1(a); 14.2, 14.5; SM p. 138].

partially agreed case

One of the types of **IRS tax-exempt organization examination** cases that may be closed is the "partially agreed case," which is a case that entails more than one issue, where the **exempt organization** agrees with the **IRS** to at least one issue and disagrees as to at least one issue, and signs the appropriate waiver and acceptance forms as to the agreed issues. [AU § 5.32(a)].

partially completed appraisal summary

The phrase "partially completed appraisal summary" is used in the context of the **appraisal rules** that apply with respect to certain **charitable contributions** of **appreciated property**. In the case of nonpublicly traded securities, the claimed **value** of which does not exceed $10,000 but is greater than $5,000, the **donor** must attach a partially completed appraisal summary form (**Form 8283**) to the **tax return** on which the **charitable contribution deduction** is claimed. [CG § 21.5; FR § 5.17(c); SM pp. 139–140].

participating loan restriction

The term "participating loan restriction" is used in the context of defining circumstances where an **exception,** from the **law** treating **income** from **debt-financed property** as **unrelated business taxable income**, is available to **qualified organizations** that make debt-financed investments in **real property** (**IRC** § 514(c)(9)(A)). Under this exception, income from investments in real property is not treated as income from debt-financed property.

This exception is available only where six restrictions are satisfied (**IRC** § 514(c)(9)(13)). One of them is the "participating loan restriction," which provides that the amount of the indebtedness or any amount payable with respect to the indebtedness, or the time for making any payment of any amount, may not be dependent (in whole or in part) on **revenues**, **income**, or **profits** derived from the property (**IRC** § 514(c)(9)(B)(ii)). This rule, however, is relaxed in this regard where (1) a qualified organization acquires the property from a financial institution that acquired the real property by foreclosure (or after an actual or imminent default), or was held by the selling financial institution at the time that it entered into conservatorship or receivership, (2) any **gain recognized** by the financial institution with respect to the property is **ordinary income**, (3) the stated **principal** amount of the seller financing does not exceed the financial institution's outstanding indebtedness (including accrued but unpaid interest) with respect to the property at the time of foreclosure or default, and (4) the present value of the maximum amount payable pursuant to any participation feature cannot exceed 30 percent of the total purchase price of the property (including contingent payments) (**IRC** § 514(c)(9)(H)). [UB § 5.4(f); EO § 24.9(c)].

participation

Generally, "participation" means taking part in some action or attempt; it is the act of participation. The **federal tax law** uses this word in a variety of settings: (1) there is no **business expense deduction** for an amount paid or incurred in connection with any "participation" in a **political campaign** involving a **candidate** for **public office** (**IRC** § 162(e)(1)(B)), (2) **tax-exempt charitable organizations** may not be a part of any "participation" in a political campaign involving a **candidate** for **public office** (**IRC** § 501(c)(3)), (3) one of the **excise taxes** imposed for acts of **self-dealing** can be assessed when a **foundation manager** had a "participation" in the act (**IRC** § 4941(a)(2)), and (4) one of the excise taxes imposed for an inappropriate participation in the making of a **jeopardizing investment** (**IRC** § 4944(a)(2)). [EO §§ 23.2, 23.7; PF §§ 5.15(d), 8.5(a); LI Q 4.62, Q 5.45, Q 8.5].

participation, units of

See **Units of participation**.

particular services

The term "particular services" generally means services that are provided by a **tax-exempt business league** to some of its **members** (or perhaps other **persons**) that are in addition to those that are **exempt functions** funded by **dues**; usually there is a separate payment for these services. The **tax regulations** indicate that provision of these types of services is a ground for loss or denial of **exemption**, although the greater likelihood is that the activity will be treated as an **unrelated trade or business**. [EO § 14.2(c); UB § 9.4(a); AS § 2.10(c)].

partisan

The word "partisan" generally means to be (or someone who is) strongly devoted to (perhaps militantly so) a particular political party. The term is also used with respect to causes and ideas. (cf. **Nonpartisan**).

partner

A "partner" is a **person** who is a **member** of a **partnership** (IRC § 7701(a)(2)). [EO § 31.1(a); SM p. 225] (also **General partner**; **Limited partner**).

partnership

A "partnership" is a form of **organization**, recognized as a separate legal **entity**. A partnership is usually evidenced by a **partnership agreement**; however, a partnership may be deemed to exist by **operation of law**. It is always a **membership organization**, with the members (individuals and/or organizations) termed "**partners**." Often, the interests of partners in a partnership are represented by **units** in the partnership. A partnership must have at least one **general partner**; it may have one or more **limited partners**. The **federal tax law** defines a partnership as including a syndicate, group, pool, **joint venture**, or other **unincorporated organization**, through or by means of which any **business**, financial operation, or venture is carried on and which is not a **trust**, **estate**, or **corporation** (IRC § 7701(a)(2)). A partnership does not pay **federal income tax**; in that regard, a partnership is a type of **tax-exempt organization**. [EO §§ 19.23, 24.7, 31.1(a); UB §§ 6.4, 8.9(a); AS § 7.1; AR §§ 3.1(rr), 3.2(rr), 11.1(f)(3), 21.1(a), 21.2(c), 21.2(f); HC §§ 22.1–22.3, 22.7, 22.8; PF §§ 4.5, 7.1(c), 7.2(b), 11.3(c); CU Q 16.37; RE Q 14.25; CG § 2.8; PG pp. 149–154; SM pp. 225–226] (also **General partnership**; **Limited partnership**).

partnership agreement

A "partnership agreement" is a document (**instrument**) that is a **contract** between two or more **persons** evidencing the existence of, and stating the terms and conditions of, a **partnership**. A document, however, need not be so formally titled to be considered a partnership agreement; a partnership may be found as a matter of **law** from a particular set of facts and circumstances, even where the parties involved did not intend or desire to have a partnership. [EO § 31.1(a)].

P

partnership restrictions

The term "partnership restrictions" is used in the context of defining circumstances where an **exception**, from the **law** treating **income** from **debt-financed property** as **unrelated business taxable income**, is available to **qualified organizations** that make debt-financed investments in **real property** (IRC § 514(c)(9)(A)). Under this exception, income from investments in real property is not treated as income from debt-financed property. This exception is available only where six restrictions are satisfied (IRC § 514(c)(9)(B)). One of them is the "partnership restrictions" rule, which provides that, if the investment in the property is held through a **partnership**, certain additional requirements must be satisfied by the partnership (IRC § 514(c)(9)(B)(vi)). [EO § 24.9(c); UB § 5.4(f)].

partnership rule

The "partnership rule" states that, generally, a **trade or business regularly carried on** by a **partnership** of which a **tax-exempt organization** is a **member** is an **unrelated trade or business** with respect to the organization. In computing its **unrelated business taxable income**, the organization must (subject to the **modification rules**) include its share (whether or not distributed) of the **gross income** of the partnership from the unrelated trade or business and its share of the partnership **deductions directly connected** with this gross income (**IRC** § 512(c)(1)). [EO § 24.7; UB § 6.4].

party

The word "party" generally refers to a **person** in a set of facts, such as a "party to a transaction." The term also is used to refer to a **plaintiff** or a **defendant** in a **lawsuit**.

pass-through

The term "pass-through" is a **federal tax law** concept describing the process of money, **property**, and/or **tax deductions** or **credits** being transferred from one **person** to another but flowing through an intermediate **entity** as part of that process. For example, in some instances, the federal income tax deduction for **depreciation** flows through a **pooled income** fund to its **income beneficiaries** in determining their federal income tax **liability**. [EO §§ 24.7, 31.1; CG § 13.7] (also **Pass-through entity**).

pass-through entity

A "pass-through entity" is an **organization** having, as one of its **principal** features, a "pass-through" function. These **entities** include **partnerships, S corporations, limited liability companies, pooled income funds**, and **charitable remainder trusts**. [EO §§ 19.23, 31.1; CG Chaps. 12, 13].

pass-through foundation

The phrase "pass-through foundation" refers to a **private foundation** which, not later than the fifteenth day of the third month after the close of the foundation's **tax year** in which **contributions** are received, makes **qualifying distributions** that are treated as distributions out of **corpus** in an amount equal to 100 percent of the contributions (**IRC** § 170(b)(1)(F)(ii)). A contributor in this context must obtain sufficient evidence from the foundation showing that it made this qualifying distribution. This is not a separate category of private foundation, but the rule facilitates preferential **tax law** treatment of the charitable gifts involved or enables a foundation **grant** to constitute a qualifying distribution when otherwise it would not so qualify. [PF §§ 3.2, 6.5(a), 14.4(a); CG § 7.5(a)] (also **Conduit foundation**).

pass-through of depreciation

See **Depreciation, pass-through of**.

passive income

See **Income, passive**.

passive rent rules

An **exclusion** from **unrelated business income taxation** is available with respect to **rent** (**IRC** § 512(b)(3)). This exclusion, however, is generally available only with respect to rent that is in the form of **passive income**. Thus, where a **tax-exempt organization** carries on leasing activities that constitute a **trade or business** or if determination of the amount of the rent depends in whole or in part on the income or profits involved, the exclusion will not apply. [EO § 25.1(h)].

Patient Protection and Affordable Care Act

Enactment of the Patient Protection and Affordable Care Act brought several substantive changes in the law of tax-exempt organizations, including additional hospital exemption requirements, tax exemption for qualified nonprofit health insurance issuers, and exemptions from the individual health insurance mandate. [HC §§ 1.0, 2.6, 13.1(f), 13.3–13.5, 26.10(a), 26.10(b); CL §§ 1.2(e), 1.2(f), 1.2(g), 4.0, 4.4; EO §§ 2.4, 7.6(a)(ii), 19.18, 26.6, 28.2(a)(i), 28.13(b)].

patriotic organization

See **Patriotism, promotion of**.

patriotism, promotion of

An organization may be **tax-exempt** under the **federal tax law** if it qualifies as a **charitable organization**; one way for an organization to so qualify is to engage in activities that "promote patriotism." These activities include the purchase and display of flags, the conduct of flag-raising and other ceremonies, and the celebration of a patriotic holiday. [EO § 7.15(b)].

payout requirement

See **Mandatory payout requirement**.

penalty

Like most forms of **law**, many of the laws directly applicable to **nonprofit organizations** have as **sanctions** for them various "penalties." A penalty is a form of punishment imposed for the violation of a law. Penalties can be **civil** or **criminal**; a penalty is usually considered to be the levying of a sum of money, rather than another form of punishment (such as imprisonment or death, despite the term "death penalty").

For example, in the **federal tax law** setting, there are penalties for failure to file an **annual information return** (**IRC** § 6652(c)(1)(A)); for failure to make an **application for recognition of exemption** accessible to the public (**IRC** § 6652(c)(1)(D)) or annual information return accessible to the public (**IRC** § 6652(c)(1)(C)); for failure to **disclose** the **nondeductibility** of a portion of a payment in the case of a **quid pro quo contribution** or for the making of a disclosure that is incomplete or inaccurate (such as an estimate not determined in **good faith** of the **value** of goods or services furnished to the **donor**) (**IRC** § 6714); for failure to disclose that certain information or services offered by a tax-exempt organization is available without charge from the federal government (**IRC** § 6711(a)); for a **substantial underpayment** of **income tax** (**IRC** § 6662(b)(2)); for a substantial income tax **valuation misstatement** (**IRC** § 6662(b)(3)); for a substantial **estate tax** or **gift tax valuation understatement** (**IRC** § 6662(b)(5)); for **negligence** (**IRC** § 6662(b)(1); for **disregard** of **rules** or **regulations** (**IRC** § 6662(b)(1); and for fraud (**IRC** § 6663).

P

The **excise taxes** that underlie the **intermediate sanctions** rules, the **donor-advised fund** rules, and the **private foundation** rules, and the prohibitions on **substantial legislative activities** and on **political campaign activities**, are forms of penalties. In a sense, the revocation of **tax-exempt status** or the denial of a **charitable contribution deduction** is a type of penalty.

The penalty for failure to timely file an annual information return, absent **reasonable cause**, is $10, payable by the organization, for each day the failure continues, with a maximum penalty for any one return not to exceed the lesser of $5,000 or 5 percent of the gross receipts of the organization for one year (**IRC** § 6652(c)(1)(A)). This penalty also applies to a failure to include any information required to be shown on the return or failure to show the correct information. An additional penalty is imposed at the same rate and maximum of $5,000 on the individual(s) responsible for the failure to file, absent reasonable cause, where the return remains unfiled following demand for it from the **IRS** (**IRC** § 6652(c)(1)(B)). An addition to tax for failure to file a federal **tax return** (including a **Form 990-T**, by which a **tax-exempt organization reports** its **unrelated business taxable income**) may also be imposed (**IRC** § 6651(a)(1)).

The penalty for failure to make a copy of an application for recognition of tax exemption available for public inspection, payable by the person failing to meet the requirement, is $10 per day, absent reasonable cause, without any limitation (**IRC** § 6652(c)(1)(D)). A person who **willfully** fails to comply with this inspection requirement is subject to a $1,000 penalty with respect to each application (**IRC** § 6685).

The penalty for failure to make a copy of an annual information return available for public inspection is $10 per day, absent reasonable cause, with a maximum penalty per return of $5,000 (**IRC** § 6652(c)(1)(C)). A person who willfully fails to comply with this inspection requirement is subject to a $1,000 penalty with respect to each return (**IRC** § 6685).

The penalty for failure to make a disclosure in the case of a quid pro quo contribution is $10 per contribution, capped at $5,000 per particular **fundraising event** or mailing, imposed on the organization involved, unless the failure was due to reasonable cause (**IRC** § 6714).

The penalty for failure to disclose that information or services being offered by a tax-exempt organization is available without charge from the federal government, which is applicable for each day on which the failure occurred, is the greater or $1,000 or 50 percent of the aggregate cost of the offers and **solicitations** that occurred on any day on which the failure occurred and with respect to which there was this type of failure (**IRC** § 6711(b)).

The penalty for a **substantial understatement of income tax** is 20 percent of the resulting **underpayment** of tax (**IRC** §§ 6662(a), (b)(2)). The penalty for an income tax substantial valuation misstatement is 20 percent of the resulting underpayment of tax (**IRC** §§ 6662(a), (b)(3)). The penalty for a **substantial estate tax valuation understatement** or a **substantial gift tax valuation understatement** is 20 percent of the resulting underpayment of tax (**IRC** §§ 6662(a), (b)(5)), The penalty for negligence in the federal tax context is 20 percent of the resulting underpayment of tax (**IRC** §§ 6662(a), (b)(1)). The penalty for disregard of the federal tax rules and regulations is 20 percent of the resulting underpayment of tax (**IRC** §§ 6662(a), (b)(1)). The penalty for the commission of tax fraud is 75 percent of the portion of the resulting underpayment of tax that is attributable to fraud (**IRC** § 6663(a)).

pension fund

A "pension fund" is a **fund** from which fixed amounts of money are periodically paid to individuals in **consideration** of their past services to the **organization** that operates the fund (usually an **employer**). Nearly all pension funds are **tax-exempt organizations** (IRC § 401(a)). [EO § 18.1; SM p. 43] (also **Employee benefit fund**).

Pension Protection Act of 2006

Enactment of the Pension Protection Act of 2006 brought several substantive changes in the law of tax-exempt organizations, including development of the law concerning **Type III supporting organizations**, **donor-advised funds**, **credit counseling organizations**, and disclosures of certain proposed actions involving **charitable organizations** to **appropriate state officers**. [EO §§ 2.4, 7.3(d), 11.8(b), 12.3(c), 12.4(c), 21.4(d), 21.4(e), 26.4, 27.7, 28.3, 28.4, 28.7, 28.13(c), 30.7(d); CG §§ 2.6, 3.4, 6.15, 9.10(e), 17.7, 21.1, 21.5; HC §§ 5.5(b), 5.5(e), 5.5(i), 20.2(b), 28.3(d), 31.2(d), 33.7(a), 36.3(f); FR §§ 5.11(c), 5.17(a)].

per donee gift tax exclusion

The phrase "per donee gift tax exclusion" means that the **federal gift tax** is inapplicable with respect to the first $14,000 **contributed** to each **donee** in a year (**IRC** § 2503). Only **present interests** in **property** are considered for this **annual exclusion**. [CG § 8.2(h)].

per se private inurement

Certain transactions or arrangements involving **tax-exempt organizations** are inherently deficient, in that a form of **private inurement** is embedded in them. This is "per se private inurement." It is thus irrelevant, in this context, that the economic benefit conferred on an **insider** is **reasonable**. [EO § 20.6; HC § 28.1(a)].

P

per se rule

The term "per se" is of Latin origin, meaning "in and of itself"; it is somewhat synonymous with "intrinsic" or "inherent." Thus, a "per se rule" is a **rule** that states that, where certain facts are present, a particular conclusion necessarily follows; in this context, the conclusion is a rule of **law**. One such per se rule, as developed by the **IRS** but no longer followed, was that the participation by a **charitable organization** in a **partnership**, where the organization is the, or a, **general partner** and private investors are **limited partners**, would automatically lead to **revocation** or **denial** of tax-exempt status on the ground that unwarranted private economic benefit was being provided to the limited partners.

The successor rule, which is still somewhat of a per se rule, is this: The participation by a charitable organization in a partnership, where the organization is a general partner and private investors are limited partners will automatically lead to revocation or denial of tax-exempt status on the private benefit ground unless (1) the charitable organization is serving a charitable purpose by participating in the partnership, (2) the charitable organization is insulated from the day-to-day responsibilities as general partners, and (3) the limited partners are not receiving an undue economic benefit from the partnership. Another illustration of this type of rule is the view of the **IRS** that certain forms of partnership arrangements (such as those where an exempt charitable organization sells a **net revenue stream** to a partnership) constitute **private inurement per se**. [EO §§ 20.6, 31.2(a); HC § 28.1(a)].

percentage-based compensation

In certain circumstances involving **tax-exempt organizations**, an individual's compensation is set, in whole or in part, on the basis of a percentage of receipts; this form of compensation is termed a **commission**. For example, it is not uncommon for a **charitable organization** to pay an individual who is assisting the organization in **soliciting contributions** a percentage of the contributions received. Although the **IRS** is rather suspicious of this practice, particularly in the context of **fundraising**, courts are quite tolerant of it. Some courts have indicated a preference for a limit on the amount of compensation paid in this manner, while others have said that this form of ceiling on compensation is unnecessary.

Attempts have been made from time to time by **associations** of fundraising professionals to maintain, in their **codes of ethics**, prohibitions against compensation based on percentages of funds raised. These prohibitions, however, technically are violations of the **antitrust laws** as illegal **restraints of trade** and thus cannot lawfully be enforced. [EO § 20.4(c); FR § 5.13].

percentage limitations

The **federal tax law**, while allowing an **income tax charitable contribution deduction** for both individuals and **corporations**, places various limitations on the amount that can be deducted, particularly in any one **tax year**. This is accomplished by means of certain "percentage limitations."

For individuals, the percentage limitations are applied to an individual's **contribution base** (which is essentially his or her **adjusted gross income**). An individual's federal income tax charitable contribution deduction for a tax year is subject to limitations of 50, 30, and/or 20 percent of his or her contribution base. The maximum federal income tax charitable contribution deduction for a tax year for an individual is 50 percent of his or her contribution base. An individual's federal income tax charitable contribution deduction for a tax year cannot exceed an amount equal to 50 percent of his or her contribution base where the **gift** (or gifts) is of money (and/or **ordinary income property** and/or **short-term capital gain property**) and the charitable recipient is a **public charitable organization** (IRC § 170(b)(1)(A)).

In general, an individual's federal income tax charitable contribution deduction for a tax year cannot exceed an amount equal to 30 percent of his or her contribution base where the gift is of capital gain property that has appreciated in value and the charitable recipient is a public charitable organization (**IRC** § 170(b)(1)(C)(i)). An individual donor can elect to have the 50 percent limitation apply, where the gift is of capital gain property that has appreciated in value and the charitable recipient is a public charitable organization, by reducing the deduction by the amount of the **appreciation element** (IRC § 170(b)(1)(C)(iii)). An individual's federal income tax charitable contribution deduction for a tax year cannot exceed an amount equal to 30 percent of his or her contribution base where the gift (or gifts) is of money and the charitable recipient is an entity, such as a **private foundation**, other than a public charitable organization (**IRC** § 170(b)(1)(B)(i)). An individual's federal income tax charitable contribution deduction for a tax year cannot exceed an amount equal to 20 percent of his or her contribution base where the gift is of capital gain property that has appreciated in value and the charitable recipient is an entity other than a public charitable organization (**IRC** § 170(b)(1)(D)(i)).

These limitations are blended where the individual donor contributes more than one type of item (money or property) in a tax year and/or gives to more than one type of charitable organization in a tax year. If a husband and wife file a **joint return**, the deduction for charitable contributions is the aggregate of the contributions made by the spouses and the percentage limitations are based on the aggregate contribution base of the spouses.

Each of these percentage limitations rules allows for contributions in excess of the limitations to be **carried forward** and deducted over the subsequent five years, in order of time. Maximum use of carried-over amounts must be made in a year.

The charitable contribution deduction for a **corporation** for a tax year is subject to a limitation of 10 percent of the corporation's **pretax net income** (**IRC** § 170(b)(2)).

There are no percentage limitations applicable in the federal **estate tax** or federal **gift tax** charitable contribution deduction context. [CG Chap. 7; AR § 19.1(a)(3); SM pp. 134–136].

percentage payout

The term "percentage payout" is used in connection with the **federal tax law** permitting a **private foundation** to pay an **excise tax** on its **net investment income** at a **rate** of 1 percent (rather than the standard 2 percent) (**IRC** § 4940(e)). The term is defined as meaning, with respect to a **tax year,** the percentage determined by dividing (1) the amount of the **qualifying distributions** made by the private foundation during the taxable year by (2) the **assets** of the private foundation for the taxable year (**IRC** § 4940(e)(3)). [PF § 10.2] (also **Average percentage payout**).

period of suspension

For purposes of the law concerning **terrorist organizations**, the term "period of suspension" means the period that begins on the later of the date of the first publication of a designation or identification described in the definition of that type of organization or November 11, 2003, and ends on the first date that all of these designations and identifications with respect to the organization are rescinded (**IRC** § 501(p)(3)). [EO § 26.8].

periodical

The word "periodical" means a publication, such as a newsletter, magazine, or journal, of which the issues appear at stated or regular intervals. For purposes of the **unrelated business income rules** applicable to periodicals, concerning the taxation of **advertising income**, material published solely on a website can be considered a periodical. [UB § 10.12; EO § 24.5(h)(ii); HC § 24.17].

permanent endowment

The **IRS** uses the term "permanent endowment" to mean an **endowment fund** that is established by a **tax-exempt organization** with **donor-restricted gifts** that is maintained to provide a permanent source of **income**, with the stipulation that the **principal** must be invested and kept intact in perpetuity, with only the income generated useable by the organization.

permanent injunction

A "permanent injunction" is an **injunction** that grants relief to a **party** to **litigation** by permanently barring another party from engaging in a form of prohibited conduct. (cf. **Preliminary injunction**; **Temporary restraining order**).

permanent insurance

"Permanent insurance" is **insurance** that does not expire after a period of time, as is the case with "term insurance." Permanent insurance can be categorized as whole life, variable life, adjustable life, and universal life insurance.

permit

See **Registration**.

permitted business holdings

The **excess business holdings** rules generally limit to 20 percent the allowable ownership of a **business enterprise** by a **private foundation** and all **disqualified persons** with respect to it (**IRC** § 4943(c)(2)(A)). If **effective control** of a business enterprise is elsewhere, a 35 percent limit may be substituted for the 35 percent limit (**IRC** § 4943(c)(2)(B)). The "permitted business holdings" of a private foundation are those that are within these percentage limitations. [PF §§ 7.1(d), 7.2; HC § 5.10; SM p. 89].

permitted sources

The term "permitted sources" is used in the context of measuring **public support** for purposes of the rules concerning **service provider organizations**. This type of organization must **normally** receive more than one-third of its support from any combination of **gifts, grants, contributions, membership fees**, and **gross receipts** from admissions, sales of merchandise, performance of services, or furnishing of facilities in activities related to its **tax-exempt functions**. Support from these sources, however, to constitute public support, must come from "permitted sources." Permitted sources are **governmental units**, the **charitable institutions, donative publicly supported organizations**, and persons other than **disqualified persons** with respect to the organization. Thus, a charitable organization seeking to qualify under this **support test** must construct a support fraction, with the amount of support from these categories of support from permitted sources constituting the numerator of the support fraction and the total amount of support received by the organization being the denominator of the support fraction. [PF § 15.5(d); EO § 12.3(b)(iv); HC § 5.3(a); SM p. 82].

perpetual care trust fund

To qualify for a **charitable deduction** for amounts distributed by a "perpetual care trust fund" to a taxable cemetery company for the care and maintenance of gravesites, the fund must be a **trust** established pursuant to local law by the taxable **entity** (**IRC** § 642(j)). [EO § 19.6].

perpetual conservation restriction

A "perpetual conservation restriction" is a form of a **qualified real property interest**, which may be the subject of a **charitable contribution deduction**. It is a restriction granted in perpetuity on the use that may be made of **real property**—including an **easement** or other interest in real property that under state **law** has attributes similar to an easement (e.g., a restrictive covenant or an **equitable** servitude). [CG § 9.7(a)].

person

The term "person" generally means either an **entity** (also termed an **artificial person**) or an individual (a human being, also termed a **natural person**). Entities include **corporations, partnerships, limited liability companies, trusts**, and **unincorporated associations**. The **federal tax law** defines a "person" to include an individual, trust, **estate**, partnership, association, company, or corporation (**IRC** § 7701(a)(1)). In some federal tax law settings (such as a failure to file an **annual information return**, or to make it or an **application for recognition of exemption** accessible to the public), the term "person" includes an officer or employee of a corporation, or a member or employee of a partnership, who as such officer, employee, or member is under a duty to perform the act (**IRC** §§ 6652(c)(4)(C), 7343).

personal benefit contract

A "personal benefit contract" with respect to a transferor is any life insurance, annuity, or endowment **contract**, if any **direct or indirect beneficiary** under the contract is the transferor, any member of the transferor's family, or any other **person** (other than a **charitable organization**) designated by the transferor (**IRC** § 170(f)(10)(B)). This term arises in the context of certain charitable split-dollar insurance plans that are essentially outlawed. [EO § 28.13(d); CG § 24.11; AR §§ 4.1(m), 4.2(h); PG pp. 193, 224–226, 251–252; SM p. 240].

personal church

The term "personal church" means an **organization** (or, sometimes, merely a **fund**) that is established, ostensibly as a **tax-exempt church**, for the private ends (including **income tax** avoidance) of one or more individuals. [EO § 10.2(c)] (also **Private inurement**).

personal expense deduction

In general, an **expense** incurred by an individual for a reason other than the economic cost of doing business is not **deductible** for purposes of the **federal income tax**. There are some exceptions to this rule, however, with the **charitable contribution deduction** being one of them. Others include the deductions for home **mortgage interest**, **medical expenses**, casualty **losses**, and state and local taxes. [CG § 2.5(b)] (also **Miscellaneous itemized deductions**).

personal property

The term "personal property" is used to describe all **property** that is not **real property**. Personal property is either **tangible personal property** or **intangible property**. [CG §§ 2.12(b)–2.12(d)].

P

personal representative

In general, a "personal representative" is a **person** who manages the affairs of another person. This relationship is evidenced by an **instrument**, such as a **power of attorney** or a **will**. Thus, the term is synonymous with the word "**executor**."

personal residence

The term "personal residence" means a dwelling in which an individual lives. The term arises in the **federal tax law** setting because of the **tax deduction** for a **gift** of a **remainder interest** in a personal residence (**IRC** § 170(f)(3)(B)(i)). This gift is not made in **trust**. To qualify, the property need not be the **donor's principal** residence; thus, for example, it includes vacation homes. The term does not include household furnishings that are not **fixtures**. [CG §§ 2.14(f), 15.2(a)].

personally liable

An individual becomes "personally liable" for a **commission** and/or an **omission** when he or she is **directly** involved in the offending act (or non-act) and cannot shift the **liability** to another **person**, such as an **employer**. In general, **corporations** are separate entities for purposes of fixing liability; however, in some circumstances, the **law** allows **piercing of the corporate veil** to cause **directors**, **trustees**, and/or **officers** to be "personally liable." An individual who is found to be personally liable may be protected by **officers'** and **directors' liability insurance**. [SM Chap. 25].

personalty

The word "personalty" is synonymous with the term **personal property**.

pet

A "pet" is an animal that is domesticated or otherwise tamed, and that is kept and cared for by one or more individuals. The **federal tax law** provides that a pet cannot qualify as a **remainder interest beneficiary** of a **charitable remainder trust** or **pooled income fund**. [CG §§ 12.2(d), 12.3(d), 13.2(b)].

petition

A "petition" is essentially the same as a **complaint**. Some courts (such as the U.S. Tax Court) use the term "petition" in their procedural rules rather than the term "complaint."

petitioner

A "petitioner" is essentially the same as a **plaintiff**. Some courts (such as the U.S. Tax Court) use the term "petitioner" rather than "plaintiff" in their procedural **rules**.

philanthropy

The term "philanthropy" is often used as a synonym for "**charity**." The term, however, has a broader meaning than the word charity and does not have the precision in **law** that the term charity has. [EO § 1.4; CG § 1.3(a)].

Philanthropy Protection Act of 1995

The "Philanthropy Protection Act of 1995" provides various **exemptions** under the **federal** securities **laws** for **charitable organizations** that maintain **charitable income funds**. [AS § 11.7; CG § 5.9].

physician recruitment program

Tax-exempt hospitals maintain a variety of "physician recruitment programs," some of which may be considered forms of **private inurement** or **private benefit**. [HC Chap. 25].

plaintiff

A "plaintiff" is a **person** who has the authority in **law** to file a **lawsuit** and who exercises this authority. (also **Action**; **Petitioner**; cf. **Defendant**).

planned

The word "planned" connotes a transaction, relationship, or some other scheme that results from a certain amount of theorizing, thinking, structuring, and implementing. It refers to the designing of an arrangement between two or more **persons**. Individuals from a variety of fields may be part of the planning process, such as a **planned gift**, which can entail the services of an **accountant**, **actuary**, **appraiser**, **fundraiser**, **insurance agent**, and/or **lawyer**.

planned gift

A "planned gift" is a **contribution** to a **charitable organization** of money and/or **property**, where one or more **planned giving** techniques are utilized.

planned giving

The term "planned giving" is a broad and loosely used phrase that covers a variety of types of **contributions** made to **charitable organizations**. While literally it applies to any contribution that is made with some "planning" involved, usually the term refers to a contribution of a **donor's interest** in money or an item of **property**, rather than an **outright gift** of the entirety of money or property. (The word "usually" is used because gifts involving **life insurance** do not neatly fit this definition and because some regard an outright gift of property, particularly **capital gain property** that has **appreciated** in **value**, made during lifetime or through an **estate** as a planned gift.) Technically, then, a planned gift is a gift of a **partial interest** in an item of property. The subject of the gift is either an **income interest** or a **remainder interest**. Often, the gift is made by means of a **split-interest trust** because that is the medium by which a property is split into its component interests. These gifts utilize a **charitable lead trust**, a **charitable remainder trust**, or a **pooled income fund**.

Other planned gifts that do not involve a split-interest trust are gifts made by means of a **charitable gift annuity**, gifts of a remainder interest in a **personal residence** or **farm**, and a **contribution** of an **undivided portion of an entire interest** in property. [CG Chaps. 5, 12–17; SM Chap. 19; PF §§ 1.1, 2.4, 14.1(a), 14.5; CU Q 12.60; RE Q 13.4; AS §§ 8.8(e), 9.2(a); LI Q 11.60].

P

planned giving program

A "planned giving program" is a series of activities by a **charitable organization** by which it starts and conducts efforts to acquire and maintain **planned gifts**. The program embraces marketing of planned giving opportunities and the **solicitation** of planned gifts. [SM pp. 244–249].

pledge, charitable

A **person** may promise to make a **contribution** to a **charitable organization** at some future date; this type of pledge is known as a "charitable pledge." The making of a charitable pledge does not give rise to a **federal income tax charitable contribution deduction**. The deduction that is occasioned, such as it may be, is determined as of the time the pledge is satisfied.

Where a charitable pledge is a binding promise, the potential recipient of the contribution is able to bring a **lawsuit** to enforce the pledge. The enforceability of a pledge is a matter of state **law**. Some states require the existence of some element of **consideration** as a prerequisite to the existence of an enforceable pledge (that is, require the arrangement to be a **contractual** one), while other states will allow enforceability of a pledge on broader, social policy grounds. [CG § 4.9; PF §§ 5.8(b), 6.2(b), 6.5(a); CU Q 1.26].

pluralism

The essence of democracy is the existence of three **sectors** of a society: A governmental sector, a **business** (for-profit) sector, and a **nonprofit** sector. The nonprofit sector, particularly the **charitable organizations** within it, offers means by which individuals can advance public policies and resolve societal problems without directly involving the governmental sector (the involvement of which on too great a scale leads to the antithesis of democracy). The array of institutions and organizations that are available for these tasks is said to produce great good for society because of their variety and function; this is termed the "pluralism of institutions" or simply "pluralism." Again, a monolithic or central approach to policymaking and problem solving is seen as contrary to the workings of a democratic state. [EO § 1.4; CG § 1.3(a); SM pp. 3–5; CL § 1.12].

point-of-solicitation disclosure

One of the essential functions of a state **charitable solicitation act** is to promote **disclosure** of information to the public. There is controversy as to the appropriate way to do this, however. Under the concept of "point-of-solicitation disclosure," certain information must be stated in the solicitation materials. Proponents of this approach assert that it is the only effective way to ensure that the public has at least minimal information about a **charitable organization** at the time the decision as to whether to **contribute** is made. Opponents of point-of-solicitation disclosure approach insist that meaningful and balanced information about a charitable organization (particularly financial data) cannot be fairly presented during the solicitation process. [FR § 3.15; HC § 31.1(b)] (cf. **Disclosure-on-demand**).

pole rental

See **Qualified pole rental**.

police organization

One type of **tax-exempt organization** is a "police organization," which is **organized** and **operated** to engage in programs in support of law enforcement officers and their work. In some states, police organizations are defined as **charitable organizations** for purposes of application of a **charitable solicitation act**. [FR § 3.2(a)].

police power

Each state and local **unit of government** inherently possesses the "police power." This power enables a state or other **political subdivision** of government to regulate—within the bounds of **constitutional law** principles—the conduct of its citizens and others, so as to protect the safety, health, and welfare of its people. The federal government legislative branch, having only enumerated powers, does not possess a general policy power.

For example, it is clear that a state can enact and enforce, in exercise of its police power, a **charitable solicitation act**. The rationale is that charitable solicitations may be **reasonably** regulated to protect the public from deceit, **fraud**, or the unscrupulous obtaining of money and/or property under a pretense that the money and/or **property** is being collected and expended for a charitable purpose. Nonetheless, constitutional law principles, such as **freedom of speech**, **procedural** and **substantive due process**, and **equal protection of the laws**, operate to confine the reach of these laws. [CL §§ 4.3(c), 4.7(a)–4.7(c), 7.3; FR §§ 4.2, 8.1(a); CG § 25.3; HC § 31.1(c); AR § 14.1(g); SM p. 153] (also **Parens patriae**).

policies, governance

The recent entry of the **IRS** into the realm of **nonprofit governance** has manifested itself in many ways, one of the most prominent being the causing of **tax-exempt organizations**, particularly **public charities**, to adopt various types of "governance policies." The principal way the **IRS** is accomplishing the adoption of governance policies is by means of the structure of the **Form 990**, which contains many instances where boxes on that **annual information return** are to be checked, indicating whether or not particular policies have been adopted (see **Shaming**). [GV Chap. 6; SM Chap. 22; LI Q 3.27, Q 3.29–Q 3.35, Q 3.45] (see **Code of ethics, Conflict-of-interest policy, Document retention and destruction policy, Executive compensation policy, Expense reimbursement policy, Fundraising policy, Investment policy, Joint venture policy, Travel policy, Whistleblower policy**).

policies, other

The federal tax law sometimes dictates the development of policies by **tax-exempt organizations**, in addition to **governance policies**. (see **Billing and collection policy, Emergency medical care policy, Financial assistance policy**).

political action committee

A "political action committee" is a type of **political organization**. The purpose of a political action committee generally is to raise money and spend it for the purpose of electing an individual to a **public office**. [EO §§ 17.1(a), 17.8; CU Q 9.17, Q 9.18, Q 9.23; SM pp. 201, 202] (also **Separate segregated fund**).

political activities disallowance rule

The "political activities disallowance rule" operates to deny a **business expense deduction** for any amount paid or incurred in connection with **participation** or **intervention** in any **political campaign** on behalf of or in opposition to any **candidate** for **public office** (IRC § 162(e)(1)(B)). [EO § 23.7].

political activity

The law of **tax-exempt organizations** uses the term "political activity" in different ways. It is a broader concept than **political campaign activity**. Political activity essentially includes the function of influencing or attempting to influence the selection, nomination, election, or appointment of any individual to any **federal**, state, or local **public office** (IRC § 527(e)(2)). This is the definition used to describe the **exempt functions** of **political organizations**. **Tax-exempt charitable organizations** and exempt **health insurance issuers** are prohibited from engaging in any political activity that constitutes political campaign activity (IRC §§ 501(c)(3), 501(c)(29)(B)(iv)). Special prohibitions in this regard are applicable to **private foundations** (IRC § 4945). Where a **tax-exempt organization** engages in a political activity, it may become subject to the **political activities tax**. [EO §§ 12.4(e), 17.1(a), 17.6, 19.18, 23.2; HC § 7.4; AU §§ 1.7, 4.4; CU Q 9.2; PG p. 123; SM pp. 201–202; LI Q 8.2] (also **Action organization; Electioneering; Political expenditures**).

political activity tax

If a **tax-exempt organization** expends an amount during a **tax year**, either **directly** or through another organization, for a **political activity**, it must include in its **gross income** for the year an amount equal to the lesser of its **net investment income** for the year or the aggregate amount expended during the year for political activities (IRC § 527(f)(1)). Generally, this amount is taxed at the highest corporate rate (IRC § 527(b)). [EO § 17.6].

political campaign

A **tax-exempt charitable organization** or exempt **health insurance issuer** is precluded by the **federal tax law** from **participating** in or **intervening** in (including the publishing or distributing of statements) any "political campaign" on behalf of or in opposition to any **candidate** for **public office** (IRC §§ 501(c)(3), 501(c)(29)(B)(iv)). The federal tax law does not define the term "political campaign." One court has written that a campaign for public office in a public election means running for office, or a candidacy for office, as that word is used in "common parlance and as it is understood by the man in the street." [EO § 23.2(e); SM p. 198].

political campaign activity

The phrase "political campaign activity" means one of a range of activities that are embraced by prohibition on **political activities** applicable to **tax-exempt charitable organizations** and exempt **health insurance issuers** (IRC §§ 501(c)(3), 501(c)(29)(B)(iv)). Thus, any activity by a charitable organization or health insurance issuer that is reflected in a **political expenditure** is a political **campaign** activity. Political campaign activities include financing of a campaign for, and an endorsement of or form of opposition to, a candidate for public office. The phrase is also used as part of the **political activities disallowance rule**. [EO § 23.2(e); FR §§ 4.3(e), 5.25; HC § 7.4; AR §§ 3.1(c), 3.2(c), 3.2(e), 10.1(c), 10.1(d), 10.2(b), 10.2(c); AS §§ 4.3, 4.5; PF § 9.2; RE Q 20.10–Q 20.13, Q 20.16–Q 20.20; CU Q 9.1; PG pp. 118–122, 341–342; SM pp. 27, 197–203; LI Q 8.1].

political campaign committee

A "political campaign committee" is an **entity** that is established and operated for the purpose of raising money and spending it on an election for the benefit of a **candidate** for office. [EO § 23.2(b)(ii); FR § 5.25(l); SM pp. 201–202].

political candidate

A "political candidate" is an individual who is a **candidate** for a **public office** and who is engaged in a **political campaign**. [EO § 23.2(d); SM pp. 197–198].

political expenditure

The term "political expenditure" generally means, in connection with the taxes on these types of expenditures by **charitable organizations**, an amount paid or incurred by a charitable organization in a participation in, or intervention in (including the publication or distribution of statements), any **political campaign** on behalf of (or in opposition to) a **candidate** for **public office**. In the case of an organization that is formed primarily for purposes of promoting the candidacy (or prospective candidacy) of an individual for public office(or which is effectively controlled by a candidate or prospective candidate and which is availed of primarily for such purposes), the term includes amounts paid or incurred to the individual for speeches or other services; travel expenses of the individual; expenses of conducting polls, surveys, or other studies, or preparing papers or other materials, for use by the individual; expenses of **advertising**, publicity, and **fundraising** for the individual; and any other expense that has the primary effect of promoting public recognition, or otherwise primarily accruing to the benefit of, the individual (**IRC** § 4955(d)). [EO §§ 23.2(b), 23.3, 23.4; HC § 7.4(f); FR § 5.25; CU Q 9.13; SM pp. 199–201].

political expenditure, tax on

The federal tax law imposes **excise taxes** on **political expenditures** by **charitable organizations** (**IRC** § 4955). An **initial tax** is imposed on a political expenditure, equal to 10 percent of the amount of the expenditure; this tax must be paid by the organization. An initial tax, equal to 2 1/2 percent of the amount of the expenditure, is also imposed on the agreement of an **organization manager** to the making of an expenditure, **knowing** that it is a political expenditure, unless the agreement is not **willful** and is due to **reasonable cause**; this tax must be paid by an organization manager who agreed to the making of the expenditure.

In a case in which this initial tax on an organization is imposed and the political expenditure is not **corrected** within the **taxable period**, an **additional tax** is imposed, equal to 100 percent of the amount of the expenditure; this tax must be paid by the organization. In a case in which this additional tax is imposed, if an organization manager refused to agree to part or all of the correction, another additional tax equal to 50 percent of the amount of the political expenditure is imposed; this tax must be paid by an organization manager who refused to agree to part or all of the correction.

If more than one person is liable for either or both of the taxes on management, with respect to a political expenditure, there is **joint and several liability**. With respect to any one political expenditure, the maximum amount of the initial tax on management may not exceed $5,000 and the maximum amount of the additional tax on management may not exceed $10,000.

If this tax is imposed with respect to a political expenditure, the expenditure cannot be treated as a **taxable expenditure** or a payment in connection with an **excess benefit** (IRC §§ 4955(a)–(c), (e)). [EO § 23.3; AR §§ 10.1(c), 10.1(d), 10.2(b), 10.2(e); CU Q 9.12, Q 9.19; SM pp. 199–201].

political organization

A "political organization" is a type of **tax-exempt organization**. A political organization is a party, **committee**, **association**, **fund**, or other **organization** (whether or not incorporated) **organized** and **operated primarily** for the purpose of **directly** or **indirectly** accepting **contributions** or making **expenditures** for an **exempt function** (IRC § 527(e)(1)). In this setting, an "exempt function" is the activity of influencing or **attempting to influence** the selection, nomination, election, or appointment of any individual to any federal, state, or local **public office** or office in a political organization, or the election of presidential or vice-presidential electors, whether or not these individuals or electors are selected, nominated, elected, or appointed (**IRC** § 527(e)(2)). A political organization is subject to the highest rate of corporate tax on its **political organization taxable income** (IRC § 527(b)). [EO § 17.1(a); SM pp. 45–46; AS § 4.7(a); CL § 5.4; CG § 8.2(g); PF § 1.6; AR §§ 10.1(c), 10.2(a); AU § 7.1(bb); CU Q 9.16; PG pp. 123–124; LI Q 8.16] (also **Newsletter fund**; **Principal campaign committee**).

political organization taxable income

The term "political organization taxable income" means the **gross income** of a **political organization** reduced by its **exempt function revenue** and allowable **deductions** that are **directly connected** with the production of its gross income (other than exempt function income (**IRC** § 527(c)). [EO § 17.5].

political subdivision

A "political subdivision" is used in connection with the **exclusion** for **gross income** generated in the exercise of an **essential governmental function** where the income **accrues** to a state or a political subdivision of a state (**IRC** § 115). A political subdivision, a court has held, denotes any component of a state made by the proper authorities, acting within their **constitutional** powers, for the purpose of carrying out a portion of the functions of a state that by long usage and the inherent necessities of government has always been considered public functions. A narrower definition of the term connotes a jurisdictional or geographical component of a state, such as a county, city, township, town, school district, or sewer district. A "political subdivision" is, in the broadest of senses, a **tax-exempt organization**, either by reason of this exclusion of gross income or the doctrine of **intergovernmental immunity**. [EO § 7.14; SM p. 47].

pooled income fund

A "pooled income fund" is a **trust** to which **charitable contributions** are made, from two or more sources, and **mingled** and invested. The fund is a type of **split-interest trust** that must be **maintained** by the **charitable organization** (which must be one of certain types of **public charities**) **to** or **for the use** of which the **remainder interests** are contributed. A **donor** receives a **charitable contribution deduction** for the **value** of the remainder interest created by a **gift** to the pooled income fund and the holders of the **income interests** created by the gifts receive the **investment income** earned by the fund. The income is **allocated** to the **income interest beneficiaries** on the basis of **units of participation** in the fund (**IRC** § 642(c)(5)). [CG § 5.5, Chap. 13; EO §§ 19.23, 29.3, 31.7; PF § 14.5; CU Q 12.66; RE Q 13.9; AS §§ 7.7, 8.3, 9.2(c); SM pp. 236–237; LI Q 11.66].

poor, assistance to

Under the **federal tax law**, a **nonprofit organization** can qualify for **tax exemption** as a **charitable organization** if it engages in **programs** designed to relieve the poor and distressed or the underprivileged. [EO § 7.1; SM p. 33] (also **Poverty, relief of**).

position of authority

In connection with the definition of the word **control**, as used in the **exception** to the definition of the term **qualifying distribution**, reference is made to circumstances whereby one or more **disqualified persons** with respect to a **private foundation** are "aggregating their votes or positions of authority." This latter phrase embraces situations where a disqualified person has control or influence over an individual who is not a disqualified person (such as by reason of being an **employee** of or **consultant** to a disqualified person), causing that individual, when a **director** or **officer** of an **organization**, to be taken into account in determining the presence of a foundation's control over that organization. Individuals in this position are regarded as de facto disqualified persons. [PF § 6.5(b)].

post

A "post" is a local **organization**, a component of a larger (usually state, regional, and/or **federal**) organization. The word is frequently used to describe local veterans' groups and similar **entities**. Some state **charitable solicitation acts exempt** veterans', **fraternal**, and other posts from some or all of an act's requirements. [EO §§ 19.4(a), 19.4(b), 19.11(a); FR § 3.5(l)] (also **Branch**; **Chapter, Lodge**).

pour-over provision

A "pour-over provision" is a provision in a **will** directing that a sum of money and/or one or more items of **property** are to be distributed to a particular **trust**. This type of provision is one way to fund a trust, including a **charitable trust**. Some **private foundations** originated as this type of trust. (also **Pour-over trust**).

pour-over trust

A "pour-over trust" is a **trust** that was or will be funded by reason of a **pour-over provision** in a **will**.

poverty, relief of

Under the **federal tax law**, a type of **tax-exempt organization** is a **charitable organization**. One of the ways an organization can qualify as a charitable organization is to engage in activities that provide relief to the poor and distressed or the underprivileged. This is the most basic and historically founded form of charitable activity. [EO § 7.1; CG § 3.2(b); HC § 1.7; SM p. 33].

power

A "power" is the **right** conferred by one **person** to another to enable the second of the **parties** to act in some capacity (or the benefit of) the other party. The relationship is memorialized in an **instrument** (itself called a "power"), and the acts represented by the scope of the power are legally binding on the **grantor** of the power. Examples of a power of this nature include **power of administration**, **power of appointment**, and **power of attorney**.

power of administration

For purposes of the **grantor trust** rules, the term "power of administration" means any one or more of the following **powers**: (1) a power to vote or direct the voting of stock or other securities of a **corporation** in which the holdings of the grantor and the trust are significant from the viewpoint of voting control, (2) a power to control the investment of the trust funds either by directing investment or reinvestments, or by vetoing proposed investments or reinvestments, to the extent that the trust funds consist of stocks or other securities of corporations in which the holdings of the grantor and the trust are significant from the viewpoint of voting control, or (3) a power to reacquire the trust corpus by substituting other **property** of an equivalent value (**IRC § 675(4)**). [CG § 3.8].

P

power of appointment

A "power of appointment" is a range of authority conferred, in writing, by one individual (the "**grantor**" or sometimes "**donor**") to another to act on behalf of the grantor with respect to his or her **income** and/or **assets**, including appointment of the **beneficiaries** of the grantor's **property** or **interest** in property. Generally, the exercise, release, or lapse of a **general power of appointment** is considered to be a transfer that is subject to the **federal gift tax** (IRC § 2514). The **gross estate** of an individual includes the **value** of **property** over which the **decedent** had a general power of appointment at the time of death. [CG § 8.3(a)].

power of attorney

A "power of attorney" is an authorization from one individual to another enabling the recipient of the **power** to act as the **agent** of the individual granting the power. The holder of a power of attorney is known as an "attorney-in-fact." The **IRS** has developed a power of attorney form (**Form 2848**) for use in the **federal tax law** context. [EO § 26.1(e); AU § 3.4] (also **Attorney**).

power to terminate

A **grantor** of a **charitable remainder trust** may retain the **power**, exercisable only by **will**, to revoke or terminate the **interest** of an **income interest beneficiary** (other than a **charitable organization**). This is done to avoid the possibility of **federal gift taxation**. [CG §§ 12.2(e), 12.3(e)].

practice

The word "practice" has various meanings, the principal one being to engage in repetitive efforts in preparation for an event or occasion. In the **law**, however, the term can mean to engage in a particular function in a business or profession, as in **lawyers** practice law. The practice of law is regulated by courts, bar associations, and government agencies. A government agency, however, can only regulate those who practice before it. This, in turn, involves the scope of an agency's **statutory** authority (**jurisdiction**). For example, the **IRS** has the authority to regulate lawyers, and other representatives of taxpayers, who practice before it. For that regulation to be valid (enforceable), however, the **IRS**'s authority is limited to regulating "practice." Courts have held that preparers of tax returns and representatives preparing and filing refund claims before commencement of any adversarial proceedings with the **IRS** or any other formal representation before the agency cannot be regulated by the **IRS** because they are not "practicing" before the **IRS**. Lawyers and other professional representatives working on behalf of **tax-exempt organizations** often practice before the **IRS**.

Preamble to Statute of Charitable Uses

The "Preamble to the Statute of Charitable Uses," written in England in 1601, contains references to a variety of **charitable** purposes, which are reflected in contemporaneous **federal tax law**. These purposes include relief of the poor and aged; maintenance of the sick; operation of schools of learning; repair of bridges, ports, havens, causeways, churches, seabanks, and highways (today, collectively known as **public works**); **education** of **orphans**; redemption of prisoners; and help for "persons decayed." [EO § 1.4; CG § 1.3(a)].

preapproval, concept of

A fundamental requirement of nearly every state **charitable solicitation act** mandates a **charitable organization** (unless **exempt** from the obligation) that intends to solicit, by any means, **contributions** from **persons** in the state to first apply for and secure permission to undertake the solicitation. This permission, which must be obtained by both **domestic organizations** and **foreign organizations**, is usually characterized as a **registration**; other such terms are "license," "permit," and "certificate." If the applicant is successful, it is authorized to conduct the solicitation; however, this preapproval may not be **unreasonably** withheld. [FR §§ 3.3, 8.7(c); SM p. 148].

preaudit precautions

The term "preaudit precautions" refers to the steps that a **tax-exempt organization** should take to maximally enhance its "public face" in advance of any **IRS examination** that may reduce the chances of, or shorten the period of, an **audit**. These precautions (informally known as "hardening the target") include review of **governing instruments**, operations, books and records, publications, correspondence, **minutes**, federal **returns**, contracts, and website(s). [AU § 3.1].

precatory provision

A "precatory provision" is a series of words in a document (usually a **will**) that constitute a recommendation on the part of the author of the words, as opposed to a direction or a mandate.

precedent

The word "precedent" is used to describe a holding in a court opinion that constitutes (or is interpreted to constitute) **authority** binding one or more courts in subsequent cases. For example, it is on the basis of precedential authority that the **common law** developed. The **federal tax law** provides that, in general, a **written determination** may not be used or cited as precedent (**IRC** § 6110(j)(3)). [CL § 1.2(d)] (also **Dictum**).

preemption

One body of **law** may "preempt" another; this means that the preempting law takes precedence over and **voids** the preempted law. For example, a **federal** law may preempt a state law (such as in the **interstate** regulation of **political campaigns**); most commonly, however, these bodies of law coexist (such as in the regulation of securities transactions). As an illustration, in some states, the **charitable solicitation act** provides that county or municipal **units of government** may adopt other and/or more stringent requirements regarding charitable solicitations and, expressly or implicitly, provide that these requirements will not be preempted by the state law. There is discussion, from time to time, about enactment of a federal charitable solicitations **statute** that would preempt the state laws in instances of interstate solicitations of **charitable contributions**. [FR § 6.3(g)].

preliminary injunction

The purpose of a "preliminary injunction" is to provide **injunctive** relief on a preliminary basis to a **party** to a **lawsuit** until the court has the opportunity to more thoroughly evaluate the merits of the case. (also **Temporary restraining order**; cf. **Permanent injunction**).

premium

A **fundraising practice** is to provide prospective **donors** with items as an inducement for the making of **charitable contributions**; these items are termed "premiums." Premiums include greeting cards, calendars, key chains, and pens. The word "premium" is also used to define payments made to secure and maintain a policy of **insurance**. [FR § 2.2(a); CG § 3.1(d); EO § 25.2(j); UB § 4.9] (also **Low-cost article**).

prepaid health care plan

A "prepaid health care plan" is a plan that provides **health care services** at the community level. One of these is the "fee-for-service" plan, which provides the administrative function of arranging for the provision of medical services by health care providers to patients constituting a "group" who subscribe for the services by prepaying **premiums** to the plan. Another is the "foundation for medical care," which is founded and controlled by physicians and provides medical care through **contracts** with physicians and other providers. Another of these health care delivery forms is the "prepaid group practice plan," also known as the **health maintenance organization**. These and like entities were once **tax-exempt organizations**, either as **charitable organizations** or **social welfare organizations**; however, this category of tax exemption generally was repealed when the rules concerning **commercial-type insurance** were enacted. [HC §§ 9.2, 13.1; EO § 7.6(f)].

prepaid tuition plan

The phrase "prepaid tuition plan" (or qualified tuition program) refers to **entities that** are **tax-exempt organizations** pursuant to the **federal tax law** (**IRC** § 529). These programs are established and maintained by a state agency or **exempt colleges** and **universities**, under which individuals may (1) purchase tuition **credits** or certificates on behalf of a designated **beneficiary** that entitle the beneficiary to the waiver or payment of certain higher education expenses of the beneficiary or (2) make contributions to an account that is established for the sole purpose of meeting these higher education expenses. [EO § 19.19; SM p. 46; LI Q 1.50].

preparatory time

The term "preparatory time" is used in connection with the requirement, that is part of the **unrelated trade or business** rules, that the **business**, to be taxable, must be **regularly carried on**. It is the position of the **IRS** that, in measuring the length of time an activity is conducted, the time the **tax-exempt organization** expended in preparing for the event must be taken into account in assessing whether or not the activity was regularly carried on. This position, however, has been rejected by an **appellate court**. This rule is of no moment if the preparatory time activities are **related**. [EO § 24.3(d); UB § 2.5(d); FR § 5.7(b)(ii); SM p. 173].

preparer tax identification number

Tax return preparers, such as **lawyers** and **accountants**, must have a "preparer tax identification number (**IRC** § 6109). The concept of a tax form in this context includes **applications for recognition of exemption** and **annual information returns**. [EO § 28.3(z); HC § 35.4(b)(xxvi)].

present interest

A "present interest" is an **interest** in an item of **property** that entitles the owner of the interest to immediate possession of the property. (cf. **Future interest**).

presently ascertainable

It is required, under the **federal estate tax law**, that the **value** of an **interest** passing to a **charitable organization** from an **estate** be "ascertainable" as of the death of the **decedent** for the estate tax **charitable contribution deduction** to be available. This means that the charitable interest must be severable from the noncharitable interest(s). This rule is often at issue where there is

vague language in the **will** and/or a **substantial** amount of discretion is vested in the **trustee** or **personal representative** of the estate. The U.S. Supreme Court has held that the standard must be "fixed in fact and capable of being stated in definite terms of money." Where the personal representative has unfettered discretion to divert an amount stated for a charitable organization to noncharitable **beneficiaries**, the charitable interest is not "presently ascertainable" and the charitable deduction will be defeated. Courts have held that this deduction will be defeated where the discretion is "sole and complete," or where the standard is based on the "well-being" or happiness" of an individual. By contrast, ascertainability has been found where language such as "comfort" or "unusual circumstances" is used. [CG § 8.7].

present value

The term "present value" is used in the context of the **charitable gift annuity**. The amount is generally equal to the cost of a similar **commercial annuity**. [CG § 14.10].

preservation of open space

For purposes of the rules concerning **deductible charitable contributions** for **conservation purposes**, one of the definitions of the term "conservation purposes" is the preservation of open space (including **farm**land and forest land) where the preservation is for the scenic enjoyment of the general public and is pursuant to a clearly delineated **federal**, state, or local government **education** policy and will yield a significant public benefit. [CG § 9.7(c)].

president

Nearly every **nonprofit organization** is required to have a "president." (The principal exception to this rule is a **trust**.) A president usually is the chief executive **officer** of the organization and, subject to the overall guidance and supervision of the **board of directors** or the **board of trustees**, has active direction and control of the affairs of the organization. He or she usually is able to sign, often with another authorized officer, any deeds, **mortgages**, **bonds**, **contracts**, or other **instruments** that the board has authorized to be executed, except in cases where the signing and execution of documents has been expressly delegated by **statute** or the organization's **bylaws** to some other individual. In general, a president of a nonprofit organization performs all duties incident to the office of a president and such other **reasonable** duties as may be prescribed by the **governing board** from time to time. [SM p. 20, PG p. 15].

presumption

A "presumption" is an inference drawn from a set of facts that leads to a conclusion as to another set of facts or as to a conclusion of **law**; the word is somewhat synonymous with "assumption." For example, the **federal tax law** presumes that a **charitable organization** is a **private foundation** (IRC § 508(b)). Some presumptions can be overcome by the proof of other facts, as a "**rebuttal**" (the presumption as to private foundation status being an example of a rebuttable presumption, as is a rebuttable presumption in the **intermediate sanctions** rules). Several of the states' **charitable solicitation acts** once contained a presumption (usually rebuttable) that a **fundraising cost** in excess of a certain percentage of total costs or total **contributions** was **excessive** and **unreasonable**, thereby precluding the organization from soliciting contributions in those states; however, this use of a presumption was struck down by the courts as being **unconstitutional** as a violation of the charitable organizations' **free speech** rights. [PF §§ 1.1, 2.6, 15.14; EO §§ 12.1(a), 21.9; FR § 4.3(a); CL § 7.4(a)].

presumption of reasonableness, rebuttable
See **Rebuttable presumption of reasonableness**.

pretax net income, corporations'
The **deduction** by a **corporation** subject to **federal income taxation** in a **tax year** for **charitable contributions** is limited to 10 percent of its "pretax net income" for the year (**IRC** § 170(b)(2)). [CG § 7.4(a); SM p. 135].

prevention of cruelty
An organization can qualify as a **tax-exempt organization** under the **federal tax law** by constituting a **charitable organization**. A way to qualify as a charitable organization is to engage in activities that prevent cruelty to children or animals (**IRC** § 501(c)(3)). [EO § 11.1; SM p. 33].

primary
The word "primary" essentially is synonymous with words such as **principal**, significant, **substantial**, or great importance. In general, an **organization** that is a **tax-exempt organization** must engage in activities that are the basis for its tax exemption as a primary portion of its total activities. This is known as the "primary purpose rule." For the most part, this rule is the **law** even where the **statute** involved uses the term "**exclusively**" (such as in **IRC** § 501(c)(3)). This rule thus allows a tax-exempt organization to engage in **nonexempt activities**, other than to a **substantial** extent, such as **unrelated business** activities. [EO §§ 4.4, 24.1; UB § 1.6; AS §§ 1.7, 2.3; AR §§ 1.6(e), 2.1(a); GV § 8.4(a); CU Q 1.35; RE Q 2.22; PG pp. 39–40, 192; SM p. 33; LI Q 1.46, Q 1.47] (also **Word of art**; cf. **Exclusively**).

primary private benefit
"Primary private benefit" is a form of **private benefit**. It is the form of private benefit that is most **directly** provided by an **organization**. For example, in the case of a **school**, the primary recipients of the benefit provided are the students (a form of benefit that would not jeopardize the **tax-exempt status** of the school). [EO § 20.11(a)] (cf. **Secondary private benefit**).

primary purpose rule
See **Primary**.

principal
In the nonprofit **law** setting, the word "principal" usually means the same as **assets** or **corpus**. That is, an **organization's** "principal" is the sum of its **capital**, the total of its **property**, usually **investment assets**. The term is also used to characterize the significance or importance of one or more activities of an **organization** for **tax** purposes; for example, an organization cannot

qualify as an **educational** organization if its "principal" purpose is the dissemination of **propaganda** (**IRC** § 501(c)(3)); likewise, one definition of the term **tax shelter** is that it is a plan or arrangement where the "principal" purpose of it is the avoidance or evasion of tax (**IRC** § 6662(d)(2)(C)(ii)). [EO §§ 8.2, 28.16(a)].

principal campaign committee

A "principal campaign committee" is a **political campaign committee** designated by a **candidate** for a seat in the U.S. Congress pursuant to the **federal election law** (**IRC** § 527(g)). This type of committee is taxed at the graduated corporate **tax rates**, rather than the highest corporate tax rate. [EO § 17.1(b)].

principal combined fund organization

The phrase "principal combined fund organization" is used in the context of the **Combined Federal Campaign**. As part of this effort, a Local Federal Coordinating Committee is responsible for organizing the local campaign, deciding on the eligibility of local voluntary **organizations**, and supervising the activities of the principal combined fund organization. This organization is the **federated group** or a combination of groups, or a voluntary agency selected by the coordinating committee to administer the local campaign under the direction of the committee and the Combined Federal Campaign. The coordinating committee selects a principal combined fund organization to administer the campaign and to serve as **fiscal agent**.

principal officer

For purposes of the heading on page 1 of the **Form 990**, the term "principal officer" is defined by the **IRS** to mean an **officer** of the reporting **organization** who, irrespective of title, has ultimate responsibility for implementing the decisions of the **entity's governing body** or for supervising the management, administration, or operation of the organization. [AR § 1.4].

prior month election rule

In the context of valuation of **income interests** resulting from **charitable gifts**, the federal midterm interest rate (**IRC** § 7520) usually used is the rate in effect in the month in which the gift is made. One can, however, **elect** to have the present **value** of the interest computed by use of the federal rate for either of the two months preceding the month in which the transfer is made (or, more technically, in which the **valuation date** falls); this is the "prior month election rule." [CG § 11.1].

Priority Guidance Plan

Toward the close of each calendar year, the **Department of the Treasury** and the **IRS** publish a compilation of their regulatory projects that are being currently developed or that are being planned, such as **regulations**, **revenue rulings**, and **revenue procedures**. These documents, known as "Priority Guidance Plans," are usually updated on a quarterly basis. A typical Priority Guidance Plan will include references to forms of guidance in connection with the law of **tax-exempt organizations** and **deductible charitable giving**.

private

The word "private" has many (and sometimes conflicting) meanings. One common meaning is "non-public," in the sense that a private **organization** (**nonprofit** or **for-profit**) is distinguished from a government **entity**. Another meaning is that, whereas a "public" organization is accessible by the **public**, a "private" organization is accessible only by specific selection. Thus, as to these two definitions, a "public **school**" is a governmentally **operated** school that is open to students from the public (within defined jurisdictions), whereas a "private school" is a nonprofit (or, in some instances. a for-profit) entity that is able to select its student body.

In the **federal tax law**, however, a "private **charitable organization**" is different from a "public charitable organization." This distinction is based on the organization's **funding** and function. A private **charity** is essentially a **private foundation**. The term "**public charity**" embraces a range of **institutions**, **publicly supported**, and other charitable organizations. Under this approach, a private school is a public charity.

Generally, a **tax-exempt organization**, particularly a **charitable** one, is expected to function in the "public" interest and not for "private" interests. To achieve this objective, however, a **beneficiary** of a charitable organization may receive money and/or **property** in a private capacity, while nonetheless furthering public ends, because the beneficiary is perceived as an instrument by which public objectives are being furthered. An illustration is the **public interest law firm**. [EO Chap. 20, §§ 6.3(b), 8.3(a)(i), 12.1(a), 12.3; PF Chap. 15, § 1.2; CU Q 2.15; AU § 7.1(d); SM Chap. 7] (also **Private benefit**; **Private inurement**).

private action

A "private action" is a **lawsuit** brought by one or more **persons** (none of whom are governments) against one or more other persons (who may be or include governments). The term is used to indicate that a **plaintiff** in an **action** can be a person other than a **governmental unit**. The ability of a nongovernmental person to bring a lawsuit of this nature is referred to as a "right of private action." For example, some state **charitable solicitation acts** authorize private actions. [FR § 3.21].

private benefit doctrine

An **organization** cannot qualify as a **tax-exempt charitable organization** under the **federal tax law** if it violates the "private benefit doctrine." This doctrine, a derivative of the **operational test**, is separate from the **private inurement doctrine**; however, it is also broader than and subsumes that doctrine (**IRC** § 501(c)(3)). The private benefit doctrine states that tax exemption on this basis is not available if the organization operates to benefit private interests to more than an **insubstantial** extent. This prohibition is not limited to situations in which the benefits accrue to an organization's **insiders** with respect to it (as is the case with the private inurement doctrine). The **IRS** occasionally applies this doctrine with respect to other categories of exempt organizations. [EO § 20.11; UB §§ 1.10, 8.14; HC §§ 4.6, 4.7, 25.4; PF §§ 5.2, 18.9(g); AR §§ 6.1(c), 19.1(g)(6), 21.1(e), 21.1(f); FR §§ 5.7(b)(iii), 5.13, 5.15(b)(iii); GV §§ 1.6(b), 5.21(g), 8.4(e); RE Q 7.2, Q 21.38; Q 21.39, Q 21.50–Q 21.54; CU Q 6.4; AS § 3.6(a); PG pp. 61, 70–71, 332–333; SM pp. 56–58; LI Q 4.5] (also **Primary private benefit**; **Secondary private benefit**).

private capacity

The term "private capacity" is used to describe circumstances in which a **person** is acting for private (personal) gain or in which money and/or **property** is accruing to a person for private use. A person functioning as an **agent**, **personal representative**, **trustee**, and the like can have **rights** and **powers** with respect to money or property, and yet not be utilizing those resources in a private capacity.

private educational institution

See **Private**.

private foundation

A "private foundation" is a type of **tax-exempt charitable organization**. It is "defined" in the **federal tax law** by means of a definition of what a private foundation is not; in essence, a private foundation is a charitable organization that is not a **public charity** (**IRC** § 509(a)). The federal tax law **presumes** that a charitable organization is a private foundation; the burden of **rebutting** that presumption (if it can) is on the charitable organization (**IRC** § 508(b)).

A private foundation generally has the following characteristics: (1) it is, as noted, a charitable **entity**, (2) it is **funded**, often in a single transaction (such as a **major gift** or **bequest** from an **estate**), from one source (such as an individual, family, or **corporation**), (3) its operating funds are in the form of **investment income** derived from investment of its **assets** (**principal** or **corpus**), rather than an ongoing flow of **contributions**, and (4) it makes **grants** to other charitable organizations in furtherance of charitable purposes, rather than fund and conduct its own **program**. (In this sense, a private foundation is very much like an **endowment fund**.) There is a form of private foundation that has the first three of these characteristics but operates its own program; this is the **private operating foundation**. The "private" aspect of a private foundation, then, principally concerns the nature of its financial support, rather than the nature of its governance.

A private foundation is subject to a battery of regulatory **rules** with which other charitable organizations need not comply: these are the **private foundation rules**. [PF §§ 1.2, 1.3, 15.2; EO § 12.1(a); CG §§ 3.4(c), 5.7(f), 12.10, 13.6, 16.7; AR § 8.1(a); AU §§ 5.33(g), 7.2; CU Q 4.2, Q 6.2; AS § 8.1; UB § 6.3; PG p. 84; SM pp. 79–80; LI Q 10.3] (also **Conduit foundation**; **Exempt operating foundation**; **Private operating foundation**).

private foundation rules

A **private foundation** is subject to a wide range of complex and restrictive regulatory **rules** with which other **charitable organizations** need not comply. These rules in effect prohibit **self-dealing**, **excess business holdings**, and **jeopardizing investments**; mandate annual **distributions** for charitable purposes (technically, **qualifying distributions** equal to the private foundation's **minimum investment return**) and a set of requirements and prohibitions concerning **program expenditures** (often termed **taxable expenditures**): and levy a **tax** on **net investment income**. Collectively, these are the "private foundation rules." [PF Chaps. 5–10; EO § 12.4; SM pp. 88–91].

private foundation status

A **charitable organization** that has been classified by the **IRS** as a **private foundation** is said to have "private foundation status." Under certain circumstances, a private foundation can **terminate** its private foundation status; this process can entail conversion to status as a form of **public charity**. [PF Chap. 13; EO § 12.5].

private gain

Most categories of **tax-exempt organizations** may not be operated for "private gain." This is a restatement of the **private inurement doctrine**, the **private benefit doctrine**, and/or the rules prohibiting extensive **commercial business activity**, with elements of the **law** concerning **excess benefit transactions** and **self-dealing** added to the alchemy. [EO Chaps. 20, 21, § 4.10; PF Chap. 5; SM Chap. 5].

private inurement

The doctrine of "private inurement" is the rule of **federal tax law** that essentially differentiates **nonprofit organizations** (particularly those that are **tax-exempt**) from **for-profit organizations**. The concept of private inurement is broad and wide-ranging; courts and the **IRS** have expanded on the concept to cause it to apply far beyond its literal meaning. The rules as to private inurement are particularly significant as applied to **charitable organizations**.

The word "**inure**" means to gravitate toward, flow to, or transfer to something, The word "private" is used in this setting to mean "nonpublic" or "**nonexempt**" (or, in the case of charitable organizations, "noncharitable") purposes or activities. Thus, the private inurement doctrine forbids ways of causing the **income** or **assets** of a tax-exempt organization (assuming it is subject to the doctrine) from flowing away from the organization and to one or more persons, that have some significant relationship with the organization (**insiders**), for their private purposes. Forms of private inurement include **unreasonable compensation**, **unreasonable rental arrangements**, **unreasonable borrowing arrangements**, **unreasonable sales arrangements**, and some involvements by tax-exempt organizations in **joint ventures** or **partnerships**.

The private inurement doctrine, as applicable to charitable organizations, is stated as follows: The organization must be **organized** and **operated** so that no part of its **net earnings** inures to the benefit of any person in his, her, or its private capacity (**IRC** § 501(c)(3)). This language also appears in the **federal tax law** definition of **business leagues, chambers of commerce, real estate boards, boards of trade, professional football leagues, social clubs, voluntary employees' beneficiary associations, teachers' retirement funds, cemetery companies**, and **veterans' organizations**. [EO §§ 20.1–20.10; HC §§ 1.2, 4.1, 4.2, 4.8, 22.7, 25.4, 28.1(a), 29.1, 36.4; AR §§ 6.1(a), 19.1(g)(6), 21.1(d); CG § 1.2; FR §§ 5.6(a)(ii), 5.13; PF § 5.1; GV §§ 1.6(a), 8.4(d); RE Q 1.1, Q 7.2, Q 21.35–Q 21.37, Q 21.39; CU Q 6.1; SM pp. 49, 56; CL §§ 1.3, 1.4; AS §§ 2.10(d), 3.1; UB § 1.10; PG pp. 59–61, 65–70, 331–332; LI Q 4.2] (also **Private inurement per se**).

private inurement per se

"Private inurement per se" occurs where the structure of the transaction is inherently deficient; that is, **private inurement** is found in the very nature of the transaction. Thus, it is irrelevant that the benefit conferred on the **insiders** in some way also furthers the **tax-exempt organization's exempt purposes** and/or that the amount involved is **reasonable**. An illustration of this type of private inurement occurred in the situation where a **hospital** became involved in a **joint venture** with members of its medical staff, where the venture was sold, by the hospital, the **gross** or **net revenue stream** derived from operation of a department of the hospital for a defined period of time; it is the view of the **IRS** that this type of transaction is private inurement on a **per se** basis, even if the terms of the sale are reasonable. [EO § 20.6; HC § 4.5].

private letter ruling

A "private letter ruling" is a **private ruling** issued by the **IRS**. A private letter ruling is a written statement issued to a **person** that interprets and applies the **federal tax laws** to the person's specific set of facts. Once issued, a private letter ruling may be revoked or modified for a variety of reasons, unless it is accompanied by a **closing agreement**. These rulings are made public, with the specific identifying features of the **taxpayers** involved redacted (**IRC** § 6110). [EO App. A; AU § 2.10] (also **Determination letter**).

private operating foundation

A "private operating foundation" is a **charitable organization** that is a **private foundation** that devotes most of its earnings and much of its **assets** directly to the conduct of its **charitable purpose** (as opposed to making **grants** to other organizations) (**IRC** § 4942(j)(3)). To qualify as a private operating foundation, the foundation must meet an **income test**. In addition, the organization must satisfy an **assets** test, an **endowment test**, or a **support test**. Generally, a private operating foundation is treated as a **public charity** for purposes of the **charitable contribution deduction** rules. [PF §§ 1.1, 3.1; EO § 12.1(b); CG § 3.4(b); AU § 5.33(h); SM p. 87] (also **Exempt operating foundation**; **Operating foundation**).

private ruling

A "private ruling" is a written determination from a governmental **agency** providing a conclusion of **law** based on a set of facts submitted by the **person** requesting the ruling. These rulings usually are binding only as to the persons specifically named in the ruling. In some instances, a private ruling is made public, albeit with the specific identifying characteristics of the persons involved redacted. (also **Private letter ruling**).

private school
See **Private**.

private shareholder

The term "private shareholder" is used in the context of the **private inurement** proscription, which states that the **net earnings** of a **tax-exempt organization** may not **inure** to a "private shareholder" (e.g., **IRC** § 501(c)(3)). This is anachronistic phraseology (few tax-exempt organizations having shareholders, in any event) that is read today as meaning **insider**.

private use prohibition

A fundamental **federal tax law** rule in the **charitable** context is that a charitable purpose cannot be served where the **property** involved or the **income** therefrom is directed to a "private use." The fact, however, that individuals or **organizations incidentally** or unavoidably derive a benefit from a charitable undertaking does not necessarily undermine the **tax-exempt**, charitable nature of the endeavor. [EO § 6.3(e)].

private voluntary organization

The term "private voluntary organization" is informally used to describe a **charitable organization** that operates internationally. The term is not used in the **federal tax** setting, but is used commonly among these organizations and by government officials in departments such as the Department of State and the U.S. Agency for International Development. [CG § 20.1].

procedural due process

The phrase "procedural due process" refers to the elements of **due process** that must be embodied in the procedures of the **federal** or other government. These elements will vary in accordance with the circumstances, but include adequate **notice** and the right to a **hearing**. These elements may also include a right to have **lawyer** present at the hearing, a right to a reasoned written statement of facts and conclusions of **law**, and a right of appeal. [CL §§ 1.1(b), 7.5; FR § 4.4].

procures

For purposes of the **federal tax law penalty** for aiding and abetting an **understatement** of **tax liability,** the word "procures" includes (1) ordering (or otherwise causing) a **subordinate** to do an act and (2) knowing of, and not attempting to prevent, participation by a subordinate in an act (**IRC** § 6701(c)(1)).

professional football league

A "professional football league" is a **membership organization**, with the members consisting of professional football teams. This type of **entity** is **tax-exempt** (**IRC** §§ 501(a), 501(c)(6)) (the teams are not). [AS §§ 2.3, 2.5(b), 2.7(b), 2.14; EO § 19.20; SM p. 40] (also **Professional sports league**).

professional fundraiser

The term "professional fundraiser" is defined in most of the states' **charitable solicitation acts**. While the term means an individual (or a company of individuals) who acts as a **consultant** to or **employee** of a **charitable organization**, to assist (but not participate with) the organization in the solicitation and receipt of **charitable contributions**, the term has accumulated various meanings. This most common definition of a professional fundraiser is a person who for a **flat fixed fee** under a written agreement plans, conducts, manages, carries on, advises or acts as its consultant, whether **directly** or **indirectly**, in connection with soliciting contributions for or on behalf of a charitable organization but who actually does not solicit contributions as a part of the services. Other terms used in this context include "fundraising counsel," "independent fundraiser," "professional fundraiser consultant," and "professional fundraising counsel." Frequently, the term overlaps or is confused with the term "**professional solicitor**." Also, the grammar varies, with use of the word "fundraiser," "fund raiser," or "fund-raiser."

Most of the state charitable solicitation laws apply to professional fundraisers, imposing accounting, **bonding**, **disclosure**, **recordkeeping**, **registration**, and **reporting** requirements. [FR §§ 4.10, 8.1(c), 8.2(a); HC § 31.1(d); AR §§ 1.6(i), 14.1(d), 14.2(a); CU Q 13.42; SM pp. 27, 29, 149].

professional fundraiser consultant
See **Professional fundraiser**.

professional fundraising counsel
See **Professional fundraiser**.

professional fundraising services
The phrase "professional fundraising services" is defined by the **IRS** to mean services performed for an **organization** requiring the exercise of professional judgment or discretion consisting of planning, management, preparation of materials (such as direct mail **solicitation** packages and applications for **grants** or other assistance), provision of advice and **consulting** regarding the solicitation of **contributions**, and **direct** solicitation of contributions, such as soliciting **restricted** or **unrestricted** grants to provide services to the public. Professional fundraising, however, generally does not include services provides by an organization's **employees** in their capacity as employees nor does it include purely ministerial acts such as printing, mailing services, or receiving and depositing contributions on behalf of a **charitable organization**. [FR §§ 3.6, 8.2].

professional society
A "professional society" (sometimes termed a "professional **association**") is a type of **tax-exempt organization** that has as its **principal** purpose the provision of services to individuals who are **members** of a profession. Examples of these organizations include medical societies, dental societies, and bar associations. Although these organizations may have some programs that are conducted for the benefit of the public, they are usually operated **primarily** to further the common **business** interests of their members, Thus, many professional societies are **tax-exempt** as **business leagues**, although some are tax-exempt as **charitable organizations**. [EO § 14.1(e)].

professional solicitor
The term "professional solicitor" is defined in most of the states' **charitable solicitation acts**. Although basically the term means an individual (or a company of individuals) who acts as a **consultant** to or **employee** of a **charitable organization**, to solicit **charitable contributions** for the organization, the term has accumulated various meanings. This most common definition

of a professional solicitor is that it is any **person** who, for a financial or other **consideration**, solicits contributions for, or on behalf or, a charitable organization, whether the solicitation is performed personally or by means of **agents** or **employees**, or through agents or employees specifically employed by or for a charitable organization, who are engaged in the solicitation of contributions under the direction of the person, or a person who, for a financial or other consideration, plans, conducts, manages, carries on, advises, or acts as a consultant to a charitable organization in connection with the solicitation of contributions but does not qualify as a **professional fundraiser.**

The other definition of a professional solicitor is a person who is employed or retained for compensation by a professional fund-raiser to solicit contributions for charitable purposes.

Most of the state charitable solicitation laws apply to professional solicitors, imposing accounting, **bonding, disclosure, record-keeping, registration**, and **reporting** requirements. [FR §§ 3.7, 3.17, 4.10, 8.1(c), 8.2(a), 8.3, 8.9; HC § 31.1(d); CU Q 13.44].

professional sports league

A "professional sports league" is a **membership organization**, the membership of which are teams performing in a particular sport as professionals, such as football, baseball, basketball, and golf. Some of these leagues are **tax-exempt** organizations (**IRC** §§ 501(a), 501(c)(6)). [EO § 19.20] (also **Professional football league**).

professional standards review organization

A "professional standards review organization" is a category of **tax-exempt charitable organization** under the **federal tax law**, with its tax exemption predicated on the fact that the organization is engaged in the **promotion of health**. These organizations are qualified groups of physicians that establish mandatory cost and quality controls in connection with medical treatment rendered in **hospitals** and financed under the Medicare and Medicaid programs, and that monitor this care. [HC § 18.3].

profit

An **organization's** "profit" is, essentially, the amount of its **gross income** less its **expenses** of operation; the term is basically synonymous with **net earnings**. The term **nonprofit organization** does not mean that the organization cannot earn a profit; it means that the profit may not be transferred to **persons** in their private capacity. Some **tax-exempt organizations** (such as **social welfare organizations, business leagues**, and **cemetery companies**) are forbidden by the **federal tax law** to earn a profit; this rule is interpreted to mean **substantial commercial business** activity. [EO §§ 1.1(a), 13.1, 14.1(a)(i), 19.6, 20.1; CG § 1.2; SM pp. 5–6].

profit motive

A "profit motive" is the conduct of an activity with an intent to derive **income**, after the payment of **expenses**, from it. Some courts are holding, as does the **IRS**, that, for an activity to qualify as a **business**, it must be conducted with a profit motive (sometimes termed a "profit objective"). Thus, under this approach, an activity that is consistently operated at a loss is not likely to be regarded as a business. [EO § 24.2(b); UB §§ 2.4, 6.1(b), 11.4(d)(i); HC § 24.2(b); SM pp. 171–172].

profit objective
See **Profit motive**.

profits interest
For purposes of defining the category of **disqualified person** known as "**20 percent owners**," where the **entity** involved is a **partnership**, the term "profits interest" of a **partner** is that equal to his, her, or its distributive share of **income** of the partnership (**IRC** § 707(b)(3)) (**IRC** § 4946(a)(1)(C)(i)). The term includes any **interest** that is outstanding but not any interest that is obtainable but has not been obtained. [PF § 4.3; EO § 12.2(c)].

program
The word "program" is used to describe a function that is conducted by a **tax-exempt organization** to further its **tax-exempt purpose**. These activities do not include management functions or **fundraising efforts**. (also **Functional accounting**).

program-related investment
A "program-related investment," a term used principally in the **private foundation law** context, is an investment the **primary** purpose of which is to accomplish one or more **charitable purposes** and no significant purpose of which is the production of **income** or the appreciation of **property** (**IRC** § 4944(c)). Also, no purpose of the investment may be the furthering of **substantial legislative** or any **political campaign activities**. [PF §§ 8.1, 8.3, 9.6(c), 11.3(b), 12.2(g); EO § 12.4(d); AR §§ 7.2(c)(13), 11.2(h); HC § 5.10; SM p. 89].

program service accomplishment
A "program service" is an activity of a **tax-exempt organization** that accomplishes its exempt purposes. These program service accomplishments are reported on **Form 990**, Part III. [AR § 2.1(h); PG p. 192].

program service expense
A "program service expense" is a financial outlay made by a **tax-exempt organization** in furtherance of a **program service**. These (and other) expenses are reported on **Form 990**, Part IX. [AR § 7.2(b)].

program service revenue
The phrase "program service revenue" is used to describe **revenue** generated by a **tax-exempt organization** from the conduct of **programs** that are **related** to the achievement of the organization's **tax-exempt purposes**. These items of revenue must be separately identified on a tax-exempt organization's **annual information return** (e.g., **Form 990**, Part VIII). [AR §§ 1.6(h), 7.2(a)(2); EO § 24.4(f); UB § 2.7; HC § 24.5; SM p. 82] (also **Exempt function revenue**).

progressivity

The term "progressivity" is used to describe the feature of a **tax** system where the amount of taxes on a **person** are levied in relation to the **taxpayer's** ability to pay. These taxes are known as "progressive taxes." For example, the **federal income tax** system is a progressive one, in that the **marginal tax rates** (of which there are five) increase as does the taxpayer's **taxable income**. The **estate tax** and the **gift tax** also are progressive taxes. Taxes that are not progressive include consumption taxes such as a gasoline tax, **sales tax**, **use tax**, and a **value-added tax**. [CG § 1.6] (cf. **Regressivity**).

prohibited act

The concept of a "prohibited act" is reflected in many state **charitable solicitation acts**. These acts may be some or all of the following: (1) a **person** may not, for the purpose of soliciting **contributions**, use the name of another person (except that of an **officer**, **director**, or **trustee** of the charitable **organization** by or for which contributions are solicited) without the consent of the other person; (2) a person may not, for the purpose of soliciting contributions, use a name, symbol, or statement so closely related or similar to that used by another charitable organization or governmental agency that it would tend to confuse or mislead the public; (3) a person may not use or exploit the fact of registration with a state so as to lead the public to believe that the registration in any manner constitutes an endorsement or approval by the state; (4) a person may not misrepresent to or mislead anyone, by any manner, means, practice, or device, to believe that the organization on behalf of which the solicitation is being conducted is a charitable organization or that the proceeds of the solicitation will be used for charitable purposes, where that is not the case; and (5) a person may not represent that the solicitation is for or on behalf of a charitable organization or otherwise induce contributions from the public without proper authorization from the charitable organization.

These prohibited acts usually apply to charitable organizations and may apply to **professional fundraisers**, **professional solicitors**, and/or **commercial co-venturers**. [FR § 8.5; HC § 31.1(i)].

prohibited benefit

A tax is imposed on the advice of an individual **donor** (or any person appointed or designated by the donor), who has, or reasonably expects to have, **advisory privileges** with respect to the distribution or investment of amounts held in a **donor-advised fund** funded by the donor, a **member of the family** of the individual, or a **35-percent controlled entity**, to have a **sponsoring organization** make a distribution from the donor-advised fund which results in the person or any of these persons receiving, directly or indirectly, a more than **incidental** benefit as a result of the distribution. This tax, which is equal to 125 percent of the benefit, must be paid by any of these persons who advises as to the distribution or who receives the benefit as a result of the distribution. A tax is also imposed on the agreement of a **fund manager** to the making of a distribution, **knowing** that the distribution would confer a more-than-incidental benefit. This tax, which is equal to 10 percent of the amount of the benefit, must be paid by the fund manager who agreed to the making of the distribution.

Neither of these taxes may be imposed if a tax has been imposed, with respect to a distribution, pursuant to the **intermediate sanctions** rules. If more than one person is liable for one of these taxes, there is **joint and several liability**. With respect to any one distribution, the maximum amount of the tax imposed on fund management may not exceed $10,000 (**IRC** § 4967). [EO § 11.8(b); PF § 16.9].

prohibited material restriction

A **private foundation** may voluntarily **terminate** its **private foundation status** by distributing all of its **net assets** to one or more **public charities** (**IRC** § 507(b)(1)(A)). In so doing, however, the foundation may not impose any **material restrictions** or **conditions** that prevent the transferee public charity from freely and effectively employing the transferred assets, or the **income** therefrom, in furtherance of its **tax-exempt** purposes; this is known as the "prohibited material restriction" rule. [PF § 13.3(a); CG § 3.1(f)].

prohibited reportable transaction

The phrase "prohibited reportable transaction" means any confidential transaction or any transaction with contractual protection (as that term is to be defined in tax regulations) that is a **reportable transaction** (**IRC** § 4965(e)(1)(C)). [EO § 28.17(f)].

prohibited tax shelter transaction

The phrase "prohibited tax shelter transaction" means a **listed transaction** and a **prohibited reportable transaction** (**IRC** § 4965(e)(1)(A)). [EO § 28.17(f); AR §§ 4.1(i), 4.2(d)].

promissory note

A "promissory note" (or "note") is a form of negotiable **instrument** by which the maker of the note agrees to pay an amount of money to another **person** at a stated time. A **tax-exempt organization** may be the holder of a promissory note. The making of a note, promising to pay money and/or transfer **property** to a **charitable organization** and **delivery** of the note to the charitable organization, however, does not give rise to a **federal income tax charitable contribution deduction**. Rather, this deduction arises (such as it may be) when the money and/or property is actually transferred to the charitable **donee** in satisfaction of the requirements of the note. [CG § 6.7; AR §§ 7.2(c)(7), 7.2(c)(23), 7.2(c)(24)].

promotion

The word "promotion" is used in the **federal tax law** as a synonym for the word "advance" (as in **promotion of health** and **promotion of social welfare**). (cf. **Advancement of education**; **Advancement of religion**; **Advancement of science**).

promotion of health

An **organization** may qualify for **tax-exempt status** under the **federal tax law** as a **charitable organization**. One of the ways to **operate** as a charitable organization is to engage in activities that constitute the "promotion of health." These activities include the establishment or maintenance of **hospitals**, clinics, **homes for the aged**, and the like; advancement of medical and similar knowledge through **research**; and the maintenance of conditions conducive to health. [EO § 7.6; HC §§ 1.7, 3.2; SM pp. 34–35].

promotion of social welfare

An **organization** may qualify for **tax-exempt status** under the **federal tax law** as a **charitable organization**. One of the ways to **operate** as a charitable organization is to engage in activities that constitute the "promotion of social welfare." These activities include lessening neighborhood tensions, eliminating prejudice and **discrimination**, defending human and civil **rights** secured by **law**, and combating community deterioration and **juvenile delinquency**. [EO § 7.11; SM p. 35].

promptly and directly made

A **tax-exempt organization** will not become subject to the **political organizations tax** when it receives **contributions** from its **members** for **political activity** and promptly and directly transfers the funds to the political organization that **solicited** them. A transfer is considered "promptly and directly made" if the organization's procedures satisfy requirements of applicable **federal** or state campaign **laws**, the organization maintains adequate records to demonstrate that amounts transferred are, in fact, political contributions, and the contributions were not used to earn **investment income**. [EO § 17.7].

propaganda

"Propaganda" is a set of principles or **doctrines** developed and advanced by a particular movement or **organization**; the spread of propaganda is usually associated with a certain amount of zealotry ("propagandizing"). The term is also associated with the propagation of particular ideas or doctrines without presentation of them in any reasonably objective or balanced manner.

This term arises in two contexts in the **federal tax law**. One concerns the prohibition, applicable to **charitable organizations**, on a **substantial** amount of activities that constitute "carrying on propaganda, or otherwise attempting, to influence **legislation**" (**IRC** § 501(c)(3)). In this setting, the propagandizing that is prohibited is that relating specifically to efforts to influence legislation.

The other context is in connection with the definition of the term **"educational,"** in which propagandizing activities are seen as the antithesis of educational activities. An organization may qualify as an educational one, even though it **advocates** a particular position or viewpoint, as long as it also presents a sufficiently **"full and fair exposition"** of the pertinent facts as to permit an individual or the public to form an independent opinion or conclusion.

Where the **principal** function of an organization is the mere presentation of unsupported opinion, the organization cannot qualify as an educational entity. [EO §§ 8.2, 22.3(b); CU Q 2.3, Q 2.4; SM p. 36; LI Q 9.3, Q 9.4] (also **Methodology test**).

property

The term "property" means anything in which a **person** may have a **right** or **interest**; it usually has an exchangeable **value**. Property held by an owner, in its totality, is expressed as **assets**, **corpus**, **estate**, or **principal**.

Property may be classified as **real property** (real estate) or **personal property** (**personalty**). Personal property is either **tangible property** or **intangible property**. All properties, or interests in or rights to property, may be the subject of a **charitable contribution**. [CG §§ 2.12, 4.2–4.4, 4.5(a); SM pp. 134, 137–138] (also **Appreciated property**).

property subject to debt

The phrase "property subject to debt" means an item of **property** against which there has been a borrowing or which has been pledged as security for a debt. This type of property is subject to a mortgage, lien, or some other form of indebtedness. If the property is purchased with borrowed money, it is **debt-financed property**.

If property subject to debt is the subject of a **charitable contribution**, the transaction may be a **bargain sale**. This type of transaction may cause **recognition** of **income** to the donor. [UB § 5.3; EO § 24.9(a); CG § 9.20].

property tax

A "property tax" is a state or local **tax** that is assessed on the basis of the **value** of the **property** involved. Most states have a tax on **real property**; some have a tax on **personal property** that is **tangible property** and some have a tax on **intangible property**. Depending on the **law** of a jurisdiction, one or more categories of **nonprofit organizations** (particularly **charitable** ones) may be **exempt** from a property tax.

prophylactic provision

A "prophylactic provision" in a document is a set of words specifically intended to prevent one or more **persons** from engaging in a particular form of conduct.

protest

A "protest" is a document that is submitted to a governmental **agency** in objection to a proposed action by the agency; this document is filed by the **person** (or persons) directly affected by the proposed action. For example, a person can file a protest with the **IRS** in opposition to a proposed adverse **ruling** issued following an **IRS** examination. This type of filing usually is required as part of the process of **exhausting administrative remedies**. [EO § 27.5(b)(ii)].

provider-sponsored organization

The term "provider-sponsored organization" is a public or private **entity** that is operated by a health care provider or provider group, which provides a **substantial** portion of the Medicare-covered services **directly** through the provider or group. These providers must have at least a majority financial interest in the PSO and share substantial financial risk. [EO § 7.6(a)(i); HC § 22.10].

proxy

Technically, a "proxy" is an individual who has been accorded the authority to act, usually vote, for another individual. This word, however, is often used to describe the **right** itself (as in the "right to vote by proxy") or the document evidencing the proxy. In most states, **directors** and **trustees** of **charitable organizations** may not vote by proxy, although **members** of the organization are permitted to do so.

proxy tax

The "proxy tax" is applied in the context of the **federal tax law** that denies a **business expense deduction** for efforts made to influence federal or state **legislation** or **participate** in **political campaign activity** (**IRC** § 162(e)(1)). A **flow-through rule** operates to disallow a business expense deduction for the portion of the **membership dues** (or voluntary payments or special assessments) paid to a **tax-exempt organization** that engages in lobbying activities or political campaign activities (**IRC** § 162(e)(3)). The general rule is that the organization (other than a **charitable** organization) (**IRC** § 6033(e)(1)(B)(i)) is required to notify its members, at the time of assessment or payment of the dues, of a reasonable estimate of the portion of the dues that are allocable to lobbying or political activities (**IRC** § 6033(e)(1)(A)(ii)). This notification requirement is not applicable, however, where the organization elects to pay a proxy tax on its lobbying and/or political campaign expenditures for the **tax year** (**IRC** § 6033(e)(2)(A)(i)). This tax is at the highest corporate **rate** of tax (**IRC** § 6033(e)(2)(A)), which is 35 percent (**IRC** § 11).

Also, this tax is applicable where an organization fails to provide its members with the notice as to anticipated lobbying expenditures and/or political campaign expenditures allocable to dues and is applicable to the amount by which the organization's actual lobbying and/or political expenditures for a tax year exceed its estimated allocable amount of the expenditures (**IRC** § 6033(e)(2)(A)(ii)). [AS § 4.5(b); EO §§ 22.6(c), 23.7; AR §§ 9.1(h)(3), 9.2(e); HC § 18.4(d); SM p. 193].

prudent person rule

The "prudent person rule" is a standard of behavior expected of individuals when they serve as **directors, officers**, and/or **trustees** of **nonprofit organizations**, particularly **charitable** ones. The rule is that these individuals are expected to act with the same degree of prudence in administering the affairs of the organization as they would in their personal affairs. Originally devised to apply in the context of investments, this rule now applies to all categories of behavior (**commissions** and **omissions**) undertaken in relation to the organization being served. [PF §§ 1.1, 8.1(a), 8.2; RE Q 2.5; SM p. 216] (also **Fiduciary**; **Jeopardizing investments**; **Liability**; **Negligence**).

P

public

The **federal tax law**, in **statutes**, **tax regulations**, court opinions, and elsewhere, often uses the term "general public." There is a whiff of redundancy in that terminology. (Somewhere, someone wrote that the "general public" are members of the public who are entitled to a salute.) Throughout this dictionary, the word "public" is used, notwithstanding that the term **general public** is utilized in the particular law.

public accountability standards

The phrase "public accountability standards" is used in the **Combined Federal Campaign** context. An **organization** that wishes to participate in this campaign must annually submit to the **Office of Personnel Management** information demonstrating compliance with these standards.

public accountant

A "public accountant" is an accountant who may or may not be licensed by a state. When a public accountant is licensed, there usually are not any examinations to pass or **educational** requirements to meet. For the most part, such an accountant can practice without experience. (also **Certified public accountant**).

public charity

A "public charity" is a **federal tax law** term meaning a **charitable organization** that is not a **private foundation**. There are four general categories of public charities: (1) the **institutional** public charity (such as a **church**, **college**, **hospital**, **medical research organization**, **school**, and **university**), (2) the **publicly supported charitable organization**, (3) the **supporting organization**, and (4) the **public safety testing organization**. With one exception, this term is not used in the **IRC**, but is used informally to mean all charitable organizations other than private foundations; the exception is use of the term "public charities" in the caption to **IRC** Subtitle D, Chapter 41, preceding the rules concerning the **excise taxes** on **excess lobbying expenditures** and on **disqualifying lobbying expenditures**. [EO § 12.3; PF §§ 1.1, 1.2, 15.1, 15.3–15.7; AR § 8.1(b); HC §§ 4.9(a), 8.1; CG §§ 3.4(a), 7.1; FR § 5.11; AU §§ 5.33(g), 7.2; CU Q 4.3, Q 6.1; AS § 8.1; PG pp. 84–86; SM pp. 80–85; LI Q 10.1, Q 10.2].

public entertainment activity

See **Qualified public entertainment activity**.

public events

See **Special events**.

public funds

The term "public funds" (or "public money") means either funds held by a **department**, **agency**, or some other component of government, or funds held by a **tax-exempt organization**, most particularly a **charitable organization**.

public inspection requirement

The **annual information return** of nearly every **tax-exempt organization** must be made available for public inspection on request (**IRC** § 6104(e)(1)). This requirement also applies with respect to applications **for recognition of exemption** (**IRC** § 6104(e)(2)). Some information is not publicly accessible, however, such as a **public charity's** list of **contributors**. There are **penalties** for violation of these requirements. [EO § 28.10; SM pp. 122–125].

public interest law firm

A "public interest law firm" is a form of **charitable organization** that has as its purpose the legal representation of important citizen interests that would otherwise go unrepresented because the cases are not economically feasible for private **law** firms. These organizations are expected to provide services—essentially **litigation**—that are of benefit to the **public**. [EO § 7.15(d); CG § 3.3(b); AU § 7.1(e)].

public office

The term "public office" is used in three contexts in the **federal tax law** applicable to **nonprofit organizations**. It is used in the limitation on **charitable organizations**, by which they are precluded from **participating** or **intervening** in a **political campaign** on behalf of or in opposition to a **candidate** for "public office" (**IRC § 501(c)(3)**). It is also used in the **private foundation rules** concerning **disqualified persons** where use is made of the phrase "elective public office" in defining a **governmental official** (**IRC § 4946(c)(1)(5)**). The third setting in which it is used is in the rules concerning **political organizations**, where the term "public office" is used in the definition of **political organization exempt functions** (**IRC § 527(e)(2)**).

The term "public office" is not defined in the first of these rules. The **federal tax regulations**, however, define the term for purposes of the other two rules by stating that it must be distinguished from mere public employment. The holder of a public office is engaged in activities that include the independent performance of policymaking functions. The definition of a "public office" is essentially the subject of a **facts and circumstances test**; the factors that are considered include the fact that the office is created by Congress, a state **constitution**, a state legislature, or a municipality or other **governmental agency** pursuant to authority conferred by Congress or a state **constitution** or legislature, and the powers conferred on the office and the duties to be discharged by the holder of the office are defined either **directly** or **indirectly** by Congress, a state constitution, or state legislature, or through legislative authority. [EO §§ 17.1(a), 23.2(f); PF § 4.8; AR § 7.2(b)(16); HC § 7.4(e); CU Q 9.10].

public policy doctrine

The "public policy doctrine" is a **federal tax law** rule, established by the U.S. Supreme Court, that an **organization** cannot qualify as a **charitable organization** (and, in some instances, a **social welfare organization**) for **federal tax law** purposes if it engages in activities that are contrary to "public policy"—that is, are contrary to the general good of a **community**. This is the case even if the organization satisfies all of the **statutory** criteria for **tax-exempt** status. Thus, an organization must satisfy the statutory requirements and demonstrably serve and be in harmony with the public interest. The organization's purpose must not be so at odds with the common community conscience as to undermine any public benefit that might otherwise be conferred. [EO § 6.2; CL § 1.8; CG §§ 1.3(a), 3.3(b), 9.31; FR § 1.1; CU Q 3.9; RE Q 8.6; SM pp. 36, 324–326; LI Q 2.5].

public safety testing organization

An **organization** may be **tax-exempt** under the **federal tax law** because it engages in **programs** that entail "testing for public safety" (**IRC § 501(c)(3)**). This term includes the testing of consumer products, such as electrical products, to determine whether they are safe for use by the public. These organizations are **exempted** from classification as **private foundations**

P

(**IRC** § 509(a)(4)). **Contributions**, **bequests**, and **gifts** to public safety testing organizations are not **deductible**. [EO §§ 11.3, 12.3(d); PF §§ 15.2, 15.13; AR § 8.1(i)].

public support

The term "public support" means either **direct public support** and/or **indirect public support**. [PF §§ 15.4–15.6; EO § 12.3(b); HC §§ 5.2–5.4; SM pp. 81–82] (also **Publicly supported charitable organization**).

public support test

Both a **donative publicly supported organization** and a **service provider publicly supported organization** must continually meet a "public support test." Although the mechanics of computing public support differ, the fundamental concept is that they generally must **normally** receive at least one-third of their support from the **public**. [PF §§ 15.4–15.6; EO § 12.3(b); AR §§ 8.1(d)–8.1(g); HC §§ 5.2–5.4; SM pp. 81–82].

public works

One of the ways to engage in **charitable** activity, for **federal tax law purposes**, is to erect or maintain public buildings, monuments, or works. This formulation of a charitable purpose, in connection with what is collectively known as "public works," is intended to provide **communities** with facilities ordinarily provided at **public** expense. It is the position of the **IRS** that the employment of engineers to build software tools that, through free and open source licensing, are dedicated to the public is not an activity amounting to the building of a public work because software is **intangible property** and is not a facility. [EO §§ 1.4, 7.7].

public, instruction of

One of the ways an **organization** can be a **tax-exempt educational organization** under the **federal tax law** is to instruct the public on subjects useful to the individual and beneficial to the **community**. [EO § 8.5; CU Q 2.2; SM p. 36].

publicly supported charitable organization

Under the **federal tax law**, there are two basic categories of **charitable organizations** that are not **private foundations** by reason of the fact that they are "publicly supported organizations." These are the **donative publicly supported organizations** and the **service provider publicly supported organizations**. Both of these types of organizations must receive at least one-third of their total support in the form of "**public support**" (although the manner of calculating public support varies); generally, this calculation is made over a five-year measuring period. This term is also used in the setting of defining an **exempt operating foundation** (IRC § 4940(d)(3)(A)). [PF §§ 15.4–15.6; EO § 12.3(b); CG § 3.4(a); CU Q 4.11–Q 4.14; PG 86–91; SM pp. 81–82; LI Q 10.8] (also **Community foundation**; **Facts and circumstances test**; **Normally**).

publicly traded partnership

A "publicly traded partnership" is a **partnership** where interests in the partnership are traded on an established securities market or are readily tradable on a secondary market (or the

substantial equivalent of a secondary market) (**IRC** § 469(k)(2)). Because of a provision in the **Omnibus Budget Reconciliation Act of 1993**, the **income** received by a **tax-exempt organization** from a publicly traded partnership is treated, for purposes of **unrelated income taxation**, the same as income from any other partnership (**IRC** § 512(c)). [EO §§ 24.7, 31.1(a); UB §§ 8.9(a), 8.11] (also **Look-through rule**).

publics

The term "publics" is used in the realm of **fundraising** to mean segments of the **public**; it is somewhat akin to the term "constituency." (also **Giving, pyramid of**).

punitive damages

"Punitive damages" (also known as "exemplary damages") are a form of **compensation** awarded to a **person** who has been injured by the action of another person. These damages—unlike **actual damages** (also known as "compensatory damages")—are set as punishment of the wrongdoer. Punitive damages are not subject to the **federal income tax**.

purely local character

The phrase "purely local character" is part of the definition of **tax-exempt teachers' retirement fund associations** and **benevolent life insurance associations**. It means confined to a particular **community**, place, or district, irrespective, however, of **political subdivisions**. Thus, the phrase means a single identifiable locality. [EO §§ 18.7, 19.5(a)].

purpose

The word "purpose" is used to describe the objective or objectives for which an **organization** was created and exists. For example, a **tax-exempt organization** must have, as a **primary** or **principal** element of its **operations**, an appropriate "**tax-exempt purpose**." Thus, a **charitable organization** is said to have a charitable purpose. [EO § 4.3(a); AR § 1.6(d); GV § 2.1(a)] (also **Mission**).

P

pyramid of giving

The "pyramid of giving" is a schematic, reflecting the various forms of **charitable contributions** and the various types and motives of **contributors**. The bottom of this pyramid is represented by the **public** and certain segments of the public. Proceeding vertically, the pyramid narrows as the sources of **gifts** are **major contributors** and **private foundations**. The **donors** at the top of the pyramid tend to make **planned gifts** and/or gifts through their **estate**. The pyramid also reflects different **fundraising** techniques. At the bottom of the pyramid are **direct mail programs**, **annual giving campaigns**, and **special events**. In the middle are **capital** and other campaigns. At the top is a **planned giving** and **bequest** program. [FR § 2.3].

Q

qualified amateur sports organization

A "qualified amateur sports organization" is an **organization organized** and **operated exclusively** to foster national or international amateur sports competition if the organization is also organized and operated **primarily** to conduct national or international competition in sports or to support and develop amateur athletes for national or international competition in sports (**IRC** § 501(j)(2)). [EO § 11.2].

qualified appraisal

Certain appraisal requirements apply with respect to **charitable contributions** claimed by an individual, a **closely held corporation**, a personal service corporation, a **partnership**, or a **small business corporation**, where the **gifts** are of various types of **property**. These requirements, which apply where the aggregate **value** of the property (and all **similar items of property**) claimed by the same **donor** in the same **tax year** is in excess of $5,000, must be complied with if the **federal income tax charitable contribution deduction** is to be allowed.

The donor must obtain a "qualified appraisal" of this type of property. This is an appraisal document that (1) relates to an appraisal that is made not earlier than sixty days prior to the date of contribution of the **appraisal property**, (2) is prepared, signed, and dated by a **qualified appraiser** (or appraisers), (3) contains a variety of required information, and (4) does not involve a prohibited type of appraisal fee.

This term is used in connection with the **reasonable cause exception** available In conjunction with **penalties** for the **underpayment** of **taxes**, where **charitable deduction property** is involved (**IRC** § 6664(c)(3)(C)). [CG § 21.5(a); HC §§ 31.2(c), 31.2(d)(i); AR § 19.1(y)(2); SM pp. 139–140] (also **Appraisal; Appraisal summary**).

qualified appraiser

In the context of the **federal income tax charitable contribution substantiation** requirements, a "qualified appraiser" is an individual who includes on the **appraisal summary** a declaration that (1) he or she holds himself or herself out to the public as an **appraiser** or performs appraisals on a regular basis, (2) because of the appraiser's qualifications as described in the appraisal, he or she is qualified to make appraisals of the type of **property** being **valued**, (3)

Bruce R. Hopkins' Nonprofit Law Dictionary, First Edition. Bruce R. Hopkins.
© 2015 Bruce R. Hopkins. Published 2015 by John Wiley & Sons, Inc.

the appraiser is not one of the **persons** excluded by the rules from being a qualified appraiser (such as by being the donor or the **donee**), and (4) the appraiser understands that an intentionally false or **fraudulent overstatement** of the value of the property described in the qualified appraisal or appraisal summary may subject the appraiser to a **civil law penalty** for aiding and abetting an **understatement** of **tax liability**, and consequently the appraiser may have appraisals disregarded.

This term is used in connection with the **reasonable cause exception** available in conjunction with **penalties** for the **underpayment** of **taxes**, where **charitable deduction property** is involved (**IRC** § 6664(c)(3)(B)). [CG § 21.5(b); HC § 31.2(d)(ii); AR § 19.1(y)(3); SM p. 141] (also **Qualified appraisal**).

qualified appreciated stock

In general, **contributions** of **long-term capital gain property** to **public charitable organizations** are **deductible**, with the **federal income tax charitable contribution deduction** computed on the basis of the **fair market value** of the property. Where this type of contribution is made to some other type of **donee**, however, the general rule is that the amount of the deduction must be reduced by the amount of gain that would have been long-term capital gain if the property contributed had been sold by the **donor** at its fair market value as of the date of the contribution. An **exception** to this **deduction reduction rule** is that it does not apply in the case of a contribution of "qualified appreciated stock."

Basically, qualified appreciated stock is any stock for which (as of the contribution date) market quotations are readily available on an established securities market and that is capital gain property (**IRC** § 170(e)(5)(B)). This exception does not extend to stock of a **corporation** contributed by a donor to a **private foundation** to the extent that the amount of stock contributed exceeds 10 percent of the outstanding stock of the corporation (**IRC** § 170(e)(5)(C)). [PF §§ 14.4(b), 15.1; CG § 4.5(b)].

qualified charitable distribution

A "qualified charitable distribution" is a distribution from an individual retirement account **directly** by the account **trustee** to a **public** (or certain other) **charitable organizations**, other than a **supporting organization** or a **sponsoring organization** for a **donor-advised fund**; distributions are eligible for an **exclusion** from **gross income** only if made on or after the date the account owner attains age 70 1/2 (**IRC**§ 408(d)(8)(B)). [CG § 9.10(e)].

qualified charitable risk pool

The phrase "qualified charitable risk pool" means an organization that is treated as a **tax-exempt charitable organization** (1) if it is **organized** and **operated** solely to pool insurable risks of its **members** (other than risks related to medical malpractice) and to provide information to its members with respect to loss control and risk management; (2) that is comprised solely of members that are exempt charitable organizations; and (3) that meets the **organizational risk pool requirements**. The body of law denying tax exemption to organizations that provide **commercial-type insurance** does not apply to qualified charitable risk pools (**IRC** §§ 501(n)(1), (2)). [EO §§ 11.6, 28.14(b); HC § 19.3].

qualified conservation contribution

The **federal tax law** contains special rules for **contributions** to **charitable organizations** of **real property** and **interests** in real property for **conservation purposes**. The subject of these rules is the "qualified conservation contribution," which is a contribution of a **qualified real property interest** to a **qualified organization exclusively** for **conservation purposes** (IRC § 170(f)(3)(B)). [CG §§ 9.7, 24.7(b)(8); FR § 5.14(d); AR §§ 11.1(b), 19.1(j)].

qualified contingency

If a **trust** would, but for a "qualified contingency," meet the requirements of the rules concerning **charitable remainder annuity trusts** or **charitable remainder unitrusts**, it would be considered as having met the requirements (**IRC** § 664(f)(1)). A "qualified contingency" is any provision of a trust that states that, on the happening of a **contingency**, the **annuity amounts** or the **unitrust amounts** (as the case may be) will terminate no later than the payments would otherwise terminate under the trust (**IRC** § 664(f)(3)). A qualified contingency is not taken into account in determining the amount of a **charitable contribution** (or the **actuarial value** of any **interest**) (**IRC** § 664(f)(2)). [CG § 12.1(a)].

qualified contribution

The term "qualified contribution" has two meanings in the **federal tax law**. One meaning defines the **charitable contribution** of **inventory** of a **for-profit corporation** (other than an **S corporation**) where (1) the use of the **property** by the **donee** is **related** to its **tax-exempt purpose**; (2) the property is to be used by the donee **solely** for the care of the ill, the **needy**, or infants; (3) the property is not transferred by the donee in exchange for money, property, or services; (4) the **donor** receives the requisite written statement from the donee confirming the foregoing; and (5) the property is subject to regulation under the Federal Food, Drug, and Cosmetic Act (if applicable) (**IRC** § 170(e)(3)).

The second meaning arises in the context of the rule that a contribution of a **split-interest** in a **copyrighted work of art** is not denied an **estate tax charitable contribution deduction** where the art work is conveyed separately from the copyright in the art work (**IRC** § 2055(e)(4)). It is a transfer of property to a **qualified organization** if the use of the property by the organization is for its **tax-exempt purpose** (**IRC** § 2055(e)(4)(C)). [CG §§ 8.3(b), 9.3(a)].

qualified convention and trade show activity

Certain **business activities** conducted by **tax-exempt organizations** are **exempt** from **unrelated business taxation**. One of these businesses is the "qualified convention and trade show activity." This type of activity is any activity of a kind traditionally conducted at conventions, annual meetings, or **trade shows**, including an activity one of the purposes of which is to attract **persons** in an industry generally as well as **members** of the public to the show for the purpose of displaying industry products or to stimulate interest in and demand for industry products or services, or to **educate** persons engaged in the industry in the development of new products and services or new **rules** and **regulations** affecting the industry (**IRC** § 513(d)(3)(A)). This exemption is available only to **charitable organizations, social welfare organizations, labor** organizations, **agricultural organizations**, and **business leagues**. [EO § 25.2(f); UB § 4.5; SM p. 176].

qualified disaster

The term "qualified disaster" means a disaster that results from a terroristic or military action; a federally declared disaster; a disaster that results from an accident involving a common carries, or from any other event that is determined by the **IRS** to be of a catastrophic nature; or, with respect to certain **qualified disaster relief payments** (IRC § 139(b)(4)), a disaster that is determined by an applicable **federal**, state, or local government or agency or instrumentality thereof (**IRC** § 139(c)). [EO § 7.2(b); PF §§ 9.3(b), 9.3(e), 17.6(d)].

qualified disaster relief payment

The phrase "qualified disaster relief payment" means an amount paid to or for the benefit of an individual (1) to reimburse or pay **reasonable** and necessary personal, family, living, or funeral expenses incurred as a result of a **qualified disaster**; (2) to reimburse or pay reasonable and necessary expenses incurred for the repair or rehabilitation of a **personal residence** or repair or replacement of its contents to the extent that the need for the repair, rehabilitation, or replacement is attributable to a qualified disaster; (3) by a **person** engaged in the furnishing or sale of transportation as a common carrier by reason of the death or personal physical injuries incurred as a result of a natural disaster; or (4) if the amount is paid by a **federal**, state, or local government, or agency or instrumentality thereof, in connect with a qualified disaster in order to promote the general welfare (**IRC** § 139(b)). [EO § 7.2(b); PF §§ 9.3(b), 9.3(e), 17.6(d)].

qualified disclaimer

Persons who hold **interests** in **property** may **disclaim** their interest without the disclaimer being treated as a taxable transfer, for purposes of the **federal gift tax**, to that person. This type of disclaimer is termed a "qualified disclaimer," meaning an **irrevocable** and unqualified refusal to accept a property interest (**IRC** § 2518(b)). To be effective, the qualified disclaimer must meet certain other prescribed form and **notice** requirements. [CG § 8.2(n)].

qualified donee income

A **person** who makes a **qualified intellectual property contribution** is provided a **charitable contribution deduction** equal to the **donor's basis** in the property in the year of the **gift** and, in that year and/or subsequent years, a charitable deduction equal to a percentage of **net income** that flows to the charitable **donee** as a consequence of the gift of the property. The net income involved in this setting is termed "qualified donee income" (**IRC** § 170(m)(3)). [CG § 9.28(b); HC § 31.2(g)].

qualified employer security

In the context of the **qualified gratuitous transfer** rules, the term "qualified employer security" means an employer security (**IRC** § 409(1)) that is issued by a domestic **corporation** that does not have any outstanding stock that is readily tradable on an established securities market and that has only one class of stock (**IRC** § 664(g)(4)). [CG §§ 12.2(g), 12.3(g)].

qualified farmer

A "qualified farmer" is a **person** whose **gross income** from the **trade or business** of farming (**IRC** § 2032A(e)(5)) is greater than 50 percent of the person's gross income for the **tax year** (**IRC** § 170(b)(1)(E)(v)). [CG § 9.7(j)].

qualified first-tier tax

A "qualified first-tier tax" is any **first-tier tax** imposed as part of the **private foundation rules** (other than the **initial tax** on acts of **self-dealing**), the rules concerning **political expenditures**, the **intermediate sanctions** rules, the **donor-advised fund** rules, and the rules concerning **hospital failures** (**IRC** 4962(b)).

qualified gratuitous transfer

The term "qualified gratuitous transfer" means a transfer of **qualified employer securities** to an employee stock ownership plan, but only to the extent that (1) the securities transferred previously passed from a decedent dying before January 1, 1999, to a **charitable remainder trust;** (2) a **deduction** for **contributions** paid by an **employer** was not allowable with respect to the transfer; (3) the plan documents contain certain provisions; (4) the plan treats the securities as being attributable to employer contributions, albeit without regard to various limitations; and (5) the employer whose **employees** are covered by the plan files with the **IRS** a verified written statement consenting to application of certain taxes with respect to the employer (**IRC** § 664(g)(1)). [CG §§ 12.2(g), 12.3(g)].

qualified health insurance issuer

A "qualified health insurance issuer" is **tax-exempt** under the **federal tax law** (**IRC** §§ 501(a)(1) and 501(c)(29)). This type of **organization** is one that has received a loan or **grant** pursuant to the Consumer Operated and Oriented Plan program but only with respect to periods for which the issuer is in compliance with the requirements of that program and any agreement with respect to the loan or grant. In addition, to be **exempt**, an issuer must seek **recognition of exemption** from the **IRS**, be in compliance with the **private inurement doctrine**, not engage in **legislative activities** to a **substantial** extent, and not **participate** in or **intervene** in **political campaigns** on behalf of or in opposition to **candidates** for **public office**. [EO §§ 19.18, 26.6; HC § 13.3; SM p. 47].

qualified intellectual property

The phrase "qualified intellectual property" means patents, copyrights (with exceptions), trademarks, trade names, trade secrets, know-how, software (with exceptions), or similar property, or applications or registrations of this type of **property** (**IRC** § 170(m)(9)). [CG § 9.28(b); HC § 31.2(g)].

qualified interest

The term "qualified interest" is used in the context of the **qualified reformation** rules to mean an **interest** for which a **charitable contribution deduction** is allowable under the **federal estate tax** law (**IRC** § 2055(e)(3)(D)). [CG § 8.6(c)].

qualified mineral interest

A "qualified mineral interest" is a **donor's interest** in subsurface oil, gas, or other minerals, and the right to access to these minerals (**IRC** § 170(h)(6)). [CG § 9.7(d)].

qualified nonprofit health insurance issuer

A "qualified nonprofit health insurance issuer" is defined in the **Patient Protection and Affordable Care Act** as being a health insurance issuer **organized** under state law as a **nonprofit membership corporation**, substantially all of the activities of which consist of the issuance of qualified health plans in the individual and small group markets in each state in which it is licensed to issue these plans. These organizations are subject to certain **governance** requirements as stipulated by that act. These organizations are required to apply for **recognition** of **tax exemption**, are subject to the doctrine of **private inurement**, cannot engage in efforts to **influence legislation** to a **substantial** extent, and man not engage in **political campaign activity** (**IRC** § 501(c)(29)). [HC § 13.3; EO § 19.18; SM p. 47].

qualified organization

The term "qualified organization" has, in relation to the **federal tax law**, three meanings.

For the **federal income tax** rules for **contributions** to **charitable organizations** of **real property** for **conservation purposes** to be available, the contributions must be made to "qualified organizations." In this setting, a qualified organization is a **unit of government**, a **publicly supported charitable organization** of the **donative** type, a **publicly supported charitable organization** of the **service provider** type, or a **supporting organization** that is **controlled** by one or more of these three types of organizations (**IRC** § 170(h)(3)(B)(ii)). Also, this type of **donee** must have a commitment to protect the conservation purposes of the donation and have the resources to enforce the restrictions.

For an **exception** in the federal tax law, which regards income from certain investments in **real property** to not be treated as income from **debt-financed property** and thus not as **unrelated business income**, to be available, the **tax-exempt organization** involved must be a "qualified organization." In this context, a qualified organization is an **educational institution**, a **supporting organization** of an educational institution, a **pension fund**, or a **multi-parent title-holding company** (**IRC** § 514(c)(9)(C)).

For purposes of defining a **qualified contribution**, a "qualified organization" is a **charitable organization**, other than a **private foundation**, but including a **private operating foundation** (**IRC** § 2055(e)(4)). [CG §§ 8.3(b), 9.7(b); EO § 24.9(c)].

qualified plan

A "qualified plan" is a type of **deferred compensation plan** that satisfies a variety of **federal tax law** requirements as to coverage, **contributions**, other **funding, vesting, nondiscrimination**, and distributions. [EO § 18.1(d); HC § 28.6].

qualified pole rental

The rules concerning the **tax-exempt status** of a **mutual** or **cooperative telephone company** state that **income** received or **accrued** from "qualified pole rentals" is to be disregarded in determining the **organization's** eligibility for **tax exemption** (IRC § 501(c)(12)(B)(ii)). The phrase "qualified pole rental" means any **rental** of a pole (or other structure used to support wires) if the pole (or other structure) (1) is used by the telephone or electric company to support one or more wires that are used by the company in providing telephone or electric services to its members and (2) is used pursuant to the rental to support one or more wires (in addition to the wires referenced in (1)) for use in connection with the transmission by wire of electricity or of telephone or other communications (**IRC** § 501(c)(12)(D)). This type of income is not subject to the **tax** on **unrelated business income** (IRC § 513(g)). [EO §§ 19.5(b), 25.2(i); UB § 4.13].

qualified public entertainment activity

Certain **business activities** conducted by **tax-exempt organizations** are **exempt** from **unrelated business taxation**. One of these businesses is the "qualified public entertainment activity." This type of activity is an entertainment or recreational activity of a kind traditionally conducted at **fairs** or **expositions** promoting **agricultural** and **educational** purposes, including any activity one of the purposes of which is to attract the public to fairs or expositions or to promote the breeding of animals or the development of products or equipment (**IRC** § 513(d)(2)(A)). This exemption is available only to **charitable organizations, social welfare organizations, labor organizations**, and **agricultural organizations**. [EO § 25.2(e); UB § 4.4; SM pp. 175–176].

qualified rancher

A "qualified rancher" is a **person** whose **gross income** from the **trade or business** of farming (**IRC** § 2032A(e)(5)) is greater than 50 percent of the person's gross income for the **tax year** (**IRC** § 170(b)(1)(E)(v)). [CG § 9.7(j)].

qualified real property interest

For the special **federal income tax** rules for **contributions** to **charitable organizations** of **real property** for **conservation purposes** to be available, the contribution must be of a "qualified real property interest." This is any one of the following interests in real property: the entire interest of the **donor** other than a **qualified mineral interest**, a **remainder interest** in the property, or a **perpetual conservation restriction** (IRC § 170(h)(2)). [CG § 9.7(a); AR § 11.1(b)].

qualified reformation

The term "qualified reformation" is used to describe a **reformation** of a **trust** to enable it to qualify as a **charitable remainder trust**; the reformation is accomplished by revising the trust document. Technically, a qualified reformation means a change of a **governing instrument** by reformation, amendment, **construction**, or otherwise which changes a **reformable interest** into a **qualified interest**, but only if (1) the difference between the **actuarial value** (determined as of the date of the death of the **decedent**) of the qualified interest and the actuarial value (as so determined) of the reformable interest does not exceed 5 percent of the actuarial value (as so determined) of the reformable interest, (2) in the case of a **charitable remainder interest**, the nonremainder interest (before and after the qualified reformation) terminated at the same time, or in the ease of any other interest, the reformable interest and the qualified interest are for the same period, and (3) the change is effective as of the date of death of the decedent (**IRC** § 2055(e)(3)). Also, a non-remainder interest (before reformation) for a **term of years** in excess of twenty years must be treated as satisfying the second of these criteria, in the case of a charitable remainder interest, if the interest (after reformation) is for a term of twenty years (*id.*). [CG § 8.6(c)].

qualified religious sect or division

The phrase "qualified religious sect or division" means an organization that (1) has established tenets or teachings by reason of which its **members** and adherents are conscientiously opposed to acceptance of the benefits of any private or public **insurance** that makes payments in the event of death, disability, old age, or retirement or makes payments toward the cost of, or provides separate services for, medical care (including the benefits of any Social Security insurance system); (2) maintains, and has maintained for a **substantial** period of time, a practice whereby its members make provision for its dependent members that is **reasonable** in view of their general level of living; and (3) has been in existence at all times since December 31, 1950 (**IRC** § 1402(g)(1)).

qualified research contribution

The phrase "qualified research contribution" means a **charitable contribution** by a **corporation** of **tangible personal property** but only if (1) the contribution is to an **institution of higher education** or a **scientific research organization**, (2) the property is constructed or assembled by the **donor**, (3) the contribution is made not later than two years after the date the construction or assembly of the property is **substantially** completed, and (4) the original use of the property is by the donee (**IRC** § 170(e)(4)(B)). [CG § 9.4; SM p. 137].

qualified scholarship

A "qualified scholarship" means any amount received by an individual as a **scholarship** or **fellowship grant** to the extent that the individual establishes that, in accordance with the **conditions** of the grant, the amount was used for **qualified tuition and related expenses** (IRC § 117(b)(1)). An amount received as a qualified scholarship is **excluded** from the individual's **gross income** when the individual is a candidate for a degree at an **educational institution** (**IRC** § 117(a)). This exclusion does not apply to the portion of an amount received that represents payment for teaching, research, or other services required by the student as a condition for receiving the qualified scholarship (**IRC** § 117(c)). [CU Q 11.6].

qualified sponsorship payment

A "qualified sponsorship payment" is a payment made by a **person**, engaged in a **trade or business**, to a **tax-exempt organization**, with respect to which there is no arrangement or expectation that the person will receive, from the **exempt organization**, a **substantial return benefit** (**IRC** § 513(i)(2)(A)). [EO § 24.6; HC §§ 24.17, 24.19; FR § 5.16(b)(2); SM p. 158].

qualified subsidiary

For purposes of the **law** concerning **multi-parent title-holding organizations**, a "qualified subsidiary" is any **corporation** if, at all times during the period the corporation was in existence, 100 percent of the stock of the corporation is held by the title-holding organization (**IRC** § 501(c)(25)(E)(ii)). [EO § 19.2(b); HC § 15.2].

qualified terminable interest property

The phrase "qualified terminable interest property" means an **interest** in **property** that is terminable; it is qualified where the surviving spouse has a right to **income** from the property (or a specified portion of the property) for life, payable at least annually, or has a life **usufruct** interest in the property (**IRC** § 2056(b)(7)). Also, no **person** may have a **power of appointment** over the property during the life of the surviving spouse, when an **election** is made, the qualified terminable **income interest** for the life of the surviving spouse is granted a **marital deduction**. [CG § 8.3(b)].

qualified tuition and related expenses

The term "qualified tuition and related expenses" means (1) tuition and fees required for the enrollment or attendance of a student at an **educational institution** and (2) fees, books, supplies, and equipment required for courses of instruction at the institution (**IRC** § 117(b)(2)). [CU Q 11.7].

qualified tuition program

See **Prepaid tuition plan**.

qualified tuition reduction

The phrase "qualified tuition reduction" means the amount of any reduction in tuition provided to an **employee** of an **educational institution** for education at the institution or another educational institution of the employee or another individual (usually a child of an employee) where the use of the tuition reduction is treated as an employee use. As long as the qualified tuition reduction is not **discriminatory** in favor of highly compensated employees, the amount of the reduction is not included in any individual's gross income (**IRC** § 117(d)). [CU Q 11.40].

qualified vehicle

For purposes of special **charitable deduction** and **substantiation** rules, the term "qualified vehicle" means motor vehicles, boats, and airplanes (**IRC** § 170(f)(12)(E)). [CG § 9.27(b); HC § 31.2(f); SM p. 138].

qualifying distribution

The term "qualifying distribution," as used in the **law** concerning the **mandatory payout requirements** imposed on **private foundations**, means (1) any amount (including a portion of **reasonable** and necessary administrative expenses) paid to accomplish one or more **charitable** purposes, other than a distribution to an **organization controlled** by the private foundation or by one or more **disqualified persons** with respect to the private foundation (with **exceptions** for distributions to a **conduit organization** or to a **private operating foundation**) or (2) any amount paid to acquire an **asset** used (or held for use) directly in carrying out one or more charitable purposes (**IRC** §§ 4940(e)(5)(A), 4942(g)). [PF §§ 1.4(e), 6.5; EO § 12.4(b); SM p. 89] (also **Grant**; **Set-aside**).

qualifying sale

The term "qualifying sale" is a **sale** by a financial institution (defined in **IRC** § 514(c)(9)(H)(iv)) if (1) a **qualified organization** acquires **foreclosure property** or certain other **property** (defined in **IRC** § 514(c)(9)(H)(iii)) from a financial institution and any **gain recognized** by the financial institution with respect to the property is **ordinary income**, (2) the stated **principal** amount of the financing provided by the financial institution does not exceed the amount of the outstanding indebtedness (including accrued but unpaid **interest**) of the financial institution with respect to the property immediately before the acquisition, and (3) the present **value** (determined as of the time of the sale and by using the applicable **federal rate** of the maximum amount payable pursuant to the financing that is determined by reference to the **revenue**, **income**, or **profits** derived from the property cannot exceed 30 percent of the total purchase price of the property (including the contingent payments) (**IRC** § 514(c)(9)(H)(ii)). These types of sales are not subject to the restrictions of either the **fixed price restriction** or the **participating loan restriction** that are part of the **unrelated debt-financed income** rules. [EO § 24.9(c); UB § 5.4(f)].

quantification, of activities

The **federal tax law** lacks a formal methodology for quantifying a **tax-exempt organization's** activities for the purposes of measuring the scope of each of them and ascertaining whether there is a sufficient combination of them to satisfy the **primary purpose test**. It is known that the **IRS**, in this regard, starts with the approach of allocating **expenditures** to an organization's various functions; other approaches are allocations of time and analyzing the way in which the organization describes itself in its dealings with the **public**. [EO § 4.5(b)].

quasi-endowment

A "quasi-endowment" is **IRS** parlance for an **endowment fund** established by a **tax-exempt organization**, from **unrestricted donor** funds and/or organizational funds, on which the organization imposes one or more restrictions as to their use; these restrictions can be temporary or permanent. [EO § 11.9(a)].

quasi-governmental entities

The concept of **tax exemption** extends to a variety of **nonprofit organizations** that are **affiliated** with one or more **governmental** departments, agencies, and instrumentalities. [EO § 19.21; AS § 1.6(t)].

Q

quid pro quo

"Quid pro quo" is a Latin phrase meaning something provided in exchange for something else. The more recent term is **consideration**. The possibility of a "quid pro quo" situation is examined in the context of determining whether a transaction involves a **gift**. Where a transaction involves consideration, so that the "**donor**" receives something of **value** approximate to the amount contributed, there is no gift. In the case of a quid pro quo situation, the transaction is not a gift (unless it is partially a gift and partially a **sale** or **exchange**). [CG § 3.1(c); FR §§ 5.4, 8.8(e)].

quid pro quo contribution

A "quid pro quo contribution" is a payment "made partly as a **contribution** and partly in **consideration** for goods or services provided to the payor by the **donee organization**" (IRC § 6115(h)). There are **disclosure requirements** that are to be adhered to in an instance of a quid pro quo contribution in excess of $75. [CG §§ 3.1(c), 9.13(e); EO § 2.3; AR §§ 4.1(k), 4.2(f), 14.1(i)(8); HC § 31.2(c); RE Q 13.24–13.27; AS § 9.5; PG pp. 239–240; SM pp. 144–146; LI Q 12.36, Q 12.37].

quorum

A "quorum" is the number of individuals of a particular group of individuals—such as a **board of directors**, a **board of trustees**, or a committee—that are required to be present so that the body can lawfully transact business. The quorum requirements of an **organization** usually are stated in its **bylaws**. In the instance of **nonprofit corporations**, the applicable state **nonprofit corporations act** is likely to contain **law** on these requirements that either overrides a provision in an organization's **governing instrument(s)** or applies where the instrument is silent on the point.

Q

R

raffle
See **Wagering**.

ratio method
The "ratio method" is a method of **allocation** of **expenses** used by an **organization** in allocating costs to **lobbying activities** or **political campaign activities**, for purposes of the rules denying a **business expense deduction** for most of these types of activities (**IRC** § 162(e)(l)). Under this method, the organization determines its costs properly allocable to lobbying activities by adding its **third-party costs** to the costs determined by using a formula where a fraction, with **lobbying labor hours** in the numerator and **total labor hours** in the denominator, is multiplied against the organization's **total costs of operation**. An organization that does not pay or incur **reasonable labor costs** for **persons** engaged in lobbying activities, however, may not use this method. [EO §§ 22.6(a), 23.7] (also **Gross-up method**; **Section 263A cost allocation method**).

real estate board
A "real estate board" is an **association** of realtors, usually operating at the local level. These **organizations**, which are **tax-exempt** (**IRC** §§ 501(a), 501(c)(6)), provide support services for realtors and information about the locality to potential purchasers of real estate. [EO § 14.5; AS § 2.13].

R

real property
The term "real property" means **property** that is land and property that is erected on, affixed to, or growing on land. The term can also include various **rights** associated with real property. One major characteristic of real property, as distinguished from other forms of property, is its permanence, its immobile nature. Real property, including things annexed to it, is permanently affixed in place. Real property (or an **interest** in it) can, of course, be the subject of a **charitable contribution**. [CG §§ 2.12(a), 3.1(d), 24.7(b)(9); AR §§ 19.1(k), 19.2(i); HC § 15.2; RE Q 17.6–Q 17.19] (also **Fixture**).

Bruce R. Hopkins' Nonprofit Law Dictionary, First Edition. Bruce R. Hopkins.
© 2015 Bruce R. Hopkins. Published 2015 by John Wiley & Sons, Inc.

realization

The term "realization" means the economic accession to wealth that is recognized in the **law**; there must be a realization of **income** or **gain** before there can be **taxation** of it. Thus, when the **fair market value** of an item of **property** increases, that gain is realized in the law. [CG § 2.14(d)] (cf. **Recognition, of gain or loss**).

reallocation of charitable contribution deduction, by IRS

The **IRS** has the authority to "reallocate" items of **income**, **deductions**, and **credits** (IRC § 482). This type of reallocation is done where necessary to prevent the evasion of **taxes** or to ensure the clear reflection of each **taxpayer's** income. The **IRS** can use this authority to reallocate, in the **charitable giving context**, in order to adjust (reduce) a claimed **charitable contribution deduction**. [CG § 10.10].

reallocation of expenses

The **IRS** has the authority to recharacterize one or more **expenses** of a **person** to state (reflect) more correctly the person's **tax** position (including **liability**). This authority also extends to reallocations of items of **income**, **deductions** (including the **charitable contribution deduction**), and credits (IRC § 482). This concept is used in determining the **reasonableness** of certain payments to **tax-exempt organizations** from **controlled organizations** (IRC § 512(b)(13)(E)(i)). [CG § 10.10; EO §§ 29.6, 30.7(d)].

reasonable

The **law** is replete with uses of the word "reasonable." There are requirements that **persons** act in a "reasonable" manner; that **charitable** and other **tax-exempt organizations** provide compensation to their **employees**, **consultants**, and vendors that is no more than what is "reasonable;" there is a rule of "reason"; and individuals can be arrested for the **commission** of a **crime** where there is **reasonable cause**.

Despite its widespread use, the term "reasonable" eludes easy definition. It is often synonymous with "rational," being derived from the word "reason," which is a faculty of the mind enabling the individual to distinguish truth from falsehood and good from evil, and to deduce inferences from facts. Other words used to define "reasonable" are "appropriate," "proper," "just," "suitable," "fair," "**equitable**," and "moderate."

When it is said that charitable and other tax-exempt organizations must confine their payments of compensation and other items (such as **rent** and **interest**) to levels that are "reasonable," what is meant is that the payments may not be excessive or immoderate (often termed "unreasonable"). [EO §§ 20.4(b), 21.4(a), 21.9; HC § 4.4(b); PF § 5.1; CU Q 1.26; RE Q 2.7; SM p. 51; CL § 1.4; LI Q 1.32, Q 5.25] (also **Private inurement**).

reasonable cause

The term "reasonable cause" is used to describe a range of circumstances as a result of which a **person** is excused from responsibility for a particular act (**commission**) or failure to act (**omission**). While the application of this term is necessarily fact-specific and somewhat subjective,

R

it can be said to mean a reliance on a set of facts and circumstances that seem at the time, to a person using average caution and care; to justify the course of action or inaction selected. Simple lack of knowledge of the law, however, is not reasonable cause. For example, the **federal tax law** often provides that an **addition to tax** or a **penalty** will not be imposed for a commission or omission, such as in connection with (1) the filing of a **tax return** or the nonpayment of a tax (**IRC** § 6651(a)); (2) the failure to file an **annual information return**, to make an annual information return accessible to the public, or to make an **application for tax exemption** accessible to the public (**IRC** § 6652(c)(3)); (3) the making of an **underpayment** (**IRC** §§ 6664(c)(1), (2)); and (4) the failure of certain **tax-exempt organizations** to **disclose** that **contributions** to them are **nondeductible** (**IRC** § 6710(b)), if the person involved acted with reasonable cause. Frequently, a reasonable cause **exception** is coupled with a requirement that the failure involved not be due to **willful** neglect or that the person acted in **good faith**. The **private foundation rules** have reasonable cause exceptions (**IRC** §§ 4941(a)(2), 4944(a)(2), 4945(a)(2), and 4962(a)(1)). For example, in the context of the rules by which an **excise tax** can be imposed on a **foundation manager** for his or her **participation** in an act of **self-dealing**, a participation is considered due to "reasonable cause" and thus not taxed if he or she has exercised his or her responsibility on behalf of the **private foundation** with **ordinary business care and prudence**. Reasonable cause exceptions are also part of the **intermediate sanctions** and **lobbying expenditures** rules. [PF § 1.10; EO §§ 21.10, 22.4; LI Q 4.65, Q 5.47] (also **Abatement**).

reasonable compensation
"Reasonable compensation" means the **value** that would ordinarily be paid for like services by like enterprises under like circumstances. A **multi-factor test** is usually employed to determine **reasonableness**. [EO §§ 20.4(b), 21.4(a), 21.9; PF § 5.15(a); CU Q 7.14, Q 7.17; SM p. 51].

reasoned
The word "reasoned" is often used to accompany and modify the term "written legal opinion," such as in the context of the **self-dealing rules**. A written legal opinion is considered "reasoned" even if it reaches a conclusion that is subsequently determined to be incorrect, as long as the opinion addresses the facts and applicable **law**. A written legal opinion is not "reasoned," however, if it does nothing more than recite the facts and express a conclusion. [PF § 5.15(e)].

reasoned written legal opinion
The phrase "reasoned written legal opinion" is utilized in the context of the **self-dealing rules**. An **initial tax** will not be imposed on a **foundation manager** when his or her **participation** in an act of self-dealing is not **willful** and is due to **reasonable cause** (**IRC** § 4941(a)(2)). In some instances, reliance on **advice of counsel** satisfies these requirements. Thus, the rule is that, if an individual. after full disclosure of the factual situation to legal counsel (including **house counsel**), relies on the advice of counsel as expressed in a "**reasoned** written legal opinion" that an act is not an act of self-dealing, although the act is subsequently held to be an act of self-dealing, the individual's participation in the act will ordinarily not be considered **knowing** or willful and will ordinarily be considered due to reasonable cause. Nonetheless, the absence

of advice of counsel with respect to an act does not, by itself, give rise loan inference that a **person** participated in an act of self-dealing knowingly, willfully, or without reasonable cause. [PF § 5.15(e)].

rebate

The **federal tax law** uses the term "rebate" to mean so much of an **abatement**, **credit**, refund, or other payment as was made on the ground that an **income tax** or an **excise tax** (including the excise taxes imposed on **private foundations**) was less than the amount originally stated in a **deficiency** (**IRC** § 6211(b)(2)). The word "rebate" is also used in defining an **underpayment** (**IRC** § 6664(a), last sentence).

rebut

The word "rebut," usually used in connection with the **law** of **evidence**, means to defeat, override, overcome, or otherwise take away the legal effect of one or more facts.

rebuttable percentage limitation

The phrase "rebuttable percentage limitation" is used to describe a feature of a **charitable solicitation act** that forbids a **charitable organization** from engaging in **fundraising** in the jurisdiction where its fundraising costs are excessive. This feature raises a **presumption** that a fundraising cost of a charitable organization that is in excess of a stated percentage is excessive, but allows the organization to **rebut** this presumption by showing that its fund-raising costs are in fact **reasonable**. This feature of **law** is **unconstitutional** as a violation of the **free speech rights** of the **soliciting** charitable organization. [FR § 4.3; CL § 7.4(a); SM p. 152].

rebuttable presumption

The term "rebuttable presumption" means a **presumption** as to the validity of one or more facts that will remain in place unless disproved or overridden (**rebutted**) by one or more other facts. For example, a **charitable organization** is presumed to be a **private foundation** (**IRC** § 508(b)), but it can **rebut** this presumption by a showing to the **IRS** that it qualifies, or is **reasonably** expected to qualify, as a **public charity**. [EO § 12.1(a); PF § 15.2; SM pp. 60, 101].

rebuttable presumption of reasonableness

As a general **federal tax law rule**, the **burden of proof** is on the **taxpayer**. In the **intermediate sanctions** law, however, a "rebuttable presumption of reasonableness" applies with respect to **compensation** arrangements and other forms of transactions between an **applicable tax-exempt organization** and a **disqualified person** with respect to it. This presumption arises where the transaction was approved by the organization's **governing board** (or a **committee** of it) that was comprised entirely of individuals who were unrelated to and not subject to the control of the disqualified person or persons involved in the transaction, the board obtained and relied on appropriate data as to comparability, and adequately documented the basis for its determination. [EO § 21.9; AR §§ 5.3, 6.1(b)(8), 6.2(c)(4); GV §§ 4.2(c), 6.3(f), 6.3(g); HC § 4.9(a)(v); CU Q 7.18; AS § 3.8(e); SM pp. 60, 101].

recapture

The term "recapture," as used in the **federal tax law**, means that a **taxpayer** must, having previously availed himself, herself, or itself of a **tax benefit**, under certain circumstances take the economic **value** of that benefit into account for tax purposes in a subsequent **tax year**. For example, when a **capital asset** is sold, the seller must, under certain circumstances, recapture prior **depreciation deductions** to convert what might otherwise be **capital gain** into **ordinary income**. Recapture provisions are in **IRC** §§ 617, 1250, 1251, and 1252. A recapture requirement can be triggered in the case of a **contribution** of an **income interest** in **property**. A recapture rule applies in the case of an **applicable disposition** of **applicable property** (IRC § 170(e)(7)(A)). [CG §§ 4.6(c), 9.3(g), 9. 22(f); FR § 5.14(e)].

recipient

In the body of **law** concerning **charitable remainder trusts**, the **income interest beneficiary** is often termed the "recipient." [CG § 1.1].

reciprocal agreement provision

One of the provisions of some of the state **charitable solicitation acts** authorizes the appropriate state official to enter into reciprocal agreements with his or her counterparts in other states to (1) exchange information about **charitable organizations, professional fundraisers**, and **professional solicitors**; (2) accept filings made by these **persons** in other states where the information required is **substantially** similar; and (3) grant **exemptions** to organizations that are granted exemptions under the other states' statutes where the laws are substantially similar. These provisions, however, are rarely utilized; some state charity officials have admitted to not knowing they exist. [FR §§ 3.16, 8.13(b)].

recognition, of gain or loss

Once a **gain** or **loss** is **realized**, there must be a determination as to whether the gain or loss will be "recognized" and subjected to taxation. Under the **federal tax law**, the general rule is that the entire amount of gain or loss on the **sale** or **exchange** of **property** must be recognized. "Recognition," in this context, is the process of taking gain or loss into account for **income tax** purposes; the gain or loss is recognized and subjected to current income taxation, unless a **deferral** of gain is permitted. As a general rule, a gain or loss is not recognized to a **donor** on the making of a **gift** of **appreciated property**, whether **outright** or by means of a **planned gift**. [CG §§ 2.14(f), 3.1(g)] (also **Nonrecognition of gain**).

recognition of public charity status

The **IRS** "recognizes" **public charity status** at the time a **determination letter** is initially issued and when there is a change in public charity status; the latter is accomplished by the filing of **Form 8940**. Although an **organization** is not required to obtain a determination letter to qualify for a new public charity classification, in order for the **IRS's** records to reflect a change in public charity status, an organization must obtain a new determination of this status. [EO §§ 3.3, 26.3].

R

recognition of tax exemption

The qualification of a **nonprofit organization** for **tax-exempt status** is a matter of **law**; that is, whether an organization is entitled to **tax exemption**, on an initial or continuing basis, is an issue of law. Thus, it is Congress that has, by **statute**, defined the categories of organizations that are eligible for tax exemption (principally, in **IRC** § 501(c)) and it is Congress that, by statute, determines whether a tax exemption should be continued. It is the role of the **IRS** in this regard to "recognize" tax exemption. Consequently, when an organization makes application to the **IRS** for a **ruling** or other **determination** as to its tax-exempt status, it is requesting the **IRS** to recognize tax exemption, not to grant tax exemption. Thus, for example, the form by which **charitable organizations** seek recognition of tax-exempt status is titled "**Application for Recognition of Exemption**" (**Form 1023**). Likewise, the **IRS** may determine that an organization is no longer entitled to tax exemption and act to **revoke** its prior recognition of tax-exempt status.

Most categories of tax-exempt organizations do not have to receive recognition of tax-exempt status from the **IRS** to be exempt. Those that must obtain this recognition to have tax exemption are charitable organizations, certain **credit counseling organizations**, certain **employee benefit organizations**, and certain **health insurance issuers**. [EO §§ 3.2, 26.1; HC §§ 34.–34.4; FR §§ 5.8(a), 5.9(k); AR §§ 2.1(f), 2.1(g), 14.1(i)(2); CU Q 3.12; RE Q 8.9; CL § 1.12; AS § 2.2; SM pp. 26, 65–66; LI Q 2.8–Q 2.12] (cf. **Self-declarer**).

recognize

The word "recognize" is used in three ways in the context of **federal tax law**. One meaning is to recognize **capital gain** for tax purposes; this is termed **recognition** of gain. The other two meanings pertain to the processes by which the **IRS** "recognizes" a **nonprofit organization** as being a **tax-exempt entity** and it recognizes a **charitable organization** as being a **public charity**. [CG §§ 2.14(f), 3.1(g)].

recordkeeping requirement

The **law** is replete with "recordkeeping requirements." **Tax-exempt organizations** must maintain certain records (**IRC** § 6001), including the records necessary to prepare filings, such as their **annual information returns** and state **annual reports** (those required by state corporate law and state **charitable solicitation acts**). **Donors** must keep records of their **charitable contributions** in compliance with the **substantiation** rules. [EO § 28.19; HR § 7.1(d); CG §§ 21.1–21.4; FR § 5.3; CU Q 17.62; SM pp. 141–142].

records

The **law** frequently requires **persons** to keep "records," which generally are documents and other writings. Audio and video recordings may also constitute records, as well as documents maintained electronically. The **federal tax law** contains many requirements for the keeping of records; one example of this is the requirement that **charitable organizations** maintain records of their **expenditures** for **lobbying**. [EO § 28.19] (also **Reliable written record**).

recreational activity

An **organization** may be able to qualify for the **federal income tax exemption** as a **charitable organization** on the ground that it promotes, advances, and sponsors "recreational" and amateur sports. If, however, the recreational activity is **substantial**, the organization may be more appropriately classified as a **tax-exempt social club**. [EO §§ 7.16(c), 11.2, 15.1].

reduction of deduction

There is a **federal income tax charitable contribution deduction** for the **gift** of an item of **long-term capital gain property** to a **charitable organization**, with the amount of this deduction usually equal to (at least prior to application of one or more **percentage limitations**) the **fair market value** of the property. There are, however, circumstances under which the amount of this deduction must be reduced by an amount equal to the **appreciation element** in the property; that is, the charitable contribution deduction is confined to the **donor's basis** in the property. These circumstances are gifts of this type of property (1) to a charitable organization where the property is **tangible personal property** and where the use by the **donee** of the property is an **unrelated use** or. in some instances, where the property is **applicable property** (**IRC** § 170(e)(1)(B)(i)), (2) **to** or **for the use of** most **private foundations** (**IRC** § 170(e)(1)(B)(ii)), (3) in the case of certain intellectual property; (**IRC** § 170(e)(1)(B)(iii)), and (4) in the case of **taxidermy property** (**IRC** § 170(e)(1)(B)(iv)). A similar deduction reduction rule applies where the property that is the subject of the gift is **ordinary income property** or **short-term capital gain property** (**IRC** § 170(e)(1)(A)). [CG §§ 4.4(b), 4.5(a), 4.6(a), 4.6(c), 9.19(c), 9.24, 9.28(b)].

reference written determination

The text of certain **written determinations** of the **IRS** are open to public inspection. The phrase "reference written determination" means a written determination that has been determined by the **IRS** as having **significant** reference value (**IRC** § 6110(b)(3)(A)). The **IRS** may not dispose of reference written determinations. [EO § 28.10(a)] (also **General written determination**).

referral

Using a most striking euphemism, the **IRS** uses the word "referral" when referencing a complaint alleging abuse of an **organization's tax-exempt status**. Although the (non-**IRS**) source of a referral will receive an acknowledgment letter, the **IRS** cannot disclose whether it has initiated an **examination** or the results of an examination. A revenue agent will analyze the allegation, then take steps ranging from taking no further action on the referral to forwarding the case for an examination. The **IRS** prefers that a complaint be submitted by means of **Form 13909**, with any supporting documentation.

reformable interest

The **federal tax law** requires that certain provisions be (or not be) in a **charitable remainder trust** if a **charitable contribution deduction** is to be available. There is a procedure, however, by which these trusts, both those created during lifetime (**inter vivos trusts**) and **testamentary**

trusts, can be adjusted to bring them into compliance with the appropriate tax law requirements, for federal **income tax, estate tax**, and **gift tax** consequences. Federal law permits a charitable contribution deduction for a **qualified reformation** of a trust, which does not meet the requirements of a **charitable remainder annuity trust** or a **charitable remainder unitrust**, for purposes of qualifying for the federal estate tax charitable contribution deduction (**IRC §** 2055(e)(3)).

The **reformation** procedure requires that the interest involved be a "reformable interest" that can be changed into a **qualified interest**. In general, a reformable interest, for federal estate tax law purposes, is any interest for which a charitable contribution deduction would be allowable at the time of the death of the **decedent** but for the requirement that the interest be in one of the specified forms (**IRC §** 2055(e)(3)(C)(i)). The term "reformable interest" does not include any interest unless, before the **remainder interest vests** in possession, all payments to **noncharitable persons** are expressed either in specified dollar amounts or a fixed percentage of the property (**IRC §** 2055(e)(3)(C)(ii)). This rule does not apply, however, to any interest if a judicial proceeding is commenced to change the interest into a qualified interest not later than the ninetieth day after the last date (including extensions) for filing the **estate tax return** (if one is required), or the last date (including extensions) for filing the **income tax return** for the first tax year for which a return is required to be filed by the trust (if an estate tax return is not required to be filed) (**IRC §** 2055(e)(3)(C)(iii)). [CG § 8.6(c)].

reformation
See **Qualified reformation**.

regional health information organization
The phrase "regional health information organization" means a **tax-exempt entity** that promotes use of health information technology to improve health care quality and reduce health care costs. This type of organization is **charitable** because it **lessens the burdens of government**. [HC § 19.5; EO §§ 7.6(k), 7.7].

registered agent
The **law** of each state requires a **nonprofit corporation** to maintain, in the state, a "registered agent." (The term, in some states' law, may be somewhat different, such as "resident agent.") A registered agent is a **person** who, as **agent** for the corporation, is the formal point of contact for anyone who is required to communicate with the corporation, such as the state sending its **annual report** form or another person seeking to deliver **service of process**. A corporation must maintain a registered agent in the state in which it is headquartered and in any other state in which it is **doing business**.

A registered agent can be an individual who is a **resident** of the state, a corporation that is authorized by the state to function as registered agent for corporations, or (in some states) a **lawyer** who is a **member** of the bar of that state. Acting only as such, a registered agent is not **liable** for actions of the corporation, as the position is not one of **officer, director**, or **trustee**.

Many of the state **charitable solicitation acts** require a **charitable organization** that is **soliciting contributions** in the state to appoint a registered agent in the state; this requirement may also be imposed on **professional fundraisers** and/or **professional solicitors**. In several states, where a registered agent is not appointed for this purpose, the law provides that where the **foreign** charitable organization (or professional fundraiser or professional solicitor) participates in a charitable solicitation in a state, the administrator of the act (usually the secretary of state) is deemed, by virtue of the solicitation activity, to have been **irrevocably** appointed its agent for service of process and similar functions. [RE Q 1.15, Q 1.16; CU Q 1.7; LI Q 1.13–Q 1.15, Q 1.26].

registered historic district

The term "registered historic district" means any district listed in the **National Register**. It also means any district that is (1) designated under a **statute** of the appropriate state or local government, if the statute is certified by the Department of the Interior to the **IRS** as containing criteria that will **substantially** achieve the purpose of preserving and rehabilitating buildings of historic significance to the district, and (2) certified by the Department of the Interior to the **IRS** as meeting **substantially all** of the requirements for listing of districts in the National Register (**IRC** § 47(c)(3)(B)). [CG § 9.7(c)].

registration

A "registration" is a filing of documents with an **agency** of government in compliance with a **law**; the purpose of submitting this information usually is to provide **notice** of an impending transaction or other undertaking, for the benefit of the **public**. The registration generally results in a license, permit, or the like, allowing the undertaking to proceed. One of the most well-known registration requirements is that of the **federal** securities laws, by which a **for-profit corporation** that desires to sell its securities publicly must obtain approval from the Securities and Exchange Commission of its registration statement. **Nonprofit organizations** have registration requirements as well: (1) state **charitable solicitation acts** usually embody a registration requirement for **soliciting** organizations, **professional fundraisers**, and **professional solicitors**; (2) the process of **incorporation** in a state is, in a sense, a registration process; and (3) the filing of an **application for recognition of exemption** with the **IRS** in request of a **determination letter** or **ruling** is a registration. [EO § 26.1(a); FR §§ 3.3, 3.22, 4.13(c), 8.10; HC § 31.1(e); CG § 25.5].

registration requirements, state

Nonprofit organizations are subjected to a variety of "registration requirements" under the **laws** of the states. Nearly every state has a **nonprofit corporation statute**, pursuant to which corporations that are formed under the state's law must register by filing **articles of incorporation** or a **certificate of incorporation**. A corporation that is formed under the law of one state and that **does business** in another state must register in that state as a **foreign corporation**. Most states require **charitable trusts** to register under their laws. Nearly every state has a **charitable solicitation act**, which requires most **charitable organizations** that are **soliciting contributions** in the state to register in accordance with that law; these laws frequently also require registration by **professional fundraisers** and **professional solicitors** [PG p. 6; SM pp. 148–151; FR §§ 3.3, 3.22, 4.13(c), 8.10; CG § 25.5; HC § 31.1(e)].

regressivity

"Regressivity" is the term given to a **tax** system where the **tax rate** does not change in relation to the amount subject to the tax. The taxes in this category principally are **excise taxes**, **sales taxes**, **use taxes**, and **value-added taxes**. [CG § 1.6] (also **Progressivity**).

regular corporation

The term "regular corporation" is used in the **federal tax law** to describe a **C corporation**. The principal type of corporation that is not a regular corporation under the federal tax law is an **S corporation**. [CG §§ 2.8, 3.2, 6.13–6.15, 7.18(a), 9.8, 24.2, 24.3, 24.7(a); EO § 19.23].

regular member

The term "regular member" is used to describe the voting **members** of an **organization**, who have the **right** to hold office in the organization. [FR § 3.5(h)] (also **Associate member; Honorary member; Life member; Member**).

regularly carried on

One of the principal features of the **law** of **tax-exempt organizations** is the **tax** on the **income** derived from the conduct of an **unrelated trade or business**. For a business activity to give rise to this tax, it must be "regularly carried on" (**IRC § 512(a)(1)**), as distinguished from sporadic or infrequent activity or transactions. The factors that determine whether an activity is regularly carried on are the frequency and continuity of the activities and the manner in which the activities are pursued. As to the latter factor, the inquiry is whether the activity is undertaken in a manner generally similar to comparable **commercial** activities of **nonexempt organizations**.

Where income-producing activities are performed by commercial organizations on a year-round basis, the performance of these activities for a period of only a few weeks does not constitute the regular carrying on of a trade or business. Similarly, occasional or annual income-producing activities, such as **fundraising events**, do not constitute a business that is regularly carried on. The conduct of year-round business activities for one day each week, however, constitutes the regular carrying on of a business. Where commercial entities normally undertake an income-producing activity on a seasonal basis, the conduct of that activity by a tax-exempt organization during a significant portion of that season is the regular conduct of that activity.

In general, a trade or business is regularly carried on if the attributes of the activity are similar to the commercial activities of nonexempt organizations. [UB § 2.5(a); EO § 24.3; CG § 3.4(c) HC § 24.3; FR §§ 5.7(a)(iv), (b)(ii); PG pp. 174–175; SM pp. 172–173].

regulation

A "regulation" is a form of **law**; it may be promulgated at the **federal**, state, or local level of government. A regulation is issued by an **agency** or **department** of an **executive branch** of government or by an **independent regulatory agency**; a regulation is never issued by a component of a **legislative branch** or **judicial branch** of government. A regulation is almost always issued in amplification of a **statute**. For example, it is common for the U.S. Congress to enact a **tax** statute, which is subsequently explained, illustrated, and otherwise amplified by a regulation written by the **Department of the Treasury** (and, within it, the **IRS**) (**IRC § 7805**).

A regulation usually has the force of law; this is particularly the case with respect to a regulation that has been in existence for some time and where the legislative body in the jurisdiction has subsequently legislated in the subject matter area to which the statute relates. A regulation is, nonetheless, subordinate to the related statute. A court is not bound by a regulation, although it will normally follow it, and can **void** a regulation where it is broader than the related statute. [EO App. A] (also **Chevron standard**; **Deference**; **Rule**).

regulatory agency

A "regulatory agency" is an **agency** of a government that has the responsibility of administering and enforcing the **laws** that pertain to a particular field of government regulation. For example, the **IRS** has regulatory responsibilities with respect to the **federal tax** system and the **Federal Elections Commission** has these responsibilities with respect to the federal election laws. [EO § 2.2(a); FR § 5.25(b)].

reinsurance

The term "reinsurance" means a **contract** of **insurance**, obtained to insure against a **loss** or **liability**, in substitution for an obligation incurred pursuant to a previously obtained contract of insurance. Thus, the **reinsurer** becomes contractually obligated to pay to the **reinsured** the amount of insurance that is required under the contract, which usually is the same amount as that required under the original insurance contract. The term "reinsurance" is used in connection with **charitable gift annuities**, in that the **charitable organization** that is the **remainder interest beneficiary** may "reinsure" the annuity obligation by purchasing a comparable annuity from a **commercial** insurance company. In this sense, the charitable organization is considered the original **insurer** and the **reinsured**. [CG § 14.1].

reinsured

A **person** who is the "reinsured" is one who procures a **contract** of **insurance** and who is an **insurer** pursuant to a previously obtained contract of insurance covering the identical **loss** or **liability**.

reinsurer

A **person** who is the "reinsurer" is one who **insures**, pursuant to a **contract** of **insurance**, another person who is an insurer under a previously obtained contract of insurance covering the identical **loss** or **liability**.

related

The word "related" refers to a relationship between two or more **persons**, objectives, or **programs**, in which there is a unique form of association or connectedness. As to individuals, they are "related" when, for example, they are married or otherwise **members** of the same family. Individuals owning **significant interests** in **corporations**, **partnerships**, or other **enterprises** are deemed "related" to these **entities**. A program of a **tax-exempt organization** may be "related" to the **exempt purposes** of the organization. [EO §§ 24.4(a), 24.4(f); UB §§ 2.6, 2.7; SM pp. 173–174] (also **Affiliate**; **Control**; **Member of the family**).

related activity

A significant factor in determining whether an item of **income** received by a **tax-exempt organization** is to be taxed as **unrelated business income** is whether the activity that gave rise to the income is "related" or **unrelated** to the **tax-exempt purpose** of the organization. If the income is to be **excluded** from taxation, the underlying activity must be **substantially related** to the tax-exempt purpose (**IRC** § 513(a)). [UB § 2.6; EO § 24.4(a); SM pp. 173–174; CL § 8.4(b)].

related organizations

Two or more **organizations** may be "related"; this can be the case irrespective of whether one or more of the organizations are **nonprofit organizations**, **tax-exempt organizations**, **for-profit organizations**, and/or **governmental units**. Frequently, the relationship is one of **control**. The **law** is replete with situations in which one or more exempt organizations are related in some manner to one or more other organizations. Instances of this are national **associations** and their **chapters**, the use of **supporting organizations**, the use of **title-holding corporations**, U.S.-based **charitable organizations** that engage in **fundraising** for charitable organizations outside the U.S., a for-profit **corporation** with a related **foundation**, and the use of **joint ventures**, **partnerships**, and **subsidiaries**.

The mechanisms by which these relationships are accomplished are manifold. One of the most common of these mechanisms is the **interlocking directorate**. Another is a procedure whereby the **board of directors** of one organization selects the board of directors of another; this procedure is usually reflected in the organization's **articles of organization**. Another is a relationship that is evidenced whereby one organization is a **member** of another. On occasion, one organization will own some or all of the stock of another. Some organizations are related, not by formal structure, but by commonality of policy positions. (also **Affiliated organizations**; **Expenditure test**; **Group exemption**; **Parent organization**; **Subsidiary**).

related person

For purposes of the **federal tax law** by which a **person** can cease to be considered a **substantial contributor** (and thus not a **disqualified person**, unless there is another basis for the classification) with respect to a **private foundation**, the term "related person" means any person who would be a disqualified person by reason of his, her, or its relationship to another person (**IRC** § 507(d)(2)(C)(ii)). In the case of a **contributor** that is a **corporation**, the term also includes any **officer** or **director** of the corporation (*id.*). [PF § 4.1].

religion

The term "religion" is used to describe a set of beliefs that assists individuals in giving meaning to otherwise unanswerable questions; it is a way that individuals orient themselves to the reality of the world. Religion often involves a ritual, prayer, **ethics**, a figurehead, a center of worship, a text, one or more practices, symbols, and a goal (an ideal state of existence). Religion usually entails a belief in a realm of existence that lies beyond humans' planetary existence, efforts to progress toward a goal, and the achievement of personal benefits through techniques such as prayer, offerings, rituals, and pilgrimages. [EO § 10.2(a); RE Q 3.1, Q 25.5; SM pp. 36–38; CL § 2.11].

religion, advancement of

One of the ways an **organization** can qualify for **tax-exempt status** as a **charitable organization** under the **federal tax law** is to have a purpose to and engage in activities to **advance religion**. This concept of "advancement of religion" includes the construction or maintenance of a **church** building, monument, memorial window, or burial ground and collateral services such as the provision of music, payment of **salaries**, dissemination of **religious doctrines**, maintenance of missions, or distribution of religious literature. [EO § 7.10; RE Q 8.5; CG § 3.2(b); SM p. 34].

Religion Clauses

The "Religion Clauses" are contained in the portion of the **First Amendment** to the U.S. Constitution that provides that "Congress shall make no law respecting an establishment of religion, or prohibiting the free exercise thereof." These clauses are respectively known as the **establishment clause** and the **free exercise clause**. Both of these clauses have as their goal the maintenance of government neutrality with regard to affairs of **religion**. [CL §§ 1.1(b), 2.1, 2.2; RE Q 3.2, Q 25.1–Q 25.3; EO § 10.1; FR §§ 4.3(e), 4.7; SM pp. 327–329].

Religious Freedom Restoration Act

The "Religious Freedom Restoration Act" was enacted in response to a 1990 decision by the U.S. Supreme Court, which held that the **Free Exercise Clause** does not relieve an individual of the obligation to comply with a valid and neutral **law** of general applicability. Congress set a standard higher than that required by the **First Amendment**, which is that the **federal** government may not **substantially** burden an individual's religious exercise, even where the burden results from a religiously neutral and generally applicable law, unless the imposition of the burden is the least restrictive means to serve a compelling governmental interest. Free exercise decisions that predate the 1990 decision remain instructive when determining the requirements of this law. [RE Q 25.3, Q 25.4].

R

religious order

A "religious order" is a **religious organization** that, according to the **IRS**, has the following characteristics: (1) the organization is a **charitable** one; (2) the **members** of the organization vow to live under a strict set of rules requiring moral and spiritual self-sacrifice and dedication to the goals of the organization at the expense of their material well-being; (3) the members of the organization, after successful completion of the organization's training program and probationary period, make a long-term commitment to the organization (normally more than two years); (4) the organization is, **directly** or **indirectly**, under the **control** and supervision of a **church**, **convention of churches**, or **association of churches;** (5) the members of the organization normally live together as part of a community and are held to a significantly stricter level or moral and religious discipline than that required of lay church members; (6) the members of the organization work or serve full time on behalf of the religious, **educational**, or charitable goals of the organization; and (7) the members of the organization participate regularly in activities such as public or private prayer, religious study, teaching, care of the aging, missionary work, or church reform or renewal. [EO § 10.6; RE Q 3.11; UB § 3.17].

religious organization

A "religious organization" is an **organization** that is **organized** and **operated primarily** to engage in **programs** of a **religious** nature. Qualifying religious organizations generally are **exempt** from **federal income taxation** (**IRC** § 501(c)(3)) and from the requirements of the states' **charitable solicitation acts**. [RE Chap. 3; EO Chap. 10; CG § 3.2(b); FR §§ 4.7, 5.18(b)(i); PF §§ 1.5, 1.6, 9.1(c); HC § 8.4; AU § 7.1(c); AS § 1.6(p); SM pp. 36–38; CL § 7.8] (also **Apostolic organization**; **Association of churches**; **Church**; **Integrated auxiliary of a church**; **Religious order**).

remainder interest

The "remainder interest" in an item of **property** is the projected **value** of the property, or the property produced by reinvestment, at some future date. That is, the remainder interest in a property is an amount equal to the **fair market value** of the property (or its offspring), at the time the remainder interest was created or when it is to be received at a subsequent point in time. The remainder interest becomes **tangibly** available to the **remainder interest beneficiary** at the time of expiration of the **income interest** (or interests) in the same property. Remainder interests in property can be created in a variety of ways, including by means of **charitable gift annuities**, **charitable lead trusts**, **charitable remainder trusts**, and **pooled income funds**. [CG §§ 5.3, 8.6(a), 12.2(g), 12.3(g), 13.2(a), 15.1, 15.2(a), 15.3; CU Q 12.61; SM p. 234] (also **Partial interest**; **Split-interest trust**).

remainder interest beneficiary

A "remainder interest beneficiary" is a **person** who is the, or a, **beneficiary** of a **trust** or **contract** arrangement pursuant to which he, she, or it is destined to receive, or has received, a **remainder interest** in a **property** (perhaps including money). On occasion, the term "**remainderman**" is used. (cf. **Income interest beneficiary**).

remainderman.

The word "remainderman" derives from the common law rules concerning charitable trusts. The person (whether or not a charitable entity) who is to receive the corpus of the trust following a period of time is said to be the "remainderman." Today, the person holding the remainder interest in a split-interest trust (usually a charitable entity) is sometimes termed the "remainderman." There are circumstances, however, where a remainder interest can be created without use of a trust. The contemporary term is "remainder interest beneficiary."

remainder trust

See **Charitable remainder trust**.

removal from jeopardy

The phrase "removal from jeopardy," as used in connection with the **jeopardizing investment** prohibition imposed by the **federal tax law** on **private foundations**, means removal of an investment that jeopardizes the carrying out of **tax-exempt purposes** from jeopardy to the extent that it is sold or otherwise disposed of and the proceeds of the **sale** or other **disposition** are not invested in a way that jeopardizes the carrying out of tax-exempt purposes (**IRC** § 4944(e)(2)). [PF § 8.5(c)].

rent

"Rent" is money paid, or some other **consideration** provided, for the occupation or other use of **property**. A **tax-exempt organization** may pay rent for the use of property or collect rent from another **person** for the use of property. In the latter instance, the rent may constitute **gross income** subject to taxation, unless it is a form of **passive income** or is otherwise **excluded** from **tax** (**IRC** § 512(b)(3)). Rental income may be subject to this tax if the acquisition of the income-producing property was **debt-financed** (**IRC** § 512(b)(4)). Rental arrangements can be forms of **exempt functions**, **private benefit**, **private inurement**, or **self-dealing**. [UB § 3.8; EO §§ 12.4(a), 20.5(a), 21.4(a), 25.1(h)(iii); HC §§ 4.4(d), 24.18, 25.7; PF §§ 10.3(e), 11.2(b); AR §§ 7.2(a)(2), 7.2(a)(3); RE Q 21.46; AS § 3.4(b)(i); SM pp. 52–53] (also **Modification**).

rental

For purposes of the rules concerning **qualified pole rentals**, the word "rental" includes any **sale** of the **right** to use the pole (or other structure) (**IRC** § 501(c)(12), last sentence). [EO § 19.5(b)].

reportable compensation

For purposes of **annual information return** reporting, the **IRS** defines the term "reportable compensation" to generally mean the aggregate **compensation** that is reported (or required to be reported, if greater) on **Form W-2**, box 1 or 5 (whichever amount is greater), and/or **Form 1099**-MISC, box 7, for the calendar year ending with or within the **organization's tax year**. If the amount reported on **Form W-2**, box 5, is zero or less than the amount in **Form W-2**, box 1 (which is the case, for example, for certain clergy and religious workers not subject to Social Security and Medicare **taxes** as **employees**), reportable compensation includes the box 1 amount rather than the box 5 amount. For foreign persons who receive U.S. source income, reportable compensation includes the amount reportable on **Form 1042-S**, box 2. For persons for whom reporting on **Form W-2, 1099**-MISC, or **1042**-S is not required (certain foreign persons, **institutional trustees**, and persons whose compensation was below the $600 reporting threshold for **Form 1099**), reportable compensation includes the total value of the compensation paid in the form of money or property during the calendar year ending with or within the organization's tax year. [AR §§ 6.2(a)(4), 6.2(a)(5)].

reportable transaction

The term "reportable transaction" means a transaction with respect to which information is required to be included with a **tax return** or statement because the transaction is of a type that the **IRS** determines as having a potential for tax avoidance or evasion (**IRC** § 6707A(c)(1)). [EO § 28.17(d)].

reporting requirement

Federal, state, and local **law** impose a wide variety of "reporting requirements" on **nonprofit organizations**. The **federal tax law** imposes reporting requirements in this context, principally by means of **annual information returns** and the reporting of **unrelated business taxable income**. Many reporting requirements, imposed on **donors** and/or **donees**, are part of the **charitable giving** rules. **Tax returns** and information returns filed by other **persons** can affect nonprofit organizations, such as the tax returns filed by individuals reflecting claims of the **charitable contribution deduction** and the information returns filed by **partnerships** reflecting the activities and rights of nonprofit organization **partners**. State laws pertaining to **charitable solicitations**, **corporations**, and **trusts** contain reporting requirements. Other persons functioning on behalf of nonprofit organizations, such as **lobbyists** and **professional fundraisers**, can have reporting requirements. [EO §§ 28.2, 28.3, 28.6–28.8; UB §§ 11.3–11.5; CG Chap. 24, §§ 9.13(g), 25.6; FR § 3.4; HC §§ 7.1(e), 31.1(f), 31.2(j); PF §§ 9.3(f), 9.6(h), 12.3(e); SM Chap. 9].

republication

The term "republication" is used to describe the re-execution (or second publication) of a **will** by a **testator**, usually after a prior will was revoked.

request a ruling

The phrase "request a ruling," in the **nonprofit law** context, usually means a written statement filed with the **IRS** asking that agency to issue a **private letter ruling** on a particular topic of **federal tax law**. Occasionally, a request for a ruling will lead to the issuance of a **revenue ruling**.

research

The term "research" means a systematic inquiry or investigation into a subject for the purpose of discovering principles or facts. This is a broad term, frequently preceded by a word such as "applied," "basic," "fundamental," or "practical"; in the **nonprofit organization law context**, the term is often preceded by the word "**scientific**." This law frequently distinguishes research from "**commercial testing**." Thus, when research is an **exempt function**, it is usually basic or fundamental research. Research can also qualify as a **charitable** or **educational** activity.

The **income** from certain categories or sources of research is **exempt** from the **unrelated business income tax**. Income derived from research for the U.S., any of its agencies or **instrumentalities**, a state, or a **political subdivision** of a state is **excluded** from taxation (**IRC** § 512(b)(7)). In the case of a **college**, **university**, or **hospital**, income derived from research for any **person** is excluded from taxation (**IRC** § 512(b)(8)). In the case of an organization **operated primarily** for purposes of carrying on fundamental research the results of which are freely available to the **public**, income derived from research for any person is excluded from taxation (**IRC** § 512(b)(9)). [EO §§ 9.2, 25.1(l); UB § 3.13; AR §§ 15.2(d)(7)(B)(vii), 15.2(i)(1)(K);

PF § 11.2(c); AS §§ 1.3(d), 5.9(i); PG p. 18; SM pp. 38, 177–178] (also **Qualified research**; **Scientific research**).

reserved life estate

The phrase "reserved life estate" is used to describe the retention by a **contributor** of **property** of an **interest** in the property for the life of the contributor. This phrase is most commonly used in relation to a **gift** of **real property**, where the contributor reserves the right to live on the property during his or her lifetime, with the **remainder interest** in the property passing to one or more **charitable organizations** following his or her death. [CG § 15.2].

residence

An individual may have one or more places of "residence"; these are places where the individual lives (has a bodily presence). An individual is, as to his or her place of residence, a "resident." **Tax liability** may be affected in relation to whether an individual is a resident or a nonresident. (also **Domicile**).

residence, gift of

See **Personal residence**.

resident agent

See **Registered agent**.

residuary beneficiary

A "residuary beneficiary" is a **person** to whom has been conveyed the **residue** of an **estate** by operation of a **residuary clause** in a **will**.

residuary clause

A "residuary clause" is a provision in a **will** conveying to one or more **beneficiaries** of the **estate** its **residue**.

residue

The word "residue" means something left over or remaining after one or more other things have been taken away (also "residuum"). This word is often used to refer to the **assets** of a **decedent's estate** after all of the **specific bequests** and **devises** have been accounted for. For example, an individual may die, leaving the "residue" of his or her estate to a **charitable organization**.

respondent

The word "respondent" essentially is synonymous with the word **defendant**. It is used in some courts (such as the U.S. Tax Court, where the **Commissioner of Internal Revenue** is always the respondent) instead of the word defendant, where the **person** initiating the **action** is termed the **petitioner**.

responsibility test

For purposes of the definition of the term **key employee**, the second of three tests that need to be satisfied is the "responsibility test." Pursuant to this test, the employee (1) has responsibilities, powers, or influence over the **organization** in its entirety similar to those of **trustees**, **directors**, or **officers**; (2) manages a discrete segment or activity of the organization that represents 10 percent or more of the activities, **assets**, **income**, or **expenses** of the organization, as compared to the organization in its entirety; or (3) has or shares authority to control or determine 10 percent or more of the organization's capital expenditures, operating budget, or compensation for employees.

responsible person

Under the **federal tax law**, the term "responsible person" is used to describe an individual, who, by reason of his or her relationship with an **organization** that is obligated to withhold and remit taxes (such as employment taxes) to the federal government, is responsible for payment of the tax if the organization fails to pay it. The law describes this individual as one who is required to "truthfully account for" a tax or who "**willfully attempts** in any manner to evade or defeat any such tax or the payment thereof" (**IRC** § 6672(a)). If the tax is not timely paid, the responsible person is liable for a **penalty** equal to the amount of the tax (*id.*). In the context of a **tax-exempt organization**, a responsible person can be a **director**, **trustee**, **officer**, or key **employee**; this is the case irrespective of whether the individual is serving as a **volunteer** or in an honorary capacity.

responsive

A **charitable organization** that intends to avoid **private foundation status** on the ground that it is a **supporting organization** must stand in at least one of three basic required relationships between a supporting organization and a **supported organization**. One of these relationships is encompassed by the phrase "**operated in connection with**" (**IRC** § 509(a)(3)(B)). Among the requirements for this relationship is that the supporting organization be "responsive" to (that is, attendant to and supportive—usually financially—of) the needs or demands of one or more supported organizations; this is demonstrated by satisfaction of the **responsiveness test**. [PF § 15.7(g)].

R

responsiveness test

An organization, to qualify as a **Type III supporting organization**, must satisfy a "responsiveness test," which requires that it be **responsive** to the needs or demands of a supported organization. This test is generally satisfied if (1) one more **trustees**, **directors**, or **officers** of the supporting organization are elected or appointed by the trustees, directors, officers, or **membership** of the supported organization; (2) one or more members of the governing body of the supported organization are also trustees, directors, or officers of, or hold other important offices in, the supporting organization; or (3) the trustees, directors, or officers of the supporting organization maintain a close and continuous working relationship with the trustees, directors, or officers of the supported organization.

Also, by reason of one of these three elements, the trustees, directors, or officers of the supported organization must, for this test to be satisfied, have a significant voice in the investment policies of the supporting organization, the timing of **grants**, the manner of making them, and the selection of recipients by the supporting organization, and in otherwise directing the use of the **income** or **assets** of the supporting organization. [PF § 15.7(g); EO § 12.3(c); HC § 5.5(d)].

restriction

A "restriction" is a form of limitation or **condition**. The word is often used in connection with a **charitable contribution**, where the **donor** restricts the **gift** for a particular use (such as construction of a particular building, **research**, or **scholarships**). [CG § 10.4].

retained interest

A "retained interest" is an **interest** in **property** which a **grantor**, **contributor**, or **person** in some other capacity creates in the property prior to the disposition of the property. The interest retained may be an **income interest** (including a **life estate**) or a **remainder interest**. If the transaction is a **contribution**, the **gift** may be of the interests in the property other than the retained interest or the gift may be of the entirety of the interests in the property, albeit to different **donees**. [CG § 9.23].

retirement plan

A "retirement plan" is an **employee** benefit program, maintained and **funded** (in whole or in part) by an **employer**, that provides retirement funding to the employee during (in whole or in part) his or her retirement. The **trust fund** that underlies this type of plan is a **tax-exempt organization** (IRC §§ 401(a), 501(a)). The law of retirement plans is substantially that enacted into law by the **Employee Retirement Income Security Act of 1974**. **Charitable contributions** may be made from these plans. [EO § 18.1; CG § 9.10] (also **Employee benefit**; **Employee benefit fund**; **Pension plan**).

retirement plan reversion

A **tax-exempt organization** may maintain a **qualified pension** or other **retirement plan** to provide retirement benefits to its **employees**. This type of plan may be terminated; if **assets** remain in it after satisfaction of all liabilities to plan participants and other **beneficiaries**, the **employer** is permitted to recover the excess assets. Where the employer is the type of **exempt organization** that is subject to the rule that all **income** other than **exempt function income** is taxable as **unrelated business income**, generally the amount of the reversion is included in the organization's unrelated business income. [EO §§ 18.1, 24.5(n); UB § 9.10].

retroactive revocation, of tax exemption

The **IRS** has the authority to **revoke recognition** of an **organization's tax-exempt status** or, absent this type of recognition, revoke an organization's tax exemption. In some instances, the tax exemption of an organization will be revoked "retroactively." This can occur where the organization omitted or misstated a **material fact** in the process of acquiring recognition of tax-exempt status, the organization **operated** in a manner that is materially different from that originally represented, or the organization engaged in a **prohibited act**. A retroactive revocation of recognition of tax-exempt status will occur as of the date the **IRS** determined that

exempt functions ceased. For example, an organization may have its tax-exempt status recognized in 2000, cease engaging in exempt functions in 2005, be **audited** in 2015, and have its tax exemption revoked in 2015, retroactive to 2005. [EO § 27.3; AU § 1.12; SM pp. 308–309].

return

A "return" is a document, usually promulgated by a government **agency**, which a **person** is required by **law** to fill out, complete, or otherwise add information to and "return" that document containing the requisite information to the agency by a specified time. The **federal tax law** defines a "return" as any return, statement, schedule, or list, and any amendment of or supplement to these documents (**IRC** § 6213(g)(1)). (also **Return, information**; **Return, tax**).

return, information

An "information return" is a **return** that must be submitted to the **IRS** by a **person** who is required by **law** to file it. It is so named because the purpose of the return is to provide information to the **IRS**; that is, it is not a **tax return**. For example, the **annual information return** that nearly every **tax-exempt organization** must file is an information return (**IRC** § 6033(a)(1)). Likewise, because **partnerships** and **S corporations** do not pay taxes, their annual returns are information returns. (also **Form 990**; **Form 990-Z**; **Form 990-PF**).

return, tax

A "tax return" is a **return** that must be submitted to the **IRS** by a **taxpayer**. The return includes the calculation of the taxpayer's **tax liability** for a particular period. Thus, most individuals, **corporations**, **estates**, **trusts**, and **unincorporated associations** must file tax returns, unless they are **tax-exempt organizations**. Even a tax-exempt organization, however, must file a tax return if it has **unrelated business income** for a **tax year** (**IRC** §§ 6012(a)(2), (4)). [AR passim; UB Chap. 3; EO § 28.8; AU §§ 5.10, 5.12, 5.19(j)] (also **Form 990-T**).

revenue

The term "revenue" means monies received, including returns on investment, **profits**, and issue from any type of **property**. The concept of "revenue" is broader than that of "income." For example, the **annual information return** filed by most **tax-exempt organizations** requires them to report their "revenue"; the term encompasses **contributions**, **gifts**, **grants**, **direct public support**, **indirect public support**, **government grants**, **program service revenue**, **membership dues** and **membership assessments**, **interest**, **dividends** and other interests from securities, net **rental** income, other investment income, gains or losses from the sale of property, net money from **special fundraising events**, and gains or losses from **sales**. [AR Chap. 7; PF § 12.1; CU Q 2.48, Q 2.50].

Revenue Act of 1913

The "Revenue Act of 1913" is the **legislation** that first established the **federal tax law**. The legislation enacted prior to that time (the **Tariff Act of 1894**) failed on **constitutional** law grounds; that legal problem was resolved by ratification of the Sixteenth Amendment to the U.S. Constitution. Both the 1894 and 1913 legislation contained provisions for **tax-exempt charitable**

organizations, the latter including the **private inurement doctrine**. [EO § 2.4; CG § 1.3(a); HC § 1.3].

Revenue Act of 1917

The "Revenue Act of 1917" caused enactment of the **federal income tax charitable contribution deduction**. [EO § 2.4].

Revenue Act of 1918

The "Revenue Act of 1918" expanded the category of **tax-exempt charitable organizations** to include those organized for the prevention of cruelty to children or animals. [EO § 2.4].

Revenue Act of 1921

The "Revenue Act of 1921" expanded the category of **tax-exempt charitable organizations** to include **community chests, funds,** and **foundations,** and added **literary organizations**. It also brought the **estate tax charitable contribution deduction**, which was made retroactive to 1917. [EO § 2.4].

Revenue Act of 1932

The "Revenue Act of 1932" caused enactment of the **gift tax charitable contribution deduction**. [EO § 2.4].

Revenue Act of 1934

The "Revenue Act of 1934" introduced the **federal tax law** prohibition on **substantial lobbying activities** by **charitable organizations**. [EO § 2.4].

Revenue Act of 1936

The "Revenue Act of 1936" introduced the **federal income tax deduction** for **corporations**. It limited that deduction to **contributions** to **organizations** established in the U.S. that used the contributions within the U.S. [CG § 18.2].

Revenue Act of 1938

The "Revenue Act of 1938" narrowed the **federal income tax charitable contribution deduction** for individuals to **gifts** to **domestic organizations**. [CG § 18.2; HC § 1.3].

Revenue Act of 1939

The "Revenue Act of 1939" altered the **federal income tax charitable contribution deduction** for individuals to make qualifying donees those that have been **organized** in the U.S. or a possession of the U.S. This remains the rule of **law** today. [CG § 18.2] (also **Conduit organization; Foreign charitable organization**).

Revenue Act of 1950

The "Revenue Act of 1950" introduced the basic **federal tax law** concerning the **unrelated trade or business rules**. [EO § 2.4; HC § 24.2].

R

Revenue Act of 1978

The "Revenue Act of 1978" brought interim relief measures to protect **employers** from the effects of misclassification of workers, under certain circumstances. [HC § 27.4].

Revenue Act of 1987

The "Revenue Act of 1987" brought **taxes** on **public charities** for engaging in **excessive lobbying** and **political campaign activities**, as well as the **fundraising disclosure** requirements for noncharitable **organizations**. [EO §§ 2.4, 22.4, 23.3; FR § 5.5; CG § 22.3].

revenue procedure

A "revenue procedure" is a statement, by the **IRS**, of its internal procedures and practices. These revenue procedures are published in the **Internal Revenue Bulletin**. For example, the **IRS** publishes revenue procedures that detail the processes for the issuance of **rulings, determination letters**, and **information letters**, and for seeking **recognition** of **tax exemption**. Revenue procedures are issued only by the **National Office** of the **IRS**. [EO App. A; AU § 2.10].

revenue ruling

A "revenue ruling" is an interpretation by the **IRS**, published in the **Internal Revenue Bulletin**, of one or more points of the **federal tax law**. It is the conclusion of the **IRS** on how the law is applied to a specific set of facts. Revenue rulings are issued only by the **National Office** of the **IRS** and are published for the information and guidance of **taxpayers**, **IRS** personnel, and other interested **parties**. [EO App. A; AU § 2.10].

revenue-sharing arrangement

To the extent to be provided in **tax regulations**, the phrase **excess benefit transaction** includes any transaction in which the amount of any economic benefit provided by an **applicable tax-exempt organization** to or **for the use of** a **disqualified person** is determined in whole or in part by the **revenue** generated by one or more activities of the organization, but only if the transaction results in **private inurement** (**IRC** § 4958(c)(3)). This type of transaction is known as a "revenue-sharing arrangement"; the **excess benefit** is the amount of the private inurement. [EO § 21.4(b); HC § 4.9(a)(iii); AR §§ 6.1(a)(4), 6.2(c)(6), 6.2(c)(7), 6.2(c)(8), 18.1(d)(4); CU Q 7.16; SM p. 59].

reversion

A "reversion" is a **property** or collection of properties, and/or interest in one or more properties, left by a **grantor** or his or her **heirs**, which **vests** or otherwise comes into being on the extinction of some other interest in the property or properties. Thus, a reversion is a form of **future interest**. A reversion occurs by **operation of law**; by contrast, a **remainder interest** arises by act of one or more **persons**.

A **charitable organization** may not be **organized** so that one or more individuals retains a reversion (or "reversionary interest"), by which the **assets** of the organization would flow to one or more persons in their **private capacity** upon **dissolution** or **liquidation**. [CG § 5.3; EO § 4.3(b)] (also **Private inurement**).

revocable

An **instrument** or transaction is "revocable" when one or more **persons** have the **right** to revoke (that is, annul, nullify, rescind, **void**) it. For example, a **will** and many **trusts** are revocable. Often, an instrument or a transaction will not have any legal effect if it is (or while it remains) revocable. Thus, a contribution by means of a revocable trust is not deductible until or unless it becomes irrevocable.

revocable transfer

A **person** may transfer **property** to another person, with the transfer structured as a "revocable" one, that is, the **transferor** retains the **right** to modify the terms of the transfer or even undo it. Property may be transferred in this fashion so that **legal title** is transferred but **beneficial title** is retained (because of the nature of the powers and rights that have been retained). Property transferred in this way remains part of the **gross estate** of the transferor. **Tax deductibility** may depend upon whether a transfer is revocable, rather than **irrevocable**; for example, there is no **federal income tax charitable contribution deduction** for a transfer of money or property to a **charitable organization** if the transfer is a revocable one. [CG § 8.3(a)].

revocation, of tax exemption

The **IRS** has the authority to "revoke" its prior **recognition** of the **tax-exempt status** of an **organization**. This may occur because of a **substantial** change in the character, purpose, or method of operation of the organization, or because of a change in the **law**. The **IRS** also has the authority to revoke the exempt status of an organization where the exemption was obtained but not recognized by it. In appropriate circumstances, the **IRS** may revoke an organization's tax exemption **retroactively**. [EO §§ 26.1(c), 27.3; AU §§ 1.12, 5.21, 5.22, 5.26, 5.33(e); HC § 36.5].

right

A "right" includes some form of **interest** in or possession by a **person**, in or with respect to money or an item of **property**, as well as some relationship to a government, another person, or a rule of **law**. For example, when a person has the right to file a **lawsuit**, the person is said to have a "right of **action**." Individual liberties are expressed as **constitutional** rights or civil rights. Other expressions using this term are "right of privacy," "right of way," "right to remain silent," and "right to work laws."

right to use property

A **person** may **contribute** to a **charitable organization** the "**right** to use **property**" (such as a **rent**-free use of office space). There is, however, no **federal income tax charitable contribution deduction** for this type of **gift**. [CG § 9.18] (also **In-kind contribution**).

rollover

A "rollover" is essentially a **federal tax law** term to describe certain transfers of money or **property** that are not **recognized** for tax purposes. For example, an individual may transfer money or property from a **retirement plan** to an individual retirement account without having to pay taxes or incur **penalties** as a consequence of the transfer. As another illustration, an individual may sell his or her principal **residence** and reinvest the sales proceeds in another principal residence within two years before or after the sale without having to **recognize gain** except to the extent the adjusted sales price of the old residence exceeds the purchase cost of the new residence (**IRC** § 1034).

Likewise, a **tax-exempt social club** enjoys a similar rule, concerning property used **directly** in the performance of the club's **tax-exempt purposes**; where this type of property is sold and the proceeds reinvested in **exempt function property**, with in a period beginning one year before the sale date and ending three years after that date, any gain from the sale is recognized only to the extent that the **sale** price of the old property exceeds the purchase price of the new property (**IRC** § 512(a)(3)(D)). [**EO** § 15.6; **CG** § 2.14(f)].

royalty

A "royalty" is a payment (a form of **income**) reserved by the **grantor** of a **property** or an **interest** in property, where the grant is for the use or development of the property or property interest by the **grantee**, with the payment based on the use made of the property by the grantee. For example, an **organization** may own a property (such as land) and transfer it to another **person** for purposes of development (such as mining); the grantee would pay a royalty to the grantor based on the production generated by the activity of the grantee.

In general, a **tax-exempt organization** can receive income in the form of a royalty and not be subjected to the **unrelated income tax** on that income (**IRC** § 512(b)(3)). Nonetheless, where the exempt organization is **actively** involved in the **business** that generates the income, such as through the provision of services, the income may be taxed (unless the underlying business activity is **related** to the organization's **tax-exempt purposes**); in this situation, the relationship between the parties is that of **joint venturers**. Also, this tax may apply where the royalty income is **debt-financed** (**IRC** § 512(b)(4)). [**UB** § 3.7; **EO** § 25.1(g); **PF** §§ 10.3(f), 11.2; **HC** § 24.18; **FR** § 5.7(b)(vi); **AR** §§ 7.2(a)(3), 7.2(b)(13); **SM** p. 177].

rule

A "rule" is a form of **law**. A rule may be issued by an **agency** of the **federal**, state, or local government. A rule usually is an interpretation of a **statute** and/or a **regulation**. Most rules are issued by a component of the **executive branch** of a government, although both legislative bodies and courts issue rules for the conduct of matters before them. For example, the U.S. Congress enacts tax statutes, the **Department of the Treasury** (and, within it, the **IRS**) promulgates **regulations** in amplification of the statutes, and the **IRS** issues rules (**rulings**) in interpretation of the statutes and the regulations (**IRC** § 7805).

A court is not bound by an executive branch rule; however, a court will normally follow a rule, in **deference** to the expertise underlying it. Nonetheless, a court can **void** a rule if it is broader than the statute or regulation to which it relates. [EO App. A].

ruling

The term "ruling," in this context of the **law**, means a pronouncement by a **governmental agency**. The term is applied to conclusions of fact and law by regulatory agencies and courts. The most common use of the term "ruling" in the law as it applies to **tax-exempt organizations** is with respect to **determination letters** issued by the **IRS**. The most common of these rulings is the ruling issued **recognizing** the tax-exempt status of a **nonprofit organization**. A "ruling" of this type is issued by the **National Office** of the **IRS**. The **IRS** issues rulings that are either **revenue rulings** or **private letter rulings**. In a generic sense, **technical advice memoranda**, **general counsel memoranda**, and **chief counsel memoranda** are also "rulings." [EO App. A, § 26.1(c); CU Q 3.20; RE Q 8.24; LI Q 2.16].

ruling request

See **Request a ruling**.

R

S

S corporation

An "S corporation" is a **corporation** that has certain characteristics that make it nontaxable under the **federal tax law**; in this sense, this type of corporation is treated, for tax purposes, in the same way as a **partnership** (IRC § 1372(a)(1)). (As corporation with this feature is so named because the tax rules with respect to it are found in the **IRC**, Subtitle A, Subchapter S.) This body of law allows the shareholders of a qualifying **C corporation** to **elect** a **pass-through** system under which corporate **income taxes**, **deductions**, and **credits** are passed through and **directly** attributed to the shareholders (IRC §§ 1361–1379). A **tax-exempt charitable organization** may be a shareholder in an S corporation (IRC § 1361(c)(6)), although that interest is treated as an interest in an **unrelated trade or business**, so that all items of income, loss, or deduction, and any gain or loss on the disposition of the stock in an S corporation, must be taken into account as **unrelated business taxable income** (IRC § 512(e)). [CG §§ 2.8, 3.2, 6.13, 6.15, 7.18(a), 9.8, 24.3, 24.7(a); EO §§ 19.23, 25.2(m), 32.8(c); UB §§ 6.3(c), 8.2; PF § 11.3(c)].

safe harbor

The concept of a "safe harbor" is derived from the thought of a safe place near land for a boat in a storm. In the **law**, a "safe harbor" is a set of rules that, when met, provide assurance to the **person** involved that a general rule has been complied with. For example, with respect to the limitations on **lobbying** by a **public charity**, compliance with the **expenditure test** is a safe harbor in relation to that limitation. [EO §§ 22.2(b), 22.3(d); HC §§ 9.2(a), 24.16, 24.17, 27.4, 30.3(c); SM pp. 189–191].

salary

The word "salary" means fixed **compensation** periodically paid to an individual for services rendered. The word usually is used in connection with work that is other than manual or menial labor. [HC §§ 25.5(a), 28.5(a)] (also **Wages**).

sale

A "sale" is a transaction where there is a transfer of **property** or the rendition of a service from one **person** to another in exchange for **consideration**. Thus, a transaction that constitutes a sale

Bruce R. Hopkins' Nonprofit Law Dictionary, First Edition. Bruce R. Hopkins.
© 2015 Bruce R. Hopkins. Published 2015 by John Wiley & Sons, Inc.

cannot qualify as a **contribution**, although a transaction may be partially a sale and partially a contribution. [CG §§ 3.1(c), 9.19; PF § 5.4; FR § 3.2(d); CU Q 18.28–Q 18.30] (also **Sale or exchange**).

sale and leaseback

A "sale and leaseback" is a transaction whereby an owner of a **property** sells it to another **person**, who immediately **leases** the property back to the prior owner of the property. It was a variety of sale and **leaseback** transactions involving **tax-exempt organizations** that caused enactment of the **tax-exempt entity leasing rules**. [EO § 28.16; SM pp. 219–220].

sale or exchange

The phrase "sale or exchange," common in the **federal tax law**, is used to refer to a **disposition** of **property** for a full and adequate **consideration**, in contrast to a **contribution** of property. A sale or exchange of property may cause a **realization** of **gain** as a result of the transaction. The word "exchange" usually is somewhat superfluous, in that the word "sale" often suffices to describe the transaction. The word "exchange" is added to be certain that all types of dispositions, other than gifts, are captured by the phrase.

sales solicitation for charitable purposes

Under the **charitable solicitation acts** of some states, the phrase "sales solicitation for charitable purposes" is used to describe what other states term a **charitable sales promotion** or a **commercial co-venture**. [FR § 3.8].

sales tax

A "sales tax" is a **tax**, levied by state and local governments, on the sale of certain items of **property** at retail. Usually, this tax consists of one **rate**. In some states, certain types of **nonprofit organizations** (most frequently, **charitable** ones) are **exempt** from payment of the sales tax (although not necessarily exempt from the collection of it). [CG § 9.13(f); FR § 8.8(f)] (cf. **Use tax**).

salvage value

The "salvage value" of an item of **property** is the estimated **value** of the property as of the time the owner of the property has finished use of it. It is the value of a property at the completion of its **useful life**.

same geographic locale

One of the requirements for **tax exemption** as a **voluntary employees' beneficiary association** is that the **members** must have an employment-related bond. The bond may be demonstrated where employees of one or more **employers** are engaged in the same **line of business** in the "same geographic locale." [EO § 18.3].

same specific subject

The phrase "same specific subject," as employed in the **same specific subject allocation rule**, means an activity or specific issue, discussed in a non-**lobbying** context, that would be **directly** affected by the **specific legislation** that is the subject of the **lobbying** message in the same **communication**. Also, a discussion of the background or consequences of the specific legislation, or discussion of the background or consequences of an activity or specific issue affected by the specific legislation, is on the same specific subject as the lobbying communication. [EO § 22.3(d)(ii)].

same specific subject allocation rule

One of the two rules under the **expenditure test** concerning **allocation** of **expenses** between **lobbying** and non-lobbying purposes pertains to nonmembership lobbying **communications**. Where this type of communication also has a **bona fide** nonlobbying purpose, the **organization** must include as lobbying **expenditures** all costs attributable to those parts of the communication that are on the **same specific subject** as the lobbying message. [EO § 22.3(d)(ii)].

same state rule

Generally, **gross income** from the **sale** of items that result from the performance of **tax-exempt functions** does not constitute gross income from the conduct of an **unrelated business** if the item is sold in **substantially** the "same state" (using the word *state* to mean corporeal form, not governmental jurisdiction) it is in on completion of the exempt functions. [UB § 2.7(c); EO § 24.4(c); HC § 24.4(b)].

sanction

The word "sanction" has several meanings in the **law**. A sanction can apply in either the **civil** or **criminal law** context. It includes a fine, one or more **taxes**, an **injunction**, and/or imprisonment. As to the law of **tax-exempt organizations**, sanctions are prevalent in the **federal tax law** and the states' **charitable solicitation acts**. For example, as to the former, the various **excise taxes** underlying the **private foundation rules** are sanctions. Indeed, the tax penalties that underlie the **excess benefit transactions rules** are termed **intermediate sanctions**. [EO §§ 12.4, 21.10; PF §§ 1.10, 5.1, 5.2; FR § 3.21; SM pp. 59, 90–91] (also **Excise taxes**).

sanctioned whaling activities

The phrase "sanctioned whaling activities" means subsistence bowhead whale hunting activities conducted pursuant to the management plan of the Alaska Eskimo Whaling Commission (**IRC** § 170(n)(3)).

sanctions, intermediate

See **Intermediate sanctions**.

Sarbanes-Oxley Act

The "Sarbanes-Oxley Act" is **federal** accounting reform and **for-profit corporate** responsibility legislation that was signed into law in 2002. This measure is focused on publicly traded companies and large accounting firms. The emergence of this **law**, however, is raising a number of questions for **nonprofit organizations** as to application of its principles to them; the leadership of these organizations often voluntarily adopts many of its precepts. [GV §§ 2.1(c), 3.2, 4.2(b), 5.10, 5.16, 5.18, 5.19, 6.0, 6.1(a), 6.3(c), 6.3(d); AR §§ 5.1(g)(1), 7.1(c); EO § 5.5; HC §§ 28.3(d), 33.3(a); CU Q 5.19; AS § 11.1; SM pp. 93, 270; LI Q 3.17, 3.18].

Schedule K-1

Income from **partnership investments**, including income received by a **tax-exempt organization**, is reported to it on "Schedule K-1," accompanying **Form 1065**, as developed by the **IRS**. [PF §§ 6.5(b), 10.3(a), 10.3(h), 11.3(c), 12.3(g); EO § 31.6].

schedules, Form 990

The "Form 990" (**annual information return**) and in some instances the **Form 990-EZ**, is accompanied by seventeen schedules; which of them have to be prepared by a filing **tax-exempt organization** depends on the type of **exempt organization** involved, the mature of its funding and other financial matters, and its program and other activities. [AR Chap. 3].

scholarship

A "scholarship" is a **grant** of money to a student to enable him or her to attend a **school, college,** or **university**. The scholarship can be for tuition, fees, books, supplies, equipment, travel, secretarial and similar assistance, meals, and/or lodging. (The latter two items are commonly referred to as "room and board"). As to the **grantee**, the amount paid as a scholarship by the **grantor** will constitute **gross income** unless the amount received constitutes a **qualified scholarship** and the recipient is a candidate for a degree at a qualifying **educational organization** (**IRC** § 117(a)). [CU Q 11.2, Q 11.3; PF § 9.3; CL § 8.6; EO § 7.8; AR § 12.1(f); SM pp. 71–72] (also **Fellowship**).

school

The word "school" means a facility, the **primary** function of which is the presentation of formal instruction, that is, where **educational** activity occurs, particularly where those receiving the instruction are children. That is, the word "school" is commonly meant to be the equivalent of the phrases "elementary school" (or "lower school") and "high school" (or "secondary school"), in that it encompasses the type of education provided at **educational institutions** other than **colleges** and **universities**. A **nonprofit** school almost always is a **tax-exempt organization** (**IRC** § 501(a), by reason of description in **IRC** § 501(c)(3)) and a **public charity** (**IRC** §§ 170(b)(1)(A)(ii) and 509(a)(1)). Most schools satisfy the **federal income tax** definition of the term, which is that the organization normally maintains a regular faculty and curriculum and normally has a regularly enrolled body of students in attendance at the place where its educational activities are regularly carried on (**IRC** § 170(b)(1)(A)(ii)). The word "school" is also used to refer to a division of a university offering courses of instruction in a particular profession, such as a school of nursing, engineering, law, or architecture. [CU Q 2.13, Q 2.14; EO §§ 8.3(a), 12.3(a), 24.5(a); FR § 5.12; AR Chap. 12, §§ 3.1(m), 3.2(m); PF § 15.3(b); SM pp. 35, 80; LI Q 9.13] (also **Institution**).

S

science

The word "science" means a branch of study in which knowledge is systematized or classified through the use of observation, experimentation, or reasoning; it also entails the formulation of **scientific** principles and rules. [EO § 9.1; SM p. 38].

science, advancement of

One of the ways a **nonprofit organization** can achieve **tax-exempt status** under the **federal tax law** is to qualify as a **charitable organization** on the basis that it is **organized** and **operated** to advance **science**. This type of **entity** usually is not one that engages **directly** in scientific **research** (a **scientific organization**) but rather engages in collateral activities, such as publishing or conferences. [EO § 7.9; CG § 3.3(b); SM p. 34].

scientific

The word "scientific" means of or pertaining to, or concerned with, **science**.

scientific organization

The phrase "scientific organization" means an **organization** that has as its **primary** purpose the dissemination of **scientific** knowledge. A scientific organization usually engages in scientific **research**. If a scientific organization is serving a public interest, rather than a private interest, it may qualify for **federal income tax exemption** (**IRC** § 501(a), by reason of description in **IRC** § 501(c)(3)). A **tax-exempt** scientific organization may also engage in activities that are **charitable** and/or **educational**, such as publishing and the conduct of seminars and conferences. [EO Chap. 9; PF §§ 1.6, 1.8; CG § 3.3(b); FR § 5.18(b)(iv); AU § 7.1(g); SM p. 38; LI 1.50].

scientific research

Although the projects may vary in terms of degree of sophistication, if professional skill is involved in the design and supervision of a project intended to solve a problem through a search for a demonstrable truth, the project usually entails "scientific research." [EO § 9.2; UB § 3.13; SM p. 38].

scientific research property, gift of

Special **federal tax rules** are applicable to **charitable contributions** of **scientific property** used for **research** (**IRC** § 170(e)(4)). To qualify under these rules, the **property** that is the subject of the gift must be **tangible personal property** and stock in trade of a **corporation** or other property of a kind that would properly be included in the **inventory** of the corporation if on hand at the close of the **tax year**, or property held by the corporation primarily for sale to customers in the ordinary course of its **trade or business**. Also, this **gift** must be a **qualified research contribution**.

The amount of this charitable deduction is determined by applying two reduction rules. The amount of the first reduction is equal to one-half of the amount of **gain** that would not have been **long-term capital gain** if the property had been sold by the donor at its **fair market value** on the date of its contribution. If the amount of the charitable contribution that remains after this reduction exceeds twice the **basis** of the contributed property, then the amount of the charitable contribution is reduced a second time to an amount that is equal to twice the amount of the basis of the property.

This deduction is generally available only for **corporations**. It is not available, however, to an **S corporation**, a personal holding company, or a service corporation. [CG § 9.4; SM p. 137] (also **Twice-basis deduction**).

scope of authority

The phrase "scope of authority" is used in the law of **principal** and **agent**. It describes a range of acts that may be appropriately and necessarily undertaken by the agent to accomplish the objective of the **agency** relationship. **Liability** can arise for the principal for acts committed by the agent if the acts were within the scope of authority of the agent.

scope of employment

The phrase "scope of employment" describes a range of acts that may be appropriately and necessarily undertaken by an **employee** to accomplish his or her employment goals. **Liability** can arise for the **employer**, and if an **organization**, its **directors** and **officers**, for acts committed by an employee if the acts were within the scope of his or her employment.

scrivener's error

Errors are made from time to time by **lawyers** in drafting **charitable remainder trust** documents, with inadvertent insertion of one or more provision that should not be in the document or failures to include one or more provisions that are required to be in the document. The **IRS** generously (and quaintly) considers mistakes of this nature to be "scriveners' errors," although correction by judicial reformation is usually required. [CG § 12.4(i)].

second-tier subsidiary

A "second-tier subsidiary" is an **organization** that is a "**subsidiary**" with respect to a **parent** organization. In this instance, however, there is not an **element** of **direct control** between the parent and the subsidiary; the control element is between a "**first-tier subsidiary**" and the second-tier subsidiary. In other words, a parent organization controls the first tier subsidiary and the first-tier subsidiary controls the second-tier subsidiary; at most, the parent entity indirectly controls the second-tier subsidiary.

second-tier tax

The term "second-tier tax" is synonymous with the term **additional tax**, as that term is used in the **black lung benefits trust**, **donor-advised fund**, **intermediate sanctions**, **political expenditures**, and **private foundations** settings. (IRC § 4963(b)).

secondary education

"Secondary education" is **education** received at the high-**school** level. It is education other than that received in the lower schools, and at **colleges** and **universities**. [CU Q 2.19] (also **Higher education**).

secondary private benefit

"Secondary private benefit" is a form of **private benefit**. It is the form of private benefit that is **indirectly** provided to an **organization**. For example, in the case of a **school** that trains individuals to be **political campaign consultants** and other professionals, the secondary recipients of the benefit provided are the **political candidates** and **political parties** that hire the school's graduates (a form of benefit that would jeopardize the **tax-exempt status** of the school). [EO § 20.11(a); HC § 4.6] (cf. **Primary private benefit**).

secretary

Nearly every **nonprofit organization** is required to have a "secretary." (The principal exception to this rule is a **trust**.) The secretary is to keep the **minutes** of the meetings of the **board of directors** or **board of trustees**, see that all notices are duly given in accordance with the provision of the organization's **bylaws** or as required by **law**, be custodian of the **records** of the organization, and see to it that any seal of the organization is affixed to all documents executed on behalf of the organization (if required). In general, a secretary of a nonprofit organization may perform all duties incident to the office of secretary of an organization and performs such other **reasonable** duties as from time to time may be assigned by the **president** or by the **governing board** of the organization. [SM p. 20; PG p. 16].

Secretary of the Treasury

The "Secretary of the Treasury" has the **principal** responsibility of administering and enforcing the **federal tax law**, in his or her capacity as the top **executive** of the **Department of the Treasury** (IRC § 7801). One of the functions of the Secretary is to prescribe the powers and duties of the **Commissioner of Internal Revenue** (IRC § 7802(a)). [EO § 2.2(a); AU § 2.1(a)].

section 263a cost allocation method

The phrase "section 263A cost allocation method" is a method of **allocation of expenses** used by an **organization** in allocating costs to **lobbying activities**, for purposes of the rules denying a **business expense deduction** for certain lobbying activities (**IRC** § 162(e)(1)). Pursuant to this method, an organization determines the costs properly allocable to lobbying activities under rules concerning **capitalization** and inclusion in **inventory costs** of certain expenses (**IRC** § 263A). Lobbying activities are considered a service department or function for this purpose. [EO § 22.6(a)] (also **Gross-up method; Ratio method**).

Section 306 stock

"Section 306 stock" is stock acquired in a nontaxable transaction which, if the stock were sold, would generate **ordinary income** (rather than **capital gain**); its name is derived from the fact that it is defined in Section 306 of the **IRC**. A **gift** of this type of stock can yield a **charitable contribution deduction**, although what would otherwise be the charitable deduction (based on the **fair market value** of the stock) must be reduced by the amount of ordinary income that would have been realized on a sale of the stock. [CG §§ 4.4(a), 9.9].

Section 501(c)(3) organization

In referencing one of the most well-known sections in the **IRC**—"Section 501(c)(3)"—the **federal tax law** encompasses **tax-exempt charitable, educational, scientific, religious**, and like **organizations (IRC § 4955(f)(1))**. (see **Charitable organization**).

sector, of U.S. society

The concept of "sectors" of U.S. society includes the thought that, in the largest sense, there are three of them. The institutions of society within the U.S. are generally classified as governmental, **for-profit**, or **nonprofit entities**. Nonprofit organizations constitute a sector that is called, variously, the "**philanthropic**" sector, "third" sector, "**voluntary**" sector, "independent" sector, or "private" sector. [EO § 1.1(b); CG § 1.4; SM pp. 4–5].

securities, lending of

Payments to a **tax-exempt organization** for the lending of securities to a broker and the return of identical securities are not items of **unrelated business taxable income (IRC § 512(a)(5))**. For this non-taxation treatment to apply, the security loans must be fully collateralized and must be terminable on five business days' notice by the lending organization. An agreement among the parties must provide for reasonable procedures to implement the obligation of the borrower to furnish collateral to the lender with a **fair market value** on each business day the loan is outstanding in an amount at least equal to the fair market value of the security at the close of business on the preceding day. [UB §§ 3.4, 5.4(e)(v), 5.4(g); EO § 25.1(d); PF § 6.2(f)].

Securities Exchange Act of 1934

The "Securities Exchange Act of 1934" is **legislation** regulating the secondary trading of securities. This **law** created the Securities Exchange Commission. [CG §§ 5.9, 14.9].

seeding, of pooled income funds

Although the **federal tax law** states that a **pooled income fund** can include only amounts received from transfers that meet the **statutory** tests, a **charitable organization** may combine its **endowment assets** with the assets of the fund for investment purposes, as long as adequate records are maintained to show the separate nature of the two categories of assets.

A charitable organization may begin operation of its pooled income fund by "seeding" the fund, in whole or in part, with its own assets. This may have to be done, for example, where the **trustee** is a financial institution that demands an initial deposit of some magnitude in the fund and there are inadequate **gifts** at the outset. Thereafter, as gifts come in, the assets can be withdrawn from the fund. In any event, **income beneficiaries** do not participate in the earnings from the non-gift assets in the fund. [CG § 5.5(h)].

self-dealing

In general, the term "self-dealing" is used to describe a transaction where a **fiduciary** acquires or makes use of **property**, which belongs to the **person** as to whom the fiduciary stands in a fiduciary relationship, for his, her, or its benefit. When Congress enacted the **Tax**

Reform Act of 1969, one of its primary goals was to eradicate transactions between a **private foundation** and those who have some special relationship with the foundation (who became termed **disqualified persons**), particularly where the transaction was or appeared to be economically disadvantageous to the foundation. Thus, one of the principal features of the 1969 legislation was introduction of the rules concerning "self-dealing" where the transaction involved private foundations (**IRC § 4941**). These rules, as **substantially** amplified by **regulations**, **revenue rulings**, **private letter rulings**, and court opinions over the ensuing years, have proven to be a formidable barrier to inappropriate transactions and arrangements between a private foundation and one or more disqualified persons with respect it. In many ways, the self-dealing rules are a codification of important elements of the **private inurement** proscriptions.

Self-dealing consists of two basic categories of transactions: **direct self-dealing** and **indirect self-dealing**. Both of these types of self-dealing are predicated on the thought that **arm's length** standards are inadequate and that it is immaterial whether the self-dealing transaction results in a benefit or detriment to the foundation. A self-dealing transaction, however, does not include a transaction between a private foundation and a disqualified person where the disqualified person status arises only as a result of the transaction.

In general, the following transactions between a private foundation and one or more disqualified persons are acts of self-dealing: the (1) **sale or exchange** of **property**, (2) **leasing** of **property**, (3) lending of money or other extension of credit, (4) furnishing of goods, services, or facilities, (5) payments of **compensation** or **expenses**, (6) transfer to or use by or **for the benefit of** a disqualified person of the private foundation's **income** or **assets**, and (7) payment of money or property to **government officials**. [PF Chap. 5; EO § 12.4(a); RE Q 6.1; PG pp. 62–63, 76–78, 335; SM pp. 89, 90; LI Q 5.9–Q 5.34, Q 5.36].

self-declarer

The **IRS** uses the term "self-declarer," in a somewhat deprecating manner, to describe a type of **nonprofit organization** that can, lawfully, be **tax-exempt** without having to obtain a **determination letter** or **ruling recognizing** its exempt status. Organizations of this nature include **social welfare organizations**, **business leagues**, and **social clubs**. [EO § 26.7; SM p. 24].

self-defense communications

The phrase "self-defense communication" is used, as an element of the **expenditure test**, to describe a **communication** that is not a **direct lobbying communication**. This means that a **charitable organization** that has **elected** the expenditure test and is in conformance with it can engage in one or more self-defense communications without having those communications taken into account in determining overall allowable lobbying.

A self-defense communication generally is an appearance before, or communication with, a legislative body with respect to a possible action by that body that might affect the existence of the charitable organization, its powers and duties, its **tax-exempt status**, or the **deductibility** of **contributions** to it (**IRC § 4911(d)(2)(C)**). A similar rule applies to a communication by a **member** of an **affiliated group** of charitable organizations or of a **limited group of organizations**. The communication can be with the entire legislative body, committees or subcommittees of it, individual legislators, members of their staffs, or representatives of the executive branch who are involved in the legislative process.

A self-defense exception is also available in the context of the restrictions on lobbying activities by **private foundations** (**IRC** § 4945(e)). [EO § 22.3(d)(v); PF § 9.1(e); CU Q 8.18; SM p. 190].

self-defense lobbying

A **tax-exempt charitable** engages in "self-defense lobbying" to the extent its **lobbying communications** are confined to **self-defense communications**.

self-perpetuating board

The phrase "self-perpetuating board" is used to describe a **governing board** of a **nonprofit organization** that perpetuates itself; that is, its **members** elect subsequent members of the board (who may be or include themselves). This type of board is distinguished from, for example, a board that is elected by a **membership** or a board whose members are appointed by another body. [SM p. 17; PG p. 10].

seller-financing restriction

The term "seller-financing restriction" is used in the context of defining circumstances where an **exception**, from the **law** treating **income** from **debt-financed property** as **unrelated business income**, is available to **qualified organizations** that make debt-financed investments in **real property** (**IRC** § 514(c)(9)(A)). Under this exception, income from investments in real property is not treated as income from unrelated debt-financed property. This exception is available only where six restrictions are satisfied (**IRC** § 514(c)(9)(B)). One of them is the "seller-financing restriction," which provides that the seller or a **person related** to the seller (or a person related to the plan with respect to which a **pension trust** was formed) may not provide financing in connection with the acquisition of the property (**IRC** § 514(c)(9)(B)(v)). This rule is, however, not violated where the financing is on **commercially reasonable** terms (**IRC** § 514(c)(9)(G)(ii)). [EO § 24.9(c)].

S

separate contribution

The term "separate contribution" is used in applying the **substantiation requirements** with respect to **contributions** of $250 or more; these requirements apply to "separate contributions." Under this **law**, separate payments generally are treated as separate contributions and are not aggregated for the purpose of applying the $250 threshold. In cases of contributions paid by withholding from wages, the deduction from each paycheck is treated as a separate payment. [CG § 21.3(a); FR § 5.3].

separate fundraising unit

One of two types of **fundraising expenditures** that are not **exempt purpose expenditures**, for purposes of the **expenditure test**, are expenditures paid to or incurred for a "separate fundraising unit" of the **charitable organization** involved or of an organization **affiliated** with it (**IRC**

§ 4911(e)(1)(C)). A "separate fundraising unit" is two or more individuals, a majority of whose time is spent on fundraising for the organization or any separate accounting unit of the organization that is devoted to fundraising. Amounts paid to or incurred for a separate fundraising unit include all amounts incurred for the creation, production, copying, and distribution of the fundraising portion of a separate fundraising unit's **communication**. [EO § 22.3(d)(iii)].

separate identity principle

The "separate identity principle" is a **doctrine** developed by courts to determine whether the activities of one **organization** should be attributed to another organization for **law**, such as the **federal tax law**, purposes. This principle is frequently applied in the **tax-exempt organizations** law context, whether both **entities** are exempt organizations or one of them is a **for-profit organization**. There will be attribution if the organization the activities of which are to be attributed lacks a business purpose or that entity is merely an arm, **agent**, or **instrumentality** of the other organization. The application of this principle often arises where the relationship between the two organizations is that of **parent** and **subsidiary**. [EO § 30.2].

separate payment

The concept of a "separate payment" is used in connection with the **disclosure requirements** that apply with respect to **quid pro quo contributions** in excess of $75. For purposes of that threshold, separate payments made at different times during a year in conjunction with separate fundraising events generally will not be aggregated. [CG § 22.2; FR § 5.4].

separate segregated fund

The **federal** election law defines a form of committee that is allowed to **solicit** and receive **contributions** from a restricted class of **donors** and, in turn, make contributions and **expenditures** to influence the outcome of federal elections. These committees are known, pursuant to this law, as "separate segregated funds," because the committee's funds are kept separate and segregated from the funds of the **organization** that is sponsoring the **fund**. These **entities** are known in the **federal tax law** as **political organizations** or, more specifically, **political action committees**. [EO § 17.1; AR §§ 10.1(c), 10.2(a)(1), 10.2(c)(3)].

separation of church and state

The passage in the **First Amendment** that "Congress shall make no law respecting an establishment of religion, or prohibiting the free exercise thereof" is often read as a mandate that there must be a "separation of church and state." The U.S. Constitution does not use that phraseology, however, and the U.S. Supreme Court interprets the **Religion Clauses** with an attitude of neutrality and flexibility. [CL §§ 2.1, 2.2; EO §§ 10.1(a)(i), 10.1(a)(ii)].

sequencing list

The **IRS** developed a "sequencing list" to assist **tax-exempt organizations** in completing the **Form 990**, including its schedules. [AR §§ 1.5(a), 1.11].

service of process

The phrase "service of process" refers to the communication of court proceedings to a party to a **lawsuit** or to another **person**. This is accomplished by actual delivery or other method, permissible under the **law**, which provides reasonable notice of the court proceedings against or affecting the person.

service provider organization

The phrase "service provider organization" is used to describe one category of **charitable organization** that is not a **private foundation** by reason of the fact that it is a form of **publicly supported organization**. The term "service provider" is used because this category of organization can include as **public support** certain types of **exempt function revenue**, that is, revenue generated from the performance of tax-exempt functions. For an organization to achieve nonprivate foundation status as a service provider charitable organization, it must **normally** receive more than one-third of its support from any combination of (1) **gifts**, **grants**, **contributions**, and/or **membership fees**, and (2) **gross receipts** from admissions, sales of merchandise, performance of services, or furnishing of facilities in activities **related** to its **tax-exempt purposes**, subject to certain limitations, as long as the support in either category is from **permitted sources** (**IRC** § 509(a)(2)(A)).

There is no limitation on the amount of support that may be taken into account in determining public support from the first of these categories, other than the requirement that the support be from permitted sources. In computing the amount of support received in the form of gross receipts (the second of these categories) that is allowable toward the one-third requirement, however, gross receipts from related activities received from any **person** or from any **bureau or similar agency** of a **governmental unit** are includible as public support in any **tax year** to the extent that the receipts do not exceed the greater of $5,000 or 1 percent of the organization's support for the year (the **1 percent limitation**) (**IRC** § 509(a)(2)(A)(ii)).

Further, an organization, to be a service provider entity, must normally receive not more than one-third of its support from the sum of **gross investment income** and any excess of the amount of **unrelated business taxable income** over the amount of the **tax** on that income (**IRC** § 509(a)(2)(B)). [PF §§ 15.5, 15.6, 15.8(a), 15.9, 15.10; EO § 12.3(b)(iv); HC § 5.3; CG §§ 3.4(a), 24.7(b)(22); AR §§ 8.1(e), 8.3; SM p. 82].

services, gifts of

An individual may **contribute** (or have contributed) to a **charitable organization**, his or her services. This is, of course, the action of a **volunteer**. There is no **federal income tax charitable contribution deduction** for the contribution of services. Unreimbursed **expenses** made incident to the rendition of services to charitable organizations, however, are deductible. [CG §§ 9.14, 20.3].

settlement

A "settlement" is the closing of a matter by action of the parties to a **lawsuit** or similar (including **administrative**) proceeding. A settlement, if it is of a judicial proceeding, may require approval of the court. [HC § 36.5] (also **Closing agreement**; **Will settlement**).

settlor

A "settlor" is a **person** who creates a **trust**. (also **Creator of a trust**).

set-aside

The term "set-aside" is primarily used as part of the law pertaining to **private foundations**. A private foundation must pay out a certain amount for **charitable purposes** with respect to each of its tax years; this amount is called the **mandatory payout amount** or, more technically, the **distributable amount**. This amount is usually equal to the foundation's **minimum investment return** and the amounts expended (or **property** transferred) by a private foundation to meet the mandatory payout must generally be in the form of **qualifying distributions**.

An **exception** to the timing of distributions by a private foundation for mandatory payout purposes is the set-aside (**IRC** § 4942(g)(2)). An amount set aside in one year for a **specific project** that is for charitable purposes may be treated as a qualifying distribution, if payment for the project is to be made over a period not to exceed sixty months. The funds set aside are credited, for purposes of the qualifying distribution requirements, as if paid in the **tax year** the set-aside is made, thus reducing the actual amount of the mandatory payout in that year.

The **federal tax law** provides two types of private foundation set-asides: those that satisfy the **suitability test** and those that meet the **cash distribution test**. The concept of the set-aside is also being utilized in connection with the **Type III non-functionally integrated supporting organization payout rule**.

The term "set-aside" is also used in the definition of exempt function income of tax-exempt social clubs, voluntary employees' beneficiary associations, and supplemental unemployment benefit trusts. Income that would not otherwise qualify as exempt function income can be converted into that type when it is set aside for charitable purposes (**IRC** § 512(a)(3)(B), as limited by **IRC** § 512(a)(3)(D)). [PF §§ 6.5, 15.7(g); EO § 12.4(b); UB § 6.1(c)].

sham

The word "sham" means a thing, such as a transaction, that is not what it purports or appears to be. It is a pretense, a cover for giving something the look of genuineness, a counterfeit; most strongly, it is a hoax. This type of sham is sometimes referred to as a "factual sham." (cf. **Economic sham**).

sham transaction

The term "sham transaction" is used to describe a transaction that is without substance. This type of transaction usually is constructed solely to circumvent, avoid, or take advantage of one or more **laws**—often, the **federal tax law**. In applying the law, a sham transaction is ignored. For example, two related **corporations** may be treated as one if there is no business purpose for one of the **entities**, the **governing boards** are the same, and the formalities of the corporate law are not followed. [EO § 30.2] (also **Circular gift**; **Loophole**).

shaming

The word "shaming" refers to one or more techniques or devices by which a person causes, or attempts to cause, another person to feel shame or be ashamed, usually with the intent of forcing the recipient of the shaming to take some type of action, in circumstances where acting under the influence of the shaming party alleviates the shame. For example, the **IRS** has peppered the **Form 990** with many references to **governance policies**, accompanied by boxes to check indicating whether or not these policies have been adopted. **Tax-exempt organizations**, fearing an **IRS examination** if certain policies are not adopted and realizing that this **annual information return** is a public document (reviewed by prospective funders, government officials, and representatives of the media) that is more presentable if it reflects the adoption of these policies, are shamed into adopting the policies, which is what the **IRS** wants them to do, so they can check the "yes" boxes. [AR passim].

sharable income policy

Some **tax-exempt scientific organizations** have developed a "sharable income policy." Pursuant to this type of policy, **royalties** and other forms of **income** received by the organization from the licensing or other transfer of the organization's patents, **copyrights**, processes, or formulae are shared with the inventors, who received a **significant** (such as one-third) percentage of the income. Likewise, **employees** of the organization who made valuable contributions to the patents and the like may receive a percentage of the income. (also **Private benefit**; **Private inurement**).

share-crop lease

A "share-crop lease" is a **contractual** arrangement between two **persons** concerning the **farming** of a parcel of **real property** (a **farm**). One of these persons is the tenant; this person manages the property, farms the land, makes necessary improvements, and pays necessary **expenses**. The other person, the owner of the property, supplies the property and the buildings and **fixtures** on it, the materials necessary for repairs and improvements on the farm, and skilled labor for making permanent improvements. Other features of the arrangement may include the following: (1) the landowner is responsible for providing a percentage of the cost of seed, fertilizer, limestone, herbicides, and insecticides; (2) the tenant is responsible for all machinery, equipment, power, and labor necessary to farm the land; (3) the parties are to confer for the purpose of planning land use and sharing certain costs; and (4) liability for all accidents relative to farming is conferred on the tenant. The amount of rent payable to the landowner is fixed at a percentage of the harvested crops. A **tax-exempt organization**, as owner of a farm, may be a party to a share-crop lease.

It is the view of the **IRS** that these arrangements are either **general partnerships** or **joint ventures**, and that the payments under the leases to exempt organizations represent a return of **profits** and are taxable. Courts, however, have held that the monies received by exempt organizations by reason of these leases are forms of **excludable rent**. [EO § 24.5(l); UB § 9.9; CU Q 16.47].

shifting the burden of proof

In certain proceedings, once a party satisfies his, her, or its burden of proof on a point of fact, the burden of proof as to another point of fact is transferred (shifted) to another party.

shipowners' mutual protection and indemnity association

Federal tax law provides that the receipts of "shipowners' mutual protection and indemnity associations" are not considered forms of **gross income**, as long as these organizations are not **organized** for **profit** and no part of their **net earnings inures** to the benefit of any **private shareholder** (IRC § 526). This type of organization, however, is taxable on **income** received in the form of **interest**, **dividends**, or **rent**. [EO § 19.13; AS § 1.6(r); SM p. 45].

short accounting period

A "short accounting period" is an accounting period of less than twelve months, which occurs when an **organization** changes its annual accounting period. This short period also can exist as an organization's initial and/or final year of existence. (also **Tax year**).

short-term capital gain

A **gain** from the **sale** or **exchange** of a **capital asset** is classified, for **federal tax** purposes, as either **long-term capital gain** or "short-term capital gain." The word "**term**" refers to the period of time a capital asset has been held by the taxpayer. Thus, "short-term capital gain" means a gain from the disposition of a capital asset held for not more than one year (**IRC §§ 1222(1), (2)**). For purposes of the **federal income tax**, short-term capital gain and **ordinary income** are usually regarded as the same. [CG § 2.16(c); SM p. 134].

short-term capital loss

A **loss** from the **sale** or **exchange** of a **capital asset** is classified, for **federal tax** purposes, as either **long-term capital loss** or "short-term capital loss." The word "**term**" refers to the period of time a capital asset has been held by the taxpayer. Thus, "short-term capital loss" means a loss from the disposition of a capital asset held for not more than one year (**IRC §§ 1222(1), (2)**). [CG § 2.16(c)].

side letter

The term "side letter" means a letter of agreement between parties, separate from the documentation concerning a transaction between the same parties. When a side letter is executed in the **charitable giving** context, between the **donor** and the **donee** (such as an agreement to return a charitable gift if a deduction for it is denied), the letter will likely be regarded by the **IRS** as a **condition** of the gift, warranting it nondeductible. [CG § 10.4].

significant disposition of assets

The phrase "significant disposition of assets" is used in the context of the **private foundation** rules. It means a **disposition** in a **tax year** of 25 percent or more of the **fair market value** of the **net assets** of a private foundation; the measurement is taken at the beginning of the tax year of the disposition (in the case of a disposition occurring in one year) or at the beginning of the first tax year of a sequence of years (in the case of a series of related dispositions occurring in more than one year). A significant disposition of assets can occur when there is a transfer of assets to one or several **organizations**; it can also occur when the recipient organization is a private foundation. The determination as to whether a significant disposition has occurred through a series of related dispositions is to be made from all of the facts and circumstances of the particular case. Thus, the phrase arises in the setting of **mandatory distributions** and private foundation **terminations**. [AR Chap. 20; PF §§ 6.7(a), 13.1].

significant disposition of net assets

A "significant disposition of net assets" occurs when a **tax-exempt organization** disposes of its **net assets** by means of a **sale**, **exchange**, or other form of transfer, irrespective of whether the organization received full or adequate **consideration**. This type of asset disposition involves (1) one or more dispositions during the organization's **tax year**, amounting to more than 25 percent of the **fair market value** of the organization's net assets as of the beginning of its tax year or (2) one of a series of related dispositions or events begun in a prior year that, when combined, comprise more than 25 percent of the fair market value of the organization's net assets as of the beginning of the tax year when the first disposition in the series was made. This type of transaction is required to be reported on Schedule N of the **Form 990** or **Form 990-EZ** for the year involved. [AR § 20.2(b)].

significant involvement

The words "significant involvement" are used in connection with the rules for **private operating foundations**, in the context of application of the **income test**. For an **organization** to qualify under this test, it must make **qualifying distributions directly** for the **active conduct** of **charitable** activities, which is to say that it must have a significant involvement in the operation of its program.

The requisite involvement is present where payments to accomplish the **tax-exempt purpose** of the private operating foundation are made directly and without the assistance of an intervening organization, and the foundation maintains a staff (such as administrators or **researchers**) that supervises the tax-exempt activities on a continuing basis. To use this meaning of the term, the foundation must have as a tax-exempt purpose the relief of **poverty** or human distress, and its tax-exempt purposes must be designed to ameliorate conditions among a poor or distressed **class** of **persons** or in an area subject to poverty or natural disaster. This involvement is also present where the private operating foundation has developed some specialized skills, expertise, or involvement in a particular discipline, and it maintains a staff that supervises or conducts programs or activities that support its work, and if the foundation makes **grants** or other payments to individuals to encourage their involvement in its field of interest and in some segment of the activities it carries on. [PF §§ 3.1(a), 3.1(d)].

significant use test

The "significant use test" is applied in the context of determining the amount of the **charitable deduction** for the **contribution** of a **qualified vehicle**. Generally, this deduction is confined to the amount of the gross proceeds received by the **donee** on disposition of the vehicle. Where there is a "significant use" of the vehicle by the **donee**, however, which means that the **organization** must significantly use the vehicle to **substantially** further the organization's charitable program, the deduction is based on the **fair market value** of the vehicle. [CG § 9.27; HC § 31.2(f)].

significant voice test

One of the requirements of the **responsiveness test** applicable to **Type III supporting organizations** is that the **trustees**, **directors**, or **officers** of the **supported organization** must have a "significant voice" in the investment policies of the supporting organization, the timing of **grants**, the manner of making grants, and the selection of grant recipients by the supporting organization, and in otherwise directing the use of the **income** and **assets** of the supporting organization. [PF § 15.7(g); HC § 5.5(d)].

similar amounts

The term "similar amounts," as used in conjunction with the concept of annual **dues**, includes voluntary payments made by **members**, **assessments** made by an **organization** to cover basic operating costs, and special assessments imposed by the organization to conduct **lobbying activities**.

similar items of property

The phrase "similar items of property" is used in the context of the **appraisal** requirements that apply with respect to certain **charitable contributions** of **property**. These requirements apply when the aggregate claimed or reported **value** of the property, and all "similar items of property" for which **deductions** for charitable contributions are claimed or reported, by the same **donor** for the same **tax year** (whether or not donated to the same **donee**) is in excess of $5,000. The phrase means property of the same generic category or type, including stamp collections, coin collections, lithographs, paintings, photographs, books, nonpublicly traded securities, land, buildings, clothing, jewelry, furniture, electronic equipment, household appliances, toys, and kitchenware. For example, if a donor claimed for a year deductions of $2,000 for books contributed to College A, $2,500 for books given to College B, and $900 for books given to College C, the $5,000 threshold would be exceeded. [CG § 21.5(a)].

sin tax

A "sin tax" is a tax imposed in connection with the conduct of what a majority of society believes is inappropriate behavior. This type of tax includes taxes on the consumption of tobacco and alcohol.

single-member limited liability company

A "single-member limited liability company" is a **limited liability** company that has only one **member**, which can be a **tax-exempt organization**. Often, this type of company is a **disregarded entity**. [EO § 32.6; UB § 8.12(b); HC § 15.1; CG § 10.9(b); AR § 11.1(f)(3)(G)(ii); PG pp. 156–158; SM pp. 22–23, 230–231] (cf. **Multi-member limited liability corporation**).

single-parent title-holding corporation

A "single-parent title-holding corporation" is a **title-holding corporation** that operates for the benefit of only one **tax-exempt parent organization**. It is an **exempt organization (IRC §§ 501(a), 501(c)(2))**. [EO § 19.2(a); AU § 7.1(a); SM p. 42] (cf. **Multi-member title-holding corporation**).

Sixteenth Amendment

The Sixteenth Amendment to the U.S. Constitution is the legal basis of the **federal** system of **income** taxation. It exempted income from the general rule of apportionment among the states and authorized the collection of **taxes** on income "from whatever source derived." Once this amendment was ratified, Congress enacted the **Tariff Act of 1913**, which began the **statutory** tax system. [CL § 1.1(b); EO § 2.4].

size-and-extent test

In determining whether an activity contributes importantly to the accomplishment of a **tax-exempt** purpose, so as to be a **substantially related business**, the "size and extent" of the activity must be considered in relation to the nature and extent of the exempt function it purportedly serves. Thus, where **income** is **realized** by an **exempt organization** from an activity that is generally related to the performance of its exempt functions, but the activity is conducted on a scale that is larger than **reasonably** necessary for performance of the functions, the **gross income** attributable to the portion of the activity that is in excess of the needs associated with exempt functions constitutes gross income from the conduct of an **unrelated business**. [UB § 2.7(b); EO § 24.4(b)].

skip person

The term "skip person" is used in connection with the law comprising the **generation-skipping transfer tax rules**. The tax is applied to a **taxable distribution**, a **taxable termination**, or a **direct skip**. A "skip person" is a **person** two or more generations below the transferor of the **interest (IRC §§ 2612(b), 2613)**. [CG § 3.16].

small business corporation

See **S corporation**.

small business investment company

A "small business investment company" is an **entity** licensed under the Small Business Investment Act; thus, it is required to comply with applicable regulations promulgated by the Small Business Administration. Under certain circumstances, this type of **organization** may qualify as a **local economic development corporation**. [EO § 7.16(e)].

Small Business Job Protection Act of 1996

The Small Business Job Protection Act of 1996 introduced **federal tax rules** pertaining to **tax exemption** for **qualified charitable risk pools** and **prepaid tuition programs**, the rules concerning **insurance income**, and the rule allowing **exempt charitable organizations** to own stock in **S corporations**. [EO §§ 11.6, 19.19, 24.9, 25.2(m), 28.14(b); HC § 27.4].

small lease

The term "small lease" is used in the context of defining the scope of the **exclusion** from the **unrelated debt-financed property** rules for investments in **real property** by **qualified organizations** (IRC § 514(c)(9)). More particularly, the term is used as part of the rule relaxing the **leaseback restriction** and the **disqualified person restriction**. For this purpose, a **lease** is small where no more than 25 percent of the leasable floor space in a building (or complex of buildings) is covered by the lease (**IRC** § 514(c)(9)(G)(i)). [UB § 5.4(f); EO § 24.9(c)].

small organization

The term "small organization" is used in a variety of settings, primarily to describe **organizations** that are not required to file **annual information returns**. As to this **exception**, the obligation to file an annual information return is inapplicable to certain organizations the **gross receipts** of which in each **tax year** are **normally** not more than $50,000. These organizations, however, are required to annually electronically **submit** an **e-postcard**. [EO §§ 26.2(b), 28.2(a)(iv), 28.2(b)(ii); HC § 35.3(e)] (also **Eligible organization**).

small solicitation

Nearly all of the state **charitable solicitation acts exempt** "small solicitation" efforts from the registration, licensing, or permit requirements. The definition as to what is "small" varies from $2,000 to $25,000. [FR § 3.5(i)].

so remote as to be negligible

A **condition** placed by a **donor** on a **contribution** may affect the **deductibility** of the **gift**. A condition is ignored for this purpose, however, if it is "so remote as to be negligible." This phrase has been defined as a chance that every dictate of reason would justify an intelligent person in regarding the condition as so highly improbable and remote as to be lacking in reason and substance. [CG § 9.7(d)] (also **Material condition**).

social club

A "social club" is a type of **tax-exempt organization** (IRC § 501(a), by reason of description in **IRC** § 501(c)(7)). This type of club is **organized** and **operated** for pleasure, recreation, and other nonprofitable purposes, **substantially all** of the activities of which are for these purposes, where no part of the **net earnings** of the club **inures** to the benefit of any **private shareholder**. Generally, these organizations are supported **primarily** by **dues**, and other **membership fees** and **assessments**. To be exempt by reason of this category, the club must have an established membership of individuals, personal contacts, and fellowship; a mingling of the members must play a **material** part in the operations of the organization. **Entities** that are exempt as social clubs include country clubs, dinner clubs, variety clubs, golf and tennis clubs, and **college** and **university fraternities** and **sororities**. There are limitations on the extent to which these clubs can make their facilities available to the public and have non-membership income. These clubs are taxable on all income other than **exempt function income**. They cannot be exempt if they have a written policy of **discrimination** on account of race, color, or **religion**. An exempt social club is a **welfare benefit fund**. [EO Chap. 15, §§ 4.9(h), 24.10; CL §§ 1.8(b), 1.12(f), 6.6, 6.8; CG § 1.3; PF §§ 1.6, 9.6(a); AU § 7.1(n); AR §§ 4.1(r), 4.2(m); AS § 1.6(f); UB § 6.1; SM p. 41; LI Q 1.50].

social enterprise movement

Among the contemporary forces shaping the **law** of **tax-exempt organizations** is the emergence of entrepreneurism: the open and accepted conduct of **businesses** by **exempt organizations**, with a **for-profit** mentality to the end of supplementing or even supplanting **charitable contributions** and **grants**. The unabashed aim of organizations undertaking entrepreneurial activities is generation of funds in advancement of the **mission**, upgrading the quality of staff and other resources, and becoming self-sufficient, that is, not dependent on external funders for financial support. This development, which clashes with elements of the **commerciality doctrine**, is known as the "social enterprise movement." [EO § 4.11(a); UB § 7.5; PG pp. 142–144].

social welfare

The term "social welfare" is used, in the **federal law** of **tax-exempt organizations**, in two contexts. The term is used to describe a type of exempt organization, namely, a **social welfare organization**. The term is also used to describe a type of exempt **charitable organization**, which has that status because it **promotes social welfare**.

In the first of these contexts, the term "social welfare" is said to be commensurate with the "common good and general welfare" and "civic betterments and social improvements." The term does not include activities that **primarily** constitute the carrying on of a **business** with the public in a manner similar to organizations that are operated for **profit**, nor does the term include **political campaign activity**. [EO §§ 7.11, 13.1; HC § 1.9; SM pp. 35, 39–40].

social welfare, promotion of

One of the ways an **organization** can qualify for **tax-exempt status** as a **charitable organization** is to engage in activities that constitute the "promotion of **social welfare**." The **federal tax regulations** state that this type of charitable activity embraces activities that further other types of purposes deemed to be charitable, lessen neighborhood tensions, eliminate prejudice and **discrimination**, defend human and civil **rights** secured by **law**, and combat **community** deterioration and juvenile delinquency. [EO § 7.11; CG § 3.2(b); SM p. 35].

social welfare organization

A "social welfare organization" is a type of **tax-exempt organization** (IRC § 501(a), by reason of description in **IRC** § 501(c)(4)). As the name indicates, this type of organization must engage in **social welfare** activities; these activities must be those that will benefit a **community**, rather than a select group of individuals. Also, these organizations are subject to the prohibition on **private inurement** and limitations on **political campaign activity**. An exempt social welfare organization may engage in **legislative activities** without restriction as long as they are in furtherance of the organization's **exempt purposes**. [EO Chap. 13; HC §§ 4.9(a)(i), 7.3, 7.8; PF §§ 1.6, 2.6, 15.9, 15.12; AR §§ 3.1(e)(1), 14.3(e); AU § 7.1(i); CU Q 1.39; AS §§ 1.6(a), 3.8(b); PG pp. 116–117, 122; SM pp. 39–41; LI Q 1.50] (also **Civic league**).

society

The word "society" is sometimes used to describe an **organization** of **persons** who are associated for some **nonprofit** purpose; in this sense, the word is synonymous with the word **association**. This term tends to be used where the **members** are individuals and the purpose of the organization is to advance the interests of those in a particular profession—thus, the term "professional society." [EO § 14.1(e); AS § 2.9].

solely

The word "solely" is synonymous with words such as "wholly" and "only." When a **law** uses that term, it would seem to not allow for any contradictory or other behavior, although the courts have a tendency to graft a de minimis standard onto these types of "absolute" requirements or prohibitions. This has been the case, for example, with use of the word **exclusively**. As an illustration, although the **federal tax law** states that a **charitable organization**, to be **tax-exempt**, must be **organized** and **operated** "exclusively" for its tax-exempt purposes, courts have ruled that the term actually means "**primarily**." (Thus, in that setting, the term "exclusively" is a **word of art**.) In one context, however, Congress stated, in the **legislative history** underlying a particular body of law, that the term "exclusively" was used to mean "solely" rather than "primarily": the rules requiring a **supporting organization** to be organized and operated "exclusively" to support or otherwise benefit one or more **supported organizations**. [EO §§ 4.4, 4.6; PF § 15.7(b)].

sole proprietorship

A "sole proprietorship" is a form of **business** conducted by one **person**, where none of the other legal forms of business are involved. If a **tax-exempt organization** operates an **unrelated business** as a sole proprietorship, the business is one of the functions of the organization itself. Thus, a private foundation that **actively** operates an unrelated business as a sole proprietorship would contravene the rules concerning **excess business holdings**, in that the private foundation would be the owner of 100 percent of the business. [PF § 7.2(b)].

solicit

As used in the states' **charitable solicitation acts**, the term "solicit" means to request, **directly** or **indirectly**, money, credit, **property**, or other financial assistance in any form on the plea or representation that the money, credit, property, or other financial assistance will be used for a **charitable purpose**. [FR §§ 3.2(c), 8.2(b), 8.11; SM p. 148].

solicitation

A "solicitation," in the context of the states' **charitable solicitation acts**, is an act by which a prospective **donor** is **solicited** for a **contribution**. A solicitation can take place by an in-person request, U.S. mail, email, other publishing, television, radio, telephone, the Internet, or other medium. The term embraces both oral and written solicitations. The term may include the pursuit of a **grant** from a **private foundation**, other **nonprofit organization**, or a **governmental unit**. [FR §§ 3.2(c), 4.13, 8.2(b), 8.11; HC § 31.1(f); SM p. 148].

solicitee

A "solicitee" is a **person** who has received a **solicitation**.

solicitor

A "solicitor" is a **person** who has made a **solicitation**. (also **Professional solicitor**).

sorority

A "sorority" is a **society** the **membership** of which is comprised of women, such as an **association** of women at a **college** or **university** (usually at the undergraduate level). In many contexts, such as at the graduate level in **higher education**, an organization of this nature is included within the definition of the word **fraternity**. For **federal tax law** purposes, a sorority is a **social club**. [EO § 15.1; CU Q 3.7, Q 3.8].

sources of the law

See **Law, sources of**.

sovereign immunity

The **doctrine** of "sovereign immunity" owes its name to the word "sovereign," which means a chief ruler with supreme power, such as a king. The doctrine means that, when a government is engaged in a legitimate governmental function, it is immune from **lawsuits** relating to that function. (A loose translation of this doctrine is that "the king can do no wrong.") A government may waive this **immunity** by **statute**.

special event

A "special event" is a function organized and operated by a **tax-exempt organization**, usually a **charitable organization**, for the purpose of enhancing community visibility and relations, and for **fundraising** purposes. As to the latter purpose, special events are typically the most expensive and least profitable method of fundraising. Some regard the fundraising function to be secondary, asserting that the primary purpose of the event is **fundraising**. Special events include auctions, dinner and theater events, formal balls, sports tournaments, **games of chance**, **fairs**, carnivals, festivals, car washes, and bake sales. In many instances, a payment for admission to and/or participation in an event is not a **gift** or is only partially a gift. Usually, the **revenue** generated by a special event is not taxable as **unrelated business taxable income** because the event, although often a **business**, is not **regularly carried on** (being annual or otherwise sporadic) or is a business conducted **substantially** by **volunteers**. Revenue from these events may be subject to unique reporting requirements on an **annual information return** (where the return refers to these activities as **special fundraising events**). [FR §§ 5.9, 5.16(a); CG § 23.2; AR § 14.2(b)].

S

special fundraising event

A "special fundraising event" is a form of **fundraising** consisting of a social, **educational**, sporting activity, or like occasion for which tickets are sold and underwriting **gifts** are **solicited**. [FR §§ 5.9, 5.16(a); AR § 14.2(b); SM p. 113].

special purpose fundraising program

A "special purpose fundraising program" is a selective **fundraising** effort designed to secure **major gifts** and/or **grants** for significant projects. These gifts are usually made on a one-time (as opposed to annual) basis, often in the context of a **capital campaign**.

specific bequest

A "specific bequest" is a **bequest** of a specific (that is, separately identifiable) item of a **decedent's estate**. This type of bequest can be satisfied only by **delivery** of the particular item referred to in the **will**.

specific deduction

To reduce the possibility of forcing payments of insignificant amounts of **tax** resulting from small amounts of **unrelated business taxable income**, the **federal tax law** provides a "specific deduction" in the amount of $1,000 (**IRC** § 512(b)(12)). Thus, by reason of this provision, a **tax-exempt organization** can receive up to $1,000 of unrelated business taxable income without having to pay tax on it, although the income must nonetheless be reported to the **IRS**. [UB §§ 3.19, 11.4(d)(xi); EO § 25.1(r); HC § 24.22].

specific legislation

The term "specific legislation" is used in connection with the **expenditure test**. A **communication** with a legislator or **government official**, or **employee** of either, is a **direct lobbying communication** only where certain standards are met, including the requirement that the communication refers to "specific legislation." The term is also used in the definition of **grass-roots communication**.

The term "specific legislation" means legislation that has already been introduced in a legislative body and a specific legislative proposal that an **organization** either supports or opposes. In the case of a referendum, ballot initiative, constitutional amendment, or other measure that is placed on a ballot by petitions signed by a required number or percentage of voters, an item becomes specific legislation when the petition is first circulated among the voters for signature. [EO § 22.3(d)(i); HC § 7.1(b)].

specific performance

The term "specific performance" is used in the **law** of **contracts**. The concept of the term is that the **person** contracting for the services of another is desirous of the performance of services by that person and not by another person, who may be the transferee of the obligation from the person who is a party to the contract. The contract will likely be breached if the specific performance requirement is violated. Thus, for example, a **charitable organization** contracting for

fundraising services may insist on the services of one or more named fundraising professionals; this requirement is a form of insistence on specific performance.

specific project

The term "specific project" is used in the context of the **set-aside** rules involving **private foundations and non-functionally integrated Type III supporting organizations**. The term includes situations in which relatively long-term **grants** or other **expenditures** must be made in order to secure the continuity of particular projects or **program-related investments** or where grants are made as part of a **matching grant program**. Examples of a specific project are a plan to construct a building to house a **tax-exempt activity** (such as a **museum**) and a plan to fund a specific **research** program that is of such a magnitude as to require an accumulation prior to commencement of the research. [PF §§ 6.5(e), 15.7(g); EO §§ 12.3(c); 12.4(b)].

specified individuals, gift for

A **fundraising** effort may be undertaken in order to **solicit contributions** for the benefit of an individual. This is usually done when the individual has incurred **substantial** medical or legal costs and lacks the resources to pay them. While these contributions are not **charitable gifts** for **federal tax law** purposes, they are frequently within the purview of states' **charitable solicitation acts**. [FR § 3.5(j)].

specified payment

For purposes of the **rules** concerning the taxability of **tax-exempt organizations** on **revenue** received from **controlled organizations**, the term "specified payment" means **interest**, an **annuity**, **royalties**, and/or **rent**. [EO § 30.7(b)].

specified public charity

A **supporting organization** must be **organized** and **operated** to support or benefit one or more "specified" **supported organizations** (IRC § 509(a)(3)(A)). This specification requirement must be reflected in the **articles of organization** of the supporting organization, although the manner of the specification is dependent on the nature of the relationship between the supporting organization and the **supported organization**. Generally, it is expected that the articles of organization of the supporting organization will designate the supported organization by name. If the relationship is one of **operated, supervised or controlled by** or **supervised or controlled in connection with**, however, designation by name is not required as long as the articles of organization of the supporting organization require that it be operated to support or benefit one or more supported organizations that are designated by class or purpose. They must also include one or more public charities for which there is at least one of these two relationships (without designating the organizations by name) or public charities that are closely related in purpose or function to public charities for which there is at least one of these relationships (again, without designating the organizations by name). Therefore, if the relationship is one of **operated in connection with,** generally the supporting organization must designate the specified supported organization by name. [PF § 15.7(c); EO § 12.3(c); HC § 5.5(c)].

S

speech, freedom of

See **Free speech**.

spin-off

The word "spin-off" essentially means the same as a **subsidiary**. In the **nonprofit law** context, the term refers to a **nonprofit organization**, almost always a **tax-exempt entity**, that removes a particular activity (or **program**) or set of activities from its base of operations and transfers it or them ("spins" them "off") to a separate **organization**. This separate organization may be a **for-profit** entity or a nonprofit one. Spin-offs may be dictated by **tax law** reasons (such as the need to place an **unrelated trade or business** in a separate organization so as not to jeopardize the **tax-exempt status** of the **parent organization**) or for management reasons. Spin-offs often arouse suspicion, particularly where the parent organization is a **charitable organization**, the entire network of organizations appears rather sophisticated, and there is an abundance of **interlocking directorates**. In fact, however, the practice is lawful and often appropriate (and unavoidable). [EO § 29.1; PG pp. 132–134; SM p. 213] (cf. **Direct outgrowth rule**).

split-interest trust

The general rule in the **federal tax law** is that there is no **charitable contribution deduction** for a contribution of a **partial interest** in **property** made to a **charitable organization** (IRC § 170(f)(3)(A)). One of the several **exceptions** to this rule is a charitable contribution made by means of a "split-interest trust" (**IRC** § 170(f)(2)).

The **trust** used to facilitate this type of **gift** is known as a "split-interest trust" because the trust is the mechanism for satisfying the requirement of the splitting of the interests (so as to result in partial interests) into one or more **income interests** and a **remainder interest** (IRC § 4947(a)(2)). That is, the trust is the medium used to split the property into its two primary component interests.

The basic forms of split-interest trusts are the **charitable lead trust**, the **charitable remainder trust**, and the **pooled income fund**.

A defective charitable split-interest trust may be **reformed** to preserve the charitable deduction where certain requirements are satisfied (**IRC** §§ 170(f)(7), 2055(e)(3)). [CG Chaps. 12, 13, 16, §§ 5.3, 21.3; PF §§ 1.9, 3.5, 3.7, 7.2(b), 14.5; AR Chap. 8, §§ 3.1(a), 3.2(a); AU § 7.3; SM pp. 234–235].

sponsor

The term "sponsor" as it relates to the **federal tax law** and state law concerning **nonprofit organizations** has several meanings. One meaning is that a sponsor is a **person** (often a **business enterprise (corporation)**) that provides money to a **charitable organization** (or perhaps other type of **tax-exempt organization**) in exchange for some form of **acknowledgement** (or **recognition**) and/or **advertising** services. The sponsorship involved is usually of some specific event or series of events, such as one or more sports events. [EO § 24.6; CG § 23.3; SM pp. 158–161] (also **Sponsorship, corporate**).

sponsoring organization

The term "sponsoring organization" means a **tax-exempt charitable organization**, that is not a **private foundation**, and which maintains one or more **donor-advised funds** (IRC § 4966(d)(1)). [EO § 11.8(e); CG §§ 3.1(f), 23.4; PF § 16.9; AR § 11.1(a)(2); SM p. 206].

sponsorship, corporate

It has become a common practice for **business corporations** to **sponsor** one or more events **organized** and **operated** by a **public charity** or perhaps another type of **tax-exempt organization**. These events are often sports events; an example is a business corporation that provides funds to a **college** bowl **association** to help underwrite the staging of an annual college bowl football game. This type of sponsorship has generated questions under the **federal tax law** as to the appropriate way to classify these funds for purposes of potentially subjecting the recipient of them to tax. The classification is dependent on the extent of benefits or services provided by the exempt organization to the sponsor. The essence of the law is that, if the sponsor is receiving mere **acknowledgement** or **recognition** for having made the payment, the payment is a **contribution**, but that if the benefits or services amounts to **advertising** or other **substantial return benefit**, the payment is subject to taxation as **unrelated business income**, unless an **exception** from the tax is available (**IRC** § 513(i)). [EO § 24.6; UB § 6.6; CG § 23.3; FR § 5.16(b); PF §§ 15.4(b), 15.5; HC § 24.17; RE Q 23.28; AS § 9.3; SM pp. 158–161; LI Q 13.48–Q 13.54].

sports, amateur, promotion of

One of the ways an **organization** can qualify for **tax-exempt status** under the **federal tax law** as a **charitable organization** is to engage in activities that promote, advance, and/or sponsor recreational and amateur sports activities. This type of organization may foster national or international amateur sports competition (but only if no part of their activities involves the provision of athletic facilities or equipment) (**IRC** § 501(c)(3)). This limitation as to facilities or equipment is inapplicable, however, where the organization is a **qualified amateur sports organization**. [EO §§ 7.15(c), 11.2].

standard mileage rate

The phrase "standard mileage rate" is used to describe a means for claiming a **federal charitable contribution deduction** for unreimbursed **expenses** incurred while providing services to a **charitable organization**, which are **directly** attributable to the operation, maintenance, and repair of an automobile or similar item (such as an airplane). Instead of itemizing these expenses, the taxpayer can use the "standard mileage rate" in calculating the charitable contribution deduction for use of a passenger automobile, which is 14 cents per mile (**IRC** § 170(i)). [CG § 9.17].

S

standard of care

The term "standard of care" means a standard of conduct that is considered in the **law** as being **reasonable** under the circumstances. Behavior that falls short of that standard may be an act or acts of **negligence**; a **person** engaging in this type of substandard behavior may incur **liability** as a result.

standing committee

A "standing committee" is a **committee** of an **organization** that has permanence in the sense of being authorized in the organization's **governing instrument** or by resolution of the organization's **governing board**, and in the sense of the nature of its duties. Typical standing committees are an **executive committee**, development (**fundraising**) committee, finance committee, and long-range planning committee. (also **Ad hoc committee**).

standing to sue

The **doctrine** of "standing to sue" requires that, for a court to have jurisdiction over a matter, a **person**, to successfully initiate a **lawsuit** complaining of some alleged unlawful conduct, must show that the conduct of one or more other persons involved in the matter has damaged some legally protected interest (an actual injury) of the person bringing the **action**, who in general must have some meaningful personal stake in the controversy. For standing to be present, a **plaintiff** must allege personal injury that is fairly traceable to a **defendant's** allegedly unlawful conduct and that is likely to be redressed by the requested relief. There are subcategories of standing, such as **establishment clause** standing, voter standing, and **equal protection** standing. [CL §§ 1.2(b), 8.12] (also **Third-party litigation**).

standstill valuation rule

In general, a **private foundation** must annually **value** its **assets**, for **minimum investment return** purposes. An interest in **real property** may, however, be valued for a five-year period, where **reasonably** made by an independent **appraiser**. The **IRS** will not disturb this valuation, despite any value changes; this is the "standstill valuation rule." [PF § 6.3(f)].

startup capital

For purposes of the law concerning **qualified charitable risk pools**, the term "startup capital" means any **capital** contributed to, and any **program-related investments** made in, the risk pool before the pool commences operations (**IRC** § 501(n)(4)(A)). [EO § 11.6].

start-up period

The phrase "start-up period" is used in connection with the type of **private foundation set-aside** that meets the **cash distribution test**. Generally, the start-up period of a private foundation is the four years following the year in which the private foundation was created. [PF § 6.5(e)] (also **Full-payment period**).

start-up period minimum amount

The phrase "start-up period minimum amount" is used in connection with the type of **private foundation set-aside** that meets the **cash distribution test**. The start-up period minimum amount that must be timely distributed, as money or otherwise, is at least the sum of 20 percent of the private foundation's **distributable amount** for the first year of the **start-up period**, 40 percent of its distributable amount for the second year of the start-up period, 60 percent of its distributable amount for the third year of the start-up period, and 80 percent of its distributable amount for the fourth year of its start-up period (**IRC** §§ 4942(g)(2)(B)(ii)(II), (III)). Under certain circumstances, distributions made during the year preceding the private foundation's start-up period and/or made within five and a half months following the start-up period are deemed part of the start-up period minimum amount. [PF § 6.5(e)].

state action doctrine

The "state action doctrine" is invoked when a **private person** is pursuing a remedy against another private person for violation of the first party's civil rights, where the potential **sanctions** involved require action by a government (the "state") or by a private party that has powers and responsibilities delegated or otherwise conveyed to it by a government. This **doctrine** enables the complaining private person to assert that the party being complained of should be regarded as a governmental **entity** for purposes of the legal proceeding. For example, the state action doctrine has been used against **tax-exempt social clubs** by complainants asserting **unconstitutional** racial **discrimination** in **membership** policies. [CL Chap. 6; EO § 4.8; FR § 9.3; SM pp. 329–330].

state interest

The term "state interest" means an interest by a government (the "state") in the results of a particular form of regulation, usually by **statute**, even though that method of regulation impinges on individual **rights**. In those instances in which the **law** is subjected to "strict scrutiny," it may be **unconstitutional** unless the state can show a "compelling" interest in having the regulation undertaken by the particular statute. For example, courts have frequently held that a provision of a state's **charitable solicitation act** is unconstitutional because it is too broad and the state lacks the necessary interest in enforcing the law in this manner. By contrast, it has been held that a state may preclude a **nonprofit membership organization** from engaging in forms of gender **discrimination**, notwithstanding the **right of association**, because the state had the necessary interest (eradication of this form of discrimination). [CL § 7.4(b); FR §§ 4.2, 4.3].

state officials, IRS disclosure to

In response to a written request by an **appropriate state officer**, the **IRS** may disclose (1) a notice of proposed refusal to **recognize** an **entity** as a **charitable organization;** (2) a notice of proposed **revocation** of **tax exemption** of a charitable organization; (3) issuance of a proposed deficiency in certain **taxes**; (4) the names, addresses, and taxpayer identification numbers of organizations that have applied for recognition of exemption as charitable organizations; and (5) **returns** and return information of organizations with respect to which information has been disclosed pursuant to the foregoing four categories of disclosure (**IRC** § 6104(c)(2)(A)). [EO § 27.8; HC § 35.6; LI Q 2.20].

state-sponsored medical care organization

Tax-exempt status under **federal law** is available for a **membership organization** established by a state **exclusively** to provide coverage for medical care on a **nonprofit** basis to high-risk individuals through **insurance** issued by the organization or a **health maintenance organization** under an arrangement with the organization (**IRC** § 501(c)(26)(A)). [EO § 19.15; AS § 1.6(n)].

state-sponsored workers' compensation entity

Tax-exempt status under **federal law** is available for a **membership organization** established before June 1, 1996, by a state **exclusively** to reimburse its members for losses arising under workers' compensation acts (**IRC** § 501(c)(27)(A)(i)). [EO § 19.16(a); AS § 1.6(o)].

status

The word "status" generally means the character, in **law**, of a **person** or other thing. For example, a **charitable organization** is said to have "charitable **donee** status" and a charitable organization that is not a **public charity** is said to have "**private foundation** status." **Nonprofit organizations** that have **tax exemption** are said to have "**tax-exempt** status."

statute

A "statute" is a form of **law** created by a legislative body and (usually) made part of a **code** of laws. Thus, this type of law is to be distinguished from law created by court opinion, **regulation**, **rule**, and the like.

Statute of Charitable Uses

The **federal tax law** definition of the term "charitable" is traceable back to the English "Statute of Charitable Uses," enacted in 1601. This **statutory law** is, in turn, based on the English common law and earlier civilizations, cultures, and religions. The preamble to this statute enumerates certain charitable purposes including relief of the aged, impotent, and poor people; maintenance of sick and maimed soldiers and mariners; establishment of **schools** of learning; repair of bridges, ports, causeways, seabanks, and highways; **advancement of education**; care of orphans; assistance with respect to marriages of poor maids; aid to young tradespersons and handicraftpersons; and provision of relief for prisoners. [EO § 1.4].

statute of limitations

A "statute of limitations" is a **law** (**statute**) that sets a period of time within which a **person** must institute a legal proceeding (**litigation**, an **administrative** hearing, or some other action to enforce a **right**) or else be barred from asserting the claim. For example, in the **federal tax law** setting, the statute of limitations governing the ability of the **IRS** to **audit** a person generally is three years (**IRC** § 6501(a). During the pendency of this period of time, it is said that the statute of limitations is "running." By agreement of the parties, however, a statute of limitations can be "extended" (that is, the period of time covered by it is elongated). [AU §§ 3.11, 5.4(f), 5.4(g), 5.10, 5.30; AS § 3.8(i); CG § 10.12].

statutory construction

"Statutory construction" (also known as "statutory interpretation") means the process of divining the meaning of a **statute**, an exercise often undertaken by a court. One of the reasons for construing the intent of the statute-writers is to determine whether a **regulation** accompanying the statue is valid. Statutory construction is accomplished by application of the **Chevron standard**.

The term "statutory construction" is utilized to describe the exercise used to ascertain ("construct") the meaning of a statute, where the meaning is not plainly evident from the statute's text. Usually, this construction is based on the **legislative history** of the statute. Occasionally, other laws and writings in existence at the time of adoption of the statute are used in this process. Also, the courts have developed principles of statutory construction.

Statutory construction is a matter of some controversy, with "strict constructionists" arguing that use of legislative history and the like is inappropriate "law-making" by an **entity** other than a legislative body (usually, a court) and "liberal constructionists" contending that application of the **doctrine** is necessary to understand and effectuate legislative intent. [CL § 8.1; EO App. A].

statutory law

"Statutory law" is a **law**, or a collection of laws, that was created by **statute**.

step transaction

The "step transaction" is a **tax law** concept, which applies where two or more ostensibly independent transactions are consolidated and treated as one. An illustration of this **doctrine** appears in connection with the law concerning the **federal income tax charitable contribution deduction**, which is that, if a **person** contributes **property** that has appreciated in **value** to a **charitable organization**, under circumstances where the **donee** is legally obligated to sell the gift property to a purchaser because of a binding prearrangement between the purchaser and the **donor**, the law will treat the donor as having transacted **directly** with the purchaser, so that the **capital gain** that was **recognized** on the **sale** is taxable to the donor. That is, the transaction will be regarded as a sale of the property by the "donor" to the third-party purchaser and a gift of the sales proceeds to the charitable organization. [CG §§ 4.8, 9.8(b), 9.19(e); CU Q 12.12; LI Q 11.12].

stepped-up basis

A "stepped-up basis" is an increase in the **basis** of an item of **property** by **operation of law**; most frequently, the basis level is reset at the **fair market value** of the property. For example, when an item of property is transferred to a **person** from an **estate** (an inheritance), the **heir's** basis in the property is increased to an amount equal to the **value** of the property on the date of death of the **decedent** (**IRC** § 1014). Likewise, when an item of properly is contributed to a **charitable organization**, the **donee** takes the **donor's** basis (although that outcome is usually irrelevant, because the donee is **tax-exempt**). [CG § 2.14(a)].

stipulation

A "stipulation" is a document containing a statement of facts that is agreed on by opposing parties, such as those to a **lawsuit**. For example, the parties may "stipulate" the facts so that the issues are wholly ones of **law**.

straight-line method of depreciation

The "straight-line method of depreciation" is a **depreciation** method by which the annual **deduction** for depreciation is ascertained. The annual deduction is determined by subtracting from the total cost or other **basis** of the **asset** its estimated **salvage value** and then by dividing that amount by its estimated **useful life**.

streamlined application for recognition of exemption

A "streamlined" **application for recognition of exemption** may be filed by an **eligible organization** seeking recognition of **tax exemption** as a **charitable organization**. This application, which must be filed electronically, is **Form 1023-EZ**. This is a three-page application, with no attachments required. The application is a series of attestations, consisting of an eligibility worksheet and checking of boxes to attest to compliance with various requirements of law.

submit

One of the meanings of the word "submit" is to "present," "refer," "supply," or "offer" something, such as a document. In the **federal tax law** context, most documents are filed, such as **annual information returns** that are filed by **tax-exempt organizations** with the **IRS**. Some of these documents are technically submitted, rather than filed. For example, the **ePostcard** must be electronically submitted to the **IRS;** it is not filed. A filing starts applicable **statutes of limitation** running; a submission does not. [EO § 28.4].

subordinate

For purposes of the **federal tax law penalty** for aiding and abetting an **understatement** of **tax liability**, the word "subordinate" is defined to mean any **person** (other than the **taxpayer** involved)—whether or not a **director**, **officer**, **employee**, or **agent** of the taxpayer involved—over whose activities the person has direction, supervision, or **control** (IRC § 6701(c)(2)).

subordinate organization

The **IRS** uses the term "subordinate organization" to describe an **organization** that is **recognized** as a **tax-exempt organization** by reason of a **group exemption**, meaning that the subordinate organization is subject to the general supervision and **control** of a **central organization**. [EO § 26.9; SM p. 78].

subscriber

Under the **expenditure test**, the amount expended for **lobbying** in the form of a **membership communication** that is also distributed to non-members may be required to include an **allocation** of costs on the basis of a variety of factors, including a determination of who the "subscribers" are. For this purpose, a **person** is a "subscriber" to a written communication if (1) the person is a member of the publishing organization and the membership **dues** expressly include the right to receive the communication or (2) the person has affirmatively expressed a desire to receive the written communication and has paid more than a nominal amount for it.

A similar requirement applies in the context of determining an amount of **unrelated business income**, for the purpose of ascertaining taxable *advertising income*, that is derived from subscribers who are members of the organization, so that a portion of their membership dues is allocated to the advertising function. [EO § 22.3(d)(v); HC § 13.1].

subsequent use rule

An activity that is not inherently an **attempt to influence legislation**, such as the creation of a publication or the conduct of **research**, may be considered a form of **lobbying** of a product of the activity is used in an effort to influence legislation. [EO §§ 22.3, 22.6].

subsequently listed transaction

The phrase "subsequently listed transaction" means a transaction to which a **tax-exempt entity** is a party and that is determined by the **IRS** to be a **listed transaction** at any time after the entity has become a party to the transaction. The term, however, does not include a transaction which is a **prohibited reportable transaction** at the time the entity became a party to the transaction (**IRC** § 4965(e)(2)). [EO § 28.17(f)].

subsidiary

A "subsidiary" is an **organization** that is owned or otherwise **controlled** by another organization. Technically, ownership of one organization by another can be manifested only by stock; a few states allow the formation of a **nonprofit corporation** using stock. (An organization that issues stock must be a corporation.) Ways by which one organization (incorporated or otherwise) controls another include an **interlocking directorate**, some other arrangement by which **directors** (and perhaps **officers**) of one organization select the directors (and/or officers) of another organization, or an arrangement where one organization is a **member** (perhaps the sole member) of another organization. These features are usually reflected in the **articles of organization** and/or **bylaws** of the controlling organization. Some organizations are controlled by another organization only as to policy positions; this relationship is usually identified in the bylaws of both organizations.

The **law** of **tax-exempt organizations** contains many situations where one or more organizations are in a subsidiary relationship to another organization. Illustrations of this arrangement include a **charitable organization** that has a separate charitable organization to act as a **fundraising** vehicle (both of these organizations may be **domestic entities** or one may be domestic and the other **foreign**), a charitable organization that is a subsidiary of a **business association** or a **professional association** (or some other form of **business league**), a **social welfare organization** that is a **lobbying** entity for a charitable organization, a **supporting organization**, a **title-holding company**, a **feeder organization**, a **for-profit** subsidiary of a **tax-exempt organization**, or a tax-exempt subsidiary of a for-profit organization.

Also, there are rules concerning subsidiaries in **partnerships** and the taxation of **revenue** from a subsidiary organization to an exempt **parent organization**. [EO Chaps. 29, 30; UB § 8.8; AR § 11.1(f); CU Q 16.1–Q 16.3, Q 16.7, Q 16.7, Q 16.12, Q 16.30; RE Q 14.1; PG pp. 131–132; SM pp. 214–215].

substantial

The word "substantial" generally means an ample or considerable amount of something; it is often synonymous with the word **material**. The **federal tax law** does not assign any specific percentage (of money or time) to this term. A guideline may be that the term means as much as 80 percent of something; the term **substantially all** has been defined by the **IRS** to mean at least 85 percent. [EO §§ 4.4, 12.3(b)(i), 22.1, 22.3(c)(ii), 24.1; UB § 1.6; HC § 31.2(f); LI Q 2.23] (cf. **Insubstantial**; also **Substantial part test**).

substantial compliance, doctrine of

The "doctrine of substantial compliance" is a form of **equity** by which a **person** can contend that a requirement of **statutory law** was satisfied because it was adhered to in a **substantial** manner. In applying this **doctrine**, a court is to determine whether the requirement relates to the substance or essence of the statute. If so, the requirement is a **mandatory requirement**. Otherwise, the requirement is considered to be a **directory requirement**. [CG §§ 12.1(c), 21.5(c); SM p. 141].

substantial contributor

The term "substantial contributor" means a **person** who **contributed** or **bequeathed** an aggregate amount of more than $5,000 to a **private foundation**, if that amount is more than 2 percent of the total contributions and bequests received by the organization before the close of the **tax year** of the organization in which the contribution or bequest is received by the organization from the person (**IRC** § 507(d)(2)(A)). In the case of a **trust**, the term "substantial contributor" also means the **creator of the trust** (*id.*). A substantial contributor to a private foundation is a **disqualified person** with respect to that foundation.

For this purpose, (1) each contribution or bequest is valued at its **fair market value** on the date it was received, (2) in the case of an organization that was in existence on October 9, 1969, all contributions and bequests received on or before that date are treated (except for purposes of the preceding valuation rule) as if received on that date, (3) an individual is treated as making all contributions and bequests made by his or her spouse, and (4) any person who is a substantial contributor on any date remains a substantial contributor for all subsequent periods, except to the extent noted in the next paragraph (**IRC** § 507(d)(2)(B)).

Nonetheless, a person ceases to be treated as a substantial contributor with respect to an organization as of the close of a tax year of the organization if (1) during the ten-year period ending at the close of the tax year, the person and any **related persons** have not made any contribution to the organization; (2) at no time during the ten-year period was the person or any related person a **foundation manager** of the organization, and (3) the aggregate contributions made by the person and any related persons are determined by the **IRS** to be insignificant when compared to the aggregate amount of contributions to the foundation by one other person (**IRC** § 507(d)(2)(C)). For purposes of the third criterion, **appreciation** with respect to contributions while held by the organization is taken into account (*id.*).

The term "substantial contributor" is also used when computing **public support** for purposes of the **service provider publicly supported charity rules** (**IRC** § 509(a)(2)), as part of the definition of an **exempt operating foundation** (**IRC** § 4940(d)(3)(C)), and in the definition of disqualified person as used in connection with the **excess benefit transaction** rules (**IRC** § 4958(c)(3)(C)(i)). [PF §§ 4.1, 15.5(d); EO § 12.2(a); HC § 4.9(a)(iii); AR §§ 18.1(c)(1), 18.1(c)(5); PG pp. 89–90, 192].

substantial estate or gift tax valuation understatement

There is a "substantial estate or gift tax valuation understatement" where the **value** of an item of **property** claimed on an **estate tax return** or a **gift tax return** is 50 percent or less of the amount determined to be the correct amount of the valuation (**IRC** § 6662(g)(1)).

substantial part test

The "substantial part test" is the standard, applicable to **tax-exempt charitable organizations** (other than **private foundations**), which states that no **substantial** part of the activities of the organization may constitute carrying on **propaganda** or otherwise attempting to **influence legislation** (**IRC** § 501(c)(3)). Although the term "substantial" is not defined in this context, the term can be applied in one of three ways: (1) as an amount in relation to (or percentage of) total annual **expenditures** of money by a charitable organization, (2) as an amount in relation to (or percentage of) the total annual expenditure of time by or on behalf of a charitable organization, and (3) as a measure of the amount of "influence" brought to bear on a legislative process by a charitable organization (irrespective of time or money spent), such as by reason of its general reputation or credibility, usually determined on the basis of hindsight.

This test likely means that a charitable organization (other than a private foundation) may, without endangering its **tax-exempt status**, annually involve itself in one or more legislative processes to an **insubstantial extent**. Stated as a percentage (of time or money), the term "insubstantial" may correlate to as much as 15 percent. This calculation is based, in part, on the percentages derived by the **IRS** in defining the term **substantially all**. [EO §§ 22.2(a), 22.3(c); HC § 7.1; CG § 3.3(b); PF §§ 9.1(a), 9.1(b); AR §§ 9.1(d), 9.2(c); CU Q 8.4, Q 8.6; PG pp. 110–111; SM p. 183] (cf. **Expenditure test**).

substantial return benefit

The phrase "substantial return benefit" is used in conjunction with the **corporate sponsorship rules** to mean a benefit, provided to a **sponsor** in exchange for a payment, that is other than certain uses or a mere **acknowledgement** or one that is **disregarded** because it is **de minimis**. [EO § 24.6; UB § 6.6(a); HC § 24.17; CG § 23.3; SM pp. 158–159].

substantial understatement

In general, a "substantial understatement" of **income tax** for a **tax year** occurs if the amount of the **understatement** for the year exceeds the greater of (1) 10 percent of the tax required to be shown on the **tax return** for the year or (2) $5,000 (**IRC** § 6662(d)(1)(A)). In the case of a **corporation** (other than an **S** corporation or a personal holding company (as defined in **IRC** § 542), "$10,000" is substituted for "$5,000" (**IRC** § 6662(d)(1)(B)).

S

substantial valuation misstatement

In general, there is a "substantial valuation misstatement" for **income tax** purposes if (1) the **value** of any **property** (or the **adjusted basis** of any property) claimed on a **tax return** is 200 percent or more of the amount determined to be the correct amount of the valuation or adjusted basis (as the case may be) or (2) (a) the price for any property or services (or for the use of property) claimed on a tax return in connection with any transaction between persons as described in the **law** concerning **allocations** of **income** and **deductions** among **taxpayers** is 200 percent or more (or 50 percent or less) of the amount determined under that law to be the correct amount of the price or (b) the net transfer price adjustment under that law (as defined in **IRC** § 6662(e)(3)) for the tax year exceeds $10 million (**IRC** § 6662(e)(1)).

substantially all

The phrase "substantially all" is used in the **federal law** of **tax-exempt organizations** in three instances. In two of these settings, the **IRS** has ruled that the term means at least 85 percent. Thus, the amount not covered by the requirement is an amount that may be as much as 15 percent.

The first context for use of the phrase "substantially all" is in the rules concerning **private operating foundations**, which require adherence to an **income test**. To satisfy this test, a **private foundation** must annually expend an amount equal to substantially all of the lesser of its **adjusted gross income** or its **minimum investment return**, in the form of **qualifying distributions**, **directly** for the **active conduct** of its **charitable** activities.

The second context for use of this phrase is in the rules concerning **Type III functionally integrated supporting organizations**, where an **integral part test** must be met. This test can be met in one of three ways, one of which is that the supporting organization engages in activities substantially all of which **directly** further the **exempt purpose** of one or more supported organizations.

The third use of the phrase "substantially all" occurs in connection with the **lobbying disallowance rule** and the **political activities disallowance rule**. These rules generally apply to **membership organizations** that engage in lobbying and/or political activities, by means of a **flow-through rule**; that is, the portion of the member's **dues** that is **allocable** to either or both of these types of activities is disallowed as a **business expense deduction**. Generally, these organizations must provide **disclosure** to their members of this allocable portion or the dues. This disclosure is not required, however, where substantially all of the organization's dues monies are paid by members not entitled to deduct the dues in computing their **taxable income**. In this context, "substantially all" means 90 percent. [PF §§ 3.1(d), 15.7(g); EO §§ 12.1(b), 12.3(c), 22.6(c), 23.7; SM pp. 87, 193].

substantially completed application

A "substantially completed application for recognition of tax exemption" is an application of this nature that is ready for processing by the **IRS**. Also, for purposes of the **declaratory judgment rules**, it is the position of the **IRS** that the 270-period does not begin until the date a substantially completed application is filed with the IRS.

A **substantially** completed **application for recognition of tax exemption** is one that (1) is signed by an authorized individual; (2) includes an **employer identification number**; (3) includes a statement of receipts and **expenditures** and a balance sheet for the current year and the three preceding years (or the years the **organization** has been in existence, in the case of a shorter period), although if the organization has not yet commenced operations, or has not completed one accounting period, a proposed budget for two full accounting periods and a current statement of **assets** and **liabilities** is acceptable; (4) includes a detailed narrative statement of proposed activities (including each of the **fundraising** activities of a **charitable** organization) and a narrative description of anticipated receipts and contemplated expenditures; (5) includes a copy of the document by which the organization was established, signed by a principal **officer** or accompanied by a written declaration signed by an authorized individual certifying that the document is a complete and accurate copy of the original or otherwise is a conformed copy; (6) if the organizing document is a set of **articles of incorporation**, includes evidence that it was filed with and approved by an appropriate state official (such as a copy of the certificate of incorporation) or includes a copy of the articles of incorporation accompanied by a written declaration signed by an authorized individual that the copy is a complete and accurate copy of the original document that was filed with and approved by the state, and stating the date of filing; (7) if the organization has adopted **bylaws**, includes a current copy of that document, which need not be signed if submitted as an attachment to the application; otherwise, the bylaws must be verified as being current by an authorized individual; and (8) is accompanied by the correct **user fee**. [EO § 26.1(b); HC § 34.1(b); RE Q 8.36; LI Q 2.28].

substantially related

A **tax-exempt organization** derives **gross income** from an **unrelated business** if the conduct of the trade or business that produces the income is not "substantially related" (other than through the production of funds) to the organization's tax-exempt purposes (**IRC** § 513(a)). This requirement necessitates an examination of the relationship between the business activities that generate the income in question (the activities of producing or distributing the goods or performing the services involved) and the accomplishment of the organization's tax-exempt purposes.

A trade or business is "substantially related" only if the causal relationship, shown in the requirement that the trade or business be **related**, is a **substantial** one. Thus, for the conduct of a trade or business from which a particular amount of gross income is derived by a tax-exempt organization to be substantially related to the purposes for which **tax exemption** was **recognized**, the production or distribution of the goods or the performance of the services from which the gross income is derived must contribute importantly to the accomplishment of these purposes. Where the production or distribution of the goods or the performance of the services does not contribute importantly to the accomplishment of the exempt purposes of an organization, the income from the sale of the goods or the performance of the services does not derive from the conduct of a related trade or business.

Whether activities productive of gross income contribute importantly to the accomplishment of any purpose for which an organization has been recognized as tax-exempt depends in each case on the **facts and circumstances** involved.

In determining whether activities contribute importantly to the accomplishment of a tax-exempt purpose, the **size and extent** of the activities involved must be considered in relation to the nature and extent of the exempt function that they purport to serve. Thus, where income is realized by an exempt organization from activities that are in part related to the performance of its exempt functions, but that are conducted on a larger scale than is reasonably necessary for performance of its functions, the gross income attributable to that portion of the activities in excess of the needs of exempt functions constitutes gross income from the conduct of an unrelated trade or business. This type of income is not derived from the production or distribution of goods or the performance of services that contribute importantly to the accomplishment of any tax-exempt purpose of the organization. [UB § 2.7(a); EO § 24.4; HC § 24.4; PF § 11.1; FR § 5.7(a)(v); SM pp. 173–174] (also **Dual use facility**; **Exploitation**).

substantiation rules

There is a battery of **rules** to which a **donor** to a **charitable organization** and the charitable organization that is the **donee** must adhere as a condition of allowance of the otherwise allowable **federal income tax charitable contribution deduction**. That is, where there is noncompliance with these rules, the donor will not be entitled to the charitable contribution deduction, notwithstanding the fact that all other applicable rules have been followed. Some of these rules are collectively termed the "substantiation" requirements.

One set of these substantiation rules provides that the charitable contribution deduction is not allowed for a **separate contribution** of $250 or more unless the donor has written substantiation from the donee of the contribution, including a **good faith** estimate of the **value** of any good or service that has been provided to the donor in exchange for making the contribution to the donee (**IRC** § 170(f)(8)).

The written acknowledgment of a gift must provide information sufficient to substantiate the amount of the deductible contribution, but it need not take any particular form. Thus, acknowledgements may be made by letter, post card, or computer-generated form. A donee **charity** may prepare a separate acknowledgement for each contribution or may provide donors with periodic (such as annual) acknowledgements that set forth the required information for each contribution of $250 or more made by the donor during that period. (A charitable organization that knowingly provides a false written substantiation to a donor may be subject to the **penalty** for aiding and abetting an **understatement of tax liability**.)

In cases where, in **consideration** for a contribution of $250 dollars or more, a **religious organization** furnishes to a contributor solely an **intangible religious benefit** generally not sold in a **commercial** transaction outside the donative context, the written substantiation must contain a statement to the effect that an intangible religious benefit was so furnished, but the substantiation need not further describe, nor provide a valuation for, the benefit.

A contributor must obtain substantiation prior to filing his or her **tax return** for the **tax year** in which the contribution was made (or, if earlier, the due date, including extensions, for tiling the return). It is the responsibility of the donor to obtain this substantiation and maintain it in his or her records. (The **income tax** charitable contribution deduction is dependent on compliance with these rules.)

The foregoing substantiation procedure is an addition to the rules that (1) require the provision of certain information to the **IRS** (on **Form 8283**) if the amount of the claimed deduction for all non-cash contributions exceeds $500 and (2) apply to non-cash gifts exceeding $5,000 per item or group of **similar items** (other than certain publicly traded securities), where the services of a **qualified appraiser** are required, and the donee must acknowledge receipt of the gift (by signing **Form 8283**) and provide certain other information.

There are additional substantiation requirements in conjunction with the making of a **qualified conservation contribution**. [CG §§ 9.7(f), 9.13(d), 21.3–21.5, 21.7, 21.8; FR §§ 5.3, 8.10(d), 8.12; AR §§ 14.1(i)(7), 19.1(y); RE Q 13.20–Q 13.23; AS § 9.4; PG pp. 237–239; SM pp. 142–144; LI Q 12.31, Q 12.32].

substantive due process

"Substantive due process" is the category of **due process** that is applied to determine whether the substance of a **law** (**legislation**) is in conformity with **constitutional** law principles. This is accomplished by ascertaining whether there is a rational state interest underlying the law in relation to individual **rights**. [CL §§ 1.1(b), 7.5].

suitability test

The "suitability test" is one of two tests by which qualifying **set-asides** are determined in the **private foundation law** context (**IRC** §§ 4942(g)(2)(A), (B)(i)). This test is met where the general set-aside rules are satisfied and where the private foundation is successful in convincing the **IRS** that the project can be better accomplished by a set-aside rather than by the immediate payment of funds. A **ruling** from the **IRS** is necessary for this type of set-aside and the private foundation must apply for the ruling before the end of the year in which the amount is set aside. The request for the ruling must include the amount of the intended set-aside, the reasons why the project can be better accomplished by a set-aside, and a detailed description of the project. [PF § 6.5(d)].

sum certain

A "sum certain" is an amount (usually, of money) that is stated, fixed, and/or exact. In the context of **charitable remainder annuity trusts**, a "sum certain" is a stated dollar amount, which is the same either as to each **income beneficiary** or as to the total amount payable for each year of the period of existence of the trust. This stated dollar amount may be expressed as a fraction or a percentage of the initial net **fair market value** of the **property** irrevocably passing in trust as finally determined for **federal tax** purposes. [CG § 12.2(a)] (also **Annuity**).

summary judgment

The term "summary judgment" is used to describe a judgment issued by a court in circumstances under which there is no issue of **material** fact as to a claim, but only one or more issues of **law**. This type of judgment is stimulated by a **motion** for summary judgment filed by one of the parties to the litigation. A judgment obtained as a result of a **declaratory judgment action** is closely akin to a summary judgment.

superparent organization

A "superparent organization" is a type of **supporting organization** that provides support to one or more qualified **supported organizations** that are two tiers below. For example, a superparent supporting organization may be **operated in connection with** two or more **hospitals**, with the organizations in the intermediate tier consisting of other supporting organizations and/or hospital systems. A superparent organization is often referred to as a **grandparent organization**. [HC § 20.2(c)].

supervised or controlled in connection with

A **charitable organization** that intends to avoid **private foundation** status on the ground that it is a **supporting organization** must stand in at least one of three required relationships between a supporting organization and a **supported organization**. One of these relationships is encompassed by the phrase "supervised or controlled in connection with" (**IRC** § 509(a)(3)(B)). The distinguishing feature of this relationship is the presence of **common supervision or control** by the **persons** supervising or controlling both the supporting organization and the supported organization to ensure that the supporting organization will be **responsive** to the needs and requirements of the supported organization. To meet this requirement, the control or management of the supporting organization must be vested in the same persons that control or manage the supported organization. An organization will not be considered to be in this relationship with one or more **public charities** if it merely makes payments (mandatory or discretionary) to one or more named public charities, regardless of whether the obligation to make payments to the named beneficiary is enforceable under local law. This is the **Type II supporting organization**. [PF § 15.7(f); EO § 12.3(c); HC § 5.5(d); SM p. 83].

super-PAC

A "super-PAC" is the informal term for a form of **political action committee**, which is more technically referred to as an "independent-expenditure only committee." This is because it may engage in an unlimited amount of **political campaign** spending independent of political campaigns; it cannot make contributions to **political candidate's** campaigns or political parties. A super-PAC can raise funds from individuals, **unions**, **business corporations**, and other **entities** without any limitations as to amount. The vehicle of choice for a super-PAC often is a **tax-exempt social welfare organization**. [SM p. 203].

supplemental unemployment benefit trust

One way for a **nonprofit organization** to qualify as a **tax-exempt organization** under the **federal tax law** is for it to be a "supplemental unemployment benefit trust" (**IRC** § 501(a), by reason of **IRC** § 501(c)(17)). This is a **trust** that is part of a **plan** providing for the payment of **supplemental unemployment compensation benefits**. The plan that includes this type of trust must have eligibility **conditions** and benefits that do not **discriminate** in favor of supervisory or highly compensated **employees** and that requires that benefits be determined according to objective standards. The trust must be part of a plan that provides that the **corpus** and **income** of the trust cannot (before the satisfaction of all **liabilities** to employees covered by the plan) be used for or diverted to any purposes other than the provision of supplemental unemployment compensation benefits. Termination of a supplemental unemployment benefit trust, with distribution of its remaining **assets** to employees covered by the plan (after the satisfaction of all liabilities) will not result in loss of **exempt status**, even though technically the assets will not be used solely for the purpose of providing benefits. These trusts are intended to provide benefits to laid-off (or perhaps ill) employees, frequently in conjunction with other payments such as state unemployment benefits. This type of trust is a **welfare benefit fund**. [EO §§ 18.4, 24.10; AU § 7.1(w); SM p. 43].

supplemental unemployment compensation benefits

The phrase "supplemental unemployment compensation benefits" means separation-from-employment benefits and sick and accident benefits that are subordinate to the separation benefits (**IRC** § 501(c)(17)(D)). These benefits encompass short-term benefits paid to employees not wholly separated from employment and relocation payments to **employees** who would otherwise be separated from employment. [EO § 18.4].

supplier's exhibit

The term "supplier's exhibit" is used in conjunction with the rules concerning a **qualified convention and trade show activity**. A "supplier's exhibit" is an exhibit at which there is display of goods or services that are supplied to, rather than by, the **members** of the **association** in the conduct of their **trade or business**. The **exclusion** from the concept of **unrelated business** that is provided by the convention and trade show activities rules is available with respect to a supplier's exhibit that is conducted by the association in conjunction with a qualified convention or trade show. The exclusion is not available, however, to a stand-alone supplier's exhibit that is not a qualified convention show. Nonetheless, **income** from a supplier's show is not taxable where the displays are **educational** and where **soliciting** and **selling** is prohibited. [UB § 4.5; AS §§ 2.8, 3.5, 5.9(n); EO § 25.2(f)].

support, financial

The type of financial support received by a **charitable organization** will determine, among other matters, whether the organization qualifies as a **publicly supported organization**. If the organization is achieving **nonprivate foundation** status as one of the **institutions** or as a **supporting organization**, the nature of its financial support is irrelevant in relation to its **public charity status**.

In this context, the term "support" that is used to describe the denominator of the **support fraction** in the case of **donative organizations** means amounts received as **gifts**, **grants**, and **contributions, net income** from **unrelated business activities, gross investment income, tax revenues** levied for the benefit of the organization and either paid to or expended on behalf of the organization, and the **value** of services or facilities (exclusive of services or facilities generally furnished to the public without charge) furnished by a **governmental unit** to the organization without charge (**IRC** § 509(d)).

The term "support" that is used to describe the denominator of the support fraction in the case of **service provider organizations** means amounts received as gifts, grants, contributions, and **membership** fees, **gross receipts** from admissions, **sales** of merchandise, performance of

S

services, furnishing of facilities as part of **related** activities, **net income** from unrelated business activities. gross investment income, tax revenues levied for the benefit of the organization and either paid to or expended on behalf of the organization, and the value of services or facilities (exclusive of services or facilities generally furnished to the public without charge) furnished by a governmental unit to the organization without charge (*id.*).

In general, a publicly supported charitable organization must **normally** receive at least one-third of its total financial support in the form of **public support** to qualify as other than a private foundation on that basis. In the case of an organization that has its public charity status based on the **facts and circumstances test**, the public support ratio may be as low as 10 percent.

An organization that is a publicly supported organization because it is a service provider organization, in addition to having to have the requisite amount of public support, has a limitation on the amount of support it can receive in the form of **investment income** and **unrelated business taxable income**: it must normally receive no more than one-third of its support from the sum of gross investment income and any excess of the amount of unrelated business taxable income over the amount of tax on that income (**IRC** § 509(a)(2)(a)). This type of organization also has a limitation on the amount of support received as gross receipts from the performance of **tax-exempt functions** that can constitute public support: gross receipts from **related activities** received from any **person** or from any **bureau or similar agency** of a governmental unit are includible as public support in any year to the extent that these receipts do not exceed the greater of $5,000 or one percent of the organization's support for the year; this is the **1 percent limitation** (**IRC** § 509(a)(2)(A)(ii)).

Another test involving financial support of a charitable organization is the **support test** that may be applicable to a **private operating foundation**. [PF §§ 15.4(b), 15.6(a), 15.6(c); EO §§ 12.3(b)(i), 12.3(b)(iv); HC §§ 5.2(a), 5.3(a), 5.3(d); AR §§ 8.1(d)(3), 8.1(e)(2); PG p. 85].

support, public

A **charitable organization** that wishes to avoid **private foundation** status on the ground that it is a **publicly supported organization** must **normally** receive the requisite amount of "public support," which usually is at least one-third of the support constituting the denominator of its **support fraction**. Public support is the amount of support constituting the numerator of the organization's support fraction. [PF §§ 15.4–15.6; EO § 12.3(b); SM pp. 80–82].

support fraction

A **charitable organization** that wishes to avoid **private foundation status** on the ground that it is a **publicly supported organization** must construct and remain in compliance with the requirements of the appropriate "support fraction." The denominator of the support fraction is total (allowable) **financial support**.

The numerator of the support fraction for **donative charitable organizations** consists of allowable **direct** or **indirect contributions** from the **public** and **grants** from **governmental units** (**IRC** § 170(b)(1)(A)(vi)). (Amounts received as **income** from the performance of an **exempt function** cannot qualify as public support under these rules.) In general, contributions (and grants) constitute public support to the extent that the total amount of contributions (or grants) from a **donor** (or **grantor**) during the **computation period** does not exceed an amount equal to 2 percent of the total (allowable) **financial support** for the period (the amount that is the denominator of the support fraction); this is one of the **2 percent limitations**. (If a donor or grantor provides an amount that is in excess of the **2 percent limitation,** the portion that does not exceed the limitation nonetheless qualifies as public support.)

Thus, the total amount of support by a donor or grantor is included in full in the denominator of the support fraction and the amount determined by application of the **2 percent limitation** is included in the numerator of the support fraction. This latter amount is support in the form of **direct contributions** from the public. Donors or grantors who are related (as defined by the **disqualified person** rules) must be treated as one source for purposes of the 2 percent limitation. Support that is received from other donative charitable organizations and/or governmental units is support in the form of **indirect contributions** from the **general** public. Support that is in the form of indirect contributions (or grants) from the public is not subject to the **2 percent limitation** (assuming the amount was not **earmarked**); that is, this type of support is, in its entirety, public support.

Where an organization is a donative publicly supported organization by reason of the **facts and circumstances test**, its support fraction is computed using the foregoing rules.

The numerator of the support fraction for **service provider charitable organizations** consists of allowable gifts, grants, contributions, **membership fees**, and **gross receipts** from admissions, sales of merchandise, performance of services, or furnishing of facilities in **related activities** (**IRC** § 509(a)(2)(A)(ii)). This support must come from **permitted sources**. Also, support in the form of gross receipts from admissions, sales of merchandise, performance of services, or furnishing of facilities, to be public support, must be that allowed by the **1 percent limitation**.

support test

The "support test" is one of the alternative tests used in determining whether a **private foundation** qualifies as a **private operating foundation**. The requirements of this test are that (1) **substantially all** of the foundation's **support** (other than **gross investment income**) is **normally** received from the **public** and from at least five **tax-exempt organizations** that are not **disqualified persons** with respect to each other or the recipient foundation, (2) not more than 25 percent of its support (other than gross investment income), and (3) not more than 50 percent of its support is normally received from gross investment income (**IRC** § 4942(j)(3)(B)(iii)). [PF §§ 3.1(d)–(f); EO § 12.1(b); SM p. 87].

supported organization

An **organization** generically is a "supported organization" when it is the qualified beneficiary of funding, services, or other operations of one or more **supporting organizations**. Technically, the term "supported organization" means, with respect to an organization that is a supporting organization, an organization that is eligible to be a supported organization, for whose benefit the supporting organization is **organized** and **operated**, or with respect to which the organization performs the functions of or carries out the purposes of. Usually, a supported organization is a **public charity** (other than a supporting organization). As the following provision clearly states, however, a **tax-exempt social welfare organization**, an **exempt labor organization**, and an exempt **business league** can also qualify as a supported organization: "For purposes of paragraph (3), an organization described in paragraph (2) shall be deemed to include an organization described in section 501(c)(4), (5), or (6) which would be described in paragraph (2) if it were an organization described in section 501(c)(3)" (**IRC** § 509(f)(3)). [PF § 15.7; EO § 12.3(c); CG § 3.4(a); SM p. 83].

supporting organization

One of the ways by which a **charitable organization** can avoid being classified as a **private foundation** is to qualify as a "supporting organization" (**IRC** § 509(a)(3)). This type of **public charity** is one that is not one of the **institutions** nor is a **publicly supported organization** but is sufficiently **related** to and supportive of one or more qualified **supported organizations**, which are usually **public charities** (other than supporting organizations), so that the requisite elements of **control** and involvement are present; it is, in essence, a **derivative public charity status**.

A supporting organization must be **organized** and, at all times thereafter, **operated exclusively** for the benefit of, to perform the functions of, or to carry out the purposes of one or more supported organizations (**IRC** § 509(a)(3)(A)). It must be operated, supervised, or controlled by or in connection with one or more public charities (**IRC** § 509(a)(3)(B)). Thus, fundamentally, the relationship must be one of these types: (1) **operated, supervised, or controlled by**, (2) **supervised or controlled in connection with**, or (3) **operated in connection with**.

There are four categories of supporting organizations. A supporting organization that is operated, supervised, or controlled by one or more supported organizations is termed a **Type I supporting organization**. The relationship of a Type I supporting organization with its supported organization(s) is comparable to that of a **parent-subsidiary** relationship. A supporting organization supervised or controlled in connection with one or more supported organizations is a **Type II supporting organization**. A Type II supporting organization is controlled or managed by the same **persons** that control or manage its supported organization(s). A supporting organization that is operated in connection with one or more supported organizations is a Type III supporting organization. A **Type III supporting organization** is either **functionally integrated** with its supported organization(s) or is not functionally integrated with its supported organization(s).

A supporting organization must meet an **organizational test** and an **operational test**. Further, a supporting organization must not be **controlled**, **directly** or **indirectly**, by one or more **disqualified persons** with respect to it (other than **foundation managers**), excluding supported organizations (**IRC** § 509(a)(3)(C)).

An organization can be a supporting organization with respect to a **social welfare organization**, a **labor organization**, or a **business league**, as long as the supported organization meets the **public support** test applicable with respect to **service provider organizations** (IRC § 509(a), last sentence). [PF §§ 1.1, 1.2, 3.5, 7.4, 15.2, 15.7, 15.8(b), 15.8(c), 15.9, 15.10; EO § 12.3(c); HC § 5.5; CG § 3.4(a); FR § 5.11(c); AR § 8.1(h); CU Q 4.18; RE Q 14.15, Q 14.24; AS §§ 8.6, 8.8(g); PG p. 85; SM pp. 82–85, 220; LI Q 10, 15].

suspension of tax-exempt status
See **Tax exemption, suspension of**.

sweepstakes
A "sweepstakes" is a **game of chance** where each of a number of **persons** contributes an identical sum of money (a "stake") and all of the contributions are taken (swept) by the winner (or winners). Some **nonprofit organizations** use a sweepstakes as a **fundraising** technique. [FR § 2.2(a); CG § 3.1(b)] (also **Lottery**).

S

tacking

The word "tacking" is used to describe a characteristic of some consequence in **law**, once held by a **person**, then subsequently transferred to or attributed to another person. For example, if a **tax-exempt charitable organization**, **organized** as a **trust**, has **public support** and the entity subsequently becomes a **corporation**, even though it must file another **application for recognition of exemption**, the **federal tax law** will allow the **incorporated entity** to "tack" onto its public support experience the public support of the predecessor organization.

tangible

The word "tangible" refers to something that can be understood by human senses, and physically possessed and moved. It is something that is corporeal and has inherent **value**, as opposed to being representative of value. For example, the items constituting the **inventory** of a **business corporation** are tangible, while the stock constituting ownership of the corporation is not. (cf. **Intangible**).

tangible property

"Tangible property" is **property** (**real property** or certain **personal property**) that is **tangible**. [CG §§ 2.12(c), 6.11] (cf. **Intangible property**).

Tariff Act of 1894

The "Tariff Act of 1894" was the first general **federal tax law** statute. It contained a provision for **tax exemption**, which stated that "nothing herein contained shall apply to . . . **corporations**, companies, or **associations organized** and conducted **solely** for **charitable**, **religious**, or **educational** purposes." This law was declared **unconstitutional** in 1895. [CL § 1.1(b); EO § 2.4] (also **Sixteenth Amendment**; **Tariff Act of 1913**).

Tariff Act of 1913

Following ratification of the **Sixteenth Amendment**, the "Tariff Act of 1913" was enacted. This statute initiated the general **federal income tax law**. **Exempted** from this tax was "any **corporation** or **association organized** and **operated exclusively** for **religious**, **charitable**, **scientific**, or

Bruce R. Hopkins' Nonprofit Law Dictionary, First Edition. Bruce R. Hopkins.
© 2015 Bruce R. Hopkins. Published 2015 by John Wiley & Sons, Inc.

educational purposes, no part of the **net income** of which **inures** to the benefit of any private shareholder or individual." [CL § 1.1(b); EO § 2.4].

tax

A "tax" represents a sum of money, imposed on a **person**, for support of a government. A tax may be levied on **income**, transactions, or **assets**. The U.S. Supreme Court observed that "taxes are the life-blood of government."

tax abatement

See **Abatement**.

tax benefit rule

The "tax benefit rule" consists of two components: the inclusionary component and the exclusionary component. The exclusionary component, which is partially codified (**IRC** § 111(a)) but which also exists outside the provisions of that section, does not become an issue unless, and until, the inclusionary component of the rule is first satisfied.

This inclusionary component provides that an amount **deducted** from a **person's gross income** in one **tax year** is included in the person's gross income in a subsequent year if an event occurs in the subsequent year that is fundamentally inconsistent with the premise on which the deduction had previously been based. The exclusionary component of the tax benefit rule, by contrast, restrains the inclusionary component by limiting the income that must be **recognized** in the subsequent year to the amount of the tax benefit that resulted from the deduction.

Thus, an amount must be included in gross income in the current year if, and to the extent that, (1) the amount was deducted in a year prior to the current year, (2) the deduction resulted in a tax benefit, (3) an event occurs in the current year that is fundamentally inconsistent with the premises on which the deduction was originally based, and (4) a **nonrecognition** provision of the **IRC** does not prevent the inclusion in gross income.

A current event is considered fundamentally inconsistent with the premises on which the deduction was originally based when the current event would have foreclosed the deduction if that event had occurred within the year that the deduction was taken. [CG § 12.4(i)].

tax credit

A "tax credit" is a feature of **tax law** (usually, an **income tax** law) that allows some or all of the amount of an **expenditure** to reduce, on a dollar-for-dollar basis, the amount which would otherwise be the tax. Examples of income tax credits include those for foreign taxes (**IRC** § 27), increasing **research** activities (**IRC** § 41), and certain rehabilitations (**IRC** § 47). [CG §§ 2.23, 2.24, 9.29; UB § 11.4(d)(vi); PF § 3.4].

tax deduction

A "tax deduction" is a feature of **tax law** (usually, an **income tax** law) that allows some or all of the amount of an **expenditure** to be subtracted from **adjusted gross income** to arrive at the sum of **taxable income**. Some of the income tax deductions for both individuals and **business** enterprises are for outlays in the form of **business expenses** (IRC § 162), **depreciation** (IRC § 167), **charitable contributions** (IRC § 170), and contributions to **black lung benefit trusts** (IRC § 192). Other income tax deductions for individuals, that are **above-the-line** deductions, include those for payments of alimony (**IRC** § 215) and moving expenses (**IRC** § 217). [CG § 2.5] (also **Business expense deduction; Charitable contribution deduction**).

Tax Equity and Fiscal Responsibility Act of 1982

The "Tax Equity and Fiscal Responsibility Act of 1982" revised the **rules** pertaining to **veterans' organizations** and amended the law concerning **amateur sports organizations**. [EO § 2.4].

Tax Exempt and Government Entities Division, IRS

The **IRS** is organized as four divisions, one of them being the "Tax Exempt and Government Entities Division" (sometimes referenced as the TE/GE Division). Within this division is the Exempt Organizations Division, which develops policy concerning and administers the **law** of **tax-exempt organizations**. [EO § 2.2(b); AU §§ 1.4, 2.2–2.4, 5.2(c); HC § 36.1(a); FR § 7.4; AS § 11.9; SM p. 294].

tax exemption

A variety of **nonprofit organizations** are **exempt** from a variety of **taxes**. These taxes may be imposed at the **federal**, state, and/or local levels of government. The types of taxes include **excise, income, sales, use, personal property**, and **real property** taxes. When an organization is excused from the payment of one or more of these taxes, it has a "tax exemption." [EO § 3.1; UB §§ 1.1, 1.2, 11.4; HC § 1.1; CG § 1.2; CL § 1.6; RE Q 8.49; SM p. 323].

tax exemption, advantage of

The one advantage shared by all categories of **tax-exempt organizations** is that, barring **revocation of exemption** or imposition of the **tax** on **income** other than **exempt function income**, the **unrelated business income tax**, the tax on **excessive legislative expenditures**, the tax on certain **political expenditures activities**, or (if **private foundations**) a variety of **excise taxes** and a tax on **net investment income**, they are spared **federal income taxation**. In some instances, **tax-exempt status** under **federal law** will mean comparable status under state and local law; in other cases, additional requirements must be satisfied. [EO §§ 3.3(a), 3.3(h); HC § 2.2].

T

tax exemption, denial of

See **Denial of tax exemption**.

tax exemption, disadvantages of

The principal disadvantages of "tax exemption" are that the **organization** involved may be precluded from engaging in certain activities (such as excessive **lobbying, political campaign activities**, or having **excess business holdings**) and that the **annual reporting** obligations may be greater than if the **entity** was taxable. [EO § 3.4; HC § 2.3].

tax exemption, forfeiture of

In general, there is no formal procedure for voluntarily forfeiting **tax exemption**, once the **IRS** has **recognized** the exempt status of an **organization**. The **IRS** generally is of the view that, having filed an **application for recognition of exemption** and received a **determination letter** or **ruling**, an organization has surrendered itself to the **law** governing **tax-exempt organizations**. The IRS, however, has adopted a procedure by which a **dual-status governmental entity** may voluntarily relinquish its **charitable status**. [EO § 26.11].

tax exemption, as government subsidy

The U.S. Supreme Court has been remarkably inconsistent when determining whether a **tax exemption** accorded a class of **nonprofit organizations** (or **charitable** deduction or **charitable tax** credit) is a subsidy, provided by the government that legislated the exemption, although concurring and dissenting opinions have been amply clear (albeit severely diametric). [CL § 1.12; SM pp. 333–335].

tax exemption, rationale for

Several rationales for the **federal income tax exemption** for various categories of **nonprofit organizations** abound. **Charitable organizations** are **tax-exempt** because of their critical role in American society and their **program** activities. Some organizations are exempt because of a similar, yet not as lofty, rationale; these include **social welfare organizations, business and professional associations**, and **labor organizations**. The rationale for exemption for organizations such as **social clubs** is that their activities do not involve **taxable events**. Some organizations have tax exemption as a byproduct of other **law** policy developments; these entities include professional **football leagues, pension funds**, and **black lung benefit trusts**. [CL § 1.7; EO §§ 1.4–1.6; HC § 1.3; SM pp. 323–324].

tax exemption, recognition of

See **Recognition of tax exemption**.

tax exemption, revocation of

See **Revocation of tax exemption**.

tax exemption, suspension of

Federal income tax exemption, and the eligibility of an **organization** to apply for **recognition** of exemption, is suspended for a particular period if it is a **terrorist organization** (IRC § 501(p)). Also, **contributions** to this type of organization are not **deductible** during the period for income, **estate**, and **gift tax** purposes. [EO § 26.8].

tax expenditure

A "tax expenditure" is a term given to a loss (or ostensible loss) of government **tax revenue** attributable to a provision of the **federal tax law** that allows a **tax deduction, tax credit, tax**

exemption, tax exclusion, preferential tax rate, or **deferral of tax liability**. Thus, tax expenditures include any reduction in **income tax liability** that results from a special tax provision that provides a tax benefit to particular **taxpayers**. The income tax **charitable contribution deduction** is currently the eleventh largest tax expenditure ($251.8 billion). [EO § 1.2; CL §§ 1.12, 1.12(g); UB § 1.3 HC § 3.1].

tax extenders

Some provisions of the **IRC**, including some that are part of the law of **tax-exempt organizations** or the law of **deductible charitable giving**, are assigned expiration dates. This is usually done because of the budgetary expense of the provision; this incremental approach allows Congress to minimize the annual cost of a provision. Typically, these provisions allow for the existence of an exception or similar provision for one calendar year. An item of tax legislation that would extend one of these provisions for another period (such as one year) is known as a "tax extender."

Tax Extenders and Alternative Minimum Tax Relief Act of 2008

The "Tax Extenders and Alternative Minimum Tax Relief Act of 2008" temporarily extended the **S corporation charitable giving basis rules**, the special rule for charitable gifts of **food** and **book inventory**, the rules for charitable gifts of computer technology or equipment, and the rules concerning **qualified charitable distributions**. [CG §§ 6.15, 9.3(h), 9.3(i), 9.5, 9.10(e); EO § 2.4].

tax fraud penalty

The **federal tax law** contains a **penalty** that is imposed when an **underpayment** of **tax** required to be shown on a **tax return** is attributable to **fraud** (IRC § 6663).

Tax Increase Prevention Act of 2014

The "Tax Increase Prevention Act of 2014," signed into law on December 19, 2014, extended various expired provisions of the **Internal Revenue Code** through 2014. These provisions include the rules allowing tax-free distributions from individual retirement accounts for **charitable** purposes, modification of the tax treatment of certain payments to **controlling tax-exempt organizations**, the special rule for **contributions** of **capital gain real property** for **conservation purposes**, the **enhanced charitable deduction** for contributions to charity of food **inventory**, and the rule concerning **basis adjustment** to **stock** of **S corporations** making charitable contributions of property. [EO § 2.4].

Tax Increase Prevention and Reconciliation Act of 2005

Enactment of the "Tax Increase Prevention and Reconciliation Act of 2005" introduced the rules taxing **tax-exempt entities** that enter into **prohibited tax shelter transactions**. [EO § 2.4].

tax preference item

A "tax preference item" (or "item of tax preference") is a **tax deduction**, tax **credit**, or similar item, the economic **value** of which is subject to the **alternative minimum tax**. [CG § 1.6].

Tax Reform Act of 1969

The "Tax Reform Act of 1969" is the most significant of the **federal tax acts** from the standpoint of the **law** of **tax-exempt organizations**. This **legislation** brought a dazzling array of **exempt organizations** laws, including rules differentiating **public charities** from **private foundations**, imposing **excise taxes** on various aspects of the operations of private foundations, and revising the **unrelated debt-financed property** rules and the tax treatment of **social clubs**. [PF §§ 1.3, 5.14, 5.15, 6.1, 6.7(e), 15.2; EO § 2.4; UB § 1.9; HC § 8.1].

Tax Reform Act of 1976

The "Tax Reform Act of 1976" brought the **expenditure test rules**, extended a **private foundation** rule relating to the **sale** of **excess business holdings** and non-excess business holdings to **disqualified persons**, definition of **agricultural**, **tax exemption** for **amateur sports organizations**, and introduced the **declaratory judgment** and **generation-skipping transfer tax** rules. [PF §§ 6.3(e), 6.8; EO § 2.4; CG § 8.5; HC § 24.3].

Tax Reform Act of 1984

The "Tax Reform Act of 1984," a component of the Deficit Reduction Act of 1984, introduced the tax-exempt entity leasing rules, made changes in the definition of an exempt operating foundation, and brought the church audit and child care organization rules and changes in the **U.S. instrumentality** rules. The occasion of enactment of this legislation enabled Congress to direct the **IRS** to fully enforce the rules concerning **private foundation annual information returns**. [EO § 2.4; PF §§ 9.6(j), 15.11(b)].

Tax Reform Act of 1986

The "Tax Reform Act of 1986" introduced the law concerning **multi-parent title-holding corporations** and provision of **commercial-type insurance**, brought law addressing **liquidations** of **for-profit entities** into **tax-exempt organizations**, and made several revisions in the **tax-exempt entity leasing rules**. [EO § 2.4; HC §§ 9.3, 30.1(a); CG § 2.16(b)].

Tax Relief, Unemployment Insurance Reauthorization, and Job Creation Act of 2010

The "Tax Relief, Unemployment Insurance Reauthorization, and Job Creation Act of 2010" temporarily extended the **S corporation charitable giving basis rules**, the special rule for charitable gifts of **food** and **book inventory**, the rules for charitable gifts of computer technology or equipment, and the rules concerning **qualified charitable distributions**, and revised the **estate tax** rules. [CG §§ 6.15, 8.4, 8.5, 9.3(h), 9.3(i), 9.5, 9.10(e)].

tax return

See **Return, tax**.

tax return preparer

A "tax return preparer" is, for purposes of the **preparer tax identification number** requirement, **a lawyer, certified public accountant**, enrolled agent, or registered tax return preparer. [EO § 28.3(z); HC § 35.4(b)(xxvi)].

tax shelter

The term "tax shelter" is used to describe a transaction or series of transactions designed to reduce (or eliminate) the **tax liability** of a **taxpayer** by the provision of tax **credits** and/or tax **deductions**. In the context of the **accuracy-related penalties**, the term "tax shelter" means a **partnership** or other **entity**, an investment plan or arrangement, or any other plan or arrangement where the **principal** purpose of the entity, plan, or arrangement is the avoidance or evasion of **federal income tax (IRC § 6662(d)(2()C)(ii))**. Most tax shelters have been eliminated by tax revision **statutes** in recent years and otherwise discouraged by the enactment of **penalties** for participating in **abusive tax shelters (IRC § 6700)**. Some forms of **charitable giving** schemes are loosely referred to as tax shelters. [EO § 28.17; CG § 1.6; PG pp. 252–254; SM pp. 208–210] (also **Listed transaction**).

tax year

The "tax year" of a **person** essentially is the same period as referenced in the **federal tax law** term "taxable year." That body of law, however, uses this term even when the person is not taxable (such as because he, she, or it is **tax-exempt**) or otherwise when no tax is due. Thus, a "tax year" is the period of time over which a **person's tax liability** is determined. This term is also used to describe the annual financial period of **tax-exempt organizations**. Generally, the tax year of an individual is the calendar year. For other persons, the tax year is either the calendar year or some other fiscal year; the desired year may be elected (**IRC § 441(b)**) and can be changed. [CG § 2.9].

tax-exempt

An **organization** is "tax-exempt" when it is, by **law**, **exempt** from the obligation of paying a particular **tax**. For example, an **organization** that is generally exempt from payment of the payment of the **federal income tax** is "tax-exempt."

tax-exempt entity

For purposes of the **tax-exempt entity leasing rules**, a "tax-exempt entity" includes any **organization** that is **tax-exempt** under the **federal income tax law** (other than a **farmers' cooperative**) (**IRC § 168(h)(2)(A)(ii)**). Governmental bodies and their **instrumentalities** are also tax-exempt entities (**IRC §§ 168(h)(2)(A)(i), (D)**), as are certain foreign organizations (**IRC §§ 168(h)(2)(A)(iii), (B), (C)**). Special rules deem certain previously tax-exempt organizations to be tax-exempt entities where they were exempt during the five-year period ending on the date the **property** involved was first leased to the organization (**IRC § 168(h)(2)(E)(i)**), with a special election for certain **benevolent** or mutual organizations (**IRC § 168(h)(2)(E)(ii)**).

For purposes of the rules taxing certain "tax-exempt entities" that enter into **prohibited tax shelter transactions**, these entities include conventionally defined **tax-exempt organizations**, **apostolic organizations**, **charitable donees** (which include **governmental units** other than the United States), **Indian tribal governments**, and **prepaid tuition plans** (**IRC § 4965(c)**). [EO §§ 28.15, 28.16].

tax-exempt entity in tax shelter, tax on

If a transaction is a **prohibited tax shelter transaction** at the time a **tax-exempt entity**, that is a conventionally defined **tax-exempt organization**, an **apostolic organization**, a **charitable donee**, or an **Indian tribal government**, becomes a party to the transaction, the entity must pay an **excise tax** for the **tax year** in which the entity becomes a party and any subsequent tax year. If a tax-exempt entity, that is in one of these four categories, is a party to a **subsequently listed transaction** at any time during a tax year, the entity must pay an excise tax for that year.

This tax generally is an amount equal to the product of the highest rate of corporate income tax and the greater of (1) the entity's net income for the year which (a) in the case of a prohibited tax shelter transaction (other than a subsequently listed transaction) is attributable to the transaction, or (b) in the case of a subsequently listed transaction is attributable to the transaction and which is properly allocable to the period beginning on the later of the date the transaction is identified by the **IRS** as a **listed transaction** or the first day of the year, or (2) 75 percent of the proceeds received by the entity for the year which (a) in the case of a prohibited tax shelter transaction (other than a subsequently listed transaction) are attributable to the transaction, or (b) in the case of a subsequently listed transaction are attributable to the transaction and which are properly allocated to the previously described period. This tax is increased in instances where the tax-exempt entity **knew**, or had reason to know, that a transaction was a prohibited tax shelter transaction at the time the entity become a party to the transaction (**IRC** §§ 4965(a)(1), (b)(1). [EO § 28.17].

tax-exempt entity leasing rules

The **federal tax law** contains a series of provisions concerning certain situations where **tax-exempt organizations** lease **real property** and/or **personal property**. These practices are known collectively as "tax-exempt entity leasing." The tax-exempt entity leasing rules impose restrictions on the federal tax benefits arising from the leasing of property to exempt organizations and places restrictions on the federal tax benefits available to investors in **partnerships** composed of taxable and exempt entities (**IRC** § 168(h)).

The essence of the tax-exempt entity leasing rules is to force investors to compute their **depreciation deduction** over a longer **recovery period** where the property is **tax-exempt use property**. Where these rules apply, the depreciation deduction must be determined by using the **straight-line method of depreciation**. [EO § 28.16; AS § 7.7; SM pp. 219–220].

tax-exempt number

There is no such thing as a "tax-exempt number," yet there is frequent and ongoing reference to it. The **employer identification number**, which is sometimes termed a **taxpayer identification number**, has no significance in relation to **tax-exempt status**. [SM p. 25].

tax-exempt organization

An **organization** is a "tax-exempt organization" when it is **exempt** (even in part) from one or more **federal**, state, or local taxes; it is an organization with a **tax exemption**. Usually, the term "tax-exempt organization" is applied to an organization that is exempt from an **income tax**. The **federal tax law** provides for exemption from federal income taxation (**IRC** § 501(a)) and enumerates in one provision (**IRC** § 501(c)) most of the types of organizations that are exempt from that tax. (The other tax exemption provisions are **IRC** §§ 501(d), 526–528.) Tax-exempt organizations include **charitable, educational, religious,** and **scientific** organizations; **social welfare organizations; labor** entities; **business leagues; social clubs, employee benefit funds, farmers' cooperatives, political organizations,** and **veterans' organizations**. In the instance of the **disclosure requirements** concerning the offering of information or services that are available from the federal government (**IRC** § 6711), the term "tax-exempt organization" means an organization that is described in **IRC** § 501(c) or (d) and exempt from taxation under **IRC** § 501(a) or is a political organization (**IRC** § 6711(c)(1)). Overall, there are seventy-four categories of exempt organizations. Despite the sweep of the term, an exempt organization may, in fact, be subject to one or more taxes, such as the tax on **unrelated business income**. [EO § 1.2; PF §§ 1.6, 2.1, CG §§ 1.2, 1.4, 1.5; AU §§ 1.5, 7.1; RE Q 8.1, Q 8.2, Q 8.3; CU Q 3.1, Q 3.2; UB §§ 1.3, 1.5; PG pp. 38–40, 63–65; SM pp. 24, 47, 65–74; LI Q 2.1–Q 2.3].

tax-exempt purpose

A "tax-exempt purpose" is the purpose (or purposes) of being for a **tax-exempt organization** and the reason that it has **tax-exempt status**. To be and to remain exempt, the organization must be **operated primarily** to serve the exempt purpose. (also **Exempt purpose expenditure**).

tax-exempt status

Where an **organization** has been granted **recognition** of **tax exemption** by the **IRS** or has a tax exemption by **operation of law**, that person has "tax-exempt status." [PF §§ 2.5, 2.7; FR § 5.26; PG pp. 41–53; SM pp. 26, 65–66].

tax-exempt use property

The term "tax-exempt use property" means that portion of any **tangible property** (other than nonresidential **real property**) that is leased to a **tax-exempt entity** (**IRC** § 168(h)(1)(A)). In the case of nonresidential real property, the term "tax-exempt use property" means any portion of the property that is leased to a tax-exempt entity by means of a **disqualified lease** (**IRC** § 168(h)(1)(B)(i)). These rules apply to property, however, only if the portion of the property leased to a tax-exempt entity by means of a disqualified lease is more than 35 percent of the property (**IRC** § 168(h)(1)(B)(iii)).

In the case of any property that is leased to a **partnership**, the determination as to whether any portion of the property is tax-exempt use property is made by treating each tax-exempt partner's share of the property as if it is being leased to the partner (**IRC** § 168(h)(5)(A)). This rule also applies in the ease of any **pass-through entity** other than a partnership and in the case of tiered partnerships and other entities (**IRC** § 168(h)(5)(B)). [EO § 28.16; HC § 16.6; SM pp. 219–220].

taxable distribution

The term "taxable distribution" means a distribution from a **donor-advised fund** to a **natural person** or to any other person if the distribution is for a non-**charitable** purpose or the **sponsoring organization** does not exercise **expenditure responsibility** with respect to the distribution. This term does not include a distribution from a donor-advised fund to a **public charity** (other than a **disqualified supporting organization**), the sponsoring organization of the donor-advised fund, or to another donor-advised fund.

A tax is imposed on a taxable distribution, equal to 20 percent of the amount, payable by the sponsoring organization with respect to the donor-advised fund. A tax is also imposed on the agreement of a **fund manager** to the making of a distribution, **knowing** that it is a taxable distribution; this tax, which must be paid by a fund manager who agreed to the making of the distribution, is equal to five percent of the amount. If more than one person is liable for the tax on fund management, there is **joint and several liability**. With respect to any one taxable distribution, the maximum amount of the tax imposed on fund management may not exceed $10,000 (**IRC §§ 4966(a)–(c)**). [EO § 11.8(b); PF § 16.9; CG § 23.4; AR § 11.1(a)(2)].

taxable estate

The term "taxable estate" is used, as part of the **federal law** of **estate taxation**, to describe the amount of money and/or **property** to which the **estate tax rates** apply. This amount is a **decedent's gross estate**, less allowable **deductions** (such as the **charitable contribution deduction** and the marital deduction) (**IRC § 2051**). [CG § 8.3(b)].

taxable event

In general, for the **federal income tax** to be applicable, there must be a "taxable event"—that is, there must be a shifting of **income** from one **person** to another. It is on this basis that **social clubs** are **tax-exempt**, where they are supported **primarily** by **membership dues**, **fees**, and **assessments**. The rationale is that the members are merely doing collectively what they could do individually, without tax.

The term "taxable event" means any act (or failure to act) giving rise to liability for tax in the **black lung benefits trust**, **donor-advised fund**, **intermediate sanctions**, **political expenditures**, and **private foundations** settings. For purposes of the **correction period** rules, however, (1) in the case of the private foundation **mandatory payout rules**, a taxable event occurs on the first day of the **tax year** for which there was a failure to distribute income, and (2) in the case of the **excess business holdings** rules, a taxable event occurs on the first day on which there are excess business holdings (**IRC §§ 4963(c), (e)(2)**).

taxable expenditure

The **federal tax law** terms an **expenditure** by a **private foundation** that is thought to be inappropriate for private foundations a "taxable expenditure." This is because, when a private foundation makes one of these expenditures, it is likely to become subject to **sanctions**, in the form of **federal excise taxes** (**IRC §§ 4945(a), (b)**). The term "taxable expenditure" is defined as an amount paid or incurred by a private foundation to engage in any of five practices. These are (albeit with a host of **exceptions**) (1) carrying on **propaganda** or otherwise attempting to **influence legislation**, (2) influencing the outcome of any specific public election or carrying on, **directly** or **indirectly**, a **voter registration drive**, (3) making a **grant** to an individual for travel, study, or similar purposes by the individual, (4) making a grant unless the recipient **organization** is one of several eligible **entities** (most notably, a **public charity**) or unless the private foundation exercises **expenditure responsibility**, and (5) making a grant for a **noncharitable purpose** (IRC § 4945(d)). There is also a set of taxable expenditures rules for **black lung benefit trusts** (IRC § 4952). [PF Chap. 9, §§ 1.4(h), 17.6(d); EO § 12.4(e); HC § 5.9; SM pp. 89–90, 91].

taxable gift

The term "taxable gift" is used, as part of the **federal law** of **gift** taxation, to describe the amount of money and/or **property** to which the **gift tax rates** apply. This amount is the total amount of gifts made, less allowable **deductions** (such as the **charitable contribution deduction** and the **marital deduction**), and less any **per donee gift tax exclusions**. Because the **federal estate taxes** and the federal gift taxes are **unified**, taxable lifetime gifts (**inter vivos** gifts) become part of the **donor's gross estate** to determine the estate tax (IRC §§ 2522–2524). [CG §§ 8.2(f), 8.2(g)].

taxable income

"Taxable income" is the amount of **income** subject to the applicable **tax rate**. For individuals, taxable income is **gross income**, less the **deductions** allowed to ascertain **adjusted gross income**, and less the amount of **itemized deductions** or the **standard deduction**, and less the **personal exemptions**. For **corporations**, taxable income is gross income less allowable deductions. [CG § 2.7].

taxable period

The term "taxable period" is used in the context of the excise taxes that are imposed as **sanctions** in various aspects of the **law of tax-exempt organizations**. In general, in the **private foundation** law setting, the taxable period begins with the event giving rise to the transgression involved (**self-dealing**, **taxable expenditure**, and the like) and ends on the earlier of the date a **notice of deficiency** with respect to an **initial tax** is mailed or the date the initial tax is **assessed** if a deficiency notice is not mailed (IRC §§ 4941(e)(1), 4942(j)(1), 4943(d)(2), 4944(e)(1), 4945(i)(2)). An **addition to tax** may be assessed at the close of the taxable period.

The term "taxable period" means, with respect to an **excess benefit transaction**, the period beginning on the date on which the transaction occurs and ending on the earliest of the date of mailing of a **notice of deficiency** with respect to the **initial tax** on the **disqualified person** or the date on which this tax is **assessed**. A similar definition is used in the context of the **political expenditures taxes** rules (IRC §§ 4955(f)(4), 4958(f)(5)). [PF §§ 5.15(d), 6.7(c), 7.6, 8.5(c), 9.10(d); EO § 21.10; HC § 4.9(a)(vi)] (also **Correction period**; **Second-tier tax**; **Termination tax**).

taxidermy property

The term "taxidermy property" is used to describe any work of art that is the reproduction or preservation of an animal, in whole or in part; is prepared, stuffed, or mounted for purposes of recreating one or more characteristics of the animal, and contains a part of the body of the dead animal (**IRC § 170(f)(15)(B)**). [CG § 9.24].

taxpayer

A "taxpayer" is a **person** who is subject to a **tax**, irrespective of whether the tax is timely paid. The **federal tax law** uses the term broadly to mean any person, including one who is **tax-exempt** (**IRC § 7701(a)(14)**). [AU § 1.9; CG § 2.1].

Taxpayer Advocate Service

The "Taxpayer Advocate Service," headed by the National Taxpayer Advocate, is an independent office within the **IRS**. The mission of this office is to help **taxpayers** resolve problems with the **IRS** and recommend changes to prevent taxpayer problems. The Service, which is available in the **tax-exempt organizations** context, is not a substitute for formal **IRS** procedures but can help in causing a **tax** matter to get "prompt and proper handling" (**IRC §§ 7803, 7811**). [AU § 2.12; SM p. 308].

Taxpayer Bill of Rights 2

The "Taxpayer Bill of Rights 2" is **legislation** that added the **intermediate sanctions rules**, expanded the **penalties** for failure to timely file complete **annual information returns**, expanded the content of these returns, revised disclosure rules, and added the **private inurement** provision to the **law** pertaining to **tax-exempt social welfare organizations**. [EO § 2.4].

taxpayer identification number

The **federal tax law** requires every **person** to have a "taxpayer identification number." This number is merely for identification purposes and does not signify anything else (such as **tax exemption**). This number is required even though the person is not, literally, a **taxpayer**. [EO § 26.1(b); SM p. 22].

teachers' retirement fund association

The **federal tax law** provides **tax exemption** for a "teachers' retirement fund association," where it is of a **purely local character**, there is an absence of **private inurement**, and where its **income** consists wholly of amounts received from public taxation, amounts received from assessments on the salaries of its **members**, and investment income (**IRC § 501(a)**, by reason of description in **IRC § 501(c)(11)**). [EO § 18.7; AS § 1.6(j); AU § 7.1(q)].

technical advice

The term "technical advice" has two meanings in the **federal tax law**. One of these definitions pertains to advice sought from the **National Office** of the **IRS**, either by a **taxpayer** or by an **employee** of the IRS, for a legal interpretation of a tax law provision.

The other meaning of the term relates to knowledge or skill in a given area; under certain circumstances, it can include the offering of opinions or recommendations. This meaning of the term is used in the context of defining one of the types of **lobbying** in which a **charitable organization** can engage. A **communication** is not a **lobbying communication** if it is the provision of technical advice (or assistance) to a governmental body, a governmental committee, or a subdivision of either in response to a written request by the body, committee, or subcommittee. To qualify, the request cannot come merely from an individual **member** of one or more of these entities. [AU §§ 1.9, 5.23; EO §§ 22.3(c)(iii), 22.3(d)(v); PF § 9.1(d); SM p. 187].

technical advice memorandum

A "technical advice memorandum" is a written interpretation of the **federal tax law** as prepared by the Office of the Chief Counsel in the **National Office** of the **IRS**, by which **technical advice** as to one or more tax law inquiries is provided. [AU § 2.10].

Technical and Miscellaneous Revenue Act of 1988

The "Technical and Miscellaneous Revenue Act of 1988" contained an authorization of the **U.S. Department of the Treasury** to promulgate **regulations** allowing **regular corporations** to provide, in the case of **charitable contributions** of **inventory**, less detailed **substantiation** than that required for other corporations. [CG § 9.3].

technology transfer

The term "technology transfer" means the transfer of technology, developed within and by the laboratories of **tax-exempt colleges**, **universities**, and other **research institutions**, to **for-profit corporations**, which refine, market, and sell the resultant products to the public. The exempt transferor usually participates in the profits from the **commercialization** of the technology by means of **royalties**. This type of transfer can generate issues as to the way in which to accommodate this practice in relation to the concepts of **excess benefit transactions**, **private benefit**, **private inurement**, and/or **unrelated business activity**. [EO § 9.5; SM pp. 38, 184].

telephone company, cooperative

Telephone companies that are operated on a **cooperative** basis may qualify for **tax exemption** pursuant to the **federal tax law** (IRC §§ 501(a), 501(c)(12)). [EO § 19.5(b)].

televangelist

A "televangelist" is the term accorded an evangelist who does his or her preaching, and otherwise extends his or her ministry, by means of the medium of television. A synonym is "media evangelist." [EO § 10.2].

temporarily restricted endowment

The concept of the "temporarily restricted endowment" is an **endowment fund** established by **donor-restricted gifts** that is maintained by a **tax-exempt organization** to provide a source of **income** for either a specified period of time or until a specific event occurs. The term also encompasses all other temporarily restricted **net assets** held in a donor-restricted endowment, including unappropriated income from a **permanent endowment** that is not subject to a permanent restriction. [EO § 11.9(a); CU Q 10.1–Q 10.3].

term

A "term" is a period of time measured by the life of an individual or the lives of two or more individuals, or a **term of years**. In certain instances, an **income interest** can be measured by a term; this is principally the case with respect to **charitable remainder trusts** and **pooled income funds**. [CG §§ 12.2(f), 12.3(f)].

term of art
See **Word of art**.

term of years
A "term of years" is a **term** that is measured by a stated number of years, rather than one or more lives.

termination assessment
If the **IRS** determines that a **taxpayer** designs quickly to (1) depart from the U.S. or to remove his, her, or its **property** from the country, (2) conceal himself or herself or his or her property in the U.S., or (3) do any other act (including, in the case of a **corporation**, distributing all or a part of its **assets** in **liquidation** or otherwise) tending to prejudice or to render wholly or partially ineffectual proceedings to collect an **income tax** for the current or immediately preceding **tax year** unless the proceeding is brought without delay, the **IRS** has the authority to immediately make a determination of tax for the current tax year or the preceding tax year (or both) and the tax thus becomes immediately due and payable (**IRC** § 6851). This means that the **IRS** does not have to wait until a tax year terminates before **assessing** an income tax for that year. A special rule allows a termination assessment where the **IRS** determines that (1) a **tax-exempt charitable organization** has made one or more **political expenditures** and (2) the expenditures constitute a flagrant violation of the prohibition against making political expenditures (**IRC** § 4955) (**IRC** § 6852). [EO § 23.4].

T

termination tax
The **private foundation status** of an **organization** may be involuntarily terminated if the **IRS** notifies the organization that it has engaged in willful, flagrant, or repeated acts or failures to act giving rise to one or more of the private foundation **excise taxes**. In this instance, a "termination tax" is imposed. This tax is an amount equal to the lower of (1) the amount that the organization substantiates by adequate records or other corroborating evidence as being the **aggregate tax benefit** resulting from the status of the organization as a **charitable entity** or (2) the **value** of the **net assets** of the organization. This tax is also known as the **third-tier tax**, because of its severity and finality. [PF Chap. 13, §§ 1.2, 1.9, 15.12; EO § 12.4; AU § 5.24] (cf. **First-tier tax**; **Second-tier tax**).

terrorist organization

An organization is a "terrorist organization" if it is designated or otherwise individually identified under the Immigration and Nationality Act as a terrorist organization or a foreign terrorist organization, in or pursuant to an executive order that is related to terrorism and issued under the authority of International Emergency Economic Powers Act or the United Nations Participation Act of 1945 for the purpose of imposing on the organization an economic or other sanction, or in or pursuant to an executive order issued under the authority of any federal law if the organization is designated or otherwise individually identified in or pursuant to the order as supporting or engaging in terrorist activity (as defined in the Immigration and Nationality Act) or supporting terrorism (as defined in the Foreign Relations Authorization Act, Fiscal Years 1988 and 1989), and the order refers to this body of tax law concerning terrorist organizations. This definition is used in connection with the rule that a terrorist organization cannot be **tax-exempt** or receive **deductible charitable contributions** during a **period of suspension** (**IRC** § 501(p)). [EO § 26.8; AR § 13.1(h)].

testamentary trust

A "testamentary trust" is a **trust** created by a **will**. It is common for a **split-interest trust** or a **private foundation** to be created as a testamentary trust. (also **Pour-over trust**).

testator

A "testator" is an individual who makes and executes a **will**. The word "testatrix" is sometimes used when the testator is a woman.

testing, commercial

In the context of **tax-exempt scientific organizations**, significant emphasis is placed on the function of scientific **research**. This type of research, however, does not include activities ordinarily carried on incident to **commercial** operations, as, for example, the testing or inspection of materials or products or the designing or construction of equipment or buildings. [EO § 9.2].

testing for public safety

See **Public safety testing organization**.

third-party costs

The term "third-party costs," used in connection with the **ratio method** of **cost allocation**, means amounts paid or incurred for **lobbying activities** conducted by third parties (such as **dues**) and amounts paid or incurred for travel (including meals and lodging while away from home) and entertainment relating to lobbying activities. [EO § 22.6(a)].

third-party litigation

"Third-party litigation" is **litigation** brought by one or more **persons** as a challenge to an **IRS** policy in administering the **law** of **tax-exempt organizations**. The persons bringing the **action** file against the Secretary of the Treasury and the Commissioner of Internal Revenue, in their official capacity. The short-range goal of the litigation is **revocation** of an organization's

tax exemption; the long-range goal is a change in tax policy. Third-party litigation has been stymied in recent years by reason of courts' strict interpretation of the law of **standing**. [CL §§ 8.11, 8.12(b)].

third-tier tax
See **Termination tax**.

30 percent limitation (money)
The general **federal tax law** rule is that an individual's **charitable contributions** made during a **tax year** to one or more **charitable organizations**, other than **public charities**, where the subject of the **gift** is money, are deductible to the extent that these contributions in the aggregate do not exceed 30 percent of the individual's **contribution base** for the tax year (**IRC** § 170(b)(1)(B)(i)). [CG § 7.8(a)] (also **Percentage limitations**).

30 percent limitation (property)
The general **federal tax law** rule is that an individual may **deduct charitable contributions** of **capital gain property** made during a tax year to a **public charity** to the extent that the contributions in the aggregate do not exceed 30 percent of the individual's **contribution base** (**IRC** § 170(b)(1)(C)(i)). [CG § 7.6(a)] (also **Percentage limitations**).

35 percent controlled entity
In the context of the **intermediate sanctions rules**, the phrase "35 percent controlled entity" means a **corporation** in which **disqualified persons** or **organization managers** own more than 35 percent of the total combined voting power, a **partnership** in which these persons own more than 35 percent of the profits interest, and a **trust** or **estate** in which these persons own more than 35 percent of the beneficial interest (**IRC** §§ 4958(f)(3), (7)(C)). [EO § 21.3].

35 percent limit
The "35 percent limit" applies in the context of the **private foundation rules** pertaining to **excess business holdings**. If **effective control** of a **business enterprise** can be shown to be with one or more parties other than the private foundation and its **disqualified persons**, a 35 percent limit on holdings may be substituted for the general **20 percent limit** (**IRC** § 4943(c)(2)(B)). [PF §§ 7.1(d), 7.2, 7.2(a); SM p. 89].

35 percent owner
A "35 percent owner" is a form of **disqualified person** for purposes of the **private foundation** rules. A corporation is a disqualified person if more than 35 percent of the total combined voting power in the corporation (including some constructive holdings) is owned by substantial contributors, foundation managers, 20 percent owners, or members of the family of any of these individuals (**IRC** § 4946(a)(1)(E)). [PF §§ 4.5, 4.6].

threshold notice rule
The "threshold notice rule" encompasses the general concept that, once the **IRS recognizes** the **tax exemption** of an **organization**, where its **application for recognition of exemption**

was filed with the **IRS** within twenty-seven months from the end of the month in which the organization was formed, the exemption is effective as of the date the organization was created. [EO §§ 26.2(a), 26.3(a)].

thrift store

The **federal tax law** provides that the phrase **unrelated trade or business** does not include a business that constitutes the selling of merchandise, **substantially all** of which was received by the organization involved as **contributions** (**IRC** § 513(a)(3)). This exception is available for thrift shops, **organized** as **nonprofit organizations**, that sell **donated** clothing, books, and the like to the public. [UB § 4.3; EO § 25.2(c); SM p. 175].

timing of charitable contribution deduction

Generally, an **income tax charitable contribution deduction** arises at the time of, and for the year in which, the amount giving rise to the deduction is actually paid or transferred. A **significant exception** to this rule is the body of tax **law** concerning **carryovers**. In determining the "timing" of a tax deduction, the law follows the concept of transfer of **title**. [CG Chap. 6].

tipping

"Tipping" occurs when a **private foundation** or other **major funder** makes a **grant** or a **contribution** to a **charitable organization**, thereby (because of the size of the amount transferred) causing the organization to lose its status as a **publicly supported organization** and to become a private foundation. This result is known as "tipping"— the charity is said to be "tipped" into **private foundation status**.

title

The word "title" means ownership of a **right** to possess and use an item of **property**. The word is most frequently used to reference ownership of **real property**, although it is also used to identify ownership of an item of **tangible personal property** (such as an automobile). Ownership of a property is often evidenced by a document, also called a "title." Ownership of an item of property passes from one **person** to another when title passes.

T

title-holding company

A "title-holding company" is an **organization** that is **tax-exempt** under the **federal income tax law** (**IRC** § 501(a)) because it engages in the **exempt function** of holding **title** to one or more items of **property** for the benefit of another type of **tax-exempt organization**. A title-holding company may operate for the benefit of one exempt **parent** (**IRC** § 501(c)(2)) or multiple parents (**IRC** § 501(c)(25)). A variety of criteria must be satisfied if the company is to qualify for **tax exemption** on this basis, particularly in the case of a multi-parent title-holding company. [EO §§ 19.2, 24.10; HC §§ 1.4, 15.1–15.3; PF §§ 1.6, 7.1(b); UB § 6.2(c); SM p. 42; LI Q 1.50] (also **Single-parent title-holding company**; **Multiple-parent title-holding company**).

to

Most **charitable contributions** are made "to" a **charitable organization** and are **deductible** on that basis. The tax deductibility can be different, however, where the **gift** is made **for the use of** a charitable organization. [CG §§ 7.13, 10.3].

top financial official

For purposes of **annual information return** reporting, the **IRS** employs the phrase "top financial official" to mean the individual who has the ultimate responsibility for managing the reporting **organization's** finances. This individual is usually the **treasurer** or chief financial officer. [AR § 6.1(a)].

top management official

For purposes of **annual information return** reporting, the **IRS** employs the phrase "top management official" to mean the individual who has the ultimate responsibility for implementing the decisions of the reporting **organization's governing body** or for supervising the management, administration, or operation of the organization. This individual is usually the **president**, chief executive officer, or executive director. [AR § 6.1(a)].

top 20 test

For purposes of the definition of the term **key employee**, the third of three tests that need to be satisfied is the "top 20 test." Pursuant to this test, the employee is one of the twenty employees (who satisfy the **$150,000 test** and the **responsibility test**) with the highest **reportable compensation** from the **organization** and **related organizations** for the calendar year ending with or within the organization's **tax year**.

total costs of operations

The phrase "total costs of operations," used in connection with the **ratio method** of **cost allocation**, means an **organization's** total cost of its **trade or business** for a **tax year**, excluding **third-party costs**. [EO § 22.6(a)].

total labor hours

The term "total labor hours," as used in the **ratio method** of **cost allocation**, means the total number of hours of labor that the personnel of an **organization** spend on its **trade or business** during a **tax year**. An organization may make **reasonable** assumptions concerning total hours worked by its personnel during the year. [EO § 22.6(a)].

trade association

The term "trade association" is loosely used to refer to a variety of **membership associations**; technically, these organizations are among the types of **entities** known as **business leagues**. The strict definition of the term is that of an association of members who belong to a certain trade. In practice, the term also embraces **organizations** the members of which belong to a certain **line of business** or profession. The purpose of an association such as this is to improve the conditions of their members through a variety of services, including conferences, publications, and **lobbying**. Usually, these organizations are **tax-exempt** under the **federal tax law** (**IRC** § 501(a), by reason of description in **IRC** § 501(c)(6)). [AS § 1.4; EO Chap. 14; PF § 15.9; CG § 1.3(b); SM pp. 40, 50, 54–55].

trade or business

The phrase "trade or business" is used in the **federal tax law** pertaining to **unrelated business activity** as the general equivalent to the term **business** (**IRC** § 513(c)). A trade or business may be **related** or **unrelated** to an **organization's exempt purpose**. The phrase includes the performance of the functions of a **public office** (**IRC** § 7701(a)(26)). [UB § 2.2(a); EO § 24.2; HC § 24.2; FR §§ 5.7(a)(iii), 5.7(b)(i); PF §§ 11.1(a)–(e); SM pp. 171–172].

trade show

A "trade show" is an event involving a display of products and services with respect to an industry or profession, usually maintained as part of an **association's** annual convention, in an effort to stimulate interest in and demand for these products and services. [AS §§ 2.8, 3.5, 5.9(n); UB § 10.6; EO § 25.2(f); SM p. 176] (also **Qualified convention and trade show activity**).

transaction of interest

The concept of the "transaction of interest" arises in the context of application of **tax shelter rules** to **tax-exempt organizations**. These rules require disclosure of **reportable transactions**, including a category of transactions known as transactions of interest, the identification of which alerts **persons** involved in these transactions that they have certain responsibilities arising from this involvement. [EO § 28.17(f); CG § 10.15].

transfer tax

A "transfer tax" is a **tax** imposed on the transfer of money and/or the **title** to **property** from one **person** to another person. These taxes include **estate taxes, excise taxes, gift taxes, generation-skipping transfer taxes, inheritance taxes, sales taxes**, and **value-added taxes**. [CG Chap. 8].

travel policy

A **tax-exempt organization** usually creates a policy concerning travel expenses when it adopts an **expense reimbursement policy**.

travel tour

A **tax-exempt organization** may have as one of its functions the conduct of one or more travel tours. If the **primary purpose** of the tour is **charitable, educational**, and/or **religious** in nature, the tour will be an **exempt function** for the charitable, educational and/or religious organization. If, however, the primary purpose of the tour is **social** or recreational in nature, the activity, if conducted by an exempt organization (other than a **social club**), will be regarded as an **unrelated trade or business** or, if it is a **substantial** part of the organization's activities, a basis for **revocation** or denial of recognition of the organization's exempt status. [UB §§ 9.1(c), 9.7; EO § 24.5(j)].

treasurer

Nearly every **nonprofit organization** is required by state **law** to have a "treasurer." (The principal exception to this rule is a **trust**.) The treasurer has charge and custody of and is responsible for all funds and **property** of the organization, receives and provides receipts for moneys due and payable to the organization, and deposits moneys in the name of the organization in financial institutions selected by the **board of directors** or **board of trustees**. In general, a treasurer may perform all of the duties incident to the office of a treasurer of an organization and may perform such other **reasonable** duties as from time to time may be assigned by the **president** or the **governing board** of the organization. [SM p. 20; PG pp. 15–16].

treasury decision

A "Treasury Decision" is an interpretation, by the **Department of the Treasury**, of one or more provisions of the **IRC**. This Department's interpretations are published in both proposed and final form. When the product is a final tax regulation, it is published as a Treasury Decision, which is cited as "T.D." [EO App. A].

Treasury Inspector General for Tax Administration

Within the **Department of the Treasury** is the office of the "Treasury Inspector General for Tax Administration." This inspector general has the sole authority to investigate the **IRS** and often does so, frequently on **tax-exempt organizations** matters. [AU §§ 1.7, 2.1(b); EO §§ 2.2(a), 2.2(b), 5.6(u), 23.2(b); HC §§ 36.3(c), 36.4(b)(iii)].

triggering event

A **charitable remainder unitrust** can convert (flip) once from one of the **income-exception methods** to the **fixed percentage method** for purposing of calculating the **unitrust amount**. This conversion is allowed, however, only if the specific date or single event triggering the flip—the "triggering event"—is outside the control of, or not discretionary with, the **trustee** or any other **person** or persons. [CG § 12.1(a)] (also **Fixed percentage charitable remainder unitrust, net-income charitable remainder unitrust, net-income make-up charitable remainder unitrust**).

true endowment

See **Permanent endowment**.

trust

A "trust" is one of the legal forms of an **organization**. It is an **unincorporated, nonmembership entity**, established by means of a **trust agreement** or **declaration of trust**. A trust is one of four forms available for a **tax-exempt organization**, and is often used to organize entities such as **private foundations** and **employee benefit funds**. Trusts are also used in facilitating **planned gifts**; most of these trusts are known as **split-interest trusts**. [CG §§ 2.8(d), 3.8, 5.3, 9.22, Chaps. 12, 13, 16; SM pp. 6, 9–10; PG pp. 4, 7; PF §§ 1.1, 1.9, 2.4(b), 2.4(c), 3.5–3.7, 5.13; AR § 21.2(d); CU Q 1.14; RE Q 1.8, Q 1.17] (also **Charitable lead trust; Charitable remainder trust; Pooled income fund**).

trust agreement

A "trust agreement" is a **contract** by which a **trust** is established. Many **split-interest trusts** are created in this manner. [SM p. 10] (cf. **Declaration of trust**).

trustee

The term "trustee" is used to describe an individual who sets and implements policy for an **organization**, and otherwise assists in the operation of the **entity**. Also, another type of **person**, such as a financial institution, may serve as the or a trustee. Technically, where a person is acting in this capacity, the organization involved is a **trust**. In practice, however, the term is also used where an organization has some other legal form. The term is often used interchangeably with the term **director**. In most instances involving **nonprofit organizations**, the term is used to describe those who oversee the operations of **charitable** and **educational organizations** (such as **universities** and **private foundations**) and **employee benefit funds**. Where there is more than one trustee of an organization, the group of them is termed a **board of trustees**. [SM p. 10; CG §§ 5.5(f), 12.4(b), 13.2(f); RE Q 5.3] (also **Fiduciary**).

tuition annuity program

A "tuition annuity program" is one use of the **deferred payment charitable gift annuity**. The **organization** that offers this program is a **tax-exempt college**, **school**, or **university**; a **donor** designates the recipient of the annuity and may designate an alternative **annuitant**. The annuitant is entitled to the **annuity** for life; however, the annuitant has the right to sell or assign his or her annuity to the **annuitor** or to a third party in return for a **lump-sum** payment or installment payments over several years. While it is contemplated that a designated recipient of the annuity will use the funds to attend the **institution** that is the **remainder interest beneficiary** under the **contract**, this outcome is not required and the annuitant will be able to use the funds for any purpose. Donors in this situation usually are making these contributions for the benefit of a child or grandchild. [CG § 14.3(b)].

tuition remission

See **Qualified tuition reduction**.

20 percent limitation

In general, a **contribution** of **capital gain property** by an individual to a **charitable organization** that is not a **public charity** is subject to a "20 percent limitation" (**IRC** § 170(b)(1)(D)(i)). This limitation is a percentage of the individual's **contribution base** for the **tax year**. [CG § 7.12(a); SM p. 135] (also **Percentage limitations**).

20 percent owner

A "20 percent owner" is a form of **disqualified person** for purposes of the **private foundation rules**. An owner of more than 20 percent of the total combined voting power of a **corporation**, the profits interest in a **partnership**, or the **beneficial interest** in a **trust** or **unincorporated enterprise**, any of which is (during the period of ownership) a **substantial contributor** to the private foundation, is a disqualified person (**IRC** § 4946(a)(1)(C)). [PF §§ 4.3, 7.1, 7.1(d), 7.2(a); EO § 12.2(c); SM p. 82].

twice-basis deduction

In the field of **charitable contribution deductions** involving **gifts** of **property**, the general rule is that the amount of the deduction is equal to the **value** of the property contributed. Some charitable deductions arising from gifts of property, however, are limited to an amount equal to the **donor's basis** in the property. In two instances, the charitable deduction arising from a gift of property may be an amount equal to twice the amount of the donor's basis.

As a general rule, when a **corporation** makes a charitable gift of property from its **inventory**, the resulting charitable deduction is confined to an amount equal to the donor's basis in the property (**IRC** § 170(e)(3)). Under certain circumstances, however, corporate donors can receive a greater charitable deduction for gifts out of their inventory. Where the tests are satisfied, the deduction can be equal to the basis in the property, plus one-half of the **appreciated value** of the property. Nonetheless, this charitable deduction may not exceed an amount equal to twice the basis in the property. A similar rule applies with respect to contributions of **scientific property** used for **research** (**IRC** § 170(e)(4)). [CG §§ 9.3, 9.4; SM p. 137] (also **Inventory, gift of**; **Scientific property, gift of**).

2 percent limitation

The "2 percent limitation" is used in computing **public support** for the **donative publicly supported charitable organization**. The general rule in this regard is that, in computing the numerator of the **support fraction**, **contributions** and **grants** from individuals, **trusts**, **corporations**, and other **entities** constitute public support to the extent that the total amount of support from any **donor** or **grantor** during the **computation period** does not exceed an amount equal to 2 percent of the organization's total support for the period. Donors and grantors who are **related** must share a single 2 percent limitation. This limitation, however, does not generally apply to support received from other publicly supported organizations of the donative type, nor to grant support from **governmental units**. [PF § 15.5; EO § 12.3(b)(i); SM p. 82].

Type I supporting organization

The phrase "Type I supporting organization" means an **organization** that satisfies the **organizational** and **operational** requirements, and the **control test**, imposed on supporting organizations generally, and which is operated, supervised, or controlled by one or more qualified **supported organizations** (**IRC** § 509(a)(3)(B)(i)). [PF § 15.7(e); EO § 12.3(c); HC § 5.5; SM p. 83].

Type II supporting organization

The phrase "Type II supporting organization" means an **organization** that satisfies the **organizational** and **operational** requirements, and the **control test**, imposed on supporting organizations generally, and which is supervised or controlled in connection with one or more qualified **supported organizations** (**IRC** § 509(a)(3)(B)(ii)). [PF § 15.7(f); EO § 12.3(c); HC § 5.5; SM p. 83].

Type III supporting organization

The phrase "Type III supporting organization" means an **organization** that satisfies the **organizational** and **operational** requirements, and the **control test**, imposed on supporting organizations generally, and which is **operated in connection with** one or more qualified **supported organizations** (**IRC** §§ 509(a)(3)(B)(iii), 509(f)(1), 4943(f)(5)(A)). [PF § 15.7(g); EO § 12.3(c); HC § 5.5; SM pp. 83–84].

T

U

UBIT

The acronym "UBIT" is frequently used to refer to the **unrelated business income tax**.

UBTI

The acronym "UBTI" is frequently used to refer to **unrelated business taxable income**.

ultra vires

The words "ultra vires" are Latin for "outside of." The term is usually applied to define an act that is beyond the authority (as defined in its **articles of organization**) of an **organization** (most frequently a **corporation**) to undertake. Thus, an act that is outside of an organization's power to commit is an ultra vires act, which thus may be deemed by a governmental authority to be void. [CU Q 1.29; RE Q 1.20; LI Q 1.35].

unagreed case

Among the situations in which a **tax-exempt organization examination** case will be closed is the "unagreed case," in which the **exempt organization** has not signed the appropriate waiver and acceptance forms or has not **corrected** ay acts or failures to act that give rise to any **excise taxes** applicable to it. [AU § 5.32(a)].

underpayment

The term "underpayment" means the amount by which a **tax** imposed by the **federal tax law** exceeds the excess of (1) the sum of (a) the amount shown as the tax by the **taxpayer** on his, her, or its **tax return**, plus (b) amounts not so shown previously **assessed** (or collected without **assessment**), over (2) the amount of rebates (such as an **abatement**, **credit**, refund, or other repayment) made (**IRC** § 6664(a)). [CG § 10.14].

understatement

For purposes of the **accuracy-related penalties** and the **tax fraud penalty**, the word "understatement" means the excess of the amount of the tax required to be shown on a **tax return** for a **tax year** over the amount of the tax imposed that is shown on the tax return, reduced by any rebate (as defined in **IRC** § 6211(b)(2)) (**IRC** § 6662(d)(2)(A)). [CG § 10.14] (also **Substantial understatement**; **Valuation overstatement**).

undistributed income

For purposes of the **mandatory payout rules** imposed by the **federal tax law** on **private foundations**, the term "undistributed income" means, with respect to any private foundation for any **tax year** as of any time, the amount by which (1) the **distributable amount** for the tax year exceeds (2) the **qualifying distributions** made before that time out of the distributable amount (**IRC** § 4942(c)). [PF §§ 6.5, 6.7, 12.2(k)].

undivided portion of an entire interest

The phrase "undivided portion of an entire interest" is used in connection with the **federal income tax charitable contribution deduction** for a **gift** of an undivided portion of an entire interest in an item of **property** (**IRC** § 170(f)(3)(B)(ii)). An undivided portion of a **donor's** entire interest in an item of property must (1) consist of a fraction or percentage of each and every **substantial interest** or **right** owned by the donor in the property, and (2) extend over the entire **term** of the donor's interest in the property and in other property into which the property may be converted. This type or deduction is available only when the gift is not made by means of a **trust**. [CG § 15.3; CU Q 12.106, Q 12.108].

unethical

The word "unethical" means contrary to one or more provisions of the **code of ethics** of an **organization**. When an individual commits an unethical act, the individual is likely to receive some sort of sanction, such as a reprimand, expulsion from **membership** in the organization, and/or revocation of a **certification**. Sometimes the word is used to reference an act that is considered distasteful, without reference to any particular ethics code. An act (or lack thereof) that is unethical is by no means necessarily illegal.

unfair competition

The words "unfair competition" often are used to mean a form of competition between a **nonprofit organization** and a **for-profit organization**. The word "competition" is used to reflect the fact that the two organizations are engaged in essentially the same type of activity. The word "unfair" is used when the nonprofit organization is a **tax-exempt organization** and does not have to pay **taxes** on the **income** earned by the competing activity, thereby enabling the exempt organization to charge a lower price for the competing good or service. [EO §§ 4.10(a)(i), 24.2(c); SM pp. 288–289] (also **Halo effect**; **Level playing field**).

unfair trade practices laws

Many states have an "unfair trade practices law." This type of **law** prohibits **fraudulent advertising** and other fraudulent or deceptive consumer practices. In some states, certain forms of **solicitations** of **charitable contributions** are considered violations of these laws. [FR § 3.23].

unfunded

The word "unfunded" means an account or plan that is established but that lacks any money or **property** (funds). Some forms of **non-qualified plans** are "unfunded." (cf. **Funded**).

unified taxes

"Unified taxes" are blended taxes. The **federal estate tax** and the **federal gift tax** are unified taxes. That is, gift and estate transfers are taxed as an integrated whole; they comprise a unified **transfer tax** system. These taxes are imposed on a **decedent's taxable estate** and on the amount of certain **gifts**. [CG § 8.4].

uniform annual report

From time to time, there have been efforts to cause the states to adopt a form of a "uniform annual report" that would be filed by **charitable organizations** in compliance with the various states' **charitable solicitations acts**. The purpose of this type of report is to offer some relief fur these organizations from the hodgepodge of state **laws** regulating charitable solicitations. Considerable progress is being made in this regard, marred somewhat by the tendency of regulators in some states to add reporting items to the otherwise "uniform" report. [FR § 8.13(c)].

Uniform Prudent Management of Institutional Funds Act

The "Uniform Prudent Management of Institutional Funds Act" is a **uniform statute** the major goal of which is application of the same standards for the investment and management of **charitable funds** to those organized as a **trust**, **nonprofit corporation**, or other type of **entity**. [AR §§ 7.2(c)(27)–7.2(c)(29), 11.2(e); PF § 8.2].

uniformity

A proposed **law** that is written as a model for adoption by one or more states is termed a "uniform law." Efforts have been made from time to time to write a uniform **charitable solicitation act** but these efforts have always failed. Examples of successful uniform laws are the "Uniform Supervision of Trustees for Charitable Purposes Act" and the "Uniform Anatomical Gift Act".

unincorporated

The word "unincorporated" is used to refer to an **organization** at a point in time when it is not **incorporated**. That is, the word is applied to describe a legal state of an organization other than a corporation. (also **Limited liability company**; **Trust**; **Unincorporated association**).

unincorporated association

An "unincorporated association" is an **organization**, usually one with a **membership**, that is not organized as a **corporation** (or a **limited liability company** or **trust**). The **articles of organization** of this type of organization are in the form of a **constitution**. [SM pp. 6, 10–11: PG pp. 4–7; CU Q 1.15; RE Q 1.3, Q 1.4, Q 1.8, Q 1.17].

union

A "union" is a type of **labor organization**. It is an **association** of individuals who are workers and has as its purpose the betterment of working conditions for its **members**. The **principal**

U

activity of a union is to bargain with one or more **employers** on behalf of their **employees**. A union can qualify for **tax-exempt status** under the **federal tax law** (**IRC** § 501(a), by reason of description in **IRC** § 501(c)(5)). [EO § 16.1; SM p. 41].

unit

Many types of investment **funds** are comprised of "units." This is the case, for example, with respect to **pooled income funds**. This type of fund is divided into units, each of which represents an **interest** in the fund equal in **value** to each of the other units. The value of a unit is determined by dividing the **fair market value** of the fund's **assets** on the **determination day** by the number of outstanding units. A bank's **common trust fund** also is divided into units. [CG § 13.3(a)].

united fund

The term "united fund" is used to describe an **organization** that raises funds in a **community** and distributes them to local **charitable** organizations. These funds may be **exempt** from a state's **charitable solicitation act**. [FR § 2.2(a)] (also **Community chest**).

unit of government

See **Governmental unit**.

united states, instrumentality of

See **Instrumentality of the United States**.

unitrust

See **Charitable remainder unitrust**.

unitrust interest

An **income interest** qualifies as a "unitrust interest" only if it is an **irrevocable right** pursuant to the **governing instrument** of a **charitable remainder unitrust** to receive payment, not less often than annually, of a **fixed percentage** of the **net fair market value** of the trust's **assets**, determined annually. [CG §§ 5.7(a), 9.23, 12.3, 12.10(b)] (also **Valuation date**).

units of participation

On each transfer of money and/or **property** by a **donor** to a **pooled income fund**, one or more "units of participation" in the fund must be assigned to the **beneficiary** or beneficiaries of the **income interest** retained or created in the property, the number of **units** of participation being equal to the number obtained by dividing the **fair market value** of the property by the fair market value of a unit in the fund at the time of the transfer. [CG § 13.3(a)].

university

A "university" is, as defined in the **federal tax law**, an **educational organization** that normally maintains a regular faculty and curriculum and normally has a regularly enrolled body of students in attendance at the place where its educational activities are **regularly carried on** (**IRC**

§ I70(b)(1)(A)(ii)). A university is a **tax-exempt** educational **institution** under the federal tax law (**IRC** § 501(a), by reason of description in **IRC** § 501(c)(3)) and is a **public charity** (**IRC** §§ 170(b)(1)(A)(ii), 509(a)(1)). [CU Q 2.12; EO §§ 8.3(a), 12.3(a), 24.5(a); PF §§ 3.5, 15.3; FR § 5.11(a); AR § 8.1(c)(3); SM pp. 35, 80, 299; LI Q 9.12].

unreasonable

The word "unreasonable" is used to describe something that is not **reasonable**. For example, **private inurement** takes place when the **compensation** paid to an **insider** is excessive; it is said to be unreasonable compensation. [EO § 20.4(b)].

unreasonable borrowing arrangement

An "unreasonable borrowing arrangement" is a lending transaction that occurs in circumstances in which (1) the **private inurement doctrine** is applicable, that is, when the transaction is between a **tax-exempt organization** that is subject to the doctrine and an **insider** with respect to the organization, and (2) the terms of the transaction are not **reasonable**. This type of transaction could be the basis for loss of the **entity's tax-exempt status**. For the transaction to not be private inurement, the terms of the loan should include a market rate of **interest**, a **commercially** conventional **term**, and adequate security. [EO § 20.5(b)] (cf. **Excess benefit transaction**; **Self-dealing**).

unreasonable compensation

A form of "unreasonable compensation" is **compensation** that occurs in circumstances in which (1) the **private inurement doctrine** is applicable, that is, when the compensatory relationship is between a **tax-exempt organization** that is subject to the doctrine and an **insider** with respect to the organization, and (2) the amount and/or terms of the compensation are not **reasonable**. This type of compensation can be the basis for loss of the **entity's tax-exempt status**. For the compensation to not be private inurement, it must not be excessive. [EO § 20.4(b); HC § 4.4(b)] (cf. **Excess benefit transaction**; **Self-dealing**).

unreasonable rental arrangement

An "unreasonable rental arrangement" is a rental arrangement that occurs in circumstances in which (1) the **private inurement doctrine** is applicable, that is, when the transaction is between a **tax-exempt organization** that is subject to the doctrine and an **insider** with respect to the organization, and (2) the terms of the transaction are not **reasonable**. This type of transaction can be the basis for loss of the **entity's tax-exempt status**. For the transaction to not be private inurement, the amount of **rent** paid by the organization must not be excessive or, if the insider is the tenant, the amount of rent paid must not be too low in relation to **commercial** standards. [EO § 20.5(a)] (cf. **Excess benefit transaction**; **Self-dealing**).

unreasonable sales arrangement

An "unreasonable sales arrangement" is a sales arrangement (such as a **sale** of one or more of the organization's **assets**) that occurs in circumstances in which (1) the **private inurement doctrine** is applicable, that is, when the transaction is between a **tax-exempt organization** that is subject to the doctrine and an **insider** with respect to the organization, and (2) the terms of the transaction are not **reasonable**. This type of transaction can be the basis for loss of the **entity's tax-exempt status**. For the transaction to not be private inurement, the amount constituting the sales price, if paid by the organization, must not be excessive, or, if paid by the insider, must not be too low in relation to **commercial** standards. [EO § 20.5(c)] (also **Excess benefit transaction; Self-dealing**).

unreimbursed expenses

In general, the **expenses** incurred by an individual in the course of assisting the work of a **charitable organization** are **deductible**; these expenses are treated as the making of **charitable contributions**. To be deductible, however, the expense must have been incurred for the benefit of the organization, rather than for the individual, involved. [CG § 9.15].

unrelated

The word "unrelated" is used to describe an activity of a **tax-exempt organization** that is not **related** to the achievement of the organization's **exempt purposes**. The word is usually used in conjunction with the phrase **trade or business** to describe an **unrelated trade or business**. [EO § 24.4(a)].

unrelated business

See **Unrelated trade or business**.

unrelated business activities

The phrase "unrelated business activities" means activities of a **tax-exempt organization** that constitute one or more forms of **unrelated business**. [UB passim; EO Chap. 24; HC Chap. 24; AS Chap. 5; AU §§ 5.33(i), 7.4, 7.6(d), 7.7(e); CG § 3.5(d); LI Q 12.43, Q 13.3].

unrelated business income

The phrase "unrelated business income" generally means **gross income** derived by a **tax-exempt organization** from the **regular conduct** of an **unrelated business** (IRC § 512(a)(1)). In the case of organizations such as **social clubs**, however, unrelated business income means all income other than **exempt function income** (IRC § 512(a)(3)). [UB passim; EO Chap. 24; PF §§ 7.1(b), 11.2, 11.4, 11.5; LI Q 13.21, Q 13.22] (also **Unrelated business taxable income**).

unrelated business income tax

The "unrelated business income tax" is a **federal income tax** that is applied to **unrelated business taxable income**. For most **tax-exempt organizations**, this tax is the regular **corporate income tax** (IRC § 511(a)); for **trusts**, the individual income tax applies (IRC § 511(b)). [UB § 11.1; EO § 24.11; HC §§ 10.3, 23.2(b); PF §§ 6.1, 6.4, 11.5].

unrelated business taxable income

The phrase "unrelated business taxable income" generally means the **gross income** derived by a **tax-exempt organization** from any **unrelated trade or business**, **regularly carried on** by it, less any **deductions** for **expenses** paid or incurred **directly** in connection with the conduct of the unrelated trade or business (**IRC** § 512(a)(1)). In the case of a tax-exempt **social club**, **voluntary employees' beneficiary association**, or **supplemental unemployment benefits trust**, however, the phrase means the gross income of the organization (**excluding exempt function income**), less any allowable deductions that are directly connected with the production of the gross income (**IRC** § 512(a)(3)). Also, in the case of a tax-exempt **veterans' organization**, the phrase does not include any amount attributable to payments for life, sick, accident, or health **insurance** with respect to **members** of the organization or their dependents which is **set aside** for the purpose of providing for the payment of insurance benefits or for a **charitable purpose** (**IRC** § 512(a)(4)). [UB § 11.1; EO § 24.11; SM pp. 174–175].

unrelated debt-financed income

The phrase "unrelated debt-financed income" means, with respect to each item of **debt-financed property**, **income** of a **tax-exempt organization** that is **unrelated business income**, in an amount that is the same percentage of the total **gross income** derived during the **tax year** by the organization from or on account of the property as the average **acquisition indebtedness** for the tax year with respect to the property is of the average amount of the **adjusted basis** of the property during the period it is held by the organization during the year (**IRC** § 514(a)(1)). [UB §§ 5.2–5.5; EO § 24.9; HC § 24.21; AS § 5.10; CG §§ 14.6, 17.5].

unrelated trade or business

The phrase "unrelated trade or business" means a **business** that is conducted by a **tax-exempt organization** under circumstances where the activity is not **substantially related** to the achievement of the organization's **exempt purpose** or purposes (**IRC** § 513(a)). There are some **exceptions** to this definition, namely, businesses conducted substantially by **volunteers**, **businesses of convenience**, and **thrift stores** (**IRC** §§ 513(a)(1)–(3)). The **income** received by an exempt organization from the conduct of unrelated business is generally reportable to the **IRS** on **Form 990-T** and is subject to the **unrelated business income tax**. [UB §§ 1.11, 2.1; EO § 24.2(a); AR §§ 1.6(g), 4.2(b), 7.1(b), 14.1(i)(4), 19.1(g)(6); CG § 3.5(b); FR § 5.7(a); CU Chap. 14; RE Chap. 23; PG pp. 169–171, 345–346; SM pp. 171–172; CL §§ 1.10, 8.4].

unrelated use

The words "unrelated use" mean the use of an item of **tangible personal property** by a **tax-exempt organization** in a way that is **unrelated** to the organization's **exempt purpose**. This type of use can have an adverse impact on the amount of the **charitable contribution deduction** arising from a gift of the property. [CG § 4.6; CU Q 12.34–Q 12.36].

unrelated use property

The term "unrelated use property" means an item of **tangible personal property** that is **contributed** to a **charitable organization** and put to an **unrelated use** by the organization. When a **charitable gift** of unrelated use property is made, the amount of the **charitable contribution deduction** that would otherwise be determined must be reduced by the amount of **gain** which would have been **long-term capital gain** if the property contributed had been **sold** by

U

the **donor** at its **fair market value**, determined at the time of the contribution. [CG § 4.6] (also **Deduction reduction rule**).

unsolicited merchandise, mailings of

A form of **fundraising** is the mailing of "unsolicited merchandise" as an inducement for **persons** to give. These items are also termed **premiums**. When these items qualify as **low-cost articles**, the activity of mailing them and collecting the resulting gifts is not an **unrelated trade or business**. [UB § 4.9; EO § 25.2(j); FR § 5.7(a)(vi)].

unusual grant

An "unusual grant" is a **grant** (or **contribution** or **bequest**), received by a **charitable organization**, that is **substantial** and was attracted by reason of the status of the organization as a **public charity**, was unusual or unexpected because of the amount, and would adversely affect the classification of the organization as a **publicly supported charitable organization**. An unusual grant may be excluded from the numerator and the denominator of the recipient organization's **support fraction**. [PF §§ 15.4(g), 15.5(c); HC §§ 5.3(c), 5.8; PG pp. 90–91].

useful life

The "useful life" of an item of **depreciable property** is the **reasonable** estimate of the **term** (life), measured in years, of usefulness of the property as used by its owner in a **business**. The useful life of a type of property, particularly for **federal tax purposes**, is usually set by **statute**.

use of property

The words "use of property" refer to a **right** of a **person** to use the **property** owned by another person for a certain purpose for a certain period of time. For example, the owner of an office building may allow a **charitable organization** to use a certain amount of office space on a rent-free basis for a set period. Under the **federal tax law**, however, there is no **charitable contribution deduction** available for a **gift** of the use of property. [CG § 9.18; CU Q 12.11].

user fee

A "user fee" is a charge by a government **agency** for the provision of a specific service to a **person**, rather than a range of services that are funded generally by taxes. For example, the **IRS** imposes a user fee for the processing of **ruling requests** and **applications for recognition of exemption**. [EO § 26.1(d); FR § 8.9] (also **Form 8718**).

U

use tax

A "use tax" is a **tax** that is imposed on an item of **property** that is purchased in one jurisdiction (usually a state) and used in another jurisdiction. This type of tax is a back-up tax in relation to a **sales tax** and almost always has the same **tax rate** as the related sales tax. In some states, certain categories of **nonprofit organizations** are **exempt** from the use tax.

usucaption

A "usucaption" is a form of acquisition of **title** to an item of **property** by reason of a long occupation of it. (also **Adverse possession**).

usufruct

The word "usufruct" means a **right** of a **person** to use an item of **property** that is owned by another person. During the period of time this right is in existence, the holder of it may enjoy the **yield** from the property and all other aspects of the property, as long as the property itself is not altered. (cf. **Income interest**).

uxorial

The word "uxorial" means pertaining to or benefiting a wife. For example, when a man executes a **charitable remainder trust**, creating an **income interest** for his spouse, he is engaging in an "uxorial" act.

U

vacation home

A "vacation home" is a home owned by one or more individuals that is not his, her, or their **principal residence**; is a **personal residence** and (usually) is used by the individual or individuals as a place for a vacation. This type of **property** may be the subject of a **contribution** of a **remainder interest** in a personal residence, even though the gift is not made in **trust**, and thus gives rise to a **federal income tax charitable contribution deduction** (IRC § 170(f)(3)(B)(i)). For this deduction to be available, the residence must contain facilities for cooking, sleeping, and sanitation. It is common for gifts of the use of vacation homes to be made in the context of **charity auctions**; there is no federal income tax charitable deduction available for this type of gift. [CG §§ 9.13(b), 15.2].

vague

A **statute**, **regulation**, or **rule** may be determined by a court to be "vague" and thus **unconstitutional**. The vagueness element is present when **persons** of common intelligence must necessarily guess as to the meaning of the **law** and differ as to its application. [FR § 4.8] (also **Void for vagueness**).

valuation

The word "valuation" is used to describe the process of ascertaining the **value** of an item of **property**. The property may be **personal property** or **real property**, **tangible property** or **intangible property**. A property may be valued in its entirety or partially.

In the context of the **law** concerning **nonprofit organizations**, a valuation is done usually to determine the value of a property for purposes of calculating the amount of a **charitable contribution deduction**, to ascertain whether there has been an **excess benefit transaction** or a violation of the **private inurement** doctrine, or for determining the value of property to be recorded on the books and records of the organization that has received the property (such as by **gift** or **purchase**). Valuation of property also occurs in the process of ascertaining the amount of a **decedent's gross estate**. A valuation is usually performed by an **appraiser**. If valuation is the subject of litigation, two or more appraisers are likely to be serving as **expert witnesses**.

Bruce R. Hopkins' Nonprofit Law Dictionary, First Edition. Bruce R. Hopkins.
© 2015 Bruce R. Hopkins. Published 2015 by John Wiley & Sons, Inc.

With respect to real property, the **fair market value** of the property is generally determined by taking into account the highest and best use of the property on the relevant **valuation date**. Three methods are generally employed to measure the fair market value of property: the market method, the income method, and the replacement cost method. Because a market for the purchase and sale of **conservation easements** rarely exists, a conservation easement's value is ordinarily determined by measuring the diminution in value of the burdened property resulting from imposition of the easement; this is known as the before-and-after method of valuation. [CG Chap. 11, §§ 2.14, 10.1(a); PF §§ 6.3(a), 6.3(b), 6.7(d), 14.6(c); AR § 19.1] (also **Appraisal requirements**).

valuation date

The term "valuation date" is used to describe a date, usually within a year, on which a **valuation** of an item of **property** or a collection of properties is to occur. For example, in the context of determining the **net fair market value** of the assets of a **charitable remainder unitrust**, that valuation may be made on a date occurring during the **tax year** of the trust. The same date must be used each year. (An alternative with respect to a charitable remainder unitrust is to use the average of valuations made on more than one date during the tax year of the trust, as long as the dates and valuation methods are used each year.) [CG § 12.3(a)].

valuation table

A "valuation table" is a chart of **factors** used to calculate the **value** of an **income interest** or a **remainder interest** in an item of **property contributed** to a **charitable organization**. This type of valuation table is usually prepared by the **IRS**, using the most recent mortality experience available (**IRC §§ 7520(a)(1), (c)(3)**). These tables must be revised at least once every ten years to take into account the most recent mortality experience available as of the time of the revision (**IRC § 7520(c)(3)**). The **IRS** tables reflect the use of a wide range of interest rates or **adjusted payout rates**. The factors involved may be used for **income**, **gift**, and/or **estate tax** purposes. Tables are available for calculation of interests arising from the making of gifts to **charitable remainder trusts**, **pooled income funds**, and **charitable lead trusts**, and in connection with the creation of **charitable gift annuities**. [CG Chap. 11].

value

The "value" of something is its inherent worth in a material or monetary sense. For example, the value of an item is determined for the purpose of calculating a **charitable contribution deduction** for a **gift** of **property**, determining the **reasonableness** of a transaction, or ascertaining the amount of a **gross estate**. The word is also used to describe the process of ascertaining that value, in that an item of property may be "valued." [CG §§ 2.14, 10.1(b)] (also **Fair market value**; **Valuation**).

VEBA

The acronym "VEBA" is popularly used to refer to a **voluntary employees' beneficiary association**.

veil, piercing the corporate

One of the finest phrases in the **law**, the phrase "piercing the corporate veil" is used to describe the act, dictated by the law, of disregarding the **corporate form** of an **organization**. In general, a **corporation** is regarded by the law as a separate legal **entity**, that is, as a **person** in its own right; the idea of "separate" means that it is not considered a part of, or its activities are not attributed to, another organization and it is distinct from its **directors** and **officers**. Nonetheless, under certain circumstances (such as where the corporation is regarded as a **sham** or where the law regards the placement of **liability** elsewhere rather than solely on the corporation as appropriate), the corporate form will be ignored ("pierced") for purposes of analysis or the assignment of liability; under this doctrine, one or more directors and/or officers or a corporation may be found **personally liable** for an act, or failure to act, undertaken in the name of a corporation. (also **Separate identity principle**).

vested

The term "vested" generally refers to something that has accrued or accumulated to the point that one or more **rights** are created. The term is often used in the context of the **law** of **employee benefits**, to describe the benefits that have become the right of (or vested in) an employee. [EO § 18.1].

veterans' organization

In general, a "veterans' organization" is a type of **tax-exempt organization** under the **federal tax law**. The precise tax law classification of a veterans' organization depends on the nature of its program activities. Thus, it is possible for a veterans' organization to be tax-exempt by reason of its status as a **charitable organization** or as a **social welfare organization**. For the most part, however, a veterans' organization is exempt because it is a **post** or other organization of past or present **members** of the U.S. armed forces, or an auxiliary unit or **society** of, or a **trust** or **foundation** for, any such post or organization, where (1) it is organized in the U.S. or any of its possessions, (2) at least 75 percent of the members of the organization are past or present members of the U.S. armed forces and **substantially all** of the other members of the organization are individuals who are cadets or are spouses, widows, or widowers of past or present members of the U.S. armed forces or of cadets, and (3) no part of the **net earnings** of the organization **inures** to the benefit of any **person** in his, her, or its private capacity (**IRC** § 501(a), by reason of description in **IRC** § 501(c)(19)).

In some states, veterans' organizations are **exempt**, in whole or in part, from the **charitable solicitation acts**.

These types of veterans' organizations are the **beneficiary** of a rule by which the phrase **unrelated business taxable income** does not include any amount attributable to payments for life, sick, accident, or health **insurance** with respect to members of the organizations or their dependents which is **set aside** for the purpose of providing for the payment of insurance benefits or for a **charitable purpose** (**IRC** § 512(a)(4)). Tax exemption is also available for an **association**—organized before 1880—where more than 75 percent of its members are present or past members of the armed forces and a **principal** purpose of which is to provide insurance and other benefits to veterans or their dependents (**IRC** § 501(c)(23)).

V

Most veterans' organizations are **charitable donees** for purposes of the **federal income**, **gift**, and **estate tax charitable contribution deductions**. For this purpose, a veterans' organization is defined as a post or organization of war veterans, or an auxiliary unit or society of, or trust or foundation for, any of these posts or organizations, that is organized in the U.S. or any of its possessions and where none of its net earnings inures to the benefit of any person in his, her, or its private capacity (**IRC** § 170(c)(3)). [EO §§ 19.11, 24.10; CG § 3.3(a); FR § 5.18(b)(iv); HC § 3.1; PF § 1.6; AU § 7.1(x); AR § 19.1(a)(2); AS § 1.6(m); UB § 6.2(a); SM p. 45; CL § 1.11; LI Q 1.50].

vicarious tax exemption

A facet of the **integral part doctrine**, applied largely with respect to **tax exemption** as a **charitable organization**, enables an organization the sole activity is an integral part of the exempt activities of a **related entity** to derive exemption on the basis of the relationship with its affiliate. Tax exemption of this nature is known as a "vicarious" exemption. [EO § 26.10(a); HC § 34.7] (also **Derivative exemption**).

vice president

A **nonprofit organization** may have, but is not usually required to have, one or more "vice presidents." A vice president acts in the absence of the organization's **president** or in the event that the president is unable or refuses to act. A vice president may perform such other **reasonable** duties as from time to time may be assigned by the president or the **governing board** of the organization.

Victims of Terrorism Tax Relief Act

The "Victims of Terrorism Tax Relief Act," enacted in 2001, introduced rules (and clarification of existing rules) for provision of assistance by **charitable organizations** to individuals who are victims of terrorism. [EO § 7.2(b)] (also **Disaster relief program**).

void

The word "void" means to render something a nullity, such as a **law** that is made unenforceable or ineffectual. For example, a court may render a **statute** void because it is **unconstitutional**.

voidable

The word "voidable" means something that is capable of being rendered **void** but remains valid until nullified. The term is often used in the **law** of **contracts**, where one **person** lacks the capacity to enter into a binding contract (for example, because he or she is a **minor**), but does so anyway, so that the contract is binding on the other person to the contract until and unless the incompetent person repudiates (voids) the contract.

void for vagueness

The phrase "void for vagueness" is used to describe a basis in **constitutional law** by which a **statute**, **regulation**, or **rule** may be rendered **void** because it is **unconstitutional** in that it is too **vague**. The **doctrine** is usually applied in the context of the **criminal law**, on the ground that crimes should be defined with certainty and precision, as a matter of **due process**. This doctrine can, however, be employed in the context of the **civil law,** including the **federal tax law** as applied to **tax-exempt organizations**. For example, a court concluded that the **full and fair exposition test** created by the **IRS** was so vague as to violate the **First Amendment** and thus voided the regulation containing the test. This doctrine is by no means uniformly applied; if it were, probably around two-thirds of the **IRC** would be rendered unconstitutional. [EO § 8.2; FR § 4.8].

voluntarism

The word "voluntarism" is used to describe that aspect of the role of **nonprofit organizations** in U.S. society that stimulates the services and **contributions** of individuals who serve these organizations, and ultimately society as a whole, as **volunteers**. U.S. society is founded on the **principle** of individual initiative, rather than governmental directives, and that principle is honored through the existence and program efforts of voluntary **organizations**. Voluntarism and **charitable giving** have contributed immeasurably to social and scientific progress in the U.S. [CG § 1.3(a); HC § 1.3; SM pp. 4, 15].

voluntary

The word "voluntary," as employed in the context of the **law** of **nonprofit organizations**, is used in defining a criterion of **tax-exempt voluntary employees' beneficiary associations**. There, **membership** in the association is considered "voluntary" if an affirmative act is required on the part of an **employee** to become a member rather than the designation as a member due to employee status. This type of association is considered to have a voluntary membership even though membership is required of all employees, as long as the employees do not incur a detriment (such as deduction from compensation) as the result of membership in the association. [EO § 18.3].

voluntary employees' beneficiary association

A "voluntary employees' beneficiary association" is a form of **tax-exempt organization** that provides for the payment of life, sick, accident, or **other benefits** to the **members** of the **association** or their dependents or designated **beneficiaries**, where no part of the **net earnings** of the association **inures** (other than through these payments) to the **private benefit** of any **person** (**IRC** § 501(a), by reason of **IRC** § 501(c)(9)). Membership in this type of organization must, as its name states, be **voluntary**.

Eligibility for membership in a voluntary employees' beneficiary association may be restricted by geographic proximity, or by objective conditions or limitations **reasonably** related to employment, such as a limitation as to a reasonable classification of workers, a limitation based on a reasonable period of service, a limitation based on maximum **compensation**, or a requirement that a member be employed on a full-time basis. Also, eligibility for benefits may be restricted by objective **conditions** relating to the type or amount of benefits offered. An exempt voluntary employees' beneficiary association must be **controlled** either by its membership, an independent **trustee** (such as a financial institution), or trustees, at least some of whom are designated by or on behalf of the membership. The life, sick, accident, or other benefits

V

provided by a voluntary employees' beneficiary association must be payable to its members, their dependents, or their designated beneficiaries. The **private inurement doctrine** as applied to these organizations means not only a prohibition on matters such as **unreasonable compensation** or **self-dealing**, but also the payment to any member of disproportionate benefits.

Generally, a voluntary employees' beneficiary association cannot be tax-exempt unless it meets certain **nondiscrimination requirements** (**IRC** §§ 505(a)(1), (b)). This type of organization constitutes a **welfare benefit** fund and therefore a **disqualified benefit** provided by it will give rise to tax liability (**IRC** § 4976(a)). These entities are subject to the **unrelated income rules**, including the special rules by which only **exempt function revenue** is **excluded** from taxation. [EO §§ 18.3, 24.8; AU § 7.1(p); AS § 1.6(h); SM p. 43].

volunteer

A "volunteer" is an individual who provides a service to a **nonprofit organization**, doing so under his or her free will, without financial **compensation**. (For this purpose, a reimbursement of **expenses** does not detract from an individual's status as a volunteer.) Thus, the services of a volunteer are **contributed** services. There is, however, no **federal income tax charitable contribution deduction** for the **value** of contribution of services. A volunteer is not an **employee**. Exempt from the scope of the phrase **unrelated trade or business** is a business in which **substantially all** of the work in carrying on the business is performed for the **tax-exempt organization** without compensation (**IRC** § 513(a)(1)). (The provision of noncash economic benefits may be treated by the **IRS** or a court as "compensation," thereby **voiding** this **exception**.) It is common for **charitable** and other types of nonprofit organizations to be served by volunteers; usually, their **directors**, **trustees**, and/or **officers** will serve as volunteers. [EO § 25.2(a); CG § 1.4; UB § 4.2; FR § 3.1(k); PF §§ 5.7(c), 11.2(d); AR §§ 9.1(d), 9.1(e), 9.2(c)(1), 10.2(a)(3)].

Volunteer Protection Act

The "Volunteer Protection Act," signed into law in 1997, limits lawsuits against **volunteers** serving **charitable organizations** and **governmental entities**. This **law**, which preempts inconsistent state law, provides **immunity** for volunteers if (1) the volunteer was acting within the scope of his or her responsibilities; (2) the volunteer was properly licensed, certified, or authorized to act; (3) the harm was not caused by willful, criminal, or reckless misconduct or gross negligence; and (4) the harm was not caused by a volunteer operating a motor vehicle, vessel, or aircraft. [RE Q 15.2].

voter education

"Voter education" activities are activities, **educational** in nature, designed to provide information to voters to enable them to cast their votes for **candidates** for **political office** in an informed manner. These activities include provision of a forum for debates by the candidates, and dissemination of the views, voting records, and the like of candidates by means of publications and mailings. These activities will constitute **charitable** and educational activities as long as they do not fall within the ambit of **political campaign activities**. [EO § 23.2(c); AR § 10.1(a)(3); CU Q 9.6; SM p. 198].

V

voter registration drive

A "voter registration drive" is an effort to secure the registration of individuals eligible to vote, prior to an impending election; most of these drives are conducted by **persons** who attempt to register voters who are likely to vote in the same manner as they will. In general, the term **taxable expenditure** includes any amount paid or incurred by a **private foundation** to carry on, **directly** or **indirectly**, any voter registration drive (**IRC** § 4945(d)(2)).

A private foundation, however, may engage in or make **grants** with respect to a voter registration drive, without making taxable expenditures, if (1) the activities of the private foundation are nonpartisan, are not confined to one specific election period, and are carried on in five or more states; (2) **substantially all** of the **income** of the **organization** is expended **directly** for the **active conduct** of its **tax-exempt activities;** (3) substantially all of its **support** (other than **gross investment income**) is received from **tax-exempt organizations**, the public, **governmental units**, or any combination of these entities, it does not receive more than 25 percent of this support from any one exempt organization, and not more than one-half of its support is received from gross investment income; and (4) contributions to it for voter registration drives are not subject to **conditions** that they may be used only in specific states, possessions of the U.S., or **political subdivisions** or other areas of any of the foregoing or the District of Columbia, or that they may be used only in one specific election period (**IRC** § 4945(f)). Therefore, other **charitable organizations** may be involved in voter registration drives, at least to the extent of these criteria. [PF §§ 9.2(c), 9.8].

voting power

For purposes of defining the category of **disqualified person** known as **20 percent owners**, where the **entity** involved is a **corporation**, the term "voting power" includes outstanding voting power and does not include voting power obtainable, but not obtained, such as voting power obtainable by converting securities or nonvoting stock into voting stock, by exercising warrants or options to obtain voting stock, and voting power that will vest in preferred stockholders only if and when the corporation has failed to pay preferred dividends for a specified period of time or has otherwise failed to meet specified requirements. [EO § 21.3; PF §§ 4.3, 4.5, 5.11, 7.1(d)].

vouch

To "vouch" is to **substantiate** by providing evidence—to verify. When a **charitable organization** complies with the **statutory substantiation rules**, it is "vouching" for the validity of the **charitable contributions** involved.

V

W

wage

The word "wage" means **compensation** paid to an individual, often by the day or week, for services rendered. The word is usually used in connection with work that is manual or menial labor. (cf. **Salary**).

wager

The word "wager" means to place a bet (that is, to stake money and/or **property** on an uncertain event) or otherwise to gamble; it also means the amount that is staked to the gamble. It is common for **nonprofit organizations** to sponsor wagering events, often in the name of **fundraising**. These events include games of **bingo**, **raffles**, and **sweepstakes**. In some instances, an activity of this nature constitutes an **unrelated trade or business**.

waiting period

A "waiting period" is a period of time that, by **law**, must expire before a **person** can lawfully pursue a **right** achieved by **contract**. These laws focus principally on **sales** of merchandise on a door-to-door basis; they are underlain with the view that an eloquent (slick) salesperson can cause a consumer who cannot afford the item being sold to nonetheless agree to purchase it. A waiting period is thus imposed as a form of consumer protection (a "cooling off" period), to enable the purchaser to rethink the merits of the transaction before consummating it. Under this approach, the right obtained by contract cannot take effect until expiration of the waiting period. A **charitable solicitation act** may embody this approach, stating that a **gift solicitation** cannot have legal effect until expiration of a waiting period. [FR § 3.3].

waiver

A "waiver" occurs when a **person** voluntarily relinquishes a **right**. Usually, the procedure or **conditions** under which a waiver may take place are determined in advance.

The concept of a waiver is used in connection with the **lobbying disallowance rule** and the **political activities disallowance rule**, as it applies to **membership organizations**. These rules contain an **exception** from the **proxy tax**, which is that an **organization** is not subject to the **disclosure requirements** of these rules or the proxy tax if it establishes to the satisfaction of the **IRS** that **substantially all** of the **dues** monies it receives are paid by **members** who are not

---

Bruce R. Hopkins' Nonprofit Law Dictionary, First Edition. Bruce R. Hopkins.
© 2015 Bruce R. Hopkins. Published 2015 by John Wiley & Sons, Inc.

entitled to **deduct** their dues payments in any event. This lack of a deduction can arise in instances such as where (1) an organization receives substantially all of its dues monies from members that are **tax-exempt charitable organizations**, (2) an organization (such as an exempt **social welfare organization**) receives substantially all of its dues monies from members who are individuals not entitled to deduct the dues payments because the payments are not **ordinary and necessary business expenses,** or (3) an organization (such as a **union**) receives substantially all of its dues monies from individuals who cannot deduct their dues because of the **2 percent floor on miscellaneous itemized deductions**. An organization in this situation, however, must, in some cases, obtain a waiver from the **IRS** (IRC § 6033(e)(3)).

want-to rule

Self-dealing can occur when a **public charity** holds a **fundraising** or other benefit event and a **private foundation** pays some or all of the cost of tickets that enable **disqualified persons** with respect to the foundation to attend the event. The **IRS** has held that, under certain circumstances, the foundation is proving an unwarranted economic benefit to its disqualified persons. Some argue, however, that it is appropriate for foundations to send their **managers** to events of entities to which they make significant grants to evidence their support. The answer probably lies in the "want-to" rule. If foundation executives truly want to attend the event (such as because of high interest in the entertainment or the popularity of the speaker), foundation payment of the tickets for their attendance probably is self-dealing. If, however, the executives really do not want to attend the event (such as one of the "rubber chicken" variety) and are reluctantly attending only out of obligation, payment by the foundation for tickets probably is not, or is merely **incidental**, self-dealing (**IRC** § 4941(d)(1)(E)). [PF § 5.8(f)].

wash

The word "wash" is used to describe a circumstance, usually in a financial setting, where one thing operates to offset another, leaving the **person** involved in the same position as was the case before the transaction. In the **federal income tax law** context, a wash occurs when, for example, an **organization's income** is the same, for a particular **tax year**, as its **expenses**.

watchdog agency

The term "watchdog agency" is used to describe a **nonprofit organization** that has as its purpose the analysis of the activities and finances of **charitable organizations** and the dissemination of that information to the public. These self-appointing agencies may also "rate" charitable organizations, such as by "approving" or "disapproving" them in relation to a **code** of ethical standards (conjured by the watchdog agency), and publicize these ratings. Quite frequently, prospective **donors** and **grantors** will rely on this information (including ratings) in deciding whether to make **contributions** and **grants**. These organizations term themselves "voluntary" agencies, meaning that charitable organizations are not legally required to submit to their scrutiny, but that approach is misleading because an organization that refuses to comply is rated as not meeting the standards for that reason alone, which will likely adversely affect **fundraising** outcomes; thus, many charitable entities "voluntarily" comply, fearing the financial consequences if they do not. These agencies are not required by law to adhere to the principles of **procedural** or **substantive due process**. [FR Chap. 9; SM Chap. 21; PG pp. 29–33].

W

wealth replacement trust

A "wealth replacement trust" is a **trust** designed to provide equivalent **assets** to one or more **heirs** of an individual who has, usually by **will**, made a **major contribution** to a **charitable organization**. Because of the **gift**, these heirs would be deprived of a significant portion of the **estate**, were it not for the wealth replacement trust. The asset of the trust is life **insurance**, the heirs are the **beneficiaries** of the insurance, and the trust is **funded** with the money saved from taxation by reason of the **charitable contribution deduction** arising from the making of the gift. [CG § 12.11].

welfare benefit fund

The phrase "welfare benefit fund" is used to encompass three types of **tax-exempt organizations** (IRC § 419(e)(3)(A)). These are **social clubs, supplemental unemployment benefit funds**, and **voluntary employees' beneficiary associations**. A **disqualified benefit** (IRC § 4976(b)) provided by a welfare benefit fund will give rise to federal **tax** liability (IRC § 4976(a)). [EO § 18.2].

whaling expenses

An individual recognized by the Alaska Eskimo Whaling Commission as a whaling captain, who is responsible for maintaining and carrying out **sanctioned whaling activities** and engages in these activities during a **tax year**, may claim a **charitable contribution deduction** not to exceed $10,000 per year for the **reasonable** and necessary whaling expenses paid in carrying out these whaling activities (**IRC** § 170(n)). The term "whaling expenses" includes amounts paid for the acquisition and maintenance of whaling boats, weapons, and gear used in sanctioned whaling activities, and the storage and distribution of the catch from the activities (**IRC** § 170(n)(2)(B)). [CG § 9.30].

whistleblower policy

The **IRS**, on the **Form 990**, asks if the filing **organization** has a written "whistleblower policy," which it describes as a **policy** that "encourages staff and volunteers to come forward with credible information on illegal practices or violations of adopted policies of the organization, specifies that the organization will protect the individual from retaliation, and identifies those staff or **board members** or outside parties to whom such information can be reported." [GV §§ 3.10(c), 4.2(b), 5.18, 6.3(c); AR §§ 5.1(i)(2), 5.2(b)(2), 5.3; CU Q 5.31; SM p. 100; LI Q 3.29].

whole-entity joint venture

A "whole-entity joint venture" is a **joint venture** usually involving two parties: a **tax-exempt organization** (most often, a **public charity**) and a **for-profit organization**, where the **exempt organization** transfers the entirety of its **assets** to the venture and the for-profit **entity** provides financing for the venture's operations. If the exempt organization cedes **control** of the venture to the for-profit company, such as by allowing the company to maintain a majority of the venture's **governing board**, the exempt organization is likely to have its **tax-exempt status revoked** for transgression of the doctrine of **private benefit**. [EO §§ 20.11(c), 31.3; UB §§ 8.12(a), 8.14; HC § 22.9; AR § 11.1(f)(3)(E); AS § 7.4; PG pp. 158–161; SM pp. 228–229].

W

widely available exception

A **tax-exempt organization** is not required to comply with requests for copies of its **application for recognition of exemption** or an **annual information return** if the organization has made the document "widely available." Essentially, this means that the organization can post the document on a webpage that the organization establishes and maintains or on a webpage containing a database of similar documents of other exempt organizations established and maintained by another entity. Various rules must be adhered to for this exception to apply. [EO § 28.8(e); AR § 1.1(e)(2); RE Q 8.21; SM p. 123].

will

A "will" is a document by which an individual expresses his or her desires as to the **disposition** of his or her **property** following his or her death. A will can pass money, **personal property**, and **real property**. Following death, the individual who executed the will is a **decedent**, the property involved is collectively known as the **estate**, and the individual (or sometimes individuals) who administer and ultimately dispose of the estate is the **executor**, or (more contemporarily) **personal representative**. A will is a **revocable instrument**. State **law** provides certain formalities that a will must meet to be legally valid. The term sometimes used is "last will and testament" (the latter word technically pertaining only to personal property), but contemporary usage is simply a "will."

A **charitable contribution** can be made by will, either as a **bequest** or **devise**. A charitable **gift** made by will can be **outright**, **partial**, and/or in **trust**. A **charitable organization** (most likely a **private foundation**) can be established by means of a will. (also **Codicil**; **Holographic will**; **Intestate**).

will contest

A "will contest" is a **lawsuit** in which one or more individuals challenge the validity of a **will**. The basis for the **litigation** is usually the **competence** of the **decedent** at the time the will was executed and/or the presence and efficacy of a prior or subsequent will. [CG § 8.6(b)].

will settlement

A "will settlement" may be the outcome of a **will contest**. It is a settlement of the case by the **parties**, often formally approved by the court. Where a will settlement involves a **contribution** to a **charitable organization** by means of a **trust**, the **IRS** may scrutinize the settlement to determine whether it was an attempt to circumvent the rule requiring, for the **federal estate tax charitable contribution deduction** to be available, that the trust be one of certain forms. [CG § 8.6(b)].

W

willful

The **law** often makes reference, such as in the context of **tax penalties**, to an act (or a failure to act) of an individual that is "willful." A willful act is one done consciously, voluntarily, or intentionally (the law may term it "willful misconduct"); it may embrace an act done recklessly. It usually does not encompass an act done wholly carelessly, thoughtlessly, or inadvertently.

Many of the **private foundation excise taxes** are excused where the individual involved did not act "willfully" (**IRC** §§ 4941(a)(2), 4944(a)(2), and 4945(a)(2)); the same is the case with respect to the black lung benefit trust excise taxes (**IRC** §§ 4951(a)(2) and 4952(a)(2)). For example, the **federal** tax **regulations** concerning **self-dealing** provide that a **foundation manager** is deemed to have acted willfully if the act is "voluntary, conscious, and intentional," and that "[n]o motive to avoid the restrictions of the law or the incurrence of any tax is necessary to make the **participation** willful." This is also the case with respect to the excise taxes on **political expenditures** by **charitable organizations** (**IRC** § 4955(a)(2)).

Sometimes the word "willful" is used in conjunction with the word "flagrant"; for example, if an individual becomes **liable** for one of the private foundation excise taxes, the black lung benefit trust excise taxes, or the excise tax on political expenditures by charitable organizations, by reason of any act or failure to act which is not due to **reasonable cause** and the act or failure to act is both willful and flagrant, the individual is liable for a penalty equal to the amount of the tax (**IRC** § 6684). There is a penalty for a willful failure to collect or pay over a tax (**IRC** § 7202) and a penalty for a willful failure to file a return, supply information, or pay a tax (**IRC** § 7203). [PF § 1.10; LI Q 4.64, Q 5.46] (also **Negligence**).

willful neglect

The **IRS** defines the term "willful neglect" to imply a voluntary, conscious, and intentional failure to exercise the care that a **reasonable person** would observe under the circumstances to see that applicable standards were observed, despite knowledge of the standards or rules in question.

wind up

The phrase "wind up" (or sometimes "winding up") is used in the context of ending the existence of a **business enterprise**, usually a **corporation** or a **partnership**. The winding-up process involves settling the accounts of the business and distribution of any **net assets** and/or **net revenue**. Often, by **statute**, the enterprise is allowed to function under its name for a stated period following the date of formal **dissolution** of the concern. The phrase is also used with respect to **nonprofit organizations**; when this type of an organization, such as a **charitable** one, has a **dissolution** clause, the winding up must be done in conformity with the terms of that clause. [EO § 4.3(b)] (also **Liquidation**).

winning the audit lottery

The phrase "winning the audit lottery" means, at least in the **tax-exempt organizations** context, being selected by the **IRS** for **examination**. [AU § 3.2].

withheld

The word "withheld" applies to sums of money that have been subject to **withholding**.

withholding

The word "withholding" describes the process, usually undertaken by an **employer**, of deducting sums of money from the **wages** or **salary** of an **employee**. This is most frequently done to withhold **federal** and state **income taxes** and social security taxes. Other items subject to with-holding may include various **insurance premiums**, contributions to a **pension fund** or retire-ment plan, and **charitable contributions** (such as those withheld pursuant to the **Combined Federal Campaign** rules). The employer is required to remit these amounts to the appropriate payees; when the payee is a government and the amount paid is for income taxes, the amount remitted is credited toward the total tax **liability** of the employee.

Also, when an individual wins a prize at a **game of chance** sponsored by a **charitable organization**, the organization is required to withhold 20 percent of the amount (when the winnings are money) or receive from the winner a payment of 20 percent of the **value** of the **property** involved, and timely remit the amount to the federal government in payment (in whole or in part) of the income tax that the winner must pay (**IRC** § 3402(q)(3)(A)). (also **Withholding tax**).

withholding tax

When the amount of money that must be **withheld** from a payment to an **employee** or other individual is for a **tax**, the amount withheld is termed a "withholding tax." The tax (or taxes) withheld are required to be timely remitted to the appropriate government.

word of art

The phrase "word of art" means a word that, while it may have a general meaning, also has a more specific meaning in the context of a particular profession or other field of endeavor. It is thus part of a terminology or vocabulary that is unique to a field (sometimes approaching or constituting jargon). The field of **law**, not surprisingly, uses words as "words of art." For example, the **IRC** states that an **organization**, to be tax-exempt as a **charitable entity**, must be **organized** and **operated** "**exclusively**" for **exempt** purposes (**IRC** § 501(c)(3)). Courts have held that the word "exclusively" is a word of art (or a "term of art") that, in this setting, means "**primarily**." [EO §§ 4.4, 4.6].

workers' compensation insurance provider

Certain "workers' compensation insurance providers," where the state involved has made a financial commitment with respect to the organization, is a **tax-exempt organization** (**IRC** § 501(c)(27)(B)). [EO § 19.16(b)].

workers' compensation reimbursement organization

A "workers' compensation reimbursement organization" that meets various conditions, including being a **membership** entity, state-sponsored, and established before June 1, 1996, is a **tax-exempt organizations** (**IRC** § 501(c)(27)(A)). [EO § 19.16(a)].

working condition fringe benefit

Certain **fringe benefits** are **excluded** from individuals' **gross income** (**IRC** § 132(a)). One category of this type of excluded benefit is a "working condition fringe" benefit (**IRC** § 132(a)(3)). A working condition fringe benefit is any **property** or service provided to an **employee** by an **employer** to the extent that, if the employee paid for the property or service, the amount paid would be allowable as a **business expense deduction** or a **depreciation deduction** (IRC § 132(d)). For example, an employee of a **tax-exempt organization** may be covered by **officers' and directors' liability insurance**, purchased by the employer, and the **value** of that coverage is excluded from the employee's gross income because that form of insurance coverage is a working condition fringe benefit. The **federal tax law** extends the tax advantages of this type of benefit to **bona fide volunteers**, who by tax regulation, are deemed to have the necessary profit motive (required for the availability of a business expense deduction) to sustain the exclusion. The value of liability insurance coverage (or **indemnification** for **liability**) is deemed to be substantially less than the value of the individual's volunteer services to the organization (required under the definition of "bona fide volunteer"), provided that the insurance coverage is limited to acts performed in the discharge of official duties or the performance of services on behalf of the exempt organization. [HC § 28.5(b); PF § 5.7(c)].

work of art

A "work of art" may be the subject of a **charitable gift**, for which there is a **charitable contribution deduction**. There are special **federal tax rules** concerning gifts of works of art, such as where the art is put to an **unrelated** use by the charitable **donee** or where the work of art that is contributed is the creation of the **donor**. Further, it is not uncommon to have controversy surrounding the **fair market value** assigned to a work of art contributed to a charitable organization. For purposes of the federal tax law concerning the federal **estate tax charitable contribution deduction** for a **qualified contribution** of a "work of art," the term is defined as any **tangible personal property** with respect to which there is a **copyright** under federal law (IRC § 2055(e)(4)(B)). [CG §§ 8.2(g), 9.1(a), 9.1(c), 24.7(b)(2); AR §§ 19.1(d)(1), 19.2(b)].

written determination

The **federal tax law** requires that the text of a "written determination" be made open to public inspection by the **IRS** (IRC § 6110(a)). For this purpose, the term means an **IRS ruling, determination letter**, or **technical advice memorandum** (IRC § 6110(b)(1)). [EO § 28.9(a); HC § 34.2].

written statement, requirement of

The **law** often requires that a **person** prepare and retain a "written statement" as a **condition** for receiving or obtaining some benefit. For example, if a **business corporation** wants to avail itself of the special **federal income tax deduction** for **contributions** of its **inventory** to those who are **needy** or are otherwise qualified **beneficiaries**, it must furnish a written statement to the **donee** or (if involved) a transferring organization. [CG § 9.3(d)].

W

xenomania

The word "xenomania" means an intense interest in the **laws**, institutions, and customs in foreign countries. The term is applicable to those who are fascinated by the extraordinary increase in the creation and operation of **nonprofit organizations** (particularly **charitable** ones) throughout the world.

xenophobia

The word "xenophobia" means a fear (or contempt) of foreigners, particularly their political or cultural views. Those who are possessed of xenomania are often frustrated with the forms of resistance to change devised by those who are afflicted with "xenophobia."

Y

yank

At least one judge has made reference to the phenomenon by which the **IRS** will "yank" the **tax exemption** of a **nonprofit organization**. This is most informal (if not coarse) terminology; the correct term, of course, is "revoke."

year

In the **nonprofit organization law** setting (as opposed to an astronomical or ecclesiastical setting), the word "year" refers to twelve consecutive calendar months. Often, an **organization**'s year is the same as the calendar year. (An individual's year is almost always a calendar year.) A year of an organization may be a **fiscal year**, if it is not a calendar year. (also **Tax year**).

year of formation

The "year of formation" is the term used by the **IRS** to mean the year in which a **tax-exempt organization** was formed in accordance with state **law**. Thus, for example, in the case of a **corporation**, the year of formation is the year of **incorporation**.

year-of-inclusion rule

A payment that is made or required to be distributed by a **charitable remainder trust**, because of certain rules applicable to **testamentary transfers**, an amendment to the **governing instrument** of certain trusts pursuant to special effective dates rules, or an **incorrect valuation**, must be included in the **gross income** of the **income interest beneficiary** of the trust in his or her **tax year** in which or with which ends the tax year of the trust in which the amount is paid, credited, or required to be distributed. This is often referred to as the "year-of-inclusion rule." (A **recipient** is allowed a **deduction** from gross income for amounts repaid to a charitable remainder trust because of an overpayment during the reasonable period of administration or settlement or until the trust is fully funded, because of an amendment or because of an incorrect valuation, to the extent these amounts were included in his or her gross income.)

yemeless

See **Negligent**.

Y

Bruce R. Hopkins' Nonprofit Law Dictionary, First Edition. Bruce R. Hopkins.
© 2015 Bruce R. Hopkins. Published 2015 by John Wiley & Sons, Inc.

yield

The word "yield" means the return on an investment; it is an amount (such as a **dividend** or **interest**) paid on the investment of **principal**. The earnings generated by an **endowment fund** are termed the "yield." The amounts received by a **beneficiary** of an **income interest**, such as from a **charitable remainder trust** or **pooled income fund**, are a yield.

Y

Z

zamindar

A "zamindar" is a **tax** collector; someone who **audits persons** and extracts taxes from them. Many **employees** of the **IRS** are thus "zamindars." The term was developed to describe officials in precolonial India who had the responsibility for collecting **real estate** taxes in various tax districts.

zeitgeist

The word "zeitgeist" means the spirit or outlook of a society at a particular time. A zeitgeist can and often does change, however. For example, there are those of the view that the zeitgeist relating to **nonprofit organizations**, where they were revered and championed, is evolving into one where they are losing the luster that underlies their **status** as **tax-exempt organizations** and, in certain instances, **charitable donees**.

zero hour

The term "zero hour" is used to describe a time when a decisive change in the course of events, such as an **IRS examination**, is impending.

zeugma

A "zeugma" is a rhetorical language device in which a word is used to modify two or more other words, although its use is logically correct with only one. On occasion, a **director of development**, having successfully designed and received a particularly creative and financially advantageous **charitable gift**, may witness a result that can be described as a "zeugma": the **donors** left the offices of the **charitable organization** in high spirits and an expensive automobile.

zillionaire

A "zillionaire" is an individual who is extremely wealthy; these **persons** are of intense interest to **fundraisers**.

zooks

A mild oath, frequently uttered upon receipt of correspondence from the **IRS**.

Bruce R. Hopkins' Nonprofit Law Dictionary, First Edition. Bruce R. Hopkins.
© 2015 Bruce R. Hopkins. Published 2015 by John Wiley & Sons, Inc.

Z

zoolatry

The practice of "zoolatry," which is the worship of animals, is a form of **religion**.

zoophilist

A "zoophilist" is an individual who is concerned with the rights of animals and their protection from abuse; a founder of a **charitable organization** engaging in activities that **prevent cruelty** to animals.

zucchini test

The **federal tax regulations** contain six discrete requirements that an **organization** must satisfy to qualify as a **tax-exempt business league**. It is insufficient, as an organization argued, that all that is required is that an organization have characteristics that are "similar to" those in the regulations. That contention, a federal court of appeals observed, "is a bridge too far." In dismissing that argument as a matter of logic, this court wrote that "simply because x has 'characteristics similar to' y does not necessarily make x a y." The court noted that a "cucumber has characteristics similar to a zucchini but it is not, in fact, a zucchini." It continued: "And, while having characteristics similar to a zucchini may be enough for some purposes (for instance, to stand in as a zucchini in an impressionist still life), it will not be enough when an object possessing all the characteristics of a zucchini—in other words, a zucchini itself—is required (say, when making zucchini bread)." [EO Chap. 14].

Z

ABOUT THE AUTHOR

Bruce R. Hopkins is a principal in Bruce R. Hopkins Law Firm, LLC in Kansas City, Missouri. He concentrates on the representation of tax-exempt organizations. His practice ranges over the entirety of law matters involving exempt organizations, with emphasis on the formation of nonprofit organizations, acquisition of recognition of tax-exempt status for them, governance and the law, the private inurement and private benefit doctrines, the intermediate sanctions rules, legislative and political campaign activities issues, public charity and private foundation rules, unrelated business planning, use of exempt and for-profit subsidiaries, joint venture planning, tax shelter involvement, review of annual information returns, Internet communications developments, the law of charitable giving (including planned giving), and fundraising law issues.

Mr. Hopkins served as chair of the Committee on Exempt Organizations, Tax Section, American Bar Association; chair, Section of Taxation, National Association of College and University Attorneys; and president, Planned Giving Study Group of Greater Washington, D.C.

Mr. Hopkins is the series editor of Wiley's Nonprofit Law, Finance, and Management Series. In addition to compiling the *Bruce R. Hopkins' Nonprofit Law Dictionary*, he is the author of the *Bruce R. Hopkins' Nonprofit Law Library*; *The Law of Tax-Exempt Organizations, Eleventh Edition*; *Planning Guide for the Law of Tax-Exempt Organizations: Strategies and Commentaries*; *Tax-Exempt Organizations and Constitutional Law: Nonprofit Law as Shaped by the U.S. Supreme Court*; *IRS Audits of Tax-Exempt Organizations: Policies, Practices, and Procedures*; *The Tax Law of Charitable Giving, Fifth Edition*; *The Tax Law of Associations*; *The Tax Law of Unrelated Business for Nonprofit Organizations*; *The Nonprofits' Guide to Internet Communications Law*; *The Law of Intermediate Sanctions: A Guide for Nonprofits*; *Starting and Managing a Nonprofit Organization: A Legal Guide, Sixth Edition*; *Nonprofit Law Made Easy*; *Charitable Giving Law Made Easy*; *Private Foundation Law Made Easy*; *Fundraising Law Made Easy*; *650 Essential Nonprofit Law Questions Answered*; *The First Legal Answer Book for Fund-Raisers*; *The Second*